FUNDAMENTALS OF SYSTEMS ANALYSIS

Using Structured Analysis and Design Techniques

3rd EDITION

Jerry FitzGerald Ph.D.

JERRY FITZGERALD & ASSOCIATES

Ardra F. FitzGerald M.L.S., M.B.A.

JERRY FITZGERALD & ASSOCIATES

John Wiley & Sons

New York · Chichester · Brisbane · Toronto · Singapore

A successful systems analyst promises no more than he or she can deliver and delivers what was promised.

Cover photograph by Paul Silverman

Copyright © 1973, 1981, 1987 by John Wiley & Sons, Inc.

Library of Congress Cataloging in Publication Data:

Fitzgerald, Jerry.
  Fundamentals of systems analysis.

  (Wiley series in computers and information processing
systems for business)
  Includes bibliographies and indexes.
  1. Business—Data processing. 2. System analysis.
I. Fitzgerald, Ardra F., 1938-   . II. Title.
III. Series: Wiley series in computers and information
processing systems in business.

HF5548.2.F476 1987   658.4'032   86-7831
ISBN 0-471-88597-5

Printed in the Republic of Singapore

10 9 8 7 6 5

About the Authors

Dr. Jerry FitzGerald is the president of Jerry FitzGerald & Associates, a management consulting firm. He has extensive experience in computer security, audit and control of computerized systems, data communications, and systems analysis. In addition to consulting, he also conducts training courses and seminars in these subjects.

Prior to starting his own firm, Dr. FitzGerald was a senior management consultant with SRI International (formerly Stanford Research Institute) in Menlo Park, California. Before that he was an associate professor in the California State Colleges and University System. Dr. FitzGerald has taught at California State Polytechnic University at Pomona, California State University at Hayward, and the University of California at Berkeley. His teaching emphasis was in data processing subjects. Prior to teaching, he was a senior systems analyst at the University of California Medical Center in San Francisco.

As a consultant, Dr. FitzGerald has been active in numerous system design projects, EDP audit reviews, new system development control reviews, EDP audit training, internal control reviews of on-line systems, and control/security of data communication networks. This work has included development of the computer security administration function within organizations, redesign of the system development life cycle process, development of data communication networks for organizations, review of the internal EDP audit function on behalf of management, and development of requests for proposals with regard to selection and purchase of computer systems.

In addition to numerous articles, he is the author of five books, two of which have been translated into Spanish. The books are *Business Data Communications: Basic Concepts, Security and Design, Designing Controls into Computerized Systems, Fundamentals of Systems Analysis, Internal Controls for Computerized Systems,* and *Fundamentals of Data Communications.*

In 1980, Dr. FitzGerald was the recipient of the annual Joseph J. Wasserman Award. This award is given by the EDP Auditors Association to the person who made the most outstanding contributions in the areas of EDP auditing, control, and security during the year.

Dr. FitzGerald's education includes a Ph.D. in Business Administration from the Claremont Graduate School, an M.B.A. from the University of Santa Clara, and a bachelor's degree in Industrial Engineering from Michigan State University. He is also a Certified Information Systems Auditor (CISA) and has a Certificate in Data Processing (CDP).

Ardra FitzGerald is a principal in Jerry FitzGerald & Associates. Her areas of expertise include technical literature searching (both paper and computerized), the design of computerized bibliographic systems with emphasis in bibliographic database searching techniques, index preparation, bibliographic citation and editing, information center organization, and seminars in literature resources for business and engineering.

Previously, Mrs. FitzGerald spent 12 years as a senior information specialist in the Library of SRI International (formerly Stanford Research Institute) located at Menlo Park, California. This position required a systems approach to problem solving and research in an international consulting environment. As the supervisor of the Library's Literature Research Section, she was responsible for implementing SRI's computerized bibliographic searching program. This program included DIALOG, ORBIT, MEDLINE, TOXLINE, DROLS, TRIS, and the New York Times Information Bank, among others. During her years at SRI International, Mrs. FitzGerald specialized in research in the areas of management, computers, accounting, systems analysis techniques to solve client problems, engineering technology, and the social sciences.

Before joining SRI International, Mrs. FitzGerald was a reference librarian and bibliographic specialist in the California State Colleges and University System. While a faculty member, she taught the use of printed resources to business and engineering students at both the graduate and undergraduate levels. Her areas of expertise as bibliographic specialist were in business management, business law, industrial engineering, civil engineering, and mechanical engineering.

Prior to joining the university, she served as a literature analyst at Lockheed Missiles and Space Company. This position involved literature searching and bibliographic compilation in the area of aerospace technology. Before joining Lockheed, she was responsible for the technical library of a small aerospace firm, as well as one for a major health care provider.

Mrs. FitzGerald's education includes a master's degree in business administration (MBA) from the College of Notre Dame in Belmont, California, a master's degree in librarianship from San Jose State University in San Jose, California, and a bachelor's degree in sociology from Wayne State University in Detroit, Michigan. In addition, she holds a lifetime California Community Colleges teaching credential and has received specialized training in all of the computerized bibliographic systems for which she was responsible while at SRI International.

Mrs. FitzGerald is a member of the American Society for Information Science and the Special Libraries Association.

Preface

Systems analysis is a course that must be taught to all college graduates, regardless of their discipline. Just as knowledge of computers and computer programming has become a basic skill needed to survive in today's information-based society, so has the design of business systems. Because the development and use of computer systems are basic to *all* business functions in today's environment, the teaching of systems analysis should be a basic university-wide course that cuts across all disciplinary lines.

This third edition of our systems analysis textbook has been modified extensively. It now contains a comprehensive and thorough explanation of structured analysis and design techniques, a workbook-style cumulative case that requires the students to perform case tasks using structured techniques, and a matrix approach to designing controls when using structured analysis and design. The primary objective of this book is to teach *systems thinking*. Along with that objective, the student will learn that work tasks are interrelated and interdependent. No action is taken independently of others; there is always a reaction. This book also teaches that the single most important ingredient in a successful business system is its *people*. Finally, in addition to being people oriented, our approach is security and control oriented.

The book is divided into three parts: The Preliminaries (Part One), The System Study Itself (Part Two), and The Tools of Systems Analysis (Part Three).

Part One (Chapters 1–2) discusses the introduction to systems analysis, how to conduct a feasibility study, the system development life cycle (SDLC), and how to use structured analysis and design techniques. Chapter 1 covers basic introductory subjects, such as the definition of systems analysis, systems and procedures, technology's effect upon systems analysis, microcomputers/distributed data processing, data communications, database, management information systems, decision support systems, and a methodology for conducting feasibility studies. Also included is a "reading data flow diagram" that offers a suggested reading flow for this book (see Figure 1-11).

Chapter 2 introduces structured analysis and design techniques and then explains how to use each of these structured techniques. May we suggest that you read the various section topics for Chapter 2 in the table of contents. This chapter first presents a 10-step system development life cycle (SDLC). The various structured analysis and design techniques are then integrated into the 10 steps of this life cycle. Figure 2-1 shows these 10 steps, along with the related structured analysis or design technique that should be used at each step of the new system development. Chapter 2 defines these structured techniques and then shows the student how to use them in a logical progression. This explanation is supplemented further by a workbook-style case that uses the structured techniques at their appropriate place within the 10-step system development life cycle. This case, Sunrise Sportswear Company, is presented cumulatively through each of Chapters 3 through 12 in Part Two of this book.

Part Two (Chapters 3–12) specifies the details of the 10-step system development life cycle. An entire chapter is devoted to what or how the analysis/design process should be carried out for each of the 10 steps. The last section in each of Chapters 3 through 12 contains the Sunrise Sportswear cumulative workbook case that utilizes structured analysis and design techniques. This case requires the students to answer various questions and complete a number of structured analysis and design tasks. The Sunrise Sportswear cumulative case is more than 150 pages in length and contains 90 student questions or tasks. For this reason, it represents a complete structured analysis and design workbook that has been integrated within this text. We hope that you will use the cumulative case in the classroom. It not only will help the student learn when to use structured techniques, but it has been written in a manner that simulates a real-life situation. The student is placed in the role of the analyst who has been hired by Sunrise Sportswear to help solve its problems. How the student deals with the people and their problems can provide a valuable classroom learning experience. The best way for you to obtain an overview of the contents of Chapters 3–12 is to read through the table of contents for these chapters or review Figure 2-1.

Part Three (Chapters 13–19) covers the tools of systems analysis that for a variety of reasons were not incorporated in the chapters that deal with the 10-step system development life cycle (3–12). Because there are so many alternative tools available to the systems analyst, some of them have to be placed separately from the SDLC steps. The most popular tools have been incorporated into the cumulative case study at their most logical point of use. Since it is unreasonable to depict numerous alternative tools during the case study, the additional tools are contained in this section of the textbook. For example, Chapters 13 to 19 cover charting, forms design, records retention, report analysis, procedure writing, techniques for the systems manager, and the research needs of the systems analyst. Our reading data flow diagram (Figure 1-11) offers a suggested way to integrate these chapters into the system development life cycle. This approach provides flexibility in the introduction of alternate tools because the most popular tools are integrated into the main discussion of the system development life cycle (Chapters 3–12). Further emphasis on alternate tools can be obtained by assignments that utilize Chapters 13 to 19.

In addition to the questions and student tasks for the Sunrise Sportswear cumulative case, there are questions at the end of each chapter that pertain to the material covered in that chapter. Also at the end of each chapter are short "situation cases" (separate from the cumulative case) for the students to complete. These situation cases depict scenarios that emphasize the material covered in that specific chapter.

By now you probably have looked at Figures 2-1 and 1-11, the SDLC, and the reading data flow diagram. May we suggest that you now examine the table of contents and make note of the material that is covered in each section of the chapters. Remember that the Sunrise Sportswear cumulative case also emphasizes the material in each chapter, in addition to the appropriate structured techniques that are used at given points within the system development life cycle. We made this a cumulative case to emphasize the continuity of the life cycle phases for the student.

We feel that this third edition provides students with a solid foundation in the fundamentals of systems analysis. Further, the cumulative case is designed to enhance the students' understanding of how to use structured analysis and design techniques in a systems situation. This book will equip students with the ability to deal with the demands of today's information society, as well as the specific business environment into which they will graduate. By applying the basics of systems thinking and a people-oriented structured techniques philosophy that fits into the 10-step system development life cycle, we feel the student will be well equipped to meet the needs and challenges of the twentieth century information-based society.

Redwood City, California   Jerry FitzGerald
                                                               Ardra F. FitzGerald

Acknowledgments

Several prominent people in the business and academic world have made contributions to this textbook. We would like to acknowledge their efforts here and thank them for their contributions. The individuals who contributed effort to this textbook are:

Logical Conclusions, Inc.
450 Kings Road
Brisbane, California 94005

Brian Dickinson, President of Logical Conclusions, spent a great deal of time instructing and critiquing portions of the material on structured analysis and design. Brian's company specializes in training and consulting activities with regard to structured techniques.

Taylor University
Upland, Indiana 46989

Dr. Leon Adkison, Director of the Systems Analysis Program, Taylor University, developed the test bank of questions that are contained in the Instructor's Manual. He also performed two reviews of the entire textbook.

The authors also would like to thank the following people for their thorough and in-depth reviews of the manuscript for this third edition of the textbook. We would like to acknowledge the fact that we utilized almost all of the comments offered. The following reviewers are listed in alphabetic sequence.

Leon Adkison, Taylor University

Angela Blas, State University of New York at Farmingdale

Gus A. King, National College

Charles Neblock, Western Illinois University

Hugh Watson, University of Georgia

J.F.
A.F.F.

Contents

Chapter 2

STRUCTURED ANALYSIS AND DESIGN TECHNIQUES   *49*

Chapter 7
DEFINE THE NEW SYSTEMS REQUIREMENTS   *281*

List of Situation Cases

The following list of cases enumerates the short situation cases that appear at the end of each chapter of this textbook. These cases depict a situation and exemplify the material that is covered within the specific chapter. The cumulative case, Sunrise Sportswear Company, is an additional workbook-style case and it appears as a major section throughout Chapters 3 through 12. This list of situation cases is in order of presentation. They are listed alphabetically by name in the index at the back of the book.

Part One

THE
PRELIMINARIES

*P*art One is concerned with the items
that are basic to a systems study. These
include an orientation to systems
thinking, the system development life
cycle (SDLC), structured analysis and
design techniques, the feasibility study,
and technology's effect upon systems.

Chapter 1

INTRODUCTION TO SYSTEMS ANALYSIS

LEARNING OBJECTIVES

You will learn how to . . .

□ Define systems analysis.

□ Understand systems and procedures.

□ See the relationships between systems and the rest of the firm.

□ Identify the functions of the systems department.

□ Incorporate philosophies of systems design.

□ Understand the basics of microcomputers, distributed DP, data communications, database, MIS, and DSS.

□ Conduct a feasibility study.

□ Follow the reading sequence of this book (Figure 1-11).

Why Study Systems Analysis?

The reason for studying systems analysis can be summed up in the occupational history of the United States. In the 1800s we were an agricultural society dominated by farmers. By the 1900s we had moved into an industrial society dominated by labor and management. By the 1950s we had moved into a service-oriented society where service-based occupations offered the greatest employment. Today we clearly have moved into an information society that is dominated by computers, data communications, and highly skilled individuals who use brain power instead of physical effort. The Industrial Revolution allowed humankind to expand its muscle power through machinery. Today our information-based society allows humankind to extend its brain power through computers and communications.

In an industrial society the strategic resource is capital. In an information society the strategic resource is knowledge. Knowledge of systems analysis and system design is more important today than ever, as satellites and other communication networks are transforming the earth into a global city. In other words, the compression of time that is achieved through high speed communications allows us to be in immediate contact with all other companies or governments and to utilize business information in an extremely timely manner. For this reason, systems analysts (those who design systems) not only will be in great demand, but they will need to know the process or methodology of designing business or government systems. The systems you will design will require not only a knowledge of system design, but also many other sorts of knowledge, such as computers, programming, basic business fundamentals/practices, data communications, database file structures, accounting/finance principles, and depending upon the specific industry, acquired knowledge in areas such as manufacturing, chemicals, and the like.

In an information society, dominated as it is by computers and communications, *value* is increased by knowledge as well as by the speed at which that knowledge moves. The mainstream of our information age is communications. It follows, therefore, that the value of any system you design would be zero if the high speed data communication network collapsed.

Finally, the transition from an industrial to an information-based society means that you will have to learn many new technologically based skills. Instead of becoming a specialist in a certain subject and working in that area for the rest of your life, it will be necessary to adapt and possibly retrain yourself several times during your lifetime. It is the rapid expansion of technology that produces premature obsolescence, thereby forcing you to retrain yourself. For that reason, the study of systems analysis is a basic tool that can be applied during this training and retraining process. Your knowledge of systems analysis can be incorporated into several careers such as programmer, business system application designer, business or government manager, and so on. Even basic job tasks in our society now require technical knowledge in the use of computers and data communications. Once the basic skills of systems analysis are learned from this textbook, you will need to keep up with state-of-the-art systems technology for the remainder of your working life.

Definition of Systems and Procedures

A *system* can be defined as a network of interrelated procedures that are joined together to perform an activity or to accomplish a specific objective. It is, in effect, all the ingredients that make up the whole. A *procedure* is a precise series of step-by-step instructions that explain

1. What is to be done.
2. Who will do it.
3. When it will be done.
4. How it will be done.

The procedures tell how the ingredients are made into the whole. Systems are often classified into the following two categories.

A *closed system* is one which automatically controls or modifies its own operation by responding to data generated by the system itself. For example, high speed printers used with computer systems usually have a switch that senses whether there is paper in the printer. If the paper runs out, the switch signals the system to stop printing.

An *open system* is one which does not provide for its own control or modification. It does not supervise itself so it needs to be supervised by people. For example, if the high speed printer used with computer systems did *not* have a switch to sense whether paper is in the printer, then a person would have to notice when the paper runs out and signal the system (push a switch) to stop printing.

Another common example of this concept is the household furnace. One with a closed system (see Figure 1-1) has a thermostat that automatically switches the furnace on when the temperature goes below a certain degree or off when the temperature goes above another degree. By contrast, an open system furnace (see Figure 1-2) is a wall heater that an individual switches on when cold or off when warm. The former (closed system) is mechanically controlled on an automatic basis, while the latter (open system) is controlled by an individual as circumstances suggest.

A twentieth-century example of an open versus closed system that affected everyone's life was dramatized in the movie *War Games*. The decision to be made

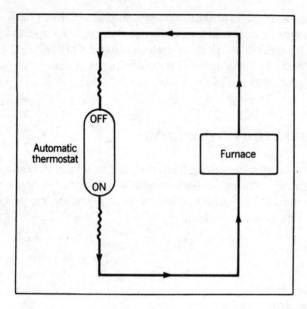

Figure 1-1 A closed system with a thermostat that automatically switches the furnace ON and OFF.

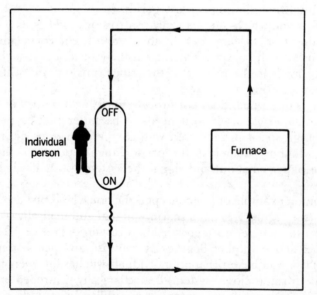

Figure 1-2 An open system showing a person that switches the furnace ON and OFF.

was: Should we launch nuclear missiles, and if so, what will trigger our launch? In the movie's first system, two human beings had to make the final decision and launch the missiles after receiving all the appropriate codes. They were instructed on the steps or procedures to follow in order to launch a nuclear-tipped missile. It was an *open* system in which the missiles would not be launched if these two individuals did not carry out their tasks. The second system that was implemented was a *closed* system in which there was no human intervention. After feeding in the secret codes and meeting certain other requirements, the computer would automatically, and unquestioningly, carry out the set of procedures to launch the missiles.

Notice, in the closed system the decision to launch the missiles was made automatically once certain conditions were met. The missiles were launched and could not be called back. In the open system, by contrast, the two people who were to carry out the procedures to launch the missiles could decide at the last second not to launch them. We could discuss indefinitely why these individuals might not act, but let us say they had information that was not programmed into the computer of the closed system and, therefore, chose to make an exception by not acting. Of course the purpose of our example is not to discuss nuclear warfare but to dramatize the difference between an open and a closed system.

In order to apply the open and closed system theory to computer-based systems, consider the following alternative approaches that could be taken in designing portions of an inventory system. In an open system (see Figure 1-3), the normal sequence of events might include

□ Customer order for parts received.
□ Computer-based system processes order to
  −update inventory master file, and
  −produce report of parts on hand.
□ Clerk reviews report and decides whether additional parts should be ordered.
□ If more parts are needed, clerk prepares a purchase order for additional parts.

In a closed system (see Figure 1-4), the normal sequence of events might include

□ Customer order for parts received.
□ Computer-based system processes order to
  −update inventory master file,
  −determine if current inventory level is below minimum level that should be maintained, and
  −automatically produce purchase order for parts if needed.

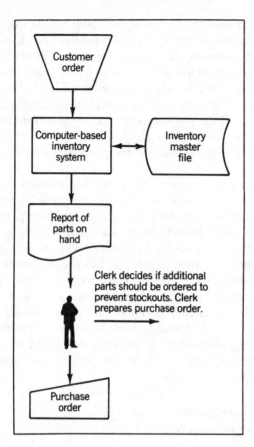

Figure 1-3 An open computer-based inventory control system showing a clerk deciding if additional parts should be ordered to prevent stockouts.

In the open system example, the control over inventory level is manual, based upon the clerk's review of the report of parts on hand. In the closed system example, the computer-based system automatically controls the inventory level by referring to a predefined reorder point for each part.

The difference in principle is the important point here. A systems analyst should consider the opportunities offered by each operation of a system for application of the closed technique, and also should understand that the open variety is appropriate to many operations.

For example, some operations in a system may have little bearing on the probability of retaining a customer's continued goodwill and business, such as the operation that routes the customer's order to one clerk or another for processing. The customer does not care which of 15 clerks fills the order, so the operation that makes the choice can be a closed type of decision generated somehow by the mechanics of the system on the basis of appropriate criteria. On the other hand, the operation that provides the customer with a special discount

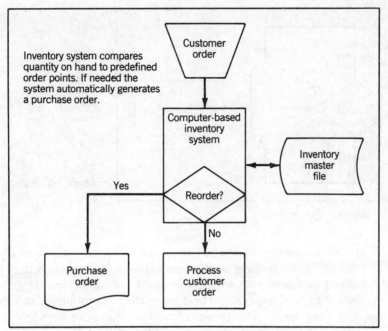

Inventory system compares quantity on hand to predefined order points. If needed the system automatically generates a purchase order.

Figure 1-4 A closed computer-based control system in which the computer program determines if additional parts should be ordered to prevent stockouts.

or other preferential treatment may be one which should have the benefit of human judgment added. It probably is an operation that should be supervised by responsible employees of the firm using the open system category.

Fully closed systems are still rarities. In the earlier example, a fully closed furnace would be one in which the temperature never varied above or below a set comfort zone. This comfort zone would be determined at the time of installation, when a program would be written instructing the computer to maintain temperature within the specified range. Progress made in the past 10 years indicates a high probability that in the future we will be able to rely significantly upon the computer for many of the decisions now supplied by people. The systems analyst plays a vital and exciting role in this transition.

Definition of Systems Analysis

Systems analysis is the process of analyzing a system with the potential goal of improving or modifying it. In other words, systems analysis involves the study

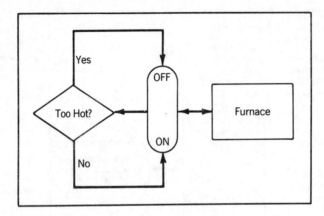

Figure 1-5 System decision point.

and design of something (a system) in order to modify it, hopefully for the better. Take the term systems analysis and dissect it. *Analysis* is the process of breaking down problems into smaller elements for study and, ultimately, solution. A *system* is a set of interrelated and interacting component parts that, when put together, function to achieve a predetermined goal or objective.

The systems analysis approach to a problem differs from a trial-and-error approach. The *trial-and-error approach* involves identifying a number of potential solutions to the problem and then testing each randomly until one alternative appears to provide an acceptable solution. In the *systems analysis approach,* all major influences and constraints are identified and evaluated in terms of their impact on the various decision points in the system. A *decision point* is that point in a system at which some person or automatic mechanism must react to input data and make a decision. A decision point may be seen in the previous Figures 1-1 and 1-2. In Figure 1-1 the thermostat is a decision point. For example, the thermostat makes the decision on whether the furnace should be turned on or turned off, depending on the temperature setting of the thermostat and the temperature in the room surrounding the thermostat. In Figure 1-2 the individual makes the decision whether the furnace should be turned on or turned off. In this case the thermostat functions only as a switch and not as the decision point. Therefore, in the systems analysis approach a system is designed around the various decision points. The system itself conveys the information or material between the different decision points and it determines the criteria with which to make the decision. Figure 1-5 shows a system decision point. The decision point is whether it is too hot or too cold, regardless of whether that decision is made by an individual or made automatically by a thermostat.

Decision points are shown in Figures 1-3 and 1-4. In Figure 1-3 the decision point is represented by the clerk's manual review of the parts on hand report to decide if additional parts must be ordered. In Figure 1-4, the decision point is embedded within the inventory system itself, which makes the decision automatically on whether to order additional parts.

As another example, a hospital's X-ray processing system would be designed around its key decision point: the doctor's evaluation of the exposed film and the alternative actions available to the doctor at that point.

A third example might be a business system used by a major stock brokerage house. As orders to buy or sell various financial instruments (stocks, bonds, commodities, certificates of deposit, government securities, and the like) arrive from individual brokerage offices around the world, a computerized system reviews them and makes various decisions automatically. Suppose an order to buy stocks is entered from the San Diego, California office. It is transmitted over the data communication network to the brokerage firm's central computer system in New York. The computer application system must look at the order and decide (the decision point) whether this is a commodity order that should go to the Chicago Wheat Exchange, a stock order that should go to the New York Stock Exchange or the Over-the-Counter (OTC) markets, an order for an industrial bond/municipal bond, an order to deposit money into a bank money market account, or an order to purchase a government security, such as a Treasury Bill. Notice that the computerized application system has to make some instantaneous decisions because this order still must be forwarded to wherever the financial instrument is traded. As you can see, you will be identifying decision points during the design of any system throughout your career as a systems analyst.

To properly understand a decision point in one system it usually is necessary to understand how other systems within (or even outside) the organization interact with and affect the decision point. As we will see, many outside influences can converge on a single decision point, which is often the reason for its existence. The decision point is a main focal point in the system. The systems analyst works to identify all such decision points. The analyst also attempts to ascertain their significance in relation to the objectives of the system before beginning any efforts to improve upon the current system.

Another important relationship that must be understood is the interdependencies or interrelationships between different component parts of a system. One part may severely restrict another part of a system. Take, for example, your automobile. If the carburetor is not operating properly, it severely restricts the operation of the engine. Notice how one component part, the carburetor, affects the operation of the engine, which totally stops the operation of the entire "system" that is the automobile. In business systems you may find that changing one small part of the system can cause a certain piece of data or a report to be produced one day later than it was prior to your system change. This seemingly insignificant one-day delay could be compounded each month and become a new vexation at year end when government regulations require a certain report be issued 10 days after the first of the new year. The interrelationship between your change and the legal requirements for a specific report has caused a problem. The point is that in real life you cannot always get the answer out of a textbook. You just have to be very clever in seeking out and understanding the relationships between parts of any system you might be designing or redesigning. Do not worry at this point because you will become more accustomed to looking for relationships as you work through this course and as you gain experience as a systems analyst.

In summary, a PROCEDURE is a set of step-by-step instructions that explains how a SYSTEM operates. Within the system there are a number of DECISION POINTS at which either one action or some other action is taken as the information or material flows through the system from start to finish. In order to be effective, the analyst must be able to understand and analyze the existing system and procedures and design new ones when required.

The Systems Analyst

The systems analyst is a person who can start with a complex problem, break it down logically, and identify the reasonable solutions. The analyst can study an ailing system and produce superior alternatives. Or given some number of objectives, the analyst can devise systematic means of attaining them. The systems analyst views a systems situation in terms of its scope, objectives, and the organizational framework.

The *scope* of a systems project is its range. What boundaries will this study encompass? In other words, the boundaries or range are the breadth that the study will encompass. We refer to this as the scope of the study. For example, the scope of a systems project to redesign the payroll system might be limited to only a redesign of the check itself and the layout of the employees' pay stub. In this case, no parts of the payroll are changed except those interacting with the check and pay stub changes.

The *objectives* of a systems study are whatever the analyst is trying to accomplish. In other words, what do we want to accomplish with this new system design and how can it be accomplished within this *organization's framework?*

The analyst also views a system in terms of the *information structure* within which that system operates. It is very important that a systems analyst completely understands the information that is used in the current system as well as the information that may be used in a proposed system.

Another very important item for an analyst to consider in viewing a systems situation is where people are involved in the operation of a system and what they do. *The basic ingredient of a system is people.* If the analyst overlooks people, the system will not be as efficient as possible. The equipment employed in a system, the forms and reports used in a system, and the responsibilities assigned to each department involved in the system are all important items to a systems analyst. An analyst who overlooks any of the above items may be jeopardizing the possibility of a good system design. The primary responsibility of the systems analyst, therefore, is not only to develop systems that meet the objectives and goals of the entire company, but also to meet the objectives and goals of the individual departments that are involved with the specific system being designed. A good systems solution meets all of its objectives. An excellent systems solution meets all of its objectives and also is tailored both to fit comfortably within the organization's framework and to take advantage of existing human resources.

An analyst can work with manual or computer-based systems techniques to creatively modify the *status quo*. Later, in Chapter 18, we will discuss the details of the analyst's job description.

Although it is common for a systems analyst to know computer programming, an analyst works with programmers who are assigned the specific programming tasks in the project. The systems analyst is more like a general manager who determines the design of the overall system, obtains the necessary technical help—programmers, forms specialists, equipment engineers—and follows the system through design, implementation, follow-up, and re-evaluation.

The analyst needs some knowledge of computer programming techniques in order to communicate effectively with the programmers; an analyst needs to be able to understand why certain things can or cannot be programmed. On the other hand, the systems analyst *must* understand the complete nature of the work being performed by the people for whom the new system is being designed. The systems analyst often is the only true liaison between the two areas, data processing and user department. Each area speaks its own language or jargon and has its own techniques; the analyst serves both as interpreter and mediator. As such, the analyst must be open-minded and willing to learn new things. Most important of all, the analyst must have the ability to deal with people at all levels of the organization.

Systems analysts will tend to perform more programming as fourth generation prototyping languages proliferate. Fourth generation prototyping is software that allows the analyst to simulate a new system and develop models of the input formats (video screen or paper), the processing, the database, and the outputs. With prototyping the user actually can see the system in operation and modify it to best fit the organization's needs. Fourth generation prototyping is described completely in Chapter 7. The use of prototyping will further eliminate the "communications gap" between business user departments and technical data processing. Another trend that will help eliminate the "communications gap" is the advent of microcomputers and distributed data processing philosophies in which some computer processing is performed on departmental microcomputers. This moves data processing out to the user business area and places it under the control of the responsible line manager.

*R*elationship of the Systems Department to the Rest of the Organization

In today's world the systems department usually is more closely related to the use of computers than to manual systems methods; however, systems analysts are concerned with both. The success of a computer-based system depends largely upon the concise definition and documentation of the relationship between it and the manual systems with which it must interface.

If the firm has a computer, the systems department may or may not have the responsibility for its use and management. There is no hard and fast rule about which department shall control the computer. In some firms the EDP (Electronic Data Processing) operation is a separate department and is considered a service organization operating for the benefit of all other departments. The systems department may operate separately on the same theory, or it may be an adjunct operation of the EDP function. Still other firms have the EDP operation under the accounting department, the industrial engineering department, or as an arm of administration. The organizational location of the EDP function probably can be traced in many cases to the first department that showed management it had a need for a computer. The need for a systems department has often not been determined until after an EDP function has gone awry. For this reason, independent systems departments are still relatively new.

Whether the systems department exists as a separate entity or as an activity within another department, it is a staff activity that renders service to all other departments. It advises and assists, rather than directs.

In today's environment, the most common location for a system design department is within the information systems department (electronic data processing department). In looking at Figure 1-6, you will see a generalized organization chart for a firm. The highest level is the Board of Directors, under which is the President of the firm. Then there are five Vice Presidents: sales, manufacturing, finance, information systems, and personnel. In our organization chart, we have expanded the detail only for the information systems department. Notice it has various organizations, such as data communications, systems design, programming, computer operations, quality assurance, and database. Each of these functions would have several employees with a supervisor or manager. Now, getting back to our hypothetical systems design department, this is where the individual systems analyst would report in the formal organization structure. Please avoid feeling that this is the only type of organization that can exist. We know of one organization in which the manager of computer operations was placed at a level equal to the vice president of information systems. In this unique case the manager of system design also was elevated to the vice-presidential level. The departments that remained within information systems

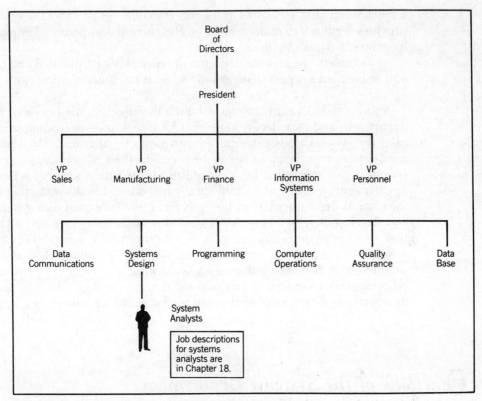

Figure 1-6 Organization chart (Figure 13-4 shows another organization chart).

then were divided between these two individuals. The guiding philosophy was that computer operations is more like a factory production environment because its function is running computer jobs and getting the output back to the business' user departments, whereas system design was a more creative, state-of-the-art task that should be separated totally from computer operations. The point is that location of the system design department may vary by organization. Figure 1-6 depicts a somewhat conservative relationship of the system design department to the rest of the organization.

The systems department can become a powerful influence in the firm because of its comprehensive involvement in most areas of the organization. It often holds the magic power of the computer, and is "in the know" about most long-range plans. The department's activities cut across organizational boundaries, because systems do. It cuts through interdepartmental networks, and involves itself in the detailed mechanics of the firm's operations. It provides management with the real-world means of implementing its plans and dreams. It also serves as a mechanism that seeks to ensure the effective use of the EDP resource and provides feedback to management on the current and potential impact systems have on the organization.

Nevertheless, the systems department remains a staff function and can design and implement systems changes only when it has authorization from line managers.

Another relationship that must be discussed is the one between the system department and user departments that have their own microcomputers. In this case, the systems analyst designs a business system that not only is used by the user department, but also is run by them on their own microcomputer. This system is not controlled by a centralized information system/data processing department. In fact, this technologically based trend really is starting to modify the systems department. User business areas now hire their own systems analyst and develop their own system design and programming capability. This means that you, the systems analyst, may be employed by a centralized information systems/data processing department, or you may be employed by an individual user business function within a major firm or government organization. Microcomputers have fostered distributed data processing, which in turn fosters distributed personnel and distributed responsibilities for designing new systems.

Functions of the Systems Department

The principal responsibility of the systems department is *systems design*. But to effectively perform this broad function, it should have strong influence in the following areas

1. The integration of information processing activities and the functions that need to be performed throughout the organization.
2. Forms design and control, such as the design of multicopy paper forms or the design of forms that are printed directly off laser/microcomputer printers, and so forth.
3. Procedure writing and procedure manual control, such as designing new procedures, printing them, and distributing updates to procedure manuals.
4. Records management, such as determining how long records should be kept, how to store them, and the method to be used for destroying obsolete records.
5. Report control, such as determining which output reports are necessary and when they might be eliminated or modified.

6. Office layout, such as redesigning floor space and work flows.
7. Work simplification studies, such as simplifying manual tasks in order to gain more efficiency and control.
8. Design systems using traditional or structured techniques.

Another function of the systems department is to perform a "needs analysis." Many times a business department knows that its system is not functioning adequately, but it does not know why or how to fix it. In this case the business department asks the systems design department to provide an analyst who can conduct a needs analysis to determine what is wrong with the current system and how to solve the problem. Basically this involves problem definition and solution proposal, although the solution may be that a full scale systems study be performed. You may think this sounds like a feasibility study, and if you do, you are right. A needs analysis is similar to a feasibility study, although it does not have to be identical. (Feasibility studies are discussed later in this chapter.)

The Systems Situation

Systems abound in nature and appear to be an essential characteristic in all things. In business and government organizations there are hundreds if not thousands of systems that, when operating together, are the corporation or government agency. No approach to organization could be more natural or rational than a systems approach.

Human organization can be viewed as a network of interdependent systems designed to perform the activities vital to human existence. If we had a static world and perfect systems, this book could end right here. But, of course, we live in an ever-changing world where "perfection" is a vague and moving target.

Our formal organizations, our businesses, government, hospitals, and so on, require a framework of systems and procedures to guide them in their day-to-day operations. In short, we live in a world of systems, whether they are biological or man-made.

Many resources may be combined for the effective operation of a system. But the most important ingredient is people—the people who operate the system and the people who use its output. Unless the system has the support of its operators, it will not work as intended. And even when it has user support, it will collapse if it fails to satisfy the needs of its users.

One of the resources of today's system is data processing. In order to meet the challenge of a world of changing business conditions, the systems analyst has learned to rely heavily on data processing as a resource for more effective and efficient handling of business data. In the past, some companies experienced significant difficulties because of ineffective use of this vital resource. In these cases, however, the fault often was with the people who determined how the data processing resource was to be used. If they set unrealistic goals, had an inadequate understanding of what was needed, or could not obtain cooperation, their efforts were doomed to failure.

Obviously, then, the human factor is a vital one in systems design. The men and women who design our systems must design them for human operation and benefit.

Every manager is responsible for systems because having systems is basic to being a manager. Each manager in an organization employs systems to carry out organizational objectives. And within each system there usually are sets of subsystems called procedures to guide the manager's team in its efforts.

The systems and procedures found in today's organizations usually are based upon a complex collection of facts, opinions, and ideas concerning the organization's objectives. In many cases, however, the systems and procedures have not been well defined or documented, and represent a collection of informal working practices. The complicated and multipurpose orientation of today's business firm makes it difficult for its members to all agree on how things should be done. Thus we may encounter departments working at cross purposes, or managers who are unable to cooperate with one another's approach to things. Unity of purpose becomes more difficult to achieve because effective communication deteriorates as the number of organizational members increases.

For example, interdepartmental competition (working at cross purposes) may not be all bad. Sales staff want low prices and ready availability of products. Manufacturing staff want long production runs that are efficient, along with complete availability of parts. Finance staff want to carry little raw goods inventory and a minimum inventory of finished goods. Personnel staff want happy, satisfied workers. Shareholders want high earnings per share. Notice, all of these goals are somewhat at cross purposes. Although there is no perfect answer to this, the correct construct might be a mild amount of tension among all the managers of the above-mentioned areas. In the final analysis you, as a system designer, are the one who must try to give all parties enough of whatever it is that will make them happy. This is the balance that you must define or achieve. The final answer to this problem cannot be learned from a textbook. You must work it out yourself by using your academic background, real-life experience, and by listening to the mandatory and wish-list requirements of each of the parties mentioned above.

For an organization to survive, it must learn to deal with a changing environment effectively and efficiently. To accomplish the making of decisions in an uncertain environment, the firm's framework of systems and procedures must be remodeled, redefined, and tailored on a continuous basis.

It often falls upon the person who is charged with designing a new system in the firm to perform the work in such a way as to redefine and refine the firm's objectives, sometimes on a very broad scale.[1] Fact must be sorted out from opinion and each used in its place. The vital must be separated from the trivial. Most important, the analyst must continue to ask *"What are we trying to accomplish?"* Only when this question is answered will a systems design effort make sense. Systems should be aimed realistically at the achievement of legitimate objectives of the organization, or they become wasted resources. In the following chapters we will discuss in detail the methods the analyst uses to develop realistic, goal-directed systems and procedures.

*P*hilosophies of Systems Design

When using structured systems analysis and design techniques, one of the key philosophies that a systems analyst must understand is the difference between logical and physical "things." The dictionary will not help you much with this distinction because with regard to "logical" it says "according to the principles of logic." With regard to "physical" it says "pertaining to material items." What you need to understand is the conceptual difference between logical and physical, rather than specific meanings. You probably already have a feeling for this concept; but let us discuss it in detail so you thoroughly understand the difference.

As an example, let us use your telephone; it has both a physical and logical address. The physical address of your telephone is where the instrument is located, your house. In order to install telephone wires between the telephone company and your house, the telephone company must know your physical address, such as 520 First Street, New York City; when the installers arrive, you show them into which room the wires will go. Your telephone is now physically installed and it has the physical address of 520 First Street. The logical address of the telephone is your telephone number, such as 555-1234. Notice, you could move to a new house that is relatively close to your current one and the telephone company would be able to change your telephone's physical address (move the telephone wires from your current house to your new one). In this case you could maintain the same logical address because they still could give you the same telephone number 555-1234. This is the difference between the physical address (location) and the logical address of your telephone.

Finally, let us relate the words physical and logical to a system as you will do when using structured analysis and design techniques. Suppose you are going to

---

[1] Firms have goals and objectives. Policies are used in order to achieve these goals and objectives. The systems analyst writes procedures (step-by-step instructions) that detail the activities required to carry out the policies. A network of such procedures constitutes a system.

describe a system. Your *logical description* would be a presentation of *what* the system is or should be doing. Therefore, the logical aspects of your system are almost the same, whether the system is a manual one or a computerized system. On the other hand, a *physical description* would show *how* the job is being performed, such as the people who are involved, forms used in a manual system or microcomputers used in a computerized system, and so on. Remember, logical descriptions describe *what* the system does, whereas physical descriptions describe *how* the job is done.

In structured analysis and design, logical and physical models of a system are built by using data flow diagrams (described in the next chapter). A *model* is a pictorial or graphic representation of a system. Using data flow diagrams, a model of a system can be developed that shows the data flows between processing steps (manual or computerized), and the various points at which data is stored and/or retrieved.

The aim of a system is coordination of managerial efforts toward the goals of the firm. The systems study must go beyond the simple paperwork studies and simple procedures. It must go far enough to include the philosophy, the objectives, the policies, the interactions, and the management thinking within the firm. It should harmonize with the style of the individual firm. By observing all aspects of the firm's organizational structure, objectives, other systems, and legal requirements, the analyst is more likely to design a system that will be accepted and used.

A system has as its objective the coordination of actions involving people, equipment, time, and money; and it should produce results such as these.

1. The right information furnished to the right people, at the right time, and at the right cost.
2. Decrease in uncertainty and improvement of decision quality.
3. Increased capacity to process present and future volumes of work.
4. Ability to perform profitable work that previously was impossible.
5. Increased productivity of employees and capital, and reduced costs.

A system may be viewed in terms of information flowing between departments. The information is continuously being recorded, processed, summarized, used, stored, and discarded. This information flow is the life blood of an administrative system. The information is necessary for making decisions and plans. It is necessary for initiating and directing actions as well as for comparing results against plans. Information also may be an objective in itself (for example, the information compiled for reports to the government).

It is important that we clarify the difference between data and information. *Data* is a general term used to denote any or all facts, numbers, letters, and symbols that refer to or describe an object, idea, condition, or other factors—such as a name, address, telephone number, or a list of such items. *Information* is

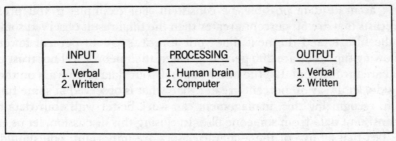

Figure 1-7 Basic input/output cycle.

a meaningful assembly of data, telling something about the data relationships—such as how many names are in the list, or how many persons live in a certain area, and so on. In essence, information can be derived from data only to the extent that the data are consistent, accurate, timely, economically feasible, and relevant to the subject under consideration. *Data processing* usually refers to the conversion of data to information.

Every systems operation consists of input, processing, and output. An *input* is the energizing element that puts the system into operation. The next activity is *processing,* which transforms the input into an output. This processing activity may be performed by an individual, by computer, or both. The *output* is the purpose for which the system was organized. Figure 1-7 shows this process, which is called the *Input/Output Cycle.*

*D*esirable Characteristics of a System (CATER)

The system should provide information that is Consistent, Accurate, Timely, Economically feasible, and Relevant. These characteristics *CATER* to the needs of the organization in which the system is used.

Consider the importance of these five characteristics. For example, information that is consistent can be trusted and utilized once a working relationship is established between the manager involved and the systems analyst preparing the information. In fact, consistency may be the most important of these five characteristics because business information is seldom totally accurate. Business information usually contains some opinions, estimates, and judgments. Business information is not the same as weighing something on a scale where a perfectly accurate answer is obtained; therefore, if the analyst is always consistent in his or her optimism or pessimism, management can learn to trust the information by applying its own "fudge factor" to the analyst's information. This does not downplay the accuracy of your data, the timely presentation or movement of your data, the economic feasibility of utilizing your system, or the relevance of your data to the problem at hand. It only says that while you are trying to obtain the most accurate data possible, be consistent. For example, if you present sales forecasts that are 50 percent greater than the final result observed some months in the future, and the next time your forecasts are 40 percent lower and the following time they are 200 percent greater, then people will not trust your data. You are inconsistent. On the other hand, if your data are always on the optimistic side, let us say 50 percent greater than what is observed at some future time, then, recognizing this, management can work better with your data than with inconsistent data from someone else. In closing this discussion, let us emphasize the fact that all five of these characteristics are important; you should strive to obtain the highest standard you can with regard to all five of them.

Other characteristics of a good system are that it

☐ Establishes standards so you can write procedures on how to do the job.
☐ Specifies each area's responsibility so that individual managers will be accountable for the work they manage.
☐ Delineates actions and decisions so the logical system can be designed with the proper physical system hardware, software, forms, and/or manual interfaces.
☐ Is easily understandable so the people who utilize it on a day-to-day basis can perform their work effectively and efficiently.
☐ Provides evaluation criteria with which to judge its performance.
☐ Identifies the decision points so the proper decisions can be made in the work flow progress.

A system must be acceptable to the organization's managers. Equally as important, it must be accepted by the people engaged in its operation. As already mentioned, the system must harmonize with company style, policy, organization structure, and external requirements imposed by custom or law. The system must also be compatible with other systems in the firm in order for it to be accepted and used.

A well-planned system has a foundation of sound procedures, and is designed and assembled in such a way that the system can be easily adjusted to changing conditions. Flexibility should be built into a good system because its environment is dynamic and not static.

*T*echnology's *Effect upon Systems Analysis*

When you go out into the operating departments of the organization to gather general information and to learn about the interactions between departments, you will find that many of the areas already are dominated by such items as microcomputers, management information systems, data communications, and database systems. While one could write a book on the numerous impacts technology has had on systems analysis, these four are the most significant. For example, the low cost and high computing power of microprocessors has started the rapid movement to distributed data processing systems. Management information systems are quite revered for their ability to facilitate decision making, as are decision support systems. Data communications allows us to interconnect or "network" our microprocessors. Finally, databases allow us to combine our data in ways never before envisioned. The following five sections, Microcomputers/Distributed Data Processing, Data Communications, Database, Management Information Systems, and Decision Support Systems will give you some insight into these very important technologically based areas.

Microcomputers/Distributed Data Processing

Ever since Intel's introduction of the microprocessor circuit chip, the microcomputer has grown to be one of the 10 or so top inventions of the twentieth century. This is because a microprocessor chip, which is the heart of a microcomputer, can control and/or run manufacturing processes, financial systems, business operations, and even augment human decision making.

A microcomputer is a small computer. Computer application systems started out on large, mainframe computers. Then a minicomputer industry was born that was dominated by a series of smaller, less powerful, and less costly computers than the large mainframe or host computers. Finally, the microprocessor chip inaugurated the microcomputer industry. Microcomputers started out as 8-bit machines[2] and have quickly moved up to 32-bit wide machines, just like their counterparts in the large minicomputer and mainframe computer world. As we see more 32-bit microcomputers that can both internally process data 32 bits at a time and transfer data into and out of themselves 32 bits at a time, we will truly have desktop computers with the power equivalent to a mainframe computer.

Today, microcomputers are establishing an entirely new concept on how much a data processing machine should cost. When you are in the information gathering phase, it is not appropriate to obtain descriptions of all the different computers that are available, nor should you cost-justify the purchase of one. At this point in your systems study, however, you might encounter microcomputers that have been installed in the various business departments that will be utilizing the new system currently under development. The impact these microcomputers might have on your system design would be in the areas of local processing, distributed data processing, and files of data.

With regard to local processing, you may find that your system design may

[2] Reference to 8-bit or 32-bit means that internal data transfers and input/output data transfers use 8-bit or 32-bit word size.

have to incorporate some of the data processing work that is done in the local department using its own microprocessor. The result of this processing then would be transmitted to the organization's central computer system (the mainframe). This may involve you in the development of numerous small computer systems for each department that has its own microcomputer. This also means that you may have to understand several different pieces of hardware, software, and/or programming languages because of the different microcomputers that are in use.

If, as described in the previous paragraph, you have to design a system that has many different microprocessors, you really may be looking at a distributed data processing function. In other words, instead of designing one system for a central mainframe computer that will be utilized by all departments of your organization, you may be designing many small localized data processing systems that will be hooked together, over data communication circuits, in order to consolidate or summarize the data processing into one centralized reporting system. A distributed system implies that we are distributing the responsibility for a business function out to that business manager; along with it *may* go the responsibility for data processing with regard to that business function. If this is the case, you will have to be clever in order to be successful because each local business manager will want his or her own system designed the way he or she sees best. Your task then will be to extract managerial compromises in order to design a way to connect the entire system together so that each of the microcomputer-based distributed systems will integrate into an overall system that serves the entire organization's policies and long-range goals.

Now that you see how local processing and distributed data processing are affected by microcomputers, you must think about the files of data. Usually, files of data are kept at a centralized site and each business organization within the company or government agency can access its information and update it as appropriate. Microcomputers, along with their inexpensive and high capacity hard disks, may move us into the world of distributed data files. The impact of technology will be easy to determine but more difficult to implement because the question is . . . do we allow each individual department with its own microprocessor to create and maintain its own files of data? Or, on the other hand, do we still maintain a central file structure where all data files are kept in central data processing but accessed by networking together the various microcomputers? Questions like these cannot be answered in a systems analysis textbook because they depend upon such factors as the desires of the organization (centralized or decentralized management); whether microcomputers, data communications, and software packages are available; personal and political opinions of the business managers involved; and outside influences such as what the competition is doing.

This section is not intended to describe what a microcomputer is or how one works. The intent is to demonstrate the close interactions between microcomputers, data communication networks, database file structures, and distributed data processing, which is the end result of all of these items working together. The next four sections expand upon data communications, database management systems, management information systems, and decision support systems.

*D*ata *Communications*

Data communications[3] describes a part of the overall system that permits one or more users to access a remotely located computer or terminal. Some questions that should be considered when designing a data communication system follow. First, what is this communications system to do for the organization? For example, the information system might be used to link together the various users and the database in a management information system, or it might be for data retrieval only, such as in an airline reservation system.

Second, consider the number of points to be involved in the transmission of information. This is when the analyst decides where to place the various locations of the input/output terminals. These terminals may be located within one plant or between two or three plants or geographically separated by hundreds of miles.

Third, the volume or total amount of information that must be transmitted within a given period of time should be considered. The analyst determines the total traffic for each terminal by taking into account the type of message, how many messages are to be transmitted, and the average number of characters per message. When this information is broken down into the number of bits per hour, it can be decided which type of communication equipment to use. For example, communication lines (telephone lines) are rated in the number of bits per second that can be transmitted over them. Other equipment such as modems and terminals also are rated as to the number of bits per second that can be transmitted over them. (This is a complicated technique and would require an entire book to do it justice.) It is with this information that the analyst decides what type of terminal is required, what type of modem is required, and what type of telephone lines are required. When deciding on the type of terminals, modems, and telephone lines, the analyst should take into account the company's future growth because it is almost always more desirable to buy or lease equipment that is able to handle next year's communication load rather than redesign the system next year.

A fourth consideration is urgency. How urgent will the messages be? Will high priority messages slow low priority messages? Will the system be able to

---

[3] See *Business Data Communications: Basic Concepts, Security and Design*, by Jerry FitzGerald (New York: John Wiley & Sons, Inc., 1984).

handle peak loads such as a large number of requests between 9 A.M. and 10 A.M. if that is when a large number of requests is expected? Will the system be used more because it is both available and quick (this is called the turnpike effect)? Will errors in the transmission of data cause so much retransmission of the same data that it either slows or stops the flow of data from a centralized database to the user?

The fifth consideration is whether operators of the individual terminals can learn the operational procedures easily and quickly. This is extremely important because if the managers who are supposed to use the system cannot quickly and easily interrogate that system through their terminal, the system will not be utilized to its fullest extent.

In summary, the data communication system is a link that connects a user to a centralized database. The analyst must determine what the communication system is to be used for, the number of terminals or points involved in the system, and the volume of information that is to be transmitted over the system. All these factors are put together in order to determine the type of equipment to be used. This is an extremely important link in any management information system or information storage and retrieval system because when the data communication link breaks down *no one* has access to the centralized data files.

Database

The *database* is the heart of any information system. It is the centralized master file of basic information that is available to any authorized person within the firm. A database should provide for rapid retrieval of accurate and relevant information. A database is a set of logically connected files that have a common method of access between them. They are the sum total of all the data that exist within the organization or within a specific department. It is essential that the database satisfy the requirements of each organization that depends on it. If it does not, each organization will continue to maintain its own information system, thus defeating the purpose of the centralized database. The key element in this concept of an information system is that each organization utilizes the same database in the satisfaction of its day-to-day information needs. The data within the database must be retrieved easily. Computer programs must be written to enable quick retrieval of the requested data.

The advent of telecommunications has enhanced greatly the ability of data processing to provide a timely service to users. It is through the on-line database systems that data processing can process and disseminate management information when it is at its peak decision-making value.

A database can be viewed as a centralized collection of all data that relates to one or more applications. The technological advances in direct access hardware technology have provided capacities and speeds that allow the data for many applications to share the same physical storage device. As a result, the cost and complexity of data redundancy can be eliminated by having multiple applications use a common, single source of data.

Once the ability to integrate the data was available, it was necessary to be able to structure data in a manner that would meet the processing requirements of each user application.

It probably is best to begin with a few definitions of data. The most basic piece of data that cannot be broken down into more detailed units is called a *data item,* a *data element,* or a *field.* Combinations of these data items, data elements, or fields make up *data structures* (also referred to as a record). For example, a meaningful set of data items is called a data structure. Also, several data elements grouped together may be referred to either as a record or a data structure. In order to simplify our discussion, we will use the terms data elements and data structures; a data structure consists of one or more data elements that offer some logical business meaning. It is helpful to remember that a data structure also can consist of another data structure and some data elements.

There are three basic ways of organizing the data within a database. Remember that the data in a database is organized in a manner that allows retrieval and use of that data by anyone needing it, hopefully, in any desired combination of data elements. The organization of the data also should ensure that there is a minimum of redundant data (the same data element occurring in two or more different data structures). The three ways to organize data are in hierarchical, network, and relational databases. Figure 1-8 shows a picture of each of these three database organizations, but you should read the following paragraphs for a description of each type as you look at the figure.

Hierarchical or tree organized databases are composed of a hierarchy of nodes. In our figure, each node is represented by a small circular symbol. Also, you should note that each of these nodes in a database really is a data structure containing whatever number of data elements are required for the data structure. In a hierarchical database, the relationship is a parent-to-child relationship. In other words, each child node (data structure) can have only one parent node (data structure). Because of this, data stored in the lower level nodes of the hierarchy can be accessed only through the parent node.

Network or plex organization allows for any child node (data structure) to have more than one parent node (data structure). In this way, data stored in the lower level nodes of the network organizational structure can be accessed by any one of several parents, which may be one or two levels higher in the overall network structure.

Relational databases are defined as a flat file (relation) in which each data structure or record (tuple) is unique because it has the same number and type of data elements. Basically a relational database looks like a table or two-dimensional matrix. Each of the nodes (data structures) that are in the hierarchi-

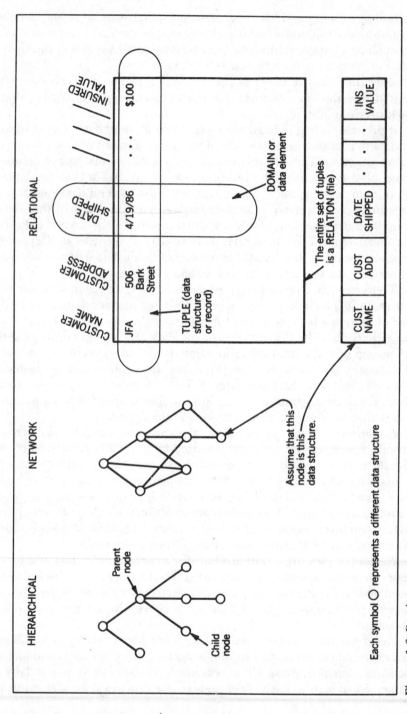

Figure 1-8 Database structures.

cal or network database are placed into a two-dimensional table or matrix. For example, we have assumed that the lowest level node of the network organization in Figure 1-8 is a seven data element, data structure. This is shown below the relational organization. Now you can see that each data structure (node) in the hierarchical or network organization would be flattened into a two-dimensional table. Therefore, relational databases are nothing more than many two-dimensional tables that can be retrieved and joined together to deliver the necessary data to the system user.

Notice that the terminology changes. In relational databases, a data structure or record is called a *tuple* (this rhymes with the word couple). Also, each vertical data element on our table is called a *domain*. Finally, the overall table that contains all of the data structures or tuples is called a *relation*. In the past we looked at this as a file. When looking at relations as a file, remember, that it may take several data structures joined together to comprise a complete record; therefore, a relation may be comprised of a set of data structures or records. If you find this confusing, it's understandable because the definitions overlap with one another. In the past when we used simple, discrete magnetic tape files, we always had records that contained fields or data elements, and the sum of all the records was a file. Now, because of direct access devices and database organizational structures, we have data elements that make up data structures. We also have data elements and data structures that may be joined together to make up other data elements or records; but, you also can have several data elements that are joined together to make a record or data structure. Therefore, what comprises a file becomes a blurred distinction.

Although this is not a course in database design, we have presented these three organizational structures because you will need to define all of the data structures and, therefore, all of the data elements that will be used in the new business system you are analyzing and designing.

Management Information Systems

A *management information system* (MIS) is a system that provides historical information, information on the current status, and projected information, all appropriately summarized for those having an established need to know. The information must be provided in a time frame that permits meaningful decision making at a nonprohibitive cost. It is a communication process in which data are recorded and processed for further operational uses. A MIS is a system that collects, processes, stores, and distributes information to aid in decision making for the managerial functions of planning, organizing, directing, controlling, and staffing a business organization. Management information systems include functions such as information storage and retrieval as well as all of the aspects of data communications. A management information system can be looked upon as the binding together of the entire organization into an effective integrated flow of information. MIS allows an information channel to serve as a means of improving day-to-day operations and future planning. Management information systems are built using

1. People, who are needed to operate the system.
2. Data processing, which provides the needed speed for information sorting and classifying.
3. Data communication, which is required in order to keep the information flowing between the different parts of the system and the people using the system.
4. Information storage and retrieval, which is required in order to store the information in its proper format and to make sure that the information can be retrieved when it is needed.
5. Systems planning, which is required in order to integrate the people, the data processing, the data communications, the information storage and retrieval, and the users of the system into an overall meaningful and well-organized management information system.

A management information system should provide information that is Consistent, Accurate, Timely, Economically feasible, and Relevant. Information with these characteristics will CATER to the needs of the user. A well-designed management information system should meet the needs of both the entire organization and each component part of the organization, and have a minimum of duplication of the stored data. It can provide reports to management that would not be feasible by other methods, and also provide them with more speed and more accuracy.

The attitudes at all the levels of management usually have to be reoriented to the fact that, when information is put into a central database, everyone who has a need to know in the organization will have access to that information. This eliminates individual pockets of information strategically located throughout the company. In preparing management for a new MIS, it may be necessary to overcome a constant fear on the part of many managers who feel they will be losing status or control. As with any other system, involving the individual manager in the project is the best method of gaining the needed cooperation.

MIS is like any other system in that it, too, needs to be evaluated in terms of its effectiveness. Answers to the following questions can help the analyst determine the effectiveness of the MIS system. Does management still make profuse use of hunches even though there is a centralized database and a management information system? Does the information from the MIS fit the plans or objectives of the organization? Does management seem to have confidence in the accuracy of the information disseminated by the MIS? Does the information meet the responsibilities of each individual manager? Are the data presented in a format that is easily understood by its users?

In summary, many organizations have computer-based systems for payroll, accounts receivable, inventory control, billing, and various other corporate activities. Very few of these organizations have fully integrated management information systems that have consolidated all these data from the independent computer-based systems into one database available to all authorized personnel. For the analyst, the future shift is away from individual computer-based systems and into improved systems designed for integrated management information systems that contain a computer-based database for management use in day-to-day business activities and for use in future planning.

Decision Support Systems

Decision support systems (DSS) are those systems that allow a manager to ask various questions that might be answered in a real-time manner based upon data stored in the databases and various, quite unique, programs to manipulate the data and re-ask questions of the manager. Decision support systems utilize fourth generation prototyping tools, high speed data communications, graphic presentations, system simulation models, and dynamic mathematical models.

Many developers refer to decision support systems as artificial intelligence (AI) or expert systems. Question and answer decision support systems using artificial intelligence can be used quite readily by physicians when diagnosing illness as the symptoms are explained, by financial analysts when analyzing various companies for prospective investment, and by lawyers when trying to determine which past precedents would affect a current legal case.

Critical to decision support systems is a knowledge base. Experts in a field are interviewed extensively, not only for facts but, more important, for a sense or understanding of the subject in which they solve problems. These general principles for solving a problem are built into various programs. They drive what is known as an inference engine, allowing the computer to make intelligent and reasoned decisions utilizing the knowledge base in the database. It is these programs containing the general principles (heuristics) that distinguish the "smart" computers from our run-of-the-mill number crunchers. Management of a large organization can use decision support systems to predict future operating results or to predict sales/marketing/inventory amounts based on given conditions supplied by experts and stored both in databases and computer programs. A disgustingly simple decision support system is the (not too intelligent) spreadsheet producing software that we use on microcomputers. A more expensive decision support system might be an economic model of the economies of the world that has a second economic model of the United States within it. This decision support system might allow us to make some predictions, based on "expert knowledge," about the interaction of the products of our company with those of other companies in the United States and throughout the world.

In summary, we might point out that decision support systems contain some sort of artificial intelligence that can make rudimentary decisions. The previously discussed management information systems (MIS) only supply the necessary data to the human decision maker, who then applies the intelligence and thus arrives at a decision. A decision support system actually can make the decision, even if it is a simple one.

What Is the "Area Under Study"?

As the systems analyst, you must attempt to determine the organizational levels that will be affected by the system design study. The purpose in doing this is to help you set the various objectives and scope. Determining the organizational levels affected by the study also offers a general road map as to the different management levels with which you may have to interact.

Your system study may involve only a small system in an obscure area of a company or government organization. Or, it may involve a system that affects the company or government organization at the highest level of management and encompass the entire firm or branch of government.

Figure 1-9 shows the five levels that may comprise the "area under study."

After looking at Figure 1-9 turn back to compare it with Figure 1-6, the organizational chart. A comparison can be made because in Figure 1-9, Level I involves the Board of Directors or President, as shown in Figure 1-6. Level II involves the Vice Presidents of sales, manufacturing, finance, information systems, and personnel. Level III involves the various departments, such as those listed under the information systems division: data communications, system design, programming, computer operations, quality assurance, and database. Level IV involves a functional area within a department, such as a functional area within the system design department. A functional area could be the training of systems analysts, the design procedures of the analysts, or the methods of documentation used by systems analysts. In other words, a functional area (Level IV) is a sub-department within a department. Finally, Level V is depicted by a specific problem within a functional area. This could be something like the office layout with regard to how documentation is stored, where the working systems analysts are seated, or the location and size of the training room for the systems analysts.

As you can see, these five levels help identify the physical areas of the company that you might need to visit. In other words, it is another use of the concepts of logical and physical. The logical division of the areas under study are

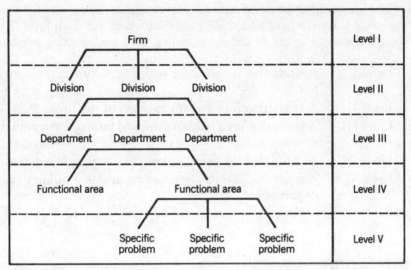

Figure 1-9 Area under study.

listed as Levels I through V in Figure 1-9. These logical subdivisions then assist you in finding the physical locations that interact and indicate the people who must be interviewed. These five levels are summarized as follows.

Level I. A problem that involves the entire organization—all its divisions and locations. Decisions on this level can have great economic and directional weight. The stakes are high. Management personnel require superior quality information. All decision points require critical treatment.

Level II. A problem that involves one division of the firm; a little less demanding, but conceptually similar to Level I. Much integration is required between the division level and the firm level.

Level III. A problem that involves departmental interaction within a firm. This is the middle management area where most systems studies are performed. Information is usually more technical and specialized here than at the division or firm level. The tasks of planning, organizing, and controlling are very detailed at the lower levels of the organization.

Level IV. A problem that involves the functions within one department. The activity to be studied is easily defined and understood. Only a small close-knit group is involved. The problems are usually easy to identify but difficult to resolve. Individual personalities and human relations play a big role at this level.

Level V. A problem that involves one specific problem within a function of a department. This is usually the smallest area studied in an organization. The problem is a specific one and is usually lacking in specific data. Only a limited number of people are involved.

The analyst must be conscious of the level which a study will affect because the nature of the objectives and tasks will be different for each level. The analyst should always be aware of the scope of the "area under study." In summary

Level I   A study that involves the entire firm—all its divisions and locations.

Level II   A study that involves one division of the firm.

Level III   A study that involves departmental interaction within the firm or division.

Level IV   A study that involves the functions within one department.

Level V   A study that involves one specific problem within a function of a department.

Feasibility Study

A *feasibility study* is undertaken to determine the possibility or probability of either improving the existing system or developing a totally new system. Something that is *feasible* is something that can be accomplished. It is feasible if it is possible within the given context and is competitive with other potential solutions.

During a feasibility study, you look at things such as *operational feasibility*. In other words, whether it is feasible to operate this system in our organization's environment. For example, is it possible to introduce an entirely new system, given our current employees? Or, is it reasonable to add an entirely new function to the workload of an already overworked staff? Incidentally, the first question recognizes that it is human nature to resist change. It is entirely possible that a new computerized system could be disastrous if current employees are fearful of computers and/or unwilling to learn about them. It is not feasible to fire an entire staff and hire all new employees. Another aspect might be *economic feasibility,* in which you examine the cost of building and operating the system with regard to what the organization can afford. Finally, you have to determine *technical feasibility.* That is, whether we are able technically to build this new system with today's environment and state-of-the-art. For example, you certainly would not have been able to build a system that required satellite data communication transmission in the year 1850; it would have been technically infeasible. Another question with regard to technical feasibility involves the required timing of the project. For example, a company may plan to implement some procedure, but because there are higher priorities, it may decide to defer this particular procedure because it involves different types of equipment than capital budgets can afford. Then one of its regulating agencies decides that this deferred procedure must be implemented by a particular date. This does not change the fact that the company does not have capital funding to purchase the necessary equipment. The procedure still is technically infeasible as far as the company is concerned. In this case, a stopgap measure may have to be utilized in the interim, until the company can implement a more desirable method. Notice that this situation is not only technically infeasible but also economically infeasible.

The feasibility study is used by management as a tool to evaluate the practicability and probable cost of developing a new system, which may not have been needed in the past but which is required now to deal effectively with the changing demands of the business environment. As we stated in the previous section of this chapter, the feasibility study is performed *prior* to embarking on the 10 steps of the system development life cycle. (These 10 steps will be defined in the next chapter in Figure 2-1, the system development life cycle.)

There are two types of feasibility studies. Up to this point we have been discussing a feasibility study that is performed before the new system development process begins. This type of feasibility study delineates the operational, financial, and technical feasibility of embarking upon a new system development project.

There is another major type of feasibility study that may be performed. This is a feasibility study to determine whether a new computer or new software package should be purchased. Feasibility studies to evaluate purchasing hardware or software usually are handled through a process known as Request for Proposal (RFP).

An RFP is written by an organization to request proposals; it is distributed to various hardware or software vendors, depending on whether the organization wants to buy hardware, software, or both. The vendors respond to the proposal and the organization evaluates their bids. Finally, one of the vendors is chosen and that piece of hardware or software is obtained. Also, the organization has the right to refuse all bids and purchase nothing. For your information, this method of using RFPs is described in Chapter 10, with a complete RFP shown in Appendix 3.

Other examples of types of questions a feasibility study can address are: What is the feasibility of putting certain manual data records into an on-line real-time format that would provide instant access by users who need this data? What is the feasibility of reselling some of our data communication network capacity in order to offset some of the costs of the network? What is the feasibility of giving user departments microcomputers so they can do some of their own data processing locally? What is the feasibility of this distributed data processing environment operating adequately after microcomputers have been placed throughout the organization? Notice that none of the above examples address the issue of *how* these things will be accomplished once the decision is made. Feasibility studies address the issue of the practicability or workability of doing something. Look at Figure 1-10. Four examples of typical business situations are shown, along with some of the types of questions addressed by a feasibility study and the

Typical Feasibility Study	Typical Areas to Examine	Constraints

Relocate to a new site	Review operations—which ones would be most affected by move
	Review financial aspects of move
	  Advantages
	  Disadvantages
	  Incentives
		Lease terminates
		Expansion assumptions

Build a civic center to revitalize the downtown area	Center's financial goals
	Markets to be served
	  Conventions
	  Trade shows
	  Consumer shows
	  Minor events
	Competition from other facilities or nearby cities
	Projections of new and repeat business
	Potential developers
		Community support
		Physical site location
		Financial risks
		Cost to develop

Market a new product	Sales potential of product
	Financial returns vs. cost to develop
	Market analysis
	  Description of market
	  Past demand
	  Present demand
	  Projected market share estimate
	Technical analysis
	  Product description
	  Product features
	  Required equipment/plant to produce
	  Cost of land
	  Cost of plant construction
	Financial analysis
	  Financial projections of costs
	  Financial projections of revenues
	  Return on investment projections
	  Sales collection forecasts
		Undesirable by-products
		Community opposition to project
		Limited development funds
		Uncertain economic climate

Need a computer	What areas would benefit? What areas would provide greatest return on investment? Would it provide needed controls? What areas would be affected adversely? Quantifiable benefits Effect on operations Effect on staff Effect on cash flow Buy or lease	Costs Staff size Availability of needed technical expertise

Figure 1-10 Typical feasibility studies and representative areas of analysis.

constraints that may affect the go/no go decision. Notice that it is quite possible that the feasibility study can demonstrate that what is desired is not workable.

Why Conduct a Feasibility Study?

A feasibility study in some form always should be conducted prior to any commitment to a large or long-term investment or change. The impact of proposed major changes must be weighed carefully because there is usually a great deal at stake. The consequences of a major change are not all felt at once. Instead, these consequences tend to unfold, for good or ill, over some period of time after the commitment is made. The impact of unwise capital expenditures, for example, can be disastrous. A firm buys another plant, only to realize later that the plant is not adaptable to the work that management thought could be done there. Such a consequence might have been foreseen if a formal feasibility study had been carried out in order to delve into the details.

Of course, our focus is systems, an area rich in the opportunities offered by the application of feasibility studies. The failure of the plant in our example above might easily have been caused by its system's inflexibility, or by a prohibitive cost required to install needed equipment and procedural routines. The right forms, the right computer system, the right personnel, and so on, are all things that must be anticipated *before* an irreversible commitment is made—or the firm may find itself in serious functional and economic trouble. Consider the airline which commits itself to a computerized ticket reservation system without a feasibility study appropriate to the size and importance of the investment. This is a dangerous road to travel. The surprises are certain to include many unhappy ones; perhaps, for example, the system quickly becomes inadequate to process increased business volume. At this point the system becomes "infeasible," and the airline probably loses its competitive ability to instantly confirm plane reservations. There may be no economical solution to such a problem and the firm may fail as a result. The feasibility study offers management the opportunity to deal with such contingencies in advance.

A well-done feasibility study enables the firm to avoid six common mistakes often made in project work. These are

1. *Lack of top management support.* Top management has to understand and support subordinate managers in their efforts to improve the firm's operations. Feasibility studies also get subordinate managers directly involved in exploring and designing the systems they will have to live with in the future. Such involvement results in increased conscientiousness, which in turn enables top management to have more confidence in subordinates' plans. The result will be top management support for such plans.

2. *Failure to clearly specify problems and objectives.* The feasibility study can be directed toward defining the problems and objectives involved in a project, after management has given the group some understanding of what they would like to accomplish.

3. *Overoptimism.* A feasibility study can be conducted in an objective realistic manner to prevent overoptimistic forecasts. The study should be conservative in its estimates of improved operations, reduced costs, and so on, to ensure that all the firm's future surprises with a new system are happy ones.

4. *Estimation errors.* It is very easy to underestimate the time and money involved in the following areas
   a. Impact on the company structure.
   b. Employees' resistance to change.
   c. Difficulty of retraining personnel.
   d. System development and implementation.
   e. Computer program debugging and running.

5. *The crash project.* Many managers do not realize the magnitude of work involved in developing new systems. Crash projects usually involve changing too quickly. A feasibility study might determine that a present system, with all its inadequacies, is superior to a crash project—assuming, of course, that the feasibility study itself is not run as a crash project.

6. *The hardware approach.* Firms have been known to get a computer first and then decide on how to use it. A feasibility study can identify, in advance, the uses to which the computer will be put and can identify the best computer for the job *before* any irreversible commitments are made.

How to Conduct a Feasibility Study

A feasibility study can be viewed as a "minisystems study" because it is preliminary to, and smaller than, a full systems study. Any feasibility study can be expanded to a full systems study if the estimated benefits are sufficient to warrant the systems study. If the feasibility study is expanded to a full systems study, the analyst will be expected to carry out the 10 steps presented in Chapters 3 through 12 of this book. These are the chapters that explain, in detail, the procedures to be followed through to completion of a full systems study.

The first order of business in conducting a feasibility study is to determine the nature and extent of the problem or problems as accurately as possible. The two main objectives of a feasibility study are first, to identify the true problem, and second, to identify a feasible approach to solving this problem. In defining the problem you must determine the subject, scope, and objectives of the feasibility study.

The *subject* is the central theme or topic that will become the problem definition. The subject of your feasibility study is the problem that you hope to solve.

The *scope* is the range, or the boundaries, of the entire study. You decide here what will be included or excluded from the feasibility study.

The *objectives* are a clear statement of what you want to accomplish. The objectives are the goals. For each objective, you should specify who is responsible for achieving the goal, how it will be achieved, what conditions may prevent success, and who will monitor the successful achievement of this objective.

If at this point you feel somewhat insecure about the subject, scope, and objectives, do not be concerned because they will be discussed in more detail at the time we cover problem definition in Chapter 3.

Incidentally, it is important that you arrive at some agreement with the managers who will be affected directly by the study, on its subject, scope, and objectives. This is important because they will be looking at your subject/problem definition in terms of their own perceptions. They also will be looking at your statement of objectives and judging whether your final feasibility study report actually met those pre-stated objectives.

Develop a To Do list that will serve as your outline or blueprint of what is going to be done in order to carry out this feasibility study. A *To Do list* is nothing more than a complete list of all the tasks or steps that you want to perform.

The following is a recommended sequence of steps to follow when conducting a feasibility study. As you conduct this feasibility study, stay flexible; modify this sequence of steps or add other steps that are appropriate within the organization for which you are working.

1. Interview key personnel to get facts about the problems they are having, or the changes and improvements they would like to see. Try to put a finger on the *real* problem and its causes. This can often be very difficult since it is natural for people in certain positions to become quite defensive if they feel you are prying. Although it is often not possible, it is good to try not to criticize a person directly. Try, instead, to focus on events rather than on personalities. Of course, all criticism should be as constructive as possible. Also, try not to assume excessive authority or status. You are there to help the people, not hurt them—and you must show them by your manner that you are trustworthy of their time and confidence. It is best to interview the key line managers first. If a line manager has staff assistants, interview them next; and, finally, interview the supervisors and clerical employees. It is often best to work from the top down; but the order can be changed to fit the situation. As in all systems work, flexibility is the key word here. This order is not always possible, nor is it always desirable. In some cases, it is

best to interview a key manager's staff assistant first in order to prepare for the interview with the manager.

Interviewing may well be your single most important tool. In other words, you must be able to conduct interviews well if you are to be a successful systems analyst. For that reason, we also cover interviewing in more detail in Chapter 3. When you realize that a feasibility study may be looked upon as a minisystem study, you can see that many of the feasibility study techniques are exactly the same as those conducted during a full system analysis and design project. As you will see later, it would be too cumbersome to cover all of these techniques in this discussion of feasibility studies.

2. Study any written procedures that exist relative to the subject of the study *before interviewing the clerical employees*. This not only will save a lot of time in learning the mechanics of the operations involved, but also will minimize interference with the firm's routine operations. Ask the area's manager about any such written procedures during your interview.

3. Try to learn the informal (unwritten) procedures while interviewing and observing the work flows. You *may* develop a data flow diagram (DFD) or flowchart of these work flows during this phase. DFDs may help here because they depict *what* is being done rather than *how* it gets done, which sometimes gets personal and political. But be careful, because informal procedures involve personalities, and the quickest way to lose cooperation is to get people upset with your tactics. Again, the analyst should try not to criticize PEOPLE. You are there to help, *not* to enhance your own status or feeling of importance. Be objective, but friendly. Never carry an attitude of superiority with you because it will show for what it is, and may wreck the project. Remember, you probably will be dealing with these people for a while, and their cooperation will be *needed*. Start selling yourself as a helpful, friendly person right from the beginning because getting cooperation is half the battle in many projects.

4. Not only must the problem be defined, but its source must be determined. Redefine the problem in light of the facts obtained from this preliminary review. Reestablish the scope and objectives, if necessary, and perhaps switch from a feasibility study to a systems study if the problem is found to be different than originally thought.

Now organize your thinking about the subject, scope, objectives, and other conclusions, so an accurate picture can be presented to the line managers when you meet with them again. Remember they will be looking for your clear understanding of the situation, and will be making decisions about whether they can trust your interpretation and recommendations.

5. Meet again with the involved line managers and go over the findings and conclusions. Give them a rough estimate of solutions, timetables, benefits, and costs. Be sure to call their attention to any changes you think are

necessary in the subject, scope, or other objectives. This step is to keep management informed and to get their tentative agreement and approval on progress to date. One sure way to hurt the success of any project is to change the definition, subject, scope, or objectives and not let management know until late in the study.

Rule No. 1 is Do not spring surprises on line managers! Rule No. 2 is Never forget Rule No. 1. Therefore, if your study develops an "odd twist" or if there is some unusual financial calculation, it is advisable to talk immediately with the appropriate manager rather than keep it to yourself. Meet privately, in a face-to-face discussion, over any issue that might be embarrassing or an unpleasant surprise. Surprises usually are taken negatively. If you embarrass a manager in front of his peers, your business career may not advance as rapidly as you might desire. The rule to follow, therefore, is no surprises, no embarrassment.

6. With management's concurrence, finish the study by analyzing and estimating the costs of performing a full systems study. Study the manpower requirements and the time that will be required to develop a new system or to modify the existing system.

At this point you may have to develop an estimate of various costs for materials that might be used in the new system. You also may have to determine some costs regarding the purchase of computers and/or software packages. In Chapter 10 we present different methods of calculating costs and a methodology for developing Request for Proposals (RFPs) with regard to hardware and software purchases.

Another cost you may be asked to estimate is the cost of conducting a complete system study, along with the time frame required to conduct it. Management might ask for some cost estimates of a new system balanced against the future benefits that might be received from such a system. In other words, all the costs are compared to the potential benefits that might be gained from the new system. Such estimates are presented to management in a feasibility study report. This feasibility study report will have recommendations in it that may or may not lead to a full system study.

*F*easibility Study Written Report

The feasibility study written report is the documentation of the feasibility study. It is the medium by which you tell management what the problem is, what you have found its causes to be, and what you have to offer in the way of recommendations. The report should

1. Define the problem in such a way that it clearly demonstrates your understanding of the problem.

2. Clearly describe the subject and scope. List the areas included *and excluded*. State the level of detail pursued and explain modifications to the original study plan.

3. State the objectives and whether they were met or not. Are the objectives technically feasible? Are they economically feasible? Are they operationally feasible? Will the objectives, if met, result in a solution or computer installation which will fit within the current organization structure or will reorganization be needed?

4. Point out special attention areas, such as unusual situations or interrelations between problems.

5. Describe the entire system or study in detail. (This is the body of the report. It is here that you must put your thoughts across.) You will want to include a description of both the existing problem and the proposed problem solution. Write a logical explanation of why you think a full system study is necessary. Alternatively, you might have found that the solution is so simple that all you need to do is make a logical explanation of the problem solution.

6. List all of the economic cost comparisons and benefits.

7. State recommendations clearly. Explain the logic behind the recommendations.

8. Provide a suggested time table for implementation of the recommendations, with appropriate milestones identified.

9. Include an appendix that shows any flowcharts, data flow diagrams, graphs, pictures, floor plans, or layouts not used elsewhere in the report.

Finally, if management accepts your recommendations, the next task is either to embark on a complete system study, drop the project (it was not feasible), or implement the final solution (it was a simple fix). Document your feasibility study well because someone else may be assigned to the full systems study.

In summary, because the feasibility study is a minisystem study, you need to use many of the tools and techniques of the full system study. It may require development of a Request for Proposals in order to evaluate hardware/software selection and purchase. Never be tempted to shrug off a feasibility study as a simple "quick and dirty" task. It may be the benchmark upon which the next year or so of your working life is based; that is, if the feasibility study is the basis of a full system study. Once that happens, you have moved into the system development life cycle that is presented in the next chapter and is spelled out, in detail, in Chapters 3 through 12.

*O*rganization *of This Book*

Take time now to examine Figure 1-11, the reading flow diagram. In it we present the relationships between the chapters in this textbook. You can use it as

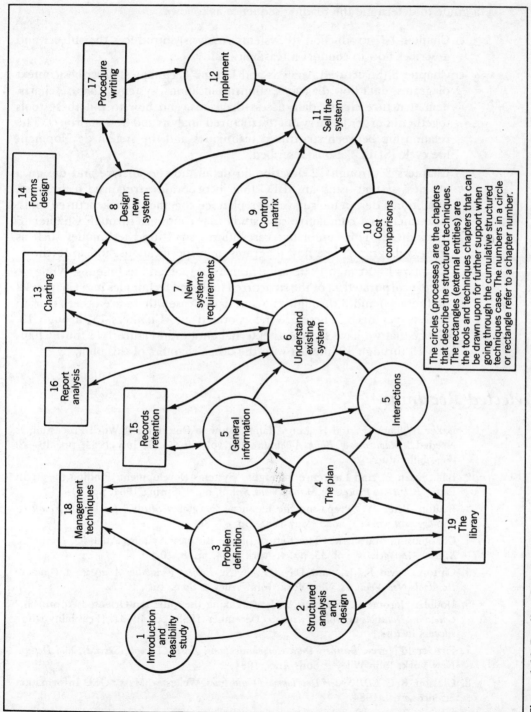

The circles (processes) are the chapters that describe the structured techniques. The rectangles (external entities) are the tools and techniques chapters that can be drawn upon for further support when going through the cumulative structured techniques case. The numbers in a circle or rectangle refer to a chapter number.

Figure 1-11 Reading flow diagram.

a guide to determine the reading sequence as follows

☐ Chapter 1 (Introduction to Systems Analysis) introduces the subject and describes how to conduct a feasibility study.

☐ Chapter 2 (Structured Analysis and Design Techniques) describes context diagrams, data flow diagrams, minispecifications, system structure charts, data structure charts, data access diagrams, and how to put these tools together in order to carry out a structured analysis and design project. The relationship between structured techniques and the system development life cycle (SDLC) also is described.

☐ Chapters 3 through 12 describe, in detail, how to analyze and design a business system using an SDLC that incorporates structured techniques. Traditional design tools have been blended together with structured tools. Also, there is a cumulative case study that continues through Chapters 3 through 12. This cumulative case utilizes structured techniques such as context diagrams, data flow diagrams, minispecifications, and so forth.

☐ Chapters 13 through 19 describe numerous tools and techniques. While we have incorporated all of the structured tools and techniques into Chapters 2 (definitions) and 3 through 12 (cumulative case), there are others that an analyst may need. These are incorporated into Chapters 13 through 19. Notice that we have shown, as external entities in Figure 1-11, how Chapters 13 through 19 interact with the other chapters of this book.

Selected Readings

1. Baker, William H., and H. Lon Adams. "How to Determine if Word Processing Is Needed," *Magazine of Bank Administration*, vol. 60, no. 7, July 1984, pp. 36–42. [Feasibility study.]

2. Ball, Susan R., and Lawrence M. Light. "Systems Development: Finding the Right Path," *ICP Data Processing Management*, vol. 9, no. 1, Spring 1984, pp. 30–32.

3. Bruton, Peter W. "Preparing the Financial Feasibility Study," *Healthcare Financial Management*, vol. 13, no. 5, May 1983, pp. 87–88.

4. Christenson, Marvin R. "The Return of the Business Systems Analyst," *Journal of Systems Management*, vol. 35, no. 4, April 1984, pp. 8–10.

5. Clifton, David S., Jr., and David E. Fyffe. *Project Feasibility Analysis: A Guide to Profitable New Ventures*. New York: John Wiley & Sons, Inc., 1977.

6. Doubler, Jerome L. "Systems Analysis: Taking the Question-Oriented Approach," *Canadian Datasystems*, vol. 15, no. 5, December 1983, pp. 40–41. [Feasibility study success factors.]

7. FitzGerald, Jerry. *Business Data Communications: Basic Concepts, Security, and Design*. New York: John Wiley & Sons, Inc., 1984.

8. Glasson, B. C. *EDP System Development Guidelines*. Wellesley, Mass.: QED Information Sciences, Inc., 1984.

9. Gorman, Michael M. *Managing Database: Four Critical Factors.* Wellesley, Mass.: QED Information Sciences, Inc., 1984.

10. Guttman, Gary. "Development Life Cycle Has 10 Milestones," *Computerworld,* vol. 18, no. 22, May 28, 1984, Special Report 42.

11. "Information Company Develops In-House Net," *Computerworld,* vol. 17, no. 13, March 28, 1983, Special Report 39–40. [Example of microcomputers impact at Zenith.]

12. Johnson, Bob. "Consultant Details 'Five Ws' of Needs Analysis," *Computerworld,* vol. 16, no. 43, October 25, 1982, p. 32. [Who, what, why, when, where.]

13. Moir, James B. "Project Methodology, Organization, and Structure," *Journal of Information Management,* vol. 5, no. 2, Winter 1984, pp. 22–38.

14. Naisbitt, John. *Megatrends: Ten New Directions Transforming Our Lives.* New York: Warner Books, Inc., 1982.

15. Shevlin, Jeffrey L. "Evaluating Alternative Methods of Systems Analysis," *Data Management,* vol. 21, no. 4, April 1983, pp. 22–25.

16. Skidwell, Joanne. "EDP: Improving the System Development Life Cycle," *CA Magazine,* vol. 117, no. 7, July 1984, pp. 62–65.

17. Weinberg, Gerald. *Rethinking Systems Analysis and Design.* Boston: Little, Brown and Company, 1982.

18. Wood, D. R. "The Personal Computer: How It Can Increase Management Productivity," *Financial Executive,* vol. 52, no. 2, February 1984, pp. 15–19.

19. Zells, Lois. "A Practical Approach to a Project Expectations Document," *Computerworld,* vol. 1, no. 35, August 29, 1983, pp. 48–61 (In-Depth pp. 1–16). [How to avoid feasibility study disillusionment.]

Questions

1. What dominates the information society?

2. Identify some of the other sets of knowledge (in addition to systems analysis techniques) that the systems analyst may require.

3. How is value increased in an information society?

4. What is the most important ingredient required for the effective operation of a system?

5. In today's organizations, what are the systems and procedures usually based upon?

6. How does the term "procedures" differ from the term "system"?

7. Explain the difference between a "closed system" and an "open system."

8. Define the term "systems analysis."

9. Define the term "decision point."

10. Why is it important to understand decision points in a system?

11. Why is it important to understand the interdependencies or interrelationships among different component parts of a system?

12. What is the primary responsibility of the systems analyst?

13. Identify some of the areas in which the systems department should have either centralized control or a very strong influence.

14. What does a "needs analysis" involve?

15. How does the logical description of a system differ from the physical description?

16. Identify some of the results that should be produced by a system that has as its objective the coordination of actions involving people, equipment, time, and money.

17. Define the terms "data," "information," and "data processing."

18. What desirable characteristics should the information produced by a system possess?

19. What level of systems analysis study requires both that all decision points necessitate critical treatment and that management personnel receive superior quality information?

20. In the context of a new system under consideration, define the term "feasibility study."

21. Define the terms "operational feasibility," "economic feasibility," and "technical feasibility."

22. How does management use the feasibility study as a tool?

23. What do you convey to management through the use of a feasibility study written report?

SITUATION CASES

Case 1-1:   Kelly's Housing Supplies

Alice Weiss, a recent college graduate, had just been hired as a systems analyst at Kelly's Housing Supplies. During her second day on the job, she was asked to perform a full systems study involving the order entry system. Because the analyst was inexperienced, she decided to sit down one afternoon to outline the entire sequence of events that would take place during the systems study.

Ms. Weiss decided to attack and carry out the systems study in the following manner. First, she would define the problem, because she knew a firm and concise problem definition would make it easier to devise an improved system. Next, an outline of the steps to be taken in performing the systems study would be undertaken. Then, she would obtain general background information on the areas under study. While in this phase, she also would endeavor to learn about the interactions between the areas being studied and the other areas of the corporation. The next step would be to define the requirements for the proposed system. This would allow her to understand what the new system must do in order to meet the current requirements of the firm as well as any future requirements. After defining the system requirements, Ms. Weiss planned a visit to each area to become thoroughly familiar with the existing system. She believed that such an understanding of the existing system would help design a better new system. Next, the analyst planned to assemble the problem definition, the definition of the new system requirements, and her understanding of the existing system in order to design a new system. This design actually would be the new system that would be presented to management.

The next step would be to sell management on the proposed system. To do this, the analyst thought she would first prepare a final written report and distribute it to all the management people involved. Then, after distribution of the final report, she would make a verbal presentation of the system. Finally, if management decided to install the new system, she would implement it (get it installed). The analyst realized she would have to go back after installation to do some follow-up work and some re-evaluation before the system project could be closed.

Question

1. Evaluate the sequence of events the analyst planned to use in performing the systems study. (*Hint:* use Figure 1-11 as a guide.)

Case 1-2: *Modern Office Products*

The Purchasing Department at Modern Office Products has been behind in its work for the past six months. The Vice President of Operations for the firm has decided to determine if the Purchasing Department needs more help or if there is a way to produce better results using only the current employees. To achieve this end, the Systems Analysis Department has been asked to assist, and an analyst has been assigned to the task.

The analyst's first step was to see the Manager of the Purchasing Department to discuss the problem. The manager felt that his staff was overworked and that he would need more clerical workers and a part-time worker until his department was caught up. He also wanted to know if it would be possible for the department to cut down on some of its "busy work" so that the staff would have more time to spend on current "productive" jobs.

After interviewing the Purchasing Manager, the analyst decided to initiate a feasibility study. The subject was too much work for the department to handle; the scope covered the entire department; and the objectives were to find out where the most help was needed and what work might be eliminated to lighten the workload.

The analyst arranged to talk with supervisors of each of the main areas in the Purchasing Department. During these discussions, he learned that each department of the firm developed its own purchase order form to send to the Purchasing Department. All the forms were different sizes, which made handling and filing a problem. The supervisors agreed they would like to see a standard form used.

The analyst then studied the written procedures of the department and found that five separate forms were filled out for each purchase order received. The purpose of these forms were: filing within the Purchasing Department, use by the Accounts Payable Department, acknowledgment of receipt for the sending department, copy for the receiving docks, and a final purchase order prepared for mailing to the vendor.

At this point, the analyst concluded that the paperwork for the department could be simplified, saving both time and money.

The analyst then interviewed the clerical workers and learned that they kept all incoming purchase orders for a period of two years, filing them by department name. He also found that they filled out another form for filing purposes. This one, used for the items purchased, was filed by the item's name. The analyst also noticed an office filled with filing cabinets and felt that some of the filing could be eliminated, thus saving both time and space.

The problem definition of the department had changed somewhat, so the analyst decided to change the subject, scope, and objectives. The subject was changed from too much work for the department to too much busy work within the department. The range was changed to encompass the filing and paperwork. The objectives were changed from finding where help was needed to eliminating much of the paperwork and filing.

The analyst met again with the Purchasing Manager. He pointed out that the department was preparing and handling too much paperwork, and estimated that 65 percent of the department's time was spent in filling out forms and another 25 percent in filing, leaving only 10 percent of the total time for research and preparation of the final purchase orders. He pointed out that the research was very important and was being neglected, with the result that the company was not getting the best buys on the goods it purchased.

The analyst then prepared a feasibility study written report from the information obtained in the study. He presented this report to the manager and his supervisors. The report included the definition of the problem, the subject, the scope, the objectives, a description of the study, and the recommendations he felt were needed.

The recommendation the analyst made was for a full systems study to standardize the incoming purchase order form, making one copy for Accounts Payable, one copy for the receiving docks, one copy for filing, and one copy for mailing to the vendor.

Questions

1. Was the report complete?
2. Did the analyst make his recommendation to the proper people?

Chapter 2

STRUCTURED ANALYSIS AND DESIGN TECHNIQUES

LEARNING OBJECTIVES

You will learn how to . . .

☐ Use structured tools during the system development life cycle (Figure 2-1).

☐ Develop context diagrams.

☐ Develop data flow diagrams.

☐ Develop data dictionaries.

☐ Normalize data structures.

☐ Develop data structure diagrams.

☐ Develop data access diagrams.

☐ Develop system structure charts.

☐ Develop minispecifications.

☐ Develop the system model.

Introduction to Structured Analysis and Design

Traditional systems analysis and design evolved over a number of decades, prior to the development of powerful computer systems. Many of these traditional techniques were developed by industrial engineers who were concerned with designing *things*. It was essentially a *physical* process. These techniques eventually were borrowed by people who designed business systems because there were no other tools available for them to use. As a result, we tended to think of business systems as moving pieces of paper from one person, desk, or file to another. This was not too far wrong until computers came on the scene.

During the early days of computers, when we were using batch systems, emphasis still was on the physical aspects, but we added tab cards and reams of computer printouts to our conceptual view of a business system. The computer was in the hands of programmers; no one else understood what it could do, much less its importance in changing how we view systems. We tended to think of systems as static. In retrospect, we now recognize that systems are, by their very nature, dynamic. That is, something always is happening in a system and outside forces sometimes require that it changes. When we viewed systems as static, we analyzed systems with such tools as flowcharts (which are discussed in Chapter 13). Flowcharts use symbols that imply sequential processing and *physical* attributes of a system. While these and other tools were acceptable to understanding movement of pieces of paper, files, and so forth, they were lacking as good communication tools for the analyst. During the analysis stage, the analyst had to make decisions as to whether storage would be on pieces of paper or tape, and inputs on disks, tape, or key entry, thereby forcing physical design decisions inappropriate to finding out *what* had to be done to make a workable system. In other words, flowcharts and similar tools do not deal very well with system logic that describes what needs to be done. Flowcharts stress *how* it is done.

During the mid-1960s, people who programmed the new and evolving computer systems needed readable and understandable code. As a result, structured programming was introduced. While this helped programmers, it still was not working toward the betterment of *systems* because it did not pull the system's parts together into a cohesive whole. By the early 1970s, people started using top-down partitioning, module development, and other conscious techniques to design flexible and maintainable systems. These techniques helped software development, but by the mid-1970s, we were seeing brilliant solutions to the wrong problems. Users found that their newly designed, expensive systems did not do what they wanted. Many of these systems were designed primarily by systems analysts and programmers, with little input from users after the initial stages. This is not too surprising because users were ignorant of what computers could and could not do. Further, users had difficulty conveying what they wanted and needed. Many of these albatross systems are still in existence because they cost so much to develop that people have been afraid to discard them.

Structured analysis came about during the late 1970s as a method of communicating more effectively with users during the entire system development life cycle. Done properly, it allows us to develop systems that are wanted by users and that can be used by them in an effective manner. Structured analysis begins with an examination of the broad picture of a system and progresses in a logical manner down to greater detail. By looking first at the overall picture, we can examine broad objectives without being hindered by details too early in the project.

We can define *structured analysis* as a systematic, top-down technique that refines goals and objectives that are presented by means of a layered model of system requirements. Put another way, it is an orderly approach that works from high-level overviews to lower-level details in which user needs are presented through the use of hierarchically arranged data flow diagrams. Structured analysis aids in defining the requirements of the new system so that users have a system they need and want. Think of structured analysis in terms of a pyramid that shows, from top to bottom, the system objective, an overview of what must be done, more detailed descriptions of what must be done, and very detailed design details of how it must be done in order to achieve the highest level goals (user objectives). Such a pyramid looks like this.

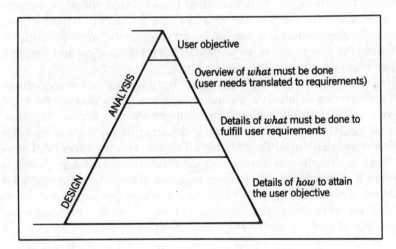

This model of system requirements is the criterion by which the success of the system is measured.

The end result of structured analysis produces a structured specification that uses several basic tools, which will be described later in this chapter. These tools are

- Context and data flow diagrams,
- Data dictionary,
- Data structure and data access diagrams, and
- Minispecifications.

The tools of structured analysis are logical models. *Structured design* is the physical implementation of these logical models, and it utilizes hierarchical partitioning of a modular structure in a top-down manner. It is the natural extension of the structured analysis process. In the context of a system development life cycle, we use *structured analysis and design techniques.*

As you will learn, analysis is a sizable part of a systems project. Because good analysis tools were not available until about 1981, we learned the hard way that less analysis means more expensive systems that do not meet user needs and that cost more in terms of long-term maintenance. The lesson of the 1970s was that it costs less to make changes early in the systems analysis, and it costs *much* more to make changes as design and implementation progress. Our goal is to design systems well during the analysis phase to avoid costly changes during design and implementation.

Another major problem during the earlier years of systems development was documentation. People tended to leave system documentation until a project was completed. At that point, they often became interested in other projects and documentation was left by the wayside. As a result, many of these systems could not be modified or maintained easily. When employees left, it often became a nightmare for others who took over their tasks because adequate documentation was not available for them to use. Since structured analysis is a self-documenting process, documentation is a natural by-product of the process. With this documentation, the system can be explained to others in a logical and understandable manner that was not possible previously.

The principal tools and documentation techniques that are used during structured systems development are context diagrams, data flow diagrams, data dictionaries, normalization, data structure diagrams, data access diagrams, system structure charts, and other processing documentation such as decision tables, decision trees, structured English, tight English, and pseudocode. Each of these is defined in this chapter and in our detailed cumulative case that is found in Chapters 3 through 12. We believe that you should first be provided with a simplified version of structured techniques before getting into the details. Before moving on to these structured techniques, however, we want to introduce the concept of the system development life cycle.

System Development Life Cycle (SDLC)

The *system development life cycle* is a methodology used to structure the application system development process, as well as any subsequent maintenance or enhancement activities, into a straightforward and easy-to-use development plan. The use of a system development life cycle establishes a standard sequence of steps with regard to development of all computer application systems, whether they are totally computerized or contain manual interface operations.

In our life cycle, we include the structured systems analysis and design philos-

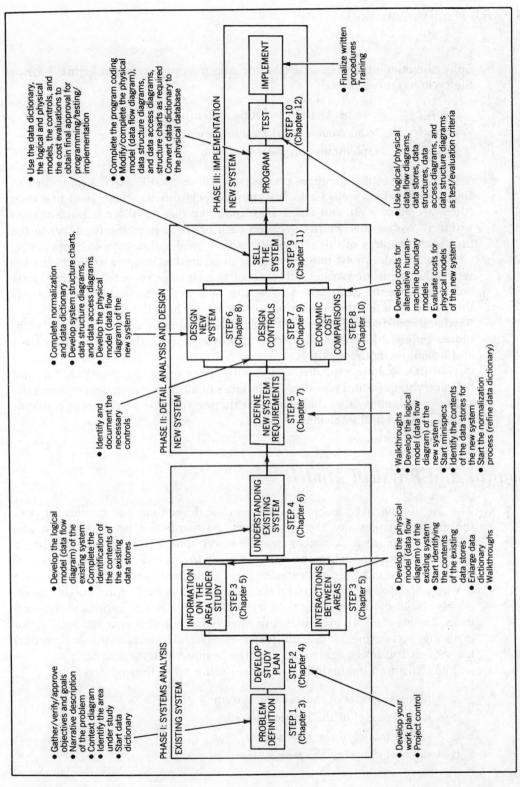

Figure 2-1 System development life cycle.

ophy (sometimes called structured techniques). As you can see in Figure 2-1, our life cycle has three phases

Phase I   Systems Analysis (existing system).

Phase II   Detail Analysis and Design (new system).

Phase III   Implementation (new system).

If you look within the three phases, you will see that Phase I is comprised of four individual job steps (tasks that must be performed), Phase II of five steps (these are Steps 5–9), and Phase III of one step that has three important tasks within it. Notice that we have related each of these steps (Steps 1–10) to the individual chapters of this textbook in which the detailed "how-to" appears.

Figure 2-1 also shows how the various structured techniques (structured analysis and design) interrelate with each of the 10 steps of our life cycle. These techniques are the descriptions related to each step in the figure. If you study this figure for a few moments, you can see that we have developed a straightforward and easy-to-use 10-step life cycle that incorporates all the structured techniques required for you to develop a new system using the structured analysis and design methodology.

Now that we have explained the importance of using structured analysis and design techniques, and how these techniques fit into the system development life cycle, we can move on to the techniques themselves. The first concept is that of logical and physical modeling.

Logical and Physical Models

The use of structured techniques involves the development of models for both the existing system and the new system. As mentioned previously, a model presents a picture of a system (see Glossary). The advantage of modeling a system is that the model can be changed easily to test different requirements of the system. For example, aircraft designers build models to test design features of wings, stability, air flows around the aircraft, and so forth. Automobile designers also build models of their vehicles so that they can test various design features. In this case, we are discussing models for business systems, such as for invoicing, accounting, or payroll. Just as the aircraft and automobile designers use models for design testing, so does the business systems analyst.

The structured methodology advocates using up to four models

☐ A physical model of the existing system
☐ A logical model of the existing system
☐ A logical model of the new system
☐ A physical model of the new system

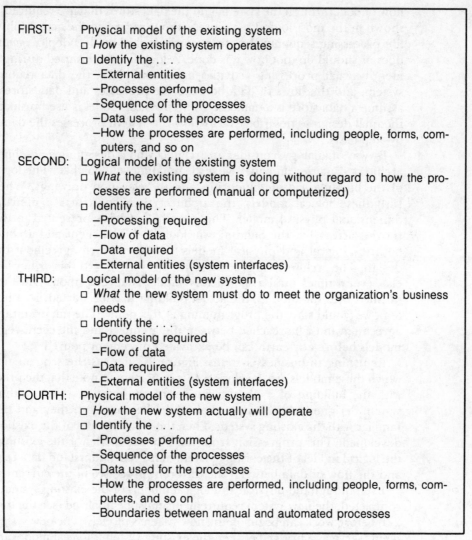

FIRST: Physical model of the existing system
       □ *How* the existing system operates
       □ Identify the . . .
        –External entities
        –Processes performed
        –Sequence of the processes
        –Data used for the processes
        –How the processes are performed, including people, forms, computers, and so on

SECOND: Logical model of the existing system
       □ *What* the existing system is doing without regard to how the processes are performed (manual or computerized)
       □ Identify the . . .
        –Processing required
        –Flow of data
        –Data required
        –External entities (system interfaces)

THIRD: Logical model of the new system
       □ *What* the new system must do to meet the organization's business needs
       □ Identify the . . .
        –Processing required
        –Flow of data
        –Data required
        –External entities (system interfaces)

FOURTH: Physical model of the new system
       □ *How* the new system actually will operate
       □ Identify the . . .
        –Processes performed
        –Sequence of the processes
        –Data used for the processes
        –How the processes are performed, including people, forms, computers, and so on
        –Boundaries between manual and automated processes

Figure 2-2 The four progressive models of structured analysis.

These models and what they accomplish are shown in Figure 2-2.

A *physical model* is a pictorial representation of the system showing how the job is performed physically, including the sequence of the operations, the people, computer processing, paper forms, and so on. The processing tasks are shown in the actual sequence in which they occur. A physical model should show *how* the processing is or will be performed. By contrast, a *logical model* is a pictorial representation of the system that shows *what* processes must be performed, the flow of data through the system, and the data stores that are required. These are shown in the most logical sequence without regard to the actual (physical) real-life processing sequence. In other words, logical models depict *what* the system does or should do, not how it is done. A logical model is used during analysis to identify what processing activities must take place, the data required by the system, and the flows of data between the processes and data stores (for now, assume a data store is a database). The physical model is used primarily during the final design to describe exactly how the system processes the data on a step-by-step basis.

By way of analogy, consider an architect who is designing a new building. The architect visualizes on paper what the building will look like. The logical models of the building are the blueprints and the elevation drawings. When satisfied with these logical models, the architect then constructs a miniature three-dimensional physical model. This physical model is presented to the client to show exactly what the building will look like. The client and architect discuss both the logical and physical models until they reach agreement on the final design. The architect may return to the drawing board (his or her logical models) several times until a satisfactory model is agreed upon. Once the client is satisfied with the models, the actual building may be started. In a business system, we would start the programming at this point. The important thing is that agreement must be reached between the architect and the client regarding the models before any earth can be excavated or cement poured.

Returning to business systems, Figure 2-3 depicts the sequential process in which these models are developed. It is important to note that the process begins with the building of a physical model of the existing system although some system designers skip this physical model because both they and the user are familiar with the existing system. Then the logical model of the existing system is developed. This progression from the physical model of the existing system to the logical model of the existing system helps you understand data requirements and the flow of data between the different processes in the current system.

Even though the physical and logical models of the existing system have been completed, the new system requirements must be finalized (see the top of Figure 2-3) before work can begin on the new system's models. The new system requirements serve as a bridge between the existing system's logical model and the new system's logical model. Without these new system requirements, there would be no difference between the existing and new logical models.

After requirements of the new system are defined, the next step in analyzing the new system is to develop a logical model for it. Notice how we have progressed down through Figure 2-2 (previous figure) to the third item. The logical model of the new system represents the data flows, processing steps, and data requirements without regard to the methods used to implement them. Finally, the physical model of the new system is developed to complete the understanding of the physical methods that will be used to implement the processing activi-

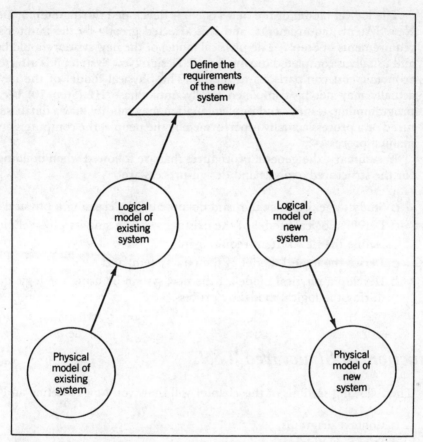

Figure 2-3 Progression from modeling of existing system to modeling of new system using structured techniques.

ties, data flows, and the sequence in which they need to occur in the actual real-life working system.

To relate this to the system development life cycle that was discussed earlier (see Figure 2-1), note that the physical and logical models of the existing system are developed during Phase I: Systems Analysis (existing system). The physical model of the existing system should be started during Step 3: Information on, and Interactions Between, the Areas Under Study. The logical model of the existing system must be completed by the end of Step 4: Understanding the Existing System.

As you move into Phase II: Detail Analysis and Design (new system), you have both the physical and logical models of the existing system to use as a basis for the development of your logical model of the new system.

The logical model of the new system is developed during Step 5: Define the New System Requirements, and it is affected greatly by the auditor's control requirements of Step 7. The physical model of the new system should be started and usually is completed during Step 6: Design New System; it is affected by the economic cost comparisons of Step 8. The physical model of the new system actually may not be completed totally until Phase III (Step 10) because the programming, testing, and implementation may modify how a database is structured or a process actually is performed by the people, the computer, and/or the manual processes.

In summary, the general procedures that are followed when building models for the structured analysis and design process are

□ Study the existing system and document it by creating a physical model,
□ Derive a logical model of the existing system using its physical model,
□ Define the new system requirements,
□ Derive the logical model of the new system, and
□ Develop a physical model of the new system by using the logic developed during the logical modeling process.

*I*ntroduction to Structured Tools

The following sections of this chapter will show you how to define and develop

□ Context diagrams,
□ Data flow diagrams,
□ Data dictionaries,
□ Data structure diagrams,
□ Data access diagrams,
□ System structure charts,
□ Minispecifications,
□ System models, and
□ Pseudocode.

We will not develop all four of the physical/logical/logical/physical models in this chapter. Instead, we want you to learn about context diagrams, the rules and methods for drawing data flow diagrams (DFDs), and how to construct and define data stores and data dictionaries. We are leaving the four models until our cumulative case (Chapters 3–12), in which you will see not only how the four models are developed, but also how to use many other tools that are complementary to the use of structured techniques.

Context Diagrams

The starting point of structured analysis is the *context diagram*. Context diagrams are constructed to show the highest level model of the system. This is the most general or broadest picture of the existing system. They are used to represent pictorially the scope or boundaries of the system, or what we call the *area under study*. Their purpose is to identify what is to be included in the area under study. They link the system to the rest of the world. In other words, the intent is to obtain a broad overview of what the system encompasses and what it does *not* encompass.

In order to illustrate how to construct a context diagram, let us consider the order processing activities of a direct sales mail order firm, Sunrise Sportswear Company. In a context diagram, the area being studied is shown as a single circle in the center of a diagram. In Figure 2-4, we see that the area under study is the circle marked ORDER PROCESSING SYSTEM. Notice that this does not say anything about whether ORDER PROCESSING is a manual system or a computerized one. That is because we are not concerned with manual versus computerized at this point.

The ORDER PROCESSING function is not an isolated island; it interacts with other entities, which are shown as rectangles on the context diagram. The scope of a system can be determined by identifying other entities which provide information to it and which receive information from it. Figure 2-4 shows that our ORDER PROCESSING SYSTEM must interface with CUSTOMERS, the SHIPPING DEPARTMENT, the ACCOUNTING DEPARTMENT, and SUPPLIERS. These areas outside our system with which we must interface are called external entities. An *external entity* is a source or destination of data. It can be a person, a supplier, a department, or another system that supplies data to, or receives data from, our system. External entities are shown as rectangles to distinguish them from the system under study.

By showing the interactions between the area under study (ORDER PROCESSING SYSTEM) and its influencing external entities, we can identify the flow of data between the ORDER PROCESSING SYSTEM and its external entities. These *data flows* are shown by lines with arrowheads indicating the direction of the flow. Data the system receives are called *inputs;* information or data it produces are called *outputs*.

Picture the flow of data between the ORDER PROCESSING SYSTEM and our CUSTOMERS (see Figure 2-4). What are the typical pieces of information

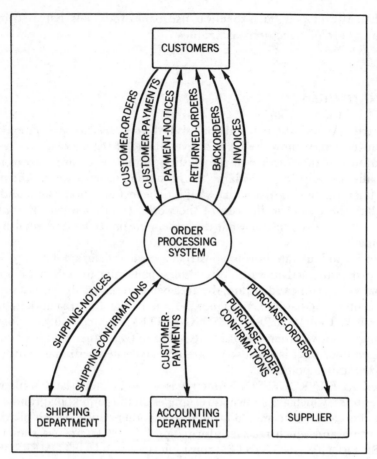

Figure 2-4 Context diagram of the order processing activity of
Sunrise Sportswear.

or data that move from the customers to the system and from the system to the
customers? Customers enter orders and make payments, while Sunrise Sportswear returns orders, notifies that the item has been backordered, and sends
invoices and payment notices. (Note that, for purposes of simplification, we are
not including merchandise movement in our example.) The other external entities also send and receive information. Sunrise Sportswear sends purchase
orders to suppliers, while suppliers send purchase order confirmations. The
Shipping Department receives shipping notices and sends confirmations. Finally, the payments received from customers are forwarded to the Accounting
Department.

Notice that these flows of information or data are indicated on our context
diagram (Figure 2-4). Inputs to the system are CUSTOMER-ORDERS, CUS-

TOMER-PAYMENTS, SHIPPING-CONFIRMATIONS, and PURCHASE-ORDER-CONFIRMATIONS. Outputs are PAYMENT-NOTICES, RE-TURNED-ORDERS, BACKORDERS, INVOICES, SHIPPING-NOTICES, PURCHASE-ORDERS, and CUSTOMER-PAYMENTS.

Did you notice that payments to SUPPLIERS and invoices from SUPPLIERS are not on the context diagram? This is because the SUPPLIERS would be dealing with the ACCOUNTING DEPARTMENT for these two items rather than the ORDER PROCESSING SYSTEM. Flows of data between external entities do not show on context diagrams because they are external to the area under study. Only inputs to, and outputs from, the system are indicated. Obviously, this is an oversimplified example because there are many other inputs and outputs in a real system. There also may be many more external entities.

In summary, context diagrams provide an overview of the area under study and the external entities with which it relates directly through the flow of data. The area under study is indicated by a circle, external entities are rectangles, and flows of data are lines with arrowheads indicating the direction of data flow. Flows of data between external entities do not show on context diagrams because they are external to the area under study.

Data Flow Diagrams

The previously developed context diagram is now made to show more detail by developing data flow diagrams from it. A *data flow diagram* is a graphic representation of a system that shows data flows to, from, and within the system, processing functions that change the data in some manner, and the storage of this data. Data flow diagrams are nothing more than a network of related system functions (processing of data) that indicate from where information (data) is received (inputs) and to where it is sent (outputs). A popular term for data flow diagrams is bubble charts. They also are referred to by their acronym DFDs.

Because they are more detailed than context diagrams, data flow diagrams are used to depict specific data flows (movement of information) from both the physical viewpoint (how it is done) and the logical viewpoint (what is done). You do not have physical or logical context diagrams because they do not depict enough detail on either how or what. In addition, context diagrams are concerned mainly with the scope or boundaries of the area under study; detailed data flow diagrams are developed using the context diagram as a high level guide.

Data flow diagrams are constructed using the symbols shown in Figure 2-5. An *external entity* is the originator or receiver of data or information. As in the context diagram, external entities are outside the boundary or scope of our area

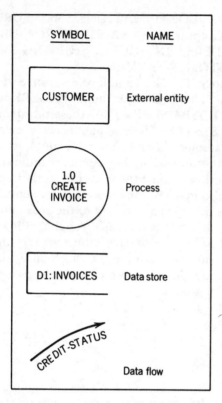

SYMBOL	NAME
CUSTOMER	External entity
1.0 CREATE INVOICE	Process
D1: INVOICES	Data store
CREDIT-STATUS	Data flow

Figure 2-5 Data flow diagram symbols.

under study and you do not look inside them or study them. They may be customers, employees, suppliers, other departments in the firm (such as accounting, personnel, purchasing, or the warehouse), government agencies, and so forth. Source data may originate from an external entity, and an external entity may be the recipient of the outputs from our system. The originator or receiver of the data is identified by writing the name of the external entity within the rectangular box. External entities also are called outside interfaces, external sources, sinks, sources, or originators by various authors. You should note also that either a rectangle or a square may be used to denote external entities; we have chosen to use rectangles.

A *process* is depicted by a circle. Sometimes it is called a bubble or a transform. Processes portray the transformation of the content or status of data. In other words, some sort of processing step takes place, such as the verification of customer credit or the billing of a customer. Processes are described by use of a strong verb (present tense, singular) and an object upon which action is taken, such as CREATE INVOICE. This process identifies the transformation of input data flows into output data flows, and it is proper to put the name of the verb–

object and a reference number for the specific process inside the circle. Each process symbol has its unique identifying number (such as 1.0, 2.0, 3.0, and so forth) that can be used to identify it clearly from any other processes in the data flow diagram. Numbering of the processes is by decimal system to facilitate layering or partitioning of the data flow diagram processes. It also helps when presenting data flow diagrams to others. The processes may be either manual or computerized, but how it is processed is not relevant until the final design stage, which is much later. *What* is accomplished by the process is of greatest importance (calculate, verify, order, create, and so forth).

A *data store* symbol portrays a file or database in which data resides. In reality, this may be the temporary storage position for data within the system itself. In a manual system, it may be paper reports, filing cabinets, microfiche (described in Chapter 15), card files, rotary files, shelves, or George's in-basket. In a computerized system, it may be tapes, disks, or any data held "in memory." A data store identifies a "time delay" for the contents of the data stored within. The name of the data store is written within the open-ended rectangle symbol and it is lettered D1, D2, D3, etc. (Some authors use two parallel lines to denote a data store.)

The fourth basic symbol (a directed line) shown in Figure 2-5 is the *data flow* symbol. This symbol is used to show the flow or movement of data between process bubbles and other processes, external entities, or data stores. You should note that a data flow always must flow to or from a process. In other words, one end of the data flow always must be connected to a process. Also, the name or content of the data flow is listed next to the arrow. Data flows can be physical, such as letters, invoices, purchase orders, vouchers, credit requests, and so forth. Data flows also can take other forms, such as telephone calls, satellite data link transmissions, program-to-program, or other electronic methods that are found in major computerized systems. Again, the format is not important. What is being moved (the data content) is of primary interest.

Occasionally, you will see other symbols used in data flow diagrams. It should be obvious by now that there are no firm standardized symbols such as in flowcharting. This is not important because data flow diagrams are used primarily to gather the requirements and demonstrate the logic of a system, not its physical attributes.

In summary, use the external entity symbol to show the people, organization, or department from which the data originally enters the system, or the point at which the data leaves the system. The process bubbles should contain both a unique identification number and a meaningful verb with an object that indicates the basic transformation or business process that takes place. The data stores should contain a name that associates closely with the data that is being stored at this point in the business process. Ideally, they also should be identified in such a manner that the users can associate with the data flow names and process verb/object names. Finally, data flows should have names that describe the composition of the data that is flowing between processes and other processes, external entities, or data stores. Data flows must either begin or end at a process bubble. A simple data flow diagram looks like this

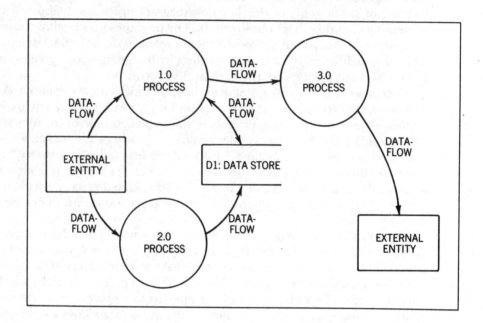

Data flow diagrams are constructed to show various *levels of detail*. When a system is too complex or too large for a single data flow diagram to depict its workings adequately, then several data flow diagrams may be constructed. Each of these data flow diagrams show a different, and successively lower, level of detail (e.g., more detail). Sometimes this expansion of the data flow diagram is called decomposition, further partitioning, Diagram 0, Diagram 1, or Level 0, Level 1 diagrams. Without regard to what it is called, you begin with the highest level (Level 0) diagram and try to depict the entire system on a single piece of paper. The Level 0 diagram is the high level data flow diagram for the system and shows all major processes and major data flows from the "area being studied" circle of the context diagram. In addition, it shows data stores which are not shown on context diagrams. We will show you how to do this, but first let us discuss this approach of top-down or hierarchical analysis.

This entire structured philosophy is a top-down approach in which you first develop a general overview of the processing for a system and then, using successively more detailed data flow diagrams, depict the unique data flows and processing steps required for the system to function. It would be no different than starting with the overall picture of an automobile. Next, you would depict a more detailed picture showing it without the exterior body, then the engine, the pistons, and so on. The automobile is our context diagram, the system without the body is the Level 0 data flow diagram, the engine is the Level 1 data flow diagram, and the pistons are the Level 2 data flow diagram. Whether you develop two or five levels depends on how much detail (decomposition) is needed to successfully describe the system you are analyzing and designing. Usually, two or three levels are more than adequate to describe a system although, theoretically, you can have as many as you need. Realistically, however, by the time you reach five levels, you generally cannot partition any further; you have reached the lowest possible level, sometimes called the *functional primitive*.

In this chapter we will develop *only* a logical data flow diagram in order to demonstrate the basic rules of data flow diagram construction. Remember, the cumulative case study in Chapters 3 to 12 depicts all four data flow diagram models that are described in Figure 2-2.

Figure 2-6 shows the first *iteration* (see Glossary) of the basic Level 0 data flow diagram that was developed from the context diagram in Figure 2-4. Sometimes it takes several iterations to complete the first, or basic, Level 0 diagram. You should work with a pencil and an eraser because you may change processes, data flows, or data stores as you learn more about the system. Do not be discouraged if you have to start over several times.

Looking at Figure 2-6, let us begin with the external entity CUSTOMER who sends an order for merchandise or a payment. The first process (1.0) verifies the details of the order or the payment and handles new customers. To verify these details, this process calls upon two data stores, D1 and D2. D1: INVENTORY is used to verify item details and price of merchandise in the inventory, while D2: CUSTOMERS is used to verify the customer's name and address. At the completion of the verification process, the data flows are dispersed because further processing varies according to several factors. CREDIT-ORDERs go to process 2.0: VERIFY CREDIT. CUSTOMER-PAYMENTs go to process 3.0: APPLY PAYMENT. NEW-CUSTOMER orders go to process 4.0: ENTER NEW CUSTOMER. Finally, the PREPAID-ORDERs have their own data flow to a process that has not been determined as yet (remember, this is the first iteration and many details still are lacking).

Did you notice that to VERIFY CREDIT (process 2.0), you must look at the D3: ACCOUNTS RECEIVABLE data store in order to get the AMOUNT-OWED? Also, notice that the data flow out of process 2.0 is to return orders (RETURNED-ORDERs) to CUSTOMERs for prepayment, and there is a second data flow that goes on to another process that has not been determined as yet in this first iteration.

When you examine process 3.0, APPLY PAYMENT, you will see that the D3: ACCOUNTS RECEIVABLE data store must be accessed to find the AMOUNT-OWED, and the D2: CUSTOMERS data store must be accessed to retrieve CUSTOMER data. Also, CUSTOMER-PAYMENT data is sent to the AC-

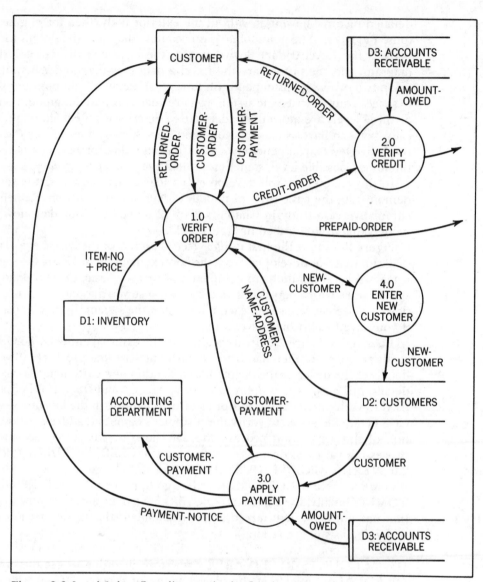

Figure 2-6 Level 0 data flow diagram in the first iteration.

COUNTING DEPARTMENT. Did you notice that data store D3: ACCOUNTS RECEIVABLE was written onto this first iteration of our data flow diagram twice? When a data store appears twice in the same data flow diagram, you use two vertical lines to the left of its number (look at the left side of D3). If the data store appeared three times, it would have three vertical lines to the left of D3. In other words, a vertical line is added for each additional time the same data store appears on the same data flow diagram. This is done so that you can avoid crossing data flows which makes the data flow diagram cluttered and confusing. Before leaving process 3.0, note that PAYMENT-NOTICEs (confirms payment received) to the CUSTOMER also are generated by this process.

With regard to process 4.0: ENTER NEW CUSTOMER, NEW-CUSTOMER data flows from it to data store D2: CUSTOMERS, making a new customer's data available to processes 1.0 and 3.0.

In order to keep our example simple, let us assume that when you returned to work the following day, you completed your second, and in this case final, iteration of the Level 0 data flow diagram (this version is shown in Figure 2-7). Notice that you completed the data flow diagram through processes 5.0, 6.0, and on to the external entities SHIPPING DEPARTMENT and SUPPLIER. The SHIPPING DEPARTMENT is the organization that actually ships the physical merchandise that the customer ordered. The SUPPLIER is the vendor from whom Sunrise Sportswear purchases its merchandise inventory.

Now look at process 5.0: VERIFY INVENTORY. This process has as its input either a VERIFIED-CREDIT-ORDER or a PREPAID-ORDER. Notice that two data stores are used by process 5.0. Data store D1: INVENTORY appears for a second time on this data flow diagram, while D4: BACKORDERS is a new data store. Notice also that data store D4 both provides information for processing by 5.0 and process 5.0 provides information to the D4 data store (arrowhead at each end of the data flow indicates data moves in both directions). Three tasks are performed during the VERIFY INVENTORY process. First, if there is not enough inventory on hand (BALANCE), the customer is told that the item has been placed on backorder (BACKORDER-NOTICE). Second, more inventory may be ordered from the supplier (PURCHASE-ORDER). Third, if there is enough inventory to fill the order, then a SHIP-ORDER notice is sent on to process 6.0: PREPARE SHIPPING NOTICE AND INVOICE. Finally, in process 6.0, a SHIPPING-NOTICE is prepared and sent to the SHIPPING DEPARTMENT external entity so the actual merchandise can be shipped to the customer. An INVOICE also is sent to the CUSTOMER. This invoice shows a zero balance if the item has been prepaid. Finally, the NEW-AMOUNT-OWED by the CUSTOMER is recorded in the D3: ACCOUNTS RECEIVABLE data store so it can be matched to the CUSTOMER-PAYMENT when it is received.

This completes the Level 0 data flow diagram, which we have shown through two iterations. We hope you have a feel for how it is done in real life. As you can see, you rarely get everything correct on the first try. Undoubtedly, in a real-life situation you would learn about more data flows and processes each time you talked with the users. Take your time at this stage, since spending a little more time now will pay greater dividends later.

Now we will choose one of the processes in Figure 2-7 and decompose it so you can see the effect of a Level 1 data flow diagram that is more detailed. Figure 2-8 shows the decomposition of process 3.0 from Figure 2-7. In real life, you also may have to decompose all of the other processes in Figure 2-7.

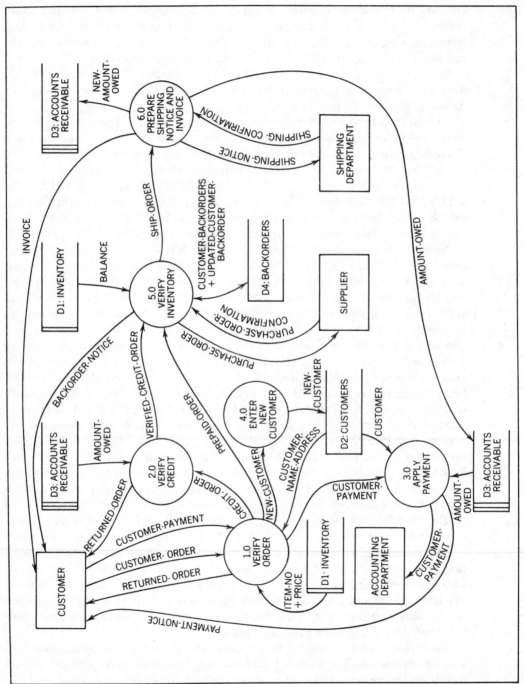

Figure 2-7 Level 0 data flow diagram after the second iteration.

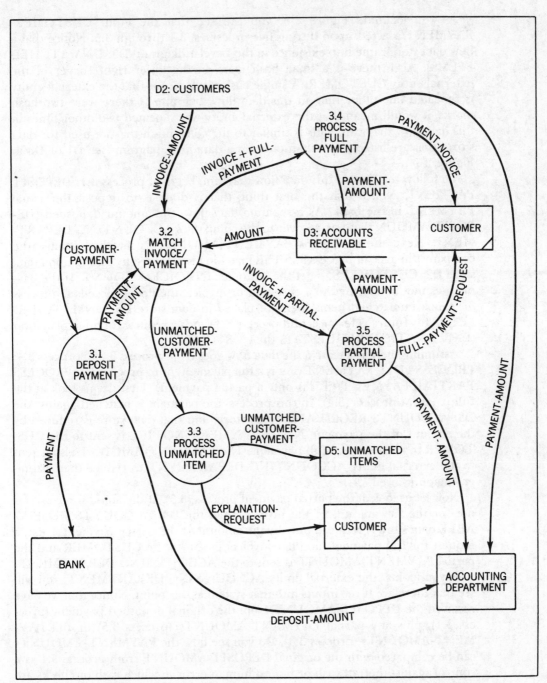

Figure 2-8 Level 1 data flow diagram from process 3.0 (APPLY PAYMENT) in Figure 2-7.

As you examine Figure 2-8, you can see that the input CUSTOMER-PAYMENT is acted upon during five processes, 3.1 through 3.5. Notice that a new data store came into existence in the Level 1 diagram (D5: UNMATCHED ITEMS). Also, there is a small hash mark in the lower right corner of the external entity CUSTOMER. A single hash mark means that the external entity is repeated one other time in this data flow diagram. If there were two hash marks, it would mean that the external entity was repeated two other times in this data flow diagram. This is similar to the convention that we used for data stores that are listed more than once on a data flow diagram (see D1 or D3 in Figure 2-7).

To follow the flow of this data flow diagram, begin at process 3.1: DEPOSIT PAYMENT. Notice that the first thing that is done is to deposit the actual PAYMENT in the bank. As a separate data flow, the amount deposited (DEPOSIT-AMOUNT) is passed over to the company's ACCOUNTING DEPARTMENT. Next, the customer's PAYMENT-AMOUNT is matched against the company's invoice in process 3.2. This matching is achieved by calling upon data store D2: CUSTOMERS to get the customer INVOICE-AMOUNT. If the payment cannot be matched to a customer or invoice, the flow proceeds to process 3.3. Such unmatched items then are placed in data store D5: UNMATCHED ITEMS for future reference, and process 3.3 sends a request for an explanation (EXPLANATION-REQUEST) to the CUSTOMER.

Assuming there is a match, the data flow goes from process 3.2 to process 3.4: PROCESS FULL PAYMENT (if it is a full payment) or to process 3.5: PROCESS PARTIAL PAYMENT (if it is only a partial payment). First, let us look at the full payment process (3.4). In this process, the payment is matched against the D3: ACCOUNTS RECEIVABLE data store, and that data store is reduced by the amount of the payment. Next, a PAYMENT-NOTICE is sent to the CUSTOMER to acknowledge full payment. The PAYMENT-AMOUNT also is sent to the external entity ACCOUNTING DEPARTMENT to reduce the customer's amount owed.

Now let us look at the partial payment process (3.5). If the amount received is not for the full amount of the invoice, then the D3: ACCOUNTS RECEIVABLE data store is reduced only by the amount of the partial payment. Next, a request for full payment (another invoice) is sent to the CUSTOMER and the partial PAYMENT-AMOUNT is sent to the ACCOUNTING DEPARTMENT.

If you look at the external entity ACCOUNTING DEPARTMENT, you will see that there are three inputs into that system at this point. Notice that we have received the DEPOSIT-AMOUNT from the original deposited payment (process 3.1), plus any partial PAYMENT-AMOUNTs (process 3.5) or full PAYMENT-AMOUNTs (process 3.4). Do you see how the PAYMENT-AMOUNTs can be compared with the original DEPOSIT-AMOUNT from process 3.1 as a control against theft of cash or honest human error in which cash or checks are lost? In a data flow diagram it is *not* proper to show data flows between external entities, but if the flow between the external entities BANK and ACCOUNT-ING DEPARTMENT were shown, that data flow would be the bank's monthly statement of deposits. This would add one more assurance against theft or errors with regard to mysterious disappearance of CUSTOMER-PAYMENTs because now you could reconcile the bank's deposits statement with the DE-POSIT-AMOUNTs from process 3.1 and the PAYMENT-AMOUNTs from processes 3.4 and 3.5. This type of reconciliation or balancing is an excellent control procedure when the system is handling cash or checks. In reality, if we were studying the accounting system instead of the payments part of the Or-der Processing system, these controls would be shown through the data flows between the BANK and the accounting system. We should point out that, in theory, controls are not shown on data flow diagrams. Real life, however, does not always conform to theory. In situations in which there are assets that need to be controlled (especially cash), there are certain processes built into the system that are not necessary to the actual conduct of the business but that are essential in order to control these assets. Auditors, for example, may mandate that such a process is necessary for them to conduct audits following Generally Accepted Accounting Principles. In such cases, the controls are a valid process and may be shown on data flow diagrams because they are user stated requirements.

As our third example of a further decomposed data flow diagram, look now at Figure 2-9. This is a Level 2 data flow diagram that was developed from process 3.1 of Figure 2-8. In Figure 2-8, process 3.1 was DEPOSIT PAYMENT. In Figure 2-9, we have exploded or further decomposed that single process (3.1) into five other processes numbered from 3.1.1 through 3.1.5. As you can see, the CUSTOMER-PAYMENT data flow enters process 3.1.1, and the PAYMENT-AMOUNT data flow leaves immediately so that this payment data can be used in an external process. In this case, the external process is process 3.2, as you can see by going back to examine Figure 2-8. Within the process 3.1.1, someone separates the cash and checks, sending the CASH to someone else for a cash count (process 3.1.2) and sending the CHECKS to yet another person for en-dorsement (process 3.1.3). When the cash count and the check endorsement are completed, the details are passed on to another process (3.1.4) in which a bank deposit slip is prepared. Once this deposit slip is prepared, it flows to process 3.1.5 as DEPOSIT-AMOUNT. Did you notice that the CASH from 3.1.2 and the CHECKS from 3.1.3 also flow into process 3.1.5? Once these three items (DEPOSIT-AMOUNT, CASH, and CHECKS) are assembled, a deposit is made at the company's BANK. The only flow left to discuss is from process 3.1.4, in which the DEPOSIT-AMOUNT is sent to the ACCOUNTING DEPART-MENT. Even though CHECKS and CASH are physical items, not logical, they can be put into a logical data flow diagram because they are system-imposed data flows. In other words, a CHECK or CASH is the data flow; you cannot separate the data from the money value of the specific check.

We suggest that you reconcile Figure 2-9 back into Figure 2-8, and then

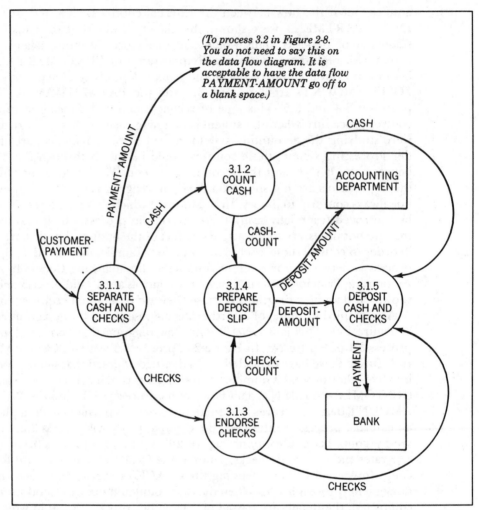

(To process 3.2 in Figure 2-8. You do not need to say this on the data flow diagram. It is acceptable to have the data flow PAYMENT-AMOUNT go off to a blank space.)

Figure 2-9 Level 2 data flow diagram from process 3.1 (DEPOSIT PAYMENT) in Figure 2-8.

reconcile Figure 2-8 back into Figure 2-7. You should be able to account for every data flow, process, and external entity as you work backward. There is a balancing rule in data flow diagramming that requires upper data flow diagrams to agree with lower data flow diagrams. Inputs and outputs must be the same in data content at both levels. Think of the balancing rule in terms of geographical maps. You may have a map of a city which shows all the streets. Suppose you are interested in following a certain road beyond the limits of that map. You go to a larger map, perhaps one of a state. You trace the city street out of the city and

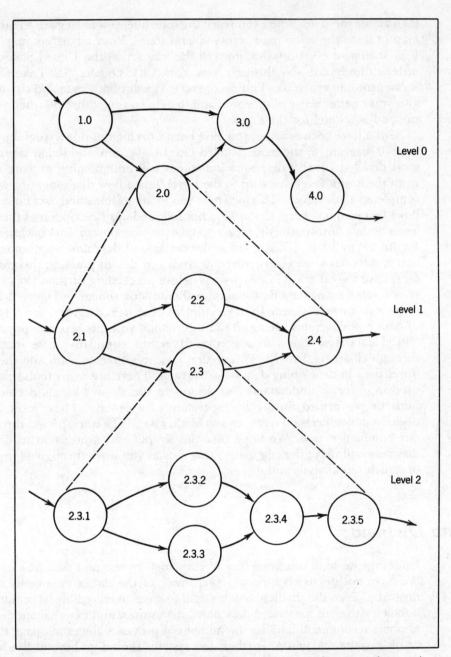

Figure 2-10 Leveled sets of data flow diagram processes demonstrating partitioning or decomposition (courtesy of Logical Conclusions, Inc., Brisbane, California).

then across the state. When you reach the state line, you must go to a higher level map to trace the same road across several states. Your city street may become U.S. Interstate 80 (I-80) that goes all the way across the United States, but in order to find your way through New York City, Omaha, Salt Lake City, and Sacramento, to reach San Francisco, you may want both state and city maps, to give you a better sense of direction and to help you relocate I-80 when you have stopped at a hotel for the night.

As you have been reading, you have been working top-down from the general Level 0 diagram, to the more detailed Level 1 diagram, and finally down to our most detailed Level 2 diagram. Sometimes it is enlightening to work upward from the lowest levels back up to the Level 0 data flow diagram after you have completed all the levels. This may help you locate mismatched data flows or data flows that lead nowhere. If you have not followed our description of these three levels of data flows perfectly, please do take the time now to work backward from Figure 2-9 to 2-8 to 2-7. A good understanding of data flow diagram construction is essential to good structured analysis and design practice; therefore, you must have a good grasp of this process before proceeding further. Conceptually, your leveled set of data flow diagrams should look similar to Figure 2-10.

Now that you have seen the development of context diagrams and three levels of data flow diagrams, we again want to remind you that separate physical and logical data flow diagrams are covered in our cumulative case that carries through Chapters 3 to 12. This section was presented to show you the procedures used in developing data flow diagrams. There are many tools that can be used in order to understand and document the various logical decisions that must be performed during the operation of a process. These tools, such as decision tables, decision trees, and so forth, also will be interspersed throughout our cumulative case. We hope that this simplified introduction to data flow diagrams will make the cumulative case easy as you work through all the details of structured analysis and design.

*D*ata Dictionary

Until now we have discussed how to construct context and data flow diagrams. We have not discussed how you keep track of the data components of these diagrams. Even the smallest systems tend to have an incredibly large number of bubbles with their associated data flows, data stores, and external entities. Practitioners recommend limiting the number of process bubbles per page to seven, or nine at the maximum. Further, few systems should go beyond five levels of decomposition. The following table[1] shows how many bubbles could result from

[1] From discussion with Brian Dickenson of Logical Conclusions, Inc., Brisbane, California.

one to five levels of data flow diagrams with anywhere from one to five bubbles per page.

Number of Levels	Number of Bubbles per Page				
	1	2	3	4	5
1	1	2	3	4	5
2	1	4	9	16	25
3	1	8	27	64	125
4	1	16	81	256	625
5	1	32	243	1024	3125

As you can see, our table demonstrates vividly why you need some method for keeping track of the data associated with the increasing number of process bubbles. The method used is called a data dictionary.

A *data dictionary* is documentation that supports data flow diagrams. It contains all the terms and their definitions for data flows and data stores that relate to a specific system. The purpose of a data dictionary is to define the contents of the data flows and data stores, with the exception of the processes that are defined separately through the use of process descriptions. It also contains definitions for data and control items on structure charts, which will be discussed later. Data dictionaries are needed because, while the data flow diagrams are useful for understanding what is happening, complete understanding of data flow diagrams is not possible until you know what is meant by the various terms (data flows) used on them. Also, you must have some method that prevents you from calling the same data flow or data store by two different names (synonyms) or two different data flows by the same names (homonyms). In other words, data dictionaries are necessary to provide consistency.

Data dictionaries are started as soon as you begin to identify data flows and data stores. This means that data dictionaries are started as early as the context diagram, and certainly by the Level 0 data flow diagram. If you go back to our context diagram (Figure 2-4), you will see that we have 11 named data flows. These 11 items would be the start of our data dictionary for Sunrise Sportswear. The Level 0 data flow diagram (Figure 2-6) adds a number of new entries to our data dictionary. Do you see how confusing it would be to have the "Payment Notice" data flow on the context diagram turn into a "Notice of Payment" on the Level 0 diagram? If you are not consistent in your use of terminology, you soon will have a chaotic situation. Some practitioners feel that the data dictionary is of primary importance in keeping a structured analysis project on the right track. In addition, it has long-term value because it is the basis for what eventually turns out to be the system's database. It provides information on data flows, other inputs, outputs, printed reports, data stores, and so forth.

During our previous discussion of data flow diagram levels, we mentioned that the lowest level is sometimes called the functional primitive level. A *functional primitive* can be defined as a process that does not need to be further decomposed to a lower level. In the data dictionary, the equivalent is a data primitive. A *data primitive* is defined as an element of data that does not need to be further defined. As you can see, functional primitives refer to processes, while data primitives refer to data flows and data stores.

Before getting into the details of data dictionaries, let us discuss some definitions. You will recall that a *data store* is a temporary or permanent storage position for data within a system. A *database* is a collection of interrelated data stored with controlled redundancy, to serve one or more applications. The most basic piece of data that cannot be broken into more detailed units is called a *data item, data element,* or a *field.* Combinations of these data items, data elements, or fields make up *data structures.* In other words, a meaningful set of data elements is called a data structure. Data flows are data structures. Also, several data elements grouped together may be referred to either as a record or a data structure. Since the multiplicity of terms makes this area confusing, *we will use the terms data elements and data structures;* therefore, a data structure consists of one or more data elements that offer some logical business meaning. It would be helpful for you to remember that a data structure also can consist of another data structure and some data elements.

In summary, a data dictionary is composed of data structures defining data flows and data stores. These data structure descriptions are comprised of data elements which, when put together to form a data structure, have meaning.

At this point we want to show you how to begin a data dictionary. To accomplish this, we want to define all of the pieces of data residing in data store D1: INVENTORY shown in the data flow diagram for Sunrise Sportswear (Figure 2-7). To keep our example manageable, we are defining only one data store, but you should be aware that a real-life system could contain many data stores which contain thousands of definitions, one for every data structure in every data flow and every data store.

When you look at Figure 2-7, our INVENTORY data store appears at two processes, 1.0 and 5.0. Our first step is to identify each of the data structures in data store D1. Then we will identify the data elements of the data structure or structures. Keep in mind, as you work on data dictionaries, that the terms used should be terms to which the users can relate. We can see that data store D1: INVENTORY must hold information on the various items of merchandise that we carry at Sunrise Sportswear.

In the following example, we will describe the physical data dictionary because you only need the "data element name" for the logical data dictionary. The physical data dictionary probably includes the description of the item, its item number, color, size, price, quantities, and so forth. Figure 2-11 shows the individual data elements that have been identified for each item of inventory in data store D1. To obtain this information, you had to interview people, read documents, observe the existing system, and identify the individual data elements that flow in and out of the inventory data store. Notice that Figure 2-11 identifies six different characteristics for each data element. The first column, Data Element Name, lists each data element by its assigned name. The second column, Approx Size, indicates the approximate size of each data element and indicates whether it is alpha, numeric, or a combination. For example, the data element EOQ consists of four numbers, while ITEM-NO has six numbers and one letter. The third column, Sample Values, translates the previous column so you will know what a specific data element looks like. For example, ITEM-DESC can have 30 letters or numbers, and in this case it looks like the item being described is a shirt. The Narrative Description column further enhances your understanding of each data element. For example, the data element PRICE is specified further to mean selling price. This column also should include any aliases or synonyms by which this data element is known to users. Aliases are nicknames such as "1040 form," "pink sheet," "purchase req," and so forth. Aliases must be identified so that they can be cross-referenced for later use if the formal data element name is not known by someone using the data dictionary. The next column is to indicate any edit checks that can be identified. Edit checks are used for control purposes. Finally, the data store in which the data element resides is listed. If the data element is in more than one data store, each one is indicated. Later in this chapter we will show you how to normalize or simplify these data elements. During this normalization process, these data store locations may change. This is because normalization is performed to reduce redundancy and the contents of data stores may be deleted entirely or moved elsewhere.

Once the list of data elements has been assembled, you can proceed to show the composition of the data structure or data structures. One data store may contain several data structures. Figure 2-12 shows a logical data dictionary of individual data elements stored in the data store D1: INVENTORY. We started with the physical data dictionary shown in Figure 2-11 so you could see the individual data elements. In a structured analysis situation, however, the physical data dictionary can be left until the design step (physical model of the new system). Usually only the logical data dictionary is developed during analysis (see Figure 2-12). It does not contain the minute details of the physical data dictionary.

Did you notice in Figures 2-11 and 2-12 that each data element and data structure was in capital letters and that multiple word data elements were hyphenated? As with data flow diagram construction, there are rules to follow in constructing a data dictionary. The terms used to describe data structures are

Data Element Name	Approx Size[1]	Sample Values (data itself)	Narrative Description	Edit Checks	Data Store
ITEM-DESC	30 AN	Shirt	Description of the item	—	D1
ITEM-NO	6N,1A	100000 to 900000	Unique ID of item 6N, plus supplier 1A	Must be numeric and only between 100000 and 999999	D1,D3,D4
EOQ	4N	500	Economic Order Quantity Alias: Buy Amount	—	D1
PRICE	8N	17.50	Selling price	—	D1
COLOR	1A	B	Color of item	Cannot be numeric	D1
SIZE	3N	12	Size of item	—	D1
QUAN	4N	175	Quantity available in inventory	—	D1
SUPPLIER	2N	16	Vendor that supplies merchandise	—	D1

[1] A = Alphabetic
N = Numeric
AN = Alphabetic & numeric

Figure 2-11 Data elements. This is a physical data dictionary for data store D1 shown in Figure 2-7.

Name of Data Store: D1: INVENTORY	
Name of Data Structure	**Name of Data Element**
INV	ITEM—DESC
	ITEM—NO
	EOQ
	PRICE
	COLOR
	SIZE
	QUAN
	SUPPLIER

Notations:
  EOQ alias: Buy amount

Figure 2-12 Data structure. This is a logical data dictionary for data store D1 shown in Figure 2-7.

always in capital letters. Multiple word names are hyphenated. Assigned names should be straightforward and user-oriented. There should be a name for each data flow, data store, data structure, and data element.

Although processes are defined through the use of process descriptions, the names of the processes and the unique identifying number may be indicated in the data dictionary because this facilitates locating related data flows and data stores. Be careful here because every time you change a process number, you have to make a corresponding change in the data dictionary. No two data flows should have the same name. The opposite also is true; no data flow should have more than one name. The name selected to describe data flows and data stores should represent the data and what we know about it. Data flows are described with nouns and adjectives that describe the contents (a data structure) of the data flow. When we discussed data flow diagram construction, we mentioned that processes should be described using a strong verb and an object. For example, in Figure 2-7, we used VERIFY ORDER for process 1.0. One trick that can be used to name output data flows is to use the past tense of the verb in the process that transforms the data. In this case, perhaps we should have used VERIFIED-CREDIT-ORDER for the data flowing between 1.0 and 2.0 in Figure 2-7. Can you find other names that could be changed to more meaningful data dictionary entries? As you can see, we were not too fussy about naming our data flows in Figure 2-7. This is because we wanted you to see how much retrospective work this would cause if this was a real-life system and you waited until later to begin your data dictionary and name your data flows. As you work through the cumulative case later, you will be expected to pay attention to such details. The use of two verbs in one process usually is an indication that you have not partitioned enough; further partitioning probably will result in two processes and two or more new data flows that must be identified and named. Finally, aliases must be discouraged; the primary name should be one that conforms to the above conventions and that the users will accept.

About now you probably are wondering exactly how you obtain these data elements so that you can describe them as a data structure in the data dictionary. Let us suppose you are studying the Shipping Department at Sunrise Sportswear. The supervisor hands you a form they call the 2211. This form is the one provided by Nationwide Parcel Service (NPS). Its formal name is Shipping Receipt and its purpose is to tell Nationwide who their customer is (Sunrise, in this case), and the destination of merchandise packages being sent from Sunrise. It is both a statement of shipments and a summary of charges for Sunrise, in addition to meeting the needs of NPS. A copy of this form is shown in Figure 2-13. By use of this form, we will demonstrate the four rules of notation that are used in compiling data dictionaries.

The *first* rule is that data structures must consist of one or more data elements. These data elements are listed vertically with plus signs (+) that indicate the terms are "anded" together. (If you have taken algebra, the following concepts

SHIPPING RECEIPT							
NAME					DATE		
STREET			CITY	STATE	ZIP		
PACKAGE	NAME				INS VALUE	COD AMT	DEL CHG
1	STREET						
	CITY		STATE	ZIP			
	NAME				INS VALUE	COD AMT	DEL CHG
2	STREET						
	CITY		STATE	ZIP			
	NAME				INS VALUE	COD AMT	DEL CHG
3	STREET						
	CITY		STATE	ZIP			
	NAME				INS VALUE	COD AMT	DEL CHG
4	STREET						
	CITY		STATE	ZIP			
	NAME				INS VALUE	COD AMT	DEL CHG
5	STREET						
	CITY		STATE	ZIP			
NATIONWIDE PARCEL SERVICE (NPS) Form 2211 (Rev. 4/86)						TOTAL CHGS	

Figure 2-13 Shipping form to be used in data structure construction.

fit into Boolean logic.) In this case, our data structure is the formal name of the form (see Figure 2-13) affectionately known as 2211. The first data element is the customer's name. The next is the address, and the next is the date that the customer shipped the package. These items appear in the data dictionary as

SHIPPING-RECEIPT = <u>CUSTOMER-NAME</u> +
<u>CUSTOMER-ADDRESS</u> +
<u>DATE-SHIPPED</u>

Notice that both the data structure name and those of the individual data elements are capitalized, multiple names are hyphenated, and the plus sign indicates that all three items must be present. The underlined data element is known as the primary key. We will discuss primary keys later, but for now it is sufficient to define a *primary key* as a data element that uniquely identifies a data structure and which is used for storage and access to and from a data store (database). The primary key is always underlined. If the data structure is a data flow that is not stored, it will not have a primary key.

The *second* rule is that data structures that consist of the same data elements repeated multiple times are shown in braces { }. In our form, we have spaces for five packages to be shipped to five destinations. The destination names and addresses are repeating elements. They are added under the previous data elements, so that now we have

```
SHIPPING-RECEIPT = CUSTOMER-NAME +
                   CUSTOMER-ADDRESS +
                   DATE-SHIPPED +
                   ⎰ DESTINATION-NAME +    ⎱
                   ⎱ DESTINATION-ADDRESS  ⎰
```

Notice that the repeating elements are indented and then braced. Each data element still has a plus sign because we are "anding" them together.

The *third* rule is that data elements requiring a selection from among several data elements are shown in brackets [ ]. Instead of using the word "or," a straight vertical line is used to separate the items from which the person would select one [|]. Now our data structure is beginning to look like this

```
SHIPPING-RECEIPT = CUSTOMER-NAME +
                   CUSTOMER-ADDRESS +
                   DATE-SHIPPED +
                   ⎧ DESTINATION-NAME +              ⎫
                   ⎨ DESTINATION-ADDRESS +           ⎬
                   ⎩ [DELIVERY-CHARGE | COD-AMOUNT]  ⎭
```

As you can see, the last addition is an either/or situation. Nationwide Parcel Service will either collect a straight delivery charge from Sunrise Sportswear, or it will collect a COD amount from the recipient of the merchandise when it is delivered. This COD amount then would be refunded to Sunrise Sportswear. Since this [DELIVERY-CHARGE | COD-AMOUNT] applies to each one of the shipped packages, it also is one of the repeating data elements; therefore, the braces have been extended to include it.

The *fourth* rule is that optional data elements are shown in parentheses ( ). In this example, only insured packages have an INSURED-VALUE data element,

Name of Data Store: D15: SHIPPING—RECORDS	
Name of Data Structure	**Name of Data Element**

SHIPPING—RECEIPT	CUSTOMER—NAME +
	CUSTOMER—ADDRESS +
	DATE—SHIPPED +
	  DESTINATION—NAME +
	  DESTINATION—ADDRESS +
	  [DELIVERY—CHARGE |
	    COD—AMOUNT] +
	  (INSURED—VALUE) +
	TOTAL—CHARGES

Notations: Alias: 2211
Repeating data elements can be repeated a maximum of 5 times.

Figure 2-14 Data store form containing data dictionary descriptions of data structure and data elements. This is part of the logical data dictionary.

which we now add to the repeating data elements. Finally, we also add the data element that shows the total charges appearing at the bottom of our form. This is the amount that Nationwide Parcel Service collects from Sunrise Sportswear.

```
SHIPPING-RECEIPT = CUSTOMER-NAME +
                   CUSTOMER-ADDRESS +
                   DATE-SHIPPED +
                  ⎧DESTINATION-NAME +              ⎫
                  ⎪DESTINATION-ADDRESS +           ⎪
                  ⎨[DELIVERY-CHARGE | COD-AMOUNT] +⎬
                  ⎩(INSURED-VALUE) +               ⎭
                   TOTAL-CHARGES
```

In summary, the symbols used in constructing data dictionaries are

= means EQUIVALENT TO

+ means AND

{ } means REPEATING data elements

[|] means EITHER one data element OR another data element

( ) means OPTIONAL data element

Sometimes a data element needs further definition. In our case, DESTINA-TION-ADDRESS and CUSTOMER-ADDRESS might have the additional data elements of STREET-ADDRESS, CITY, STATE, and ZIP. If a data element is fully understood by everyone who sees the system, it is called a *self-defining term*. Examples of such self-defining terms are birthdate, Social Security number, ZIP code, and so forth.

The data dictionary entry that we just identified can be placed on a data store form such as we show in Figure 2-14. These data store forms are assembled later, and together they comprise the data dictionary.

Data Structure Diagrams

Now that you have learned how to compile a data dictionary, the next step is organizing the data structures for use. To do this, we organize the data structures into a model that shows the business objects and their relationships for all stored data in the system. This modeling of data structure relationships is called by a variety of names, including data structure charts, schema/subschema, data structure diagrams, or data models. For structured analysis, we will use the term *data structure diagrams*. They are a graphic representation of relationships between separate, unique data structures with emphasis upon access paths between data structures in various data stores. In other words, it is a graphic means of showing access relationships between data structures. The data structure diagram shows how data stores relate to other data stores. In order for these access relationships to be modeled, the data structures must first be put into what is called third normal form. This is accomplished through a logical process known as normalization.

Normalization is the decomposition of complex data structures into "flat" files called relations. There are three levels of normalization. The *first normal form* (1NF) is any data structure without internal repeating groups. The *second normal form* (2NF) is a data structure in which all non-key data elements are fully functionally dependent on the primary key. The *third normal form* (3NF) is a data structure in which the following two conditions are met: all the non-key data elements are fully functionally dependent on the primary key (e.g., 2NF), and no non-key data element is functionally dependent on any other non-key data element in the system. In other words, no data element can be derived from another data element. We will explain these forms as we move through the normalization process, but first we should use our common sense to reduce any redundant (duplication, triplication, etc.) data elements within our data structure. As we look through the data elements that comprise the data structure in Figure 2-11, we can identify one redundant data element. Notice in the Narrative Description column that one of the data elements is SUPPLIER, and another data element ITEM-NO contains the supplier code within its seven digit size (6N,1A). By removing the data element SUPPLIER, we ultimately will have a more simple and smaller data store (less redundancy) with less risk of error in case the data element SUPPLIER somehow did not match the ITEM-NO supplier code. Now go to Figure 2-12 and circle the data element SUPPLIER. Put an explanation next to it: Removed because of redundancy.

You might remember something that usually is true for both manual and computer systems: it may be easier and less expensive to change the logic of a process than to change the structure of a data store. The more simple the data structure, therefore, the easier and cheaper it is to make changes to the data in the future. This may not be true in a very large system in which a data element is used in many places. In such a situation, if you want to change a process, you have to identify and change many data structures or data elements in the data dictionary.

With obvious redundant data elements removed, we now can move to normalization. The most simplistic definition of first normal form is that it reorganizes the contents of a data store to remove internal repeating groups. Let us begin by looking at an example of what an inventory file might look like. We will use the inventory file in Figure 2-15 to explain terms used in normalization and relational databases. A relational database is one composed of two-dimensional arrays of data elements; it is a set of files in normalized form. Some of the differences in terminology arise from the fact that, in place of the term file, the

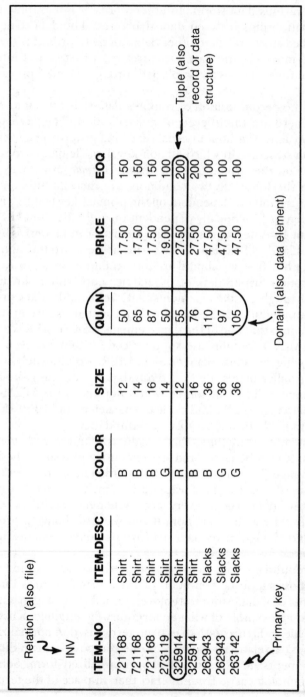

Figure 2-15 Inventory file listing, showing relational terminology. It relates to the information in Figure 2-11.

word relation is used. In place of the term data element, the word domain is used. Each individual data structure (also called record) is a tuple (rhymes with couple). This is confusing because sometimes a data structure refers to a file/relation, and sometimes a data structure refers to a record/tuple. Since our goal here is to demonstrate data structure relationships and not to teach you about relational databases, try not to let the terminology get in the way of understanding the concepts.

Every tuple in a relation (like every record in a file) must have a *primary key* by which the tuple can be identified. It is possible that a unique or primary key can be formed by *concatenating,* or chaining together, two or more data elements; therefore, a *concatenated key* is composed of more than one data element that uniquely identifies a tuple (data structure). In other words, a data structure can be accessed by using two or more data elements linked together to form a primary key. These concepts will fall into place as we proceed through the normalization process.

Let us begin with the first normal form (1NF). Any data structure without internal repeating groups is automatically in the first normal form, regardless of how complex its key is or what interrelationships there may be among its data elements. The left side of Figure 2-16 shows our original data structure from Figure 2-12 (some of the data elements are in a different sequence from the previous figure). This data structure has some repeating groups (those in braces); therefore, it is not yet in the first normal form. A repeating group is a group of data elements that are repeated a number of times. In our case, the primary key, <u>ITEM-NO</u>, has a repeating group denoting colors, sizes, and quantity available in inventory.

In the center of Figure 2-16, we have decomposed or split our original data structure, INV, into two other data structures, INV-ITEM and ITEM-CS, neither of which contains repeating data elements. Also, the data structure ITEM-CS now has a concatenated primary key, <u>ITEM-NO + COLOR + SIZE</u>. As you undoubtedly have figured out from Figure 2-16, the primary key is underlined and the repeating groups are shown by braces (remember our four rules for construction of data structures from the Data Dictionary section). We now have our data structure decomposed to the first normal form, no internal repeating groups. Data structure names should be descriptive of the data elements grouped under them. Thus, in Figure 2-16, ITEM-CS is descriptive of the data structure <u>ITEM-NO + COLOR + SIZE</u> + QUAN. Also, it makes it clear if you indent, as we did in Figure 2-16.

The next task is to get our data structures into the second normal form. Remember, a normalized relation is in second normal form if all of the non-key data elements are fully functionally dependent on the primary key. A data element is *fully functionally dependent* only if it is dependent on the entire key. It is only functionally dependent (not fully) if the value of any data element can be determined using only part of the key. This immediately tells us that any data

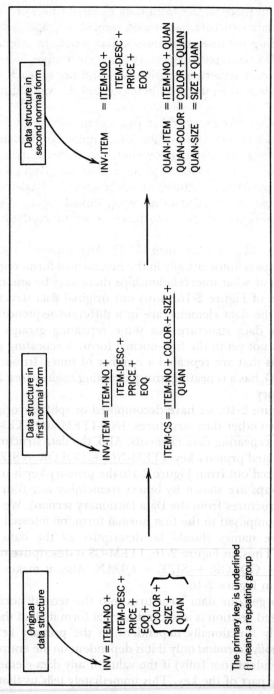

INV = ITEM-NO +
ITEM-DESC +
PRICE +
EOQ +
{COLOR +
SIZE +
QUAN}

Original data structure

INV-ITEM = ITEM-NO +
ITEM-DESC +
PRICE +
EOQ

ITEM-CS = ITEM-NO + COLOR + SIZE + QUAN

Data structure in first normal form

INV-ITEM = ITEM-NO +
ITEM-DESC +
PRICE +
EOQ

QUAN-ITEM = ITEM-NO + QUAN
QUAN-COLOR = COLOR + QUAN
QUAN-SIZE = SIZE + QUAN

Data structure in second normal form

The primary key is underlined
{} means a repeating group

Figure 2-16 Original data structure decomposed (normalization).

structure with a primary key, using only a single data element, is already in the second normal form. Thus, INV-ITEM is in the second normal form.

We do have a candidate for change, however, because the data structure ITEM-CS (see Figure 2-16) has a concatenated key. The question we must ask is: Can any of the data elements, QUAN in this case, be uniquely associated (identified) with only part of the key, either ITEM-NO or COLOR or SIZE? If they can, they are not fully functionally dependent on the whole key. In other words, they would be only functionally dependent on part of the key. QUAN can be identified using only one part of the concatenated key, ITEM-NO + COLOR. Also, QUAN can be identified by using ITEM-NO + SIZE. The question now becomes: Can we assume that QUAN and ITEM-NO without COLOR and SIZE are useless because a customer always wants a certain size and/or certain color? Not necessarily! If a customer always wants both a size and a color, knowing ITEM-NO (unique ID of an item) and COLOR is not enough. Also, knowing ITEM-NO and SIZE is not enough. Perhaps we cannot separate SIZE and COLOR. If we assume this is so, our data structure that is shown in first normal form in Figure 2-16 is also in second normal form even though it has a concatenated key. What we want to emphasize here is that you may have to question the user as to the use of the data element before you start the normalization. There are two somewhat opposing theories at work. One is to try to reduce the second normal form to single keys even if logical meaning is impaired, letting the physical database designer reassemble some of them together later. The other theory is to reduce the second normal form only to the point of a logical and meaningful data structure. In other words, reduce the data structure only to the point of a logical and meaningful data structure necessary to support the users' needs. In real life you will have to normalize as it is done at your place of employment.

As you can see in Figure 2-16, by looking at the data structure ITEM-CS, QUAN appears to be only functionally dependent (not fully functionally dependent). This is because a value of QUAN can be determined by using only part of the key; for example, ITEM-NO + COLOR. The problem is, what good is ITEM-NO (a shirt) + COLOR (blue) without the SIZE?

On the other hand, you could reduce the first normal data structure to three data structures containing only primary keys with no attached non-key data elements. If that is the case, the second normal form would be as shown in Figure 2-16. It all depends upon which theory you choose to follow.

Now we have to ensure that our data structures are in the third normal form. Remember, a normalized relation is in the third normal form if all non-key data elements are fully functionally dependent on the primary key (this is what we did in the second normal form), and also no non-key data element is functionally dependent on any other non-key data element. Another way of saying this is that all non-key data elements in a data structure are mutually independent of one another. To transform the data structure that is in second normal form to a data structure that is in third normal form, we therefore must examine each of the non-key data elements to see that they are mutually independent of each of the other non-key data elements. We must remove any such mutual dependents. One of the things that might show dependence is a non-key data element that can be derived from another non-key data element. Our data structures already are in the third normal form because there is no dependence (ability to calculate or derive one data element from the others). Go back to look at the data structures INV-ITEM, QUAN-ITEM, QUAN-COLOR, and QUAN-SIZE. Within INV-ITEM you will see that one of the data elements is EOQ (economic order quantity). If EOQ could be computed from the other two data elements (ITEM-DESC or PRICE) in that data structure, then we would have to remove it. Coincidentally, our example in Figure 2-16, after being reduced to second normal form, already is in third normal form (3NF).

At this point, you need to have one more review of the data structure to further eliminate any redundant data elements among the various data structures. Remember, we have been working with only one data store, D1: INVENTORY. If you look back to Figure 2-7, you will see that our Order Processing system has four different data stores (D1–D4). At this point, you would check to see if any of the data elements in the other data stores are the same as in data store D1 after also being reduced to third normal form. It is possible that some of the data elements from our D1 data structures can be combined with others or eliminated because of duplication of data elements in the data structures of other data stores.

The importance of third normal form is that it is the smallest possible representation of all relevant data (no redundant data). Because the normalized data dictionary eventually becomes the system's database, it must be as clean and uncomplicated as possible so that it is easy to maintain. Finally, because of more sophisticated computers, the trend is away from older network and hierarchical databases and toward relational databases. Current computers allow us to implement relational databases even though they are complex in their structure. Relational databases do not impose artificial implementation structures on a data storage problem. Normalization is the technique that provides a logical model to assist in the implementation of a physical database.

Now that you have a basic understanding of how data structures are organized, you will be able to understand how data access or data structure diagrams contribute to a modeling of data structure relationships. At the completion of the normalization process, you should have data structures that are free of redundancy. These third normal form data structures represent your refined, or final, data requirements. They can be documented graphically by using a data structure diagram.

A *data structure diagram* shows the relationships among the data structures and their possible access paths. Figure 2-17 is our example of how a data structure diagram shows these relationships. The names of data structures are written

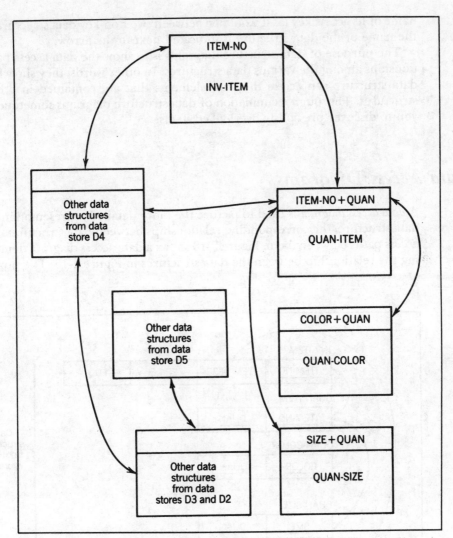

Figure 2-17 Data structure diagram showing data store D1 relationships to other data structures in other data stores.

inside the rectangular boxes of a data structure diagram. The primary key used for gaining access to a particular data structure is shown at the top of the box. As you can see, however, not all arrows lead to the primary key. The access path can be between two primary keys, between one primary key and a non-key item, or between two non-key items. All three possibilities are demonstrated in Figure 2-17. If the name of the data structure being pointed to is different from the name of its access key (as it would be between two non-key data structures), then the name of the data structure is indicated next to the arrow.

The purpose of data structure diagrams is to show the data access path relationships among the various data structures. In other words, they show how one data structure can access the data elements that are contained in other data structures. Thorough examination of data structure diagrams sometimes allows you to discover previously overlooked items.

*D*ata Access Diagrams

A *data access diagram* is used to picture the more detailed representation of each data structure, the corresponding relationships between data structures, and the access paths between them. Figure 2-18 shows a data access diagram demonstrating the relationship between the data structures in Figure 2-16. The purpose of

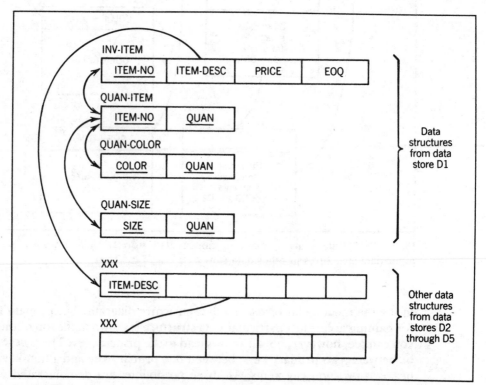

Figure 2-18 Data access diagram derived from Figure 2-16 and Figure 2-17.

the data access diagram is to show the formats of the data structures and the corresponding relationships (access paths) for the system.

Notice in Figure 2-18 that each data structure is shown along with each of its individual data elements. Any of the data elements that are utilized as the primary key are underlined. Also, the name of the data structure is shown above it at the left side. The individual name for each data element is in each component section of the data structure.

The arrows shown in Figure 2-18 indicate the access paths from one data element in a data structure to another data element in a different data structure. These data access paths may go directly to the primary key (underlined) or they may go to one of the other data elements. The purpose is to show, in a detailed fashion, the data access paths between the various data structures. Notice how the data access diagram in Figure 2-18 shows more detail than our data structure diagram of Figure 2-17. The data access diagram is documentation used to support the transition from logical file design to physical file design. Its purpose is to tell the person who is creating the physical file design (database) the exact data structure, including the data elements, the data access paths between data structures, and, therefore, the accessing capabilities that are required by the new business system.

In summary, we began with the concept of naming data flows in a logical, structured manner at the time of drawing the context diagram and through the data flow diagram levels. These named data flows became the basis of the data dictionary. Once the data dictionary was compiled, we followed four rules to place the data elements properly within their appropriate data structure. First, we eliminated obvious redundant data elements. Second, we normalized our data structures into the third normal form, which is the smallest possible representation of the data. Third, after the data was normalized, it was possible to model the data structure interrelationships through the use of data structure diagrams. Fourth, the data access diagrams were used to picture the complete details of access paths that were shown previously in a more graphic form in the data structure diagrams.

Throughout this process, our primary concern has been with data; how it flows through a system, and how one piece of data can be shown to relate to others. To learn more details about these techniques, we suggest you consult some of the structured analysis books cited in the Reading Selections at the end of this chapter.

*S*ystem Structure Charts

A *system structure chart* is a hierarchy diagram that shows the control structure we impose on the system's processes. Any system has both procedural (sequential) and hierarchical (subordination) characteristics. A data flow diagram shows the sequential order of the processes. A system structure chart shows the subordination or the hierarchical levels of rank between processes. The objective is to show which module is the boss and which is the worker. In other words, it demonstrates the boss to subordinate structure of the system.

The system structure chart looks much like the organization chart of a business. Figure 1-6 in Chapter 1 depicted an organization chart. As you already know, the president of a company is at a higher level than the vice presidents, and the vice presidents are at a higher level than the managers. In this same way, a system structure chart has a top level box that represents the top level system process. Subordinate to that top level box is the next level of processes to be performed and so on, down to the lowest level process to be performed. In other words, the top level manager is responsible for all of the activities performed by all of the individuals in subordinate positions (levels) on the organization chart. A single box at the top of a system structure chart represents the top control module (the boss) in the same way. Subordinate to that box are all of the functions that comprise the tasks to be performed. The top level and the middle level functions serve to control the functions below them in the hierarchy. It is the bottom level functions that are the real workers of the system.

As you convert your lowest level data flow diagrams to structure charts, keep in mind that the modules (boxes) deal with rank (order of importance) rather than sequence, as is the case with data flow diagrams. A rectangular box on a system structure chart is a module. A module has a name and it becomes a collection of program statements. The name of a module describes its function, such as what it does. For example, the program statements in COBOL may become a program, a section, or a paragraph, and in FORTRAN may become a subroutine or a function. In COBOL you might visualize a module as a separately compilable program on a performed paragraph. The large arrows that in'erconnect modules represent an invocation, such as a PERFORM or a CALL. The small arrows that show direction, but do not touch each module box, represent communications between modules. The box in Figure 2-19 defines the two types of small arrows used for communication between the modules.

To create system structure charts, you first identify a functional partitioning of the lowest level data flow diagrams (functional primitives). Next, take the most important process or processes (called the central transform) of a functional set of data flow diagrams and convert it or them into the heart of a system structure chart. In a small system, perhaps only one structure chart may be developed, but a large system may have several structure charts, based on the functional partitioning of one or more data flow diagrams.

Remember, the structure charts are used by programmers to write the program code. Each rectangular box on a structure chart is a module, and each module becomes a compilable set of program code. System structure charts guide what the programs must do. This is similar to the development of data

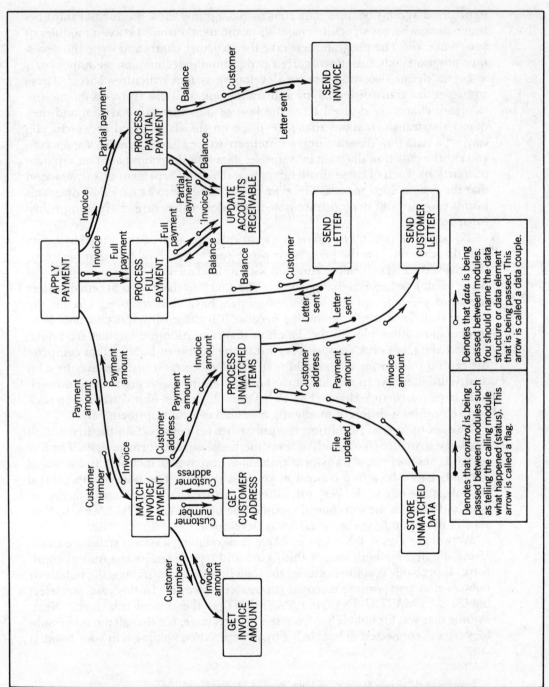

Figure 2-19 System structure chart derived from the Level 1 data flow diagram in Figure 2-8.

structure diagrams because data structure diagrams show the relationships between data, whereas structure charts show the relationships between modules of program code. The programmers take the structure charts and write the necessary program code (using structured programming techniques, we hope).

Let us define two strategies for developing system structure charts.[2] These strategies are transform analysis and transaction analysis. In *transform analysis,* structure charts are derived from the flow of data through a system and they depict the transformations that take place on the data. In other words, you convert a data flow diagram into a system structure chart. In *transaction analysis,* you cut the data flow diagram into smaller data flow diagrams based on separate transactions. Each of these smaller data flow diagrams represent one transaction that the system must process. Since we do not have complex data flow diagrams in this case, we will demonstrate how to develop a structure chart using transform analysis.

To begin, the *central transform* is the primary process of the functional data flow diagram set. It is the process, or processes (several bubbles), that performs the major data transforming function within the data flow diagram or diagrams being used. Further, it is that portion of the data flow diagram that remains after the input, editing, and output streams of data have been removed. Usually the central transform can be identified because it is the most important bubble or combination of bubbles on the data flow diagram. All other bubbles feed data, prepare data, or check data with regard to the bubble or bubbles that comprise the central transform. You should note that the central transform may be a bit difficult to identify. In real life, it cannot be identified with mathematical precision. If your structure chart seems to have an illogical set of hierarchies, go back and reconsider a different or slightly modified central transform.

Now let us look at two different approaches for constructing the first rough draft of a structure chart. Both of these methods use transform analysis. The *first* method uses the central transform as the boss (top control module). In the *second* method, a new boss (top control module) is created. The boss or top control module is the box at the very top of any structure chart. Look again at Figure 2-19 and see that the top control module (the boss) is APPLY PAYMENT. Now we will show you how Figure 2-19 was developed.

We will use Figure 2-8 as our example in developing a system structure chart. Using the first method, look at this figure and try to identify the central transform. It probably is at the center of the data flow diagram and it is the bubble or bubbles that perform the essential process or processes. In this case, we select bubble 3.2: MATCH INVOICE/PAYMENT as the central transform. Next, assume that you lift bubble 3.2 from the printed page, but that all the other bubbles are still connected to bubble 3.2 by strings. When holding it in your hand, it

---

[2] For more detail, see Meilir Page-Jones' book, Chapters 9 and 10.

looks like a mobile. Holding it in the air, you get a rearranged data flow diagram as shown below

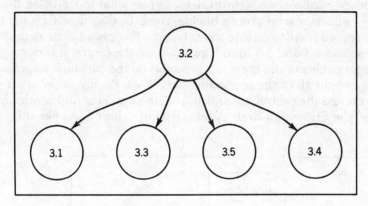

This is the first rough draft of a system structure chart. By using this method, you have decided that process 3.2 (MATCH INVOICE/PAYMENT from Figure 2-8) is the boss (top control module). At this point, do not be concerned about the fact that we still are using circles instead of rectangular boxes. We will convert to boxes in the next draft of the structure chart.

For our second method, in which a new top control module is created, we again have to identify the central transform. Instead of lifting the central transform off the page as we did previously, this time a line is drawn around it. In other words, draw a large circle or oval around the central transform on the data flow diagram. In our example, this is bubble 3.2. Next, assume that you use a pair of scissors to cut off all of the strings (data flows) that attach any other bubbles to the central transform. Cut these data flows at the point where your circle or oval surrounds the central transform. If you draw a "new boss" rectangular box as the top control module and hang the strings from it, your first rough draft structure chart appears as follows

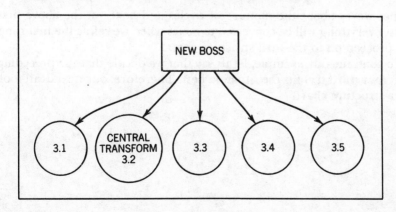

Notice that in this case, you attach each data flow (string that was cut), including the central transform, to the new boss module.

As another example, we want to demonstrate what to do when the central transform contains several process bubbles from the data flow diagram. It is best to use the second method (create a new boss) in this case. Let us assume that we decide processes 3.4 and 3.5 from Figure 2-8 are the central transform. We first draw a larger circle around these two processes on the data flow diagram (Figure 2-8). Next, we cut all of the connecting data flows. Finally, we connect or hang each process and the central transform from the new boss (top control module). Therefore, the first rough draft system structure chart looks like this

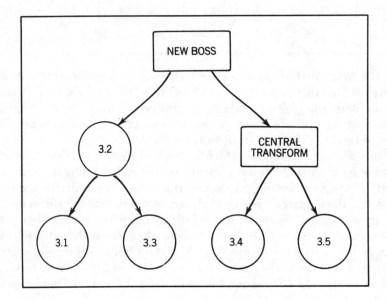

Do not worry about the mixture of circles and boxes in the above first rough draft. Everything will be converted to boxes when we refine the first rough draft and proceed on to the final structure chart.

To continue our example, let us say that we decide that the preceding rough draft (our third try) fits the situation best. Therefore, our next draft looks more like a structure chart

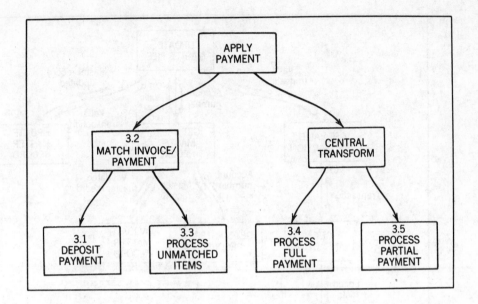

Now we must refine and develop the final system structure chart. Incidentally, in the above draft structure chart, we borrowed the name for the new boss (top control module) from bubble 3.0 in Figure 2-7.

In the final structure chart, we probably would eliminate the module DEPOSIT PAYMENT (3.1) from the above draft because it is not a programmable task. In reality, it is the movement of money and checks to the bank.

Actually, our final structure chart, developed from the above draft, is shown in Figure 2-19. First look at the central transform (PROCESS FULL PAYMENT and PROCESS PARTIAL PAYMENT modules). We added modules such as UPDATE ACCOUNTS RECEIVABLE, SEND LETTER, and SEND INVOICE in order to show the programmer what must be programmed. With regard to the modules MATCH INVOICE/PAYMENT and PROCESS UNMATCHED ITEMS, we also added a few modules, such as GET INVOICE AMOUNT, GET CUSTOMER ADDRESS, STORE UNMATCHED DATA, and SEND CUSTOMER LETTER.

The large arrows that interconnect each module show an invocation or CALL to the module below it. The small arrows show the data that is passed up or down between modules. Small arrows also can show control status (see box in Figure 2-19). At this point, you have a structure chart that shows each programmable module, the data that is passed between modules, and the control status that is passed between modules. In other words, you have a graphic picture of the programs.

Structure charts may show even more detail than we show in Figure 2-19. For example, a structure chart could go down through the hierarchies as follows

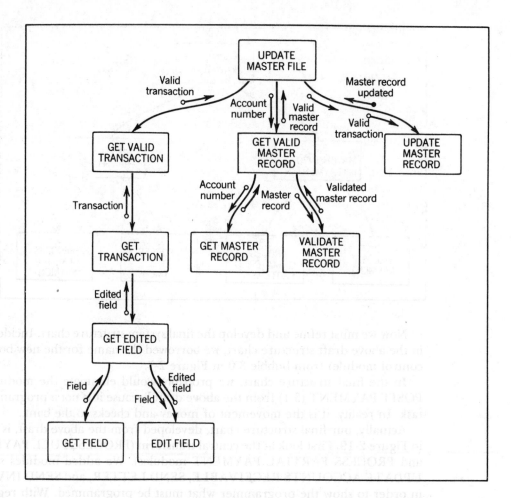

Notice that there are several levels between UPDATE MASTER FILE and GET FIELD in the above general example.

Finally, each module must be documented so the programmer will know what is to be programmed. This can be done in several ways. First, you can write pseudocode for each module (pseudocode is described later in this chapter). Second, you can use English narrative or structured English to describe what must be done within each module. Third, you can define each module in the minispecifications. Both structured English and minispecifications are covered in the next section of this chapter.

Some users of structured techniques feel that the lowest level data flow diagram processes automatically becomes the modules that the programmers use to implement their program code and/or program modules. In fact, programmers do use these to guide the program code, but design is modified for flexibility and maintainability. It is always better, therefore, to convert the lowest level data flow diagrams into structure charts. This makes it clear which are control modules and which are worker modules (the boss/subordinate relationship).

The system structure chart[3] also can be used as a document for controlling and monitoring the final programming, testing, and implementation of the system because you are able to determine which program modules have been coded, which have been tested, and so forth. Do not let us confuse you here; *all* modules on a system structure chart are automated. Only automated processes are put onto system structure charts; manual operations are left until after the analysis is completed and they are defined in the procedure manuals. Actually, the manual process procedures may not be written into procedures until Step 10, the implementation (installation).

Minispecifications

During the discussion on data flow diagrams, we indicated that processes are the points in the system at which data is transformed in some way. An input to a process may be transformed into several outputs. The fact that one input can be transformed into several outputs implies that decisions are made during the data transformation process. How these decisions are made in processes is the concern of the minispecification.

Most of us have encountered situations in which we have heard the terms "good or bad credit risk," "poor customer," and so forth. Have you ever thought about what constitutes a "good" or "bad" credit risk? Frequently these ambiguous terms are used in such places as procedure manuals. In the past, it frequently was based on the decision maker's experience. For example, by talking with a person requesting a loan, a bank loan officer would make a value judgment that the loan seeker was either a good or bad credit risk. If asked how the decision was made, the loan officer probably could not say in specific terms. If this same loan officer had to write a procedure telling other people how to evaluate a loan request, it probably would be a lengthy narrative full of ambiguous directions, and listing each exception to the general rules set forth. The reason it would turn out this way is that the loan officer, in fact, made the decisions based on what we call "gut feel." Obviously, this is not a very logical method, but if the loan officer had a low rate of bad loans, no one would bother to question the person or try to get a written policy.

Notice that we used the word policy. You should look upon the transformation of data in a process as an implementation of policy. In reality, the *minispecification* defines the policy rules that govern the process of data transformation.

---

[3] See Eckols' book for another approach on system structure chart creation.

These policy rules can be specified in a variety of ways. For example, they can be written into policy and procedure manuals such as we discuss in Chapter 17. In this age of computerization, however, we have learned how to structure these rules so that the computer can make many decisions for us. As it turns out, the way we structure these rules for computers also are very useful for manual systems. These tools include decision tables, decision trees, structured English, precise narratives such as tight English, and even pseudocode, although pseudocode is more related to programming. We will give a brief overview of how these tools are used and how they relate to one another. They also will be covered in later chapters.

Briefly, *decision tables* are a two-dimensional matrix that show all possible criteria that may be involved during a process, along with the action to be taken for any combination of situations. A *decision tree* also shows all possible conditions and actions, but it resembles the branches of a tree. *Structured English* is derived from structured programming; it uses procedural logic of structured programming (IF, THEN, ELSE, SO, REPEAT, UNTIL) along with English language that is restricted in vocabulary and syntax. It consists only of imperative verbs, data dictionary terms, and the logic terms mentioned above. *Tight English* follows the logical constructs of structured English, but eliminates the clumsy and unfamiliar notations in favor of more familiar, but logically tight English; tight English is derived from structured English. *Pseudocode* uses programming-type logic in an English-like form, but it does not conform to any one programming language. It may be used both during and after the physical design to specify physical program logic, but without any actual coding.[4]

There are times when one procedure is better than another. Decision tables are used when policy selection (carrying out the process) depends on combinations of conditions. They are helpful in prompting users to make decisions for combinations of conditions that show on the matrix as a blank space (instead of yes/no). They are good for showing as many as five or six conditions, but tend to be unwieldy with more than that. They are good for logic display and verification, and programming related tasks; however, users may be intimidated by them, and the tables may have to be reconstructed completely if the policy they interpret changes.

A decision table is another method (besides program flowcharts which are discussed in Chapter 13) of describing the logic of a computer program. The table is divided into two main parts. The upper part contains the questions and rules, and the lower part contains the action to be taken.

In the example shown in Figure 2-20 the upper part of the decision table contains the questions and rules in the sequence in which they are to be considered in reaching a decision. The lower part (below double horizontal line) contains the prescribed action to be taken when a given condition is either met or

---

[4] Gane and Sarson describe these decision making tools in detail.

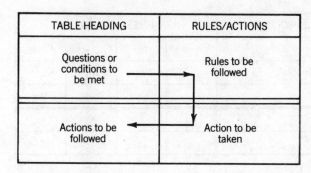

Figure 2-20 General format of a decision table.

not met. The *table heading* is the name of whatever the decision table is defining. The *questions* are the specific conditions that the analyst must choose between; it is for these questions that the decision table is constructed. The *rules* are the different situations such as YES, NO, >, <, =, ≥, ≤, TRUE, FALSE, or whatever rule fits the particular situation. The actions to be followed are the specific actions that the analyst will carry out depending upon the rules. The *action* to be taken shows which of the actions will be followed explicitly.

In reading a decision table the analyst first looks in the upper left corner "Questions or conditions to be met." The analyst reads the first question and then reads the upper right section "Rules to be followed." If the answer to the first question is yes (see Figure 2-21) then the analyst reads straight down that column to the "Action to be taken" section. From there the analyst reads left to the "Actions to be followed" section. In the example, the order would be approved. If the answer to the first question is no, then the analyst looks at the second question. If the answer to the second question is yes, then the analyst again reads down to the appropriate X in the "Action to be taken" section, reads left, and discovers that the order should be approved. Again, if the answer to the second question is no, then the analyst reads the third question. If the answer to the third question is yes, the order is approved; if no, the order is rejected. In summary, the analyst using a decision table like the one in Figure 2-21 would not reject an order unless a no answer was received to all three questions.

A decision table can be viewed as another method of describing the flow of data through a system. Decision tables are most often used for describing the logic of a computer program; but where numerous and complex conditions affect the logic flow in a system, decision tables can be used. Whenever there are situations involving numerous combinations, conditions, and actions, it is easy to overlook the occurrence of any one given combination. Decision tables provide a precise method of ensuring that every possible combination is included. If using traditional systems techniques, however, never allow a decision table to replace a system flowchart (discussed in Chapter 13), because a decision table should only be used to supplement systems flowcharts. One final warning: the analyst must

ORDER ACCEPTANCE PROCEDURE	RULES/ACTIONS			
1. Is credit limit okay?	Yes	No		
2. Is pay experience favorable?		Yes	No	
3. Is D. & B. rating AAA?			Yes	No
Approve order	X	X	X	
Reject order				X

Figure 2-21 Decision table.

remember that decision tables are complex and, therefore, a lower-level clerical employee may reject the use of decision tables. It is important to make sure that employees who must use decision tables can in fact understand them thoroughly. The reader who is unfamiliar with decision tables should work with some until their logic is well understood. Decision tables can be extremely useful to the systems analyst because they subtly force management into defining routine policies.

Decision trees also are used when combinations of conditions need to be presented; however, they fall short of decision tables if the actions resulting from the combinations of conditions total more than about two dozen. Decision trees work particularly well with users because everyone is familiar with tree branches (think of your family tree). They also are fairly good for logic and programming tasks, but do require a human translator (unlike decision tables which can be machine readable). When policies change, trees are easier to change than tables. Structured English is good for the presentation of clear logic, but its structure is awkward and unfamiliar to users. By revising it into tight English, it can be made readable and actually can be made quite usable for procedure manuals. Structured English is most useful when action sequences and loops must be taken into account; these are not well done with decision trees and tables. While it takes more time to learn to use it, structured English can be used during the entire system development life cycle, it can be automated, and it fits well into the data dictionary concepts.[5] In actuality, the primary thing you must remember with any of these tools is that, once used, they *are* the policy. This is perhaps the most difficult concept for you to present to managers who assume that their memos and other written materials are the policy. Their memos may state policy, but these decision making tools implement the policy into a working procedure that employees and/or the computer will use as guidelines. Incidentally, we also should point out that you can use any or all of these tools at various times during a project, and you can use decision trees or tables in conjunction with structured or tight English if it helps make the policy interpretation more clear.

---

[5] DeMarco has an excellent chapter on structured English.

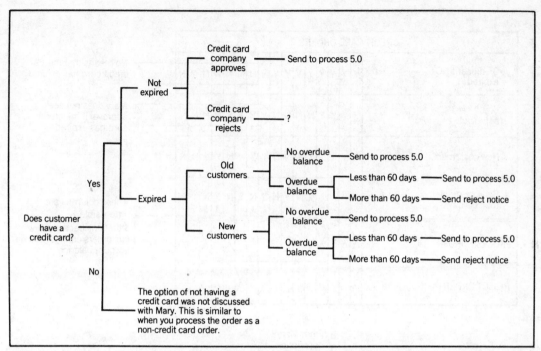

Figure 2-22 Decision tree showing process bubble 2.0, VERIFY CREDIT from Figure 2-7.

As an example of how these procedural tools are used in the decision making process, let us return to Figure 2-7 to look at process 2.0: VERIFY CREDIT. Let us assume that, when you talked to the person responsible for verifying credit, you were told the following

> *When Mary receives orders without any payment enclosed, she forwards them to us. We look at the order to determine if the customer wants to pay by credit card. If so, we have to check with the credit card company to make sure we'll get paid. If the credit card company says their credit is OK, then we go ahead and process the order. If the credit card has expired, we turn to our internal system and handle it like a regular credit purchase.*
>
> *If it's a new customer, I'd say about a year with us, and if there's no overdue balance, we process the order. But if they owe us money, then we have to determine whether the overdue balance is more or less than 60 days. If it's over 60 days, we reject the order. As for old customers, there's no problem if there's no overdue balance. But if there is, and the balance is over 60 days late, then we reject the order.*

As you can see, this narrative is not very clear. You need some method to document it. While this person is talking, you could be sketching out a decision tree such as the one shown in Figure 2-22. It is easy to use, and the person could

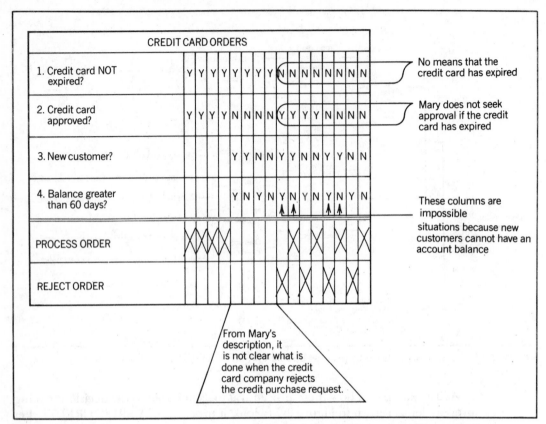

Figure 2-23 Decision table from Mary's description and the decision tree in Figure 2-22.

see that no provision has been made in case the credit card company rejects the person's credit. Is the order returned to the customer, do we call the customer to find out what to do next, or do we check our own files to see if we consider the customer a good credit risk and process it as a regular credit order? Also, if you examine Figure 2-22, you will see that in all cases, old and new customers are treated identically. Is it possible that old and new customers are treated differently? Or, if they are treated the same, have we discovered an extra step in the procedure that can be eliminated when the new system is designed? In either case, this is something that needs to be discussed with the person responsible for the credit verification area.

Now, if we want to guarantee that all possible conditions have been taken into account, we can set up decision tables such as in Figure 2-23. In our decision table there are 16 different yes (Y) or no (N) answers. This is because there are

```
IF credit card order
   and–IF credit card not expired
      THEN call credit card company
         and–IF credit card company approves
            THEN send order to process 5.0
         ELSE (credit card company does not approve)
            SO [not clear what to do, no policy statement]
   ELSE (credit card has expired) locate customer file
      IF old customer
         and–IF no overdue balance
            THEN send order to process 5.0
         ELSE (if overdue balance)
            and–IF less than 60 days overdue
               THEN send order to process 5.0
            ELSE (more than 60 days overdue)
               SO generate reject notice
      ELSE (new customer)
         and–IF no overdue balance
            THEN send order to process 5.0
         ELSE (overdue balance)
            and–IF less than 60 days
               THEN send order to process 5.0
            ELSE (more than 60 days)
               SO generate reject notice
```

Figure 2-24 Structured English example. Compare it with Figure 2-22. It uses specified logic words, verbs, objects and qualifiers (only from the data dictionary), conjunctions, and relational terms (described in the data dictionary section).

four different questions or conditions and only two answers, yes or no. In this case, raise 2 to the fourth power to get 16 possibilities ($2^4 = 16$), or all possible conditions. Notice that we cannot answer what to do with orders in which the credit card was not approved. This also was unclear in our previous decision tree. This demonstrates how decision tables and trees can help you when an employee does not know how to handle a policy decision. The decision table presents all of the possibilities so that you can return to the work area to obtain a policy decision on any unanswerable parts of the decision table.

We mentioned earlier that structured English was more difficult to learn and use with other people. As an example of this, process 2.0 is written in a structured English format in Figure 2-24. You will see that it is both very logical and concise, but also takes some reading to learn to interpret. If you choose to delete the confusing logic words and turn Figure 2-24 into a tight English format, then you would have a procedure such as the example in Figure 2-25.

As you already know from the discussion on data flow diagrams, each lower level bubble must balance its inputs and outputs with the level above it. By using

```
To verify credit:
Step 1:   Check credit card expiration date.
Step 2:   If not expired, call credit card company.
      2.1:   If credit ok, send to process 5.0.
      2.2:   If credit not ok, [not clear what to do, no policy statement]
Step 3:   If expired, locate customer file.
      3.1:   If old customer has:
            3.1.1:   No overdue balance, then send to process 5.0.
            3.1.2:   Overdue balance of:
                  3.1.2.1:   Less than 60 days, send to process 5.0.
                  3.1.2.2:   Over 60 days, send REJECT-NOTICE to customer.
      3.2:   If new customer has:
            3.2.1:   No overdue balance, then send to process 5.0.
            3.2.2:   Overdue balance of:
                  3.2.2.1:   Less than 60 days, send to process 5.0.
                  3.2.2.2:   Over 60 days, send REJECT-NOTICE to customer.
```

Figure 2-25 Tight English example derived from structured English example in Figure 2-24.

decision trees and tables, you may discover previously overlooked details. In our case, we learned that process 2.0 calls upon another external entity called CREDIT CARD COMPANY. If there is an input (a credit verification number) from this new external entity, perhaps there is a new output as well. In fact, it is likely that there is a new output, which is the credit card slip that the credit card company receives and uses to bill the customer.

Now that you have learned how to determine what policies govern a process, you can begin to compile your minispecification. You will recall from our earlier discussion of data flow diagrams that functional primitives are processes that cannot be decomposed further. There should be one minispecification for each functionally primitive bubble. Incidentally, if you developed system structure charts, each minispecification should correspond to the boxes on the system structure chart instead of the data flow diagram functional primitives. Since minispecifications are policy statements that govern processing of inputs and outputs, then your one-page minispecification form should include the name of the process, its number, a brief description of what data is transformed, inputs, outputs, and any problems that need to be resolved before the design phase. Figure 2-26 is our minispecification for process bubble 2.0 in Figure 2-7.

Your objectives in these process minispecifications should be to reduce ambiguity, have concise descriptions of what is accomplished, make sure that all processes have both inputs and outputs, that valid names are used, and that they describe the content and transformation of data inputs and outputs.

PROCESS MINISPECIFICATION

Process Name: VERIFY CREDIT

Process Number: 2.0

Description:

  Determines if credit card information is valid and if order can be shipped. If not, determines if customer credit is acceptable and order is processed or returned to customer for prepayment.

Inputs:

  CREDIT-ORDER from 1.0
  AMOUNT-OWED from data store D3: ACCOUNTS RECEIVABLE
  CREDIT-APPROVAL from CREDIT CARD COMPANY

Outputs:

  VERIFIED-CREDIT-ORDER to process 5.0
  RETURNED-ORDER to CUSTOMER

Logic:

  Verify data with credit card company. Good credit, ship order. Bad credit, check accounts receivable. Good credit, ship order. Bad credit, return order for prepayment.

Attachments:

  See attached decision tree, decision tables, and written procedures.

Unresolved Problems:

  No policy on credit card company reject.
  Are old customers given preferential treatment?
  Is there output to credit card company?

Form 4891 (rev. 9/84)

Figure 2-26 Minispecification documentation for process bubble 2.0 in Figure 2-7. Supporting logic is from Figures 2-22 and 2-25.

System Model

We started with the broadest possible overview of a system, the context diagram. From there you saw how to use data flow diagrams to model the flow of data among processes, data stores, and external entities. You now should understand the basics of how to trace data, assign names to data elements, construct these data elements into a data dictionary, normalize data structures so that redundancy can be eliminated, develop system structure charts, and show data structure relationships by means of data structure diagrams and data access diagrams. When these processes that describe the composition of data are completed, they are ready for assembly into the system database. Also, from the data flow diagrams, we showed you how to describe system processes logically and format the compiled information into minispecifications that describe processing. These steps are the basis of structured analysis techniques. By looking at Figure 2-27, you can see how these techniques parallel one another to form a

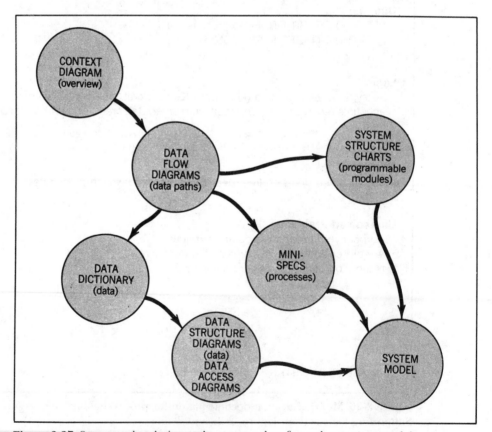

Figure 2-27 Structured techniques that are used to form the systems model.

structured analysis model. By now you probably have guessed that structured techniques are used primarily for the analysis and design of information systems because these techniques stress the transfer and composition of data. They also are used in any system that is dynamic. Since few business systems are static, structured techniques can be applied particularly well to them.

*P*seudocode

Pseudocode is used to specify physical program logic without getting into the detailed syntax of any particular programming language. You can specify the program logic by using the conventions of the previously mentioned structured English.

To do this, you need a few more verb statements. You need to be able to handle program initialization and termination, for example. Other things that must be handled are end of file, reads, writes, the ability to set up counters, and to flag items. You also need to be able to handle loops.

Pseudocode can be a replacement for the flowcharting of a program. It is used in conjunction with structured programming. The logical instructions of a structured design are written in pseudocode. As an example, the following logical instruction may appear

```
PERFORM...UNTIL or DO...WHILE
   This indicates a loop that will be performed until a fixed condition is met.
IF...THEN...ELSE
   IF a certain condition exists, THEN perform a specific task, ELSE perform some
   other task (that is, if the first condition does not exist).
```

You already have seen an example of structured English. If you were to add a few other statements such as the above two, you could use structured English as pseudocode.

A somewhat different example of using pseudocode to specify physical program logic is

```
Initialize program
Read a record, At end move 99 to end of file
PERFORM...UNTIL end of file = 99
   Process record
   Move record to print area
   Write a line
   Read a record, At end move 99 to end of file
END PERFORM, 99 = end of file
End job
Stop run
```

Pseudocode does distinguish between the PERFORM...UNTIL and the DO ...WHILE loops. The DO...WHILE loop assumes that the termination test is made before the loop starts. The PERFORM...UNTIL loop assumes that the termination test is made after the loop has been executed.

Another technique used for designing structured programs involves the use of Nassi Shneiderman charts. These charts are described in Chapter 13.

Using Structured Techniques in Analysis and Design

Early in this chapter we referred you to Figure 2-1, which shows how structured techniques are used during the system development life cycle. We also provided a brief overview of the steps in Figures 2-2 and 2-3. At that point, however, you did not have an understanding of what these steps involved, and so perhaps could not see how they related to one another.

Now that you have this understanding, we want to show you more detail so you can see their natural progression. We break this description into system analysis and then system design. During the 10 steps of the system development life cycle, we will guide you through these procedures by means of a cumulative case. You already have become familiar with some of what Sunrise Sportswear Company does, and we will continue with Sunrise as our case. These are the basic steps that you will be following

    I. Systems analysis using structured techniques
- Build basic model: context diagram
- Start data dictionary
- Build physical model of existing system (DFD)
- Build logical model of existing system (DFD)
- Define new system requirements
- Build logical model of new system (DFD)
- Develop process minispecifications
- Refine data dictionary:
  - Document data elements
  - Document data structures
  - Normalize data structures

    II. Systems design using structured techniques
- Build physical model of new system (DFD)
- Develop data structure diagrams
- Develop data access diagrams
- Develop system structure charts

        ☐ Convert data dictionary to database

        ☐ Program new system

        ☐ Test new system

        ☐ Implement new system

Before proceeding into the first step of the system development life cycle, we want to remind you that the above procedure is greatly simplified. In a real system situation, you may have to iterate through some of these steps several times. The most practical example of what we mean was in our discussion of decision trees when we found that there were some steps in process 2.0 that were not resolved (no policy on credit card company rejection of credit purchase requests) and output to the credit card company. The problems mean you have to go back to the user group to find more details, clarify policy, and perhaps even get them to set a new policy that they did not recognize they needed. If you find new outputs, this affects your data flow diagram, your minispecification, and perhaps the data dictionary (add new data elements and data structures). We hope that you understand now why good and thorough analysis in the beginning is of vital importance. It is not unusual to have one-half of the project effort be the analysis phase because it is so important. If the analysis is partitioned through the use of the leveled data flow diagrams, and if the accompanying structured tools are used (along with any traditional systems analysis tools that apply), then so much analysis effort produces a superior and more maintainable system.

Selected Readings

1. Bytheway, A., ed. *Structured Methods: State of the Art Report.* Maidenhead, Berkshire, England: Pergamon Infotech, 1984.

2. DeMarco, Tom. *Structured Analysis and System Specification.* Englewood Cliffs, N.J.: Prentice-Hall, Inc., 1979.

3. Dickinson, Brian. *Developing Structured Systems: A Methodology Using Structured Techniques.* New York: Yourdon Press, 1980.

4. Eckols, Steve. *How to Design and Develop Business Systems: A Practical Approach to Analysis Design and Implementation.* Fresno, Calif.: Mike Murach & Associates, Inc., 1983.

5. Gane, Chris, and Trish Sarson. *Structured Systems Analysis: Tools and Techniques.* Englewood Cliffs, N.J.: Prentice-Hall, Inc., 1979.

6. Golden, Donald G. "An Experience-Based Study of a Structured Analysis," *Journal of Data Education,* vol. 24, no. 3, Spring 1984, pp. 22–23.

7. Inmon, William. "Data Flow Charts Not for Everyone," *Computerworld,* vol. 18, no. 20, May 14, 1984, pp. 87, 99.

8. Martin, James. *Principles of Data-Base Management.* Englewood Cliffs, N.J.: Prentice-Hall, Inc., 1976. [Relational databases.]

9. Page-Jones, Meilir. *The Practical Guide to Structured Systems Design.* New York: Yourdon Press, 1980.

10. Shank, T. A. *Structured COBOLer's Guide.* Englewood Cliffs, N.J.: Prentice-Hall, Inc., 1984.

11. Steward, D. V. "Lost in the Forest Primeval," *Computerworld,* vol. 18, no. 12, March 19, 1984, pp. ID1–16. [Structured programming tools.]

12. Vitalari, N. P. "A Critical Assessment of Structured Analysis Methods: A Psychological Perspective," *IN Beyond Productivity: Information Systems Development for Organizational Effectiveness, Proceedings of the IFIP WG 8.2 Working Conference, 22–24 August 1983, Minneapolis, Minnesota.* Amsterdam, Netherlands: North-Holland Publishing Company, 1984, pp. 421–433. [Limitations in structuring the problem solving behavior of systems analysts.]

13. Yourdon, Ed, and L. L. Constantine. *Structured Design.* Englewood Cliffs, N.J.: Prentice-Hall, Inc., 1979.

*Q*uestions

1. Define structured analysis.

2. Can you name several of the tools used in structured analysis and design?

3. Is it logical that an analyst working in Phase II of the system development life cycle would be identifying information on the area under study and learning about the interactions between the different areas? Discuss.

4. In what step of the system development life cycle would you start developing the physical model (data flow diagram) of the new system?

5. The structured methodology advocates using up to four different data flow diagram models. Can you give a short definition of each of these four models?

6. What specific task, and a very important one, is performed between the development of the logical model of the existing system and the logical model of the new system?

7. How would you show data stores on the context diagram?

8. Draw and define an external entity, process, data store, and data flow.

9. Look at Figure 2-6. Why was the Accounting Department not connected with the customer with regard to the payment notice?

10. Looking at Figure 2-7, you will notice that data store D1 and data store D3 have been repeated more than once on the data flow diagram. Can you think of a good reason why this was done?

11. Draw a leveled set of data flow diagrams showing at least Level 0, Level 1, and Level 2.

12. Define a data dictionary.

13. Define a database.

14. Define a data structure.
15. When you are defining these data dictionary items, for what reason would you use braces?
16. Define first, second, and third normal form.
17. What is a concatenated primary key?
18. What is a data structure diagram?
19. What is a data access diagram?
20. What is a system structure chart?
21. Name some of the items that might be included in the minispecifications.
22. When using pseudocode, are the PERFORM...UNTIL and the DO...WHILE loops the same?

SITUATION CASES

Case 2-1:   *Mighty Bank*

Jack and Carol are bank tellers assigned to a new service called the "customer quick deposit teller." From a customer they accept deposit slips, the actual deposit, and inquiries about the customer's current balance. When something is wrong, Jack or Carol pass the deposit slip and the deposit over to the customer service section of the bank. They then tell the customer to go over to customer service to have their problem solved.

Questions

1. How many external entities are there in the above?
2. Draw a context diagram of the "customer quick deposit teller" system.

Case 2-2:   *Mighty Bank (continued)*

Now that you know about the "customer quick deposit teller," let us learn more about Jack and Carol's specific duties. Jack accepts the deposit slip and the actual deposit from the customer. The deposit can be cash, personal checks, company/government checks, or travelers checks. This quick deposit window cannot accept checks that are third party, out-of-state, post-dated, or past-dated (more than five days), nor does it handle "less cash" transactions when the customer gets some cash back from his or her deposit. Jack checks to make sure that the name and account number are written on the deposit slip. He then checks that the account number is on file in the customer master index and that the name matches the deposit slip. If everything is in order, he gives the deposit slip, along with the deposit, to Carol. If anything is wrong, he gives the deposit slip and the deposit to customer service and sends the customer to customer service.

Carol makes sure that the deposit amount compares to the amount on the deposit slip. She uses an adding machine if there are multiple items. If the transaction is valid, she enters the deposit amount into the customer's account and stores the money and checks, along with the deposit slip, in her cash drawer for later auditing. She then gives the customer a receipt for the amount of the deposit.

Question

1. Draw a Level 0 data flow diagram for Mighty Bank.

Part Two

THE SYSTEM STUDY ITSELF

*P*art Two describes how to conduct a full systems study. Each of the 10 steps of our system development life cycle (SDLC) are described thoroughly in Chapters 3 through 12. Each of these chapters also has a cumulative case, Sunrise Sportswear Company, which demonstrates the use of structured analysis and design techniques.

Chapter 3

PROBLEM DEFINITION

LEARNING OBJECTIVES

You will learn how to . . .

☐ Begin to use the system development life cycle.

☐ Define a problem.

☐ Conduct an interview.

☐ Use interview questionnaires.

☐ Identify problem sources.

☐ Start the cumulative case using structured techniques.

☐ Draw and use context diagrams.

☐ Start a data dictionary.

*P*hase I: Beginning the Systems Analysis Phase

You are now embarking upon the analysis of a new system. As you can see from Figure 3-1, there are four steps in this phase. This chapter covers Step 1, Problem Definition.

During this phase you also will be completing Step 2, Develop a Study Plan; Step 3, Gather General Information and Interactions; and Step 4, Understand the Existing System. You should note that Step 3 covers two tasks that are done simultaneously. In other words, you will be gathering information on the area under study and, at the same time, you will be learning about the interactions between the area under study and the other areas within or external to the organization.

If you would like to see the overall picture a little more clearly, review Figure 2-1 in order to see how the system development life cycle (SDLC) guides your design effort.

The cumulative case, Sunrise Sportswear Company, starts at the end of this chapter. This case presents a systems analysis and design project using structured techniques.

*H*ow Do You Know You Have a Problem?

Before we discuss whether or not an organization has a problem, let us discuss the difference between whether a problem truly exists, or whether the people working in the organization only perceive that a problem exists. You must be clever enough in understanding people to be able to separate the actual physical existence of a problem from a person's *perception* that a problem exists. An actual or physical problem must be perceived in order to be recognized and then finally identified. A difficulty arises when a problem is perceived where none exists. The perception that a problem exists may be more difficult to correct than if the physical problem truly exists. For example, a person might perceive that a problem exists because of personal dissatisfaction with the current job, or the simple fact that the work cannot be completed each day. In reality, if this person performed his or her work in accordance with the current work procedures he or she might easily complete the work each day. We all tend to find outside excuses when things do not go as they should; therefore, you must learn to be perceptive enough when a person is describing a problem to determine whether it is a perceived problem, or an actual physical problem that can be corrected.

One idea that you might use is to try to identify both the problem (it may be actual, or just a perception) and the person's expectations in this area. In this way you can identify the problem, as stated by whoever is reporting it to you, and

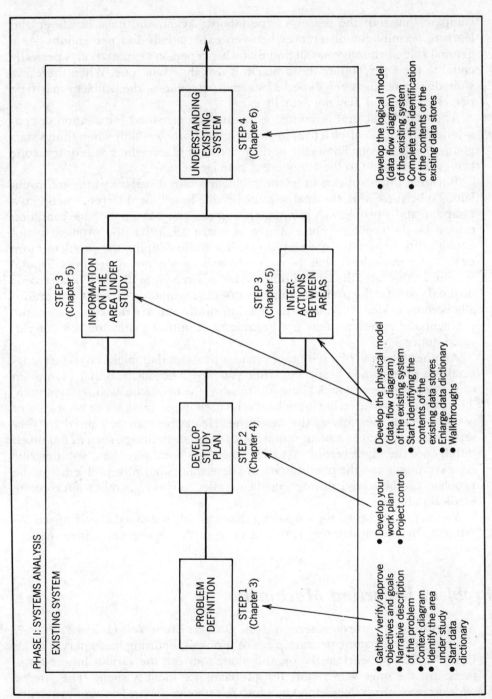

Figure 3-1 Phase I—Systems analysis.

compare that with the person's expectations. Again, you must be clever and learn to account for differences between expectations and perceptions. As a general rule-of-thumb you will find that when a person's expectation is perfectly equal to their perception, the problem is usually a valid one. When there is a wide divergence between expectations and perceptions, the problem may be a perceived one and may not actually exist!

The word "problem" is defined as "a question proposed for solution or consideration." All too often a firm finds out it has a problem only when things start going wrong. No one knows the problem exists until something fails or someone brings the problem to the attention of management.

But what often appears to be the problem is only a *symptom* of the *real* problem. To be successful, the analyst must be able to tell the difference between a symptom and a problem. A symptom is best described as a noticeable condition caused by the problem. For example, it might seem that the problem is not enough office space for the employees. But while defining the problem more exactly, one might learn that the *real* problem is the absence of a records disposal system. In this case, the lack of office space is a symptom; the lack of a records disposal system is the problem. In many cases the symptoms of a problem gradually become evident. Because they develop slowly and are difficult to spot, the problem and symptoms may not be connected until the situation has deteriorated noticeably.

Another example of a symptom versus a problem that might be more recognizable is the common headache. When you have a headache, is that a symptom or is that a problem? Think about it! Probably, the headache itself is a symptom. The pain you are suffering is the headache itself. Now, think about what kind of problem might be causing the headache. Headaches can be caused by very serious things, such as a brain tumor, or by temporary things, such as too much indulgence the night before. Actually, when you see a physician, you describe your symptoms and the physician tries to determine what your problem is so the problem can be solved through medicine, diet, surgery, or other appropriate medical practices.

You may have heard the old saying that a problem defined is half solved. In systems work one learns the truth and value of this saying many times over.

*T*he Problem Reporting Machinery

After reading the previous section, How Do You Know You Have a Problem?, you now realize that the primary piece of problem reporting machinery is PEOPLE. People who work in the organization, and with the various business systems, are the ones who report the problems, or identify them. The *problem reporting machinery* is the method by which the systems analyst learns of problems.

Within the business firm, problems may be top-down (from upper management) or bottom-up (from people who use the system in the conduct of their day-to-day activities). As you think about this, you should realize that we are talking about the true (actual) or perceived problems that you, the systems analyst, may be able to analyze, redesign, and, therefore, "fix." If you are the systems analyst assigned the task of correcting a problem, you must go back to the people in the various areas in order to define the problem.

The problem reporting machinery may involve a verbal message given to a systems analyst, or it may be submitted on a written form similar to the one shown in Figure 3-2.

The systems analyst often faces a constant barrage of problem reports from both internal and external sources. In general these sources are

From the External Environment	*From the Internal Environment*
Management consultants	Data processing
Professional associations	Financial records
State and federal agencies	Management
Crediting agencies	Informal organization
Community relations	Formal line organization
Outside auditors (public)	Employees
Competition	Company auditors (internal)
Customers	Systems department
Unions	Budgets
Regulatory agencies	Compliance auditors

*W*here Problem Signals Come From

Problems are reported through the problem reporting machinery. But the question is, where do problem signals originate? It's still another one of those questions of the symptoms versus the true problem itself. Written or verbal descriptions of a problem that are passed through the problem reporting machinery by an employee in a specific department come from that person's perception of the problem or that person's clear, concise, and factual assessment of the true problem. What we are saying here is that the financial records department, from the internal environment, may report a problem because of dwindling profits or market share. Remember, the department or the people who report the problem are only part of the problem reporting machinery. The problem may be exogenous. You must go out to identify where the problem originated (problem signal). It is when you are out there interviewing people to identify the problem

---

PROBLEM REPORT FORM

STATEMENT OF THE PROBLEM:

The area is overcrowded with records and forms. There is not enough space for the employees to work.

INCIDENTS SURROUNDING THE PROBLEM:

There are records here from 1951 to the current day. Workers appear to be dissatisfied with the clutter. We were unable to find a specific record from July, 1981.

WHY YOU ARE REPORTING THIS PROBLEM:

To propose that we start/study the possibility of a records retention and disposal system.

NAME Carol Thompson	DEPARTMENT Payroll	
TITLE Payroll Clerk III	PHONE X–4356	DATE 7/16/87

Figure 3-2 Typical Problem Report form.

signal that you must be clever enough to separate symptoms from problems and perceptions from actual physical problems. The systems department must be sensitive to changes in the firm's operating environment, so it can anticipate problems and deal with them early. A systems department that is right on target will sense problems even before they are reported officially. The alert systems department will constantly monitor and review activities throughout the firm. For example

Activities to Monitor/Review

Relocation of work areas.

New equipment installation and use, such as computers.

New system implementation and use.

Product change.

Management policy decision.

Customer, supplier, or employee feedback.

Employee morale.

Project budgets.

Number of people required for tasks.

With regard to the specific problem signals, there are a number of kinds of problems that occur within any business organization. Some of the problems that may occur range from security of the organization's data or finances, to areas such as who will have access to what information and what purpose this information might serve. Problems frequently arise when the business systems of an organization are inefficient, their accuracy is not high, they do not produce consistent data, or their reliability is constantly put to question. Finally, you can look at problems from the viewpoint that a system does not offer the speed of throughput necessary, or it is too costly to operate. The point that you should be aware of is that the above-mentioned items, starting with security and ending with operating costs, are problem signals that you must be able to identify in a more detailed fashion. The specific problem signals that you must look for are items such as those listed below. For example, do not look for problems of efficiency; but do look for evidence of it through low morale, which could be evidenced by high employee turnover and/or many complaints and hard feelings stated by the employees. For example

Problem Signals

Work or processing is too slow.

Too many people required for a task.

Too few people performing a task.

Indirect problem reports from managers.

Delays in new equipment installation and use.

Delays in new system implementation and use.

Customer, supplier, or employee complaints.

Dwindling profits or market share.

Low morale evidenced by high employee turnover.

Budget slippage on projects.

Develop a To Do List

It is often useful for the analyst to develop a habit of utilizing a To Do list to use as an aid in task planning. The To Do list is a common planning method that is nothing more than a variation of the old shopping list. It simply helps the analyst plan in an organized manner. Although there are many variations, two types of To Do lists are especially useful.

The first type is a list of all the tasks to be done tomorrow. It is prepared late in the work day. Any tasks that went unfinished today are the items that should come first on tomorrow's To Do list. Then, any new tasks are added to the list. Each day a new To Do list is prepared for the following day.

The second type of To Do list is an outline of how you are going to carry out the project at hand—in this case, the problem definition study. List in order the tasks that have to be accomplished and how they are going to be done.

Following are some of the areas that are most important to the problem definition study To Do list.

1. Have preliminary discussions with management and attempt to identify problem areas.
2. Study written procedures and attempt to identify procedural problems.
3. Observe the current system.
4. Interview the personnel involved and attempt to identify organizational problems.
5. Gather other data, for example, facts and figures.
6. Evaluate the findings.
7. Come to a conclusion on the definition of the problem; decide not only what the problem is, but also what it is not.
8. Rediscuss the findings with management.
9. Issue Problem Definition Written Report.

These major headings will be discussed more completely in the next section, Define the Problem . . . Subject . . . Scope . . . Objectives. The list should have subheadings and sublists which specify the particular departments, people, records, equipment, and so on, that you intend to see. The To Do list is the analyst's written plan of action. The better the plan, the more likely the analyst is to arrive at a correct problem definition.

The To Do list can be changed to the situation or to the personal liking of the analyst. In any event, if the analyst approaches people in an efficient and organized manner, it will be recognized, and the needed cooperation might be more easily forthcoming.

*D*efine the Problem . . . *Subject* . . . *Scope* . . . *Objectives*

Let us suppose that you as an analyst have detected the symptoms of a problem, and are ready to begin the all-important phase of concise problem definition. In this phase you must define three important things.

First, define the *subject*. The subject is the central theme or topic of your systems study or problem definition. It is simple to say, but quite difficult to do because you can state your subject only when you have a clear understanding of the problem. Obviously, you already can see the difficulty because a clear and true statement of the problem assumes that you have separated symptoms and perceptions of a problem from the actual problem that exists. You may be troubled by this now, as you are learning to be a systems analyst; but, once you get some actual experience to blend with your academic learning, you will feel more comfortable writing the subject/problem definition.

When the subject is clearly defined, you automatically have a title for the problem definition report. For example, the subject of a problem definition study might be "employee payroll complaints."

Second, define the *scope*. Now that you have described the subject/problem definition, you have to determine the boundaries of the study. In other words, state where it will start and where it will end. You must specify which departments, people, and/or organizational areas will be included. The scope is the area or range that the study will encompass. Sometimes it is limited by time, dollar resources, or organizational boundaries. It is always limited by the subject. If the subject is not adhered to, your frame of reference will be lost and you will be unable to focus on the problem area indicated by the subject. For example, if the subject is "employee payroll complaints," then the scope should include only activities that are relevant to payroll. It should not be allowed to wander into other unrelated complaints.

Third, define the *objectives*. The objectives are the things you will be trying to accomplish. In our example, the subject is "employee payroll complaints." The scope includes payroll-related complaints only. The objectives, then, must fit the subject and scope. The objectives should not be too ambitious nor, on the other hand, too limited. Remember, objectives should be measurable so management can judge whether you achieved the objectives. In short, they must express exactly what things you intend to accomplish in the problem definition study. Two objectives in our "employee payroll complaints" study might be

☐ Review timekeeping system methods and forms for adequacy.
☐ Determine whether check writing system (manual or computerized) is up-to-date relative to workload and techniques.

In order to define the subject, scope, and objectives, hold preliminary discussions with whoever raised the problem and with key management personnel involved with the problem. Get their interpretations of what the problem is, what needs to be done, and what the subject, scope, and objectives should be. Work to arrive at common definitions of the subject, scope, and objectives.

Read any pertinent written procedures that relate to the subject of the problem definition study. Ask key management personnel which written procedures pertain to the study.

Go out and observe the system in action. Talk with the employees who operate it. Interview the personnel who are affected directly by the problem. Try to get as many opinions as possible. Study any written procedures that are available. Gather any other data such as quantities, times, amounts, numbers of failures, and so on, that may be significant. Throughout this process, any important information should be recorded for future reference. These notes might include names of people who appear most knowledgeable and from whom further help might be expected, anything historically significant such as other approaches that were tried unsuccessfully, or any procedures that appear to be unnecessary or outmoded. This "observing the system in action" can serve as a check on management's perception of the problem.

After all the preliminary data has been gathered, analyze the findings in order to arrive at a precise definition of the problem. Then go back and talk again with the people who raised the problem or the key management of the area in which you are working to advise them of the findings. The point is that you should discuss the findings with the proper management *before* issuing the final problem definition report.

*I*nterviewing

Your personal ability to talk with other people and to listen to their comments is probably the most important asset you have for getting along in the business world. As a systems analyst, the most important tool for gathering data is the personal interview. Before we go into the details of how to conduct a successful interview and what to ask during the interview, we want to present three rules of thumb for the "game" of interviewing. If you can commit these three rules to memory, they will help you throughout life whenever you are trying to gather information by interviewing others.

□ First, moral judgments by you, the systems analyst, are relevant only when they are in accord with the recognized moral standards of the various participants in the interview. Our own moral standards apply only when we are predicting what our own actions, or counteractions, might be. You should try to identify the moral background of the person you are interviewing, as well as the morality of the company and/or department that an interviewee represents. Will their answers be affected by their own moral judgments or their company's moral judgments? Remember, people's moral judgments may not allow them to dump poisonous chemicals on the ground, but if the company does it, it may be okay to them. Once you have identified the moral judgments, let it go at that. Do not label them as good or bad, just recognize the moral judgments that may affect the answers to your questions.

□ Second, you should assume, unless it is already proven otherwise, that the interviewee's first objective is to stay in power or, if he or she cannot do that, to retire from the position of power with a minimum of personal loss (however he or she views loss) to themselves. You need to recognize also that there may be people throughout the organization about whom such an assumption is unjustified because they would unhesitatingly sacrifice their position in the organization's interest. In the majority of cases, your predictions from the data you receive from interviews will come out much better when you remember this second rule.

□ Third, you should assume, unless it is proven otherwise, that the person being interviewed will act in the organization's best interest as *he or she* sees it, and that this person sincerely believes he or she has a good case as it is being explained to you. Remember, try not to label people as "good guys" or "bad guys." During your interviews there will be numerous people who are trying to promote their ideas or their case according to what constitutes "winning" in their own environment.

Even though you may think the above three rules are harsh and might not apply to everyone, the real world is sometimes quite different from the case studies utilized in teaching interviewing. In case studies, people tend to be nice.

As an analyst, develop an interviewing approach that best fits *you*. You can use a "formal" approach. This approach is very businesslike and follows a step-by-step logical plan with no idle talk or undue friendship. Just business! The next might be the "legalistic" approach. This is a rules approach. For example, this type of person always goes "by the book." In other words, he or she always follows the rules. The "political" approach is next. It is based on doing favors for people, performing only the jobs that make you look good, and acting in a prudent, shrewd, and diplomatic fashion. The last approach is the "informal" or play-it-by-ear approach. This approach follows a plan, but the analyst is able to deviate as required without losing control of the situation. You should be aware, however, that the informal approach can be dangerous because it may appear to the interviewee that you are unstructured and disorganized. With this approach you must avoid looking as though you are unprepared for the interview.

The best approach is one in which the analyst is able to combine the above four approaches. If the analyst can be "formal" when necessary, "legalistic" when challenged, play "politics" with deftness when necessary, and be "informal" in unknown situations, there is a built-in flexibility which cannot help but contribute to the analyst's success. You might remember the acronym FLIP for formal, legalistic, informal, and political.

Systems interviewing simply is talking with people in order to find out how things operate now, and how they might like to see things operate in the future. Interviewing should be used throughout the systems study because it usually produces the most up-to-date information of all the sources available to the analyst. Organization charts and written procedures are often six months behind the times, a condition which can cause the analyst many headaches if they are used in place of interviews. During an interview the analyst has a chance to observe not only the current details of how the system works, but also the personality and attitudes of the employee. The latter can be the more important of the two in many situations. For example, the analyst may discover that a certain file clerk will be the one who will offer the strongest opposition to change. The actual influence the clerk will be able to exert over others must then be assessed, along with various methods of dealing with the situation.

Of course, the analyst should realize that one's own personality and approach will have much to do with the extent of cooperation received from those interviewed. A sloppy appearance, argumentative disposition, or an attitude of superiority can wreck the analyst's chances of getting the help of the employees. Word spreads fast if the analyst appears to be incompetent, disorganized, or untrustworthy. Operations personnel will retain this first impression and will withhold their cooperation as a group, making it nearly impossible for the analyst to ever successfully design and install a system for them.

The wise analyst will study the techniques of interviewing and will always have a planned approach to each interview. Above all, the analyst should bear in mind at all times that the function of an analyst is to *help* the people, not to enhance his own status at their expense. The analyst should have an honest respect for people at *all* levels in the organization, and they should be able to sense this through the analyst's approach.

As we implied, the interview is the best way to get the informal view. Interviews may be of a formal nature with a list of specific questions or they may be informal. The informal interview is one in which the analyst has a list of ideas to explore. The analyst talks informally with the manager or operating personnel in such a way as to get insight into these ideas, as opposed to getting answers to specific questions.

There are many interviewing techniques which the analyst can use to be effective in getting the needed information without wasting time, interfering with the firm's operations, or making a bad impression. At one extreme is the focused interview, in which the aspects of a situation have been preanalyzed and the analyst has arrived at certain conclusions. The analyst develops an interview guide as an outline to the major areas of inquiry. The interview is then focused on the subjective experiences of the interviewee. Responses of the interviewee enable the analyst to test the validity of the conclusions previously mentioned.

At the other extreme is the nondirected interview, where an unstructured approach is taken. The interviewee is encouraged to discuss relevant experiences, define what is significant to him, and express any opinions as he sees fit. Whatever the approach, there are certain aspects to consider for a successful interview.

First, have a plan. Prepare ahead of time some of the guidelines that you will want to follow. Perhaps this will be in the form of an outline, or it may be some specific questions. Define the purpose of the interview and explain why the interviewee's opinions are needed.

Always make an appointment; do not just drop in! Schedule your interview for a time when you can get the full attention of whomever you are interviewing.

It usually is desirable to interview in this order: first, the highest level of management that is involved in the area under study; then, the middle and supervisory managers; and finally, the operational employees in the area under study. In other words, try to work from the top down. This allows you to frame questions to lower level staff that are related to management's goals or objectives.

In the world of business and government, if you go into a working department without getting permission of the supervisory management within that department, you may find yourself rudely cut off and effectively thrown out of the department. Remember, when you are trying to conduct an interview, you are going into another manager's "home." The department is that manager's line responsibility. You must get that person's permission, or at least an acknowledgment of your presence in that area, before interviewing employees. At the least, the management will want to know why you are there, who authorized your activity, what you will be doing, and with whom you will be talking. It is almost mandatory to have the higher level personnel give you a "letter of authorization" to introduce you to their subordinates, although sometimes there is no choice but to work upward. Try to interview people who may have differing perceptions of the same situation so you will have the benefit of contrasting points of view.

Obtain facts in advance. Whenever possible, gather background information both on the person to be interviewed and on the problems to be discussed. Try to determine what policies or personalities might be involved in the subject matter of the interview. How does the person whom you are going to interview fit into this picture? Can you determine any probable biases?

Two or three shorter interviews are better than a marathon because people get bored and lose interest during a long interview. Scheduling shorter interviews at intervals also allows both the analyst and the person being interviewed time to think between interviews. Each can go over his or her questions and answers, and perhaps decide to modify some of them. Such modification of ideas brings the analyst closer to a precise understanding of the system.

A *second* aspect of successful interviewing is knowing how to conduct yourself during the interview.

Follow the plan or outline, but try not to stifle productive conversation with excessive rigidity. Try to get the needed information in a tactful way, without sounding as though you are grilling the person. Never allow the interview to sound like an investigation of something suspicious. (With the current rising trends in white collar crime, however, it is always possible that you may stumble upon some dishonest or illegal activities during a study.) Since you probably will want this person's help in the future, try not to give the impression that you are checking up on the person by comparing the person's opinions with the opinions of others. You do need to dig, however, to get to the problems and answers, so you might employ the technique of suggestion to see what reaction you get. It also is wise not to quote people directly by name since it is almost certain to get back to them. Instead, frame a hypothetical question or use some other indirect approach.

Relax and be flexible. Deviate from the outline if you think it will be more profitable. During the interview, be aware of body language on the part of the interviewee. There are many subtle involuntary reactions that can aid the interviewer. Among these are a slight change in facial expression, a change in the pitch or tone of voice, hesitancy in answering a question, or the tensing of a muscle.

There are two possible extremes to the personality of the area under study. In one, the people are relatively happy with their work, their surroundings, their manager, and their co-workers. For the analyst this is an ideal situation because happier people tend to be more cooperative—they want to right a wrong in their system.

At the other extreme is the group of people who are unhappy with themselves, their surroundings, their manager, and their co-workers. This attitude will be reflected in their acceptance of the analyst. They will either tend toward complete rejection, or they may open up to the analyst and pour out their troubles. Should the latter occur, try not to become involved in the group's day-to-day problems unless they pertain to the study. However, you will not want to turn them off entirely. Listen, for as short a time as possible. Then explain that you are sorry you cannot help them now on those points, but perhaps if they will complete a Problem Report form, then someone can begin taking action. Or if those points are completely out of your control to remedy, suggest another approach, if you can; and then get down to the business at hand.

Ask for opinions and hunches, as well as for facts. All are equally important in learning about the existing system. Subjective evaluations are often closer to the person's true assessment of present and future realities.

Keep the interview moving, but do not fill periods of silence with idle chatter. Always allow the person lots of time to think! And while doing so, use the time to phrase the next question, or to rephrase a previous one if it did not get the results you wanted. Phrase your questions clearly. If it appears that the person has sidestepped an important question, try to think of another source for the answer. If none exists and you do need an answer, explain why it is so important to have an answer, or explain some of the background or problems that led to the question. Perhaps you will get your answer, or perhaps you will learn there is something wrong with your approach to the subject.

Listen to answers; do not anticipate answers by helping the person choose words. Allow people to answer in their own words at their own speed. If the answer is unclear to you, ask for clarification. If the person is one who obviously has difficulty expressing ideas, you may assist during this clarification stage, but do not put words in the person's mouth during the first answer to a question. Be alert to hidden meanings in answers.

Documentation of interviews is an important feature which should not be neglected. After all the data gathering has been completed, a "weeding out" process takes place during which the documentation is sifted for what is relevant and what is not.

Documentation of an interview takes many forms. Ask the people being interviewed if they object to a tape recorder. If there are no objections, a tape can then be transcribed for more accurate documentation. Notes may be handwritten or they may take the form of drawings or flowcharts. The written document then becomes a permanent record for the phase Understanding the Existing System.

A *third* aspect of successful interviewing is summation. At the close of the interview verbally summarize the points covered, and verify any agreements you think you have reached with the person on important or controversial points. The object of stressing points of agreement is to verify that they do in fact exist and to end the interview in an "agreeable" mood.

Immediately after concluding the interview, summarize the interview notes in your office. Evaluate yourself! Were you really successful? Write down all the mistakes you made and decide how to avoid these mistakes in the future. Do not be discouraged. Interviewing takes practice; even the experts run into people with whom they cannot deal in interviews. The wise analyst responds by finding other ways to obtain the needed information and cooperation without succumbing to discouragement.

The Interview Questionnaire

Your use of questionnaires will most likely take one of three forms

- ☐ Fixed format questionnaires that can be answered by the recipients without your presence.
- ☐ Open-ended or free format questionnaires that you can utilize during a face-to-face interview.
- ☐ A combination of fixed format and open-ended, sometimes called a "structured" questionnaire.

Fixed format questionnaires are very much like a multiple choice test. For example, a question is framed and the recipient is asked to check the appropriate box as follows

What Is Your Age?
- ☐ Less than 15 years old
- ☐ 16–19 years old
- ☐ 20–24 years old
- ☐ 25–30 years old
- ☐ 30–40 years old
- ☐ Greater than 40 years old

Another type of fixed format questionnaire is one in which a statement is made and the recipient checks his or her agreement or disagreement with the statement, as follows

The average age of a college freshman is 19 years old.

☐	☐	☐	☐	☐
Strongly agree	Agree	Disagree	Strongly disagree	Have no opinion

As you can see, a fixed format questionnaire is one in which a question is asked and you offer *all* possible answers to that question. The possible choices should be delineated and specific so the results can be tabulated. Fixed format questionnaires lend themselves to computers because of the ease in tabulating the results.

The questions asked should be tested on a sample group of people to ensure that the question is understood, that the answer is relevant, and that the proper questions are being asked with regard to the results that will be reported upon.

The open-ended interview questionnaire is used most often by the systems analyst at the time he or she is conducting a face-to-face, personal interview. In this questionnaire, you are able to write down a specific question for which there is no predetermined set of answers. For example, you might ask the person in charge of data entry for an accounts receivable system, "What do you think is the best method for reentering erroneous data after the data entry people have corrected inputs?" Notice, there is no preset list of correct answers. This type of question allows the interviewee to give his or her opinion as to which is best. Recall our previous discussion and take into account both the perception of this person, as well as what is the actual problem. It is best if you go into a personal, face-to-face interview with a specific list of questions in writing.

The following general ideas are adaptable to most systems type open-ended questionnaires for face-to-face interviews. These examples are indicative only of the types of questions that should be asked. To ask the right questions in any systems study, you must develop them from the study's stated problem and objectives. It is here that a little originality and creativity separate the highly successful systems analyst from the ordinary systems analyst.

For the *operations* in the existing system, the analyst should

1. Determine what is done, who does it, when it is done, how it gets done, where it gets started, and why.
2. Determine how much time it takes: per day, per hour, or per unit of work (average figures or minimum/maximum times should be obtained).
3. Gather ideas, opinions, and intuitive feelings on the system's objectives from the most experienced personnel.
4. Learn the customs and decision rules followed in the area under study, both the formal and informal views.
5. Identify the controls that ensure accuracy and completeness of processing operations.

For the *inputs* of the existing system, the analyst should determine the following.

1. When and how is input received, and in what format?
2. From where and from whom is it received?
3. Is the input used as is, or is it checked, reworked, or just passed on?

4. What is the ultimate use, retention time, filing procedures, and disposition of all copies?
5. What are the controls that ensure accuracy and completeness of the inputs?

For the *outputs* of the existing system, the analyst should determine the following.

1. What information is transmitted and what is the destination of that output?
2. What is the purpose of each copy and the routing of each copy of a form?
3. How is the output compiled, filled out, sorted, reproduced, checked, and what are the various times required for each?
4. What errors and omissions are referred back to the area under study, and what are the corrective action procedures for these errors?
5. How is the output controlled to ensure that it is accurate, complete, timely, and only delivered to appropriate personnel?

For the *computer* or related equipment, the analyst should determine the following.

1. Identification and description of the computer and its related equipment.
2. A list of the applications being run on the computer that pertain to the area under study.
3. Workload: amount of work, and the time required to do it.
4. Capability: unused capacity, programming, and systems capability.
5. What controls are in place to ensure a secure computer system?

Verbal Presentation

After you have successfully defined the problem, management may decide that a verbal presentation of the general findings is appropriate. If so, the following discussion may help you be more effective in getting your ideas across.

The first step before making a verbal presentation is to make an outline of what you want to talk about. It should follow the outline of the written report you intend to make on the problem study. Remember that management does not have time for lengthy and dull presentations, so make the talk short and meaningful.

Summarize how you came to be aware of the problem, its subject, scope, objectives, and finally the definition of the problem. Outline the departments and/or important people interviewed (so management will feel free to point out anyone missed). As precisely as possible, note the findings, both pro and con. Describe any proposed changes and how successful or unsuccessful you feel they would be and why. You will probably want to include known cost factors. Any impending changes of standards, for example, also should be noted to give management a chance to postpone a decision until the needed information arrives. You also may point out whether any need exists for outside consultants. Above all, demonstrate a clear understanding of everything you are talking about. They will be looking for it.

For those who would like to incorporate a more thorough discussion on the verbal presentation at this point, there is more information in Chapter 11, Selling the System. It has enlarged sections titled, Gaining Acceptance through the Verbal Presentation, The Presentation Itself, Visual Aids, and Ending the Presentation. This abbreviated discussion on the verbal presentation was placed here because it may be needed at the end of your problem definition.

*P*roblem Definition Written Report

The written problem definition report is a short report that sets the stage for an advanced feasibility study or a major systems study. It is mandatory that this written report on the problem study be made, not only for communication now, but also for future use in further studies. Again, we must stress that the analyst should demonstrate a clear understanding of the problem. Failure to do so will cause management to lose confidence in the analyst's ability to handle the situation.

Management quite often makes a judgment on whether the work has been done correctly and completely, based on management's *impression* of the systems analyst who did the work. If you appear unsure of yourself or your work appears to be incomplete, then management may assume that the work was not done correctly. Remember, correctness is easy to measure if you are working with a known mathematical formula, but it is very difficult to measure when you are putting together different business opinions and building a new system. *Your* personal confidence factor, *your* verbal presentation, and *your* report will be used by management to judge the problem definition as presented.

Remember, the outline for the verbal problem definition report may be the basis for the written problem definition report. The written problem definition report outline will vary with the situation, but in general it should contain the following.

1. Introduce the problem: subject, scope, objectives.
2. Explain any modifications to the original plan.

3. Indicate which areas of business were included or excluded.
4. Clearly define the problem.
5. State which objectives were met and which ones were not, and why not.
6. Point out interrelation between problems, or any unique situations.
7. Make recommendations.
8. Explain your logic if need be.
9. Use any charts, graphs, DFDs, pictures, floor plans, or layouts required.

*O*ther *Considerations*

There are many pitfalls that can be the undoing of a systems analyst. Of these, the following tend to cause the most damage.

1. Improper problem definition by management, accompanied by the lack of a problem redefinition by the analyst. (The world's best solution to the wrong problem has a net value of zero.) It is in the problem definition/ redefinition phase that the analyst and management agree to agree on the subject, scope, and objectives.
2. Excessive ambition, leading to the consideration of the analyst's favorite alternatives only. The analyst tries to force a favorite solution as the last word on the situation.
3. A solution oriented more toward the technical peculiarities of a computer than to the objectives of the people who will use the system. If a system fits the computer but not the users or the organizational framework, the system will not be the solution to your problem. It will be a new problem.
4. Straying from the objectives of the problem study and becoming preoccupied with techniques or equipment for their own sake. Do first things first. Stick to the objectives.
5. Always be ready to restructure your original or current approach. Avoid setting your approach to solving the problem in cement. Be flexible and be ready to listen to other people. Remember that you can use their ideas to restructure your approach, perhaps making it more successful than the original approach.
6. Be careful not to draw incorrect conclusions from your interviews. The best thing that you can do to avoid drawing incorrect conclusions is to find out why a person gave you a specific answer to a specific question. You might go back and re-read our three tentative rules for the "game" of interviewing. Remember also that it is your job to extract *reliable* information. Other means of determining the validity of information acquired are

to cross-check against other interviewees, search for commonality in the interviewee statements, validate against history files or procedures, determine the interviewee's competence and reputation for veracity, and determine the degree to which the interviewee feels threatened by the interviewer.

SUNRISE SPORTSWEAR COMPANY

CUMULATIVE CASE: Problem Definition (Step 1)

The Sunrise Sportswear Company is a medium-size mail order clothing firm that specializes in good quality casual clothing. It was established 25 years ago and is located in a small southern city. Its location is quite advantageous because it is in the heart of the southern textile industry. Also, because of its location in a small city, and because it has a reputation for being a good employer, many of its employees have been with the firm for a number of years. It is a family-owned business whose employees are looked upon as members of the family.

Although Sunrise Sportswear has experienced moderate growth through the years, rapid expansion has not been considered to be a desirable goal by the owners. Instead, they preferred to maintain their image as a supplier of quality clothing. This image has served them well because many customers have been with them for quite a few years. Over the last two years, however, Sunrise has experienced a surge of growth for which the owners were unprepared. This growth has led to some customer-related problems that are causing the owners some concern. They value their long-term customers and want to match their service to their product. The problems caused by the upsurge in new customers, however, have caused Sunrise Sportswear's owners to seek the assistance of a consultant.

The Casper Management Consultants firm specializes in solving business problems. CMC, as it is known, is located in a large city near Sunrise Sportswear. Since it also is in the heart of the textile industry, many of its clients are textile-related firms. In fact, one of Sunrise Sportswear's suppliers suggested that CMC might be able to help solve some of its vexing customer service problems.

You are a systems analyst with Casper Management Consultants, and you are making your first visit to Sunrise Sportswear. The managing owner, Stanley Reynolds, greets you warmly. He tells you something about the background of the company and then begins to describe his problem.

Sunrise Sportswear does its business primarily through catalog mail order sales. Customers send in orders three ways. If the customer is a catalog recipient, the normal method is to fill out one of the catalog order forms and then either send a check or indicate that it is a credit card order. Mr. Reynolds calls this a prepaid order. He notes, however, that some customers are in a hurry for their merchandise and call in their orders. In this case, the customers are asked for a credit card number, but if they do not have one of the three major credit cards, then credit is extended by Sunrise Sportswear. Also, if a customer places an order by letter and does not know how much money to send because no catalog is available, that becomes a credit order. When the order arrives at Sunrise, prepaid orders are processed right away. Credit card and other credit orders take a little longer because credit orders have to be verified before the merchandise is sent. As Mr. Reynolds sees it, there are two problems. The first is that credit verification is taking too long and Sunrise Sportswear is losing valued customers who get impatient and cancel their orders. The second problem is that a growing number of people are getting their merchandise on credit orders, but Sunrise Sportswear is not getting paid. These credit customers really seem to be placing an undue strain on Sunrise Sportswear's resources, but the firm also wants to keep its good customers. Mr. Reynolds wants you to help him find some solutions to the problems in Sunrise Sportswear's Order Processing operation.

You ask Mr. Reynolds if his staff is aware that he has hired a consultant and if you are free to meet with people in the Order Processing operation who might be able to help you. He assures you that everyone is aware of your visit, and they all want to cooperate, since they have a great deal of loyalty to the firm and also are dismayed by the problems they seem to be encountering. He then takes you on a brief tour of the facility, stopping last in the Order Processing area. While there, you are introduced to the following people

Valery Brunn, Manager of Order Processing.
Jon Gray, accepts customer orders.
Rosemary Dunlap, handles customer payments.
Lynn Porter, handles credit card orders.
Bob Thompson, handles other credit orders.
Suzanne Wolfe, handles new customer records.

After the tour and introductions, the employees' work day is nearly over, so you cannot begin any interviews. Instead, since Mr. Reynolds has indicated that the problems appear to be in the order verification area, you ask both Lynn Porter and Suzanne Wolfe to fill out CMC's Problem Report form so that you can get an idea of what they feel is causing the problem. You ask them to have the forms ready when you return the following day, and they agree. Also, you ask Valery Brunn for a copy of the Sunrise Sportswear customer order form (Figure 3-3). You also ask if any other forms are used during the Order Processing operation. Ms. Brunn provides a copy of the Order Verification form (Figure 3-4) and explains that most people call it the "Blue Sheet" because of the blue colored paper on which it is printed. She explains that this form is attached to

SUNRISE SPORTSWEAR
CALL US TOLL-FREE (800) 555-1212

Sold to:

Place peel-off mailing label here. Please correct if incorrect.

Ship to: (only if different from "Sold to")

☐ Mr. ☐ Ms. First Name Initial Last Name

Address

City State Zip Code

Page	Item No.	Description	Size	Color	How many	Price	Total

Amount Enclosed	Total Price of Items	
Credit Card Number	Add 5% sales tax if state resident	
Circle one American Express Visa MasterCard	Shipping, Packaging & Handling	
Expiration Date	TOTAL	
Form 73 (7/85)		

Figure 3-3 Sunrise Sportswear catalog order form.

PREPRINTED ORDER NUMBER

ORDER VERIFICATION

DATE/TIME STAMP

ORDER INFORMATION VERIFICATION

Customer Name & Address
☐ in file   ☐ not in file
address changed (if applicable)

Inventory
☐ in stock   ☐ not in stock

Gift card enclosed
☐ yes   ☐ no
(if yes, put number on envelope)

Payment method
☐ check   ☐ credit card
☐ money order   ☐ credit order
☐ other (specify) _____

ROUTED TO
☐ Credit card verification
☐ Credit order verification
☐ New customer
☐ Inventory
☐ Backordered
☐ Returned to customer
   Reason returned _____

INVENTORY
☐ All merchandise sent
☐ Partial order sent
☐ Gift card enclosed (if applicable)

SHIPPING
☐ COD   ☐ Federal Express
☐ UPS   ☐ Other (specify)
☐ USPS

CREDIT CARD VERIFICATION
☐ Expired   ☐ Not expired
Credit card no. _____
☐ American Express
☐ Visa
☐ MasterCard
Card approval no. _____

CREDIT ORDER VERIFICATION

Old customer
Overdue balance
   ☐ yes   ☐ no
If yes
   ☐ less than 60 days
   ☐ more than 60 days

New customer
Overdue balance
   ☐ yes   ☐ no
If yes
   ☐ less than 60 days
   ☐ more than 60 days

CREDIT ACTION
☐ Approved, to Inventory
☐ Not approved, returned to customer
☐ Reason for return _____
☐ Invoice, to Accounting
☐ Approved, gift certificate sent

SUNRISE SPORTSWEAR

Figure 3-4 Sunrise Sportswear Order Verification form. Also known by employees as the "Blue Sheet."

each incoming order and follows it all the way through the process until the merchandise has been shipped. It is their means of making sure that each task is performed.

That evening you examine the forms. You also fill out a CMC Problem Report form on behalf of Mr. Reynolds (Figure 3-5) because you hesitated to ask him to do it. After that you fill out CMC's Interview Notes form (Figure 3-6) so that you can put your impressions down on paper while the interview is still fresh in your mind.

The next morning you meet with Valery Brunn. She spends some time explaining how the Order Processing area operates. She explains that when the orders first arrive, a "Blue Sheet" with a preprinted order number is time and date stamped. That form is matched to the customer's order by writing the Blue Sheet's preprinted order number at the top of the customer's order form or letter. That way, if the order gets separated, it can be traced. If the order is telephoned, the telephone order clerk fills in the catalog order form, just as the customer would have done. The telephone order clerk then turns the completed order form over to the person who does the time and date stamping. From then on, telephone orders are treated just like any other order.

They designed the Order Verification form (the real name of the "Blue Sheet") so that it could be attached to the customer's order form and be checked at each step of the process. For example, Jon Gray is the first person to handle the order. He time and date stamps the next prenumbered Order Verification form and attaches it to the order. He also writes the Order Verification number on the customer's order. Then he checks to see if the customer is in our files, checks to see if the merchandise is in stock or not, checks to see if the ordered merchandise has the correct item numbers and description, indicates whether a gift card is enclosed (writes the order number on the envelope, if there is one), then indicates how the customer paid, or intends to pay, for the merchandise. If Jon cannot match the order to our merchandise, or if he sees that we are out of stock, he returns the order to the customer for clarification or re-order. After those things have been checked off on the Order Verification form, he indicates where the order is to go next and routes it to the appropriate person.

If checks or money orders have been enclosed, they are checked against the amount on the order form to be sure the amount is correct. Then payments are forwarded to Rosemary Dunlap, who actually applies the payment to the invoices or otherwise applies the checks to the customer's account.

If the customer's name is not found in the current customer file by Jon Gray, then the order goes to Suzanne Wolfe, who enters the new customer's name, address, and date into her system. If it is a customer that Jon can locate in our file, and if it is a credit order, then he passes it to one of the credit verifiers. If it was prepaid, it is sent on to the inventory group so the items can be pulled from inventory.

The credit verification process is fairly straightforward. Ms. Brunn then gives

---

PROBLEM REPORT FORM

STATEMENT OF THE PROBLEM:
Credit verification takes too long.
Credit customers not paying their bills.

INCIDENTS SURROUNDING THE PROBLEM:
Customer orders have been held up while credit verification takes place. Some customers have cancelled orders because of this. Accounts Receivables have been increasing and credit customers not paying Also, some old customers have called because their orders were rejected for bad credit.

WHY YOU ARE REPORTING THIS PROBLEM:
We can't afford to lose valued customers. But we also cannot allow uncollected accounts to grow any more.

NAME *Stanley Reynolds*	DEPARTMENT *Executive*	
TITLE *Owner*	PHONE *X371*	DATE *3-25-86*

Casper Management Consultants   CMC Form 986 (rev 9/85)

Figure 3-5 Problem Report form you filled out on behalf of Stanley Reynolds.

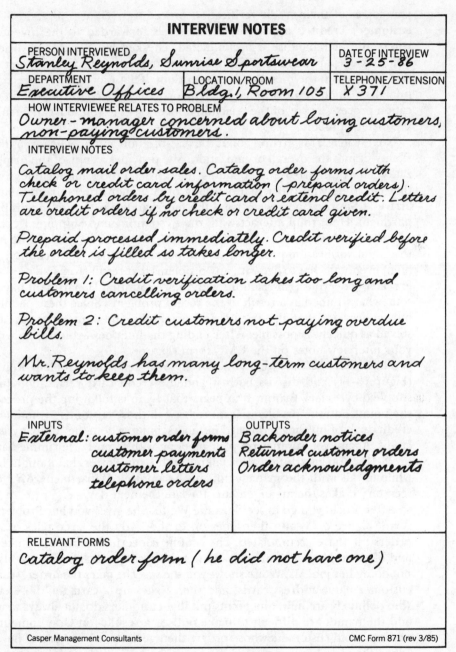

INTERVIEW NOTES

PERSON INTERVIEWED
Stanley Reynolds, Sunrise Sportswear

DATE OF INTERVIEW
3-25-86

DEPARTMENT
Executive Offices

LOCATION/ROOM
Bldg. 1, Room 105

TELEPHONE/EXTENSION
X 371

HOW INTERVIEWEE RELATES TO PROBLEM
Owner-manager concerned about losing customers, non-paying customers.

INTERVIEW NOTES

Catalog mail order sales. Catalog order forms with check or credit card information (prepaid orders). Telephoned orders by credit card or extend credit. Letters are credit orders if no check or credit card given.

Prepaid processed immediately. Credit verified before the order is filled so takes longer.

Problem 1: Credit verification takes too long and customers cancelling orders.

Problem 2: Credit customers not paying overdue bills.

Mr. Reynolds has many long-term customers and wants to keep them.

INPUTS
*External: customer order forms
customer payments
customer letters
telephone orders*

OUTPUTS
*Backorder notices
Returned customer orders
Order acknowledgments*

RELEVANT FORMS
Catalog order form (he did not have one)

Casper Management Consultants   CMC Form 871 (rev 3/85)

Figure 3-6 Your notes of the interview with Mr. Reynolds.

you copies of their credit verification procedures (Figures 3-7 and 3-8). If the customer's credit is approved, the order is forwarded to the inventory area, where the merchandise is accumulated, checked, and then forwarded to the Shipping Department. The Shipping Department returns the Order Verification form when the merchandise is sent out. That way we have a record on the final disposition of the order. Also, if an order is rejected during the credit verification process, a copy of the rejection notice is sent to Jon so it can be matched to the order number.

Next, you ask Ms. Brunn about the organization and how her areas of responsibility fit into the overall organization. She provides a copy of the firm's organization chart (Figure 3-9), explaining that Order Processing includes everything that has to do with the actual handling of customer orders, from the time they arrive at Sunrise Sportswear until the merchandise is sent to the Shipping Department. Her group interacts with the Accounting and Shipping Departments, as well as with suppliers who stock their merchandise inventory. She notes that the credit verification process is very important because the Accounting Department eventually has to live with any problems that result from bad credit customers. Her concern is that relations with the Accounting Department have become somewhat strained as a result of the recent problems. Since these people are not only co-workers, but also friends and neighbors, she wants to get the problems solved as quickly as possible. After ending the interview, you stop to write down your interview notes on the CMC form (Figure 3-10).

Your next visit is with Lynn Porter. You read her Problem Report form (Figure 3-11) and discuss both it and the credit card verification procedure supplied by Valery Brunn. It appears that Lynn is following the procedure. As she points out, the problems seem to be with those customers who have invalid credit cards or invalid credit card numbers, but to whom the company still grants credit. Again, you summarize your meeting with Lynn Porter immediately (Figure 3-12). You also decide after talking with Lynn Porter that it might be worthwhile to talk with the manager of the Accounting Department. Mr. Reynolds' secretary makes the arrangements for late the next day.

After lunch, you go to see Suzanne Wolfe. She gives you her Problem Report form (Figure 3-13) and then goes on to show you the large piles of customer orders that have accumulated. She is quite concerned because she likes her job and likes working at Sunrise Sportswear, but she is afraid of being blamed for not doing her job. Ms. Wolfe shows you the way she takes the order, searches the customer name/address cards, and then writes up a card for those customers who definitely are new. She points out that customers do not always write clearly and the names are difficult to make out. As a result, Jon Gray sometimes does not locate old customers whose orders then get delayed because of her backlog. When Suzanne has completed writing up the new customers, she forwards prepaid orders to inventory and credit orders to either Lynn Porter or Bob Thompson. As before, you complete your Interview Notes form immediately after the

To verify a customer's credit card, you should:

First, check to see if the credit card has expired. If it hasn't, then the second step is to call the credit card company to see if the customer's credit is acceptable. If it is approved, the credit card company will give you an approval number which you write on the Order Verification form (Form 57). Then you can forward the order to the inventory area where they will pull the merchandise and complete the order. But if the credit card company does not approve the customer's credit, then you should forward the order to our credit orders person who will see if we can extend credit to the customer.

If the credit card has expired, you should locate the customer's file. If it is an old customer who has no overdue balance, then approve credit and send the order on to inventory. If there is an overdue balance of less than 60 days, you also can approve the order and forward to inventory. But, if the overdue balance is more than 60 days late, send a reject notice to the customer.

If the credit card has expired and it is a new customer, locate the customer's file. If it has no overdue balance or one of less than 60 days, then you can forward the order to inventory. If there is an overdue balance of more than 60 days, however, you should send a reject notice to the customer.

Figure 3-7 Procedure to verify credit card customer credit.

To verify non-credit card credit orders:

First, determine if it is an old or new customer.

If it is an old customer, locate their file and see if they have an overdue balance. If they don't, then you can approve the order and forward it to inventory where they will fill the order.

But, if they have an overdue balance, then you have to determine if it is more or less than 60 days overdue. If it's less than 60 days, then you can extend credit and send the order on to inventory. But if it's more than 60 days, you should send a reject notice to the customer.

If it's a new customer, you locate their file. Check to see if they have an overdue balance of less than 60 days. If so, you can extend credit and pass the order on to inventory. But if it's more than 60 days, send out a reject notice.

Figure 3-8 Procedure to verify non-credit card customer credit.

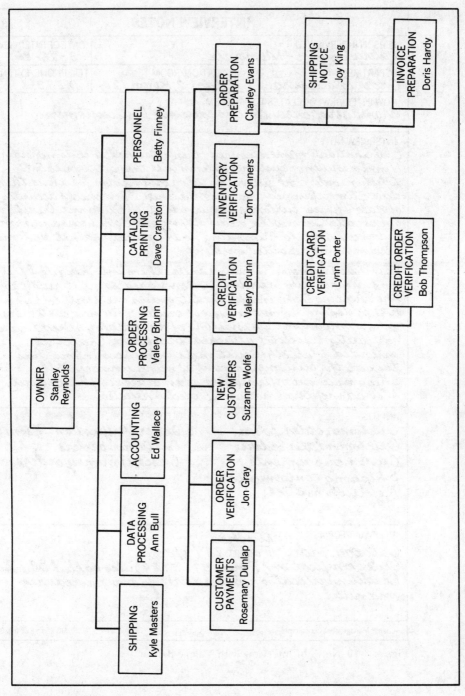

Figure 3-9 Organization chart for Sunrise Sportswear Company.

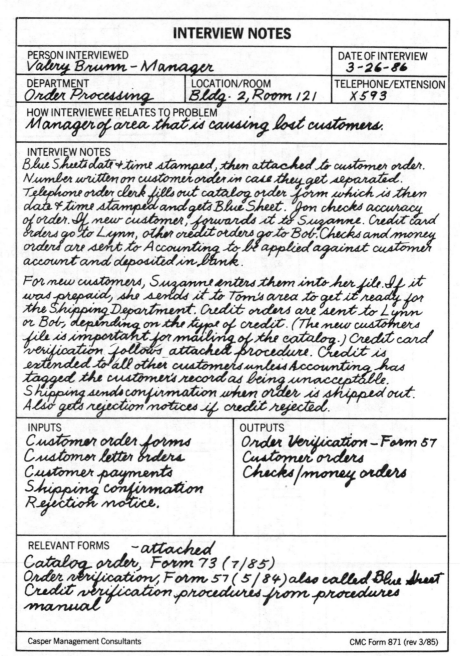

INTERVIEW NOTES

PERSON INTERVIEWED
Valery Brunn – Manager

DATE OF INTERVIEW
3-26-86

DEPARTMENT
Order Processing

LOCATION/ROOM
Bldg. 2, Room 121

TELEPHONE/EXTENSION
X593

HOW INTERVIEWEE RELATES TO PROBLEM
Manager of area that is causing lost customers.

INTERVIEW NOTES
Blue Sheets date & time stamped, then attached to customer order. Number written on customer order in case they get separated. Telephone order clerk fills out catalog order form which is then date & time stamped and gets Blue Sheet. Jon checks accuracy of order. If new customer, forwards it to Suzanne. Credit card orders go to Lynn, other credit orders go to Bob. Checks and money orders are sent to Accounting to be applied against customer account and deposited in bank.

For new customers, Suzanne enters them into her file. If it was prepaid, she sends it to Tom's area to get it ready for the Shipping Department. Credit orders are sent to Lynn or Bob, depending on the type of credit. (The new customers file is important for mailing of the catalog.) Credit card verification follows attached procedure. Credit is extended to all other customers unless Accounting has tagged the customer's record as being unacceptable. Shipping sends confirmation when order is shipped out. Also gets rejection notices if credit rejected.

INPUTS
Customer order forms
Customer letter orders
Customer payments
Shipping confirmation
Rejection notice.

OUTPUTS
Order Verification – Form 57
Customer orders
Checks/money orders

RELEVANT FORMS   *– attached*
Catalog order, Form 73 (7/85)
Order verification, Form 57 (5/84) also called Blue Sheet
Credit verification procedures from procedures manual

Casper Management Consultants

CMC Form 871 (rev 3/85)

Figure 3-10 Notes of interview with Valery Brunn.

PROBLEM REPORT FORM

STATEMENT OF THE PROBLEM:

A lot of customers write down the wrong credit card number or send numbers that have expired. We usually give them credit anyway and a lot of these people aren't paying their bills. If the persons' credit looks really bad, we return the order.

INCIDENTS SURROUNDING THE PROBLEM:

Ed Wallace, the Accounting Dept. manager, says the number of bad accounts is rising and wonders if we are checking credit the way we're supposed to. Also a couple of angry customers have called Mr. Reynolds lately. They've bought from Sunrise for a long time and don't see why their orders were returned.

WHY YOU ARE REPORTING THIS PROBLEM:

I'm doing my verification tasks the way I've been instructed. Since it's not working, we need to find another way to do it so we don't have all these problems.

NAME	DEPARTMENT	
Lynn Porter	Credit Card Verification	
TITLE	PHONE	DATE
Verification clerk	X287	3-26-86

Casper Management Consultants   CMC Form 986 (rev 9/85)

Figure 3-11 Lynn Porter's Problem Report form.

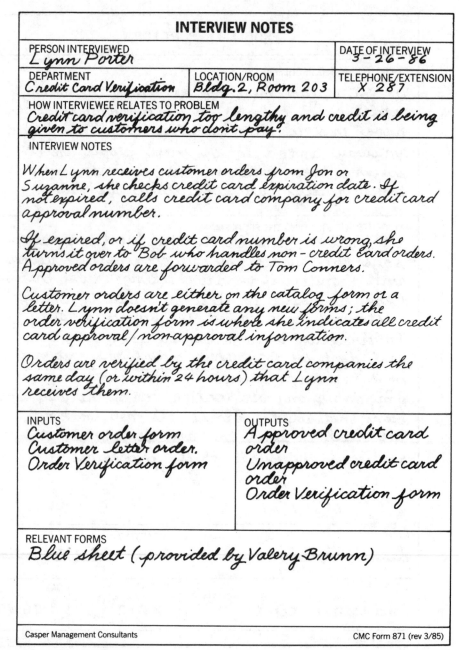

Figure 3-12 Your notes of interview with Lynn Porter.

PROBLEM REPORT FORM

STATEMENT OF THE PROBLEM:

My job is to enter new customers' names and addresses into the system. We've gotten a lot of new customers in the last couple of years and I can't handle it anymore by myself. There are just too many to process. We need to hire another person so we can check the names against the cards and complete the filing

---

INCIDENTS SURROUNDING THE PROBLEM:

We've lost some new customers, before we even got their orders processed. The reason was because we are so backed up and the processing got delayed. When the people started tracking down their orders, they were right here in my area.

WHY YOU ARE REPORTING THIS PROBLEM:

I'm frustrated because I have so many cards to check and file. We need another full time person if we're ever going to get caught up and stay that way. Also, I feel real bad that we lost customers because my area is so backed up.

NAME	DEPARTMENT	
Suzanne Wolfe	New Customers	

TITLE	PHONE	DATE
New Customer Clerk	X 473	3-26-86

Casper Management Consultants   CMC Form 986 (rev 9/85)

Figure 3-13 The Problem Report form completed by Suzanne Wolfe.

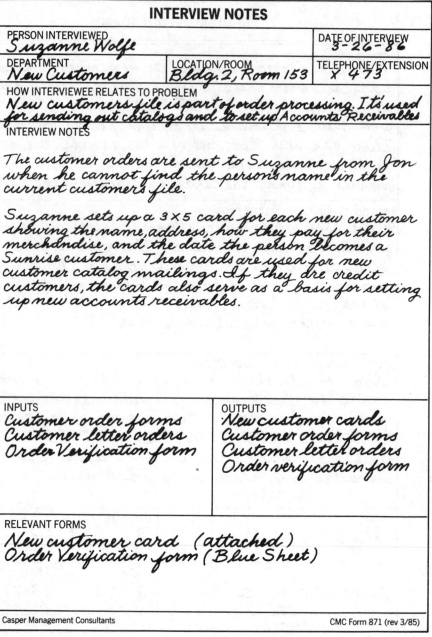

INTERVIEW NOTES

PERSON INTERVIEWED
Suzanne Wolfe

DATE OF INTERVIEW
3-26-86

DEPARTMENT
New Customers

LOCATION/ROOM
Bldg. 2, Room 153

TELEPHONE/EXTENSION
X 473

HOW INTERVIEWEE RELATES TO PROBLEM
New customers file is part of order processing. It's used for sending out catalogs and to set up Accounts Receivables

INTERVIEW NOTES

The customer orders are sent to Suzanne from Jon when he cannot find the person's name in the current customer's file.

Suzanne sets up a 3 × 5 card for each new customer showing the name, address, how they pay for their merchandise, and the date the person becomes a Sunrise customer. These cards are used for new customer catalog mailings. If they are credit customers, the cards also serve as a basis for setting up new accounts receivables.

INPUTS
Customer order forms
Customer letter orders
Order Verification form

OUTPUTS
New customer cards
Customer order forms
Customer letter orders
Order verification form

RELEVANT FORMS
New customer card (attached)
Order Verification form (Blue Sheet)

Casper Management Consultants   CMC Form 871 (rev 3/85)

Figure 3-14 Notes of your interview with Suzanne Wolfe.

KIRKPATRICK, Lyle M.

307 Mockingbird Lane, Apt. 116
Louisville, Kentucky 40397

credit card
5-7-85

Figure 3-15 New customer record supplied by Suzanne Wolfe.

interview (Figure 3-14). Also, Suzanne Wolfe has given you one of her new customer record cards (Figure 3-15). Then it is time to visit Accounting.

The manager of Accounting is Ed Wallace. His first comment is, "Well, it's about time we got some help. Those people over in Order Processing have no business giving credit to some of the deadbeats we've been dealing with."

He then goes on to explain that they expect payment of invoices within 30 days. At this time more than 10 percent of their customer accounts are more than 60 days overdue, and of these 10 percent, about half are 120 days overdue. He considers five percent over 60 days late to be excessive. Mr. Wallace tells you that he has been looking into using a collection agency to collect the aged accounts receivable. He also mentions that Mr. Reynolds is not inclined to use a collection agency because he wants to keep valued customers, and he is afraid it will hurt Sunrise Sportswear's reputation. On the other hand, Mr. Reynolds also is concerned that something be done to improve the situation because they are beginning to have some cash flow problems. As Ed Wallace sees it, if the problem gets much worse, the cash flow problems are going to be severe.

You ask Mr. Wallace about the flow of information between his department and Order Processing. He tells you that all of the credit work is done by Order Processing. Accounting is provided with customer payment data and is expected to collect on unpaid invoices. The Accounting Department's primary function is to handle payments to merchandise suppliers and vendors who supply other

INTERVIEW NOTES

PERSON INTERVIEWED *Ed Wallace*		DATE OF INTERVIEW *3-26-86*
DEPARTMENT *Accounting*	LOCATION/ROOM *Bldg.1, Rm. 206*	TELEPHONE/EXTENSION *X 325*

HOW INTERVIEWEE RELATES TO PROBLEM
Handles overdue customer accounts

INTERVIEW NOTES

More than 10% of their customer accounts are overdue by more than 60 days: Considers 5% excessive. Says 50% of the overdue accounts are 120 days overdue. He wants to use a collection agency, but owner against the idea. Overdue accounts starting to cause cash flow problems. Sunrise cannot afford situation to worsen.

All credit verification done by Order Processing. Before Order Processing got so lax about granting credit, Accounting didn't handle customer accounts at all. These problems have just started in the last year or so. They are causing major problems in his department.

INPUTS *Customer payment data* *Checks, money orders*	OUTPUTS *Bank deposit* *Overdue account* *notices*

RELEVANT FORMS
Customer payment form sent with checks and money orders.

Casper Management Consultants   CMC Form 871 (rev 3/85)

Figure 3-16 Your notes of interview with Ed Wallace.

INTERVIEW NOTES		
PERSON INTERVIEWED *Valery Brunn*		DATE OF INTERVIEW *3-27-86*
DEPARTMENT	LOCATION/ROOM	TELEPHONE/EXTENSION
HOW INTERVIEWEE RELATES TO PROBLEM		

INTERVIEW NOTES

Follow-up of yesterday's interview, re: computers.

Data Processing Department has a mainframe computer. They provide batched updates daily on inventory in stock and accounts receivable.

INPUTS	OUTPUTS

RELEVANT FORMS

Sample inventory printout
Sample accounts receivable printout.

Casper Management Consultants	CMC Form 871 (rev 3/85)

Figure 3-17 Notes of follow-up interview with Valery Brunn.

non-merchandise items (such as forms and pencils). Accounting also sends customer payments to the bank and produces the payroll checks. Since Sunrise Sportswear deals with catalog sales and provides directions to customers, it was not expected that Accounting would become involved in customer collection problems. He indicates it has become quite a burden. The summary of the interview with Mr. Wallace is shown in Figure 3-16.

While visiting the different areas of Sunrise, you have noticed that it seems to be primarily a manual operation. That evening, as you go over the day's events, you wonder if Sunrise has any computer capabilities. As a result, the next morning you again talk with Valery Brunn. She tells you that the company does have a mainframe computer in the Data Processing Department. Any computerized work done for her area is batched. The inventory listing is updated every night so that Jon Gray and Tom Conners both have up-to-date inventory information each morning. Also, the accounts receivables are batched and updated daily. She confirms that the rest of Order Processing is performed manually. You gain the impression that Ms. Brunn would just as soon not talk about computers. Her main interest is getting better credit verification faster, which has nothing to do with computers. Again, you make notes of this second interview with Ms. Brunn (Figure 3-17).

At this point, you feel you have talked with everyone who can contribute to your understanding of the problem. You feel that now you are ready to work on the Problem Definition Report. You have completed Problem Report forms, your interview notes are complete, and you have copies of the most relevant forms.

NOTE TO STUDENT: IGNORE MERCHANDISE IN THE FOLLOWING EXERCISES. We have arbitrarily chosen not to include merchandise as a Sunrise Sportswear data flow. You should be aware that some practitioners believe that structured techniques should be used only for *data*. Others contend that physical items or commodities flowing through the system should be included. In this case, we have done both. We have included customer payments (checks are physical items) because they are part of the troubled processing stream. We have excluded merchandise (a physical commodity which is essential to Sunrise Sportswear's existence) because merchandise handling is not part of the problem. We have opted to exclude this extra flow (merchandise) to avoid cluttering the figures. In a real situation, you would have to determine whether such physical commodities are legitimate data flows that should be recognized in context diagrams and data flow diagrams.

Student Questions

1. What are the problem signals?
2. What is the subject of this study?
3. What is the scope (boundary) of this study?

4. What are your objectives?

5. Has Mr. Reynolds defined the problem correctly?

6. Do you see any communication problems at Sunrise Sportswear?

7. Do you wonder when a customer ceases to be a valued customer?

Student Tasks

1. Draw a context diagram representing Sunrise Sportswear's Order Processing situation. (*Hint:* you learned about context diagrams in Chapter 2.)

2. Start your data dictionary by defining each data structure and its narrative meaning, for each data flow in your context diagram.

3. Prepare a written problem definition. Include problem signals, subject, scope, and objectives. Discuss what you know of inputs, operations, and outputs.

4. Are you beginning to see things at Sunrise Sportswear that could be improved upon? If so, have you begun making notes about them for future reference?

5. There are a number of mail order clothing firms. You may receive some of their catalogs. Begin collecting them now because they may be of use to you later in the case.

6. Make a list of only the people you have been dealing with at Sunrise Sportswear. Include their title or area of responsibility if their title is unknown.

Selected Readings

1. Albert, Kenneth J. *How to Solve Business Problems: The Consultant's Approach to Business Problem Solving.* New York: McGraw-Hill Book Company, 1983.

2. Andriole, Stephen J. *Handbook of Problem Solving.* Princeton, N.J.: Petrocelli Books, 1983.

3. Bloom, Naomi Lee, and Richard Schneider. "Avoiding the 'Package Trap': Caution Advised," *Computerworld,* vol. 18, no. 5, January 30, 1984, Special Report 2. [Understanding the business problem before buying software.]

4. Friant, Ray J., Jr. *Preparing Effective Presentations, revised edition.* New York: Pilot Books, 1978.

5. Gause, Donald C., and Gerald M. Weinberg. *Are Your Lights On?* Cambridge, Mass.: Winthrop Publishers, Inc., 1982. [Art of problem definition.]

6. *How to Improve Your Listening Skills: Desk Top Seminar.* New York: John Wiley & Sons, Inc., 1983. (Includes two cassettes.)

7. Jackson, K. F. *The Art of Solving Problems.* New York: St. Martin's Press, Inc., 1975.

8. MacMullin, Susan E., and Robert S. Taylor. "Problem Dimensions and Information Traits," *Information Society,* vol. 3, no. 1, 1984, pp. 91–111. [User problems and their dimensions.]

9. Nirmal, Barry, and Vi Sadler. "Structured Approach to Solving Systems Problems," *Journal of Systems Management,* vol. 35, no. 3, March 1984, pp. 26–27. [Isolating the problem.]

10. Ratliff, Richard L., and Al W. Switzler. "Preplanned Meetings Reap Dividends," *Internal Auditor,* vol. 41, no. 1, February 1984, pp. 47–52. [How to achieve interview objectives.]

11. Spence, J. Wayne. "Software Development Dilemma: A Case of Perceptual Bias," *Journal of Systems Management,* vol. 35, no. 8, August 1984, pp. 34–39. [Real versus perceived with eight zones of nonconcurrence.]

12. VanGundy, Arthur B. *Techniques of Structured Problem Solving.* New York: Van Nostrand Reinhold Company, 1981.

13. Weinberg, Gerald M., and Daniela Weinberg. "The Fuzzy Early Stages," *Journal of Information Systems Management,* vol. 1, no. 1, Winter 1984, pp. 71–75. [How to conduct early systems analysis interviews that are successful.]

Questions

1. What is one of the ways to determine whether a problem is perceived or if an actual physical problem exists?

2. What is a "symptom"?

3. By what method does the systems analyst learn of problems?

4. Identify four activities that the analyst can monitor/review during the problem definition.

5. Identify four typical problem signals.

6. What are the two types of To Do lists?

7. What are the three important things that must be identified during the problem definition phase?

8. What is the analyst's most important tool for gathering information?

9. Name the four approaches to use in interviewing.

10. What are the advantages of scheduling two or three shorter interviews instead of a single long interview?

11. What is the difference between a "focused interview" and a "nondirected interview"?

12. Name three aspects to consider for a successful interview.

13. Identify the two most widely used formats for questionnaires.

14. Under what circumstances are each of the two questionnaire formats most often used?

15. What techniques should be used to gather information on the subject, scope, and objectives of the problem?

16. Discuss what the analyst should determine in exploring the inputs of the existing system.

17. After successfully defining the problem, what should your verbal presentation to management cover?

18. The systems analyst typically falls prey to many pitfalls. Name six.

SITUATION CASES

Case 3-1:   *Anchor Fence Company*

The systems analyst at Anchor Fence Company was asked to simplify the clerical jobs in a department. Carol Thompson had gone through the steps of reviewing the feasibility study. Her major task now was to gain a complete understanding of the existing system. By doing this she would be able to make a comparison between the existing system and the new system that she was about to design.

The first thing she did was interview the employees. Her first appointment was with the accounting clerk. She observed the work that the clerk was performing, the daily routine, and several other small jobs done only at certain times of the week. After the accounting clerk told Carol what he did, she collected all the written procedures for his job. After reviewing the written procedures, Carol found that a few of the duties actually performed by the clerk were unnecessary, and also that the accounting clerk had left out several tasks that the procedure said should be performed. In order to sound friendly, and also to use up more of the time she had allotted for the interview with the accounting clerk, Carol asked how things were at home. He told her all about his family problems.

After the interview she decided to prepare some questions for the supervisor, based on the accounting clerk's interview. That afternoon, feeling it was the best time, she dropped in on the supervisor. She had her questions prepared ahead of time, so there was no empty interviewing time as there had been earlier with the accounting clerk.

The interview began to run into the weekly scheduled conference time for the supervisor, but Carol continued both because of the quantity of her questions and the importance of interviewing this person. She conducted her questions very formally, limiting his discussion to only her questions. In this interview she was very straightforward and businesslike. The supervisor, however, did not agree with some of the duties the clerk said he performed. At the end of the interview with the supervisor, Carol made a short summation of the questions asked in order to stress areas of agreement.

After completing interviews with all of the personnel involved, she decided to go back to her office to summarize everything learned. She reviewed the questions and answers from the interviews, making sure she understood all the answers and remembered all that needed to be answered. While evaluating herself, she reexamined all the written procedures to make sure everything was clear; she determined that everything needed had been covered. At this point, she felt that she knew the existing system very well. She made a written summation of the interviews. In this summation she also made a note to change the following: revise the signature authorization portion of the written procedures, change the local billing procedure from batch to on-line, utilize window-type envelopes for sending the bills, and preprint all return addresses. Carol Thompson was now ready to define the problem of the system.

Questions

1. Were Carol Thompson's interviews scheduled correctly?
2. Can you comment upon the scheduling of the interview with regard to Carol Thompson and the supervisor?
3. For which interview was Carol Thompson prepared?

Case 3-2:   *Questionnaire Consultants*

Assume that you are using an interview questionnaire that will be mailed to each of the respondents. You do not have time to interview them personally; therefore, you have decided to send a questionnaire. Two types of questionnaires are shown below. Comment upon these questions as to their appropriateness and clarity with regard to your questionnaire. In other words, if these were your questions, are they appropriate?

1. Overdue bills should be sent to a collection agency after 60 days.

☐	☐	☐	☐	☐
Strongly agree	Agree	Disagree	Strongly disagree	No opinion

2. Which is best, send overdue bills to a collection agency after 60 days or after 90 days?

Case 3-3:   *A. A. Feather Company*

A systems analyst received the following problem report from the supervisor of the Accounts Receivable Department

---

PROBLEM REPORT FORM

STATEMENT OF THE PROBLEM:

Because of the lack of office space, it has become increasingly difficult for accounting clerks to work comfortably. The recent growth of our workload has brought with it an increase in the number of new files.

INCIDENTS SURROUNDING THE PROBLEM:

Since clerks have to endure the tedious task of searching through outdated files when referring to previous accounts, processing time has been greatly increased.

WHY YOU ARE REPORTING THIS PROBLEM:

I have become aware of a general morale problem within the department arising from the employees' lack of confidence in the present filing system and from the overcrowding. I genuinely feel that a solution to this problem can greatly improve our performance in processing accounts more quickly and accurately.

NAME Gene Nelson		DEPARTMENT Accounts Receivable	
TITLE Department Supervisor		PHONE Ext. 1457	DATE 2-25-87

The following day the analyst discussed the situation with the department supervisor. They decided that the analyst should observe the department in action.

While speaking briefly with a few of the clerks, he noticed occasional trips to massive filing cabinets where several minutes were spent finding material. As a result, the filing area became congested at times.

After mentally assembling the details surrounding the problem, the analyst felt ready to begin the all-important phase of concise problem definition. He knew that three important things must be defined.

First, he defined the *subject* of the problem being studied as a lack of space. Second, he defined the *scope* as being limited to the three local divisional offices. Third, the *objectives* were defined as

1. Determine if a larger office is needed.
2. Develop better employee morale.

Question

1. Has the analyst in this situation successfully defined the problem? Why or why not?

Case 3-4: *Martins Mailorder*

An analyst was asked by the president of Martins Mailorder to define an existing problem. The problem, as seen by the president, was that it took too long to process an order from a customer. In the past it had taken only three hours to process an order. This time had increased to seven hours, more than double the old time.

The department receiving the orders had six telephone operators because all orders were by telephone. The proper order forms were filled out by these telephone operators. The completed forms were sent periodically to the other side of the building where the orders were filled and shipped. The time involved in sending the orders to the Shipping Department (no matter by whom) was insignificant.

The analyst first defined the subject as the time required to process customer orders. Next, the objectives of the problem were defined as

1. Improve order receipt methods.
2. Improve order forms.

After defining the subject and objectives, the analyst arranged for a meeting with the supervisors of the area under study. At this meeting he received their interpretation of the problem and what they thought should be done to correct it. The analyst then observed the department in action to see if anything out of the ordinary occurred. He also interviewed the operators receiving the orders to find out their interpretation of the problem. The analyst gathered such information as the average number of orders taken each day, the time involved in taking the orders, and the time needed for completion of the appropriate forms.

The analyst then assembled all the information he had obtained and determined the real problem. At that point, he returned to the Receiving Department and informed the employees of his findings. He told them that the real problem was with the order form, and that the process time was only a symptom of the problem. Because the company had expanded, the operators were required to take more information for each order. Sometimes the operators were not sure where to put the extra information, causing the order form to be inadequate and obsolete. A new form was needed. If each of the six operators wasted 20 seconds on every order form, and each operator received 100 calls a day, they would waste over three hours a day filling out forms. Therefore, the analyst reasoned that if he redesigned the form and corrected the problem, it would reduce the process time from seven hours to four hours.

$$6 \text{ operators} \times 100 \text{ calls} = 600 \text{ calls}$$
$$600 \text{ calls} \times 20 \text{ seconds} = 12{,}000 \text{ seconds}$$
$$12{,}000 \text{ seconds}/60 \text{ seconds} = 200 \text{ minutes}$$
$$200 \text{ minutes}/60 \text{ minutes} = 3\tfrac{1}{2} \text{ hours}$$

The analyst drew the following to show order flow.

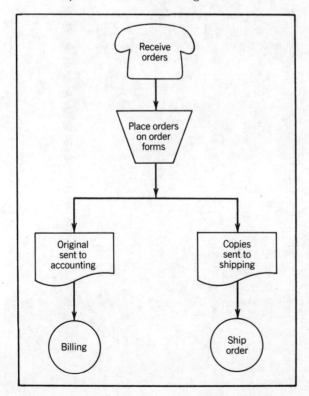

Questions

1. Did the analyst thoroughly define the key terms in the first phase of the problem study?

2. Did the analyst investigate all sources of information in the company pertaining to the department receiving the orders?

3. Should the analyst have reported his findings to the employees of the Receiving Department? Why or why not?

Chapter 4

PREPARE A PLAN OF THE SYSTEMS STUDY

LEARNING OBJECTIVES

You will learn how to . . .

□ Plan your study.

□ Use Gantt charts.

□ Organize the major areas into a plan.

□ Develop an outline.

□ Plan your attack to succeed.

□ Incorporate structured techniques into the system study plan.

Plan for the Study

The system development life cycle (SDLC) is the overall or master plan for your systems study. We want to introduce here the detailed, step-by-step action plan that you should follow. This plan will change many times as you carry out each step of the SDLC. In fact, you may re-do this action plan at each of the 10 steps of the SDLC. Basically, it is an outline of "what you are going to do." Before starting your study, this organized approach is mandatory so you can identify what you are going to do as well as structure a time frame to sequence when you will do what and who you will interview to achieve your goals.

This plan also is necessary in order to manage all of the forms, notes, data flow diagrams, data dictionary, and other structured "stuff" that are gathered or developed during the systems analysis and design steps.

The plan can be arranged in any way the analyst chooses. It may be arranged in order of target dates with each phase delineated by time. Or the analyst may prefer a subject approach with each type of task being a phase.

At this point in time the systems analyst should have a clear and concise problem definition that is understood and agreed upon by all key persons involved in the project. The analyst also may have a feasibility study to help guide in the preparation of the plan. There probably is a context diagram as well.

There are many approaches to a plan, but two excellent ones are Gantt charts and the basic outline. First we will describe Gantt charts and then we will show you how to organize your study into its major areas and develop an outline.

Gantt Chart

Gantt charts are a general form of scheduling tool and a specific form of project management control activity. Gantt charts portray performance against a time requirement. They are a very effective charting technique because they present a project overview or, in their more detailed form, a task overview which is understandable immediately to both systems and non-systems personnel. They allow anyone to review project status quickly and easily.

Figure 4-1 is an example of a Gantt chart. As you can see, the horizontal axis represents units of time in hours, days, weeks, months, or whatever units are appropriate to your project. The left vertical axis can list different projects, or the Gantt chart may be for a single project, with each of the items listed down the left vertical axis being tasks or steps of the overall project. In our example (Figure 4-1), we have titled the left vertical axis "Project Name." You could just as easily title yours "Task Name." To the right of the left vertical axis, Project Name, you will see a column that is titled "S or C." The S or C stand for

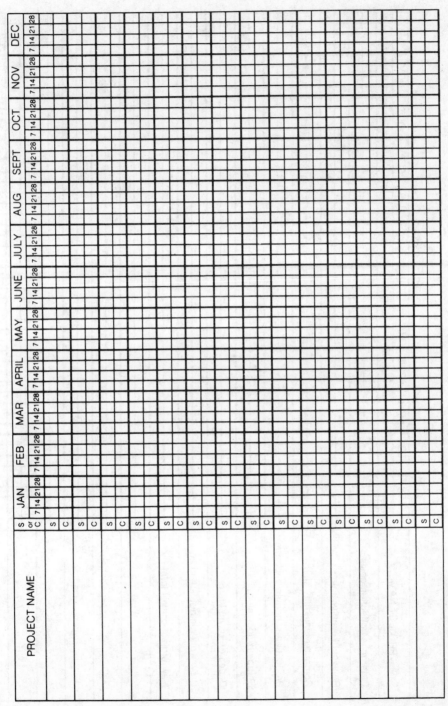

Figure 4-1 Gantt chart.

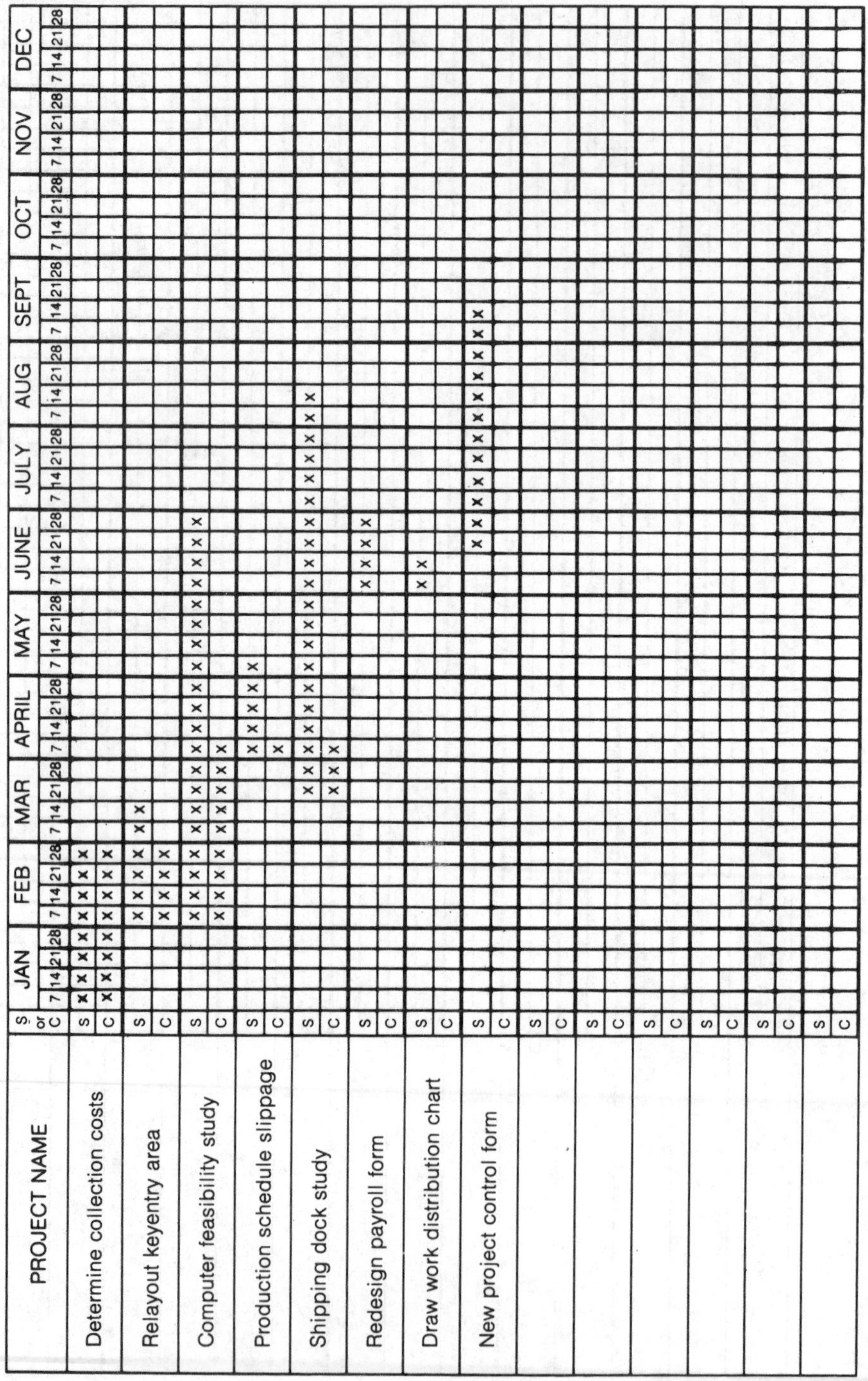

PROJECT NAME	S or C	JAN 7 14 21 28	FEB 7 14 21 28	MAR 7 14 21 28	APRIL 7 14 21 28	MAY 7 14 21 28	JUNE 7 14 21 28	JULY 7 14 21 28	AUG 7 14 21 28	SEPT 7 14 21 28	OCT 7 14 21 28	NOV 7 14 21 28	DEC 7 14 21 28
Determine collection costs	S	x x x x	x x x x										
	C	x x x x	x x										
Relayout keyentry area	S		x x x x	x x									
	C		x x x x										
Computer feasibility study	S		x x	x x x x	x x x x	x x x x							
	C		x x	x x x x									
Production schedule slippage	S				x x x								
	C				x								
Shipping dock study	S			x x	x x x x	x x x x	x x x x	x x x x	x x x				
	C			x x									
Redesign payroll form	S					x x x x	x						
	C					x x x							
Draw work distribution chart	S						x x						
	C												
New project control form	S							x x x x	x x x x	x x			
	C												
	S												
	C												
	S												
	C												
	S												
	C												
	S												
	C												
	S												
	C												

Figure 4-2 Project scheduling using a Gantt chart.

"Scheduled" or "Completed" respectively. For example, if a project or project task is scheduled for June, the analyst puts Xs in the S row under June 7, 14, 21, and 28. As the project is completed, the analyst puts Xs in the C row to show the state of completion. Look at Figure 4-2 which is an example of the scheduling of eight projects. The project "Redesign payroll form" is scheduled for June 7, 14, 21, and 28. Notice that there are eight projects shown in Figure 4-2 and that there are Xs showing the beginning and completion dates in the S rows, for each project. There also are some Xs in the C rows that show the work completed to date. If you assume that today is the first week of April (April 7), then you can see that the first project, Determine collection costs, has been completed. The second project, Relayout keyentry area, is sadly behind schedule because it should have been completed two weeks ago. The third, fourth, and fifth projects are right on schedule. Finally, the sixth, seventh, and eighth projects have not been started yet because they are not scheduled to begin until sometime during June. As you can see, the systems analyst puts Xs in the C row to show the state of completion of a given project or task.

We suggest that you use Figure 4-1 to schedule any or all of the system tasks that you have to complete for this course in systems analysis. You also might use Figure 18-1 to schedule systems projects.

If you want to utilize a much more rigorous method of project planning and scheduling, Chapter 13 describes in minute detail the Program Evaluation and Review Technique (PERT).

Organize the Study into Major Areas

The primary purpose of the systems study outline is to aid the analyst in organizing the study into its major sections. The sections to be used are determined from the subject, scope, and objectives set forth in the problem definition phase.

The 12 areas listed below are *representative* of areas the analyst might consider (depending on the scope of the systems study) when preparing the outline. You may need some of them, all of them, or you may add new ones of your own.

1. *Organization Structure.* Identify the current formal organization structure, and, if possible, the informal organization structure. Determine how the various parts of the current system relate to the different areas and levels of the organization structure. For example, you may be given an organization chart (see Figure 1-6) that depicts the department's formal reporting relationships. While studying the informal workings of the department, you may learn that both the reporting relationship and the internal power structures are different from those depicted in the formal organi-

zation chart. You must be ready to work within the informal organization boundaries, as well as recognize the formal organization boundaries.

2. *Products*. Which products, if any, are going to be studied? Is the firm a profit maximizer, a market share maximizer, is it growth oriented, or is it the type of firm that tries to optimize between profits, market share, and growth? Take into account the products of each department that will be studied. Remember that products can take many forms; even government organizations can have products in the form of services rendered to the public. For example, the product of a department could be a finished good that is sold in the marketplace, such as typewriters or automobiles. A department's product also might be a service, such as data processing (data processing is a service performed for the other departments in the organization). Other examples of products might include further completion of a form, the development of a report, data entered into an on-line computer system, or a management decision.

3. *Marketing*. The firm must adhere to its marketing goals, and you must identify these goals. How does the system relate to the consumers' needs and to the need for internal control within the organization? For example, does the system provide sufficient information on consumer/customer activity in order to carry out successfully its market planning and, ultimately, the marketing of whatever product is the system's output. In some system studies marketing may not be one of the criteria, such as in a payroll system where it is not necessary to market payroll checks.

4. *Communication*. Poor communication between independent areas is a major cause of system failure. Try to determine the patterns of communication within the area under study and the reasons for any apparent communication failures. Organizational conflict is very often indicated by poor or nonexistent communication channels. Determine to what extent formal communication channels are identified within the current policies and procedures of the organization. For example, the formal organization may delineate the official reporting relationships, but the informal organization may identify the actual reporting/working relationships within a department.

5. *Space or Layout*. Evaluate the present space allocations and the layout relative to personnel, equipment, and work flow. Office layout can have a significant impact on interpersonal relationships. For example, cramped space or poor layout may be at the root of the problem in your system study.

6. *Personnel*. Evaluate the personnel involved relative to the current system. Consider sources of job assignments, responsibilities, authority, or job related skills. For example, personal job relationships can be a cause of problems within a department, and you must be able to identify the

differences between symptoms, actual problems, and perceived problems (these were presented in the second section of Chapter 3).

7. *Physical Facilities.* Consider equipment, buildings, telephones, electrical outlets, bathrooms, furniture, maintenance, computer related items, and so forth. For example, your systems study may involve physical facilities, because, as your study evolves, you may determine that new equipment or facilities should be among your recommendations.

8. *Procedures.* Review the current operational procedures; that is, the *what, who, when,* and *how* of the system. Determine to what extent the current procedures are documented and identify key control points and supervisory responsibilities. For example, you must be able to identify and see the difference between the procedure as it is documented (how the job should be performed), and what the people are actually doing (how they actually perform the job on the day you observe them). Chapter 17 discusses procedures more fully.

9. *Policies.* Review management policies. Include the basic policies (long range at the corporate or government level), general policies (short range at the department level), and local policies (everyday at the department level). For example, companies or major government branches have overall policies for their operations and individual departments are expected to follow these policies. You need to review these in order to determine whether they are being followed. Incidentally, individual departments usually write specific procedures on how the work is to be performed, in order to demonstrate conformance with the basic policies of the company or major branch of government.

10. *Records.* Examine the records in the area under study. Note the various reasons for filing, the storage methods, and whether they are manual or computerized. Determine to what extent organizational and governmental records retention requirements are applicable. For example, do not forget that most systems today have computerized record storage (database or sequential methods) as well as manual records, most likely stored on forms within a file cabinet, or on microfilm.

11. *Data Processing.* Interface with the data processing department from the very start of the study. Are you designing around an existing database, or are you planning for a new one? For example, if you are computerizing a manual system or further computerizing a system that is half-manual and half-computerized, you must consult representatives from both the data processing department and the user department for whom you are developing this system. Today it also is advisable to have on the study team representatives from the audit department who can advise on areas of internal control.

12. *Security.* Make sure that you take into account all aspects of security and

control for the new system, whether it is manual or computerized. For example, you need security in the computerized files, manual files, the application programs, and in the manual interfaces where company employees have access to the computerized system. It is advisable to consult the organization's internal audit department with regard to security and control procedures.

The above 12 areas are some of the more important items that must be considered when formulating a system study plan. You may not need to use all 12 of these in each system study, but consider them as an overall checklist and guideline to make sure you cover all the key areas. A short discussion of these 12 items with another systems analyst will clarify which ones are important in the systems study that you have been assigned.

The plan itself should be organized in an outline following the sequence in which the needed information will be gathered. It actually will be a chronological sequence of events that can be followed in carrying out the study. This is important because, if you can develop your outline in the sequence in which you need to gather information, it automatically becomes your day-to-day working plan. It is a guide that can be followed and changed as needed. Remember, flexibility is one of the primary prerequisites of a good systems analyst. Always be ready to modify your system outline (system plan) when necessary, in order to accommodate situations that are revealed as you design a new system.

The system study outline may be nothing more than a detailed To Do list. In reality, it is the working plan of your system study.

Another idea that might help in outlining the plan is to remember that any study may be divided into one or more of the "five levels under study." These five levels were discussed in Chapter 1. For example, if the study involves several departments within a firm (Level III), it also might involve a functional area (Level IV) within each department, and possibly a specific problem (Level V) within that functional area. You might review these five levels as they were described in Chapter 1. An outline of a simple system study is shown in Figure 4-3.

It is important to develop as detailed a plan of action as possible. Include a timetable that specifies both calendar time and chargeable time. Calendar time is the overall time from start to finish, from the first day to the last day. Chargeable time is the actual number of hours to be spent in developing the new system. Since an analyst may be working on several systems projects at one time, chargeable time per week may amount to only 10 hours. It is obvious that if an analyst is supposed to be working 15 hours per week each on four different projects, the analyst either is working many hours overtime or slippage will occur on target dates.

Each activity on the outline should fit into a timetable. Gantt charts are good

Outline of a Systems Study

I. Department X, which involves a subfunction (Level IV) and a specific problem (Level V).
   A. Subfunction within department X.
      1. Study any written procedures and charts.
      2. Interview personnel involved.
      3. Observe current system.
      4. Gather hard data, for example, facts and figures.
   B. A specific problem within the subfunction.
      1. Study any written documentation.
      2. Interview personnel involved.
      3. Observe problem.
      4. Gather hard data, for example, facts and figures.
II. Department Y, which involves the entire department (Level III).
   A. Study any written documentation.
   B. Interview personnel involved.
   C. Observe current system.
   D. Gather hard data, for example, facts and figures.
III. Learn the general background and interactions between departments X and Y.
IV. Evaluate the following from departments X and Y.
   A. Understand the current system in departments X and Y.
   B. Define each department's systems requirements.
   C. Design a system compatible to both.
   D. Develop economic cost comparisons.
V. Sell the system and implement it.

Figure 4-3 Sample outline of a simple systems study involving Levels III–V.

for estimating calendar time, whereas chargeable time can be shown in one number (the number of hours required to complete a task). PERT charts also may be used for more accurate time estimations and are described thoroughly in Chapter 13, along with other charting techniques. We mention this because you might find an alternate charting technique that works better within your organization. Remember, organizations have their own culture. Because of political interactions, organization structure, and personality differences, you may have to adopt a charting technique that, while not your favorite, is acceptable to the group with whom you are working.

An example of a more specific outline for a system study follows. Notice that it is similar to the one in Figure 4-3, but it contains more detail. Suppose an analyst is designing a new order entry system for a company. Also suppose that this study encompasses the following areas: sales branches, order entry department, credit control department, and the production control department. The analyst might structure the outline as follows.

I. Study the Order Entry Department.
  A. Interview key personnel in order to obtain general information on the area under study and interactions between this area and the other areas within the firm.
  B. Study written procedures and observe the current system in operation.
  C. Search through any records and perform any estimating or sampling that must be done.
  D. Understand the existing system as it pertains to this department.

II. Study the Credit Department.
  A. Interview key personnel in order to obtain general information on the area under study and interactions between this area and the other areas within the firm.
  B. Study written procedures and observe the current system in operation.
  C. Search through any records and perform any estimating or sampling that must be done.
  D. Understand the existing system as it pertains to this department.

III. Study the Production Control Department.
  A. Interview key personnel in order to obtain general information on the area under study and interactions between this area and other areas within the firm.
  B. Study written procedures and observe the current system in operation.
  C. Search through any records and perform any estimating or sampling that must be done.
  D. Understand the existing system as it pertains to this department.

IV. Study various sized Sales Branches from different geographical areas.
  A. Interview key personnel in order to obtain general information on the area under study and interactions between this area and the other areas within the firm.
  B. Study written procedures and observe the current system in operation.
  C. Search through any records and perform any estimating or sampling.
  D. Understand the existing system as it pertains to this department.

V. Tie together the general background, the interactions, and the understanding of each individual department's system in order to develop a complete understanding of the entire system as a whole.

VI. Define the new system requirements.

   A. Study the long-range plans for each department, if available, and for the entire organization when it is appropriate for the scope of the systems study.

   B. Define the specific requirements of the new system.

      1. Define the outputs, the inputs, the operations, and the resources.

      2. Take into account the current requirements, the future requirements, and the management-imposed requirements.

      3. Document the new system requirements.

   C. Develop evaluation criteria for the new system.

VII. Design the new system.

VIII. Develop economic cost comparisons, write the final systems report, and implement the new system if management so desires.

Most of us were taught in grade school how to take notes on index cards for a report and then arrange the cards into a report outline. Today, this task of organizing the gathered information can be done using outline processing software developed for microcomputers. These programs allow you to make notes on the computer screen, assign headings and subheadings, and rearrange the material into an outline, much as you once did on index cards.

*P*lan the Attack to Succeed . . . *Techniques*

The most important factor in your favor is a positive mental attitude. Think positively and do not become a cynic because any systems study tends to take on the analyst's personality. Establish the outline in the sequence that the information is needed and seek the required data in a well-organized, efficient manner.

Aim at achievable results. Decide what the constraints are and develop the system within those constraints. For example, if upper management has decreed that they want only a computerized system in spite of the feasibility study recommendation for a manual system, *do not* design an elaborate *manual* system. They will not agree to a manual system. Even though you feel it unwise to proceed on a computerized system, you *must* do so—or perhaps begin looking for another job if you feel you cannot live with management's decision. If you are forced to design a system which you have recommended against, your best defense is to be so well organized that you can report to management what is going to go wrong next—before it happens!

This leads to another success consideration: *try to develop salable approaches.* If you cannot sell the new system to management, all of your effort has been wasted. "Blue-sky" plans are good for long-term conceptual planning, but if you never present down-to-earth, practical, usable *now* plans, management will question your ability.

You should remember that a salable approach takes into account the fact that the system must work within the culture of the organization. By culture we mean the whole set of social norms and responses that condition the organization's behavior. Culture is acquired and inculcated. It is the set of rules and behavior patterns that develop within an organization. For example, the organization operates within a cultural environment made up of folkways, mores, customs, traditions, cultural values of a country or society, and values acquired through the political/economic system in which it operates. In other words, a system that operates beautifully in the United States may not work at all in another country because some feature of the system violates a cultural norm of that country.

Another example is the differences in cultural environments between lawyers, engineers, and teachers. Each may respond differently to your approach. Do not label these responses as good or bad; just learn to work within whatever constraints they create.

For a system to be salable, therefore, you should ensure the following five principal features.

- ☐ *Technical feasibility.* Will this system really work? Sometimes a design on paper will not work in real life. This is why engineers build prototypes; simulation or emulation may not provide correct answers due to hidden tolerances or dependencies.
- ☐ *Operational feasibility.* Will this system work within the environment in which it must operate? This environment (culture) is influenced by the government, the corporate structure, local state or city laws, and the folkways and mores of the individuals who work in the area under study.
- ☐ *Organizational feasibility.* Can this system operate within both the formal organization structure and the informal organization structure of our firm or government agency?
- ☐ *Political feasibility.* Can this system operate given the existing political interactions, if any, among the organization's personnel?
- ☐ *Economic feasibility.* Can the organization afford the new system? Consider the gross cost figures; for example, you cannot spend $1,000,000 developing a new system when the organization's gross revenues are only $500,000.

It is imperative that you realize the importance of selling your ideas on the new system *during* each of the steps when conducting a full systems study (see Chapter 11 on Selling the System).

Confine the limits of the study to the "area under study." Do not get carried away with including too much in your study. Successful completion of a few small to medium-sized systems projects gives an analyst self-confidence and shows management a proven success record. It is desirable to start with small studies and confine the scope to achievable results only.

Develop tentative timetables, both calendar time and chargeable time. Forecast approximate costs, both to carry out the systems study and to install and operate the proposed system. Always be prepared to give management periodic progress reports on your progress to date, cost to date, and any slippage in the time to completion. It usually is a good idea to submit regular, simple, written progress reports which contain the following four important elements.

1. A very short written description of the progress to date.
2. Approximate cost to date compared with estimated budgeted amount to date. (Are you overspending or underspending the estimated budget?)
3. Work completed to date compared with the estimated completion schedule. (Are you ahead or behind schedule?)
4. Report *all* unexpected problems as soon as they are encountered. Do not make excuses later!

Keep the progress report simple because management wants only enough information to evaluate your general progress on the project. Do not burden them with elaborate expositions of project detail, unless they specifically ask for it (Chapter 18 covers progress reports, including a sample).

SUNRISE SPORTSWEAR COMPANY

CUMULATIVE CASE: Prepare a Plan (Step 2)

After your written Problem Definition Report was prepared, you gave a copy to Mr. Reynolds and asked him who he would like invited to your verbal presentation. It was decided that Valery Brunn and Ed Wallace should attend because they were the two managers most involved with the problem. In addition, he wanted Jon Gray, Lynn Porter, Suzanne Wolfe, and Bob Thompson to attend. He explained that each of them would be affected directly by the outcome of the study, and he wanted them to be involved with it from the beginning. Also, he felt they might be able to contribute more information since they worked most closely with the actual processing. You agreed and explained that you believe strongly that users must be involved with the system analysis and design effort all the way through the process. You told him that user acceptance is a part of each major milestone of a systems project. As a result of his requests, you provided each participant with a copy of the written Problem Definition Report (Student Task 3 in Chapter 3) and a meeting time was agreed upon.

You noticed that they all listened carefully to your verbal presentation. None had seen a context diagram (Student Task 1 in Chapter 3), but all thought it was an excellent means of focusing upon the problem areas. They discussed whether any other external entities were involved and decided the context diagram was accurate. Mr. Reynolds was interested in the fact that no provision had been made for what he called prepaid orders. You explained that what constituted a prepaid order varied, and it changed as the order progressed further down to the actual processing. After you pointed out that some of the so-called prepaid orders became credit orders later in the process, and on occasion even became overdue credit accounts, he agreed that it was a term that should be dropped. The terms you chose more closely resembled reality.

The discussion over credit policy was most lively. They had all been under the impression that old customers had a favored status, but when they saw the two policies side-by-side, it became clear that this was not the case. Mr. Wallace indicated that the credit policy was too lax and argued strongly to change it. The people working with the policy agreed that there were many problems working with it. Although Mr. Reynolds had some reservations, he agreed that the problem should be addressed in more detail and he would consider a change.

Everyone seemed surprised that the new customer record cards were so time-consuming. Mr. Reynolds agreed at the meeting to hire a temporary assistant to get the orders up-to-date, but he was strongly in favor of a more viable long-term solution. He wondered if it would be possible to put "some of that simple stuff" onto a computer. You fielded the question by explaining that it was still too early in the process to commit to a solution, but that you would keep the idea in mind for later.

Valery Brunn was in favor of streamlining her operation if it would speed up customer order processing. You also could see that she was surprised that one solution might be to delete some steps entirely or to transfer them to another area that would be better equipped to handle them. You mentally noted that any solution of that nature might cause a "turf battle."

All-in-all, reaction was favorable, and Mr. Reynolds told you to proceed with your analysis. You explained that you would prepare a plan, setting up specific tasks and time frames. This plan would guarantee that everyone would know what to expect in terms of visits to their areas, time needed for interviews, and so forth. You also explained to the group what you had mentioned previously to Mr. Reynolds; that you wanted their involvement throughout the entire system study because it is their system and you want them to like it. Mr. Reynolds said he would like to have some recommendations by the end of May, and you agreed to plan around that date.

After the meeting, you begin to jot down some of the areas you want to investigate. It starts out as a To Do list, but gradually enlarges to an outline. You have a time frame for accomplishing the tasks. Once you know what you need to do, you have the necessary ingredients to develop a scheduling tool.

You jot down the following subjects as *possible areas you may want to pursue.* You recognize that some will be more important than others, and some may turn out not to be relevant at all. Nevertheless, you want to make sure you do not miss anything vital to the outcome of the project, so you write them all down anyway.

A. Organization structure.
   1. Current organization chart up-to-date.
   2. Current organization chart complete.
   3. Current organization chart accurate.
B. Products of the system—service is a product.
C. Marketing concerns—new customer data.
D. Communication.
   1. Interpersonal.
   2. Interdepartmental.
E. Work area layout.
F. Facilities—available resources.
G. Policies.
H. Procedures.
I. Long-range plans.
J. Relevant records.
K. Data processing capabilities.
L. Controls and security.
M. Culture of the group.
N. Feasibility of change.
   1. Technical, including timing.
   2. Operational, including human factors, organizational, and political.
   3. Economic.

Next you jot down some of the *methods you may want to use.* You recognize that some of these methods are used in a specific sequence, while others are used concurrently. You write them all down, however, so that you do not forget anything.

A. Physical data flow diagrams—existing physical model of system.

B. Existing data store contents.

C. Data dictionary—data flows.

D. Logical data flow diagram—model of existing system logic.

E. Logical data flow diagram—model of new system logic.

F. Minispecifications—processes.

G. New system data store contents.

H. Refine data dictionary.

    1. Add new data flows.

    2. Delete unneeded data flows.

    3. Normalization.

I. User requirements.

J. User acceptance.

K. Physical data flow diagrams—physical model of new system.

L. Data structure diagrams.

M. Data access diagrams.

N. System structure charts.

O. Completed system model with documentation.

P. User walkthroughs.

Q. Implementation plan.

R. Implementation, including forms design, procedure writing.

S. Follow-up.

T. Transition to maintenance operation of system.

Now you begin to combine the two lists. The first one is what you want to study, the second is how you intend to do it. You want them both to conform to the general system development life cycle. After working it over several times, you are satisfied with the following study plan outline.

SUNRISE SPORTSWEAR
ORDER PROCESSING SYSTEM
STUDY PLAN

I. Introduction

    A. This mail order firm wishes to provide the right merchandise to the right person at the right time.

    B. To achieve this goal, the Order Processing system must operate in a smooth and timely manner.

    C. The firm also wishes to achieve this goal in a manner that does not jeopardize its financial viability.

    D. To achieve this secondary goal, the entire credit policy framework must ensure that bad credit risks are minimized.

    E. Also to achieve this goal, valued customers must be treated fairly and equitably.

II. Current problems to be addressed

    A. Determine current overall order processing time (average)

    B. Determine critical factors in order verification time as it relates to credit verification

    C. Determine critical factors in new customer data collection as it relates to order verification time

    D. Reduction of credit verification time

    E. Reduction of overall order processing time

    F. Examine credit policies to

        1. Eliminate bad risks

        2. Maintain long-term customers

    G. Reduction of overdue credit accounts

    H. Determine processes that can be combined, deleted, or added

III. Gather general information on the existing Order Processing system

    A. Interviews with affected personnel

        1. Document specific customer complaints to verify that problem definition is correct

        2. Accuracy of existing organization chart

        3. Policies

            a. Credit acceptance versus risk

            b. Credit rejection—extent of human involvement in rejection process

            c. Old customer versus new customer credit

            d. Need to grant credit versus cash or credit card only policy

        4. Written procedures—policy implementation

        5. Long-range plans that may affect area

        6. Records that pertain to problem area

        7. Interactions with other areas

            a. Accounting Department

            b. Data Processing Department

            c. Catalog Printing Department

            d. Shipping Department

e. Customers

f. Suppliers

g. Credit card companies

8. Collect forms, especially customer related

a. Credit rejection notice

b. Returned orders

c. Backorders

B. Sampling

1. Average time to process orders

2. Percentage of check/money order orders

3. Percentage of credit card orders (approved)

4. Number of credit card rejections

5. Percentage of credit card rejections that become overdue accounts

C. Cultural (subjective)

1. Attitudes toward automation

2. Interpersonal conflicts

3. Interdepartmental conflicts

4. Personnel open/not open to change

D. Facilities

1. Layout of order processing stream

2. Physical nearness of contiguous processes

3. Physical nearness of closely interacting people

E. Marketing

1. Importance of new customer data

2. Availability of new customer data elsewhere

IV. Develop physical model of existing system

A. Physical data flow diagram—how

1. Verify inputs

2. Verify processing

a. Verify policies

b. Map policies—decision trees/tables

c. Check for split functions

d. Check for multiple functions listed as functional primitives

3. Verify outputs

4. Identify existing data stores

5. Balance leveled data flow diagrams

     B. Verify existing data dictionary

     C. Enlarge data dictionary

     D. Start data store contents

     E. Start process descriptions

     F. Refine boundaries

     G. User validation of model (walkthroughs)

V. Develop logical model of existing system

     A. Logical data flow diagram—what

        1. Processes

           a. Include those that are

              (1) Policy related

              (2) Essential to the business

              (3) Judgmental in nature

              (4) Essential controls

           b. Eliminate those that

              (1) Merely move data around

              (2) Purely housekeeping

              (3) Non-vital controls

              (4) Exist only to support the old system design

        2. Data flows

           a. Resolve aliases

           b. Balance leveled data flow diagrams

        3. Complete data store contents

     B. User validation (walkthroughs)

VI. Define user requirements

     A. Develop logical model for new system—what

     B. Examine model in view of long-range plans—viability

     C. Start minispecifications

     D. Start new data store contents

     E. Start normalization

     F. User walkthroughs

     G. User acceptance

VII. Develop physical model of new system (design the new system)

     A. Physical data flow diagram—how

        1. Based on logical model of new system

        2. Top-down approach

        3. Define human-machine boundary

B. Convert logical data dictionary to physical data dictionary
C. Complete normalization
D. Data structure diagrams
E. Data access diagrams
F. System structure charts
   1. Top-down approach
   2. Modular
G. Complete minispecifications for all functional primitives
H. Assemble pertinent logic process documentation
   1. Decision tables
   2. Decision trees
   3. Structured/tight English
I. Prototyping for user verification
   1. Screen formats
   2. Report formats

VIII. Assemble control matrices
A. Threats
B. Components (process bubbles)
C. Controls

IX. Assemble cost comparisons
A. Alternatives available
B. Feasibility of alternatives
   1. Technical
   2. Operational
   3. Economic
C. Cost effectiveness of alternatives

X. Present the new system
A. User walkthrough
B. User acceptance

XI. Schedule for implementation
A. Gantt or PERT charts
B. Calendar time
C. Chargeable time

XII. Implementation
A. Program
B. Test
C. Install

XIII. Follow-up
    A. Old system phased out
    B. New system working properly
    C. New procedures in writing
XIV. Transition to maintenance operation

Student Questions

1. Based on your current knowledge, does it appear that any of the external entities will *not* be relevant to your analysis? Explain.
2. Name at least two areas that you can see already that should be targets for improvement.
3. Since you are dealing with a manual system, why would you bother to include such things as data dictionary, normalization, data structure diagrams, and data access diagrams in your outline?
4. Does this study plan fit into your system development life cycle? Why or why not?
5. Can you match the steps of the study plan to the chapters you will be reading later?
6. In Chapter 1, we discussed Levels I–V of the area under study as they pertain to systems studies. What Level is this study?

Student Tasks

Assume that today is March 31st. You must complete your analysis phase and have recommendations prepared by the last week of May.

1. Based on this date and the above study plan, what must you have completed by the last week of May?
2. Your primary task in this chapter has been for you to learn how to plan. The basic study plan has been outlined for you so that you can see how to put together *what* you want to accomplish with *how* you want to accomplish it. Now you must complete the second part of planning, which is scheduling for the project. Use the Gantt chart in Figure 4-1 to help you control the work phases so that the tasks can be completed on time. Gantt out the tasks that must be accomplished by the end of May.
3. We suggest that you use a copy of Figure 4-1 to Gantt chart your work tasks for the remainder of your school term.

Selected Readings

1. Delp, Peter. *Systems Tools for Project Planning*. Bloomington, Ind.: International Development Institute, 1976.
2. Gido, Jack. *An Introduction to Project Planning*. Schenectady, N.Y.: General Electric Company, Technical Promotion & Training Services, 1974.
3. Mills, Chester R. "Strategic Planning Generates Potent Power for Info Centers," *Data Management,* vol. 22, no. 2, February 1984, pp. 23–25.

Questions

1. Why is it important to prepare a plan for the systems study?
2. What do your system study plan and the charting techniques provide?
3. Identify the two basic ways an analyst can choose to arrange the outline of the system study.
4. Identify six of the typical areas the analyst might consider when preparing the outline of the system study.
5. What is the advantage of organizing the outline plan by the sequence in which the needed information will be gathered?
6. From a planning perspective, what are the differences between "calendar time" and "chargeable time"?
7. Of the two types of time (calendar and chargeable), which is best represented by Gantt charts?
8. What are some of the reasons that may cause an analyst to adopt a charting technique that is not a personal favorite?
9. With regard to systems, what must a salable approach take into account?
10. There are five principal features that must be considered to make a system salable. What are they?
11. Why is it important to keep progress reports simple?
12. Discuss the differences between operational feasibility and organizational feasibility.
13. What do Gantt charts portray?

SITUATION CASES

Case 4-1:   *Waters Rug Company*

After developing a very thorough plan (outline of the system study), Mary Watts reviewed this plan with the appropriate people in departments that interact with one another. With regard to the three departments that this new system would affect, she reviewed her plan with two of the three department managers and the first-line supervisor of the third department. The first-line supervisor of the third department was consulted because he seemed to make all of the important decisions for the manager of that department. She convinced the three of them that the system was feasible, both technically and operationally. Technically, the microcomputers were available. Operationally, they fit together very well, and the personnel could be trained easily to use this microcomputer-based on-line system.

Further, the budget was there to purchase the equipment and software, and the organizational feasibility was perfect. This was because, organizationally, the work flow progressed smoothly from department to department.

Mary chose to review the outline with the two managers and the one first-level supervisor for another reason; she had observed that whenever the three managers were all in the same room, a political squabble always seemed to be raised by the third manager. Politically, he appeared to be an empire builder who was out to get the other managers. For this reason, she reviewed the feasibilities of success for the new system by reviewing the outline of the system study (the plan) with the people whom she viewed as appropriate.

Question

1. Comment upon any future problems that might be encountered because of Mary's approach.

Case 4-2: *Daniels Service Bureau*

The Systems Manager assigned one of his analysts to a small payroll project. According to the information given by the Payroll Manager to the Systems Manager, the problem was caused by the large number of time cards that were rejected by the Data Entry Department.

With this in mind, the analyst developed the following outline as an aid in correcting the existing situation.

   I. The Payroll Department
     A. Study any written procedures regarding time cards and their handling.
     B. Interview the payroll clerks.
     C. Observe how the payroll clerks conduct their work in relation to the current system.
     D. Study the format of the time card.

II. Data Processing Department
   A. Study any written procedures regarding time cards and their handling.
   B. Talk to key entry supervisor.
   C. Talk to key entry operators.
III. Learn interactions between the Payroll Department and the key entry section.

When the analyst had completed his outline, he reported to both the Systems Manager and the Payroll Manager. He estimated that he would spend approximately 20 hours of time on the project.

When the analyst finished studying the Payroll Department, he could find no way of correcting the time card errors because they were normal everyday errors made while adding and multiplying. The analyst then set out to study the key entry aspects of the problem. While interviewing the Key Entry Supervisor, he learned that approximately 15 percent of the time cards had errors in either hourly or overtime wages. At this point he became frustrated because he had failed to correct the situation.

Later that month the Systems Manager talked with the analyst and expressed disappointment because the analyst already had taken over two weeks of time on a 20-hour project. The analyst tried to explain that he had allocated only 1½ hours per day to the project. Two weeks later the analyst determined that he had not really understood the problem. The real problem was found to be a lack of calculators in the Payroll Department, which made it necessary to figure over half of the time cards by hand. The cards figured by hand were found to contain a very large percentage of the errors.

Questions

1. How could the analyst have avoided disappointing his manager with regard to the project's time of completion?
2. Which of the 12 considerations in this chapter would have aided the analyst in his outline and would have helped the analyst understand the problem regarding the calculations?

Case 4-3:   *Herzog Pharmaceuticals Company*

Top management at Herzog Pharmaceuticals sought the assistance of a consultant to help them correct a problem in the Final Finishing Department of the plant. It appeared that units were not only backlogged and jammed up in the department, but much breakage and waste also occurred during handling and packing. Since the problem was occurring only in one subsection of the department, management requested that the consultant focus the entire study on that section. They said they were positive the other sections were efficient and did not need to be examined.

Because the problem already had been defined roughly and a feasibility study was not necessary, the consultant began by preparing an outline of the systems study. The areas that she wanted to consider when preparing the outline were: the organization structure, both formal and informal within the department; products to be studied; communication within the department; the space or layout of the equipment and work flow; physical facilities and other related items within the department; current procedures including the "who, what, when, and how" of the current system; management policies; and data processing within the department, if any.

After careful consideration of these items, the analyst prepared the following outline.

I. Final Finishing Department
  A. Packing and Handling Section in the Final Finishing Department
    1. Study any written procedures for packing and handling
    2. Interview personnel involved
      a. Department supervisor
      b. Foreman of the section
      c. Workers
    3. Observe current system
    4. Gather data, facts, and figures
  B. The jam-up and backlog of products in the department, including breakage and waste
    1. Observe the problem
      a. Do the employees arrive at work on time?
      b. How many actual hours and minutes are spent on the job?
      c. Do workers promptly return to work or are they slow in starting after lunch or coffee breaks?
      d. Are machines in perfect working order and arranged to fit the work flow?
      e. Are boxes being padded adequately?
      f. Do boxes have to be carried manually? If so, how far?
      g. Are the conveyors that transport the products too fast or too slow?

        h. Is responsibility distributed evenly among the workers so that one person is not working too fast and mishandling products while another is working too slow and being clumsy?

        i. Perform work sampling study

    2. Gather hard data, facts, and figures, and submit progress report to management

  II. Evaluate the Final Finishing Department

    A. Understand the current system

    B. Define the department's requirements

    C. Design new, more efficient system

    D. Submit cost analysis of the project

  III. Sell the system and implement it

  IV. Submit chargeable and calendar timetables to management

As an experienced analyst, she knew that it would not be wise to try to accomplish too much, so she aimed at achievable results and developed salable approaches that management could accept reasonably.

Questions

1. Did the analyst have a sound foundation upon which to begin the systems study?

2. Which "area" was left out?

Case 4-4: *Micro Disks, Inc.*

Berry Roberts, an experienced systems analyst, was assigned the project of identification, evaluation, and selection of a new accounts receivable (A/R) software package for Micro Disks, Inc. Being experienced, Berry started out by developing a Gantt chart to schedule his project. Knowing that there would be a major corporate meeting on September 23rd, he recognized that the project would have to be completed and his final results ready for both oral and written presentation on that date. Also, Berry had scheduled his vacation for the last two weeks of June, so he had to schedule around that as well. Assume that today's date is May 15th and that Berry started his project on February 1st.

Berry completed his Gantt chart by using the following project name and 10 separate tasks. To schedule his overall project from start to finish, he used the project name "A/R Software." The individual tasks that he performed were preliminary review, develop bid document, bidder's conference, evaluate mandatories, evaluate exceptions, evaluate hardware, evaluate costs, on-site vendor visit(s), final report, and choose the winner. The preliminary review was to be completed by March 1st; although, he had to start developing the bid document during the last week of February in order to get it in the mail by the first of April. The reason he had to have it in the mail by the first of April is that the bidder's conference was to be held sometime during the first week of May. He had to give the bidders the month of April before the conference and three more weeks after the conference because they needed that much time to prepare bids that would be due by May 30th.

The evaluation of the mandatories and exceptions would take place during the two weeks immediately following receipt of the bids. Immediately after his return from vacation, Berry would have to spend the next two weeks evaluating the hardware and the two weeks following that evaluating the costs. This would mean that he would be available for an on-site vendor visit sometime during the first two weeks of August. Assuming the vendor visit was completed by August 14th, this left Berry the next four weeks to prepare and complete his final written and verbal reports. Finally, Berry had one more week before the deadline to choose the winner and award the project. As of today's assumed date, Berry is right on schedule.

Question

1. Use the above information to prepare a Gantt chart showing both the scheduled and completed status. Copy Figure 4-1 for a blank Gantt chart.

Chapter 5

GENERAL INFORMATION ON THE AREA UNDER STUDY AND ITS INTERACTIONS

LEARNING OBJECTIVES

You will learn how to . . .

□ Pinpoint the area under study.

□ Gather background data.

□ Use long-range plans.

□ Identify legal requirements.

□ Work through the formal and informal organizations.

□ Identify interactions between departments.

□ View the interrelationships between outputs, inputs, and resources.

□ Handle company politics that may affect your analysis and design efforts.

□ Identify critical success factors.

□ Draw the physical data flow diagram of the existing system.

□ Identify data stores.

□ Decompose data flow diagrams to their lowest levels.

The Progression of Business Systems

While human organizations all have their similarities, they all have their unique characteristics as well. These characteristics are important to the systems analyst. They are the keys to the objectives that will satisfy the users of the system. No department or function within the organization should be an island unto itself. Rather, it must interact with, and serve, other parts of the organization. An understanding of these interactions will guide the analyst in designing appropriate business system dynamics. This chapter begins by reviewing the progression of business systems over the last 20 or 30 years.

Business systems started out as *manual* systems in which all activities were recorded on paper, such as forms or ledgers. As the modern era of computerized business information systems started, business converted to what we call *batch*-oriented business systems. These were systems in which the business department gathered the input data and put it together. This batch of information was then submitted to the data processing department, where data entry personnel keypunched it for entry into the computer.

The computer system processed this batch of data, and the output was returned to the originating business department. These systems used *discrete files,* which were files of year-to-date data that pertained only to a single business system.

Our next advancement came with the development of *data communication* (sometimes called telecommunication) circuits. These data communication circuits allowed us to move business data from the original batch systems to *on-line batch.* These on-line batch systems still operated in the same manner as a typical batch system, except the data entry function was now performed directly by the user department because it had input terminals.

The next advancement was a major one because we moved to *real-time* systems. These real-time, on-line systems differed from the original batch systems in that they would accept a single input transaction and process it immediately, giving a response to the user within a matter of seconds. In other words, we finally moved from the era of batching large quantities of input data for processing to the era of immediate single transaction processing.

The movement from separate, discrete files to *database* files was the next stage of development. These combined files allowed us to co-mingle the data from several different systems into one file structure. For example, you might have the banking data from the checking account system, passbook savings account system, and certificates of deposit system co-mingled into a single database.

The next advancement was the movement into *integrated systems.* Integrated systems are those in which the input transactions from one system automatically trigger, in the computer program, other transactions to numerous other business systems. For example, when a purchasing agent enters data into the system that acknowledges the purchase of some product, the system produces a purchase order, sends a transaction to the cash flow system so it will acknowledge a future payment, sends a transaction to the accounts payable system so it will set up a matching file to pay for the product (the purchase order, invoice, and receiving dock ticket must be matched), and sends a transaction to the receiving dock so personnel there will anticipate arrival of the goods.

The combination of the above factors and the advent of microcomputers currently is moving us into the world of *distributed systems*. Distributed data processing is when user departments have their own data processing capability; they are able to enter their own data into the system, process it, and develop their own output reports. In other words, instead of having a central data processing function, we now may have hundreds of small distributed data processing functions located within the business areas of the corporation or government agency.

Finally, on the horizon we are beginning to anticipate the move toward *distrib-*

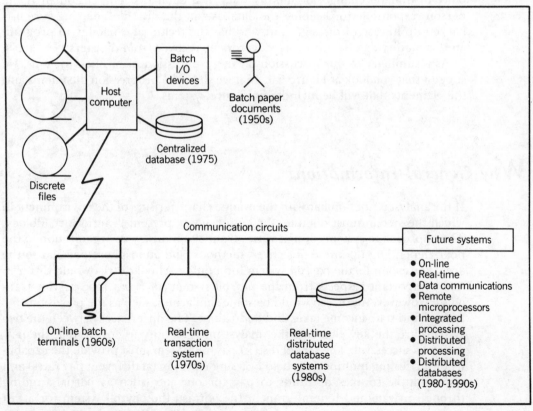

Figure 5-1 The progression of business systems.

uted database systems. This is a situation in which we not only have entered the world of distributed data processing and given user departments their own computer, but we also are distributing the files of data that previously would have been held in a central database.

Our reason for describing how systems have progressed is so you can recognize whether the system being studied is a batch system or an on-line, real-time system. You must determine this when gathering background information on the area under study. Does it use discrete files or database files? Are there data communication circuits? Is this an integrated system interacting automatically with other systems? Is it part of a larger distributed data processing system in which there are microcomputers or minicomputers distributed throughout the organization and interconnected with data communication circuits? (Incidentally, when computers are interconnected by data communication circuits, it is called a network.) Finally, are we dealing with a system that has distributed databases in which user departments are both the owner and the custodian of their own database files? (The owner is the department that "owns" the responsibility to update, change, or modify data in a database. The custodian is the person responsible for keeping the database on the disk files, making sure it is backed-up in case of disaster, and who has the technical capability to program and/or modify databases to correct errors or recover from disasters.)

As a summary to our discussion on the progression of business systems, we suggest that you look at Figure 5-1. In it we show the progression of systems and the elements that will be included in future systems.

Why General Information?

If the analyst is not familiar with the unique characteristics of the environment in which the system must operate, the design phase presents a serious roadblock. The approach to systems design varies from one industry or organization to the next, depending upon the objectives, methods, and atmosphere peculiar to the area. For example, the payroll system for a public school district would differ in many important respects from the payroll system for a fast food service franchise. However, there also would be some similarities, such as the provisions for federal and state income taxes and deductions. The differences between the two systems are the key elements the analyst must identify to ensure that the new system is successful. The school district payroll system must provide the capability of processing multiple jobs held by a single person (at different pay rates) and also multiple sources of funds to pay for one job (such as partial funding through private and federal grants). In contrast, the payroll system for a fast food service franchise must provide for the more traditional wage rate and time card driven capabilities. The hours worked may vary per pay period for each employee, and the wage rates may vary according to the shifts worked or by job assignment.

Beginning with this broad perspective on the environment of the study, the analyst should attempt to obtain the information needed to become familiar with each general level of the organization's operation, down to the specific area that is the detailed focus of the study.

This approach enables the analyst to both speak and understand the language of the "natives," and hence do a far better job on their system. In this sense, the systems analyst is similar to the anthropologist; both must enter into unfamiliar cultures and extract reliable information from which reasonable conclusions can be drawn.

Identify the Area Under Study

Even though the topic identifying the area under study is so important that it was described in Chapter 1, it must be reintroduced here as a point of reinforcement. We cannot stress enough that you must be able to identify clearly the levels at which you will be working, such as: the firm, division, department, functional area, and/or a specific problem (Levels I–V). At this point you should review Figure 5-2 and perhaps go back to Chapter 1 to reread the section titled What Is the "Area Under Study"?

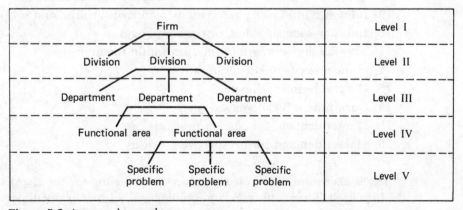

Figure 5-2 Area under study.

*B*ackground of Industry, Company, and Area Under Study

Depending on the particular study, you may or may not be interested in the background of the *industry* itself. The industry background places the firm in perspective within its environment. It also may explain why the firm does something in a certain way. For example, if the industry has been using a certain accounting procedure for 50 years, that should warn you that any change may be vigorously resisted because people are used to and feel comfortable with the long-standing procedures. In addition, you may find some very good reasons why the system has weathered the tests of time. Nevertheless, firms that wish to survive in today's uncertain environment must prepare for survival through the use of contingency planning. This concept implies that management expects the unexpected and is ready to shift directions when the external environment, contingencies that may or may not be under management's control, changes. Contingency planning may be used at any of the above five levels.

Within the industry, some of the factors that might be considered are

1. Products and services of the industry
2. Growth or decline in the industry
3. Technological trends
4. Industry-wide sales volumes and profit margins
5. Type of industry, such as oligopoly, monopoly, or nearly perfect competition
6. Effects of foreign and domestic competition
7. Effects of unions
8. Effects of legislative restrictions and reporting requirements
9. Influence of industry associations, standards groups, and so forth
10. Industry-wide subsidies, or tax advantages
11. The size and strength of the firm within the industry
12. Human needs the firm can satisfy
13. General business climate
14. Government fiscal policies
15. Market demand for current products
16. Market demand for prospective products

The background of the *company* gives one a feeling for the characteristics of the firm itself. Ideas, attitudes, and opinions of key management personnel are very important to the analyst. Knowledge of the company's background will make its goals and style more understandable. Knowing why certain employees are where they are and how the company has grown over the years helps in understanding the present direction of the business. Within the firm some of the things that might be looked for are

1. Management and employee attitudes: how do they harmonize in the area under study?
2. Patterns of growth over the years and expectations for the future
3. Products and services important to the firm's future
4. Sales volume and profit margin trends
5. Expansion or curtailment of any segment of the business over the years
6. Involvement in mergers, spinoffs, or purchases of, or by, other firms
7. Effects of foreign competition, domestic competition, government intervention, and unions
8. Type of market: oligopoly, monopoly, nearly perfect competition, and so forth
9. Effect of technology on the firm
10. Past and present goals and objectives
11. Long-range plans

Obtaining the background of the *area under study* is a mandatory step. Industry and company backgrounds are not required in many systems studies, but the background of the area under study is required for *all* studies. If one does not know the background of the specific area about to be studied, one cannot appreciate its guiding policies, atmosphere, or the day-to-day problems faced by the personnel in that area. Within the specific area under study, some of the things to look for are

1. Attitudes of all involved personnel, toward the system and toward management
2. Past and present objectives
3. Past and present policies and procedures
4. Increasing or decreasing budgets
5. Growth or decline in quantity of work in the area
6. Importance of the area to the rest of the business enterprise
7. Apparent morale problems
8. Power struggles between this area and other areas
9. Respect for the manager of this area by both peers and subordinates
10. Attitudes of personnel outside the area under study toward the area under study

The above lists are useful as reminders. This means that not all of the items are relevant in all cases. You must choose which ones are relevant to the system study you are performing.

Do not forget to look at background in the context of the *culture* of the industry, company, or area under study. The cultural environment was first described in the previous chapter. You may want to take it into account again at this point in your system study. When you take into account the customs, traditions, cultural values, folkways, mores, and the like, some of the factors that might be considered are

1. The laws and beliefs of the country in which this organization operates
2. Various environmental impacts
3. Issues posed by discrimination and/or equal employment
4. Consumerism or consumer protection
5. Government regulatory agency controls
6. Military-type authority structures
7. The influence of professional organizations
8. The ethics of the business itself and/or its officers and directors
9. International legal or political considerations
10. Influence of religious entities
11. The influence of internal politics within the organization
12. Economic policies at the national level and/or local level
13. The influence of unions
14. Mode of behavior. A company may have its own mentality and mode of behavior that is different from other companies. Do not label it good or bad, just recognize it.

Long-Range Plans

If the analyst has not done so already, the long-range plans should be reviewed at this time. Decisions must be made concerning which work operations and activities will be retained, modified, or eliminated. This requires an investigation of any long-range plans directly affecting the area under study. An understanding of any such plans is necessary before the new system's requirements can be properly defined. This approach enables the analyst to define system requirements that will not be made obsolete by later implementation of long-range plans which were not available at the time of system design. For example, if the firm intends to extend more lenient credit terms in the future, the system must be capable of processing the attendant increase in overdue accounts, data, and paperwork flow. Otherwise, the new system will be obsolete soon after the new credit terms are put into effect. Other examples of long-range considerations are

1. Changes in company goals and policies
2. Development plans for new products or new services
3. Projections of changing sales, manpower, or cash flow
4. Research and development projects
5. Major capital expenditures: new plants, computer, and so forth
6. Possible changes in product mix
7. A new level of file security

The term "long-range plan" may have a different meaning to different people. In practice, some people view long-range plans as making long-run forecasts and then adjusting to them, defining what the company should be, or developing a long-range program for the entire company. An analyst who makes decisions based simply on reading a long-range plan is not totally fulfilling his or her commitment to the company. Elements that distinguish a good analyst in this respect are: (1) Instead of defining the new system's requirements on the assumption that present conditions will continue, the analyst should try to read the future, challenge the *status quo*, and apply imagination in evaluating the systems requirements for the years to come. (2) The analyst should attempt to fit the implications of the requirements of the system into some kind of consistent pattern that fits the company's long-range plans.

The long-range plan of a company is its "road map" of the future. The long-range plan points to the direction that the company will be moving in the future. As we already have stated, the analyst looks at the long-range plan in order to make sure the new system's requirements fit in with the direction that the company will be taking. Another possibility is that the long-range plan itself might be affected by the results of a major system study. The analyst always should be alert to the fact that a system study evaluating something as big as the acquisition of another company may affect the long-range plans of the parent company. Therefore, usually the long-range plans affect the requirements of the new system, but in some cases the system study itself may affect the long-range plans of the company.

It may seem absurd that a system could actually be designed and implemented, only to become useless to the firm shortly thereafter because of the implementation of previously made plans. The fact is that it happens *often* in moderate to large organizations. The usual reasons are complexity of the organization, communication problems, lack of an organized knowledgeable approach, or the analyst's difficulties in learning of all the activities and information that may affect an area under study.

As an example, the analyst may receive approval to locate the customer record files in an area strategically related to other components of the system, and proceed to design the new system and office layout around the location of the files. Then, to everyone's dismay, it is learned that the person who gave authorization did not know about the new blueprint files that already were approved for eventual placement in that location. Another example is the analyst who designs exception routines into the system to handle certain special requirements, only to learn later that the firm will not be dealing with that type of situation by the time the system gets into operation. Suppose we are designing a new collection system. The analyst might design a routine to process the overdue accounts of a wholly owned subsidiary. This easily could require the inclusion of numerous inconvenient steps in what might otherwise be a smooth system. That is, if we had only our own accounts to process, things would be much simpler—but with the subsidiary's bills to do, too, we have to design "exception" routines to handle their differences. This could require a redesign of many forms, new files, and dozens of other problems. Without asking any questions about future plans for the subsidiary, we design the necessary exception procedures, at the cost of considerable time and effort. If only we had asked the right person the right question, we could have learned that the subsidiary company will have been sold by the time our new system goes into operation!

One warning is appropriate at this point. You sometimes may find that small to mid-size firms, non-profit organizations, government agencies, or even larger firms often do not have any written long-range plans. When this occurs, identifying the organization's long-term objectives is very difficult. Occasionally, by interviewing the "proper personnel," you can assemble a picture of the organization's long-range plans. If the organization obtains its first written long-range plans as a by-product of your system study, you may be remembered for a long time as one of the new "up and comers." One means of being recognized as an exceptional systems analyst is to identify a "hole" in the organizational fabric and then fill it. For example, suppose you embark on a system study only to discover that the organization has no long-range plans. You then should try to interview top management in order to gain an understanding of the organization's plans and commit these plans to paper. Finally, you should use the plans to guide your system study. Along the way you also get recognition from top management as being both an exceptional systems analyst and an excellent employee.

The analyst's step of checking for existing plans or anticipated changes is a mandatory one! And above all, the information received regarding such plans and contingencies must be reliable information. The analyst should investigate the possible existence of conflicting plans or contingencies for every major aspect of the system being designed.

Legal Requirements

Governments at the local, state, and federal levels have many laws which affect company operations. In the search for general information on the area under study, remember that businesses need licenses, they must pay taxes, and they must observe the laws of the nation.

Many types of business are controlled in some way by one level of government or another. If the study is involved in public utilities, insurance, aviation, stocks and bonds, railroads, television or radio, banking, unions, or pollution, one must understand the legal requirements that govern the area (if any). For example, government regulations play an extremely large role in the aerospace industry. Nearly every function in an aerospace firm is subject to direct government regulation. The same is true in the meat packing industry, and several others.

The investigation of legal requirements should answer three basic questions. First, which government regulations help the company? The following may help the company: direct subsidies, import quotas or tariffs, protection as a monopoly, special tax incentives, franchises, labor laws, and civil rights laws.

The second question is, which government regulations restrict the company? These may include excise taxes, export limitations such as with military hardware, utility regulations, safety laws, antitrust laws, pollution laws, restrictions on the sale of stocks and bonds, privacy legislation, restrictions on corporate dealings in foreign countries, and laws that restrict a company from selling a product or freely changing the price of its product.

The third question is, which government regulations affect the recordkeeping and reporting practices of the company? The following may increase recordkeeping for the company: withholding taxes of employees, social security, workmen's compensation, corporate taxes, Federal Communications Commission reports, Federal Reserve Board requirements, Securities and Exchange Commission reports, privacy legislation, restriction on corporate dealings in foreign countries, pollution control laws, regulated utility reports, civil rights laws, affirmative action programs and court rulings, safety records, and cost data to defend a possible contract renegotiation by the government.

Another method of approaching legal requirements is to identify all of those government agencies (federal, state, county, or city) that may have regulatory agencies and/or laws affecting the system that you are designing. For example, the Federal Communication Commission has laws affecting data communications and voice communications between states and between local access transport areas. There also are state public utility commissions that control or enforce laws pertaining to data communications, voice communications, and control of public monopolies, such as public utilities within a single state. The Federal Drug Administration controls new drugs and various matters pertaining to internal medicine. The Securities and Exchange Commission helps shape the strategies of organizations with regard to stocks or bonds, and their sale or trade. Business systems and the companies that use them are so widely diversified that you must be clever in trying to identify any government agency that will affect your company's business system and take into account how that will affect your design, if at all. One of the best sources to determine which regulatory agencies affect your company and/or its business systems might be the corporate legal counsel. Another is the contracts department because its personnel are familiar with compliance factors.

*T*he Organization (Formal/Informal)

Before we discuss the organization itself, let us examine *organization structure* and *organization charts.* The organization structure in a business represents the formal recognition or formal hierarchy for decision making, responsibility, and authority. For example, all organization structures should have some type of organization chart that depicts the various sub-areas of responsibility, along with what tasks exist and who carries them out. Figure 5-3 depicts the formal organization structure of the data processing department at a bank. It shows the formal organization structure, along with the specific computer systems that are under the responsibility of the managers of systems analysis and programming.

There are two types of organization to consider. One is the *formal* organization and the other is the *informal* organization. These two organizations are more or less independent of each other and both must be considered when designing a new system.

The formal organization is built around the company's goals, upper management's policy statements, and the written procedures that carry out these policies. In order to see the formal organization, all the analyst has to do is look at the company organization chart. The organization chart is a who's who of each department or functional area. The normal flow of information can be written or verbal, but it usually is passed up and down the chain of command in the organization. Formal information usually includes items about the company, its operations, products, policies, procedures, and specific situations that arise, such as a change in management or pay raises.

The informal organization is built around the job at hand. When the system does not work, the written procedures are outdated, or a manager loses control of a department, the informal organization takes over. In this case, the employees perform the job at hand in the way they see as best. Written procedures are not followed or are only partially followed. The work usually gets done but not necessarily in the most efficient manner. When the informal organization takes over, consistency is lost, and consistency is extremely important. For example,

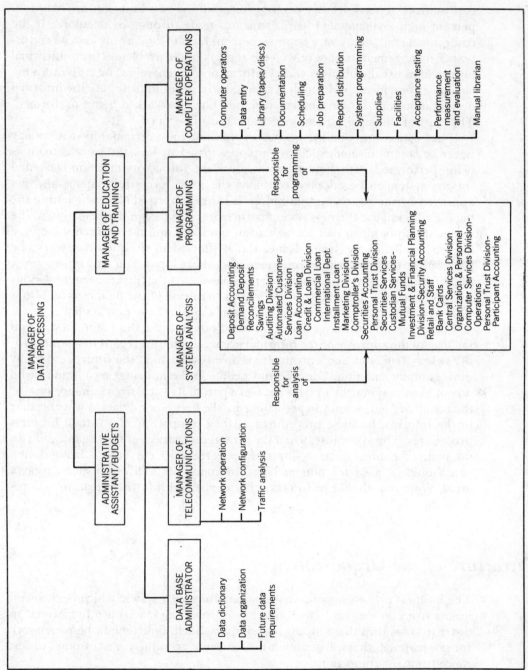

Figure 5-3 Formal organization of a bank data processing department.

cost estimate reports are not perfect; but if all the cost estimates are about 10 percent high, management learns to compensate through its decisions. If the cost estimates suddenly vary from 10 percent high to 20 percent low (no consistency), management cannot rely on the reports, and a problem is born. Informal information usually involves verbal information exclusively. The employees exchange gripes, ideas, and problem solutions. In order to penetrate the informal organization, one should observe carefully how the work is being performed. The trust of the involved employees also must be gained.

If one concentrates on the formal organization only, certain information may never be communicated, such as employee gripes or how the work actually is being performed. Although the approval of the formal organization is needed for the system to be adopted officially, the most successful systems also get approved by the *informal* organization. Informal approval comes by letting the people who will use the new system participate in its design. Participation in the design does not mean that you ask a few questions and then return some time later to install the new system. It means that after asking the questions, you come back with a rough draft and request ideas for more input. You may return many times for more input, and whenever possible discuss the final recommendations with the potential users of the system prior to release of the final report. This is what gets the informal organization to tacitly approve the new system.

There are two key things that you should remember at this point. First, if you fail to gain the approval of the informal organization with regard to operation of the new system, you may encounter passive resistance in the future, especially during implementation. You will find people in the informal organization who do not like the system or who do not feel a part of it . . . passive resistance may be the result. Second, when you are gathering the background data, always be alert to the informal business procedures as they compare to the formal business procedures. This is because, when the formal procedures of the organization do not match the informal procedures (the way the work currently is being done), you should be alert for potential improvements, as well as possible problem areas. Your goal should be to make the formal and informal work procedures coincide.

Structure of the Organization

The business process may be viewed as an integrated system which begins with inputs from the external environment on which operations are performed in order to transform these inputs into outputs. Such inputs might be paperwork for raw materials that will become a new consumer product, or a customer order, cancellation, or complaint.

There is a continuous flow of inputs, operations, and outputs, such as

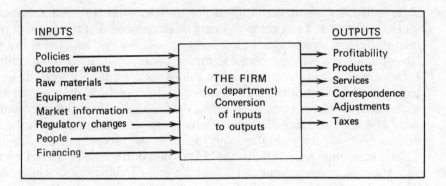

This is a general picture of any organization that yields a product or service to its users. The inputs and outputs may vary, but the principle is the same for any organization: it exists to produce products or render services to its members and customers. It accomplishes its work through dynamic interaction of its members to convert inputs to outputs.

The analyst's purpose in this scheme is to calculate the members' interactions via systems which are appropriate to the objectives and goals of the organization.

After obtaining a general familiarity with the background and environment of the area under study, the analyst can proceed to examine the area's interactions with other parts of the organization.

The internal environment of the typical business firm is composed of many departments, each with its own purposes and its own problems. Each of these internal departments accepts inputs, processes them, and passes on its outputs to other departments. There is an identifiable chain of events within the firm. The analyst must look up and down that chain of events to ensure that any contemplated changes will mesh with, or improve, the flow of business operations. A perfect system for one department might require another department to add personnel or revise its routines, perhaps at excessive cost, thus negating any savings or other expected benefits.

Since the analyst's purpose is to facilitate interaction and efficiency, a system must be designed which ensures that the benefits for a specific area will be achieved while also harmonizing with other areas and systems in the chain of operations. It must be remembered that the purpose of any one area is to render service to the other areas, all of which interact to accomplish the objectives of the organization as a whole.

The analyst should be able to detect and correct, or prevent, the functional isolation of any member or segment. If part of an organization is not serving the rest in its efforts toward attainment of overall organizational objectives, it is in need of renovation or elimination. The experienced analyst can expect to find many such fragmented areas in the organization being studied. The existence of such ineffective segments is often the source of the problems the analyst is seeking to resolve. For example, it may be discovered that the cause of delays in manufacturing sophisticated electronic devices for the military is caused by a labor intensive testing process and timing problems in scheduling components for assembly. This may be further traced to a testing process that requires tedious manual computations and a lack of timely information on the expected availability of related components for final assembly. Management often is unaware of such imbalances in the work-in-process environment until the systems analyst discovers the symptoms and identifies the related problems.

The basic interactions that should be studied are those between employees, departments, management personnel, or any combination of these elements. The analyst should start with the firm's current organization charts to view the formal relationships between the area under study and other areas. Flowcharts sometimes exist that show the work flow pattern through and between departments. These should be examined. Interviews with management also tell the analyst a lot about interactions. Job descriptions and observation of work flow will reveal more of these interactions. Finally, the informal organization, the employees who carry on the area's daily activities, can pinpoint the actual day-to-day interactions: who does what, when, how, and *why*.

In a large system study, the interactions for two or three departments up and down this chain of events must be studied. The analyst may have to go all the way to the *external* environment to understand the way some source or original input is received, or to get approval to change such an input or an output.

*I*nteractions between Outputs, Inputs, and Resources

This section discusses the interactions between outputs from the system, inputs to the system, and the system's resources, such as financial, personnel, inventory, and facilities. These interactions also might be referred to as interfaces between systems, or sub-system interfaces. At this point, we want to define the inputs, outputs, and resources, but we are doing it without depicting the specific methodology used to define them. For example, if you were using the structured design methodology with data flow diagrams, you already may have identified decision points or system interfaces, or even sub-system interfaces. What we want to discuss here, however, is what you should look for and where you should look for it. This is necessary regardless of whether structured or traditional systems analysis techniques are used.

Outputs can consist of completed paperwork, processed computer files, reports, or semifinished or finished products. One department's output may be another department's input, except when the paperwork or the product goes out of the firm and into the external environment.

The analyst should examine the outputs from a general viewpoint in order to determine how these outputs relate to other inputs and outputs up and down the chain. The methods used by the area under study to produce its outputs must be understood and related to all departments within the overall area under study. Using a public utility as an example, the following interactions could apply.

1. Customer requests electrical service through main office
2. Customer completes service request
3. A copy of the request is forwarded to the responsible field unit to schedule installation
4. An additional copy of the request goes to the billing department for processing
5. The last copy of the request goes to credit department for approval
6. The credit department notifies all departments of final approval
7. The field unit initiates service and notifies the billing department of the date
8. The billing department begins sending regular customer monthly statements

The analyst should learn the "product line" of the area under study, that is, what service they render to the firm, and how that service fits into the general scheme of operations up and down the chain. Finally, it should be determined where all the outputs go and how they are used.

Inputs consist of raw data, raw materials, paperwork, processed computer files, reports, and semifinished products. One department's input is usually another's output.

As with outputs, the analyst should obtain a broad view of the inputs to the area under study, and should relate these inputs to other inputs up and down the chain of events. The source of each input and the reason it comes into the area under study should be determined. However, at this stage of the study only the major inputs should be observed, and trivial inputs should be avoided. The analyst should learn the characteristics of the inputs, such as manual or computer generated, approximate quantities, availability (time factor), and cyclic needs. This knowledge will be of help in determining the interactions between the area under study and the rest of the chain.

Resources are those items that are used in the day-to-day operations to convert inputs to outputs. A firm will view its resources as assets because it has an investment in them. There are four categories of resources that may require analysis in order to obtain a clear picture of the interactions between the areas being studied and the rest of the organization. The four kinds of resources are financial, personnel, inventory, and facilities.

The *financial* resources of the area under study consist of the budget for that area and the area manager's ability to get financial backing for new projects and systems. Is the area under study financially stable or is it a declining segment of the firm? This is a key question for the analyst to answer because it will aid in understanding the weights and priorities appropriate to the area, and to the system which will be designed.

The *personnel* resources consist of the key managers and other skilled and able personnel in the area under study. The analyst should study the personnel by skill, location within the area under study, and current function. The personnel resources may limit or enhance a system and the analysis of personalities and talents may reveal much about why the area has its current status, and why it interacts with other areas as it does.

The *inventory* resources can be looked at from two viewpoints. First, the "stock-in-trade," such as raw materials, parts, supplies, semifinished products, by-product utilization, and finished products; and second, the "files of information" or data that have been collected over the years. While studying interactions, the analyst might check the files of information throughout the area under study for the following.

1. Completeness of the file; extensiveness; why it is kept
2. Sources of the filed documents
3. Duplication in other departments
4. Flow of documents within the area under study and between other areas
5. Age, that is, how old is the oldest item in the file, and how long until new items get into the file?
6. Is the file actually used? Does it contain obsolete information?
7. How often is the file accessed? How is it indexed?

The *facilities* resources of the area under study may consist of land, buildings, data processing equipment, or other capital equipment. Carefully note which area manages the computer (if there is one) and the interactions between that area and the other areas. Also note any excesses or shortages of floor space, desks, supplies, and so forth. The analyst needs to determine physical capacity. Finally, identify and document distributed microcomputer systems that may affect your systems study.

Company Politics

In business there is a taboo against formally recognizing that politics may be a factor in success. Political maneuvering takes place within the informal organization. Although no one advertises their personal strategy to achieve success, merit alone does not always guarantee success. The ability to understand and recognize a political situation is *critical* to the analyst who is attempting to understand the area under study.

Politicking tends to be light in rapidly growing companies and heavier in older, well entrenched companies. Of course, there are situations with new, highly profitable ventures where everybody wants to get in "on the ground floor." Vicious in-fighting often occurs in such situations, to an extent that a nonpolitical person is either left behind or is simply replaced. The analyst is wise to remember that an office under stress usually brings out the worst in office politics. Two of the most typical situations in which this stress occurs involve rapid growth situations. In one case, rapid growth means new management, which in turn causes changes in management styles to which employees must adapt. An example of this type of situation is a merger in which one firm ousts another firm's managers and brings in its own people. Such situations are chaotic for employees who must adapt, quite often, overnight. The second situation is one in which new methods are adopted. Computerization of all financial and purchasing tasks in a firm is a typical example of new methods. Usually there is some confusion and uncertainty when new methods are introduced. The one thing that the analyst can be sure of is that office politics are always fluid. Just about the time you think you have the situation figured out, it changes. Sometimes politics reach beyond your office, spilling over to suppliers, purchasers, and so on. In other words, nothing is certain but change.[1]

Whether you as the systems analyst will want to participate in this game of company politics will depend to a great extent on your own value system. It is advisable to keep in mind, however, that if you become too politically involved, your impartiality, and hence your effectiveness, will be lost.

We are including below some suggestions for "getting ahead" frequently made by company politics experts. They are included not to help you become a company politician but *to aid you in recognizing others* who may be politically motivated. Some might be considered "good," others might be considered "bad," while others are simply common sense.

Be visible to the people above you. Meetings are an excellent opportunity to make yourself visible since you can ask questions or put forth new ideas. Taking up an extracurricular activity is another way of attracting notice.

Always look good. Learn your superior's value system. Join in with the group and ask advice. Endear yourself to a star in the company who is on the way up.

Perform your work thoroughly and efficiently. Never complain about work either verbally or in writing. Accept even the less desirable assignments cheer-

---

[1] Some of the ideas in this section and the next have been adapted from a lecture by Pat Port, consultant in office politics, 912 Laurel Avenue, Menlo Park, California 94025.

fully. Do not tell your troubles (either professional or private) to your co-workers.

Be loyal. Always ask *first* what you can do for the company and *second* what the company can do for you.

Show respect. Call superiors by their title until they indicate a first-name basis is appropriate. Do not usurp authority; it usually creates antagonism.

Think about what you say *before* saying it. Reveal only what is necessary and what should be said. Hold your beliefs until the right time.

Keep a positive outlook since nothing new will ever be attempted if all possible objections must first be overcome.

Always do things to better yourself, but do not brag about it to others. Let it be revealed in subtle ways.

If you discover the prevailing weakness of any colleague, whether intentionally or by accident, remember never to trust him where that weakness is concerned. For example, if you know a fellow worker is a talkative drinker, do not tell that person anything you do not want to become public knowledge.

Gratitude for favors done is always in short supply in office politics. When someone owes you something, make sure that person knows he or she owes you in return.

When in a situation of conflict, do not try the same approach over and over again. In other words, do not try harder; try something different.

When you volunteer to do something, it becomes your job from that point onward. Never set precedents you do not intend to pursue.

Work for one, and only one, direct supervisor. Working for two supervisors places you in a most vulnerable position, especially if the supervisors are in conflict with one another.

You never get promoted if no one else knows how to do your current job. The best basis for being advanced is to organize yourself out of every job into which you are put. Another is to convince superiors that you can do the job you want better than anyone else.

When angry, do not write a letter condemning someone. If you must do something about it, do it verbally. Aristotle put it this way

> *Anybody can become angry—that is easy; but to be angry with the right person, to the right degree, and at the right time, and for the right purpose, and in the right way—that is not within everybody's power and is not easy.*

Most managers will not openly condemn another manager, and neither should the analyst. Open condemnations can be very dangerous, especially if in writing. Criticism, if given at all, should be constructive and directed at things or procedures, not people. The analyst who thinks that criticizing people will get the system installed may win the battle for that system but may lose the war called survival. If criticism is direct and unconstructive, people will think the analyst is out to get them and will be afraid to have further dealings with the analyst. Thus, the ability to obtain the needed cooperation will be lost and the analyst will not be able to function effectively.

Remember that no kindness is ever wasted. If you harm people, they may hold grudges. These same people may appear 10 years later in your life and be in a position to do you serious harm. Using the company grapevine can be productive, but be careful to use positive information since negative information probably will harm you in the long run.

Perhaps politicking is not your style. That is fine. But remember not to knock the political strategist too hard, because this is your competition; and the chances are good that this same person may have authority over you some day. Whether we like it or not, events occur that way sometimes and it is realistic to accept these situations for what they are.

*D*epartmental Interactions

Interactions between employees and supervisors or between departments are very important interactions for the analyst to observe.

Within a department the analyst should observe how the manager interacts with subordinates. What management "style" is employed? Perhaps the manager has already decided "whether it is better to be loved-than-feared or feared-than-loved." It is important to learn whether a manager tends to extremes, that is, whether "fear" or "nice-guy" techniques are used. If ruled by fear, the personnel involved in the day-to-day activities may not accept the analyst and may not cooperate unless directly commanded to do so by their manager.

It is also important for the analyst to carefully observe and understand the management styles of the managers, and the resulting differences between the area under study and other areas. Such knowledge helps the analyst understand how these managers interact with one another and how each might react to system design features.

For example, some people, when placed in an organizational climate, will behave in a particular manner based on the assumptions of the "Theory X" versus "Theory Y" philosophy.[2] Douglas McGregor called his two theoretical constructs on the nature of man Theory X and Theory Y.

Theory X is identified as management's conventional conception of harnessing human energy to organizational requirements. Theory X assumptions are that

☐ The average human being has an inherent dislike of work and will avoid it if possible.

___
[2] Douglas McGregor, *The Human Side of Enterprise* (New York: McGraw-Hill, 1960).

□ Because of man's dislike of work, he must be coerced, controlled, directed, or threatened with punishment to get him to put forth adequate effort toward the achievement of organizational objectives.

□ The average human being prefers to be directed, wishes to avoid responsibility, has relatively little ambition and, above all, wants security.

McGregor further stated that the assumptions that comprise Theory X have caused management to conceive of its mission in terms of two extreme positions: "hard" management or "soft" management. He dismissed both of them as neither wrong nor right, but as irrelevant.

McGregor's construct of Theory Y was based on the accumulation of knowledge about behavior and motivation that has emerged within this century. Theory Y is the embodiment of a set of assumptions about people that is quite different from traditional management philosophy. The assumptions include

□ The expenditure of physical and mental effort in work is as natural as play and rest.

□ External control and the threat of punishment are not the only means of getting people to work toward the organization's objectives. People do exercise self-direction and self-control toward achieving objectives to which they are committed.

□ Commitment to objectives is a function of the rewards associated with their achievement (esteem, self-actualization).

□ Under proper conditions, people learn not only to accept but also to seek responsibility.

□ Most people are capable of a relatively high degree of imagination, ingenuity, and creativity in solving organizational problems.

□ Under the conditions of contemporary industrial life, the average person's intellectual potentialities are being utilized only partially.

The interaction between managers who view management style from these opposite viewpoints is the important focus of our discussion. The analyst must study these interactions in preparation for the role of objective intermediary. During the system design phase, the opinions of two or more managers with divergent theories of human nature have to be considered, since a balance between these views needs to be achieved. The analyst should be alert to a manager's style, especially when working on a system that involves only that manager's department or personnel.

The analyst should bear in mind, as operational personnel are evaluated, that individual workers also vary widely in their reactions to management style. Some employees agree that heavy-handed, close controls are necessary, while others prefer an atmosphere of permissiveness to enhance creative thinking and new ideas. In short, some employees believe in Theory X and some in Theory Y—and, of course, there are those in between. In other words some employees *do* want to be closely controlled while others prefer considerable freedom.

Another way of viewing departmental interactions might be through the department managers themselves. You might consider the viewpoint expressed by a well known psychologist, Abraham Maslow. Maslow postulated a hierarchy of five needs. As shown below these are self-actualization, esteem, love, safety, and physiological.

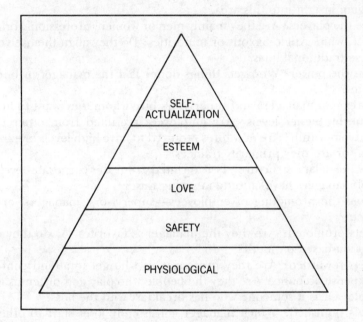

Source: *Motivation and Personality,* 2nd ed., by Abraham H. Maslow. New York: Harper & Row, 1970

The lowest order of needs, physiological, encompasses peoples' biological demands, such as hunger, thirst, sex, elimination, and so on. The next level, safety, involves relief from certain physical threats in the environment. Specifically in our case, these are exemplified by possible threats from the job place, such as loss of job, loss of income, and the like. The next need, love, usually is expressed as a person's need for warm, supportive relations with others such as family, friends, and business associates. We all have a need to have our ideas accepted. The need for esteem is dual in nature because we need the self-esteem that comes from mastery of a job, and we also have the need to have our accomplishments recognized by others. Said another way, esteem involves our mastery of some type of job or task, as well as having others recognize our personal accomplishments. Finally, at the highest level of Maslow's hierarchy is the need for self-actualization. This is where we become what we are capable of becoming. It is at this level that a person finds the key to the meaning of fulfillment. Any department manager who feels he or she has failed in self-actualization may themselves be part of the problem. The point we want to make in presenting Maslow's five needs is that if you recognize these, you can use them during your systems analysis/data gathering to evaluate the person who is giving you answers. In other words, ask yourself: What is motivating this person as he or she answers my questions?

The analyst can learn to recognize who has the power within a specific department or division in an organization. Asking some of the following questions can help you gain insight into this area.

Who are the players? Are they mainly men or women, professional or clerical, line or staff, white Anglo-Saxons or minorities? Do they align themselves along any of these traditional lines?

Who has the power? Who gets things done? Is it the manager or one of the subordinates?

Who hires? Do managers and supervisors hire whom they want to hire, or is hiring done by higher levels? Are employees recruited from other firms or promoted from within? Are new hires required to have high levels of experience or training, or are they primarily trainees?

What is the salary structure? Is it dictated from the corporate level, or do lower level managers have latitude in giving raises?

Who does the promoting of employees—supervisors, managers, or higher management?

Who gets promoted? Are they the manager's "favorites" or do they deserve the promotion based on merit?

Who gets rewarded? Are they professionals who get to attend conferences and use expense accounts? Are they the people who play golf or tennis with the right people? Or is it someone who has breakfast with the boss?

Who gets punished? Which manager consistently loses staff to other managers? Which manager is not allowed to fill job vacancies when they occur? In the area of reward and punishment, it is wise to remember that some things may look like rewards, but in fact are not. For example, the person who is given a plush new office may look on this as a reward, but if it is isolated from the rest of the group, it may in fact be a punishment.

What is the mission of this office? Does it "just" supply information to line personnel and thus is held in low esteem? Or is it the "real" producers of the organization who have more prestige internally?

What are the taboos? Who can be trusted? With whom do employees not dare disagree? Who has what pet projects that cannot be criticized? Who gets into trouble for speaking out of turn?

Between departments the analyst should determine, for example, if any department is in the "empire-building" category, since an empire-building manager may not accept a system that curtails the department's power in some way, such as reducing its span of authority and control. Empire builders may be seeking personal power, prestige, and recognition, or they may be pushing causes that they genuinely believe are vital to the firm. The systems analyst is advised to avoid taking sides when a project leads to such a power struggle. The analyst may become a pawn in the battle and end up sacrificed prior to the checkmate! Systems designed in the midst of such struggles tend to be very compromised where objectivity and quality are concerned.

The systems analyst also should stay alert to the effect any individual's personality may have on the interactions between other operations personnel, managers, and departments. For example, if a particular employee is known to be demanding and unpleasant in requesting assistance from other departments, that person should not be put in a position requiring constant contact with other departments. Some people are not suited to particular types of jobs, and the analyst needs to recognize this in designing a new system.

There is one final, subtle point that may be indicative of in-fighting between the various departments and the area under study. In areas in which fending for power is common, the managers tend to take their vacations a few days at a time so they can always defend their past, present, and future actions.

In summary, to understand the area under study, the analyst must be able to identify not only the formal characteristics of the area but also, perhaps even more importantly, the informal characteristics. By understanding both, the analyst is more likely to design a workable and acceptable system.

Critical Success Factors[3]

The new system you are designing must support the attainment of both the organization's goals and those of the individual department. As you are gathering background information on the industry, company, or area under study, and identifying its long-range plans, consider the identification and documentation of the *critical success factors* that support attainment of organization and department goals.

If you choose to use the critical success factor approach, you will be helping the management of your organization define its key or significant information needs and/or actions to be undertaken. Surprisingly, this is not very well defined in many organizations. Identification of the critical success factors involves a set of two or three interviews with high-level executives or managers. There are three steps to follow with regard to these interviews. *First,* identify the executive's or manager's goals and discuss the basic or underlying information or actions

[3] "Chief Executives Define Their Own Data Needs," by John F. Rockart. *Harvard Business Review,* March–April 1979, pp. 81–92.

(critical success factors) that are needed to meet these goals. For example, if one of your personal goals is to obtain high grades while at the university, then some of your critical success factors might be: an excellent ability to read, good nutrition and adequate sleep, a quiet study area, reasonable retention capabilities, and excellent time management so study time is separated effectively from other segments of your life. This first step of identifying goals and defining critical success factors is the purpose of the first interview.

In the *second* interview, the results of the first session are reviewed. This session is used to tidy up the list, possibly adding or subtracting from the original list of critical success factors.

During the *third* session, which may not be necessary, obtain final agreement on the overall goals and, specifically, on the exact critical success factors (information or actions) that will assure attainment of these goals. Notice that critical success factors are similar to the evaluation criteria that you might use to evaluate the success of one of your projects.

At the completion of these interviews, you should be able to focus on three to six critical success factors that will determine the success or failure of the new system you are designing. These critical success factors are the key items of information or action areas where the system *must* work in order for the organization to meet its goals. The fact is, if the system does not meet the identified critical success factors, it may not be accepted by management who must depend on its output/information.

At this point, you may wonder why we have not identified these critical success factors. It is because the critical success factors for one company or government agency may be quite different from one company or agency to another. Some examples of these differences are

- □ The Japanese automobile manufacturers identified quality control as a critical success factor early. Now, American automobile manufacturers also have come to recognize its importance.
- □ Not until the tremendous increase in oil prices did the airline industry recognize the cost of jet fuel as a critical success factor.
- □ The large increase in worldwide international debt has forced banks to recognize that the debtor's ability to pay back the principal amount is a critical success factor with regard to the bank's survival as a business entity.
- □ The PATCO air traffic controllers' strike forced unions into recognizing that obedience of the law (no strike) is a critical success factor in union survival. (NOTE: Each controller signed a no strike agreement as a condition of employment when they were hired originally.)
- □ University professors recognize that meeting their classes is a critical success factor with regard to holding their jobs.
- □ Your personal ability to maintain an adequate grade level average is dependent upon your ability to manage time, which is a critical success factor. We

suggest that you examine your own critical success factors with regard to maintaining an adequate grade point average. This will help you understand the concept better.

Notice in the first two examples above that quality control may be a critical success factor for both the automobile industry and the aircraft industry (aircraft maintenance). By contrast, as the general public adjusts to higher gasoline costs, fuel costs become a higher priority critical success factor for the airlines than to the automobile companies, with regard to sales of fuel efficient cars.

Another point should be made regarding identification of critical success factors. This involves the manager's perception of criticality (we discussed perceived versus actual problems in Chapter 3). The reason for interview sessions (the third one is to obtain agreement on the critical success factors) is so your system will address those critical success factors that are *perceived* by the managers as being key to their particular organization or the job at hand, as well as the *actual* ones. Remember that critical success factors may be different from one organization to another and from one manager to another.

In order to tie critical success factors to the previously mentioned background of the industry, company, and area under study, the analyst needs to consider the following four primary sources of critical success factors. *First* is the background of the industry itself. Each type of industry has its own critical success factors that differ from other industries. For example, a large consumer products company may have a very large advertising budget, whereas a manufacturing company that wholesales its products to two or three retail concerns may have zero advertising, but it might spend an equally large amount of money maintaining personal business relationships with its two or three primary retail customers. Another example is the microcomputer manufacturer that ignores one of its critical success factors, which is the necessity of continually producing new or upgraded products. On the other hand, a lawnmower manufacturer might be quite successful by continuously upgrading its only lawnmower model so that it is stronger, has better durability, and is of a higher quality.

The *second* source of critical success factors involves the firm's position within its industry. For example, if an industry is dominated by one or two large companies and your firm is one of the smaller ones, yours might take more and greater risks to increase market share, while the larger companies do not need to take these risks. Identification of critical success factors may be enhanced by knowledge of the competitive strategies between companies, such as how new microcomputers might be introduced, and even more important to your system, what basic information is needed from your system in order to support these new product introduction strategies.

Environmental factors and time factors are the *third* and *fourth* prime sources for identifying critical success factors at your company and for the system being designed. Environmental factors involve such things as the state of the economy and its predicted state at some point of time in the future, international tensions or embargoes between countries, transborder data flow restrictions between countries, and even state or local laws that affect the environment in which your firm operates. Some of the time factors that might lead to the identification of critical success factors include recent or possible changes in management at your company, severe losses or other financial upheaval that make time a more critical factor, leading the competition in the use of new computerized management information systems, or future cost avoidance in which some basic product costs have risen drastically in a short period of time. You will recall that the last situation occurred with both the airline and automobile industries in the mid-1970s when the Middle Eastern oil producing nations significantly raised the per barrel price of oil exports. Today, this situation has reversed itself.

The identification of critical success factors is used to highlight special information needs, actions that must be taken, or needed management controls. Used during the design of the new system, critical success factors assist in the design of a system that meets the needs of management and, therefore, one that will be accepted positively by the company or government agency. There are many benefits to be derived from this approach, namely

- ☐ It helps the executive or manager identify the critical success factors in the area for which they are responsible. They are now part of the new system.
- ☐ It develops measures by which attainment of the organization's goals can be measured.
- ☐ It ensures that the newly designed system collects the proper data, produces usable reports, and stimulates management to take the proper actions.
- ☐ It helps you build a system that meshes with the background of the industry, company, or department for which it is designed, while at the same time meeting competitive, environmental, and time factors.
- ☐ It is a tool that helps you, the analyst, be more competent. It helps you assist management in its planning processes, while improving communications between individual executives/managers in the company or government agency.

SUNRISE SPORTSWEAR COMPANY

CUMULATIVE CASE: General Information on the Area
Under Study and Its Interactions (Step 3)

Now that Mr. Reynolds has approved continuation of your systems analysis project and your tasks have been scheduled, it is time to begin the real heart of the study.

One of the first things you want to do is learn even more about the problem. Both Mr. Reynolds and Ms. Brunn have files of letters written by irate customers, so you examine these files. Customers do indeed seem to be disturbed by both the delayed processing of orders and the credit rejection notices. Several customers said they were "humiliated" by the credit rejection notices. With that in mind, you make a note to check with the employees who send out the reject notices so you can determine what they contain and how they are handled.

You also ask Mr. Reynolds if there are any long-range plans that might affect your study results. He says his main concern is to provide quality merchandise to customers and not to grow so fast that they lose sight of this goal. You inquire about any plans for facilities expansion and are told they just built the new warehouse last year because increased business required them to broaden their line of merchandise and keep a larger inventory. He also admits that some of the employees have begun to complain about lack of space and the necessity of running back and forth between buildings. Some of them have started suggesting that they would like to be closer to the people and files they need. Mr. Reynolds tells you that he had been starting to think about this, but in view of your study, now thinks he should wait until it is completed, in case your recommendations are related to that issue. You agree that this might be a good idea.

Because credit verification appears to be of major concern, you ask Mr. Reynolds if he knows how other direct mail firms handle credit. Even though Sunrise Sportswear is a member of the Direct Marketing Association, you are told they do not interact much with other members and really do not know much about how other mail order houses operate. As he points out, Sunrise Sportswear has done very well until recently and, being one of the older mail order houses, he has not seen the need to have much contact with his competitors. He supposes that it might be a good idea to start finding out more about the competition because he is aware that there has been a significant rise in the number of mail order houses over the last couple of years. You tell him that you think it is important to take the competition into account when making such major decisions as the handling of credit, and you will inform him of anything you may learn.

While talking with Mr. Reynolds, you note that the organization chart appears to be organized by process and you ask if it is accurate. He says it is and tells you that it really grew out of what started as a small mail order operation. Shipping had been the old mail room. Data Processing came about because Accounting wanted to mechanize about the same time the inventory started to grow so large. You ask about why there are no departments for such things as marketing, advertising, sales, market research, finance, or quality control. He explains that Catalog Printing really is the whole marketing operation. They handle everything along those lines, because the catalog printing really is their whole advertising campaign. Quality control is done by the Order Preparation people under Valery Brunn because they check to make sure the order is filled properly before sending out the invoices.

When Mr. Reynolds mentions invoices, you use that as an opportunity to inquire about whether he has ever thought of having the Accounting Department do such things as invoicing and collection of customer payments. He indicates that he never gave it much thought because Valery Brunn has been running that operation for quite a while, almost even before there was an Accounting Department. You tell him that many firms organize along more functional lines and explain that in such firms the Accounting Department handles everything to do with invoicing customers, paying bills, extending credit, and so forth. Since Mr. Reynolds does not seem interested in pursuing the subject, you drop it for the time being.

Your next interview is with Ann Bull, the manager of Data Processing. When you explain that you are studying the Order Processing system, she says she has not had much interaction with the people in that area, with the exception of Tom Conners for whom they produce batch inventory listings. You explain that you may encounter possible computer applications as you study the Order Processing area, and you would like to know what kind of computer capacity the firm has, in case the need arises. Ms. Bull explains that it is an older computer and is near capacity with all the batch runs they do for Inventory, Accounting, Personnel, and Catalog Printing. She is not sure that they could be of much help for anything major, but perhaps some smaller tasks could be handled. You ask about real-time capability and are told that it would not be possible because of the computer's limited capacity. She suggests, however, that microcomputers might be a possibility. The newer ones have significant capabilities—almost more than her large mainframe. She says she would be happy to help if Order Processing can use her services.

When you visit Catalog Printing, you are surprised to see that it is a sizable operation. As Mr. Reynolds mentioned, Catalog Printing does all the market research, works closely with Inventory in planning future lines of merchandise, and plans all advertising in addition to the catalog. Dave Cranston, the manager, tells you that they advertise in many publications, such as women's magazines and some sports-oriented magazines. You ask him how important the new customer records are to his operation. He explains that, while they are not the only source of information for their catalog mailings, they are important because they have no other means of obtaining the new customer information. He and Mr. Reynolds both feel it is important that new customers have positive reinforcement (in the form of another new catalog soon after their first purchase) so that they will continue to order Sunrise Sportswear products, rather than those of competitors. As far as he is aware, there is no other way to get lists of new customers than the way they do it from Suzanne Wolfe's cards.

You then inquire what they do with the cards and are told that they are put into the computer along with the other names for their mailing lists. You ask how this is done and learn that one of his staff enters the data on a keyboard that goes directly to magnetic tape. This tape is read into the computer and Data

Processing updates their customer listings when they are ready for a new mailing. You are very much interested in this detail and hope it can be useful in your problem solution.

The Shipping Department is your next stop. You explain to the manager, Kyle Masters, that you have been asked by Mr. Reynolds to study the Order Processing Department and ask if he can explain how they interact with Order Processing. He tells you that they receive boxes of merchandise from the Order Preparation people. The boxes are ready to be shipped, except for tape and labels. The reason the labels are not affixed yet is because the tape might cover them up, especially with smaller boxes. He explains that the boxes are accompanied by the original customer order, the Order Verification form, and the label which has been prepared by Order Preparation. Since you are interested in knowing whether any other department captures the new customer information, you inquire about whether Shipping fills out any forms having to do with customer names and addresses. Mr. Masters tells you that they fill out the Nationwide Parcel Service (NPS) Shipping Report (see Figure 2-13 in Chapter 2) and it has this information. Shipping attaches their copy of the NPS form to the customer's order form and the Order Verification form. When Shipping returns these three items to Order Verification, the loop is closed. Shipping also sends a copy of the Shipping Report to Accounting so amounts can be matched against the customer's account. Shipping does not keep any file copies, since Order Verification has the master file of customer orders. Shipping's primary responsibility is to package, label, and arrange for package pickups. They occasionally deal with other package delivery services, and these have forms similar to NPS. Shipping handles these other services' forms in a manner similar to those of NPS.

Since you have been talking about Shipping, you decide to backtrack one step to the Order Preparation area. You meet Charley Evans, who heads that area, for the first time. You tell him that you had been under the impression that he worked for the Inventory area until you saw the organization chart. He explains that he worked for Tom Conners for a number of years. As the inventory grew larger and Tom had to spend more time with suppliers and Catalog Printing, he (Charley) took over more of the day-to-day responsibility for the actual filling of orders. At the same time, business was expanding and the order filling process also was growing. After a while, Mr. Reynolds decided Inventory and Order Preparation should be divided into two groups. He was fortunate enough to be promoted to head of the newly formed Order Preparation section.

You learn that the Inventory staff actually pulls the merchandise from the shelves and then modifies the inventory records accordingly. They place the merchandise in a boxing area, where Charley Evans' staff goes over the order to verify that the correct merchandise has been pulled; they locate appropriate boxes, pack them, and move them to a holding area. The next step is for his staff to prepare mailing labels that are affixed to the original customer order and the

Order Verification form. Also, if it is a credit order, they prepare invoices, sending one to the customer and a copy to Accounting. When all this has been accomplished, the boxed merchandise, customer order form, Order Verification form, and the label are sent to Shipping to complete the packaging and mailing.

You mention that you have heard about Shipping Notices and wonder what purpose they serve. Mr. Evans explains that several years ago they had an unusually large number of complaints from customers who said they never received their merchandise. As a result of these complaints, they devised a postcard-type form that is filled out and sent to the customer to advise that the merchandise is being shipped. Now customers can expect their merchandise by a certain date and can notify Sunrise Sportswear sooner if it does not arrive. He says they do not seem to have many lost orders now that NPS is their shipping agent. Mr. Evans verifies what you have already observed, that all this work is performed using typewriters and without the aid of computers. Before leaving the area, you meet Joy King, who handles Shipping Notices and Doris Hardy, who prepares invoices.

Although you feel fairly confident that the suppliers are not a major concern to your study, you have a short interview with Tom Conners in Inventory. He tells you that Sunrise Sportswear has good relationships with its suppliers; they are responsive to Sunrise Sportswear's needs and provide significant assistance in planning for new merchandise lines. He confirms that stockouts are well within expected percentages and that notification of backorders to customers is not a significant problem. He explains that most backorders are caught early in the Order Verification process. Most of the ones that slip through have to do with the fact that the merchandise was in stock when the order was verified, but by the time the order gets to his area, previous orders have depleted the stock.

Mr. Conners tells you he does wish they could have more up-to-date inventory information. Even though the inventory listings are updated every night, the volume of orders is such that the listings sometimes are out-of-date by mid-morning, when there is high volume ordering of certain popular items. He tells you that this usually happens the first week after the new catalogs are mailed. You ask what the backorder notification to customers looks like and are shown a post card. It is nothing more than a preprinted notice that tells the customer that ordered merchandise is out of stock. There are lines to indicate what merchandise is being backordered, the customer's name and address, the Order Verification number, and when Sunrise Sportswear expects to have the merchandise available to ship. Mr. Conners' staff fills in a date that is based on suppliers' expected delivery dates. This post card has a copy which they use for the backorders file.

After talking with all these people, you feel you have a fairly accurate overview of how the Order Processing area interacts with other areas. You have detected a prevailing attitude in the other departments that implies the Order Processing area has prestige within the firm. You have heard several people comment that without Order Processing, Sunrise Sportswear would not exist and neither would the rest of their jobs. You now feel that it is time to go back to the beginning of the Order Verification procedure to learn more details about how they actually operate. You realize you met Jon Gray briefly the first day, but everything you know about his procedures has been gleaned from other people.

Jon Gray is the first person to have contact with customer orders, with the exception of orders that are telephoned. He tells you that the first thing he does, after time and date stamping the Order Verification form and writing the pre-printed number on the customer order, is verify that the ordered merchandise is available at Sunrise Sportswear. He says this is not much of a problem with catalog orders because customers use the order form that is bound into the catalog. These orders obviously belong to Sunrise Sportswear. Letters and tele-phoned orders, however, frequently are based on the customer's recollection that they saw merchandise in a catalog and hope it was the Sunrise Sportswear catalog. Mr. Gray shows you several of these orders and walks you through the process he uses to verify the order. If he is lucky, the customer has provided an item number and that speeds up the process quite a bit. He uses inventory printouts to verify provided item numbers. Normally, however, he has to check the name of the merchandise first, such as shirt, sweater, trousers, skirt, and so forth. Sometimes he has to second-guess what the customer really is requesting.

You inquire about what happens when he cannot identify the merchandise as being that of Sunrise Sportswear. You are told that a form letter is attached to the order, the reason the order is being returned is checked off, and both are sent to the customer. When this happens, he keeps the prenumbered Order Verification form on file so that they know what happened to the order if there is a further question from the customer. When he is successful in identifying the merchandise, he notes whether it is in stock. If not, the customer is notified and provided with enough information to re-order at a later date. He uses the same form letter, since it is a multi-purpose form that includes a variety of reasons why the order is being returned. It includes both "merchandise cannot be identified" and "temporarily out of stock."

If the order can be filled, Mr. Gray's next step is to determine whether it is an old or new customer. If it is a new customer, he forwards the order to Suzanne Wolfe so that she can make up a new customer record. If it is an old customer, he next determines the method of payment. When it is a prepaid order, he verifies that the amount on the order is correct and that the amount of the check or money order agrees with the order amount. He tells you that many careless arithmetic errors cause discrepancies in these amounts, so they need to verify these amounts early. Often the customer simply writes in the wrong amount from the catalog or multiplies incorrectly when ordering several of the same item.

At the end of each day, Mr. Gray totals all the payments received. The total is placed on a two-part transmittal slip. One copy is forwarded to Rosemary Dunlap, along with the payments. She applies the amounts to the customer's accounts. The second copy is sent to Accounting. After Rosemary Dunlap records all the payments, she forwards the payments with the transmittal slip to the Accounting Department so they can deposit the money in the bank. Also, Jon Gray notifies Accounting of any discrepancies between the amount received from the customer and the amount the customer has shown on the order form. This is done so Accounting can either reimburse customers who overpaid, or request further payment from those who have not paid enough. You then ask what happens to orders received without a payment.

When Mr. Gray receives credit orders, he checks to determine whether a credit card number has been provided. If it is an old customer who provides a credit card number, he passes the order to Lynn Porter. If it is an old customer who has not provided a credit card number or who asks to be invoiced, the order is given to Bob Thompson. All new customer orders go first to Suzanne Wolfe so she can make up her new customer records, after which she passes the orders to either Lynn Porter or Bob Thompson, based on what Mr. Gray has indicated on the Order Verification form. Jon Gray tells you that the only orders that are not held up in some manner are those for which checks or money orders have been received; these are sent to Inventory for filling of the order.

By this time you are wondering how many orders are from new customers. Mr. Gray estimates that probably half the orders he handles are sent to Suzanne Wolfe because he cannot locate the customer's name in his files. You ask how he locates the customer information and are told that when the customer's order and Order Verification form are returned from Shipping, they are separated. The actual customer orders are filed alphabetically by the customer's last name, while the Order Verification forms are filed by their prenumbered order number. One of the other Order Verification clerks writes the customer's name on the form before it is filed. That way, both forms are cross-referenced and can be located by either name or order number if needed.

After learning this latest information, you understand why there are so many file cabinets in the Order Verification area. It seems very crowded and you comment about it to Mr. Gray. He tells you that space has become very critical, and that he has been talking with his manager, Valery Brunn, about getting some more space. They have been considering the idea of splitting the Order Verification form files so that only the latest three to five years are maintained in the area, with older records being placed elsewhere in storage. They have not made a decision on this, however, because of their continuing need to determine whether a customer is old or new. They are afraid that if the files are split up, they will not be able to obtain this information as effectively as now and will end up with a lot of duplicate records in the customer files. There does not seem to be space anywhere else for the entire operation to be moved.

Because new customers are such a significant portion of the orders, you now realize that creation of these new customer records could be a major bottleneck in the entire Order Processing stream. You decide to visit Suzanne Wolfe one more time. You want to walk through the process so that you can obtain a more accurate picture of what she does. You observe that the orders are grouped so that the older orders are handled first. Ms. Wolfe takes each order and checks it first against large computer printouts of customers. You ask her how the printouts are obtained, and she answers that they are sent to her from Data Processing after each updating. You ask how often these updates are produced and are told that it is at least quarterly, but sometimes it is more often if they decide to put out some kind of special catalog that features a particular type of merchandise. You inquire about how Data Processing gets the information for the updates and Ms. Wolfe says that as far as she knows, when Catalog Printing finishes with her new customer cards, they forward them to Data Processing which somehow gets them into the computer. She further explains that it was being done that way when she was hired for the position two years ago.

You then go to the next step. If the customer's name is not located on the computer printouts, Ms. Wolfe then goes to the new customer cards that have been accumulating since the last update. She tells you that it is not so difficult to check right now because they just updated the last batch a couple of weeks ago; but when the cards have been accumulating for most of a quarter, it can be very tedious. She also thanks you for bringing up the backlog of new customer records with Mr. Reynolds because she was hesitant to ask for help for fear they would think she was not working hard enough. She is to have some extra help by next week. You tell her that you are pleased to hear this and ask exactly how old the oldest orders are. You are shown a stack that you examine and learn that some were received at Sunrise Sportswear almost two weeks ago. Ms. Wolfe also tells you that the orders are brought to her at the end of each morning and each afternoon, so each stack represents half a day's orders that have been brought to her from Jon Gray's area. This information allows you to calculate that the oldest orders have now been in Sunrise Sportswear for 11 days, with another batch of orders expected within an hour. You begin to feel guilty for taking up so much of Suzanne Wolfe's time and proceed to the next person.

Your next visit is with Lynn Porter who handles the credit card orders. You want to know if the credit card companies give a reason for rejecting a person's request for a credit purchase. You are told that they indicate whether the person's credit limit has been reached or if uncollected amounts have been sent out for collection by an outside agency. Ms. Porter confirms that if the credit card company approves the amount, the order is forwarded to Inventory. Otherwise, she turns it over to Bob Thompson who handles other credit requests.

When you go to see Bob Thompson, you follow him through the steps of checking customer credit. He uses a printout of accounts receivable to look for the person's name. These printouts are delivered to his area each morning by Data Processing. It is a listing of all the customers who owe money to Sunrise Sportswear. If the name is not located on the printout, credit is granted, and the

---

SUNRISE SPORTSWEAR COMPANY

Dear Customer,
   We have received your request for merchandise. We regret to inform you that your order cannot be filled because of the following reason:

☐ Credit card company rejected credit.
☐ Your account with Sunrise is more than 60 days in arrears. Please contact our Accounting Dept.

If you would send a money order for $____, we would still like to fill your order. If so, simply return this card with your money order, and we will complete your order as soon as possible.
   We value your continued patronage.

Sincerely,
Credit Orders Section

Figure 5-4 Credit rejection notice sent to Sunrise Sportswear's customers.

order is forwarded to Inventory for filling. If the name is located, they follow the rule of giving credit if the account is less than 60 days overdue. You ask him whether he uses the old/new customer information that is provided on the Order Verification form. He replies that it really does not pertain to his procedure even though it is written in the procedures as something important. Mr. Thompson says that he was surprised to learn that everyone thought old and new customers were handled differently with regard to extending credit. He tells you that the rules have been the same ever since he took over this job several years ago; it was just a detail he ignored because it did not seem relevant. He says that whether the account was more or less than 60 days overdue seemed to be the most important factor in extending credit to customers. Based on your reading of the procedures (Figures 3-7 and 3-8 in Chapter 3), you agree.

   Your next question has to do with what happens when a customer's request for credit is rejected. Mr. Thompson tells you that he is the only person who sends out credit rejections. These are in the form of a post card, which also has been in use since before he took the job. You examine this card, a facsimile of which is shown in Figure 5-4. When this card is sent out, the customer's order and the Order Verification form are returned to Jon Gray's area for filing. Orders that are approved for credit are forwarded to Inventory for filling. You ask Mr. Thompson if they ever use any outside credit agencies to determine a potential credit customer's credit rating. He answers that he does not really know anything about such groups and has never been asked to do any checking outside of Sunrise Sportswear.

   At this point, you have spoken with people at each step of the Order Process-

Company	Cash, Check, Money Order	Credit Card	COD	Credit
A	yes	yes	no	no
B	yes	yes	yes	no
C	yes	yes	no	yes, but only for letter orders
D	yes	yes	no	no
E	yes	yes	no	no
F	yes	yes	no	no
G	yes	no	no	no
H	yes	yes	no	no
I	yes	yes	no	no
J	yes	yes	yes	no
K	yes	yes	no	yes
L	yes	yes	no	no
M	yes	yes	yes	yes, limited to preferred customers
N	yes	yes	no	no

Figure 5-5 Summary of credit policies of Sunrise Sportswear's competitors.

ing routine. You have one other thing that you want to do before starting to document the existing system in detail. While conversing with the people at Sunrise Sportswear, you have learned the names of some similar mail order houses which they consider to be their competitors. You decide to go to the local public library to locate more information on two specific areas. The first task is to locate the names of other potential competitors. You have decided that you want a representative sampling of these competitive firms, along with their location and telephone numbers. With that information, you are able to perform a quick telephone survey to learn how these other firms handle credit orders. The second thing you want to learn while at the library is whether you can find any articles on how credit is handled in the mail order industry.

After your library search, you make a number of telephone calls to other mail order houses that specialize in clothing. You ask only about their credit policies. You want to know if they accept credit cards, if they accept COD orders, and if they accept orders on credit if a customer does not have a credit card. A summary of this survey is shown in Figure 5-5. As you can see, the majority of mail order houses do not extend credit. Many do not even accept COD orders. In other words, most of Sunrise Sportswear's competitors accept only cash, checks, money orders, or credit cards.

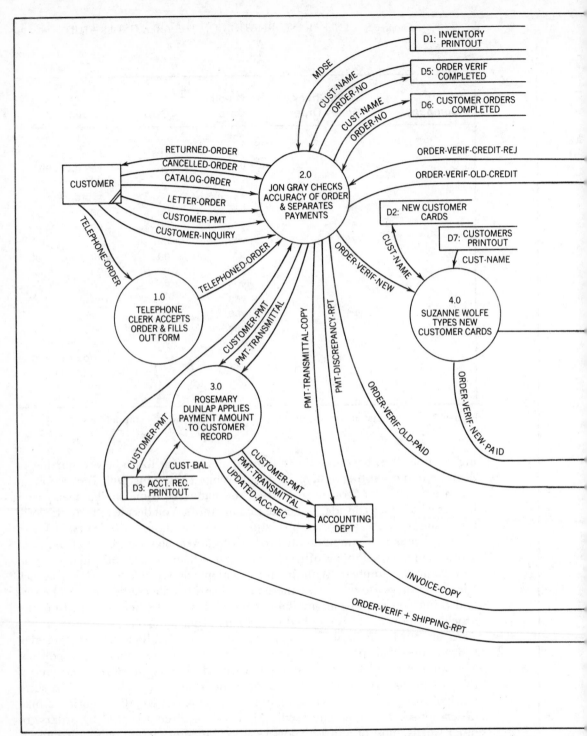

Figure 5-6 Physical data flow diagram (Level 0) showing sequence of *how* Sunrise Sportswear's existing Order Processing system works. Note that ORDER-VERIF is both the "Blue Sheet" and the customer's original order.

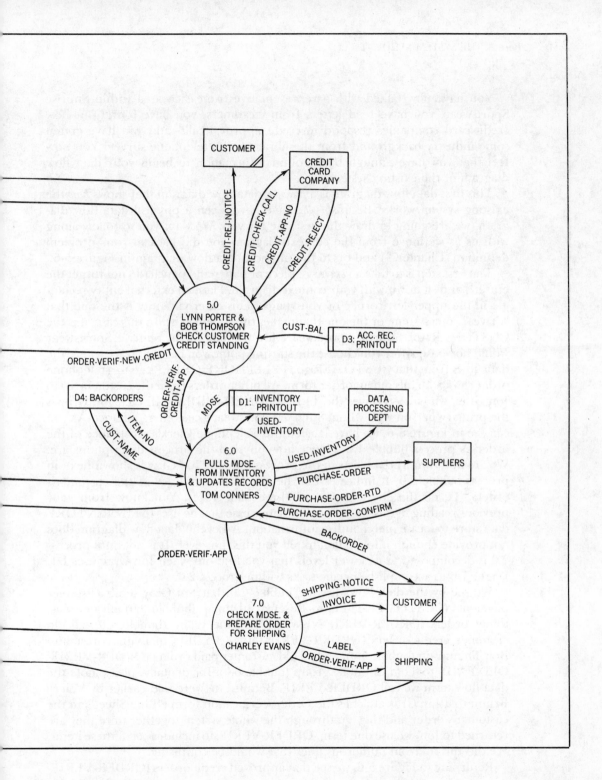

CUSTOMER

CREDIT
CARD
COMPANY

CREDIT-REJ-NOTICE

CREDIT-CHECK-CALL

CREDIT-APP-NO

CREDIT-REJECT

5.0
LYNN PORTER &
BOB THOMPSON
CHECK CUSTOMER
CREDIT STANDING

CUST-BAL

D3: ACC. REC.
PRINTOUT

ORDER-VERIF-NEW-CREDIT

ORDER-VERIF-
CREDIT-APP

D4: BACKORDERS

MDSE

D1: INVENTORY
PRINTOUT

DATA
PROCESSING
DEPT

USED-
INVENTORY

ITEM-NO

CUST-NAME

6.0
PULLS MDSE.
FROM INVENTORY
& UPDATES RECORDS
TOM CONNERS

USED-INVENTORY

SUPPLIERS

PURCHASE-ORDER

PURCHASE-ORDER-RTD

PURCHASE-ORDER-CONFIRM

BACKORDER

ORDER-VERIF-APP

7.0
CHECK MDSE. &
PREPARE ORDER
FOR SHIPPING
CHARLEY EVANS

SHIPPING-NOTICE

INVOICE

CUSTOMER

LABEL

ORDER-VERIF-APP

SHIPPING

You have now talked with a representative from each area within Sunrise Sportswear, you have read letters from customers, you have found out how credit card companies respond to credit approval calls, and you have gotten some industry background from the library and a telephone survey. You now feel that you have enough background information to begin your data flow diagram of the existing system.

This first data flow diagram is a *physical* data flow diagram that shows *how* the existing system works. Because you have never seen a physical data flow diagram, we are going to draw the first one for you. We want you to follow along with us as we move from the context diagram you did back in your problem definition (Chapter 3) and on to the physical data flow diagram in Figure 5-6.

The first step is to take a *very* large piece of paper and pencil (do not forget the eraser!) and sit down with your context diagram. Place an external entity rectangle in the upper left corner of your page. This external entity is the one that "drives" your system, or the one that makes the system exist. In this case, it is the CUSTOMERs of Sunrise Sportswear, for without them, Sunrise Sportswear would not exist. After you choose the starting point, you begin to trace where the data flows from that CUSTOMER go. TELEPHONE-ORDERs go to a telephone order clerk who fills out an order form. All other orders from the customer go to Jon Gray, who also receives the TELEPHONED-ORDERs. In fact, Jon Gray is the primary person with whom Sunrise Sportswear's customers interact. As you can see in Figure 5-6, we have labeled the Telephone Clerk's acceptance of the order as process bubble 1.0. Notice how physical the process descriptions are. We are not using verb/objects in the process bubbles. Jon Gray is shown next, in process bubble 2.0. It indicates that he checks the accuracy of the customer's orders. To do this, he uses one of three data stores. You know from your previous reading in this chapter's cumulative case that he uses the INVENTORY data store to locate merchandise information. A Level 0 data flow diagram does not provide enough information to tell you this, however. It is not until process 2.0 is decomposed to its lower levels that you find out when Jon Gray uses D1, D5, or D6 to accomplish specific tasks within process 2.0.

We see by the data flows leaving bubble 2.0 that Jon Gray sends customer payments (CUSTOMER-PMT) to Rosemary Dunlap (bubble 3.0), all new customer orders (ORDER-VERIF-NEW) to Suzanne Wolfe (bubble 4.0), all old customer credit orders (ORDER-VERIF-OLD-CREDIT) to Lynn Porter and Bob Thompson (bubble 5.0), and all old customer paid orders (ORDER-VERIF-OLD-PAID) to Tom Conners' group (bubble 6.0). Incidentally, please note the data flow term we call ORDER-VERIF. Because we were told earlier by Valery Brunn that Jon Gray attaches the Order Verification form ("Blue Sheet") to the customer's order and they go through the whole system together until they are returned to Jon, we use one term, ORDER-VERIF, to include *both* of these items. We did this to avoid numerous lines that would be confusing.

Returning to Figure 5-6, we see that approved credit orders (ORDER-VERIF-

CREDIT-APP) are sent on to process bubble 6.0, but if the customer's credit is rejected, the customer is notified (CREDIT-REJ-NOTICE), and the ORDER-VERIF-CREDIT-REJ is returned to Jon Gray. When the approved orders reach process 6.0, the merchandise is pulled from the shelves and the inventory records are adjusted accordingly. Notice that we do not show the movement of the merchandise out of process 6.0 (even though merchandise is the essence of Sunrise Sportswear's business) because we decided in Chapter 3 to concentrate on *data,* not merchandise. Instead, we see that the approved Order Verification (ORDER-VERIF-APP) moves out to process bubble 7.0. The people in bubble 7.0 check to make sure the correct merchandise has been pulled, and prepare the order for shipment. When it is ready, the ORDER-VERIF-APP and a LABEL for mailing move on to the last external entity SHIPPING.

As you can see, we have progressed somewhat sequentially through the Sunrise Sportswear Order Processing system. We have moved from left to right and from top to bottom on the page. We show the external entities from the context diagram. What we have added is each individual process in the system and the data stores needed to perform each particular process. Since the users must verify the accuracy of this first physical data flow diagram, it is done in a manner that is familiar to them. For example, we have used the names of the people at Sunrise Sportswear so that they can relate to who does what and how. Later, when you move to the logical data flow diagram, these names will be dropped and the whole data flow diagram "cleaned up."

In examining Figure 5-6, did you notice that it is based only on what we have been told so far by the employees of Sunrise Sportswear (cumulative case in Chapters 3 to 5). You recall from Chapter 2 that rectangles are external entities, open-ended boxes are data stores, and circles are processes in which data is transformed in some way. Every data flow is connected at one end to a process, and data flows are labeled. If necessary, review the section of Chapter 2 in which we described the rules of data flow diagram construction. Now examine Figure 5-6 in more detail. It is the highest level, or Level 0, data flow diagram. If you do not follow what is happening in a process, go back to the narrative about Sunrise Sportswear in the cumulative case for Chapters 3–5.

Student Questions

1. Do you think the employees of Sunrise Sportswear view what they do in the same way as management? Explain.
2. Why would customers refer to the Rejection Notices as humiliating?
3. Have you learned anything more about the Sunrise Sportswear Order Processing system's inputs and outputs since you drew the context diagram back in Chapter 3?
4. How successful would you be if you wanted to determine how long it takes

for an order to go through each one of the Order Processing steps? Explain.

5. Why are the following items not shown on the data flow diagram in Figure 5-6? The Shipping Report that goes to Accounting; the magnetic tape input used to update customer printouts.

6. Are you surprised that the management of Sunrise Sportswear does not seem to know much about its competitors?

Student Tasks

1. Update your list of people with whom you have been dealing at Sunrise Sportswear.

2. Go to the library to learn what you can about Sunrise Sportswear's competitors and how others in the mail order business handle credit, order processing, and so forth. Is it a large industry? Pick one or two things that Mr. Reynolds should know about and report back to him.

3. Modify your data dictionary for terms since drawing the context diagram. What terms should be added? Modified? Deleted?

4. Draw a Level 1 diagram of process bubble 5.0 from Figure 5-6. When you asked the user to validate the physical data flow diagram shown in Figure 5-6, you learned that when Lynn Porter gets approval for a credit card purchase, she has to fill out a credit card charge slip. The master is sent to the customer, along with the merchandise. The copy is sent to the credit card company. Sunrise Sportswear does not keep a copy. Show this new information on your Level 1 data flow diagram, and modify your data dictionary if necessary. Be sure to balance the inputs and outputs against the higher Level 0 data flow diagram.

5. Identify your data stores. Relate them to figures and narrative in the text. In one or two sentences, summarize what you know about each one of them. Add the names of the data stores to your data dictionary.

Selected Readings

1. Bell, Robert. *How to Win at Office Politics: Step-by-Step Plans for Coming Out Ahead.* New York: Times Books, 1984.

2. Dickinson, Roger A., Charles R. Ferguson, and Sumit Sircar. "Critical Success Factors and Small Business," *American Journal of Small Business*, vol. 8, no. 3, Winter 1984, pp. 49–57 + .

3. Dimino, S. A. "Corporate Politics and the System's Process," *Journal of Systems Management*, vol. 34, no. 9, September 1983, pp. 6–9.

4. Drake, Miriam A. "Information and Corporate Cultures," *Special Libraries*, vol. 75, no. 4, October 1984, pp. 263–269.

5. Drucker, Peter F. *Management: Tasks, Responsibilities, Practices.* New York: Harper & Row, Publishers, 1973.

6. Hall, David E. "Winning at Office Politics," *Credit & Financial Management*, vol. 86, no. 4, April 1984, pp. 20–23.

7. Leidecker, Joel K., and Albert V. Bruno. "Identifying and Using Critical Success Factors," *Long Range Planning* (U.K.), vol. 17, no. 1, February 1984, pp. 23–32.

8. Machiavelli, Niccolo. *The Prince.* Written 1513, first published 1532.

9. Newman, Michael. "User Involvement: Does It Exist, Is It Enough?" *Journal of Systems Management*, vol. 35, no. 5, May 1984, pp. 34–38. [Problems of non-cooperation, alienation, or overt resistance as related to designer priorities.]

10. Priest, George E. *The DP Executive's Guide to Microcomputer Management and Control.* Wellesley, Mass.: QED Information Sciences, Inc., 1984. [Strategies for management control and critical issues in the use of microcomputers.]

11. "Trainers Gauge Organizational Communication," *Training,* vol. 21, no. 6, June 1984, p. 72. [Frequency and effectiveness of formal and informal communications, communication to facilitate change, and superior–subordinate communication.]

12. Vickery, Hugh B., III. "Tapping into the Employee Grapevine," *Association Management,* vol. 36, no. 1, January 1984, pp. 59–63.

13. Vincent, David. "Corporate Culture," *Computerworld,* vol. 18, no. 45, November 5, 1984, pp. ID21–22, 26–28, 30. [Effect of information on the corporate culture.]

14. Wakin, Edward. "The Many Faces of Corporate Politics," *Today's Office,* vol. 18, no. 11, April 1984, pp. 36–45.

Questions

1. How do "real-time systems" differ from "batch systems"?

2. What did the movement from "discrete files" to "database files" allow us to do?

3. Describe what an integrated system does.

4. What capabilities does the user department have when distributed processing exists?

5. How does a distributed database system differ from distributed processing?

6. Why is it important for the analyst to gather general information on the area under study?

7. Identify some of the things to look for within the specific area under study.

8. What three basic questions should the investigation of legal requirements answer?

9. What does the organization structure in a business represent?

10. Identify what the formal organization is built around.

11. What can happen if you fail to gain approval of the informal organization?

12. With regard to the organization's structure, what basic interactions should be studied?

13. Why is it important for the analyst to observe and understand the management styles, and their resulting differences, between the area under study and other areas?

14. How is Theory X identified?

15. Identify at least three of the assumptions about people that are made with regard to Theory Y.

16. Why is it useful for an analyst to understand Maslow's five needs hierarchy?

17. Why should the analyst review long-range plans during the process of defining new system requirements?

SITUATION CASES

Case 5-1: *Robin Generators*

You have been asked to help a new systems analyst become familiar with the Systems Department and with Robin Generators in general because you are the most senior analyst to have any free time this week. This new employee needs to learn about organizational procedures and, especially, internal sources of information that can be used to learn about the interactions between and among different organizations within the firm. Your goal is to give this new analyst ideas on specific sources of information for outputs, inputs, and resources.

Questions

1. Write down some sources of information with regard to outputs.
2. Write down some sources of information with regard to inputs.
3. Write down some sources of information with regard to resources.

Case 5-2: *Takahashi Manufacturing*

You work for Takahashi Manufacturing, a large manufacturing firm, and you have been asked to perform a system study on the possibility of using a new microcomputer in the Order Processing Department. This department has many clerical employees who process purchase orders that are then sent to the warehouse for the issuance and shipment of products. Management has expressed concern that costs for operating the department are too high and that a microcomputer possibly could save money and increase efficiency. Currently, there is a three-week time lag between receipt and processing of purchase orders in the department.

Directing your analysis solely on the operations of the Order Processing Department, you have devised a detailed economic cost comparison between the existing system and the proposed new microcomputer-based system. Your data show that a microcomputer would save the company several thousand dollars per year and increase both the output and efficiency by 50 percent, thereby eliminating the three-week time lag. Obviously pleased with your own results, a meeting was scheduled with management to present your findings.

About half way through your presentation, the Warehouse Manager jumped to his feet and objected to the proposed change. The Warehouse Manager complained that his department already was operating at peak capacity and also peak employment. If your proposed 50 percent increase in output of purchase orders were to take place, it would necessitate the hiring of several more warehouse workers, more storage space, more equipment (such as material handling equipment), and a general increase in his department's overhead. Realizing that this problem would more than make up for the savings in the Order Processing Department, you had no choice but to terminate the meeting and have further study of the problem.

Questions

1. How did you get yourself into this situation?

2. Specifically, what should you have done to avoid this particular situation?

Case 5-3: *Ace Microcomputer Company*

The Ace Microcomputer Company has been considering offering its product line on the European market. They do not wish to manufacture the product overseas; however, they would set up overseas warehouses and sales offices for their merchandise. They have hired an analyst to determine whether their proposed overseas expansion would be profitable. At this point, the analyst already has defined the problem, made an outline for the study, and has been gathering background information for the study.

To begin, the analyst looked into the background of the industry in both the United States and Europe. He studied numerous library resources to learn about the products and services of the industry, its growth, technological trends, sales volumes, profit margins, unions, industry standards, foreign competition, and the size and strength of the firm within the industry. The analyst then went on to gather information on the background of the company itself. He examined its products, patterns of growth, sales volume, profit margins, the effect of technology on the firm, expansion during the past, goals and objectives, and long-range plans. Since the overseas expansion would affect all departments, he evaluated each department individually and familiarized himself with what each did in relation to the other departments. The analyst looked at each department's records, policies and procedures, departmental budgets, quantity of work in each area, the relative importance of the area, and so on.

Questions

1. Did the analyst examine all aspects of legal requirements as they might affect Ace Microcomputer Company?
2. Were any other items overlooked?

Case 5-4:   *Cleveland Bicycle Company*

The Systems Manager of a large midwestern bicycle manufacturing company was asked to examine a problem that existed in the Marketing Research Department. He assigned several analysts to the project, giving each analyst two or three functions of the study.

One analyst received the task of gathering general information on the area under study. This analyst decided that the first step was to go to the Marketing Research Department, gather information, and try to detect any unusual characteristics.

Upon visiting the area, the analyst overheard some employees discussing problems they felt existed in the department. One complaint that surfaced was that friction existed between the employees and the manager. The analyst noted this and continued to examine the area under study. Both formal and informal organizations were studied in great detail, substantiating the conversation overheard earlier by the analyst.

The analyst concluded that the informal organization had not accepted the authority of the manager, and in order to combat the negativism, the manager over-exerted his authority. This situation caused employees to choose sides, and political maneuvering was extensive in the department.

The analyst wanted more information to substantiate her conclusions. In order to accomplish this, people outside the department were asked their attitudes toward the Marketing Research Department. Their answers further corroborated her findings. The analyst went over the notes she had collected and formulated a summary statement.

In a summary to the Systems Manager, the analyst criticized the Marketing Research Manager for his power tactics. She suggested that a department meeting be held to iron out the existing problems. This also would allow the Marketing Research Manager to get to know the employees, and vice versa. She submitted the summary to the Systems Manager with the false satisfaction that she had done an excellent job.

Questions

1. Can you identify three mistakes the analyst made?
2. Was the analyst's summary objective? Why or why not?

Chapter 6

UNDERSTANDING
THE EXISTING SYSTEM

LEARNING OBJECTIVES

You will learn how to . . .

□ Understand the existing system.

□ Draw and use layout charts.

□ Search records.

□ Estimate or sample data.

□ Prepare a summary description of the existing system.

□ Translate the physical data flow diagram of the existing system into the logical data flow diagram of the existing system.

□ Describe data stores.

Why Understand the Existing System?

The fundamental problem of the systems analyst is not whether to emphasize structured analysis techniques, but how best to adapt these structured techniques to the changing and challenging needs of business. New technology is "driving" system design techniques. The techniques are changing because of the fast pace of technological development. The analyst, however, still must understand the existing system thoroughly before designing an improved version! For example, as a college student you may ask yourself, how can I get through the system at college? Upon reflection, the answer is obvious; you must understand how the system works before you determine how to get through it.

The objective of this phase of the systems study is a complete understanding of the present operations of the area under study. It provides a "benchmark" for measurement: a clear picture of the present sequence of operations, processing times, work volume being handled, and existing costs.

A benchmark is a surveyor's mark that is used as a reference point for comparison during subsequent measurements. The analyst must obtain an understanding of the existing system for use as a benchmark or reference point in determining how much improvement can be made with a new system. Many people understand specific operations within the system, but few understand the entire system. It is the analyst's task to learn the entire system *before* making any changes. Later, in order to sell a new system to management, a comparison must be made between the existing system and the one that has been proposed. A comparison of benefits cannot be made unless all aspects of the old system can be compared accurately with all aspects of the new one. Then, and only then, can management estimate the benefits of converting to a new system.

The analyst should first learn how the existing system came into being. How was the system designed and installed? By whom? Did it just evolve? Who, if anyone, has a stake in it? Is it someone's pet, or folly? Will anyone try to justify or defend the existing system, and thus slow up the change to a new system? What were some of the conditions that influenced the design of the system? Are they relevant now? These are questions that the analyst should try to answer in preparation for understanding the reasons behind the old system's detailed operations. In addition, special attention must be paid to identification of control strengths and weaknesses within the existing system so that requirements for controls in the new system can be defined.

There are several other reasons why you must understand the existing system. *First,* is to understand how the job is carried out currently to avoid backtracking later. This is a situation in which you have to go back to re-create various work steps or data in order to explain a previously unexplainable error. *Second,* sometimes several people perform a job task that is so closely related that it really is an overlap of the same function or duplication of the same effort. You, therefore, need to identify any task duplications that currently exist. *Third,* is to identify actual or perceived inequities in work distribution. For example, sometimes people may be overworked, or they may perceive that they are overworked. This may be the cause of some of the problems in the current system that can be corrected in a new system. *Fourth,* is to identify duplicate sets of records or data that are kept because people do not trust the current system. You should be forewarned that, after you install *your* new system, some people still may duplicate the current system's records or data. *Fifth,* is to determine if the people are well trained and if they know how the current system *should* operate. Do not let yourself be trapped into designing a new system because the current system is unworkable when, in fact, the current system would work if the people used it properly. *Finally,* the last reason is to identify the controls in the existing system. If there are very few controls in the current system, this will alert you to areas that can be improved as you design the new system.

Gaining the Confidence of the Area Under Study

People, as a general rule, do not accept change readily. Since they may view the systems analyst as a threat to their security, communication is the key to gaining their confidence. If the analyst is able to communicate sincere willingness to help operations personnel, they will be more apt to give the needed cooperation. Every effort should be made to inform the workers of the project objectives, plan, and progress.

The methods for doing this are only as limited as your imagination. Look for skeptics; convert them, involve them, loosen up the ones with set ideas, and try to understand their problems. Circulate rough drafts of proposals and request written comments. You may not understand clearly all the ramifications of something until it is in writing, and it is best to learn of these things early! If possible, have some simulated exercises which can quickly point out any deficiencies. Ask the users to identify these deficiencies.

You must try to make the users of the system feel that they are taking an active part in the development of this new system. Their ideas should be sought out and focused upon, so they can see that they have a "vested interest" in the new system. This will help you in the future because, if the users feel they are a part of the new system, feel they have contributed to it, and can see their ideas implemented, they are much more likely to accept the new system and, therefore, use it. Remember, any new system must be accepted by two distinct classifications of people within the organization. First are the managers who use the output of this system in their decision making and other tasks. The other classification includes the workers who use the system on a day-to-day basis in carrying out the daily business tasks that must be performed. As you can see, management must accept its outputs and the workers must be able to use it. Remember that the most probable cause of a system's failure is people. By this we mean the non-acceptance of the system and, therefore, the philosophy and method of going around or "beating" the system.

To avoid such an uncooperative situation, the analyst should involve the staff as much as possible through department meetings or any other possible way. The analyst should entertain any reasonable suggestions and attempt to explain why others do not fit the study objectives. Since the analyst is responsible for the final decision on what design elements eventually are presented to management, the analyst's role is that of a leader. It is the analyst, in the final analysis, who hears the many viewpoints and combines them all into a feasible system.

The users of the system know the existing system and can contribute many valuable suggestions for its renovation. If the analyst heeds their suggestions and performs in a reasonable manner, the operations personnel will accept a new system more readily. They will, in fact, be obligated to make it work.

Searching Records

Searching the business records is the easiest way of obtaining formal information. Informal methods usually are not documented. Therefore the analyst should remember that searching records is for learning formal information, whereas interviewing can give both formal and informal information.

The first, and most important, records that the analyst should examine are the written policies and procedures of the area under study. They tell the analyst how the area's work should be done, providing the procedures are reasonably up-to-date. However, discussions with the operating personnel usually reveal deviations for various reasons, both good and bad. (Remember, the wise analyst should not criticize people directly.)

We can refer to files maintained by the area under study as "internal" files to differentiate them from files maintained in other areas of the firm or outside the firm.

The analyst should obtain a list of the internal files while interviewing key personnel. Then it should be determined which of these files are used in the existing system.

Such files normally contain the up-to-date forms and data used by the area in the existing system. The analyst should study the documents carefully to note the various differences between transactions.

For example, it may be discovered that a form has been completed in several different ways at different times. It may be noted that on one form all spaces were filled in, and on another only some of them were used. Or there may be variations in routing, special instructions written in, and so on. This usually indicates that the routine in which the form is involved is subject to several variations and exceptions.

The analyst might go through such a file to list such variations and exceptions, and the reasons for them (as explained by area personnel). These variations and exceptions reveal a great deal about the existing system, and alert the analyst to the various conditions which the new system must improve or deal with. Since this is admittedly a very time-consuming process, it is acceptable in most cases to use a random sample approach (see the next section for a discussion on sampling).

Internal records or files that the analyst might examine are operating files such as purchase orders, invoices, sales orders, shipping forms, and so forth, memoranda files, computer files, and files maintained by individuals for protection or improved efficiency. Usually the files that are the most valuable to the analyst are the ones which are in active use in the operation of the existing system. (See Appendix 1 for an in-depth list of considerations on how to improve file operations.) Of course, any files that are not used also are subject to question. The analyst should review the area's records retention policy (see Chapter 15).

External records or files are those files that are maintained outside of the area under study or outside of the firm. External files often affect the area's systems in various ways. Files maintained by customers, vendors, governments, and so forth, can be considered "active" to the extent that they might be used for, with, or against the firm. The situation varies widely from one industry to another. The analyst should attempt to compile a list of such files and study their potential bearing on the existing system and the proposed system.

Estimating and Sampling

Estimating and sampling can be used to predict costs, quantities, time periods, and other parameters that are relevant to the existing or proposed system. These techniques are appropriate when internal and/or external records are inaccurate or incomplete. *Estimating* is the art of predicting, and therefore is uncertain to some degree. Any estimates made by the analyst should be checked against some known or reasonable overall total.

There are three kinds of estimating procedures which generally are useful in systems work. These are conglomerate estimating, comparison estimating, and detailed estimating. In *conglomerate estimating,* the representatives from each functional area within the area under study confer to develop estimates based on past experience. In *comparison estimating,* the analyst meets individually with anyone, inside or outside the firm, who has a similar system. The analyst then evaluates comparable operations and derives estimates. In *detailed estimating,* the analyst makes a detailed study of the costs, times required, and any other pertinent factors for each step of each procedure within the system. When extreme accuracy is required, perhaps because of the importance of the decisions involved, detailed estimating should be used.

Sampling is the collection of a limited quantity of data. In sampling, one collects only a fraction of the total existing data, for the purpose of studying that fraction to infer things about the total. The fractional data is the sample. The size of the sample required for such inferences varies according to the desired accuracy and certainty. There are several approaches to determining the sample size. The following is a simple and reliable method for most applications

$$\text{Necessary sample size} = 0.25 \left(\frac{\text{Desired certainty}}{\text{Acceptable error}} \right)^2$$

Desired Certainty	
For 97% certainty	Use 2.170
95% certainty	1.960
90% certainty	1.645
80% certainty	1.281

The "desired certainty"[1] is defined as how sure you want to be that your answer is less than an "acceptable error." The acceptable error might be defined as how far off the data can be or how much inaccuracy can be tolerated. You will find above a list of various levels of desired certainty that range from 97 percent down to 80 percent.

As for "acceptable error," you have to choose the acceptable error that can be tolerated. Obviously the higher the desired certainty, such as 97 percent, and the lower the acceptable error, such as 1 percent (0.01), the larger the sample size will be.

The best way for you to look at this is to pick a reasonable target; for instance, 95 percent of the time I do not want my sample data to vary from the actual results (this is the acceptable error) by more than 5 percent. If the systems analyst wants to be 95 percent certain that the sample data will not vary (acceptable error) by more than 5 percent (0.05) from the actual data, the sample size should be 384

$$\text{Necessary sample size} = 0.25 \left(\frac{1.96}{0.05} \right)^2 = 384$$

[1] Available from any introductory statistics book.

As you can see, by using the above formula, the needed sample size is 384. This means that you would have to go out and take 384 observations or samples of whatever you were sampling. Let us assume that you are taking physical observations as to how often the door to the computer center is locked when you observe it. Let us also assume that you walk by the computer center 384 times during a one-month period (this constitutes your 384 samples). Next, let us assume that the results of this sample show that 80 percent (8 out of 10 times) of the time the door to the computer center is locked. This means that of your 384 samples, 307 times the door was locked and 77 times it was unlocked (307/384 × 100 = 80%). Now, suppose someone asks how accurate you think your findings are that the computer center door actually is locked 80 percent of the time. Your response would be, "I am 95 percent certain that the sample data did not vary from the actual data (acceptable error) by more than 5 percent." In other words you are 95 percent sure that you are within 5 percent of what the true answer would be if you were to check the door every day, many times a day, for possibly months or years. In fact, it is questionable whether you could check enough times to have all possible conditions of locked versus unlocked because you would have to check the door every time someone either entered or exited the computer room. Since this is an impossible situation, you can see that you never could be 100 percent sure of your sample data.

The 0.25 is a constant and is always used. The desired certainty is chosen by the analyst and is given above. The acceptable error in the above case was 5 percent (0.05), but the analyst can choose any percentage desired, such as 2 percent (0.02), 10 percent (0.10), or 1 percent (0.01), and so forth.

For example, after determining the necessary sample size, the analyst can *randomly* collect a sample of 384 purchase orders to analyze. If there are an average of 2.5 mistakes per purchase order, the analyst can be 95 percent sure that the average of 2.5 mistakes per purchase order does not vary by more than 5 percent from the average for *all* the purchase orders. Obviously, sampling allows the analyst to learn things about the existing system with only a fraction of the effort that 100 percent evaluation would require.

The systems analyst usually is not required to perform time studies, motion studies, or methods-time measurement studies. These are functions of the industrial engineer. However, the systems analyst may wish to perform a *work sampling study* in order to understand the existing system. A work sampling study consists of a large number of observations taken at random intervals. At each observation the analyst notes what the employee is doing and records it into one of a number of predefined categories. Work sampling may be carried out in the following fashion.

1. Sell the idea of work *sampling* rather than continuous observation of the job. Convince management that sampling will enable you to get the desired results in a fraction of the time required for continuous observation.

2. Define the operations of the job. (These are the "predefined categories" for recording.) Make an Observation Recording Form (Figure 6-1) for recording observations that will be made during the study.

3. For nonrepetitive jobs it is better to make many observations. If you need 2401 observations for the desired accuracy,[2] divide them by the number of days allotted to the study to get the number of observations required per day.

4. Make sure the observations are made at random times. Do not observe the people or events at the same time each day since you may not get a reliable sampling of their complete routine.

5. After making 2401 or more random observations on each item, person, or event being observed, you can compute the percentages for each predefined category, as illustrated for item 1 below (data are from Figure 6-1).

Predefined Categories	Item Being Observed	
	1	Percentages
On telephone	241	241/2401 = 10%
Reading	501	501/2401 = 21%
Writing	362	362/2401 = 15%
Conference	831	831/2401 = 35%
Walking	345	345/2401 = 14%
Elevator	30	30/2401 = 1%
Idle	91	91/2401 = 4%
Total observations	2401	100%

6. Calculate the percentages as in step 5 above for the other items (2 through 7) from the Observation Recording Form (Figure 6-1) and you have the percentage of time spent on each predefined category of work for each person or event (items 1 through 7).

Once the analyst has computed and studied the percentage of time spent in each category of work, there is an excellent basis for evaluating the existing system, and a benchmark for comparison with the new system design. The information gained from a work sampling may be used to realign job duties among employees, to set work standards for office employees, or to eliminate unnecessary procedures.

[2] $N = 0.25(1.96/0.02)^2 = 2401$ (95% certain that the sample data will not vary from the true data by more than 2%). If 2401 are too many observations, use either a lower desired certainty or a higher acceptable error.

OBSERVATION RECORDING FORM							
Predefined Categories	**Items Being Observed: People or Events**						
	1	**2**	**3**	**4**	**5**	**6**	**7**
On telephone	III	THL		II			I
Reading	I	III	THL	IIII	THL	I	III
Writing	THL	III	III	II	THL	II	
Conference	II			THL			
Walking	III	II	IIII	THL	III	I	I
Elevator	I	I				THL	
Idle	THL	II					I
Total observations	2401	2401	2401	2401	2401	2401	2401

Figure 6-1 Observation Recording form.

Develop a Method to Document the Data

As you go through the process of understanding the existing system, a method of documenting the collected data must be developed. The cumulative case (Sunrise Sportswear) demonstrates the use of data flow diagrams and other structured techniques to document some of the findings. Other documentation methods also may be useful. For example, flowcharts are appropriate when the system study uses traditional design methodologies or later in the structured design process when the physical minispecifications are developed for the new system. Also, the Area Cost Sheet can be used during structured design to document costs. Some of these alternate methods are presented below.

As the analyst interviews, searches records, and makes estimations or samples, the collected data must be recorded, summarized, and evaluated so it will make sense. The job is to understand the existing system; it must be documented so it can be compared with the proposed system, especially for cost comparisons. One possible example of developmental system documentation follows, but the analyst should be able to modify this example to fit the specific situation. Since it is used to define and analyze the existing system, another method altogether may be required for the application faced by the analyst. A data documentation example follows.

The first piece of documentation is the Area Cost Sheet. It fits each area under study into its larger context. The purpose of the Area Cost Sheet is to document the formal organization and economic data pertaining to the area under study. Specifically, the Area Cost Sheet does the following.

1. Shows the formal organization.
2. Permits a rapid analysis of the overall structure into which the area under study fits.
3. Shows the cost impact of the area under study with respect to the overall cost structure.

The Area Cost Sheet is divided into three sections (see Figure 6-2).

1. *The formal organization chart.* This organization chart must be broad enough to cover the entire area under study. Each box shows the number of full-time equivalent employees (F.T.E.s) in that area, except that the lowest box gives the total F.T.E.s from that level down.
2. *The budget breakdown section.* These are the annual or monthly costs for each organization in the lowest level of the organization chart. The upper level costs are prorated into this tabulation. In this example, personnel, equipment, supplies, miscellaneous, and training are used as categories. The

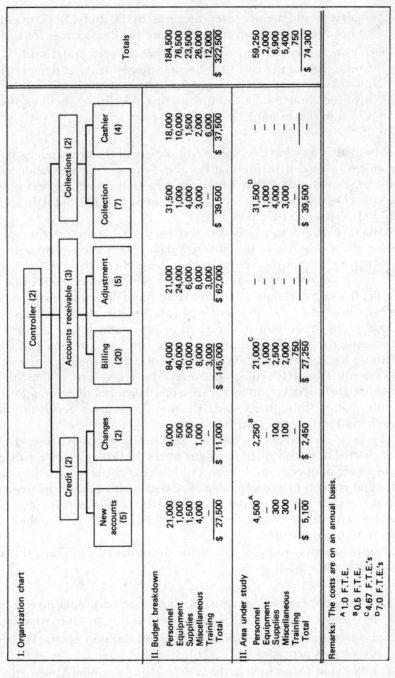

I. Organization chart

	Totals

Controller (2)

Credit (2) — Accounts receivable (3) — Collections (2)

New accounts (5) | Changes (2) — Billing (20) | Adjustment (5) — Collection (7) | Cashier (4)

II. Budget breakdown

	New accounts (5)	Changes (2)	Billing (20)	Adjustment (5)	Collection (7)	Cashier (4)	Totals
Personnel	21,000	9,000	84,000	21,000	31,500	18,000	184,500
Equipment	1,000	500	40,000	24,000	1,000	10,000	76,500
Supplies	1,500	500	10,000	6,000	4,000	1,500	23,500
Miscellaneous	4,000	1,000	8,000	8,000	3,000	2,000	26,000
Training	—	—	3,000	3,000	—	6,000	12,000
Total	$ 27,500	$ 11,000	$ 145,000	$ 62,000	$ 39,500	$ 37,500	$ 322,500

II. Area under study

	New accounts (5)	Changes (2)	Billing (20)	Adjustment (5)	Collection (7)	Cashier (4)	Totals
Personnel	4,500 [A]	2,250 [B]	21,000 [C]	—	31,500 [D]	—	59,250
Equipment	—	—	1,000	—	1,000	—	2,000
Supplies	300	100	2,500	—	4,000	—	6,900
Miscellaneous	300	100	2,000	—	3,000	—	5,400
Training	—	—	750	—	—	—	750
Total	$ 5,100	$ 2,450	$ 27,250		$ 39,500		$ 74,300

Remarks: The costs are on an annual basis.

[A] 1.0 F.T.E.
[B] 0.5 F.T.E.
[C] 4.67 F.T.E.'s
[D] 7.0 F.T.E.'s

Figure 6-2 Area Cost Sheet.

analyst should use whatever categories fit the study. Departmental budgets or historical costs from accounting are the best sources for these costs.

3. *The area under study section.* Assume that the area under study is Collection Costs, that is, the cost of collecting money from customers who charge purchases. Using cost data and the judgment of the supervisory personnel involved, isolate only those costs that pertain to the area under study, which in this example are collection costs.

The analyst now has a complete cost picture of the area under study. Include the organizational structure that lies above the specific area being studied plus the overall costs and specific costs of the area under study. For example, the New Accounts Department has a total annual cost of $27,500, but only $5,100 of that $27,500 pertains to collection costs.

Data flow diagrams, which were discussed in Chapter 2, are an excellent way to document any system that involves data. Their use is demonstrated in the cumulative case (Sunrise Sportswear) at the end of Chapters 3 through 12.

It also is appropriate to present the traditional methodology of flowcharting. If you are using data flow diagrams to document the existing system, you do not necessarily need to use this documenting technique, although you might review it briefly just to see how it works. Also, you might review a shorter form of flowcharting called HIPO diagrams. They are both presented in Chapter 13. Charting has had an evolutionary progression. First there was the flowcharting of a system. Then HIPO diagrams were a shortened form of flowcharting. Now we have data flow diagrams which are a more pictorial representation of the flow of information through a system. Chapter 13 contains details on the types of flowcharts and how to construct them.

A general method of documenting the existing system is to use a Documented Flowchart. The documented flowchart traces the flow of a single activity through its sequence of operations. It begins with whatever starts the sequence of operations and goes on to its completion. The documented flowchart (see Figure 6-3) is just a typical systems flowchart, but there are numbers in each box. These numbers are used to cross-reference each flowchart box back to the Documentation Section (Figure 6-4).

In the documentation section of the documented flowchart, the analyst records such items as

1. What is done, with what resources (financial, personnel, inventory, or facility), under what conditions, how often, and to produce what results.
2. Elapsed time, frequencies, volumes, and decision points. It should be as detailed as necessary.
3. Collect any forms used in the system. Using a standard instruction sheet (if one exists) for each form, fill in the form with sample data. Attach the forms to the documentation section to which they fit (Figure 6-4).

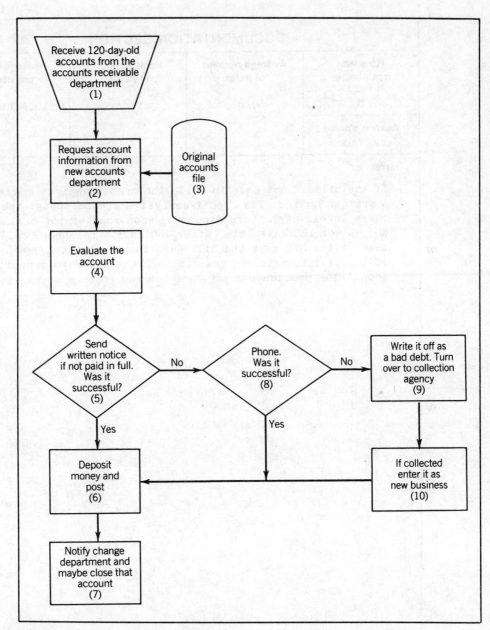

Figure 6-3 Documented flowchart.

DOCUMENTATION SECTION

Flowchart box number	Average number of items	Peak number of items	Average time per item
5	34/day	55/day	10 minutes
Analyst's name Jack Thomas			

Narrative:

If the bill is not paid in full, the credit analyst sends
a written notice. The credit analyst's microcomputer has
three levels of letters depending upon whether the bill is
60, 90, or 180 days late. After 180 days a telephone call is
used. After 270 days the bill goes to a collection agency.
If the bill is paid, it goes through the standard deposit/
accounting procedures.

Figure 6-4 Documentation section of the documented flowchart.

The documentation section is almost a narrative of the flowchart and is cross-referenced into the flowchart by the individual box numbers that are in the flowchart itself. The narrative and numerical values collected are recorded in Figure 6-4 (documentation section) and attached to the flowchart. The set then becomes the documented flowchart. One of these documentation sections should be used for each box in the flowchart.

Both the Area Cost Sheet and the documented flowchart are excellent methods of documenting the existing system and/or the proposed system. More documentation ideas are offered in Chapter 7.

Layout Charts

We have been discussing documentation of what is in the system. Sometimes it also is useful to picture the physical proximity or nearness of one process or person to another. One way of demonstrating how people, who are near one another or far away, have to move to interact with one another is shown through the use of layout charts.

A layout chart shows the floor plan of an area. It also may show the flow of paperwork or the flow of goods as well as the location of file cabinets or storage areas. Layout charts are used effectively to show the before and after layouts of the area under study. The analyst draws the area as it is in the existing system and traces in the flow of work. For comparison, the analyst draws the area as it will be in the proposed system and traces in the more efficient flow of work (Figure 6-5).

It is advisable to use scale model layouts. Draw the outside boundaries of the area under study in ¼-inch to 1-foot scale, and cut paper models (top view) of the equipment needed in the area, to the same scale. Draw in all permanent interior walls and other permanent features. Then play a game with the equipment cutouts by moving them about in order to get the most efficient layout.

Observe simple office common sense. The manager will not want the secretary 200 feet away. The manager's assistant and other supervisory personnel should be located in such a way that it is obvious that they are the supervisors. Those who need partitioning around their desk or a door to their office should get it, unless the economic situation prohibits it. It usually is a mistake to give one supervisor partitioning and a peer none.

Do not make the error of forgetting to provide electric wall sockets for those personnel who have microcomputers, and so forth. Remember to arrange for telephones to be repositioned. Each employee should keep the same extension number, if at all possible.

The layout must meet local fire safety and other emergency procedure requirements. City hall usually can provide the needed information.

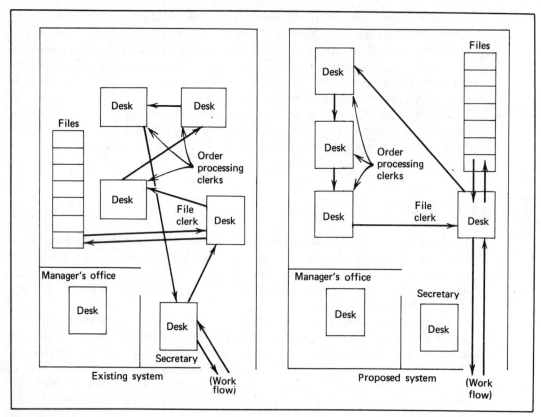

Figure 6-5 Layout charts.

*P*repare a Summary on the Existing System

Although the developmental documentation already prepared is an excellent summary of the existing system, a summary of findings still needs to be prepared. This summary should include everything of importance learned during this phase of the study. It is, in fact, the analyst's written understanding of the existing system.

The summary should include any design ideas, notes on whether currently used forms are adequate or inadequate, who was helpful, who hindered progress, and overall impressions. Notes on all aspects of the study should be included, whether gained from interviews, meetings, records, flowcharts, or work sampling.

In general, what is needed here is something that can be referred to later for data when defining the system's requirements and designing the new system. It is the "benchmark" to be used for later comparisons.

A sample outline for the summary of the existing system may look like this.

I. Description of the existing system
   A. Inputs
   B. Operations
   C. Outputs
   D. Resources
      1. Personnel
      2. Inventory
      3. Financial
      4. Facility
   E. Operational and accounting controls

II. Documentation
   A. Interviews
   B. Records
   C. Data flow diagrams
   D. Layout charts
   E. Flowcharts
   F. Sampling
   G. Cost analysis

III. Positive benefits of existing system

IV. Weaknesses in existing system capabilities and controls

V. Any other items relevant to the existing system

SUNRISE SPORTSWEAR COMPANY

CUMULATIVE CASE: Understanding the Existing System (Step 4)

During the previous steps you learned quite a bit about Sunrise Sportswear and the people who work there. You know by now that Mr. Reynolds is a Theory Y leader who allows his managers to run the operation the way they see fit. Valery Brunn has been with Sunrise Sportswear for many years and has built "an empire" during that time. Like many family-owned and run firms, procedures have been in place for many years without much thought to improving how things get done. It is a reactive atmosphere in which no one does anything unless a customer complains, at which time they react. This is in direct opposition to a professionally run organization which plans for meeting customer needs and competitors' efforts.

Several undercurrents of dissatisfaction have surfaced. Suzanne Wolfe was afraid to speak up about the increased problems with regard to her workload. Ed Wallace openly criticized the credit policies of Valery Brunn's operation. Jon Gray complained about the lack of space and, indirectly, about the lack of a decision regarding the storage of records. Tom Conners would like more adequate computer capability. By this time you probably have concluded that Sunrise Sportswear is outmoded in its approach to doing business during the Information Age. Finally, it appears that many of Sunrise Sportswear's procedures are based on doing things in the least expensive way. While this may be admirable in many things, it is not always the best way to do business. For example, the post cards that are being sent out to inform customers that Sunrise Sportswear is not extending credit to them are alienating customers. Perhaps the Order Verification form that follows an order through the entire process was useful when Sunrise was a smaller operation, but now it may have outlived its usefulness (this has not been established as yet, however). If management took a more positive approach to saving money by doing their tasks in a cost-effective manner, they might be farther ahead. Nevertheless, "pennypinching" seems to be part of the culture at Sunrise Sportswear.

Valery Brunn wants you to find out why the credit verification process is taking so long, but has no means of showing how long it actually takes. She was not aware of the most time-consuming step in the process—that of creating the new customer cards.

It is now time to try to obtain some hard facts about what is happening in Sunrise Sportswear's Order Processing system. To do this you have to search some records. One of the major problems is the large number of customers who are not paying their bills. You learned during your survey of other mail order firms that most of them do not extend credit. You also know, based on your discussion with Ed Wallace in Accounting, that Mr. Reynolds thinks he has to extend credit to customers in order to keep them. Mr. Wallace also told you that Mr. Reynolds does not want the overdue accounts sent out to a collection agency. Now that you have made them aware that they do not have a "preferred credit status" for older customers, you need to perform some sampling in order to have a basis for making later recommendations. You also might want to draw some charts to document various parts of the existing system. At this point, we are interested in the physical aspects of the system, although we will be moving toward its logical aspects by the time we finish this step.

One very physical aspect of the situation at Sunrise Sportswear has to do with how close people are to one another. While you were working on your physical data flow diagram in the last step, you became aware that you had to move quite a bit between the various buildings and floors. It seemed to you that people who had to interact with one another, especially in exchanging physical pieces of data

Brunn, Valery. Order Processing Mgr., x593, Bldg. 2, Rm. 121
Bull, Ann. Data Processing Mgr., x154, Bldg. 2, Rm. 106
Conners, Tom. Inventory, x224, Bldg. 3
Cranston, Dave. Catalog Printing Mgr., x353, Bldg. 2, Rm. 230
Dunlap, Rosemary. Customer payments, x436, Bldg. 1, Rm. 147
Evans, Charley. Order Preparation, x235, Bldg. 3
Finney, Betty. Personnel Mgr., x217, Bldg. 1, Rm. 120
Gray, Jon. Customer orders, x389, Bldg. 1, Rm. 210
Hardy, Doris. Invoice preparation, x333, Bldg. 3
King, Joy. Shipping notices, x385, Bldg. 3
Masters, Kyle. Shipping Mgr., x277, Bldg. 3
Porter, Lynn. Credit card orders, x287, Bldg. 2, Rm. 203
Reynolds, Stanley. Managing owner, x371, Bldg. 1, Rm. 105
Thompson, Bob. Credit orders, x275, Bldg. 2, Rm. 215
Wallace, Ed. Accounting Mgr., x325, Bldg. 1, Rm. 206
Wolfe, Suzanne. New customers, x473, Bldg. 2, Rm. 153

Credit clerk, Bldg. 2, Rm. 209
Telephone order clerks, Bldg. 1, Rm. 234

Figure 6-6 Sunrise Sportswear personnel and locations.

(forms), went up and down stairs and between buildings quite a bit. At this point you decide to amend the list of people who are involved in, or interact with, the Order Processing activity. The result is an updated list, such as we show in Figure 6-6.

Based on this figure, you mentally examine who is located where and find it is confusing. To overcome this confusion, you draw a layout chart of the Sunrise Sportswear property. It is not really a layout of the property, but a facsimile that shows both floors of Buildings 1 and 2 as well as the general layout of Building 3, which is a large warehouse area without any real offices. This layout chart is shown in Figure 6-7. As you can see, we have shown where people are located physically, the data flow diagram process number from Figure 5-6, and also where they have to take data to transmit it to another person. In the case of Sunrise Sportswear, this is an important chart to use because their operation currently is very much a physical system. As you undoubtedly determined during your discussion with Mr. Reynolds, Sunrise more or less "just grew that way." The layout chart proves that it is indeed a haphazard system in terms of the physical proximity of people who must interact with one another.

Because of your concern over the procedures by which credit is granted to customers, you now decide to perform some sampling. You have many things you would like to sample, but find most are impossible because of Sunrise

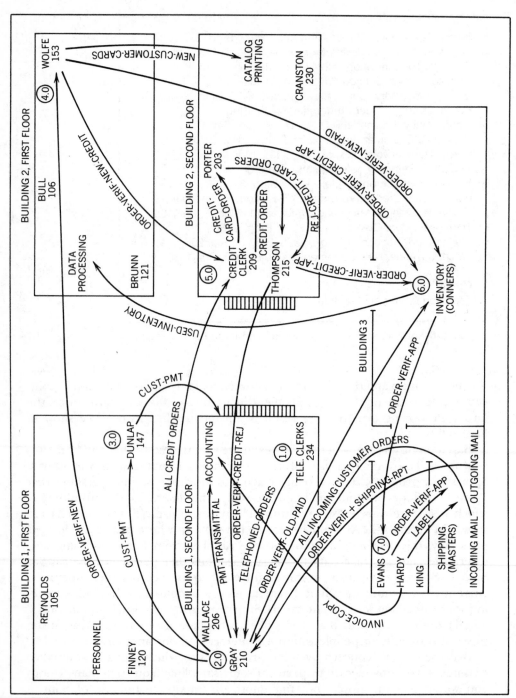

Figure 6-7 Building and personnel layout chart of Sunrise Sportswear. Stairs show access to second floor. Arrows indicate physical movement of data as shown in physical data flow diagram (existing) in Figure 5-6. Not all flows are shown and some have been combined. Notice the process number next to key people.

Sportswear's poor recordkeeping. Knowing that any sampling will be tedious because of the poor recordkeeping, you decide to go with the most critical question. You want to determine what percentage of credit card rejections that are extended credit by Sunrise eventually become overdue accounts.

To determine how many records you must locate in order to have a viable sample, you use the formula shown earlier in this chapter

$$\text{Necessary sample size} = 0.25 \left(\frac{\text{Desired certainty}}{\text{Acceptable error}} \right)^2$$

Because you want to be 90 percent certain that the sample results will not vary from the actual results by more than 5 percent, your calculation shows a sample size of 271

$$\text{N.S.S.} = 0.25 \left(\frac{1.645}{0.05} \right)^2 = 271$$

Now you know that, if you obtain a sample of 271 credit card rejections, you will be 90 percent certain that the sample results will not vary from the actual data by more than 5 percent.

Mr. Wallace is your first stop. He says that he has no records that show which accounts were credit card rejections. Actually, you had suspected this would be the case, but wanted to confirm it. Knowing there are no shortcuts to this answer, you go to Jon Gray's area to use the file of completed Order Verifications. You know from studying the Order Verification form previously (see Figure 3-4 in Chapter 3), that it is a relatively complete record of credit information. Overdue accounts at Sunrise Sportswear are recognized as being those over 60 days old. The last month of Order Verification forms are too recent to be considered, so the sample you select covers the period from two to five months ago. Older forms are not wanted in the sample, because they may have been paid and will no longer be found in the current overdue accounts. Going back further would restrict the results to seriously overdue accounts only. Although this would be interesting, it would not get the needed information.

To make it as valid a sample as possible, you first determine how many drawers of Order Verification forms cover the needed time period and then judge that every tenth form should be enough to obtain a sample of 271. Of the Order Verification forms chosen, you write down the customer's name, whether it was originally a credit card rejection or other credit, and the customer's zip code (to be used later to verify that the correct customer account is being examined). Once 271 names have been gathered, it is time to return to Accounting to examine individual customer accounts. It is fortunate that Accounting has a printout of overdue accounts that is updated every night. The printout indicates whether an account is 30, 60, 90, 120, or more days overdue. When you examine the 271 accounts and match them to the printout, you find that 163 originally were rejected by the credit card companies and are now more than 60 days overdue. By using this sample data, you can now conclude that 60 percent of the overdue accounts are those of customers who were rejected originally by the credit card companies. The calculation is: $163/271 = 0.60 \times 100 = 60\%$. By estimating the number of customers on each page of the overdue accounts printout and multiplying that by the number of pages, you calculate that there are approximately 2,000 overdue accounts. If 60 percent of these were credit card company rejections, there are 1,200 customers to whom Sunrise Sportswear should not have extended credit. The calculation is $2,000 \times 0.60 = 1,200$.

With this new information in hand, you seek out Ed Wallace. He says he is not at all surprised by the results (remember, earlier he called these people dead-beats). In fact, he does not believe Sunrise Sportswear should extend credit at all, and is pleased to learn that the sample results are so high. It seems he has been trying to convince Mr. Reynolds for some time that Sunrise Sportswear should not place itself in the position of being a creditor. His personal opinion is that mail order firms should deal only in checks or credit cards. Your telephone survey and sampling of overdue accounts vindicate his position. You caution Mr. Wallace not to say anything to Mr. Reynolds about the sampling just yet because you are not ready to present your results of this next phase. You indicate that your purpose in telling him this information is to verify that he thinks the sample is accurate. He says he believes it is correct.

At this point, most everything has been accomplished that contributes to your understanding of the existing Order Processing system. It is now time to convert this physical information into a logical data flow diagram and work on the existing system's data stores.

The first step is to return to the physical data flow diagram constructed during the last step (see Figure 5-6 in Chapter 5). Since drawing the diagram, you have learned of two more things that must be added to it. The first of these is that when Lynn Porter gets a credit card purchase approval, she fills out a credit card charge slip. The original is sent to the customer along with the ordered merchandise. When she completes this form, the customer's copy is attached to the Order Verification form when it is forwarded to inventory. The credit card charge slip copies are accumulated and sent each evening to the credit card companies. This means there are two new data flow names to be added to the data dictionary. They are CREDIT-CARD-CHARGE-SLIP and CREDIT-CARD-CHARGE-SLIP-COPY.

The second pertinent thing you learned was from talking with Tom Conners in Inventory. When new inventory arrives at Sunrise Sportswear, they count the merchandise and modify the inventory printout just as they do when the inventory stock is depleted. This means there is a third new data flow called NEW-INVENTORY. It is sent to Data Processing every night along with USED-INVENTORY.

These three new data flows are added to the physical data flow diagram and the three new data flow names are added to the data dictionary. You feel confident that all data flows have been identified, and proceed to translate the physical data flow diagram into a logical data flow diagram. Taking another large piece of paper, you again begin with the CUSTOMER external entity in the upper left corner. Look at Figure 6-8 and you will see that we have drawn the Level 0 logical data flow diagram for you. The CUSTOMER still telephones an order, and it is accepted by the telephone order clerk. Notice, however, that the description inside the process bubble (1.0) has been changed to read ACCEPT TELEPHONE ORDER. It has a strong verb (accept) and an object (telephone order). The fact that it is a telephone clerk who accepts the order has been dropped. It also does not show that this person fills out the order form because that is something physical. Perhaps it is even something that could be done using a computer terminal.

Before going further into this logical data flow diagram, let us discuss the naming of this particular process and the data flows. Some people might say that we should have combined processes 1.0 and 2.0 and simply called it "Accept Orders." We have not done that because you always must do what is realistic. In the case of Sunrise Sportswear, you were not asked to computerize the Order Processing system. With the information that you have now, it is fairly obvious that process 1.0 is not going to change. Purists might say, yes, but you should be showing only logical processes on this data flow diagram. For the same reason, they might say that TELEPHONE-ORDER, CATALOG-ORDER, and LETTER-ORDER should all be combined into one data flow called ORDER-ENTRY. We acknowledge that this would be desirable in either very large systems or those that are highly mechanized. In this case, however, we suggest that a middle ground between theory and reality must be achieved. Figure 6-8 reflects more accurately what flows into the Sunrise Sportswear Order Processing system and what happens to those data flows once they are in the Sunrise Sportswear system. You may be sure that if you were hired to solve Sunrise Sportswear's credit problem and instead revised the order entry system, Stanley Reynolds would be very unhappy with your work and Casper Management Consultants would get a bad reputation.

Moving on to process bubble 2.0, we find that information has been shortened to read only VERIFY ORDER. In other words, we have chosen the most important thing that occurs at that step as the title of the process.

As we move out of bubble 2.0, we observe the next major change. In the physical data flow diagram we showed that the various processes were more or less in a sequential order. In the logical data flow diagram, we observe that processes occur in parallel and are governed by the flow of data. That is, process

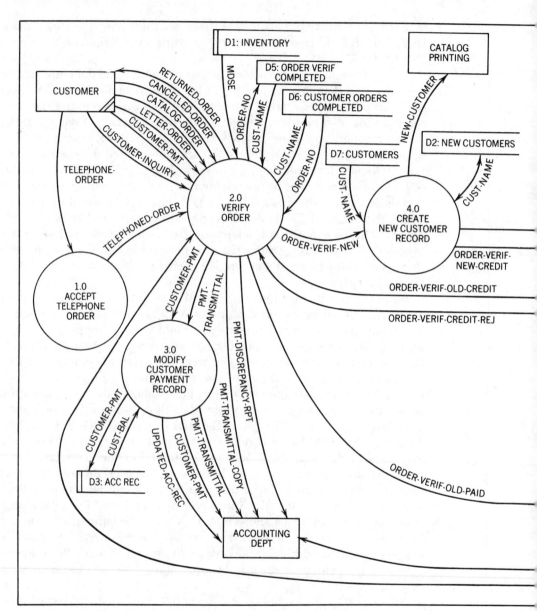

Figure 6-8 Logical data flow diagram (Level 0) showing *what* happens in Sunrise Sportswear's Order Processing system. Note that ORDER-VERIF is both the "Blue Sheet" and the customer's original order. The left-to-right flow of this DFD is not perfect because it had to be fit across two pages.

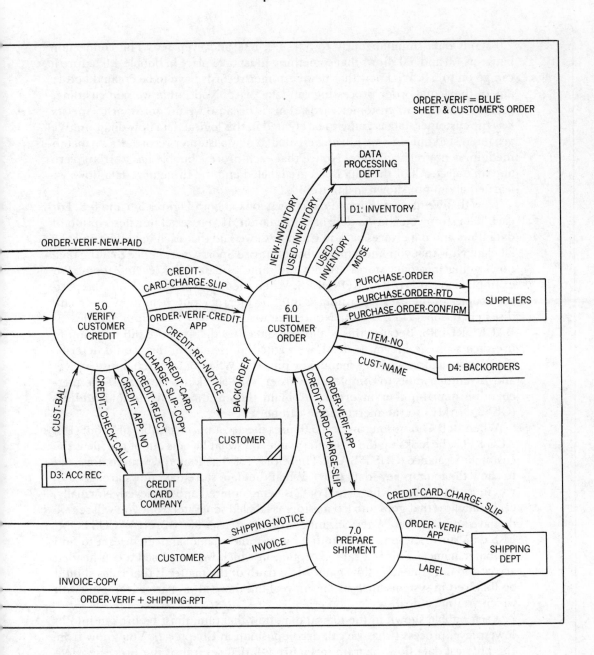

2.0 sends data simultaneously to 3.0, 4.0, 5.0, and even 6.0. The connection between 4.0 and 5.0 shows that something must take place in bubble 4.0 before it can go on to 5.0. We know that new customer records have to be created before any of the actual order processing can take place. Notice that we said customer records rather than customer cards. This is because we do not want to specify *how* the customer data is going to be created in this logical data flow diagram. We are interested only in *what* is being created: a new customer record. Its format or medium is not relevant here. Notice that each process bubble has a strong verb and an object. All of the data flows are labeled and the three new data flows we learned about are shown in Figure 6-8.

Now that we have mentioned data flows, look at both Figures 5-6 and 6-8. For each data store you show a flow of information. If you recall our description of data flows and data stores back in Chapter 2, we said that each data flow must be labeled. Now that you know more about Sunrise Sportswear, notice that the data flows going into data stores are not the same as data flows leaving them. For example, look at D4: BACKORDERS. When the inventory people put the post-card copies of the backorder notices into the file, they put them in by merchandise item number (ITEM-NO). Notice that we did not label the input data flow as BACKORDERS. Because this is a logical data flow diagram, we did not want to use such a physical term. Instead, we wanted to use a term that would describe the data structure, whether manual or physical. When new merchandise arrives and Inventory wants to complete the order, they check the file against the merchandise item number in order to obtain the customer's name and address (CUST-NAME) so the merchandise can be sent.

When Bob Thompson (process 5.0) uses the accounts receivable printout (D3: ACC REC), he looks up the customer name, but what he gets out of the file is the customer's balance (CUST-BAL). Therefore, for data lookups, you do not need to show the lookup key (data flow). When the data store data flows are labeled, you must think about what actual data is being entered and retrieved. Normally, each data flow that goes into a data store is labeled separately, but you will see we do have an exception. When Suzanne Wolfe (4.0) uses her D2: NEW CUSTOMERS data store, she puts cards into it by customer name, and she uses it to find customer names. This is a rare exception in which we have used a two-headed arrow and only one data flow name. The truth of the matter is that rules should be followed in systems analysis, but in real life there always are exceptions with which you must deal.

Each bubble shown in the logical data flow diagram, must be broken into its lowest level process (what we call decomposition in Chapter 2). You know from the physical data flow diagram in Figure 5-6 that several of the processes definitely had multiple tasks, specifically 2.0, 5.0, 6.0, and 7.0. Although 1.0 and 4.0 appear to have only one task, they too will have to be examined in more detail to determine if they are at their lowest level. Let us use process bubble 4.0 of Figure 6-8 as an example. When Suzanne Wolfe receives the Order Verification form, the first thing she does is check the D7: CUSTOMERS printout to see if the person's name is on it. Next, she checks her second data store, D2: NEW CUS-TOMERS. If she does not find the name in either of these places, she types a customer card. After the card is typed, it is put into the card file of new customer names. When this is done, she separates the orders so that those already paid for can be taken to Inventory (6.0); credit orders are forwarded to Lynn Porter and Bob Thompson (5.0). As you can see, there are four separate tasks Suzanne Wolfe performs: Check Names, Type New Customer Cards, File Cards, and Separate Orders. Right? Well, not quite. What we have just described is physical. When it is translated into a logical Level 1 data flow diagram, it becomes three steps, such as you see in Figure 6-9. CHECK NAMES is acceptable. Type New Customer Cards is not, so we change it to CREATE NEW CUSTOMER REC-ORD. Look what happened to File Cards; it disappeared. Remember, we are looking at it *logically*. If the person was sitting in front of a computer terminal, the file would be created, but it certainly would not be filed like the cards. Finally, we keep SEPARATE ORDERS (4.3) even though no data is transformed in it; someone must make a decision as to whether it is a paid or credit order. If this process was in a computer, code would be written for it.

Once all the process bubbles have been decomposed, you need to finish iden-tifying the contents of the existing data stores. So far, the data stores have been described briefly, but you do not know what individual data elements are in them. It is now time to get out some blank Data Store content sheets, such as we showed in Figure 2-14. You will need seven, one for each data store. We will develop one for you. Go back to Chapter 3 and look at Figure 3-15. You will recall that this is what Suzanne Wolfe's new customer record looks like. Let us put that into a reasonable format

Customer name	= CUST-NAME
Street	= CUST-STREET
City	= CUST-CITY
State	= CUST-STATE
Zip code	= CUST-ZIP
Payment method	= PMT-METH
Date	= DATE-ENTERED

When we enter this onto a data store form, it looks similar to what we have in Figure 6-10. Remember, as you work on these data store contents, you must take into account the data that flows into them and out of them. The most important data element is the primary key, and it is underlined. Now you are ready to complete the other data stores. By the way, data store forms may be used to document data flows, too.

You have accomplished quite a bit and now have a good understanding of the

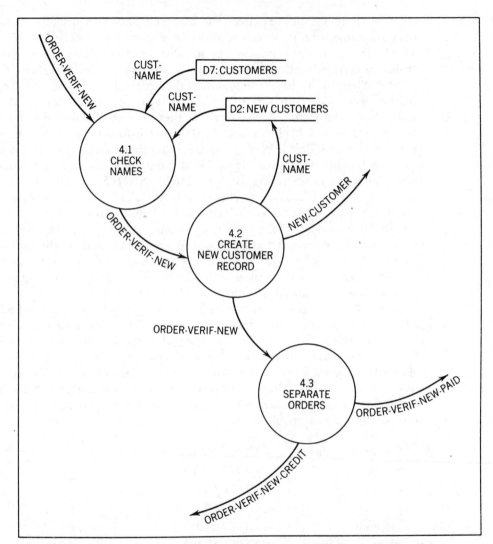

Figure 6-9 Process bubble 4.0 from Figure 6-8 further decomposed to Level 1.

existing Order Processing system at Sunrise Sportswear. It is time now to have some user walkthroughs. To do this, you go to each of the people involved in the process and go through each data flow diagram that has one of their processes in it. The users must validate that you have analyzed their process properly. Also, validate the contents of the data stores and data flows. At this point, we want to make one additional comment with regard to data stores. You, as an outsider, cannot hope to understand the data stores completely, although you must do

Data Store Name: D2: NEW CUSTOMERS	
Name of Data Structure	**Name of Data Element**
NEW-CUSTOMER	CUST-NAME + CUST-STREET + CUST-CITY + CUST-STATE + CUST-ZIP + PMT-METH + DATE-ENTERED

Notations: Currently on 3 × 5 cards. Street can be post office box number, rural route number, etc. State can be Canadian province. Needs provision for other countries.

Figure 6-10 Data store contents for data store D2: NEW CUSTOMERS.

your best to do so. The users are the only people who can understand them completely. It is for this reason that having users validate data store contents is an extremely important step.

When you are satisfied that the logical data flow diagrams and data store contents are both complete and accurate, it is time to gather all of your documentation together to explain to Mr. Reynolds and Ms. Brunn what you have found: Hopefully you would have been talking with them all along; if so, they already have seen the physical data flow diagram. Now you want to show them how you translated it into the logical data flow diagram, you want to tell them the results of your telephone survey (remember to have it documented into a tabular format or some other visual method they can identify with), and you want to explain what you found out about the Accounting records you sampled.

You have reached a major milestone in this systems analysis and design effort because Phase I of the system development life cycle (Steps 1–4) has been completed. At this point (the end of Phase I), Sunrise Sportswear's management could decide to cancel or postpone the continuation of this effort. This is because it is a logical point to terminate the entire study if they are not satisfied with your findings to date. For this reason, it is very important that you obtain management's concurrence with your data flow diagrams, layout charts, and other findings. Your next task is to begin Phase II of the system development life cycle if Mr. Reynolds wishes to continue the study.

Student Questions

1. What are some of the more obvious conclusions that you have presented to Mr. Reynolds and Ms. Brunn?
2. How large a sample size would you need if you wanted to be 97 percent certain that the sample would not vary from the actual data by more than 3 percent?

Student Tasks

1. Decompose process bubble 6.0 (logical data flow diagram of the existing system in Figure 6-8) into a Level 1 diagram. (*Hint:* We identified five processes, 6.1–6.5.) Also, analyze each of the bubbles in the Level 1 diagram. Not all of them can be decomposed further. Either decompose each of these bubbles into a Level 2 diagram or describe why it cannot be decomposed further.
2. Describe data store D4: BACKORDERS using a data store contents form. (*Hint:* You may use some of the data element names from Figure 2-15 in Chapter 2.)

Selected Readings

1. Briefs, U., et al., eds. *Systems Design For, With, and By the Users.* New York: Elsevier Science Publishing Company, 1983.
2. Hession, William, and Malcolm Rubel. "Benchmarking Business-Modeling Software," *Byte,* vol. 9, no. 5, May 1984, pp. 127–132. [Use of benchmarks when selecting software for business models.]
3. Maynard, Harold B. *Industrial Engineering Handbook, 3rd edition.* New York: McGraw-Hill Book Company, 1971.
4. Sepah, Dary. "Work Sampling and Micro Computers," *MTM/Journal of Methods-Time Measurement,* vol. 11, no. 1, 1984, pp. 9–13. [Bank of America's work sampling program in PASCAL to establish job standards.]
5. Wilburn, Arthur J. *Practical Statistical Sampling for Auditors.* New York: Marcel Dekker, Inc., 1984.

Questions

1. What does obtaining a complete understanding of the present operations of the area under study provide?
2. Why is it important to gain the confidence of the area under study?
3. Identify three things the analyst can do to help gain the confidence of the area under study.
4. How does the information that can be gained from searching records differ from the information that can be gained from interviewing?
5. With regard to understanding the existing system, how can estimating and sampling be used?
6. Identify the three types of estimating procedures that are useful in systems work.
7. In which type of estimating procedure does the analyst make a detailed study of the costs, times required, and any other pertinent factors for each step of each procedure within the system?
8. Define the terms "desired certainty" and "acceptable error."
9. Of what does work sampling consist?
10. How can the information gained from a work sampling be used?
11. What does the Area Cost Sheet specifically show?
12. As a general method of documenting the existing system, what does the documented flowchart trace?
13. Why is a summary of the existing system prepared?
14. What does a layout chart show?

SITUATION CASES

Case 6-1:　*Incom Telecommunications*

A new, highly technical telecommunications company was having difficulty keeping the books of available equipment up-to-date because the orders were not being processed quickly enough. The microprocessor-based computerized switchboards were being sold long before they were manufactured. An outside consulting systems analyst was hired to find out what was delaying the order processing and/or the manufacturing.

Let us assume the consulting analyst already has defined the problem and prepared a detailed plan for the systems study. Also, he has gathered the general information on the area under study and learned about the various interactions between order processing and the manufacturing areas. Now, today's task is to understand thoroughly the existing system, which is the analyst's "benchmark" for understanding this system.

In order to gain the confidence of the area under study, the analyst first attempted to contact the Manager of the Order Processing Department, but he was not in his office. Not wanting to waste any time, he proceeded to interview the clerical workers in an effort both to understand the informal procedures and to observe the work procedures in the office. One thing he learned is that the manager of the department personally developed the current system.

When the manager arrived later in the day, he was somewhat irritated to learn that the analyst had been interviewing his staff without his permission. The analyst was able to smooth this over by reviewing the various objectives of this study with the Order Processing Manager. He also was able to point out *all* of the bad points, or unworkable and uneconomical parts of the system. Actually, the analyst thought the manager would be pleased, but he seemed a bit gruff and ended the interview at that point.

For the next couple of days the analyst searched through records and performed some sampling in order to verify figures that he had located while searching the records. After documenting the data on an area cost sheet, the analyst returned to review this area cost sheet with the Order Processing Manager. The next task was to review the manufacturing process in order to learn how it operated.

Question

1. Comment upon the actions of the analyst within the Order Processing Department, specifically with regard to gaining the confidence of the people in that area.

Case 6-2:   *Kone Auto Parts Corporation*

The Kone Auto Parts Corporation requested that a team of analysts conduct a study of the existing system for the purpose of projecting labor costs to be used during upcoming labor–management contract negotiations. After having defined the problem, the team went on to develop an outline, gather background information, and study the interactions between areas. To gain a clear picture of the present sequence of operations, processing times, volume of work, and existing costs, the team began a thorough study of the existing system.

One analyst was delegated the responsibility of work sampling, in which he was to collect only a limited quantity of the total existing data to make inferences about the total. Specifically, the analyst was to study five secretaries and make observations about their duties.

To begin the sampling study, the analyst used the following method to determine the necessary sample size

$$\text{Necessary sample size} = 0.25 \left(\frac{\text{Desired certainty}}{\text{Acceptable error}} \right)^2$$

Since he wanted to be 90 percent certain that the sample data would not vary by more than 2 percent (0.02) from the actual data, he submitted the following values

$$N = 0.25 \left(\frac{1.645}{0.02} \right)^2$$

Therefore, the necessary sample size was 1,692 observations.

Next, the analyst defined the operations (job duties) of the secretarial job itself. These predefined categories included typing, taking dictation, filing, talking on the telephone, walking, on the elevator, writing, and idle time. He then developed an observation form for recording the observations to be made during the study.

The next step was to schedule the number of observations to be made each day. The total number of observations (1,692) were divided by the number of days he was allowed to spend on the study (18). His schedule, therefore, required 94 observations per day. Since the analyst was occupied with other work each morning, all observations were made between the hours of 2:00 and 4:15 P.M.

After making the required number of observations for each secretary (Figure 6-11), the analyst was able to compute the percentages for each predefined category, as illustrated in Figure 6-12.

SUMMARIZED OBSERVATION RECORDING FORM

Predefined Categories	Secretaries under Observation				
	1	2	3	4	5
Typing	541	795	592	677	575
Dictation	305	271	338	254	204
Filing	169	85	270	204	321
On telephone	51	67	101	117	85
Walking	170	135	85	168	86
Elevator	50	102	51	87	49
Writing	338	220	169	151	339
Idle	68	17	86	34	33
Total observations	1692	1692	1692	1692	1692

Figure 6-11 Summarized Observation Recording form.

COMPOSITE PERCENTAGE COMPUTATIONS

Predefined Categories	Secretaries under Observation				
	1	2	3	4	5
Typing	32%*	47%	35%	40%	34%
Dictation	18	16	20	15	12
Filing	10	5	16	12	19
On telephone	3	4	6	7	5
Walking	10	8	5	10	5
Elevator	3	6	3	5	3
Writing	20	13	10	9	20
Idle	4	1	5	2	2
	100%	100%	100%	100%	100%

$$* \ 541/1692 = 32\% = \frac{\text{Category observations (541)}}{\text{Total observations (1692)}}$$

Figure 6-12 Percentages table.

Once the analyst had computed and studied the percentage of time spent in each category of work, he felt there was an excellent basis for evaluating the existing system. However, when the team of analysts later presented its findings to management in a detailed system report, management discounted the validity of the sampling study and rejected the team's new system proposal.

Questions

1. What errors were made at the beginning of the study that resulted in management's unfavorable reaction to the sampling study?

2. Did the analyst conduct the observations according to the correct steps of sampling?

Chapter 7

DEFINE THE NEW SYSTEMS REQUIREMENTS

LEARNING OBJECTIVES

You will learn how to . . .

□ Identify operational goals for an area under study.

□ Define the requirements of a new system.

□ Develop evaluation criteria for a new system.

□ Document the new system's requirements.

□ Use prototyping to assist in defining the user requirements.

□ Summarize the requirements for use during the detail design step.

□ Convert the logical data flow diagram of the existing system to the logical data flow diagram of the proposed system.

□ Refine the data dictionary by the process of normalization.

□ Complete process descriptions.

*P*hase II: Beginning the Detail Analysis and Design

The conversion of ideas to realities requires the use of real methods and resources. Thus, the systems analyst must define the methods and resources that are required to transform the system from the analysis stage to actual operation. To accomplish this, you must define clearly what it is that the new system must do. These are the new system requirements.

Now you are beginning the detail analysis and design phase of the system development life cycle. As you can see in Figure 7-1, Step 5, Define the New Systems Requirements, is your next priority. During Phase II, you also complete Step 6, Design New System; Step 7, Design Controls; Step 8, Perform the Economic Cost Comparisons; and Step 9, Sell the System. You should note that Steps 6, 7, and 8 are performed simultaneously. In other words, you design the system, design controls into that system, and evaluate costs at the same time. You iterate among these three steps during the design phase. Notice how they are shown in parallel in Figure 7-1.

As you begin to work on the new system requirements, start by reviewing what the current system does and how it performs these operations. Then, relate what the system is supposed to do 'to carry out the required operations. Although it may sound simple, it can be very difficult to define the requirements of the new system. Remember, this is the point at which you begin converting the logical model of the existing system to the logical model of the new system.

*W*hy Define Requirements

The object of defining the *new* system requirements is to assemble an overall picture of the inputs, outputs, operations, and resources required by the system to meet the present and future needs of the organization. Another activity of this phase is to outline the evaluation criteria that will be used to evaluate the new system's performance. In this chapter we discuss the broad performance criteria that are required to design the new system. We do not include here the technical aspects of the system which will be included in Chapter 8, Designing the New System. In other words, we are not yet designing the new system; we are *preparing* to design it.

At this point in the systems study, there is usually a problem definition, perhaps a feasibility study report, an outline, some general information on the area under study, and an understanding of the existing system. Now all of this information should be pulled together. The first objective is to define what the new system must be able to do. The second objective is to determine criteria that can be used to evaluate the performance of the new system.

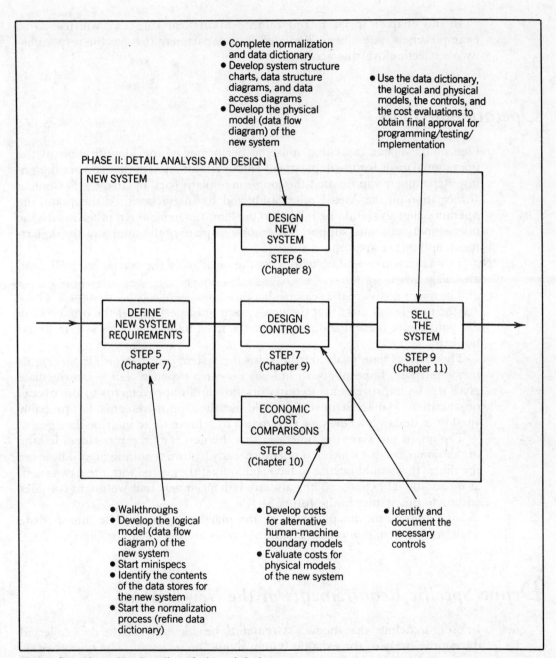

Figure 7-1 Phase II—Detail analysis and design.

In this chapter (prior to our Sunrise Sportswear case), we will use as an example a new system being designed for a department that has the responsibility of collecting overdue accounts.

Operational Goals

One of the major tasks that must be performed is the identification of the operational goals for the department and/or specific system that you are designing. Remember, you defined the long-range plans back in Chapter 5, General Information on the Area Under Study and Its Interactions. At this point, the operational goals should be related to the long-range plans. In other words, the operational goals must support the long-range plans of the company, the department, and/or the area under study.

To do this you should try to identify the *major* goals, the *intermediate* goals, and any *minor* goals.

The major goals are the reasons that this new system is being designed. These are the mandatory tasks that the new system must perform. If the organization did not require these mandatory tasks, the need to design a new system would not exist.

The intermediate goals are the gains the system can make while serving its major purpose, hopefully with little or no extra expense. These intermediate goals will be improvements to our work flow and improvements to the overall organization. Management really would like these improvements, but probably would not design a whole new system just to achieve these intermediate goals.

The minor goals are the functions that the new system can perform for the organization, but for which it is not quite ready (future requirements). These are the things that would be nice to have, but only if they come with the new system at no additional expense. They also are enhancements that we might consider adding to this system in the future.

In summary, the major goals are the mandatory items. The intermediate goals are the desirable items. The minor goals are the "wish list" items.

Define Specific Requirements of the New System

In order to define what the new system must be able to do, all the data collected during the study of the existing system should be reviewed. The objectives set during the problem definition phase also should be analyzed and refined. This information, and any other relevant information, such as long-range plans affecting the area under study, should be used as a basis for developing the new system requirements.

The analyst must be very careful when defining the new system requirements because these requirements are the analyst's "road map" that will be used to design the new system. The requirements must be broad enough to cover each and every detail of the system. They must be flexible so the analyst can mold them or modify them during the design phase (Chapter 8). The system requirements are the "heart" of the new system that the analyst will be designing. The purpose of the new system is to carry out and achieve the system requirements that are defined during this phase of the systems study.

While the new system requirements are being determined, they should be summarized continually in a write-up that outlines the objectives of the new system and spells out the requirements for each activity or job procedure involved in the new system. The analyst should determine the requirements of the new system in terms of

1. Outputs it must produce
2. Inputs it needs to produce the outputs
3. Operations it must perform to produce the outputs
4. Resources it must use to produce the outputs
5. Operational and accounting controls

Define outputs first. Then define *inputs.* Next define *operations* and *resources.* Also define *controls.* Because we cannot describe everything simultaneously as we go through the text of this book, you should note that defining the controls is discussed thoroughly in Chapter 9, Designing New System Controls. At this point you would set up your initial controls matrix by identifying the various threats to your system and the individual component pieces of your system. This technique is described in the Chapter 9 section titled Introduction to Control Matrices.

By working from the anticipated end product (outputs) *backward* into the system, the analyst can be assured of a clean design unencumbered by existing system routines. Put another way, the analyst can be innovative in the use of new approaches, because the only concern with the existing system will be at those points that interface with other systems. When defining outputs, inputs, operations, resources, and controls for the new system, four general questions should be considered.

1. What are the *current requirements* of the new system?
2. What are the *future requirements* of the new system?
3. What are the *management-imposed requirements*, such as time limits, or other restrictions on money expenditures?
4. What are the key operational and accounting *control points?* Your Chapter 9 matrix will be valuable here.

Other considerations you must take into account are batch versus on-line and batch versus real-time systems. Will there be data communication circuits in the system? Will the system be using discrete files (where each system has its own set of files), or will it be using a database file structure? Also, will the database be centralized or have we begun to think in terms of distributed database systems? Is the system an integrated system that automatically interacts with other systems within the organization? You will recall that these items were discussed in the first section of Chapter 5, the Progression of Business Systems.

As you define the outputs you must take into account

☐ Scheduled, overnight reports that will be delivered on a daily basis to the users. These may be detailed reports presenting all of the data content, or they might be summary reports that show accumulated totals.

☐ Exception reports that are designed to call attention to a predefined condition and printed only if that condition is met.

☐ On-line query responses that might be requested at any time and received in a matter of seconds from on-line real-time systems.

☐ Turnaround type reports that are output documents, which also serve as future input documents to re-enter data in order to correct an erroneous situation or to notify someone of a condition that allows them to re-enter their response.

Once the type of report is determined, you will have to identify the content of each output report. The content, of course, includes the exact items of data that will be printed on the output report and the format/location of that data on the piece of paper or video screen. Besides this data content, which should be identified by the business' user department, there are various other questions you should answer: Are any items of data missing? Is the same information to be included in other outputs? What is the time sequence, or how often should this output be produced? Who will use this output? How will the output be used? How many copies are needed? What is the best format/layout for presentation of this data?

Finally, we again refer you to a different chapter for a more in-depth review on output reports. Please examine Chapter 16, Report Analysis. This chapter identifies points to consider when reviewing a report, introduces the criteria of a good reporting system and discusses characteristics of a good report, common weaknesses of reports, and techniques for reviewing management reporting systems.

With regard to defining inputs, the two major alternatives you will want to consider are whether to batch the data together and enter it all at once or whether to use on-line real-time entry on a transaction-by-transaction basis. For batch entry, the user department might batch the data and send it off to a separate data entry department. Alternately, the user department may have on-line terminals with which it can enter the data during normal business operations and have the data held in batch at the data center on a disk device. The other alternative is an on-line real-time system in which the data is entered on a transaction-by-transaction basis. Of course, with such a system, users receive a response back to their transaction almost immediately (real-time). Other input methods that are beginning to be utilized are voice, touch screen, a mouse, light pen, and optical reading devices that can read a previously prepared page.

With regard to what data should be entered into this system, you already have defined this because you have defined the outputs. Take the data that will be output to the output reports, then work backwards to determine which items of data must be entered into the system in order to prepare those final output reports.

In defining the operations, you have to identify the individual processing steps that are required in order to convert the inputs into the required outputs. At this point you will be very concerned with data flow diagrams or other methods to help determine how to process the data. Always remember to answer the question: What needs to be done in order to process the inputs that will give the user the desired outputs?

Along with defining operations, you need to identify various resources. Resources in this case could be such items as computers (mainframes, minis, or micros), the type of file structure (discrete or database), the possible use of packaged software, various components of data communications, and the like. Microcomputers, data communications, and databases were discussed in Chapter 1.

*D*evelop Evaluation Criteria for the New System

Finally, as the definition of the new system's requirements task draws to a close, some evaluation criteria need to be developed. By developing these evaluation criteria *prior* to design of the new system, management is provided with a valid method of measurement that can be used to evaluate the new system's performance. In other words, evaluation criteria provide a benchmark by which to judge performance.

Evaluation of the new system is very important. A new system should never be installed without a valid set of evaluation criteria. This means that performance standards must be devised for key characteristics of the system. The performance standards should be geared to the objectives set for the system. For example, in our collections system, one of the objectives should be to pay for the cost of the new system with increased collections. That is, we wish to add more to revenue than to cost. Therefore, one criterion of evaluation is the net revenue of the new system compared with the net revenue of the old system. This requires that we carefully analyze (and document) the costs and collections of each.

Perhaps the disorganization and confusion that characterized the old system caused frequent errors in mailing the collection letters. Perhaps good customers were often mailed strongly worded letters by mistake. We should set an objective to reduce these errors, and should define to management how we will measure our success in doing so.

The analyst will always be ahead if valid, reasonably accurate, conservative standards and measurement criteria for the system can be devised. Once the analyst is convinced of the validity of the standards and measurement criteria, concurrence from management must be obtained so that everyone can judge the system's performance in the same terms.

Usually, if the analyst does not provide such evaluation criteria, management will adopt its own. This can have very unfavorable implications for the analyst's future with the firm. Managers are busy people and may lack sufficient time to analyze the validity of their adopted criteria of the system's merits. They have not had the advantage of the analyst's comprehensive overview of the system, nor do they have the analyst's technical skills. The analyst owes it both to management and himself or herself to provide the necessary system evaluation criteria.

We do not mean to imply that a firm's management is unqualified to decide the merits of a system. Quite the contrary, theirs should be the final word. Our point is that no matter how good the new system is, the analyst must explain and justify its *relative* merits so that management can agree or disagree with a minimum of effort. If the new system costs more than the old one (which is usually the case), the analyst must point out the system features that appear to justify the higher cost. There are many system characteristics that must be evaluated when assessing the overall merit of a system. Some of these evaluation criteria are

- □ *Goals.* Does it do what it was designed to do? Does it meet the users' major goals? Does it meet any intermediate or minor goals? If so, which ones?
- □ *Time.* This could be elapsed time, transaction time, overall processing time, response time, or other operational times.
- □ *Cost.* This may be the annual cost of the system, per unit cost, maintenance cost, or other cost items such as operational, investment, and implementation.
- □ *Quality.* Is a better product or service being produced? Is there less rework because of the system? Has the quality of data or information improved?
- □ *Capacity.* This involves the capacity of the system to handle workloads, peak loads, and average loads, as well as long-term future capacity to meet the organization's needs in the next decade.
- □ *Efficiency.* Is the system more efficient than the previous one?

□ *Productivity.* Has productivity of the user (information provider) and management (information user) improved? Is decision making faster and more accurate because of the information provided by this system?

□ *Accuracy.* Are there fewer errors? Can management rely on this system more than the old one?

□ *Flexibility.* Can the new system perform diverse operations that were not possible before?

□ *Reliability.* Are there fewer breakdowns of this system compared with the previous one? Is uptime very high with this system? The reliability/uptime of an on-line network is probably the number one criterion by which to judge its design and development.

□ *Acceptance.* Evaluate whether both the information providers and the information users have accepted the system.

□ *Controls.* Are adequate security and control mechanisms in place in order to prevent threats to the system such as errors and omissions, fraud and defalcation, lost data, breaches of privacy, disastrous events, and the like?

□ *Documentation.* Does the system have adequate written/pictorial descriptions documenting all of its hardware, protocols, software, circuits, and user manuals?

□ *Training.* Are training courses adequate and are they offered on a continuous basis, especially for terminal operators? Are training manuals adequate and updated on a regular basis?

□ *System Life.* Is the life of the system adequate? When two to five years are spent designing and implementing a system, the system life should be of adequate duration to take advantage of the economies of scale.

*D*ocument the Requirements for the New System

Once the analyst has answered the above questions satisfactorily, a system requirements model can be developed. Figure 7-2 depicts one of these models in general terms. Note that it is concerned only with the new system requirements, not the existing system.

The level of detailed description will vary from one item to another, but the system requirements model ensures that *all* requirements (current, future, management-imposed, and controls) of the new system are taken into account. It provides a checklist which ensures that the analyst has not forgotten any of the outputs, inputs, operations, controls, or resources that will be necessary in operating the new system. It is an excellent device also for communicating the picture of a system to others. The model always should be checked for completeness by the personnel in the area under study. Figure 7-3 shows the detail of Figure 7-2.

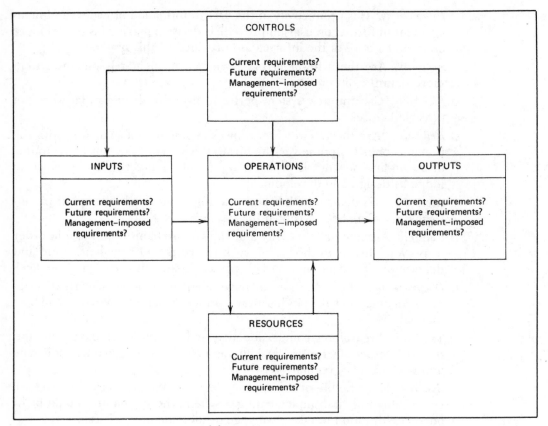

Figure 7-2 System requirements model.

An Input/Output (I/O) Sheet (Figure 7-4) should be used to document the *inputs* and *outputs* that will be different from those used in the existing system (usually new forms or changes in existing forms). At this stage the I/O sheets probably will be used only in general terms since actual design of the system has not yet taken place. In the analyst's mind, however, the two steps defining the new system requirements and design of the new system often are so closely related that the two steps cannot be separated. Obviously, if a very good idea occurs to the analyst, it should be documented immediately lest it be forgotten entirely. The I/O sheets will not be completed, of course, until the new system is completely designed.

Perhaps some of the input and output formats of the old system will be used "as is" in the new system. Others, however, will require changes, and still others must be completely redesigned. The analyst's documentation package should be composed of samples of the I/O formats, which will be used "as is," in addition to I/O sheets for the changed or new formats.

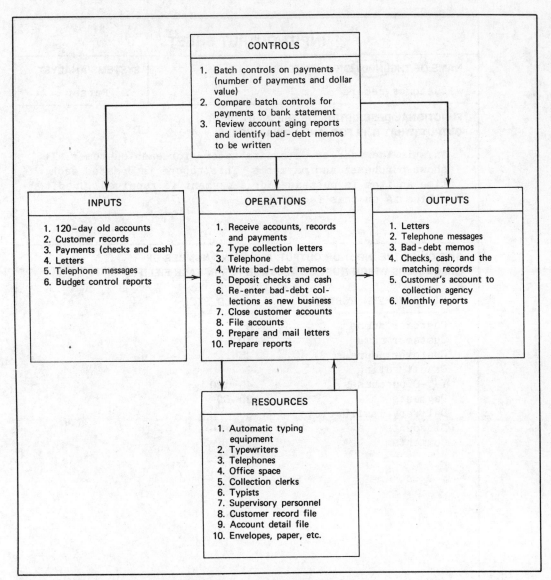

Figure 7-3 System requirements model for collection costs.

The I/O sheet should bear a *functional description* of the input or output and describe its purpose and use, and whenever practical, a *sketch* of the input or output. For example, in our new collection system we may need more data on the input *Customer record* (see Figure 7-4) so we can supply some extra details on our monthly reports to management. Possibly we will need to revise or redesign completely the form on which these data are received. For example, we may

INPUT/OUTPUT SHEET

NAME OF THE ⬭INPUT⬭ OR OUTPUT	SYSTEMS ANALYST
Customer record	A. Purser

FUNCTIONAL DESCRIPTION OF THE INPUT OR OUTPUT (WHAT IT IS FOR, AND HOW IT WORKS)

This is the year-to-date data record for each customer. It shows purchases and payments. This record is updated each time an item is purchased or a payment is received. Credit status is on this record.

SKETCH OF THE INPUT OR OUTPUT, INCLUDING NUMBER OF CHARACTERS WHICH MUST BE ALLOWED FOR IN EACH FIELD

VIDEO SCREEN FORMAT	FIELD SIZE
Customer number	9
Customer name	30
Customer address	45
Credit rating	2
Y-T-D purchases	40-120
Payments	20-60
Delivery instructions	50
Discounts	15
Comments	75

Figure 7-4 Input/Output (I/O) Sheet.

decide that we need data on the customer's financial standing, such as the firm's present Dun & Bradstreet (D & B) rating, current ratio, and whether discounts are being taken with other creditors. We need these data to compute the probability that we will be paid the overdue amount owed us. (We wish to include this probability figure in our monthly report to management.)

The existing form does not supply the data to us, so we design some changes, or a new form, or some means of securing the needed input.

We must be specific about our new requirements

☐ What specific data items are needed?

☐ How are they to be expressed—in words? numbers?

☐ If the data are to be processed with electronic equipment, the maximum number of characters must be specified for each data item. Also, we must specify whether the item is numeric (all numbers), alphabetic (all letters), or alphanumeric (mixture of numbers, letters, and possibly other special characters).

We would describe the purpose and function of the data items in the upper portion of the I/O sheet. Of course, as the title indicates, the input/output sheet is used to record either input or output data. Also, Input/Output Sheets can be cross-referenced to the activity symbols on your data flow diagrams in order to further define specific outputs and/or inputs. Incidentally, these I/O sheets are an alternative to the Data Store Contents form used earlier in the Sunrise Sportswear case.

In defining the input and output requirements for a new system, the analyst must be able to identify potential applications where a video display terminal (VDT) or Cathode Ray Tube (CRT) can be used in place of the traditional input documents and printed output reports. In the past, CRTs were used primarily as an input device for cardless data entry. Today, however, CRTs are being used by management and staff much more frequently as an on-line inquiry device. For example, a bank teller can enter a customer's account number and display the balance in the savings and checking accounts. As an output device the CRT can display standard computer reports, respond to specific inquiries, and, when needed, function as a sophisticated graphics terminal capable of displaying charts and diagrams designed to facilitate management decision making.

When the requirements of the new system warrant the use of microcomputers as a medium for input or output and possibly local processing, the analyst must explore thoroughly the pertinent hardware considerations and define the microcomputer requirements as well as the microcomputer software requirements. The computer hardware must be able to support data communications and provide adequate response times needed by users.

Once the analyst has identified how the microcomputer or CRT is to be used, explored the hardware implications, and determined the terminal requirements, the foundations have been laid for the input and output design phase. Chapter 8, Designing the New System, includes a section on designing input and output screens.

You also might have to describe, in detail, each transaction or message so it can be related to a data flow diagram. Each message that is entered into the system or received from each application system at each terminal/microcomputer location should be identified. Also, each message field (item of data) must be identified, along with the average number of characters for each field. It may be necessary to identify message length and the volume of messages. If the system is manual, these messages might be forms in the current system, although they already might be electronically generated messages or video screen formats. Your goal is to have a complete list of all messages (these could be input items or items of data that are already in the database files) so that you can follow the flow of each transaction through the data flow diagrams.

To document the required *operations* of the new system you can use flowchart segments, data flow diagrams, decision tables, or narrative descriptions. A description of each one follows.

Use of a *flowchart segment* is shown in Figure 7-5. The flowchart segment enables the analyst, and others, to get a comprehensive view of the operation. It provides a format that is easy to use when working out the design for the new system. Flowcharting templates with standardized symbols are available at most office or drafting supply companies. In Figure 7-5 the two diamond-shaped figures contain decision criteria which lead to one or the other actions specified in the boxes. (Conventions and methods of flowcharting are covered in Chapter 13.)

Use of a *decision table* in our new collection system is illustrated in Figure 7-6. This example parallels the flowchart segment example (Figure 7-5). Note that the decision criteria and actions are the same in both examples. The logic is also the same. Decision tables are very useful for listing all the possible decision criteria that might be involved in an operation. As such a list is compiled and entered into the table, the analyst (with the help of management and operations personnel) can specify the action to be taken in each situation. Thus the completed decision table is an excellent communication and coordination device. It can be used to verify inclusion of all possible situations that will require decisions in the system. More important, it also can be used to compel managers to decide exactly what their policy will be in each situation. (Decision tables were introduced in Chapter 2.)

A *narrative description* of the operations is a description written in story form. It is a verbal model in which the analyst details the sequence of steps involved in the necessary operations. The narrative should begin with whatever starts an operation, and follow through each step to the completion of the operation.

A description of the operational and accounting *controls* should be prepared

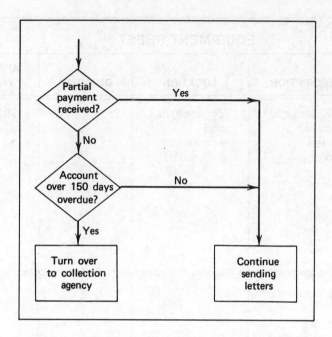

Figure 7-5 Flowchart segment.

using the "control matrix approach." This is presented in Chapter 9 because all of the analyst's working tools cannot be covered in a single chapter. For now, assume that you should start the control matrix when you define the new system requirements, or even earlier if possible.

Document the required *resources* of the new system with Equipment Sheets, Personnel Sheets, or File Sheets. A typical Equipment Sheet appears in Figure 7-7. Equipment sheets are used to describe needed equipment such as typewriters, copy machines, desks, telephones, computers, and so on. Usually, only relatively major items are listed.

A typical Personnel Sheet appears in Figure 7-8. The analyst should specify

PARTIAL COLLECTION PROCEDURE			
Partial payment received? (Condition)	Yes	No	
Account over 150 days overdue? (Condition)		Yes	No
Continue sending letters (Action)	X		X
Turn over to collection agency (Action)		X	

Figure 7-6 Decision table.

EQUIPMENT SHEET			
NAME AND DESCRIPTION	**LOCATION**	**QUANTITY**	**APPROX. VALUE**
IBM—PC, 512K memory, two disks, color monitor, modem, matrix printer, and cable	Purchasing and Accounts Receivable	2	$9,350

Figure 7-7 Equipment Sheet.

PERSONNEL SHEET			
JOB TITLE	NUMBER OF POSITIONS	JOB DESCRIPTION	APPROX. PAY RANGE
Microcomputer operator (These are for Purchasing and Accounts Receivable)	2	See personnel job description A-279	$14,000–$19,000

Figure 7-8 Personnel Sheet.

FILE SHEET	
FILE NAME (1) Student grades	**LOCATION** (2) #3 Data center

STORAGE MEDIUM (3) Removable disk pack	**AGE OF FILE** (4) 6 Years	**HOW CURRENT** (5) 3 Months

SEQUENCED BY
    (6)
Student number—Primary key
Secondary keys—Name, major, and GPA

COMPLETE BELOW FOR COMPUTERIZED FILES

FORMAT
   (7)
Student number—9 numeric
Name—30 alpha
Street address—45 alphanumeric
City, State, Zip—27 alphanumeric
Gender—1 alpha
Major—15 alphanumeric
Current quarter GPA—4 numeric
Y.T.D. GPA—6 numeric
Y.T.D. classlist—100 alphanumeric per quarter completed (this
   will grow in size depending upon how many quarters have
   been completed).
....and so forth for each data item...

       (8)   (9)

CHARACTERS PER RECORD		RECORDS PER FILE	
AVERAGE	PEAK	AVERAGE	PEAK
1,700	16,200	6,000	9,000

Figure 7-9 File Sheet.

the job description, job title, number of positions available, and approximate pay range for each needed position in the system. The personnel department can be consulted regarding pay scales for the various classifications involved.

A typical File Sheet appears in Figure 7-9. The file sheet describes a collection of information, that is, a file. Each item on the file sheet is described below.

1. *File name:* unique name of this file
2. *Location:* physical location of the file
3. *Storage medium:* tub file, computer disk drive, magnetic tape, file cabinet, three-ring binder, and so forth
4. *Age of file:* age of the oldest record in the file or the retention time before items are to be removed from this file and sent to a records retention area
5. *How current:* age of the record when it is first entered into the file
6. *Sequenced by:* sequencing item of the file, for example, customer name, part number
7. *Format:* a character-by-character layout of any record to be processed by tabulating or electronic equipment
8. *Characters per record:* an estimate of the average number of characters per record and of the maximum number possible
9. *Records per file:* an estimate of the average number of records per file and of the maximum number

The analyst may use all or some of the devices described for documenting the new system requirements, or entirely new methods may be devised. In any case it is necessary to document the requirements of the new system in some clear manner.

System requirements vary widely from one situation or firm to another. The analyst is encouraged to be creative in defining the system requirements and documentation. And it is important to keep not only the present requirements in mind, but the future requirements as well. New systems can be very expensive to develop; thus a prime objective should be long life.

*P*rototyping

Prototyping is one of the newest system design tools. With it a new system is simulated through the use of a model that is constructed using a fourth generation software language. User requirements go directly to the final computerized system using these specially developed software tools for the modeling/ simulation. In prototyping, systems analysts, programmers, and users work together to develop new operational systems, using special software tools that function in a manner similar to program generators, but which are much more powerful. A prototype actually is a working system, although it is not a production system that could go on-line. The words prototype and model, as used in system design, mean the same thing and can be used interchangeably. Prototyping is one of the best ways of getting users to divulge what they want from a system (e.g., the specifications).

Rather than data processing experience, fourth generation prototyping languages require applications experience and knowledge in order to be effective. Prototyping sometimes does not start until the physical model of the new system, although it may be best to prototype the logical model of the new system.

The steps of defining the new system requirements, designing the new system, and creating the final design are carried out or completed by using a prototype of the new system. The prototype is developed through the use of a fourth generation prototyping software language.

Before providing an overview of the steps involved in prototyping, you need to understand one major difference between prototyping and structured design. Go back and look at Figure 2-2. You will see that in structured design you build formal logical models (what needs to be done) and formal physical models (how something is done) for the system being designed. In prototyping, by contrast, you usually build only physical models. Yes, you do have a plan or idea which is your logical model, but it is not as extensively documented as it is in the structured logical model of the new system. This is because fourth generation prototyping languages make it so easy to modify the final physical model that you, the system designer, can work with a loosely defined logical model of the new system. For example, you and the user department representatives can play "what if" games, such as: What if the data were to be presented on the video screen using either of two different formats. With the use of prototyping, you can experiment with either format, actually see the simulated output, and choose the desired output format. In other words, you keep revising the logical model until the user department is satisfied with the format of the output report. Changes in the concept of the logical model can be inserted immediately into the final physical model by the fourth generation prototyping software. If this is not yet clear, assume that you use fourth generation prototyping software to build a logical model of the current system (while interacting with user department representatives who ultimately will utilize the system you are building) and to define the new system requirements. Next, you enter these requirements into the final physical model of the new system. This process may allow you to skip the development of formal logical models for a new system, which dramatically speeds up the overall system design process. It also allows users, who learn how to use fourth generation languages, to design their own systems (fourth generation prototyping software is now available for microcomputers).

In prototyping, a fourth generation software program allows you to build a system model. This software can create/store files of data, interact between these files, perform processing activities, output to video screens or to batch reports, accept data inputs, and so forth. Once you know how to use the fourth generation prototyping software package, you can develop the new system using the following steps.

- ☐ Define the problem.
- ☐ Gather general information and study interactions.
- ☐ Understand the existing system.
- ☐ Develop a model of the system.
  - –Create a mock-up of video screens and printed reports.
  - –Create a mock-up of the database.
  - –Develop the interaction of processing and on-line activity/printed reports.
- ☐ *Involve the system users* and develop the new system requirements by adding the requirements to your working model one at a time. The user can evaluate the results of each change as you progress.
- ☐ Evaluate alternatives and complete your new system prototype (model). Provide for the iterative (see Glossary) approach as you complete the model.
- ☐ Complete programming and integrate the new system into the overall data processing operations of the organization.

For today's fourth generation prototyping, there are languages such as Ramis II, Focus, and Nomad II. These languages have embedded database management systems, video screen generators, statistics, graphics, and links to other database packages. They can perform complex logic operations, use English-like statements, and even optimize the database access and processing steps.

As an example, suppose your assignment is to develop a system to prepare purchase orders on a microprocessor-based distributed system (Focus works on IBM PCs). Within a couple of days, you can produce enough programs, along with the necessary database, to produce a few purchase orders at a time. Now the users can sit with you in front of their own microcomputers and "play" with your newly prototyped system. After a number of iterations, you and the users have developed not only the new system requirements, but you also have built the requirements into the new system as you "played" with the system model (the prototype).

Prototyping languages do not have to be elaborate or costly. For example, two excellent prototyping tools are electronic spreadsheets and screen painting, both available on many microcomputers. Think about this. As you build the original spreadsheet, you are building the physical model or prototype. Then, as you modify the data items in the spreadsheet cells, you are iterating toward a final solution. The final solution is the final physical model or prototype of the new system. If at this point you save the spreadsheet data and program, you have completed the development and integrated your new system into your personal data processing library.

This text stresses structured analysis and design techniques, along with the traditional systems approach. As a result, prototyping is not integrated into our cumulative case. You will have enough to learn with the structured technique, and both structured and traditional tools. We discuss prototyping here because it is a superb means of getting the user involved in the new system's requirements step. We would be remiss if we also did not tell you that prototyping can be used exclusively to develop a new system, although a better and more complete system is developed when prototyping is used in conjunction with structured techniques.

Preparing a Summary of the New System Requirements

The analyst should summarize the notes and documentation package as a memory aid for the future. The summary should include the important points from both the *existing system* documentation (Chapter 6) and the *new system requirements* documentation (Chapter 7). The summary should be structured in such a way that it will remind the analyst of all key design considerations that must be observed during the detailed design. Thus the summary should be written as a comprehensive overview of all work done by the analyst so far on the project, and not as a report to others. It is an exercise that compels the analyst to make many necessary decisions on the procedures to be followed during the detailed design of the new system.

The deliverable document that you should prepare at the end of the step, "Define the New System Requirements," is the system design specification. There are many ways of writing this design specification, including defining the requirements through the use of prototyping. Basically, the purpose of the specification is to have a detailed list of the new system requirements. This may be the most critical step of the whole process. The seeds of failure are more often planted here than at any other point. The most important caveats are

☐ Distinguish between requirements and desirable features. Be sure you know and state both what is a mandatory and what is a desirable item, or even a "wish list" item. It is important to list desirable and wish list items, but be sure to label them as such.

☐ Be quantitative, precise, and performance oriented. Avoid using terms such as "a large number of messages." Use instead "a minimum of 1,000 messages containing 150 characters in average length will be transmitted during the peak hours."

- ☐ Distinguish between requirements and solutions. Solutions do not yet belong here; however, since it is impossible to ignore them, you probably have recorded or identified several solutions. Solutions are addressed during the actual design of the system (Chapter 8). For example, printing that can be read easily by a person with normal eyesight under normal office lighting conditions may be a requirement. But, a statement that printing shall be 0.1 inches high in italic font is not a requirement; it is simply a solution masquerading as a requirement. The designer who does not make this distinction must accept responsibility that the solution may not really solve the underlying problem.
- ☐ Be sure to include requirements for
  - –Outputs/inputs
  - –Processing
  - –Hardware/software
  - –File structures/database
  - –Communication circuits
  - –Interfacing with other systems
- ☐ Include all of the evaluation criteria that were mentioned previously in this chapter.

As you commit the new system requirements to paper or, in other words, actually write the system design specification, take into account all of the items listed below. Some may not apply to the specific system being designed, but these must be weeded out until only those relevant to the type of system being designed are left.

- ☐ Use the original feasibility study in order to provide a framework of justification over the entire project.
- ☐ The problem definition should be restated in a very concise fashion.
- ☐ An option is to include a short section on the general information, interactions, and your understanding of how the existing system currently operates.
- ☐ Describe the goals and objectives of the new system. Differentiate between the major, intermediate, and minor goals. Describe what the new system will accomplish.
- ☐ Describe the outputs.
- ☐ Describe the inputs.
- ☐ Describe the processing and resources.
- ☐ Describe file structures, data communication links, and/or the use of microcomputers.

- □ Describe user interfaces and the flow of transactions through the system, using data flow diagrams if that is your methodology.
- □ Describe the control and security levels that will be in the new system.
- □ Describe the performance criteria against which the new system is expected to perform. Match it against your list of evaluation criteria so management can judge whether your goals are achieved with the new system.
- □ If there are any unique long-range goal or policy considerations that affect this system, describe them here.
- □ Describe any special technical support that might be required, as well as the interface between computer operations and the department that will be utilizing the new system.

The system specification should be written in a non-technical manner, because concerned people in the user department must be able to understand it. Normally, the user department for whom you are designing the system will "sign off" on this system specification. Their approval is your signal to proceed with the detail design and programming. In other words, they are agreeing to accept a system with the above-mentioned specifications.

SUNRISE SPORTSWEAR COMPANY

CUMULATIVE CASE: Define New System Requirements (Step 5)

The presentation to Mr. Reynolds and Ms. Brunn on your understanding of the existing system begins with a review of the objectives that were stated during the Problem Definition (Step 1). The most important aspects of the problem in the Order Processing system at Sunrise Sportswear involve the elimination of poor credit risks, the location and modification of system bottlenecks, and the reduction of overdue credit accounts. The requirements of the new system can be categorized as follows:

Major

- □ Reduce overdue credit accounts to 5 percent or less
- □ Eliminate poor credit risks
- □ Reduce order time to 48 hours by reducing current bottlenecks
- □ Key new customer information only one time
- □ Provide for updating old customer addresses when necessary

Intermediate

☐ Move people who need to interact closer to one another
☐ Reduce old customer record storage
☐ Reduce filing time of old customer records
☐ Reduce filing and search time of new customer records
☐ Provide control records of merchandise sent

Minor

☐ More up-to-date inventory (wish list because it involves new computer)

You show them the logical data flow diagram of the existing system (Figure 6-8 in Chapter 6) and point out the line you have drawn around the steps that have been identified as essential to the actual filling of customer orders. This bounded version of the logical data flow diagram is shown in Figure 7-10, and it shows that two processes have been identified as non-essential to filling customer orders. These are processes 3.0 (the application of payment amount to customer record) and 4.0 (typing of the new customer cards). As you point out, while both are needed and wanted processes, neither is essential to the filling of customer orders. You add that, in a sense, process 5.0 (credit verification) also falls in the non-essential category, except that credit card purchases cannot be filled unless the credit card company approves them. As a result, process 5.0 cannot be removed from the processing sequence. Processes 3.0 and 5.0 are what we call system-imposed requirements. In reality, even though customer payment (process 3.0) is non-essential, it cannot be removed because customer payments must be handled in some manner. Likewise, the credit card verification is system-imposed. Process 4.0 could be eliminated because it is a management-imposed task. Since management has no other means of obtaining new customer names and addresses, however, it cannot be ignored. Instead, you hope to find a better means of dealing with what has become a major system bottleneck.

The next item of discussion is the final logical data flow diagram for the existing Order Processing system (see Figure 7-11). You explain how you removed the names of individuals, stressed the most important task that occurs at each processing step, modified the process bubbles to stress those tasks, and added newly discovered data flows and data stores. Since the new system design cannot begin until the existing system's logical data flow diagram is approved, you walk Mr. Reynolds and Ms. Brunn through it step-by-step. They are not able to find any flaws in the logic and approve it.

Part of your explanation involves the data dictionary. At this point, you have the terms shown in Figure 7-12, and explain how some of the terms changed because you have a more accurate understanding of the system as it now exists.

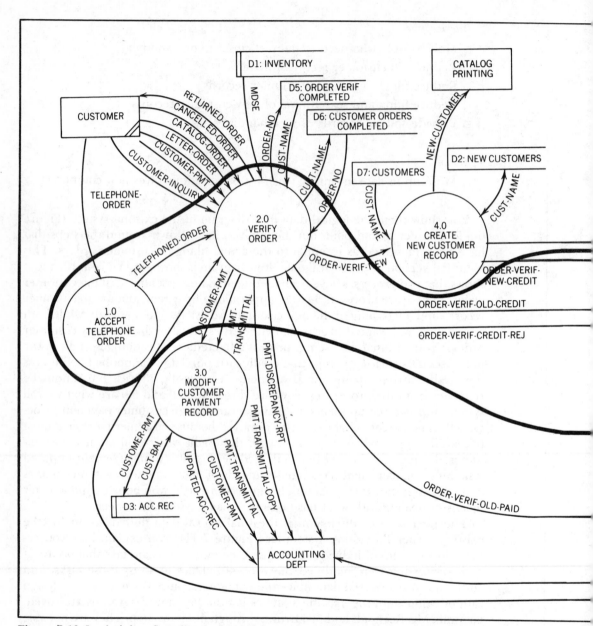

Figure 7-10 Logical data flow diagram (Level 0) emphasizing processes essential to filling orders in Sunrise Sportswear's existing system. Based on Figure 6-8 in Chapter 6.

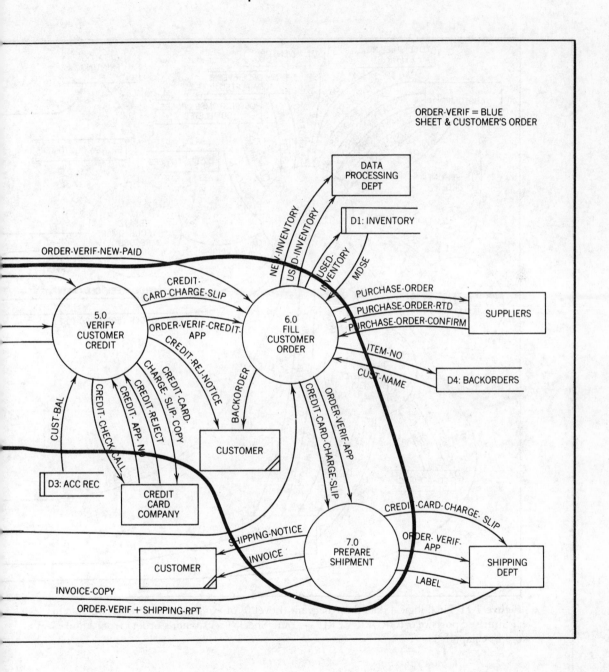

ORDER-VERIF = BLUE
SHEET & CUSTOMER'S ORDER

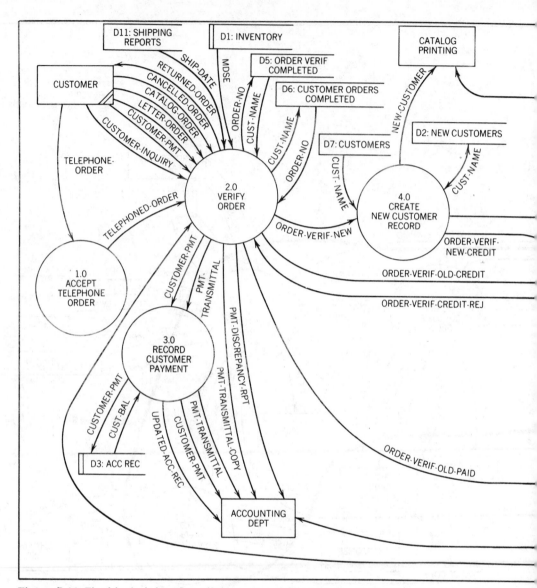

Figure 7-11 Final logical data flow diagram (Level 0) of *existing* Order Processing system at Sunrise Sportswear (ORDER-VERIF = Blue Sheet + customer's order) from Figure 6-8 in Chapter 6.

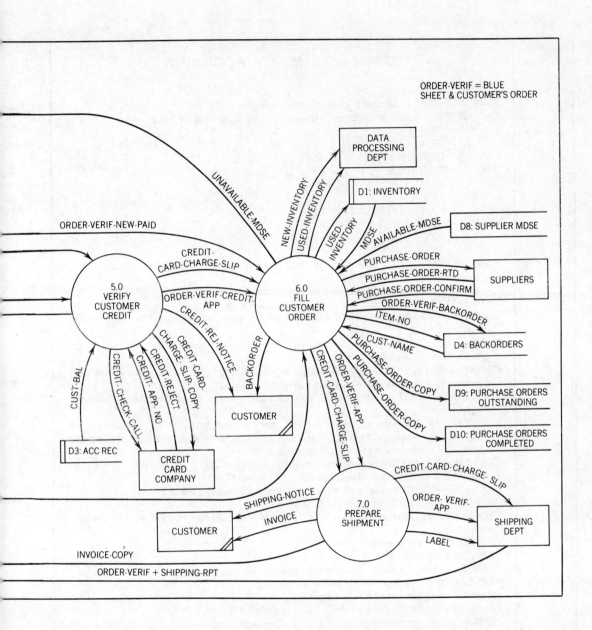

SUNRISE SPORTSWEAR DATA DICTIONARY

ACC REC—data store D3

AVAILABLE-MDSE—merchandise identified by supplier in D7

BACKORDER = notice to customer that merchandise is out-of-stock but on order.

     = <u>ITEM-NO</u> +
       ITEM-DESC +
       ORDER-NO +
       CUST-NAME +
       [CUST-STREET | RR-NO | PO-NO] +
       CUST-CITY +
       [CUST-STATE | CUST-PROV] +
       [CUST-ZIP | CUST-POSTAL] +
       (CUST-CTRY) +
       SHIP-DATE

BACKORDERS—name of data store D4. Data structure is BACKORDER.*

BLUE-SHEET—alias for ORDER-VERIF

CANCELLED-ORDER—cancellation of order by customer

CATALOG-ORDER—customer order on catalog order form

CREDIT-APP-NO—number given by credit card company when credit card purchase is approved

CREDIT-CARD-CHARGE-SLIP—form that is filled out when a credit card purchase is approved. Goes to customer.

CREDIT-CARD-CHARGE-SLIP-COPY—copy of form that is filled out when a credit card purchase is approved. Goes to credit card company.

CREDIT-CHECK-CALL—telephone call to credit card company to verify that credit purchase can be made

CREDIT-REJ-NOTICE—notification to customer that Sunrise Sportswear cannot extend credit

CREDIT-REJECT—notification that credit card company will not approve credit purchase (credit limit reached, credit card bill not paid, etc.)

CUST-BAL—balance due in customer's account, data store D3

CUST-NAME—customer name recalled from data stores D2, D4, D5

CUSTOMER-INQUIRY—questions from customers that relate to their orders

CUSTOMER ORDERS COMPLETED—data store D6

CUSTOMER-PMT—check or money order received from customer in payment for merchandise

CUSTOMERS—data store D7

INVENTORY—data store D1

INVOICE—notice of amount due sent to customer

INVOICE-COPY—copy of invoice sent to customer

ITEM-NO—filing term used for data store D4

LABEL—mailing label prepared by Order Preparation

LETTER-ORDER—customer order by letter, no form attached

MDSE—merchandise information recalled from data store D1

NEW-CUSTOMER—new customer name, address, and start date

NEW CUSTOMERS—data store D2

NEW-INVENTORY—list of new merchandise received for next update of data store D1: INVENTORY

---

* Each entry in the data dictionary must have its data elements defined as we did with BACKORDER.

ORDER-NO—filing term for data store D5; what is recalled from data store D6

ORDER-VERIF—Order Verification form; alias is Blue Sheet. Used from time order is received until it leaves Shipping Department.

ORDER-VERIF-APP—order that has gone through the approval process

ORDER-VERIF-BACKORDER—order that has been placed on backorder because of temporary stock outage

ORDER VERIF COMPLETED—data store D5

ORDER-VERIF-CREDIT-APP—order that has gone through the credit approval process

ORDER-VERIF-CREDIT-REJ—order that has been rejected by the credit approval process

ORDER-VERIF-NEW—new customer's order

ORDER-VERIF-NEW-CREDIT—new customer's credit order

ORDER-VERIF-NEW-PAID—new customer's paid order

ORDER-VERIF-OLD-CREDIT—old customer's credit order

ORDER-VERIF-OLD-PAID—old customer's paid order

PMT-DISCREPANCY-RPT—report to Accounting of discrepancy between amount paid and amount of order

PMT-TRANSMITTAL—transmittal slip for checks and money orders received

PMT-TRANSMITTAL-COPY—copy of transmittal slip for checks and money orders received

PURCHASE-ORDER—purchase order for merchandise to replenish inventory

PURCHASE-ORDER-CONFIRM—confirmation from supplier that merchandise order is being filled.

PURCHASE-ORDER-COPY—copy of purchase order that is filed in data store D9 or D10

PURCHASE-ORDER-RTD—purchase order returned from merchandise supplier (out-of-stock)

PURCHASE ORDERS COMPLETED—data store D10

PURCHASE ORDERS OUTSTANDING—data store D9

RETURNED-ORDER—order returned to customer, not our merchandise or temporarily out-of-stock

SHIP-DATE—date merchandise shipped, from data store D9

SHIPPING-NOTICE—notification to customer that merchandise is being shipped

SHIPPING REPORTS—data store D11

SHIPPING-RPT—copy of shipper's report of the packages sent to customers

SUPPLIER MDSE—data store D8

TELEPHONE-ORDER—customer order by telephone

TELEPHONED-ORDER—order form filled out by telephone order clerk for customer's order by telephone

UNAVAILABLE-MDSE—merchandise that is no longer available and should be excluded from future printing of catalog

UPDATED-ACC-REC—updated accounts receivable listing

USED-INVENTORY—was updated inventory listing

The following terms have been deleted.

CREDIT-AMT—inaccurate term from context diagram

ORDER-VERIFICATION—changed to ORDER-VERIF

PURCHASE-ORDER-RETURNED—changed to PURCHASE-ORDER-RTD

SHIP-APPROVAL—inaccurate term from context diagram

SHIP-CONFIRM—inaccurate term from context diagram

UPDATED-CUSTOMERS—inaccurate term replaced by NEW-CUSTOMER

UPDATED-INVENTORY—inaccurate term from context diagram

Figure 7-12 Version of data dictionary at final logical data flow diagram step of existing system.

If you examine Figure 7-12, you will see that one entry is different from the others. Look at the term BACKORDERS. You will see that it includes much more information than the other terms. This is because each data store now must have a complete description of its contents. In Student Task 2 of Chapter 6, you had to fill out a Data Store Contents Form. The data elements that were defined in that task should be put into the data dictionary. Further, each data dictionary term should have its individual data elements described completely in the data dictionary. It is acceptable to have a descriptive note for entries such as we show in Figure 7-12, but contents are mandatory. For example, if you change the title of the data store contents form, it can be used to describe the data elements on the Order Verification form. Also, you would not wait until this point to develop the data structure contents; ideally, you should begin when the first data flows are defined and you begin collecting forms. Further, you should indicate whether the data dictionary term is a data element, a data flow, a data store, a data structure, or a process name. In our BACKORDER example, the BACKORDER data structure should have each data element within it listed under the BACKORDER entry. Further, each one of its data elements (ITEM-NO, ORDER-NO, etc.) should be listed in the alphabetic data dictionary lists of terms. For example, CUST-ZIP should be listed in the "C" section and identified as to the fact that it is a data element in data store D4. When the data dictionary is completed, it may show that CUST-ZIP is in several different data stores. Each data element also must be described in physical terms (physical data dictionary is described in Chapter 8).

Returning to your presentation to Mr. Reynolds and Ms. Brunn, the next documentation is the layout chart that you developed during the previous step (see Figure 6-7 in Chapter 6). They want to know why you developed it. You explain that, while learning about the existing system, it seemed you had to walk back and forth between buildings a great deal. Also, it was necessary to go up and down the stairs frequently. It became obvious after a while that employees who need to be near one another are not, and that the "real" work at Sunrise Sportswear is performed primarily on the second floor of the buildings. This means that people frequently have to go downstairs and then upstairs to deliver data to the next process. Of course, for the round trip, they have to go downstairs and upstairs twice. Knowing that Mr. Reynolds has received some employee complaints about this up-and-down/back-and-forth movement, you mention that a solution to this problem may be found as a by-product of your solution to the major problems. Mr. Reynolds and Ms. Brunn indicate that they now have a clearer picture of why people are complaining and agree that something must be done about it.

Finally, you reach the point of telling them about the telephone survey in which other mail order houses were called to find out what their credit policies are with regard to extending credit to customers. While talking, you realize that Mr. Reynolds suddenly seems distant and unresponsive. You outline how the names of the various companies to call were located and remind Mr. Reynolds that you had promised to keep him informed of anything learned about the competition and their handling of such problems.

While talking about credit, you also explain the sampling done on Sunrise Sportswear's customer records. You go into detail about the process used to determine sample size, how records were searched, and the conclusions. Just as you reach the main point you wish to make about the sampling results, Mr. Reynolds interrupts and says he already knows about them. Wondering how he found out, you inquire about his source of information and are told that Ed Wallace came to see him about it. You are quite understandably upset that Mr. Wallace violated your confidence, and explain that you are sorry Mr. Reynolds had learned about the sampling from someone else and that you only told Ed about it as a means of double-checking the sample results for reasonableness. Mentally, you make a note to avoid such internal political squabbles in the future.

Recognizing the importance of the telephone survey and the sampling, you steer the conversation back to the conclusions. They are

1. As a general rule, other firms that are successful and growing in the mail order business do not extend credit to customers.

2. Most clothing-oriented mail order firms deal only in checks/cash/money orders and credit cards.

3. Few mail order firms accept COD orders.

4. Sunrise Sportswear does not give older customers a preferred credit status as they had believed.

5. Old and new customers are treated equally with regard to credit, whether credit card or otherwise.

6. Credit card customers expect their purchases to be handled by credit card, not by Sunrise Sportswear extending credit to them. This is a cause of some customer complaints.

7. Based on sampling results, 60 percent of the overdue accounts are those of customers whose credit cards were rejected by the credit card companies as either having reached the credit card dollar limit or for not having paid amounts owed and to whom Sunrise Sportswear granted credit.

8. Sunrise Sportswear extends credit to everyone who does not have an account that is more than 60 days overdue.

9. No outside credit checks are made on customers who request credit, so there is no means to verify a customer's credit-worthiness.

10. Performing credit rating checks with outside credit rating companies would be time-consuming and costly when compared with the number of customers gained by doing it.

11. It is necessary and desirable to do business with credit cards; however, it is not necessary to do business by extending credit to anyone who asks or whose credit card does not pass credit card company approval. This is proven by the large number of successful firms that are now competitors of Sunrise Sportswear.

12. By eliminating credit purchases, Sunrise Sportswear would relieve its Accounting Department of an unnecessary burden that is costly in terms of both labor and paperwork filing and storage.

13. Invoicing can be eliminated.

Once these conclusions have been outlined, you propose that Sunrise Sportswear discontinue extending credit to its customers. The reasoning is that current credit policies are without any credit rating controls, and the policy is vague. It is costing Sunrise Sportswear in the following ways.

1. The Accounting Department has had to hire extra people to handle the increase in overdue accounts. These people were needed to send out the extra invoices and to handle the filing of invoices.

2. The Order Preparation section also has a person who types invoices.

3. Customers have been alienated because of the current credit situation. What was intended originally to help customers, has backfired.

4. The current accounts receivable has to be checked by two different processes. These are during the recording of customer payments (process 3.0) and when verifying customer credit (process 5.0).

5. Extending credit has increased the cost of doing business for Sunrise Sportswear, thereby reducing net profits.

6. Credit is causing overdue accounts to increase.

Because of these costs, you again recommend that extending credit to customers be suspended, and volunteer to help them make the transition as effortless as possible.

Going on to the second major problem area, that of the new customer cards, you explain that it appears 50 percent of the orders now have to go through this process before orders can be filled. Because Sunrise Sportswear's new customer base has grown so rapidly, orders for new customers are being held up at this time by approximately two weeks. This process definitely is a major bottleneck. Also, both Jon Gray and Suzanne Wolfe check customer records for names, but there is no consistency between the two checking processes because two different files (data stores) are used. Jon Gray uses completed customer orders, while Suzanne Wolfe uses the printout of customers provided by Data Processing. Jon Gray has a whole room full of these old customer order records because none have ever been discarded. As far as you can determine, there are no legal requirements to maintain these old records. It appears that their main purpose is to determine whether a customer is new or old. Recent records are needed to handle problem inquiries, but these usually are no more than six months to a year old. You mention the fact that they have been considering storing some of the older records in another area. Since storing so many files of old records is costly, it is hoped that part of the final solution to the other problems will help find a method that makes storage of all but the most recent records unnecessary.

Finally, you mention that you have learned of still another duplication of effort. Suzanne Wolfe types the new customer information onto 3 × 5 cards. She then sends those cards to Catalog Printing. They have a person who again keys this information so that it can be put onto magnetic tape. It would be desirable for new customer information to be keyed only once. Also, because there does not appear to be any formal means of capturing old customer address changes, you would like to incorporate that into any new system. Mr. Reynolds and Ms. Brunn agree that both are desirable goals.

You next call their attention to the handling of orders for inventory that is temporarily out-of-stock; they are handled in two different ways at two different steps in the process. When Jon Gray initially checks the order, any out-of-stock items are marked as such on a returned order form. This assumes the customer will re-order later. Since Mr. Gray returns these order forms to the customer immediately, without determining if the customer is old or new, a second negative by-product of this step occurs as new customer information for catalog mailings is lost. The second time out-of-stock merchandise is handled is the step at which the Inventory staff pull merchandise from the shelves. At that time, out-of-stock merchandise is marked as a backorder, and the customer is notified of when to expect the order. Since Inventory has more complete information on when to expect incoming merchandise, you recommend that only Inventory should handle backorders. Jon Gray should return orders only when he cannot identify the merchandise as that of Sunrise Sportswear. Mr. Reynolds and Ms. Brunn agree that they were not aware of this situation and that the recommendation is a sound one. In fact, since it will not interfere with your work, it is agreed that Ms. Brunn will tell Jon Gray immediately to stop returning temporarily out-of-stock orders. You make a mental note to forewarn Tom Conners in Inventory that this may mean an increase in their backorders.

Something has been bothering you during the entire study, and it is now time to bring it up. You have not been able to find any files documenting what merchandise actually gets sent to customers. When asking questions of the staff, no one seemed to know of any records that would do this. As far as you can tell, the only proof of merchandise sent to the customer is the customer order form on which the items are checked off as it goes through the Order Preparation process. The Shipping Report is the only proof that a box of merchandise was sent. You ask if this is correct, and are told that they depend on the customers to let them know if there is a problem with the order. You wonder what happens if the customers have not kept copies of their orders but think they ordered something that was not in the box. Mr. Reynolds and Ms. Brunn say they assume Jon Gray checks the completed customer order file in such a situation.

Based on this information, you tell them that most mail order operations today include a packing list with the merchandise. You note that Sunrise Sportswear does send a shipping notice to customers, but that it only includes an order number and the date the merchandise is to be shipped. You point out that a less-than-honest employee could remove merchandise from the box between Order Preparation and the Shipping Department (remember, the boxes are not sealed until they reach Shipping), and Sunrise Sportswear has no proof of anything except the fact that a box of something was shipped to a particular customer on a specific date. Because of this situation, another desirable requirement of the proposed system is to use packing lists, instead of shipping notices. You point out that there are very few problems with packages not being received and that sending the current post cards is expensive. Sunrise Sportswear has more to gain with packing lists.

To summarize this session, you say you would like to continue with the new system requirements by eliminating credit orders, invoices, and shipping notices. You plan to find another method to deal with new customer information, and you would like to add packing lists and a method to obtain old customer address changes as new requirements. Mr. Reynolds agrees for you to proceed on this basis.

Back in your office, you complete a Required Inputs/Required Outputs form which looks like Figure 7-13 when it is completed. Remember, we said early in this chapter that you should work with required outputs first, then required inputs. The outputs are based on the requirements of the various processes and external entities that were identified previously. The inputs are based primarily on what the customer initiates, although suppliers also initiate quite a few inputs. These outputs and inputs are determined by using the final logical data flow diagram of the existing system (Figure 7-11).

Once the required outputs and inputs have been decided upon, your next task is to set up a system requirements model based on what operations have to take place in order to process the inputs and produce the outputs, what resources are available to accomplish these processes, and the controls needed for the system. (Perhaps you also can begin Step 9 at this time.) Your system requirements model is shown in Figure 7-14. Notice that it does not contain those inputs and outputs that you plan to eliminate in the new system. Also note that the Figure 7-13 inputs and outputs use the appropriate data dictionary terms, while everything in Figure 7-14 is in plain English. This is because you want the system requirements model to be understood by the users who must approve it.

All the preliminary steps have been performed, and now the logical data flow diagram for the new system can be drawn. Figure 7-15 shows the logic of the proposed system. Notice that processes 1.0 and 2.0 remain the same, except that

Required Inputs	Required Outputs
AVAILABLE-MDSE	ADDRESS-CHANGE (add)
CANCELLED-ORDER	BACKORDER
CATALOG-ORDER	CREDIT-CARD-CHARGE-SLIP
CREDIT-APP-NO	CREDIT-CARD-CHARGE-SLIP-COPY
CREDIT-REJECT	CREDIT-CHECK-CALL
CUSTOMER-INQUIRY	CREDIT-REJ-NOTICE
CUSTOMER-PMT	CUSTOMER-PMT
LETTER-ORDER	INVOICE (delete)
ORDER-VERIF-COMPLETED	INVOICE-COPY (delete)
PURCHASE-ORDER-CONFIRM	LABEL
PURCHASE-ORDER-RTD	NEW-CUSTOMER
SHIPPING-RPT (delete)	NEW-INVENTORY
TELEPHONE-ORDER	ORDER-VERIF-APP
	PACKING-LIST (add)
	PMT-DISCREPANCY-RPT
	PMT-TRANSMITTAL
	PMT-TRANSMITTAL-COPY (delete)
	PURCHASE-ORDER
	RETURNED-ORDER
	SHIPPING-NOTICE (delete)
	UNAVAILABLE-MDSE
	UPDATED-ACC-REC (delete)
	USED-INVENTORY

Figure 7-13 Required inputs and outputs for Sunrise Sportswear's Order Processing system (based on Figure 7-11).

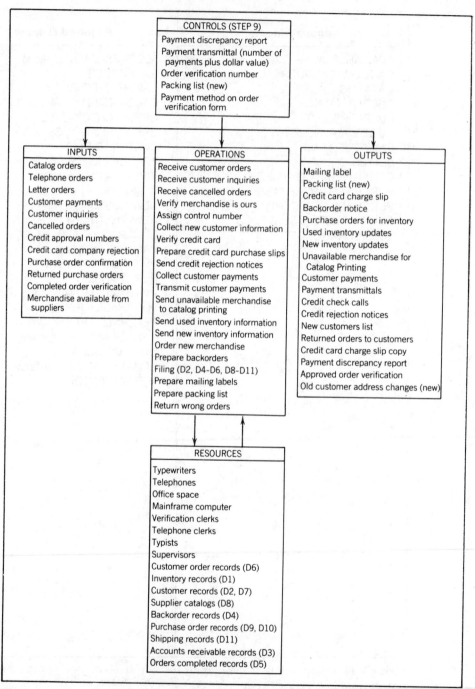

Figure 7-14 System requirements model for Sunrise Sportswear's Order Processing system.

2.0 has been reduced in scope. The new process 3.0 now assigns the order number, and while doing that, processes new and old customer information. We have begun to think about the physical implementation (even though still in the logical phase) because our new design logic must be something that can be accomplished. In this case, we think we have found a way to help them do what they are doing now, but in a more efficient manner. Notice that none of the data flows refer to old or new customers except during the lookup use of data store D7 by process 3.0.

As the orders leave process 3.0, notice that they are split into two streams. Those orders for which cash, checks, or money orders are enclosed go to process 4.0. There the payments are verified, batched, and forwarded to the AC-COUNTING DEPARTMENT. Do you see how an Accounting Department function has been removed from Order Processing? The second stream that leaves process 3.0 is credit card orders. What happens in process 5.0 has been streamlined because only credit cards are involved now. Both process 4.0 and 5.0 then forward the orders as previously to process 6.0. The merchandise is forwarded, along with the appropriate paperwork, to PREPARE SHIPMENT (7.0) and then on to the external entity SHIPPING. As you can see, the logical data flow diagram for the new system is very similar to the logical data flow diagram for the existing system (Figure 7-11). This is because the same basic processes still have to be done. We have simply rearranged a couple that are causing problems.

Once again, you are ready for a user walkthrough. When the new logical model is approved, you can identify the contents of the data flows and data stores you will be dealing with, refine the data dictionary by normalizing the data structures, and write the minispecifications.

Student Questions

1. What Accounting Department functions have been removed between the logical data flow diagram for the existing system (Figure 7-11) and the new system's logical data flow diagram (Figure 7-15)?

2. Whose jobs are going to be affected most by the proposed changes? Explain.

3. Do you think Ed Wallace is going to be happy with your new system? Valery Brunn? Stanley Reynolds? Explain.

4. What processing currently takes place in the Order Processing system that is inappropriate to Order Processing but which is outside of the scope of the current problems and will not be changed?

5. At this point in time, do you think Sunrise Sportswear has gotten its money's worth with your efforts?

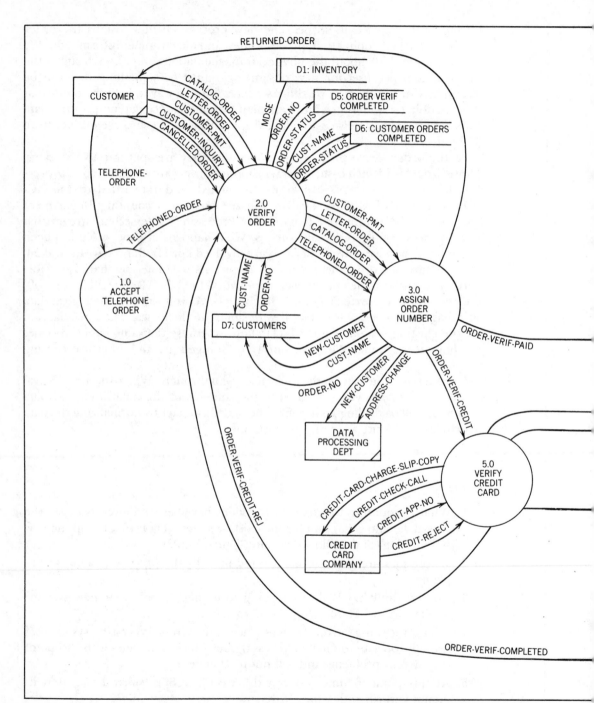

Figure 7-15 Logical data flow diagram (Level 0) of new system proposed for Sunrise Sportswear.

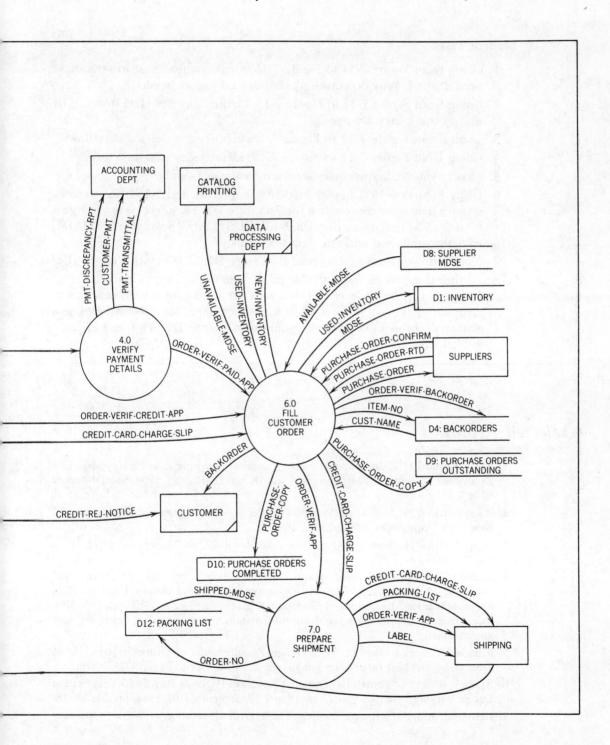

Student Tasks

1. Going from Figure 7-11 to Figure 7-15, identify any data stores that have been deleted. Why do you think they are no longer needed?
2. Going from Figure 7-11 to Figure 7-15, identify any new data stores. Why do you think they are needed?
3. Going from Figure 7-11 to Figure 7-15, identify any deleted data flows.
4. Going from Figure 7-11 to Figure 7-15, identify any new data flows.
5. Modify your data dictionary according to tasks 1–4 above.
6. Using Figures 3-15 (Chapter 3), 6-10 (Chapter 6), and 7-15 (this chapter), set up a data store contents list for data store D7. The object is to arrange it in such a way that data stores D2: NEW CUSTOMERS and D7: CUSTOMERS are combined into one data store.
7. Normalize your newly combined data store D7: CUSTOMERS.
8. Assume that process 5.0 in the logical data flow diagram in Figure 7-15 is at its lowest functional level and that your knowledge of the process now is complete. Fill out a process minispecification sheet for process 5.0. Use a simple decision table to show your logic. (*Hint:* Use Figure 2-26 as a guideline.)

Selected Readings

1. Boar, Bernard H. "Alleviating Common Concerns of Application Prototyping: The Experience Difference," *Computerworld*, vol. 18, no. 22, May 28, 1984, Special Report 66–67.
2. Boar, Bernard H. *Application Prototyping: A Requirements Definition Strategy for the 80s.* New York: John Wiley & Sons, Inc., 1983.
3. Boar, Bernard H. "Prototyping," *Computerworld*, vol. 17, no. 37, September 12, 1983, pp. ID37–47.
4. Bourne, T. J. "Business Information: Defining the Requirements," *IN International Conference on Networks and Electronic Office Systems, 26–30 September 1983, Reading, England.* London: Institution of Electronic & Radio Engineers, 1983, pp. 185–189. [Identification of functions requiring information system support, examples, and applications.]
5. Bracchi, G., and B. Pernici. "The Design Requirements of Office Systems," *ACM Transactions on Office Information Systems*, vol. 2, no. 2, April 1984, pp. 151–170.
6. Bradley, Robert J. "Fourth-Generation Tools Slash Highway Patrol's 10-Year System Design Backlog," *Computerworld*, vol. 18, no. 37, September 10, 1984, pp. 55, 76–78.
7. Desmond, John. "Language Barrier: The Fourth Generation at Work." *Computer-*

world, vol. 19, no. 44, December 11, 1985, pp. 1, 55, 61–62. [Problems of defining the meaning of fourth generation software, includes chart for IBM mainframe environment.]

8. Gallant, John. "Fourth-Generation Language Use Must Be Planned, Report Says," *Computerworld*, vol. 18, no. 18, April 30, 1984, pp. 67, 74.

9. Johnson, J. R. "A Prototypical Success Story," *Datamation*, vol. 29, no. 11, November 1983, pp. 251–256.

10. Kaniper, Carol A. "Prototyping: New Tools for Cutting Through the Applications Backlog." *Computerworld Focus*, 1985. [How prototyping is changing the systems development life cycle for applications.]

11. Orr, Ken. *Structured Requirements Definition*. Wellesley, Mass.: QED Information Sciences, Inc., 1981. [Expands use of Warnier/Orr diagrams and shows how to determine what the user wants.]

12. Palmer, John F. "Of Time and Analysis," *Computerworld*, vol. 18, no. 33, August 13, 1984, pp. ID1–12. [Effective requirements definition.]

13. Shamlin, Carolyn. *A User's Guide for Defining Software Requirements*. Wellesley, Mass.: QED Information Sciences, Inc., 1984.

14. White, C. C., III, A. P. Sage, S. Dozono, and W. T. Scherer. "Performance Evaluation of a Decision Support System," *Large Scale Systems: Theory and Applications* (Netherlands), vol. 6, no. 1, February 1984, pp. 39–48. (U.S. Copyright Clearance Center Code 0167-420X/84/$3.00.)

Questions

1. What is the reason for defining the new system's requirements?

2. It is important that you identify the major operational goals of the department and/or system that you are designing. Why?

3. There are four general questions that should be considered when defining outputs, inputs, operations, resources, and controls for the new system. What are these questions?

4. What factors should be taken into account when defining the type of outputs?

5. After considering the data content of each output report, what other questions should be answered?

6. With regard to defining inputs, what are the two major alternatives that must be considered?

7. Why is it important to develop new system evaluation criteria prior to design of the new system?

8. Once the analyst is convinced of the validity of the standards and measurement criteria for the new system, why must management concur?

9. Name eight typical evaluation criteria for systems.

10. What is the system's requirements model intended to ensure?

11. What should the Input/Output Sheets be used to document?

12. To what can the I/O sheets be cross-referenced on the data flow diagrams?

13. In what ways must the information recorded on the I/O sheets be specific with regard to new requirements?

14. Identify the techniques that can be utilized to document the required operations of the new system.

15. What can a decision table be used for after it has been completed?

16. Name at least two benefits you gain if prototyping is used.

17. Define the term "direct access."

18. What is the deliverable product at the end of the Define the New System Requirements step?

19. What are some of the most important caveats that must be considered when preparing the system design specification. Can you name five?

20. Who normally signs off on the system specification?

SITUATION CASES

Case 7-1: Aero Delivery Service

You have been assigned the responsibility of defining the system requirements for a new computerized application system. Aero Delivery Service has been using its central computer center mainframe for two eight-hour work shifts.

You have researched Aero's operational goals and long-range plans and have concluded that the proposed computerized application system is consistent with the progressive and growth-oriented outlook of management. First, you interviewed key management personnel to determine the most usable form for the outputs required by management. From the interviews you also were able to develop input formats consistent with the users' needs. You then defined what operation would be necessary to maintain and use the new system. Preliminary calculations indicated that the average inquiry would require about two seconds of computer time to process. Management has estimated that about 300 daily inquiries will be made when the system is fully operational.

Next you documented all of the outputs and inputs using I/O sheets. Using narrative descriptions, decision tables, and data flow diagrams, you documented the operations of the new system. You then prepared a summary containing key points of the new system. Your set of evaluation criteria was very acceptable to management, and they were impressed with it.

Question

1. Assuming that the above is a description of your work, discuss any items that you may have overlooked in defining the new system requirements.

Case 7-2: *Nor Cal Computer Sales*

Nor Cal Computer is a small firm that sells computer equipment. An opportunity has arisen for it to take over the Northern California Regional Sales and Service Departments of another company. This acquisition would require the maintenance of a very large inventory of spare parts and it would increase substantially the number of employees. The other company wants to sell this branch as a trial project in divesting all of its sales and service outlets in the United States. Your company has as its goal the acquisition of as many of these dealerships as is feasible.

One of the tasks assigned to a Junior Analyst was to set up a payroll department for the new company. The analyst had a feasibility study report, a problem definition, an outline plan, some general information on the area under study, knowledge of interactions with other departments, and an understanding of the existing system.

The new company already has a computerized payroll system with the EDP and payroll departments located in Chicago. Your own firm's payroll is not going to be computerized.

The new company would have four major classifications of employees

1. Salaried managerial, paid monthly.
2. Sales staff, base salary plus commission with the base salary paid on the 15th and the commission paid on the 1st of each month.
3. Nonmanagerial salaried personnel paid on the 1st and 15th of the month.
4. Hourly employees, paid weekly.

The analyst proceeded to define the inputs of the payroll department. They would be in the form of weekly time cards, bimonthly commission reports, monthly salary authorization reports by department managers, payroll change reports, W-4 forms, and authorized deductions for bonds, uniform rental, and insurance.

Outputs would be checks to employees, reports to management and Accounts Payable, W-2 forms, and reports to various government agencies.

Operations would include

1. Weekly: Receive time cards, compute total time, calculate gross pay, make deductions, compute net pay, enter information on the payroll report,

prepare checks and check stubs, present information to Treasurer for approval, file data, and make out required reports.

2. By the 15th of the month: Compute the pay for the sales staff and non-managerial salaried personnel, following the directions outlined above.
3. Monthly: Receive sales staff commission information, compute pay, and follow the directions outlined above.
4. Prepare reports for various government agencies when due.
5. Prepare W-2 forms yearly for all employees.

Last of all the analyst defined resources as the following.

1. Checkwriting equipment
2. Typewriters
3. Telephones
4. Office space
5. Clerical staff
6. Supervisory personnel
7. Employee record files
8. Payroll file
9. Time card file
10. Envelopes, paper, forms, etc.

In considering the requirements for the new system, the analyst took into account the current requirements and management-imposed requirements.

Questions

1. In defining the specific requirements of the new system, has the analyst taken into consideration sequence logic?
2. Is there any tool the analyst could have used to ensure that all of the requirements were taken into account?
3. In setting up the new payroll department, did the analyst adequately research the new system's requirements? If not, explain.

Case 7-3: *Printer Mafco*

The systems analyst at Printer Mafco, a medium-size manufacturing business, was requested to develop and implement a new system to handle all purchases automatically. Along with the request, management allowed a budget of $5,000 for the development and implementation of the system.

After defining the major goals and objectives of the new system, the analyst interviewed the Controller and key people in the Purchasing and Accounting Departments. From these interviews, the analyst was able to finalize the problem definition, which was accepted by management.

Next, the analyst organized a plan in the form of an outline of the study. The analyst then delved into the area under study, the Purchasing Department. Extensive interviewing in the Purchasing Department supplied the analyst with the necessary information for understanding the existing system as well as background information and the interactions between Purchasing and other departments.

The analyst then had a clear understanding of all outputs, inputs, operations, and resources of the Purchasing Department. After researching the operational goals and the long-range plans of the company, a new system requirements model was developed in which the management-imposed, present, and future requirements of the system were defined. The new system requirements were documented using Input/Output Sheets, system flowcharts, Personnel Sheets, and File Sheets. At this point, the analyst prepared a summary of the system for personal use.

Based on the analyst's system requirements, the new system was designed and implemented with little trouble. The analyst was pleased with the system design and implementation because the entire project developed smoothly in a well-organized manner. When evaluating the system, the analyst was especially proud of the fact that the project was completed in a reasonable time and five percent under the budget imposed by management.

Several weeks later, the analyst, much to her dismay, learned that when management evaluated the new system, they were not at all pleased with the new automated purchasing system. The Purchasing Department was not saving the 10 percent time and cost expected by management. Also, because the analyst had overlooked several outputs, the Purchasing Department was not accepting the new system as an aid; they looked upon it as a hindrance to their operation.

Question

1. Why did Printer Mafco's management and the analyst disagree on the success of the new system? What steps should have been taken by the analyst to avoid this situation?

Chapter 8

DESIGNING THE NEW SYSTEM

LEARNING OBJECTIVES

You will learn how to . . .

□ Use previously gathered data for design.

□ Distinguish between problem solving and decision making.

□ Evaluate tradeoffs during design.

□ Combine design background and systems concepts.

□ Stimulate your creativity to conceptualize and create the new system.

□ Recognize roadblocks to clear thinking.

□ Understand video screen design.

□ Make the transition to the physical data flow diagram.

□ Devise alternative human–machine boundary designs.

□ Compile the physical data dictionary.

□ Complete minispecifications.

□ Draw data structure and data access diagrams.

□ Draw system structure charts.

The Design

To improve things we usually must have clear concepts of where things stand at present and what the objectives and requirements are for the future. We then can pull all of our ideas together into a design that will accomplish our purposes. By the time you reach this step, designing the system, you probably have been using structured analysis with data flow diagrams. We too have been doing this through the steps of our system design, which is demonstrated in our cumulative case.

When you reach this point, you will be doing more than just designing; you will be performing three parallel steps simultaneously. If you review our system development life cycle (described in Chapter 2, Figure 2-1), you will see that during Phase II, Design the New System, Design Controls, and Economic Cost Comparisons are done in parallel. In practical terms, this means that you will be designing a system, designing controls into that system, and evaluating economic cost comparisons with regard to hardware/software decisions. We wanted to mention these parallel steps at this point because design really is not complete until you have designed the controls and made the economic cost comparisons.

As you move forward into the system design process, you must remember that now you are moving from "*what* the system must do" (Chapter 7) to "*how* the system will do it" (Chapter 8).

Problem Solving versus Decision Making

A problem is defined as an unsettled matter demanding solution or decision and usually requiring considerable thought or skill for its proper solution or decision.[1] The process by which one finds the solution to the problem is called problem solving. Technically, *problem solving* is the process of recognizing the symptoms of a problem, identifying exactly what the problem is, determining what is causing the problem, and providing a solution to the problem.

Decision making, on the other hand, is choosing the best solution to the problem based upon the alternatives identified. In current business practice, a systems analyst is primarily a problem solver and a manager is primarily a decision maker.

This is not meant to imply that the analyst *never* makes a decision. To the contrary, the analyst constructs a new system by considering the alternative solutions and then evaluates the solutions according to established criteria. Decision making is inherent in this process. The difference is more in the interaction

---

[1] *Webster's Third New International Dictionary* (Springfield, Mass.: G & C Merriam Company, 1976).

between the two processes. That is, the analyst provides solutions to the problem and recommends that solution which appears to be the most favorable. Management then makes a decision based on the considered judgment of the analyst.

Design Background

By the time the analyst is ready to begin designing the new system, certain items already should be established. There should be a problem definition, general background information on the area under study, a feeling for the interactions within the area under study and with other areas, a good understanding of the current system, and a set of requirements for the new system. It should be noted at this point that few companies today have a formal systems development process that encompasses the above phases.

Systems design is a highly creative process which can be greatly facilitated by the following.

1. Strong problem definition.
2. Pictorial description of the existing system.
3. Set of requirements of the new system.

By definition, *design* means to map out, to plan, or to arrange the parts into a whole which satisfies the objectives involved. Systems design is concerned mainly with the coordination of activities, job procedures, and equipment utilization in order to achieve organizational objectives. The systems designer is faced with choices. There is a "choice-set," which is the set of all available alternatives. Each alternative is a different system or a slightly modified version of another system alternative. The analyst in the design phase

1. Determines the choice-set, that is, all possible systems.
2. Divides the choice-set into the attainable and the unattainable sets. The attainable set contains only those alternatives that have a reasonable chance of acceptance by management.
3. Places in order the alternatives in the attainable set, from the most favored to the least favored.
4. Presents the most highly favored alternatives to management for review and, hopefully, approval of one of the alternatives.

The designer, at this point, should know already whether the proposed system is going to be maximizing something, optimizing something, or satisficing something. To *maximize* is to get the highest possible degree of use out of the system without regard to other systems. To *optimize* is to get the most favorable degree of use out of a system taking into account all other systems; an optimal system does just the right amount of whatever it is supposed to do, which is not necessarily the maximum. To *satisfice* is to choose a particular level of performance for which to strive and for which management is willing to settle.

When you maximize something there are tradeoffs to consider; you may be hurt in other areas. For example, if your personal goal is to maximize your grades, then you may suffer loss in other areas, such as the loss of friends, little or no social interaction, loss of work experience because you cannot work part-time, or poor health caused by lack of sleep and inadequate nutrition.

When you optimize you take into account those tradeoff items such as nutrition, sleep, social interactions, part-time jobs and the like. You then might choose to optimize for a B average, while also gaining work experience, making friends, and maintaining your health.

Finally, if you choose to satisfice, you might arbitrarily choose to attain a B average. All of the logical considerations that are considered if you use the optimization methodology are ignored. But in this case, most of your friends are earning Bs and your parents, who are financing your college education, are willing to settle for B performance levels. Many times people satisfice in order to emulate or copy someone or something else. Satisficing is like following the old saying, "If it's good enough for them, then it's good enough for me."

Another important consideration that will help you, the system designer, is to think in terms of tradeoffs. Politicians call this compromising. Many tradeoff situations are encountered during the design of a system. For example, a classic one is the tradeoff between the cost of the system versus the operational quality of the system and its outputs. An example that might be more *apropos* to you would be, "Should I buy a low cost video monitor for my microcomputer system or should I buy a high cost, high resolution monitor?" Obviously, the lower the cost the lower the resolution and, thus, the poorer the quality of the images on the video screen. Other examples of tradeoffs are

- ☐ Time required to write the program and the programming language utilized (assembly language versus high level macro language versus fourth generation prototyping).
- ☐ Cost versus performance, with regard to hardware.
- ☐ In-house programming versus purchase of a software package.
- ☐ Response time versus numerous considerations such as hardware/software/ data communication networks.
- ☐ One user's satisfaction with the system when measured against another's.
- ☐ Management acceptance of the system versus the local department's acceptance of the system.

We could cite many more types of tradeoffs; but the point is that you should be ready to trade off or compromise your ideas with those of other people.

The designer also must be aware that the job procedures within the new system have four levels of dependence.

1. Random dependence: a procedure is required because of some other procedure.
2. Sequential dependence: one procedure *must* precede or follow another procedure.
3. Time dependence: a procedure is required at a *set time* with regard to another procedure.
4. Parallel: two procedures may be performed simultaneously.

The analyst should look at these procedures during the design phase in terms of their flexibility, maintainability, and expandability. Put another way, the system's procedures should be able to meet new needs over a period of time; they should not be so rigid that they are ignored; and they should be open-ended to allow for growth.

By the time you reach this step, you probably have already started your matrix of controls. If not, you *must* begin it now. We realize that you do not yet know what a matrix of controls does, but do not be concerned about that now since it will be discussed in the next chapter. The control matrix description is deferred until Chapter 9 because it is a step performed in parallel with the one described in this chapter. In a real life situation, if you already had started your matrix, then you would just continue identifying the necessary controls for the new system. Most of the controls are designed and entered onto the matrix during the design process, although they are programmed into the system during programming, and implemented into the system during its implementation (installation).

*P*atterns of Systems Design

The pattern of systems design follows an iterative technique. Systems design is a creative process in which the analyst iterates through various activities or job procedures, one at a time, mentally tracing through the entire system. You, as the analyst, should keep these two very important points in mind.

1. Solve one problem at a time. Do not let your mind get clogged with too many problems at the same time.

2. Your new system must conform with the overall objectives and goals of the area under study and the firm itself.

The *first logical step* in designing a system is to define the problem accurately (this should be done already). Many problems never get solved because they never are defined correctly. Keep an open mind because the definition of the problem may need refinement as the steps toward solution are completed.

The *second step* is to assemble the facts that seem to pertain to the problem. Examine your feasibility study, problem definition, outline, general information, interaction between areas, understanding of the existing system, and the new system requirements. The object is to have *all* of these facts in your mind so you can put them together in a better design than the original system.

The *third step* is to THINK! The designer can use vertical thinking or lateral thinking.[2] Vertical thinking starts with the most promising method of approaching the problem and proceeds from that point to a solution. Lateral thinking explores all of the different ways of looking at the system.

For example, suppose you are to play a game of chance with a person of questionable honesty. You are to pick a marble from a hat and if the marble is red, you lose; if it is blue, you win. (The hat is supposed to contain one blue marble and one red one.) The problem is your opponent's dishonest character. Your objective is to win a fair game. But your opponent is to be the one who puts the two marbles into the hat.

What are the vertical and lateral approaches for verifying your opponent's honesty? The vertical approach is to make sure that there is one red and one blue marble in the hat *before* choosing. This is a perfectly acceptable solution! But lateral thinking might further suggest that the first marble drawn will be discarded (thrown away) and its color determined by the color of the remaining marble.

Notice that vertical thinking started at the *beginning* of the event when the marbles were first put in the hat. Lateral thinking usually starts at the *end* of an event (when the marbles were picked out of the hat). Starting with the systems outputs and working backward through the system is a good example of lateral thinking. Vertical thinking goes from inputs to the outputs, whereas lateral thinking goes from outputs to the inputs.

One of the toughest problems to overcome in either vertical or lateral thinking is the preoccupation with a dominant idea. Dominant ideas tend to block out creative thinking. The designer cannot fruitfully search out all of the alternatives. Some suggestions for dealing with this problem include: stop thinking about that idea for 24 hours, carry the idea to its extremes in order to make it

---

[2] *New Think; the Use of Lateral Thinking in the Generation of New Ideas,* by Edward de Bono (New York: Basic Books, Inc., 1968).

appear foolish, or write down the idea so your mind does not have to hold it "in memory."

There are many methods available to the analyst to help stimulate the creative aspects of design work. Just talking with other people, either to use them as a "sounding board" or to "pick their brains" can be beneficial, although the analyst has to learn to recognize the plateau that occurs when nothing new is being said. Then it is time for the talking to taper off and the designing to pick up!

Group brainstorming can be very effective as long as people are stimulated. If the group is too large and little cliques break off, it can evolve into a gab session.

Another method is to prepare lists of all the ideas and then try to rank them according to objectives, inputs, outputs, or any other criteria.

The manipulation of data collected to discover any recurring patterns can be especially effective if a computer is available. The computer can manipulate the data in such a way that one factor can be balanced against another. This technique is called *factor analysis*. And, of course, the computer can manipulate the data thousands of times faster than a human.

For extremely large systems where many people are working on the design, each alternative can be given to a different team for analysis.

The important thing is to try to think in pictures rather than words. Visualize the activities and job procedures as well as the various ideas of design. Begin to see pictures instead of words. No matter how ridiculous an idea, try to visualize it. Do not immediately discard an idea because it seems wrong or foolish. The desire to be perfectly correct in each step of the design process is a great barrier to creative thinking. Let your mind roam. You may discover a whole new approach to a section of the design—one which may provide new benefits. One such benefit will be the establishment or reinforcement of your image as a creative thinker in the minds of your evaluators, that is, your manager! One idea is to listen to yourself on tape; the bad or good ideas may stand out.

Always review the unresolved design problems each day to stimulate the subconscious mind's ability to solve them. The subconscious mind has a way of putting things together on its own while your conscious mind is busy with other problems. It will announce its progress by "striking" you with bright ideas.

The *fourth step* is to evaluate the ideas or systems that have occurred to you. Without being too rigid, or as they say, "without setting your ideas in cement," do the following:

Decide what the system will do, working from what inputs to what outputs (vertical) or from what outputs to what inputs (lateral), through what operations, using what resources. Go back and talk to the management in the area under study in order to get a tentative approval on the alternatives or on the design itself.

In summary, then, the points to follow when designing a new system are

1. Examine all of the available data.
2. Think hard, and think creatively!

3. Devise various input, output, operation, control, and resource techniques.
4. Evaluate the most important procedures first.
5. Examine various alternatives.
6. Do not spring the final result on management since surprise endings usually are rejected.

Another consideration in the design phase is the amount of control to be exercised from within the system. Some controls will be determined by various system parameters such as the applications and inputs. Certain quality controls may need to be designed into the system. For instance, all inputs should be prepared in a consistent manner to maintain reliability, a built-in check and balance system may be desirable, or a special error section may be developed.

*H*ow to Think Clearly

In the previous section we discussed thinking as it relates to the system design phase. Now let us discuss the many roadblocks that prevent people from thinking clearly. These roadblocks distort how they look at new situations so their relationships with co-workers and supervisors are affected adversely. Let us look at an example of such a distortion. Suppose you, Bill, and Charles have agreed to meet at 2:00 P.M. to discuss a problem. At 2:05 Bill has not arrived. You say, "Bill is five minutes late." Charles replies, "Yes, Bill is always late." This may be a true statement; however, more than likely Charles knows that Bill has been late on one or two occasions and jumps to the conclusion that Bill is *always* late. This is an illogical conclusion based on twisted logic. Such distortions make it difficult to think clearly. Let us examine some distortions that are barriers to clear thinking.[3]

Overgeneralization is like our example of Charles and Bill above. People take one or two things that happen and overgeneralize so that statements become *every* time, *every*body, *every*where, or *always*. What is in fact a "sometimes" becomes an "always." During a system design, do inputs sometimes come from Source A, or do they always come from Source A? If they always come from Source A, you do not need to worry about other areas that may be affected, but if they only sometimes come from Source A, then other sources must be examined as well.

Poisoning the Positive discourages friendships and promotes distrust. An example is when Charles compliments George on a report George has written.

---

[3] Some of the ideas in this section have been suggested by Earl Ubell in his article "How to Think Clearly," *Parade Magazine*, October 7, 1984, pp. 12–15.

George thinks to himself that Charles is a lousy writer, so the report cannot possibly be very good. George finds reasons to dismiss friendly overtures and converts compliments into distrust. He does not know how to accept a compliment gracefully and turns what is meant to be positive into a negative.

The *Shoulds* are those people who always set impossible standards, either for themselves or for others. The Should person always knows what should or must be done. Every statement is said in such a positive manner that failure is almost guaranteed. This person is unreasonable. Suggestions from reasonable people are more tentative; "Such and such *might* be better" rather than "Such and such *is* better." In the system design process the analyst needs to avoid such "must" situations because there may be better ways of doing something. If the analyst is always overly positive, this has a tendency to inhibit other people who may have perfectly good ideas to contribute. These people refrain from contributing their ideas because they may feel intimidated by the Should or Must person. Another way of looking at the Should or Must person is that he or she is an "idea killer." Ideas are acceptable only if they fit into that person's conception of what must be.

The *All or Nothing* person tends to look at everything in either black or white terms and does not recognize that gray areas may exist. Have you ever walked through a real maze? You can get to a junction where you must make a decision of where to go next. Do you turn right or left? The All or Nothing person thinks there are only two alternatives. In reality, there is a third. Perhaps you should turn around and retrace your steps until you locate another junction. In system design, the All or Nothing person thinks another person's suggestion is either good or bad, when it may have some good features and some bad features. In other words, the suggestion is neither black nor white. Do not label it all good or all bad, but somewhere in between. The successful designer recognizes this and tries to utilize the good aspects of the suggestion. Many people in business suffer from seeing things in terms of extremes.

The *Preconceived Notions* person looks at all situations in terms of his or her own presumptions. This set of presumptions is the person's "frame of reference." That is, through the years the person has received stimuli from the environment, which, when taken together, have meaning. An example of this frame of reference is taken from a typical American childhood experience. On summer days, children playing outside often hear the sound of a bell tinkling a block or two away. They know from the sound that an ice cream truck is approaching. A child who has never seen, heard, or read about American ice cream trucks would not have that perception or frame of reference. In the context of the design situation, we tend to hear what we want to hear, see what we want to see, and screen out other information that contradicts our preconceived notions. To illustrate this situation, some years ago researchers had 23 managers read and evaluate a long case problem about a steel company. The managers, who were from sales, production, accounting, and eight miscellaneous areas, all tended to identify the steel company's most critical problem as the one most closely related to their own specialty.[4] This also occurs during systems analysis and design. The people with whom the analyst must interact see the problem and solutions from their own preconceived frames of reference. The analyst must be alert to preconceived notions so that solutions are not channeled too narrowly. That is, the area under study needs to have its solutions, but perhaps the needs of other interrelated areas also must be considered. Finally, the analyst also must avoid the trap of his or her own preconceived notions. The analyst may have preconceived notions about what the accounting department does to justify its existence. Since the analyst's frame of reference may be too narrow, he or she must be open to learning about new tasks or functions that the accounting department carries out, but which the analyst does not think of in accounting terms.

The *Mind Reader* always knows what another person is thinking. The analyst Mind Reader *knows* that the area under study wants a new computer, even though they asked for a new software program that would handle several other tasks the current software cannot handle. When you act on what you believe rather than verifying reality, you get into trouble. Mind reading usually has a low success rate. Never design a new computer system when all the user wants is a new software program!

Catastrophizing is when you view everything as a catastrophe. Having one system design vetoed is a signal to the Catastrophizer that this is the end of a good system design career. Catastrophizing is a fear that everything is for the worst; it paralyzes. Unfortunately, some people grow up in families in which catastrophe is a way of life and thinking. If you were reared in such a family, recognize it and deal with it so that it will not inhibit your career as a systems analyst and your ability to think clearly. The Mislabeler is closely related to the Catastrophizer.

In *Mislabeling,* you may think you are a failure when all you really did was make a mistake. The person who mislabels paints a picture of reality picturing what is wanted or feared rather than what actually exists. This can be dangerous in a systems situation because you can mislabel the initial problem statement; therefore, what people say to you during interviews may lead you to solve the wrong problem.

The *Thoughts as Things* person takes what exists only in his or her head and turns it into something real. This is another type of mislabeling. You may *think* that your manager is giving you all the most difficult design projects, when this is not the case. Look around and you probably will discover that other analysts also have difficult projects; you may even find others more difficult than yours.

People tend to *Magnify or Minimize* situations which can affect a system design

---

[4] "Selective Perception," by Dewitt C. Dearborn and Herbert A. Simon. *Sociometry,* vol. 21, 1958, pp. 140–143.

outcome. At one extreme, the manager of the area under study may view the problem in such an exaggerated way that you, the analyst, are sure it is a major problem. At the other extreme, the Minimizer tends to downplay the problem. In this situation, the analyst may be led to think some aspect of the problem is not important enough to warrant much effort. The Magnify/Minimize person is akin to the All or Nothing person because the situation is not viewed in a moderate and realistic way. These people unwittingly mislead others.

The *Jumping to Conclusions* person can be especially troublesome because important areas may be overlooked. For example, this person, during interviews, allows the interviewee to say something and, at the first pause, jumps on to another question. This type of interviewer jumps to the conclusion that the person is finished when the most important point has not yet been stated. Because the important point is never heard, the Jumping to Conclusions person may miss vital information that should be taken into account during the design process. A strong interviewee can stop the Jumping to Conclusions person by saying, "Just a moment please, I need to make an important point with regard to your last question."

If you recognize yourself in any of our distorted thinking types of people, you are a victim of illogical thinking. You can retrain yourself. To think clearly, you need to confront your belief with reality. How many catastrophes have you really had? How many times out of all the times you have met with Bill was he really late? Has anyone else complimented George on the report he wrote? Many people are trapped by their own distortions, which they learned by copying the style of thinking used by parents, peers, and teachers. By learning to recognize your own distorted thinking patterns, you can overcome them by retraining your own thinking style. The next time you catch yourself in one of these traps, stop, and look at the facts and reality. Reality is a necessity if you are going to look realistically at inputs, processing, and outputs so that you have a good system design. Can you identify yourself in any of the above distortions to thinking clearly?

*V*ideo Screen Design

Before we continue with our cumulative case, we want to introduce some ideas for the physical design of video screens. Remember, it is during this step that the logical model of the new system is converted to the physical model of the new system. Video screen design uses physical design ideas. Until now, we have been concerned only with logical analysis ideas, such as data flows and data structures, without regard to *how* they will be presented on a video screen.

During the design step, one of the difficult tasks is to develop the actual layouts for the inputs and the output reports for the new system. You should use the "specific requirements of the new system" and the "Input-Processing-Output models" that you developed earlier (these were discussed in the previous chapter). These "requirements" and "models" are the basis for the video screen forms, hard copy multipart forms (if paper), and the computer printed outputs.

Remember that Chapter 14, Forms Design, contains much more detail on

☐ Video screen data structures.

☐ Layout form for computer printers.

☐ Techniques of forms design and layout.

As you read the following section on video screen design, it will give you ideas on how to handle the data for presentation. Even though video screens are the topic, you can transfer some of these ideas to paper forms, such as computer printers or multipart paper forms. For now, let us quickly review 10 different ideas on how video screen data can be handled.

Simple input queries are ones in which the terminal operator keys in an employee number, a bank account number, a document number, or the like, and the relevant items then appear on the screen. The data items of records that appear on the screen should be in a simple straightforward left-to-right format in the most frequently requested sequence as needed by the business' user departments.

Mnemonic queries are those designed with simple two- or three-character abbreviation codes (mnemonic) that, when keyed in by the terminal operator, generate the requested information on the screen. What appears on the screen depends upon whether numeric or graphic data is being requested.

English language queries are those in which the terminal operator enters the entire English word or phrase in order to retrieve the requested data. In this case, the system may prompt the terminal operator by first indicating what should be entered, such as name, and then accepting the entered data.

Transaction code entries are those in which a business system has a two- or three-digit transaction code for each input transaction programmed into the application system. In this type of system, terminal operators must know which transaction code goes with which request. For example, if you cash a check at the bank, the teller might enter a three-digit transaction code that identifies his or her query as one that first checks the balance in your account and, second, puts a hold on the amount of money for which you are cashing the check. Obviously, a different transaction code would be used to tell the computer that you are making a deposit.

Scroll/paging techniques are used when a display retrieved from the files is too big for the screen. In this case the video screen "scrolls" up or down; it appears that the data is being moved continuously up or down the screen. It is as if the data were on a long piece of paper that is rolled by the video screen. In paging, the system displays the first "page" of data, stops for it to be read, and then displays the second page of data on command, and so forth.

Interactive instructions are those in which the computer and the terminal operator have an interactive dialog. The operator makes a request, the computer answers the request, and then instructs or prompts the terminal operator on what to do next. An alternative is to provide a HELP screen which is used to instruct or lead the terminal operator through the interactive dialog.

Menu selection is a technique in which a limited set of valid questions/answers are used to lead the operator through the input process. For example, an operator may be entering a new car order from an automobile dealer to the automobile manufacturer. The operator can use either mnemonics or full English statements in the query. The computer system asks, "What kind of car?" and the terminal operator answers, "Lincoln." The computer system then displays a "menu" of all possible models of the Lincoln from which the terminal operator chooses one. Then the system lists all possible engine options for the chosen car model and the operator again chooses one. This process continues until all possible choices are made and, thus, the order has been entered.

Telephone directory methods are used when there are too many items (hundreds) to use a menu selection approach. This method is similar to menu selection except it lists items alphabetically and the operator scrolls/pages through them rapidly in order to choose the desired option.

Form completion is where the analyst duplicates filling out a paper form but does it on a video screen. When forms are moved from paper to video screens, you should never have more than one item to complete on a single line. For example, some paper forms have two items per line. Therefore, you would have to change how the data is listed on the video screen, with one item per line and in the sequence that is most convenient for the terminal operator to fill in (enter the data).

Text editing techniques deal with narrative texts that can be modified. Items that have to be changed may be done directly. For example, changing the character "A" to the character "R" involves typing an "R" right on top of the already displayed "A." Deleting also can be done directly. Inserting involves shifting or moving data and/or text and then typing in the new items.

The above ideas can be used when designing for inputs or retrieval of data from a computerized application system. Following the basic techniques of forms design when you lay out video screens will help you design successful screen formats. For example, first develop a list of all data items that need to be available for retrieval or to appear on the screen. Only after doing that should you engage in the design of the layout or positioning of these items on the video screen. As with any forms design (detailed in Chapter 14), when you talk with people about form layout or positioning, they may become so entranced with the graphics that they omit key pieces of data (data items) that are required in your new system.

Now that we have learned patterns of design, clear thinking, video screens, and so forth, we can start Step 6 of our cumulative case.

SUNRISE SPORTSWEAR COMPANY

CUMULATIVE CASE: Designing the New System (Step 6)

Once again you meet with Mr. Reynolds and Ms. Brunn. This time, however, other key people who are concerned with the Sunrise Sportswear Order Processing system also are invited. The primary purpose of this meeting is to have everyone approve the new logical system as shown in the logical data flow diagram for the proposed system (see Figure 7-15 in Chapter 7). Much to your delight, both Mr. Reynolds and Mr. Wallace are enthusiastic about the changes, although Ms. Brunn and some of the others do not appear as well pleased. You reiterate the problems that need to be solved, the steps you have gone through to reach this point, and how you moved through the steps of the physical data flow diagram of the existing system (Figure 5-6), to the logical data flow diagram of the existing system (Figure 7-11), and now to the logical data flow diagram of the proposed system (Figure 7-15). You seek their approval of it before beginning the physical data flow diagram for the new system.

One of the major points of discussion is the elimination of credit to Sunrise Sportswear customers. Prior to the meeting, you spoke with Bob Thompson, Doris Hardy, and Joy King because it appears from the logical data flow diagram that their jobs may be eliminated. Your purpose in talking with them was to provide reassurance that they would still have jobs, but that their duties undoubtedly would be changed. You wanted to tell them this in private rather than surprise them with it in the meeting. Even with this reassurance, you can see that some of the people are nervous about the changes. You explain the various alternatives that were considered before settling upon this proposal. The alternatives relating to credit are

1. Leave the credit system as is. Because one cause of the current problem has been determined to be the current system of extending credit, this does not seem to be a viable alternative.
2. Move credit verification activities to the Accounting Department. This also does not seem like a good answer to the problem because it would not change the fact that customers are not paying their bills.
3. Use outside credit rating agencies to check new customer's credit standing. This is a costly and time-consuming process. Although it might result in

fewer overdue accounts, the large number of relatively small balances does not appear to make this a worthwhile alternative. Also, it might make the order processing still slower, which Sunrise Sportswear cannot afford to do.

4. The most viable alternative appears to be that of eliminating credit entirely. Sunrise Sportswear's competitors operate, for the most part, on a check or credit card basis. You describe the results of the telephone survey and the sampling of the Sunrise Sportswear overdue accounts.

There is a lively discussion of the pros and cons of these alternatives, and you can see that both Mr. Reynolds and Mr. Wallace seem to be strongly in favor of the alternative you have chosen.

You also discuss what you learned about the new customer cards prepared by Suzanne Wolfe. One of your key points is that this process has become a major bottleneck because of the increase of Sunrise Sportswear's new customer base; you are careful to avoid making it appear as though Ms. Wolfe has not been doing her job. You stress such things as the duplication of keying the data, as well as Jon Gray and Suzanne Wolfe using two different customer files to determine whether it is an old or new customer. You stress that this duplication of effort is costly and a serious roadblock to getting the customers' orders filled promptly. The alternatives for this situation are

1. Leave the new customer system as is. This is one of the worst alternatives because it has the potential of becoming still a worse bottleneck if it is not changed.

2. Hire more people to do the work. This is only a temporary solution to the problem. It would not stop either the keying duplication or the checking of different records to determine old/new status.

3. Since a customer's old/new status is not relevant to the Order Processing stream *per se*, but what is called a management-imposed requirement, a better method of doing the work must be found. One way would be to have copies made of the orders, continue with the processing of the orders, and have the new customer records made from the copies. This alternative would get the new customer cards out of the main processing stream, but it would not eliminate any of the other undesirable aspects of the problem. In fact, it would be a costly alternative because of the labor cost to make the copies and the cost of the copies themselves, which you estimate would be a minimum of $0.08 per copy.

4. Since new customer records must be maintained, it is more desirable to have it be a part of the main Order Processing stream, but to do it in a more logical and efficient manner.

You explain the logical data flow diagram (Figure 7-15) in which one step is verifying orders (2.0), the next step is assigning the order and customer numbers and checking the customer status (3.0), and then the orders are passed on to the people who verify payments (4.0) and credit cards (5.0). As you show them on the logical data flow diagram, when the order verification person needs to locate customer information, it now can be done using the same file (D7: CUSTOM-ERS) as the person who assigns the order numbers. This has the added benefit of having only one person verify customer status. The order verification person would need customer information only when trying to solve specific customer problems. You explain that you hope to devise a system in which they will no longer have to have all of the old files of completed customer orders.

There are many questions about *how* you are going to accomplish all this. You find this is a problem because the users are accustomed to thinking in terms of *how* things happen, rather than in terms of *what* happens. It is necessary to explain that, once the logical data flow diagram of the proposed system is approved, you will begin to work out the details of how the system will operate, at which point everyone will be brought together again. You stress that the old way of doing things may have worked a few years ago; but, because Sunrise Sportswear's competitors have computerized their operations and streamlined their processing, Sunrise Sportswear must be willing to make changes now or be overtaken by the competition. You emphasize this point by stating that it is better to go through some trauma and upheaval now than to be faced with the possibility of a plant shutdown in the future. You also try to reassure them that you will make every effort to see that the transition is as easy as possible for all concerned. One technique that you use to make them more enthusiastic about the changes is to tell them that it is natural not to want change—that is human nature—but we all need to learn how to do things in new ways in order to grow personally. You ask them to view the new system as a way to help them reduce job stress caused by some problems that can be eliminated, and as a means of making their lives more interesting. You also stress that there is still plenty of work for everyone because of Sunrise Sportswear's continuing growth.

As the meeting draws to a close, you expect Mr. Reynolds to say that he wants to think about it. Instead, he tells you to proceed. He is anxious to get on with the changes because they are needed. You are very pleased and say you will get right to work on it.

Now you have reached the critical point at which you stop analyzing and start designing. As you must realize by now, the use of structured analysis and design techniques implies what Gane and Sarson referred to as the spiral approach.[5] Prior to structured analysis and design, it was assumed that a systems project was performed in a straight line that went from feasibility, through analysis, on to coding, testing, and finally to implementation. This classical approach is demonstrated by Figure 8-1.

---

[5] The idea for this discussion of the straight-line versus spiral approach to systems development is from the book, *Structured Systems Analysis: Tools and Techniques,* by Chris Gane and Trish Sarson (Englewood Cliffs, N.J.: Prentice-Hall, Inc., 1979).

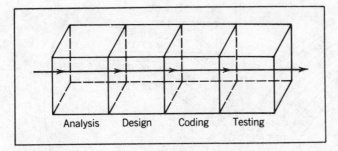

Figure 8-1 The classical approach to systems is one that progresses in a straight line (Gane and Sarson, p. 224).

As Gane and Sarson pointed out so aptly, the straight line approach is an ideal which does not match reality. Instead, they saw the system development project in terms of a spiraling effect in which the analyst iterates through the steps, with the users providing input at each step. This spiral approach changes the system development project to look like Figure 8-2. By now, you should see that our situation at Sunrise Sportswear is a simple one. There is much more to systems development than talking to a few people, designing a new system, having them approve your plans, and then implementing the changes. In reality, at this point in the system development life cycle, you will have talked with everyone at Sunrise Sportswear many times.

Now it is time to convert the logical model of the new system into a physical model. Contrary to what you may think, this new physical model is only a slightly modified version of your logical data flow diagram. Your new system's physical data flow diagram, along with other structured documentation, becomes the physical model of the proposed system. As you did previously, the logical model is used to achieve this physical model. In the process, decisions are made regarding tradeoffs. Do you want to maximize, optimize, or satisfice?

The physical data flow diagram of the proposed system looks like Figure 8-3.

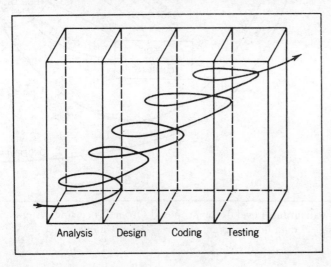

Figure 8-2 The structured analysis approach to systems development progresses in a spiral in which steps are iterated as users provide more input to what is needed (Gane and Sarson, p. 225).

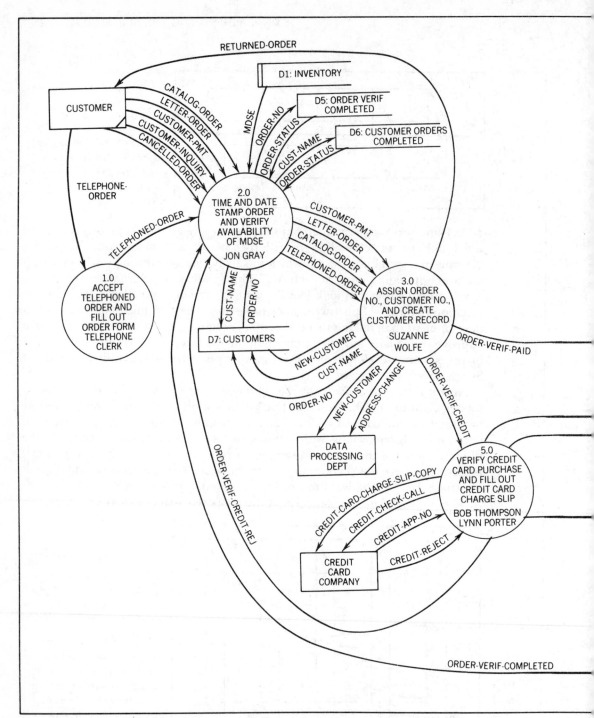

Figure 8-3 Physical data flow diagram (Level 0) for proposed Order Processing system at Sunrise Sportswear. Derived from logical data flow diagram (Figure 7-15 in Chapter 7).

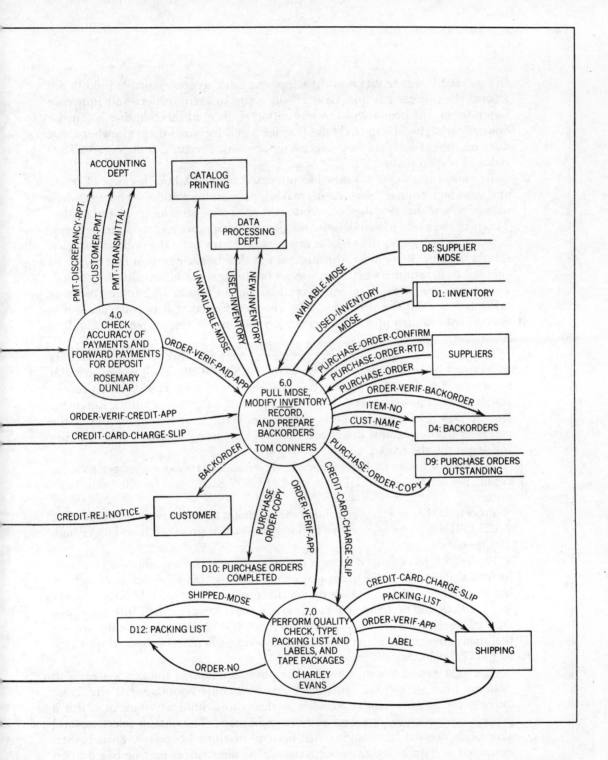

ACCOUNTING DEPT

CATALOG PRINTING

DATA PROCESSING DEPT

D8: SUPPLIER MDSE

D1: INVENTORY

SUPPLIERS

D4: BACKORDERS

D9: PURCHASE ORDERS OUTSTANDING

4.0 CHECK ACCURACY OF PAYMENTS AND FORWARD PAYMENTS FOR DEPOSIT
ROSEMARY DUNLAP

6.0 PULL MDSE, MODIFY INVENTORY RECORD, AND PREPARE BACKORDERS
TOM CONNERS

CUSTOMER

D10: PURCHASE ORDERS COMPLETED

D12: PACKING LIST

7.0 PERFORM QUALITY CHECK, TYPE PACKING LIST AND LABELS, AND TAPE PACKAGES
CHARLEY EVANS

SHIPPING

PMT-DISCREPANCY-RPT
CUSTOMER-PMT
PMT-TRANSMITTAL

UNAVAILABLE-MDSE
USED-INVENTORY
NEW-INVENTORY
AVAILABLE-MDSE
USED-INVENTORY
MDSE
PURCHASE-ORDER-CONFIRM
PURCHASE-ORDER-RTD
PURCHASE-ORDER
ORDER-VERIF-BACKORDER
ITEM-NO
CUST-NAME

ORDER-VERIF-PAID-APP
ORDER-VERIF-CREDIT-APP
CREDIT-CARD-CHARGE-SLIP
BACKORDER
CREDIT-REJ-NOTICE

PURCHASE ORDER-COPY
ORDER-VERIF-APP
CREDIT-CARD-CHARGE-SLIP
PURCHASE-ORDER-COPY

SHIPPED-MDSE
ORDER-NO
CREDIT-CARD-CHARGE-SLIP
PACKING-LIST
ORDER-VERIF-APP
LABEL

347

In process 1.0, we see that now the telephone clerk accepts an order and fills out a form. In process 2.0, Jon Gray is still going to verify orders and time/date stamp them. His primary task is to verify that ordered merchandise is Sunrise Sportswear's. He no longer checks payments and forwards them elsewhere, nor does he split the orders into processing streams. Process 2.0 appears to have reduced responsibilities.

By contrast, process 3.0 now has increased responsibilities because of order and customer number assignment, making old customer address changes when necessary, and dividing the orders into two processing streams (paid and credit). This may seem odd to you because the new customer process has been the major bottleneck; increasing the tasks at this process seems to be the opposite of what should be done. Remember, this process was slow because two sources had to be checked to determine whether it was an old or new customer, and the records were typed on cards. If a better method can be found to handle customer information, then the process can be speeded up. Also, it is quite likely that process 3.0 will turn into a two-person job with one of the people being shifted from another process.

Process 3.0 then splits the order processing stream in three directions. Orders that cannot be verified are returned to the CUSTOMER, credit orders are sent to process 5.0, and the "real" prepaid orders go to process 4.0. This process' responsibilities have changed. Instead of updating customer accounts, Rosemary Dunlap now does what Jon Gray used to do: verifies the dollar amount of the customer's order against the check. She still forwards payments to Accounting for deposit in the bank.

Process 5.0 has been halved because Sunrise Sportswear no longer extends credit. We see that a CREDIT-CARD-CHARGE-SLIP must be filled out, however.

Process 6.0 has not changed much except that it now mentions preparation of BACKORDERs, which are more important now that process 2.0 no longer handles them.

Process 7.0 has changed quite a bit. We now see that a quality check is performed at this point in the order processing stream. Actually, it was done before, but no one knew it. Also, we see that in this process, they type PACKING-LISTs and LABELs and then tape packages. When the boxes are closed with appropriate enclosures, they are forwarded to SHIPPING. You see, there really are not that many changes from the logical data flow diagram of the proposed system to its physical data flow diagram.

The next step in the shift over to the physical model of the new system is to examine what we call the tentative human–machine boundary. As the name implies, the *human–machine boundary* is the point within a system at which a process is automated, or taken away from humans. The analyst selects several alternative designs by changing this human–machine boundary. Each is then examined in light of its cost-effectiveness. The alternatives may be based upon computerizing an entire system, getting a computer to perform some of the major functions, or getting microcomputers to perform some of the smaller processes only. After one alternative has been selected by the users (remember, it is *their* system), the parts that are to be computerized are put into physical models. These physical models are the lower level physical data flow diagrams, data structure diagrams, data access diagrams, and system structure charts. This step of the new system design is the point at which you settle upon what the inputs and outputs will look like and whether they are some type of computer output report, a video screen, or a paper form. Both input and output decisions may be made by the use of prototyping. In fact, prototyping lets the user experience how his or her new system actually will function.

In a system that utilizes both computerized and manual methods, drawing the human–machine boundary helps clarify what processes need to continue as part of the structured design process and what processes need to be developed using traditional systems design. In other words, the automated processes are described by lower level data flow diagrams, the data dictionary, and the minispecifications for the processes. The manual processes are described by support documentation such as decision tables, flowcharts, written procedures, and so forth. The difference between structured and traditional techniques becomes most evident at this point in the system development life cycle. In traditional systems analysis, documentation generally is left until the end of the project, with the exception of tools such as flowcharts and layout charts that are part of the new system design. When structured techniques are used, all documentation is well under way at this point, and the same documentation can be used for both the manual and automated processes (e.g., data flow diagrams and decision logic tools).

As we already know, Sunrise Sportswear is not a very computer-oriented company at this point in time. We can guess that Mr. Reynolds would not be very interested in a major new computer system. Nor would it be appropriate to recommend one if the scope of the problem does not call for it. Let us return to our physical data flow diagram of the proposed system (Figure 8-3) and examine it in view of its human–machine boundary.

Process 1.0 appears to be a manual operation. A telephone order clerk accepts a telephone call and fills out a form. If your job was to find a better way to make process 1.0 a more efficient operation, we could say that this process could be computerized. Many order-taking telephone operators today are, in fact, order entry operators. They enter the information onto a CRT and thereby start an entire sequence of events that is computerized completely. We will keep this in mind for our alternatives, but it may be too much for Sunrise Sportswear to handle at this point. Also, you have been hired to solve some specific problems; redesigning the entire Order Processing system to computerize it is beyond the scope of what you have been asked to do, even though it may be a desirable thing.

Process 2.0 involves checking inventory to establish that the ordered merchandise is that of Sunrise Sportswear. The INVENTORY data store currently is batched every night by DATA PROCESSING and given to users in the form of a computer printout the next morning. Tom Conners expressed a desire earlier to have more up-to-date inventory information, but this also is outside the scope of the current problem. You have not been asked to study the inventory system.

The completed Order Verification file (D5) currently is a paper file. It could be computerized if Sunrise Sportswear wanted to computerize its entire Order Processing system. This would be a nice thing to do, but again, it is beyond the scope of the current problem. The other major file used by process 2.0 is data store D6. This is the actual customer order and probably will remain as a paper file unless Sunrise Sportswear someday becomes so computerized that customers can send orders over data communication networks. For Sunrise Sportswear, that is not very realistic for the near term.

Going on to process 3.0, we can see a place for real improvement. This step currently is the major bottleneck that needs to be removed or improved. Because it cannot be removed (remember, it is a management-imposed requirement), you will have to improve it. With the improvements in microcomputers, this is a very likely starting place for modernizing Sunrise Sportswear. By using a microcomputer instead of a typewriter, Suzanne Wolfe can check her computerized file to determine whether it is a current customer, make address changes, key in new customer information, flag new customer records for later transfer to DATA PROCESSING, assign a customer identification number, and assign the next order number. Providing this step of the process with a microcomputer allows you to eliminate the data store that was 3 × 5 cards of customer records. It also allows the process to have access to one up-to-date list of customers with the capability of printing out all new customers within a certain time period, all from one state, all from outside the United States, or other "fancy" things as yet unrecognized by those nice people at Sunrise Sportswear.

Finally, providing a microcomputer at this step of the process (3.0) has another benefit. It allows the person at process 2.0 to have access to this new file of customers if a microcomputer is put in that area as well. This would allow Sunrise Sportswear to eliminate most of a room full of paper customer files that would no longer be needed. This is not to say that all of the paper files would disappear. Sunrise Sportswear would have to determine how far back they would need to keep files in order to handle current customer problems and inquiries. Probably six months to a year are adequate for such a use. Of course, you would have to convince them of this because these people are used to paper files, and feel most comfortable with them. Initially, they might not want to eliminate any; but, as they see files being unused and taking up needed space, this will change—especially if you show them some tricks that will prove the files are no longer being used. (If you are curious, go to Chapter 15 and read the part about storage box labels; these can be converted to use on file drawers as well.)

Moving on to process 4.0, this is an unlikely area to computerize. It involves someone totaling the customer order prices to verify their accuracy and then making sure the customer's payment matches the total. These checks and money orders then are forwarded to the ACCOUNTING DEPARTMENT for depositing in the bank. When there is a discrepancy between the customer's order and the payment amount, this must be reported so that some decision can be made as to either billing the customer for the extra amount or providing a refund. This is an area that you will have to get some policy decisions on at a later time. In any event, computerization of this process is unlikely.

Process 5.0 is another area that probably does not need to be computerized. There are two potential aspects that should be examined, however. With a microcomputer, the customer rejection notices could be personalized. Instead of saying "Dear Customer," they could be addressed to the correct person. Since there could be a computerized file of customers at process 3.0, perhaps it could be used to accomplish this. Also, if a way could be found to have the computer type out the CREDIT-CARD-CHARGE-SLIPs, that would be a great time-saver. Process 5.0 then is a possible area to computerize.

Process 6.0 is a manual process since it involves pulling merchandise off shelves and reducing current stock in the INVENTORY file. Again, you were not asked to study the inventory system, so this is not an area that would be changed. There is, however, one potential aspect of the inventory area that is a possibility. The placing of BACKORDERs can be time-consuming. Since Jon Gray no longer handles out-of-stock returns, handling of BACKORDERs by the Inventory staff probably will increase. If they have access to the CUSTOMERS data store and a microcomputer, perhaps they can print the BACKORDERs more quickly. It is even possible that the paper BACKORDERS file could be eliminated. Of course, given the right equipment, it might even be possible to computerize the PURCHASE-ORDERs, but that really is getting away from the scope of the problem defined back in Step 1!

Finally, in process 7.0, there are several areas that could be speeded up with the help of a microcomputer. The first and simplest is that of LABEL typing. Again, if they have a microcomputer and the proper type of printer, someone could access the CUSTOMERS data store and print the information needed to complete the LABEL for that order number.

A second use of a microcomputer in process 7.0 is the preparation of PACK-ING-LISTs. The CUSTOMERS data store would again provide the necessary name, address, and order number information. The Order Preparation staff could enter in whatever information they want to add that pertains to the merchandise sent, the number of boxes, weight of the shipment, and so forth. If the Order Preparation people do all this, they could pack the merchandise in the box, place the PACKING-LIST (and gift card, if applicable) in the box, tape the box, and place the LABEL on it. If this was done, the management of Sunrise Sportswear would have a good record of what left the Order Preparation area and the possibility of theft would be lessened.

Now that each process has been examined in view of its potential computerization, the human–machine boundary can be drawn. Actually, several can be drawn. Remember, you want to provide Mr. Reynolds with some alternatives. Also, the alternatives must meet the users' perceptions of decreased processing time, flexibility, and control. Three alternatives are shown in Figures 8-4, 8-5, and 8-6.

Figure 8-4 is the minimal automation (Alternative A) for the Sunrise Sportswear Order Processing system. Process 3.0 must be automated if they wish to maintain new customer records. Since it is a key point in the entire system, getting it automated will permit the dissolution of data store D2: NEW CUSTOMERS (the 3 × 5 cards), create a more up-to-date and reliable system for tracking both old and new customers, and eventually make the data store D7: CUSTOMERS available to other processes such as 2.0. Providing process 7.0 with automated capability allows them to have PACKING-LISTs for the first time and to maintain them in a data store (D12: PACKING LIST). It also allows them access to data store D7.

In Figure 8-5, we show a middle-of-the-road approach to what could be automated (Alternative B). In addition to processes 3.0 and 7.0, we have added processes 2.0, 5.0, and 6.0. Making data store D7 available to process 2.0 would enhance Jon Gray's ability to respond quickly to customer inquiries regarding orders. Perhaps more important, it would allow Sunrise Sportswear to dispense with all but the most recent records in data store D6: CUSTOMER ORDERS COMPLETED. Since this is a paper file and contains *all* old customer orders, it has grown beyond the bounds of reasonableness. It is time to discard it in favor of newer and more efficient methods.

Process 5.0 could make effective use of a microcomputer and printer to handle the credit rejection notices in a more personal manner. Also, this process could gain access to the D7 data store when needed.

Process 6.0 was added, not to modernize the Inventory system (remember, that is beyond the scope of your problem statement), but to enable the employees to handle what will be an increased load of BACKORDERs. If the people in Inventory get enthusiastic and learn ways to handle the shipped and new inventory items more effectively, so much the better. The primary reason for giving them a microcomputer, however, is to handle the BACKORDERs.

In Figure 8-6 (Alternative C), only one other process, 4.0, has been added. This process might need only a relatively unsophisticated microcomputer configuration, but it may be able to use data store D7 as well. This leaves only process 1.0 without any automation. The only reason this process would be automated would be if Sunrise Sportswear decided to computerize its entire Order Processing system. Since this is highly unlikely, and because you were not hired to do that, this alternative is not shown.

Incidentally, notice that some of the data stores were left out of the human–machine boundary. The reason is that they are data stores that have been supplied by other groups (e.g., external entities) over which the Order Processing system has no control. That is, the D1 data store exists because Inventory inputs to it; however, nothing can be done to change it unless Data Processing gets new equipment to handle expanded capabilities.

These three figures of the alternative human–machine boundaries are your choice-set. Taking tradeoffs into account, Figure 8-6 maximizes what could be accomplished. This is in the context of the problem as defined. If you really wanted to maximize, you probably would say that the entire system should be computerized and Sunrise Sportswear should invest in a major new computer system. That is not why you were hired, however, so to maximize in this case means dealing only with what can be accomplished within the Order Processing system. Taken in this context, Figure 8-5 recognizes the optimal solution because it does what it is supposed to do (speed up the order processing and reduce overdue accounts) and assists in three other areas as well (streamlines order verification, speeds up backorder handling, and produces needed packing lists and labels efficiently). Figure 8-4 is the choice to satisfice. It achieves the two major goals but little else except for eliminating some paper records in process 2.0 and enabling automated packing lists in process 7.0. This minimal human–machine boundary chooses a level of performance for which management may be willing to settle. At this point, you do not *know* whether Mr. Reynolds will choose to maximize, optimize, or satisfice because you do not know how much money he is willing to spend in order to correct the problems. We have already guessed that he probably will not be ready for an entire computerized order processing system. He may be willing to choose the middle-of-the-road approach; however, you recognize some penny-pinching traits that may mean you will have to satisfice. In fact, it is important to recognize, when you are dealing with other people's money, that your "satisfice" may be their "optimize." What we mean is that your minimal choice may be to provide processes 3.0 and 7.0 with microcomputers. Mr. Reynolds, on the other hand, may think even this is excessive and want only 3.0 computerized. There even is a chance that he may love the idea, but hate spending the money to set up an adequate system. Some people cannot be convinced to spend a large sum of money "up front" to achieve long-term gains. People like this tend to select the approach of making copies of customer orders so someone like Suzanne Wolfe can be more efficient. Such people "nickel and dime" themselves out of existence and never understand why. We hope you never have such a situation, but the possibility always exists.

Returning to the human–machine boundary, you know you must have a concrete plan in mind when the alternatives are presented to Sunrise Sportswear's management. If two or more areas are designated to be automated, you plan to install a local area network (LAN) at Sunrise Sportswear. A local area network is a communications network in which a variety of electronic equipment are interconnected so that they can communicate among themselves at high speed. The local area network is what makes the automated office function.

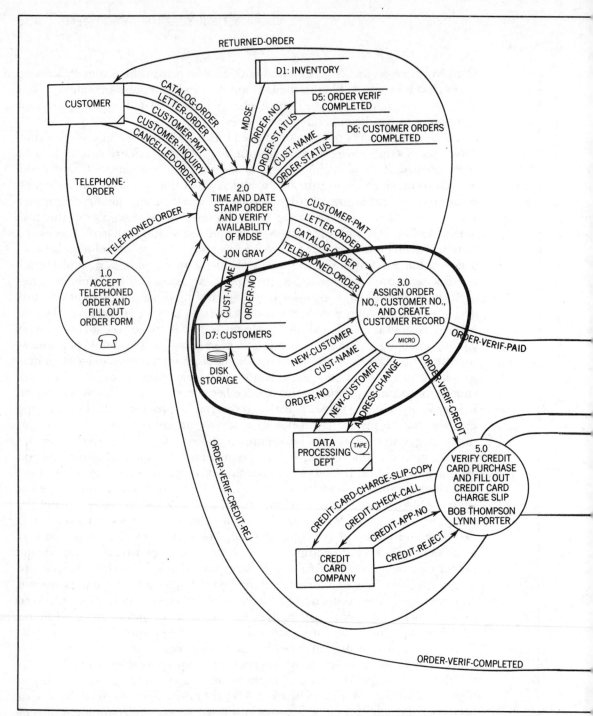

Figure 8-4 Physical data flow diagram showing minimal human–machine boundary (Alternative A).

354

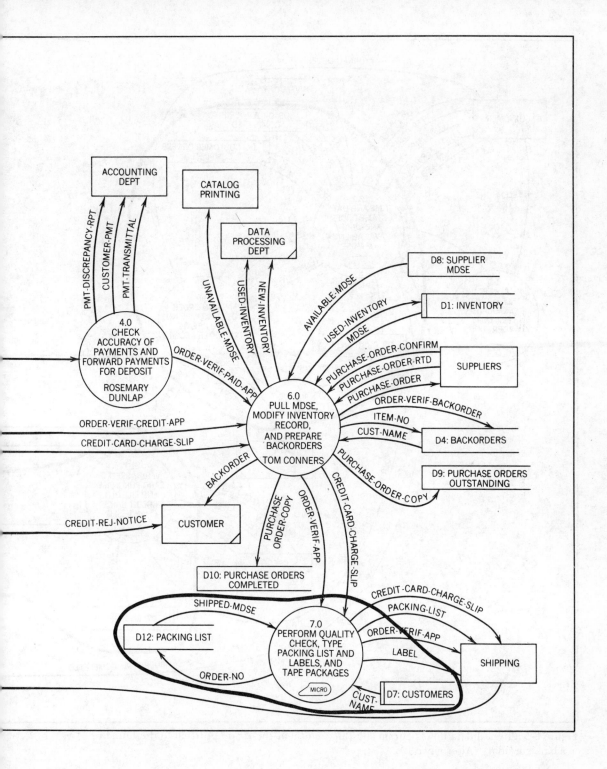

ACCOUNTING
DEPT

CATALOG
PRINTING

DATA
PROCESSING
DEPT

D8: SUPPLIER
MDSE

D1: INVENTORY

SUPPLIERS

PMT-DISCREPANCY-RPT

CUSTOMER-PMT

PMT-TRANSMITTAL

4.0
CHECK
ACCURACY OF
PAYMENTS AND
FORWARD PAYMENTS
FOR DEPOSIT

ROSEMARY
DUNLAP

UNAVAILABLE-MDSE

USED-INVENTORY

NEW-INVENTORY

AVAILABLE-MDSE

USED-INVENTORY

MDSE

PURCHASE-ORDER-CONFIRM

PURCHASE-ORDER-RTD

PURCHASE-ORDER

ORDER-VERIF-BACKORDER

ORDER-VERIF-PAID-APP

6.0
PULL MDSE,
MODIFY INVENTORY
RECORD,
AND PREPARE
BACKORDERS

TOM CONNERS

ORDER-VERIF-CREDIT-APP

CREDIT-CARD-CHARGE-SLIP

ITEM-NO

CUST-NAME

D4: BACKORDERS

D9: PURCHASE ORDERS
OUTSTANDING

CREDIT-REJ-NOTICE

BACKORDER

CUSTOMER

PURCHASE-ORDER-COPY

PURCHASE-
ORDER-COPY

ORDER-VERIF-APP

CREDIT-CARD-CHARGE-SLIP

D10: PURCHASE ORDERS
COMPLETED

SHIPPED-MDSE

D12: PACKING LIST

ORDER-NO

7.0
PERFORM QUALITY
CHECK, TYPE
PACKING LIST AND
LABELS, AND
TAPE PACKAGES

MICRO

CREDIT-CARD-CHARGE-SLIP

PACKING-LIST

ORDER-VERIF-APP

LABEL

SHIPPING

CUST-
NAME

D7: CUSTOMERS

355

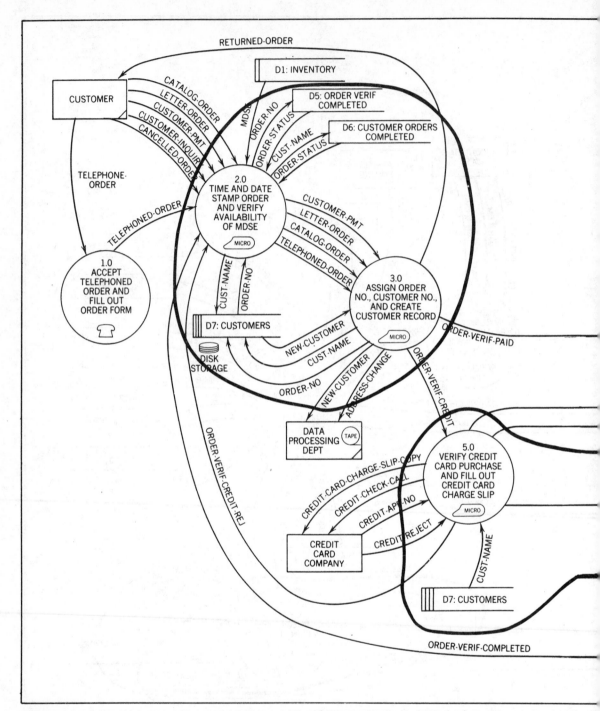

RETURNED-ORDER

D1: INVENTORY

D5: ORDER VERIF COMPLETED

D6: CUSTOMER ORDERS COMPLETED

CUSTOMER

CATALOG-ORDER
LETTER-ORDER
CUSTOMER-INQUIR
CUSTOMER-PMT
CANCELLED-ORDER

MDSE
ORDER-NO
ORDER-STATUS
CUST-NAME
ORDER-STATUS

TELEPHONE-ORDER

TELEPHONED-ORDER

2.0
TIME AND DATE STAMP ORDER AND VERIFY AVAILABILITY OF MDSE
MICRO

CUSTOMER-PMT
LETTER-ORDER
CATALOG-ORDER
TELEPHONED-ORDER

1.0
ACCEPT TELEPHONED ORDER AND FILL OUT ORDER FORM

3.0
ASSIGN ORDER NO., CUSTOMER NO., AND CREATE CUSTOMER RECORD
MICRO

CUST-NAME
ORDER-NO

D7: CUSTOMERS

DISK STORAGE

NEW-CUSTOMER
CUST-NAME

ORDER-VERIF-PAID

ORDER-NO
NEW-CUSTOMER
ADDRESS-CHANGE

ORDER-VERIF-CREDIT

DATA PROCESSING DEPT
TAPE

5.0
VERIFY CREDIT CARD PURCHASE AND FILL OUT CREDIT CARD CHARGE SLIP
MICRO

CREDIT-CARD-CHARGE-SLIP-COPY
CREDIT-CHECK-CALL
CREDIT-APP-NO
CREDIT-REJECT

CREDIT CARD COMPANY

ORDER-VERIF-CREDIT-REJ

CUST-NAME

D7: CUSTOMERS

ORDER-VERIF-COMPLETED

Figure 8-5 Physical data flow diagram showing middle-of-the-road approach to the human–machine boundary (Alternative B).

356

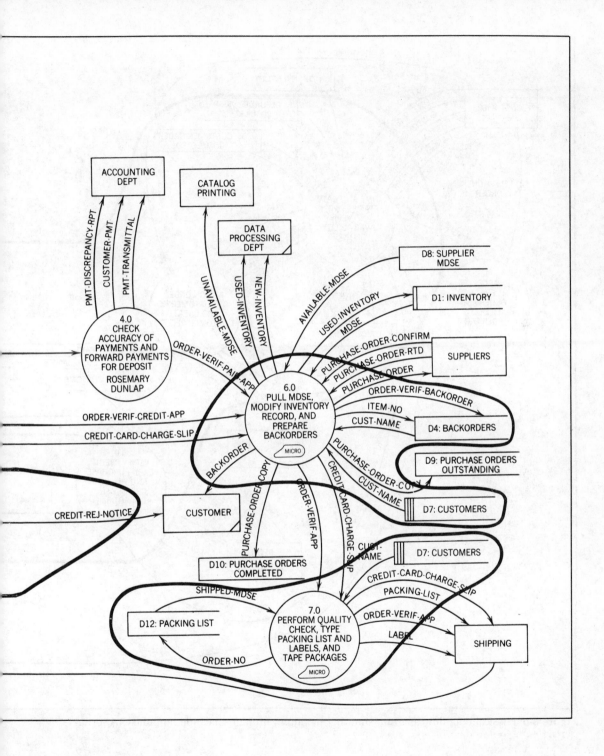

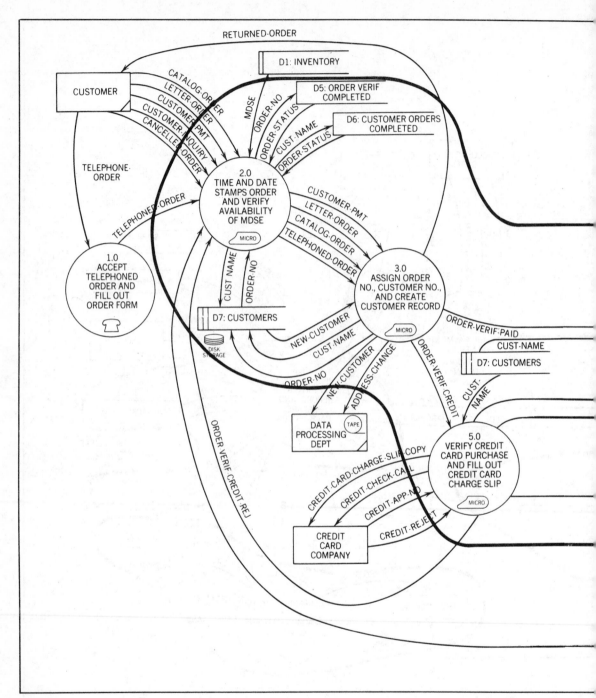

Figure 8-6 Physical data flow diagram showing maximum human–machine boundary (Alternative C).

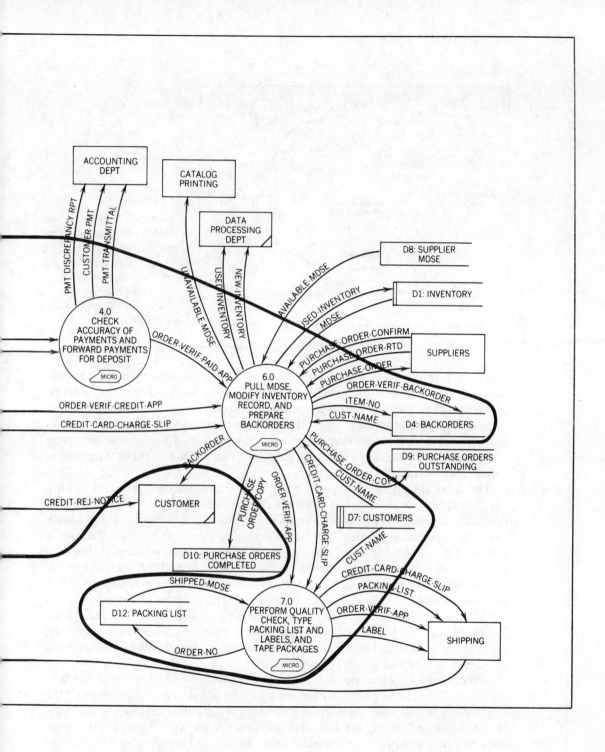

ACCOUNTING DEPT

CATALOG PRINTING

DATA PROCESSING DEPT

D8: SUPPLIER MDSE

D1: INVENTORY

SUPPLIERS

PMT DISCREPANCY RPT

CUSTOMER PMT

PMT TRANSMITTAL

UNAVAILABLE MDSE

USED INVENTORY

NEW INVENTORY

AVAILABLE MDSE

USED INVENTORY

MDSE

4.0 CHECK ACCURACY OF PAYMENTS AND FORWARD PAYMENTS FOR DEPOSIT

MICRO

ORDER VERIF PAID APP

PURCHASE ORDER CONFIRM

PURCHASE ORDER RTD

PURCHASE ORDER

ORDER VERIF BACKORDER

6.0 PULL MDSE, MODIFY INVENTORY RECORD, AND PREPARE BACKORDERS

MICRO

ORDER VERIF CREDIT APP

CREDIT CARD CHARGE SLIP

ITEM NO

CUST NAME

D4: BACKORDERS

D9: PURCHASE ORDERS OUTSTANDING

PURCHASE ORDER COPY

CUST NAME

BACKORDER

PURCHASE ORDER COPY

ORDER VERIF APP

CREDIT CARD CHARGE SLIP

CUST NAME

CREDIT REJ NOTICE

CUSTOMER

D7: CUSTOMERS

D10: PURCHASE ORDERS COMPLETED

SHIPPED MDSE

D12: PACKING LIST

7.0 PERFORM QUALITY CHECK, TYPE PACKING LIST AND LABELS, AND TAPE PACKAGES

MICRO

CUST NAME

CREDIT CARD CHARGE SLIP

PACKING LIST

ORDER VERIF APP

LABEL

SHIPPING

ORDER NO

359

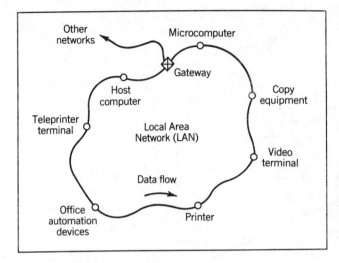

Figure 8-7 A local area network configuration. (Source: *Business Data Communications: Basic Concepts, Security, and Design,* by Jerry FitzGerald. New York: John Wiley & Sons, Inc., 1984, p. 139).

Figure 8-7 shows how a local area network might be configured. LANs are installed within a small area such as a building or several buildings on a single property. They connect word processors, computers, and so forth. When the need exists, these small networks can interconnect to outside telephone networks (called long-haul interexchange channels). The point of interconnection with these outside networks is called the gateway. The LAN at Sunrise Sportswear will be on a smaller scale.

The local area network you envision for Sunrise Sportswear begins with a microcomputer at process 3.0. This microcomputer can be a "file server" that enables a large number of files to be stored at this microcomputer. It has intelligent software that separates each user file so that other users access the files at process 3.0. A hard disk of 20–50 megabytes will be adequate to handle the data stores of the Sunrise Sportswear Order Processing system. With such a configuration, other processes designated for automation can be provided with either microprocessors or "dumb" terminals, depending on the need. Processes 5.0 and 7.0 will need microprocessors with text-editing capabilities, for example. Process 7.0 could use two printers. One would feed continuous form labels while the other could be used to print continuous form packing lists (continuous forms are described in Chapter 14 on Forms Design).

We still have much to do with structured tools, however, before we get into such details. At this point, all we have is a Level 0 physical data flow diagram. In reality, you would have decomposed the logical data flow diagram to its functional primitives during the last step, when you were working with the logical data flow diagram of the proposed system. You should now be converting these lower level processes to their physical form, just as we did earlier with Figure 8-3. In a system that is as manually oriented as the one at Sunrise Sportswear, it is easy to make this shift over from logical to physical. The reason is that the logic for each process is so close to being physical that it is difficult to keep it at the logical level. In a heavily computerized situation, the opposite may be true.

When all of the data flow diagram processes have been reduced to their lowest level, you will need to complete a minispecification for each one as we described in Chapter 2 (Figure 2-26) and Student Task 8 in Chapter 7. Remember that each minispecification must be accompanied by its pertinent logic documentation for the process. This logic documentation can be in the form of decision tables (Figures 2-20, 2-21, and 2-23 in Chapter 2), decision trees (Figure 2-22 in Chapter 2), structured English (Figure 2-24 in Chapter 2), or tight English (Figure 2-25 in Chapter 2). When we were talking about possible areas that could be automated, we mentioned that process 4.0 (payments) would have to have a policy on whether to bill or refund customers for discrepancies in the amount of payment sent. We do not know how Sunrise Sportswear has been handling this situation. Before the minispecification for process 4.0 can be completed, someone must make a policy decision on this matter. The question is, at what dollar amount do we issue an invoice or a refund check. If an order is $0.50, $1.00, or $1.50 off, do we ignore it, or process an invoice/refund check. A firm amount must be stated as a guideline. You will have to ask Sunrise Sportswear's management whether it is worth it to issue an invoice for $0.25 or $1.00; only they can make this decision.

Once the data flow diagrams are at their lowest level and the minispecifications and logic are complete, the terms in the data dictionary should be checked to make sure all have been taken into account (added or deleted). The data dictionary should be fairly well completed by this point and should not change much more. Remember, the data dictionary must have each of its data structures, data stores, or data flows defined completely as to the individual data elements that comprise each of them. For example, return to Figure 7-12 and refresh your memory on how the data structure BACKORDER was defined. Notice that each data element in the BACKORDER data structure was defined. By this time, you must have identified completely the individual data elements that make up each data structure in the data dictionary; that is, each data structure's contents must be defined by now.

After the data flow diagrams have been functionally decomposed to their lowest level, all data stores should be double checked as well. Did you find any new ones? Can you account for every data store number? Each time you shift from one of the Level 0 data flow diagrams to another, it is a good idea to arrange each data store in a numerical sequence to verify that any deleted ones are in fact deleted, and any new ones are in fact added. It is *very* easy to misnumber data stores or forget to put them on higher level data flow diagrams! For example, at this point in our Sunrise Sportswear case, we have data stores D1, D4–D10, and D12. We have deleted D2, D3, and D11. Our last data flow diagram (Figure 8-6) has all the data stores it is supposed to have. If you found any new ones during process decomposition, make sure they are added at this time.

When you are sure that all data stores have been taken into account, the normalization process can be completed. Remember that normalization is considered to be a *logical* process. Once the logic of the data dictionary has been described by the process of normalization, the physical data dictionary can be completed. The data store D1 physical data dictionary was shown in Figure 2-11 in Chapter 2. Describing the physical data dictionary is necessary. This physical description enables you to know how large each data element can be, which in turn tells you the maximum number of characters that must be taken into account for a specific data element. For example, consider street addresses. The number of the address can range all the way from "1" to what? In a large city, it is not at all unusual to have a five-digit street address; therefore, you must leave at least five spaces. Perhaps you should leave even more. The street name also can vary widely. "Maple St" takes only eight characters (you must include the space between the words), but "Massachusetts Ave, NW" takes 21 characters. In other words, you must obtain the users' help in determining what each data element looks like and what it's possible maximum character size may be.

As was pointed out in Chapter 2, structured analysis is network oriented while structured design is hierarchical. During the analysis phase, you developed network-oriented data flow diagrams. Now you are nearing the end of the system design and preparing for eventual implementation. To make this transition, you develop modular and hierarchical system structure charts, in addition to the data structure diagrams and data access diagrams. This is done by converting the final data flow diagrams to system structure charts (you may wish to reread the Chapter 2 section on System Structure Charts). As we did previously, we will help you through this process by converting the Figure 8-8 data flow diagram to a system structure chart. Figure 8-8 was developed from process bubble 3.0 of Figure 8-3, and it is the functional primitive level. Also shown is the manual (non-automated) versus the computerized (automated) boundary.

To obtain the first rough draft of the system structure chart, the central transform in Figure 8-8 must be identified. Then a decision must be made on whether to create a new top control module (new boss) or use the central transform that is identified as the top control module. When examining Figure 8-8, recall that the primary reason for its existence is to assign customer numbers and then to obtain information on new customers so that the Sunrise Sportswear catalog can be sent to a wider base of customers. In addition, we learned that Sunrise Sportswear has never had any formal means of collecting address changes for its old customers. Since Mr. Reynolds and Valery Brunn agreed to centralize the checking for new customers, it is logical to place old customer address changes at the same process as new customer record creation. As a result, the central transform in Figure 8-8 is process 3.8.

Now assume that process 3.8 was chosen as the central transform. Also assume that we decided to use the central transform as the top control module (the boss). We now lift bubble 3.8 off the printed page (remember the example of the mobile in Chapter 2). The other bubbles hang down from the central transform so that the first rough draft looks like this.

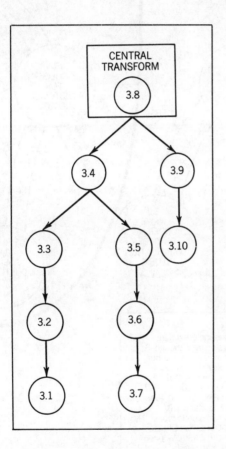

Now, as we proceed toward the final system structure chart, we must refine and develop detail from the above draft structure chart. Using this draft, processes 3.1, 3.2, and 3.3 are eliminated because they are manual operations (assigning order numbers and writing the order number on checks and on the Order

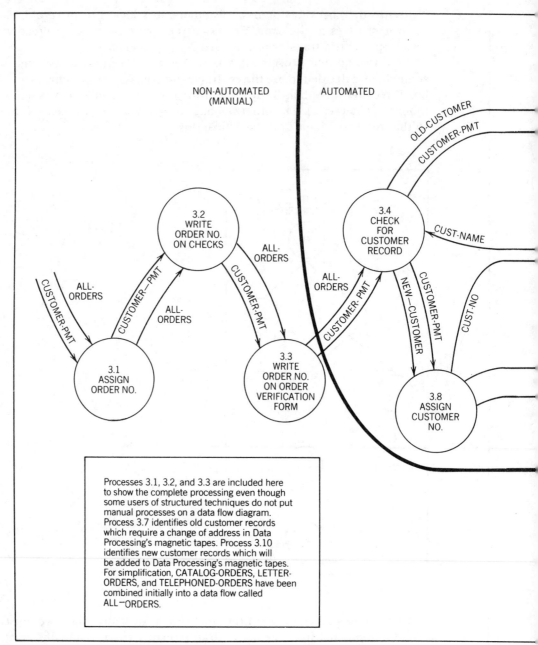

NON-AUTOMATED
(MANUAL)

AUTOMATED

Processes 3.1, 3.2, and 3.3 are included here
to show the complete processing even though
some users of structured techniques do not put
manual processes on a data flow diagram.
Process 3.7 identifies old customer records
which require a change of address in Data
Processing's magnetic tapes. Process 3.10
identifies new customer records which will
be added to Data Processing's magnetic tapes.
For simplification, CATALOG-ORDERS, LETTER-
ORDERS, and TELEPHONED-ORDERS have been
combined initially into a data flow called
ALL–ORDERS.

Figure 8-8 Decomposition of process bubble 3.0 from Figure 8-3.

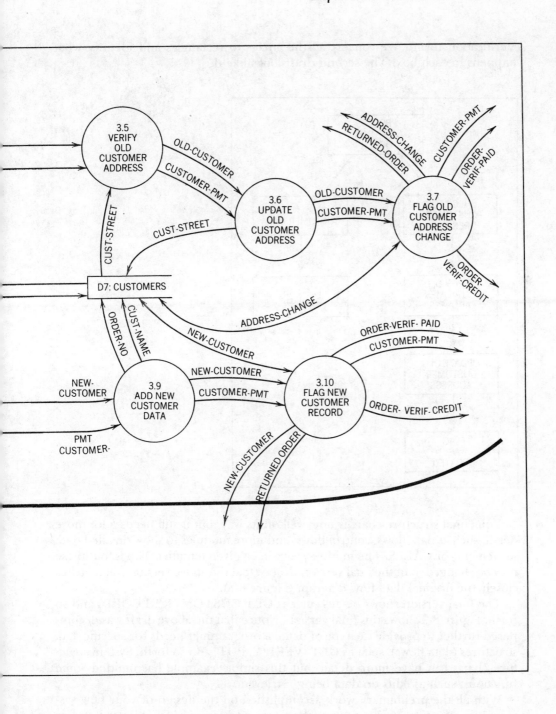

Verification form). We convert all the circles to rectangles and identify what happens in each box. The second draft looks like this.

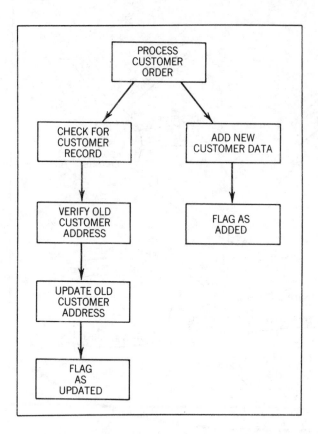

Your final structure chart is now well on its way, but it still needs a lot more detail, such as data flows, control flows, and more modules to show detailed data movements or CALLS. The modules have been given tentative names, but these may be changed to fit the final version. Notice that the above version still matches closely the original data flow diagram (Figure 8-8).

The final version shows details such as GET CUSTOMER RECORD, and so forth. Figure 8-9 shows this final version. Notice that the above draft was decomposed further to provide the type of detail a programmer needs for specific data structures (data flows), such as GET, VERIFY, PUT, and so forth. System structure charts can have more detail, but this simple example has omitted some functions, such as edits on data being retrieved.

With all the preliminary work accomplished on the design of your new system, you now can work on what the users want their video displays and/or

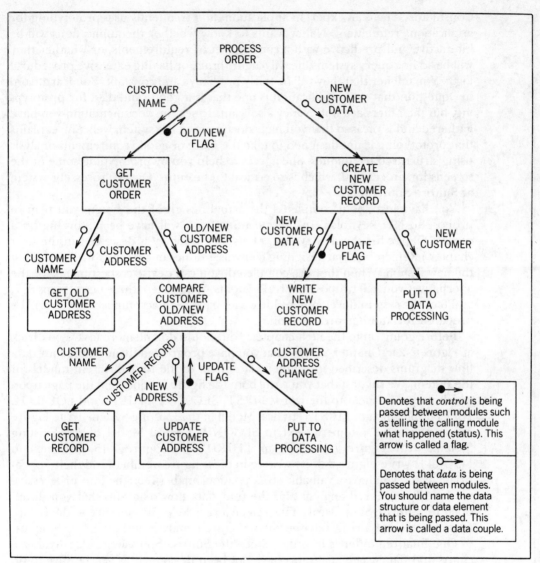

Figure 8-9 System structure chart for process bubble 3.0.

computer-generated reports to look like. If prototyping is unavailable, you do this by purchasing pads of CRT Layout Forms. Such forms provide 80 to 132 characters per line for 24 lines, plus a line for status control. You lay out each screen format on this form. There is one form per screen, so if the system is menu-driven, each menu selection should have a layout form.

You decide to consult with your friend Nancy back at Casper Management

Consultants. She is an expert in applications and frequently uses prototyping for applications refinement. Nancy wants to know whether the applications will be interactive and predictive with a constant set of requirements, or whether they will be ad hoc query systems, heavily algorithmic, or having extensive procedural logic. You tell her that they will be fairly predictive and constant. You learn from her question that your application is one that is a good candidate for prototyping, but the others are not. Nancy also wants to see the documentation you have gathered and is pleased that you have documented the system well. She explains that prototyping is not designed to take the place of good requirements analysis using structured techniques. She agrees to help you by prototyping some of the screens for process 3.0, which is so critical to the entire Order Processing system at Sunrise Sportswear.

You have just about completed the actual design of the system you plan to propose to Mr. Reynolds. In the meantime, you will have been working on a control matrix for the new system. (This methodology is described in the next chapter.) Remember that designing controls is done concurrently with designing the new system. When they are completed, you can devise cost estimates for the alternatives you will propose to Mr. Reynolds. When these three tasks (Steps 6, 7, and 8 of the system development life cycle) have been accomplished, you will be prepared for another presentation.

Before going on to the next chapter, you should do one more task. Look back at Figure 2-2 in Chapter 2. Now that you have progressed through the four data flow diagrams described in it, interrelate them to the four different models of the system. We suggest that you write both the figure number and the page upon which it appears next to the words FIRST, SECOND, THIRD, and FOURTH. For example, next to FIRST: Physical Model of the Existing System, write Figure 5-6 and its page number. Next to SECOND: Logical Model of the Existing System, write Figure 7-11; next to THIRD write Figure 7-15, and next to FOURTH write Figure 8-3. By writing in these figure numbers and their appropriate pages, you have a valuable cross-relationship between the four progressive models of structured analysis and the four data flow diagrams that you developed for Sunrise Sportswear. This will be a very helpful reference in the future when you design a real system using structured analysis and design techniques.

One final reminder is in order. Since the Sunrise Sportswear data structure charts and data access diagrams have not been developed as yet, be sure to do Student Tasks 2 and 3 for this chapter so that your documentation will be complete.

Student Questions

1. There always are two alternatives to solving problems such as those at Sunrise Sportswear. Name them.

2. What is the primary change that takes place when you make the transition from the logical data flow diagram of the proposed system to the physical data flow diagram of the proposed system?

3. What is the purpose of drawing the human–machine boundary?

4. Of what does the logical model of the proposed system consist? Contrast the logical model with the physical model.

5. Name the steps required to compile a data dictionary. Put them in their natural sequence.

6. Name the steps required to convert processes from the existing system to a proposed system that is ready for implementation.

Student Tasks

1. Using the data store contents list that you developed in Student Task 6 of Chapter 7, compile a physical data dictionary for data store D7: CUS-TOMERS.

2. Using your normalized data store D7 (from Student Task 7 of Chapter 7), draw a data structure diagram that shows the interrelationships between D7 and other automated data stores.

3. Using your normalized D7 data store (from Student Task 7 of Chapter 7) and any other data store information, draw a data access diagram.

4. Complete a File Sheet (Figure 7-9 in Chapter 7) to show data store D2 which you will be combining with data store D7. Also complete one for D7. What are the differences between the contents of the two data stores?

Selected Readings

1. Auerbach Publishers, Inc. *Auerbach Computer Technology Reports* (formerly *Auerbach Standard EDP Reports*). Pensauken, N.J.: Auerbach Publishers, Inc., 1962– . [Updated monthly.]

2. Campbell, Gordon. "Proponents of Data, Function Design Schools Battle It Out," *Computing Canada,* vol. 10, no. 16, August 9, 1984, p. 4. [Advantages and disadvantages of output-driven and function-driven structured design.]

3. Cohen, Henry B. "Developing User-Friendly Systems," *Journal of Information Systems Management,* vol. 1, no. 1, Winter 1984, pp. 32–39.

4. Datapro Research Corporation. *Datapro Research Reports* series. Delran, N.J.: Datapro Research Corporation, 1969– . [Updated monthly.]

5. DeBono, Edward. *New Think: The Use of Lateral Thinking in the Generation of New Ideas.* New York: Basic Books, Inc., 1968.
6. Hansen, H. Dines. *Up & Running: A Case Study of Successful Systems Development.* New York: Yourdon Press, 1984. [Demonstrates real-world applications of structured techniques.]
7. Martin, Merle P., and William L. Fuerst. "Communications Framework for Systems Design," *Journal of Systems Management,* vol. 35, no. 3, March 1984, pp. 18–25.
8. Plunkett, Lorne C., and Guy A. Hale. *The Proactive Manager: The Complete Book of Problem Solving and Decision Making.* New York, John Wiley & Sons, Inc., 1984.

Questions

1. Name the three parallel steps that are performed simultaneously during this stage of the SDLC.
2. Define the terms "problem" and "problem solving."
3. Identify three factors that can facilitate the system design process.
4. With what is systems design mainly concerned?
5. What does the analyst do during the design phase?
6. Identify three of the levels of dependence among individual job procedures within a new system.
7. Identify the four logical steps that are used in designing a new system.
8. Identify at least five different video screen design formats that can be used.
9. Identify the typical ways in which a terminal can be used as an output device.
10. When would the telephone directory method be used instead of the menu selection method when designing a video screen format?

SITUATION CASES

Case 8-1:   *Data Network Corporation*

The Data Network Corporation manufactures and distributes data communication hardware, such as modems, multiplexers, and intelligent terminal controllers. The organization has been in business for 14 months and employs 11 people. Its sales area primarily consists of the western United States.

The network sales manager felt that market conditions were such that sales could be doubled, or even tripled, if production was increased. The manager of production, however, indicated that she was having some difficulties expanding production. As a result, the people who put up the venture capital money hired a consultant systems analyst to help decide the best approach for expanding production, or determine if they should hold the same production levels and forego the expansion.

The first thing the analyst did was identify all of the problems and write them down in a list so he would be more inclined to solve only one problem at a time. After learning the background, interactions, and understanding the existing system, the analyst then identified all the new requirements that would be necessary in order to expand production. Next, he divided the remaining design effort into three major steps as a means of following a logical step-by-step approach toward finding the most cost-effective alternatives. The analyst's first step was to pursue a line of lateral thinking which involved system outputs and working through the system. The next step was to evaluate the ideas that had been identified.

In checking with the production manager, the analyst noted that the four different machines used throughout the manufacturing process were all more than five years old (they had been purchased in the used market) and, therefore, the assembly line operation for circuit boards had reached its assembly capacity. At this point, the analyst began to explore possible alternatives. With the close cooperation of the production manager, four alternatives were identified. First, the company could keep the existing machines. Second, they could add one more final assembly machine and increase production marginally. Third, they could sell all the other machines and purchase newer high speed equipment. Fourth, they could extend operations to three shifts instead of the current two-shift operation.

Next, the analyst divided the different alternatives into attainable and unattainable sets. During this process, the analyst noted that because of cash-flow problems, the company was not in a position to purchase new equipment and, as a result, his attainable set included only three alternatives.

Since the company's labor force was unionized, it could be difficult to obtain approval for running a third or midnight shift. Also, technical assembly personnel were difficult to hire in this work area. The first alternative was considered to be the least favored alternative because of the president's desire to expand production. This was followed closely by the fourth alternative. The analyst decided that the second alternative was the most favorable and began further discussions with the production manager to get her tentative approval before making a final recommendation to the president and the people who raised the venture capital money for the organization. Knowing that this approval was very important, the analyst described the favored alternative in a very positive approach. He told the production manager that this alternative was the only one. The favored alternative was presented in black and white terms, which totally eliminated the other three. If the alternative was not accepted, the firm would meet a catastrophe down the road.

Questions

1. Discuss the analyst's approach or actions in trying to gain the production manager's prior approval before going to the president and venture capitalists.

2. What else should the analyst have done first in following the logical step-by-step approach?

Case 8-2:   *Micro Manufacturing Company*

A systems analyst who was employed by the Micro Manufacturing Company was given a high priority assignment directly from top management. They wanted a system that would increase the delivery time of disks to their customers.

In meeting with the marketing manager for Micro, the analyst learned that customers were not receiving their goods on time. This repetitive discrepancy was causing Micro to lose many loyal customers. It was the analyst's task to perform a systems study and report back to management within three weeks with a proposal for a new system design.

After performing the first five steps of a full systems study, the analyst approached the design phase by first assembling all the facts pertaining to the problem. For example, by the end of the first week he had gathered general information, investigated interactions between the related areas, and analyzed the existing system.

After a thorough review of this information, the systems analyst accurately defined the problem and its causes. It seemed that Production was unable to comply with the schedules given to them by the Order Entry Department, but the source of the problem was in the Sales Department. The salespeople were making promises to customers without any knowledge of the production workload. The analyst decided to design a communication system that would coordinate the efforts of the Sales, Order Entry, and Production Departments.

With all the facts in mind, the analyst decided to just THINK about the problem. He concentrated his thoughts in searching for a "choice-set" of all available alternatives to produce a system that would satisfy the on-time efficiency of production.

First he applied lateral thinking, or exploring all the different ways of looking at the system. This method seemed to be unsuccessful, so he switched to a vertical approach. The major drawback the analyst encountered in using vertical thinking was the occurrence of dominant ideas. He was familiar with these hindering thoughts and knew how to cope with them. When the analyst felt an idea persisting, he would write the idea on paper. For him, this was all that was required to free his mind and open channels for creative thinking.

Because time was a problem, the analyst immediately discarded all ideas he believed to be irrelevant or foolish and at the end of each day he briefly reviewed all unresolved problems. He also tried to be perfectly correct at each step when visualizing designs for his new system. In doing so, the analyst believed he would achieve maximum creativity.

Two weeks passed and the analyst was one week ahead of management's time schedule. He decided to take advantage of being ahead of schedule by reporting to management without any further delay. In doing so, he thought management would be impressed with his promptness.

With a feeling of confidence the analyst took what he had designed and sought management's approval on his new design for a communications system.

Questions

1. Did Micro's systems analyst follow the correct sequence, using a "step-by-step" approach in the design of his new system? Explain.
2. What were the two mistakes the analyst made during his THINK process which may have limited creativity?
3. At the end of the case, was the systems analyst really ready to seek management's tentative approval or was there something he forgot to do immediately before that?

Chapter 9

DESIGNING NEW SYSTEM CONTROLS

LEARNING OBJECTIVES

You will learn how to . . .

□ Construct a matrix of controls.

□ Evaluate the controls in your new system design.

□ Relate a controls matrix to the data flow diagrams of structured analysis.

□ Identify the specific controls required for the new system.

□ Develop audit (transaction) trails.

□ Convert data flow diagram processes for use in a controls matrix.

The Need for Controls

A successful new system in today's sophisticated, rapidly changing business environment must be built upon a solid framework of operational and accounting controls. The management of a firm is responsible for establishing and maintaining adequate internal controls. In fact, the establishment and maintenance of such a system of internal controls is a significant management obligation.

To emphasize the need for controls further, it should be noted that in recent years, organizations increasingly have become dependent upon computer hardware, software, and data processing personnel. This commitment to computerization has changed the potential vulnerability of the organization's assets because the traditional security, audit, and control mechanisms take on a new and different form in a computer-based system.

A complex on-line data communication-oriented system consists of various combinations of hardware, software, facilities, people, and the policies and procedures that interrelate these components. The many diverse components and potential entry points into a complex on-line system make it possible for a person with sufficient technical or applications knowledge to enter the system to make unauthorized manipulations of data, programs, or operational procedures. Furthermore, control procedures for an on-line system cut across many lines of responsibility within an organization, creating a control problem in itself. For instance, several departments within an organization may share in the exercise of the control procedures and each department may be responsible for only one segment of the overall control plan. The integration of controls among the various components of such a complex on-line system is the infrastructure upon which a secure on-line data communication-oriented system must be based.

This increased reliance on computers, the consolidation of many previously manual operations onto computer systems, the shared responsibility between different departments for control procedures, and the fact that on-line systems cut across many lines of responsibility have increased management's concern about the adequacy of the present control mechanisms in use in the EDP environment.

While the use of computers is rising, it is also evident that a far greater potential exists to control errors and omissions, disastrous events, fraud, and other adverse occurrences in automated systems than in the manual systems they have replaced. Finally, management's concern over adequate controls will be negated if the data processing system designers, EDP auditors, and their managers do not have the proper training and control techniques to utilize when designing or reviewing the internal controls associated with on-line computerized systems.

The systems analyst must be able to appreciate both systems and application controls in order to design and implement effective, efficient, and well-con-

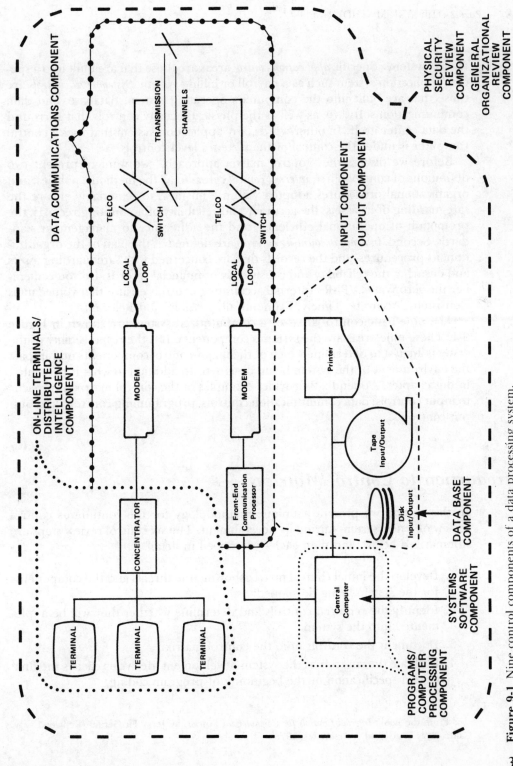

Figure 9-1 Nine control components of a data processing system.

PHYSICAL SECURITY REVIEW COMPONENT

GENERAL ORGANIZATIONAL REVIEW COMPONENT

DATA COMMUNICATIONS COMPONENT

TRANSMISSION CHANNELS

TELCO SWITCH

LOCAL LOOP

MODEM

TELCO SWITCH

LOCAL LOOP

MODEM

Front-End Communication Processor

CONCENTRATOR

TERMINAL

TERMINAL

TERMINAL

ON-LINE TERMINALS/ DISTRIBUTED INTELLIGENCE COMPONENT

Printer

Tape Input/Output

Disk Input/Output

INPUT COMPONENT OUTPUT COMPONENT

DATA BASE COMPONENT

Central Computer

SYSTEMS SOFTWARE COMPONENT

PROGRAMS/ COMPUTER PROCESSING COMPONENT

trolled systems. Specific *application control* areas are those that are built into a specific application system such as a payroll or billing system. *System level controls* are those that are built into the computer's operating system, database, and data communication software, as well as the physical security controls that surround the data center itself. In other words, any application system that uses a central computer is under the control of the system's level controls.

Before we discuss the "control matrix approach," we want to present two definitions of control. First, *internal control* refers to all the methods, policies, and organizational procedures adopted within a business to reasonably ensure the safeguarding of its assets, the accuracy and reliability of accounting records, the promotion of operational efficiency, and the adherence to management standards. Second, *internal accounting controls* are defined as the plan of the organization, its procedures, and the records that are concerned with safeguarding assets and ensuring the reliability and consistency of financial records. Do you remember the acronym CATER? Internal accounting controls ensure that your data is Consistent, Accurate, Timely, Economically feasible, and Relevant.

The nine basic control areas of a computerized system are shown in Figure 9-1. These nine areas are the system's components. It is the responsibility of the systems analyst to determine which of the major control components may impact the environment of the system being designed. In addition to what is presented in this chapter, Appendix 2 provides examples of the control matrix approach[1] to input controls, data communication controls, programming controls, and output controls.

Introduction to Control Matrices

In this section we present a unique methodology for the continuous control review of a new system during its development. The six control review steps are summarized below, and then each is described in detail.

1. Develop the initial control matrix showing the threats and the components for the system being developed.
2. Identify the required controls and determine whether they will be implemented into the system.
3. Document the controls onto the control matrix.
4. Evaluate the controls as the system development life cycle reaches the final system specification or the beginning of program coding.

---

[1] From the book, *Internal Controls for Computerized Systems,* by Jerry FitzGerald (Redwood City, Calif.: Jerry FitzGerald & Associates, 1978).

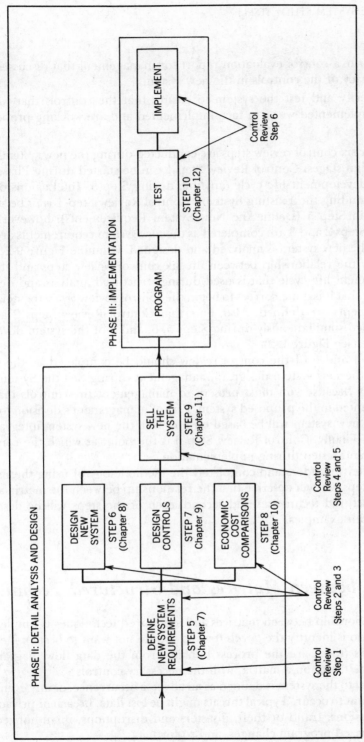

Figure 9-2 Control review steps related to the system development life cycle.

379

5. Write a control evaluation report for management that discusses the adequacy of the controls in the new system.
6. Verify and test the system to ensure that the controls that were to be implemented were, in fact, implemented and are working properly.

These six control review steps are conducted during the new system's analysis and design stages. Control Review Step 1 can be started during Phase I of the system development life cycle (anytime during Step 3: Interactions or Step 4: Understanding the Existing System). Control Review Step 1 *must* be started no later than Step 5 (Define the New System Requirements), however. Control Review Steps 2 and 3 are completed as the new system requirements are defined and as the new system is analyzed and designed. Examine Figure 9-2, in which we show the relationship between the six control review steps and the system development life cycle that is used during structured analysis and design. Remember that it is quite correct to begin the control review *before* the new system's requirements are defined. Also, note that Control Review Steps 2 and 3 are performed simultaneously during Steps 5, 6, and 8 of the system development life cycle (see Figure 9-2).

Steps 4 and 5 of the control review should be completed by the time you present the new system design to management during Sell the System. This is necessary because you must present to management the controls that will be implemented in the proposed system. Part of management's decision to proceed with the new system will be based on how well the new system integrates these controls. Finally, Control Review Step 6 is the point at which the controls are verified and tested during implementation.

In order to understand completely the methodology of using the six control review steps, we will describe first the relationship between the matrix approach and structured techniques and second, each of the steps will be described in detail, with examples.

Relationship between Matrices and Structured Techniques

The relationship between matrices and structured techniques is simple. All you need to do is identify the *threats* (events you do not want to occur), identify the *components* (these are the process bubbles from the data flow diagrams), and interrelate them, on a matrix, with the necessary controls.

A *threat* to the system is defined as an adverse occurrence, or any event that we do not want to occur. Typical threats might be lost data, breach of privacy, errors and omissions, fraud or theft, disasters and disruptions, unauthorized access, unauthorized program changes, and so forth.

A *component* is one of the individual parts or pieces of the system that, when assembled together, make up the entire system. In our case, the components are the process bubbles that have been defined already in our data flow diagrams. If you look back to Figure 2-7 in Chapter 2, you will see that the components for that system are (1.0) VERIFY ORDER, (2.0) VERIFY CREDIT, (3.0) APPLY PAYMENT, (4.0) ENTER NEW CUSTOMER, (5.0) VERIFY INVENTORY, and (6.0) PREPARE SHIPPING NOTICE AND INVOICE. For those systems analysts who do not use structured analysis and design techniques, the process symbols from system flowcharts can be used. Another alternative to using process bubbles might be to identify the major components (individual pieces of a system), such as terminals, data communications, central computer, application programs, systems programs, terminal operators, management personnel, paper forms, data files (database), reports, and so forth.

Because we are using structured techniques, our matrix uses the threats that we relate to our new system and the components are the processes from our data flow diagrams. Figure 9-3 illustrates an initial matrix built upon Figure 2-7 from Chapter 2 (ignore the numbers 1 and 3 in the cells for now).

Control Review Step 1

This step begins during the defining of the new system's requirements or before, such as during the understanding of the existing system. At this point, the *control review team* identifies all of the threats and components (process bubbles) that face our new system. The term "control review team" is used because the systems analyst should get some assistance at this point. The control matrix should be identified and documented by a team that represents three viewpoints. These viewpoints are the data processing department, the user department, and the audit department. It does not matter whether the systems analyst leads the control review part of the project or whether the auditor does this. In fact, it often is better to have a member of the internal audit department lead the task of developing controls.

To identify the threats facing a new system you should assemble the control review team and conduct a two- or three-hour brainstorming session. The purpose of this session is to identify all of the threats to the system that is being developed. In other words, the user, the data processor, and the auditor identify those events that they do not want to occur (the threats). At this point, write the name of each threat in a list and add a one- or two-sentence description to define the meaning of each threat.

One thing that may help identify the threats is for you to use the list of components (the individual processes that were identified in the data flow diagram). During this brainstorming session, discuss a process and list all of the

COMPONENTS	THREATS					
	ERRORS AND OMISSIONS	THEFT	UNAUTHORIZED ACCESS	BREACH OF PRIVACY	LOST DATA	DISASTERS AND DISRUPTIONS
1.0 VERIFY ORDER	1					
2.0 VERIFY CREDIT	1					
3.0 APPLY PAYMENT	1	3				3
4.0 ENTER NEW CUSTOMER	1					
5.0 VERIFY INVENTORY	1					
6.0 PREPARE SHIP NOTICE AND INVOICE	1					

Figure 9-3 Initial matrix without controls.

possible threats to that process. After discussing each process individually, along with its related threats, assemble them together into one master list of all the threats. It is important that you pick a short one- or two-word name for each threat. It is this name that goes across the top of the matrix as you saw in Figure 9-3. Remember, each threat must have a unique name as well as a definition.

At this point, if you are not using structured techniques, the design review team has to identify all of the component parts of the system. Remember, the component parts can be taken from the flowchart symbols (if you use system flowcharts) or they may have to be identified during the brainstorming session. When the component parts have to be identified during the brainstorming session (because you do not have data flow diagrams) the control review team identifies them from their perceived knowledge of the system. We introduced this idea earlier in this chapter when we listed component parts such as terminals, data communications, central computer, application programs, system programs, terminal operators, management personnel, paper forms, data files (database), reports, and so forth.

Once the control review team has identified all of the threats and the components (process bubbles from the data flow diagrams), you have the initial matrix that is used for the identification, documentation, and evaluation of the system of internal controls that is to be implemented in the new system. Go back and look at Figure 9-3 because this is what your initial matrix looks like before identifying the necessary controls (again, ignore the numbers 1 and 3 in the cells for now). Notice that you have put a descriptive name for each threat and each component along the appropriate axis of the two-dimensional matrix. You also should have a complete definition for each threat and each component written on a separate piece of paper.

Using the example in Figure 9-3, the threats might be defined as follows.

□ *Errors and omissions.* The accidental or intentional creation of error during processing of the data, including data omissions. This includes errors and omissions in the application programs, data communications, microcomputers, software, or human mistakes made during manual processes.

□ *Theft.* Refers to safeguarding the organization's assets (including information assets) from their unauthorized removal, either by persons trusted by the organization (employees, vendors), or by outsiders who are not related directly to the organization. Includes embezzlement, fraud, and outright theft.

□ *Unauthorized access.* Refers to unauthorized access to the database, data center, microcomputers, and so forth. It allows most users to have access to specified areas, while a few may have full access to all areas.

□ *Breach of privacy.* Protects against the accidental or intentional release of personal information about an individual that is improper to the normal conduct of business. It also refers to the protection of private data with regard to the organization.

☐ *Lost data.* Refers to the failure of restart and recovery of application programs, data communications, and software that causes lost data.

☐ *Disasters and disruptions.* This refers to a major interruption (natural or intentional) that would disrupt the database, data center, data communications, microcomputers, and the like.

We are not going to define what is meant by each of the components at this point because their definitions depend on what happens in the process bubbles in any given situation. When all threats and components have been defined, you are ready to proceed to Control Review Step 2.

Control Review Step 2

This step is the longest of the entire process because it is paced by the speed of the analysis and design. This is the step at which you identify those controls that may be appropriate for this system and, hopefully, get the concurrence of the entire control review team that these controls will be implemented into the new system.

It is during this step that you have to be very creative; you must possess the skills to work effectively with other people in order to gain their concurrence on the necessary controls. During this step, the matrix is used like a questionnaire. For example, look at the matrix in Figure 9-3. Find the intersection cell for the threat, Errors and Omissions, and the component, (1.0) VERIFY ORDER (this cell is in the upper left corner of Figure 9-3). The question you pose with regard to the cell is, What controls can we implement to mitigate or stop errors and omissions from occurring during the order verification process?

As another example, look at the cell intersection of the threat, Lost Data, and the component, (5.0) VERIFY INVENTORY. With this one you might ask the question, What controls can we implement to mitigate or stop lost data during the process of verifying the inventory? Do you see how, if you were to lose data during the process VERIFY INVENTORY, you probably would lose customer orders and/or lose control of the amount of inventory that you currently have in stock?

You now can see that each cell of the matrix is an individual question to be proposed to the entire design team. In other words, your goal is to identify enough controls for each cell in order to achieve an overall system of controls that is acceptable for the system being designed.

The object of a control matrix is to ensure that there are adequate controls in each cell, or to have good justification for the lack of adequate controls in each cell. Obviously, good justification includes such reasons as: the control is too costly, there are no known controls that we can utilize in this cell, or the risk factor is so low that it is not worth implementing controls for that individual cell.

The controls identified in each cell may be recommended by auditors, user department personnel, or data processors. User personnel usually are good at suggesting logical controls. A *logical control* is one that pertains to the logical framework of the business system being computerized. Data processing personnel usually are best at suggesting technical controls. A *technical control* is one that pertains to the computer hardware, software, application programs, data communication network, or other data processing facilities to be utilized in the new computerized business system. Auditors are best at suggesting management-oriented controls and controls that are effected through legal requirements. *Management-proposed controls* are those controls that are required by middle and upper management. Middle and upper management personnel look for overall financial controls and controls that will enhance the operation of a system to make it more efficient. The legal aspect involves those controls that are necessary because of some law or regulatory agency requirement.

As the controls are identified, write them down in a list. In other words, each control that you have *discussed seriously* should be on your list. This list starts with number 1 and goes on through however many controls you identify. The purpose of writing the complete description of each control on a list is so you can place the appropriate number that corresponds to each control onto the matrix. You can see already that it would be impossible to include the full narrative description of each control in each of the small cells of our matrix; therefore, we place the number of a control in the appropriate cell of the matrix instead.

Let us look at Figure 9-4 to see a typical controls list. Notice that the controls are numbered 1–41, or however many you have identified. Also notice that there is a narrative that describes each control. The disposition of the control is indicated at the end of the narrative description. For example, you should note whether the control has been accepted for implementation, rejected for cause, or deferred until later in the system development process.

When a control is accepted for implementation, it is wise to determine at that time who or which department is responsible for the implementation (installation) of the accepted control. Further, when a control is rejected for cause or deferred until later in the system development process, you should write down the reasons for rejection of the control, or a future date when the temporarily deferred control can be reevaluated.

As you can see now, Control Review Step 2 involves identifying controls that can be placed into each of the cells of our original matrix (Figure 9-3). When you are discussing potential controls, many of them will be rejected for a valid cause. We suggest that you include these rejected controls in your overall list of controls to provide future documentation as to what was discussed and what was rejected.

SAMPLE CONTROLS LIST

1. Let the system perform automated and/or preprogrammed editing for all input such as: reasonableness checks, test for blanks, check for consistency between fields, conduct a limit test, checking for completeness, sequence checking, self-checking numbers, or dual entry of critical data. (Accepted for implementation; 12/15/86). To be implemented by the application programmers.

2. Develop listings for erroneous data and use these to ensure that the entries have been corrected and reentered into the system. Consider having this be an on-line file that would operate in a real-time fashion. (Rejected because of high programming cost; 12/20/86.)

3. Keep a count on the number of program instructions executed, run time, any other application-oriented data, sensitive programs, or sensitive program interfaces. These can be compared periodically with similar data from a prior period to reveal irregularities and track automated transactions. (Accepted for implementation; 1/14/87.) To be implemented by the system programming department.

41. Utilize a minicomputer-based badge recording system to restrict access to and from the major central terminal areas as well as the central computer site itself. (Deferred until decision on new building is final; 1/29/87.) Check next December.

Figure 9-4 Controls list.

Most system methodologies only keep what was accepted for implementation. At a future date, it may be very important to be able to know or justify why you did not implement a certain control. The point is, if you took the time to discuss a control and rejected it, why not write the description of that control on the master controls list in case it is needed later?

Control Review Step 3

As the various controls are identified and discussed (during Control Review Step 2), and their disposition is determined, the control review team next places these controls within the appropriate cells of the matrix. It is always obvious into which cell the control should be placed. This is because you would have been discussing a specific cell, such as Errors and Omissions versus (1.0) VERIFY ORDER, when you identified a potential control candidate. As you add a new control to your list and give it the next number in sequence, you write that number into the cell that you currently are discussing. Placing each control into its so-called primary cell is not enough. You must place the appropriate control (actually its number from the list) into *all* of the cells to which it offers some sort of protection. In order to place a specific control into the proper cells of the matrix, you must ask yourself two specific questions about each control. These questions are

1. Which threat or threats would this control help mitigate? In other words, would it, hopefully, stop the threat?
2. Which component or components will this control safeguard? In other words, will it safeguard the components?

Let us look at the first control on the sample controls list in Figure 9-4. Read that control and identify into which cell it should be placed in the matrix of Figure 9-3. By asking ourselves the first question (Which threat or threats would this control help mitigate?), we might decide that automated editing would help mitigate only one of the threats, Errors and Omissions. Now ask the second question, Which component or components does this control safeguard? By looking at the components of Figure 9-3, it appears that automated editing would offer us some protection for control with regard to all six of our components. Therefore, the number 1 is placed in each of the six cells below the threat Errors and Omissions. Now you see why we already have placed the number 1 down the Errors and Omissions column in Figure 9-3. For another example, look at control number 3 in the sample controls list of Figure 9-4. In control 3 we maintain a count of the number of program instructions for security purposes. If we ask ourselves the first question with regard to control number 3 (Which threat or threats would this control mitigate?), we might be able to say that this control would help mitigate both the threats of Theft and Disaster and Disruptions. Now look at the second question, Which component or components does this control safeguard? In this case it appears that keeping a count of the number of program instructions for security purposes applies primarily to component 3.0 and, secondarily, to any other component that has an automated program function. In this example, let us assume that our final decision is that it applies only to component 3.0. In that case the control number 3 appears in our matrix (see Figure 9-3) as shown.

As you can see, your task is to identify appropriate controls (Control Review Step 2) and then to place these controls into their proper cells (Control Review Step 3). As you discuss a particular cell as it relates to a control, you always know that the control number goes into that cell, although you do not know how many other cells should have this same number. You determine this by asking yourself the two key questions that we have been discussing.

At the conclusion of Control Review Step 3 you will have a matrix of controls that looks like the one shown in Figure 9-5. Notice that there are some empty cells. This may come about because there are no known controls for that cell or the cost of the known controls is too great for the new system. Also, notice that there are breaks in the numbering system. In other words, it appears that there

THREATS

COMPONENTS	ERRORS AND OMISSIONS	THEFT	UNAUTHORIZED ACCESS	BREACH OF PRIVACY	LOST DATA	DISASTERS AND DISRUPTIONS
1.0 VERIFY ORDER	1,7	11,19	17	11	4	5,14
2.0 VERIFY CREDIT	1,2	2	2	2,13	13	5,14
3.0 APPLY PAYMENT	1,20	3,16,21	17,20			3,14
4.0 ENTER NEW CUSTOMER	1	9		10	10	10,14
5.0 VERIFY INVENTORY	1,8	8,19	8	8	8,25	8,14
6.0 PREPARE SHIP NOTICE AND INVOICE	1	9,15	A	12,24	15,24	14
			← New recommendation			

Figure 9-5 Matrix at end of Control Review Step 3.

are some missing numbers. In fact, there are missing numbers because we did not copy onto this matrix the numbers of any of the controls that were either rejected or deferred. This matrix contains only the numbers for controls that were accepted for implementation.

As the analysis and design effort approaches the completion of the written system specification, the beginning of program coding, or the formal design freeze point, the matrix should have all of the control numbers that pertain to the controls that have been accepted for implementation. The matrix may have some new or modified threats too. Remember, at the beginning of this control matrix effort, you may not have been able to identify all of the specific threats to the exact level of detail that may have been required. In that case, you may have added new threats or made some of them more detailed. Also, you might have developed some detailed micro matrices.

A *detailed micro matrix* is a separate matrix that is built by using components from one of the more detailed data flow diagrams. In this case, you might build a micro matrix using the components (process bubbles) from a Level 1, Level 2, Level 3, or lower, data flow diagram. You build such a micro matrix using lower level data flow diagrams *only* if you need extra control detail. You might even build a specialized micro matrix utilizing the same components from your original (Level 0) data flow diagram, but expanding one of the threats into its micro detail. For example, you could take the matrix from Figure 9-5 and use the exact components listed on it but expand the single threat Errors and Omissions into half a dozen or more unique and highly detailed "Errors and Omissions" threats. Micro matrices are developed only when there is a need for an in-depth review of controls.

Our next step is to evaluate the adequacy of the controls in each cell of the matrix.

Control Review Step 4

At this point, the new system's specification has been completed. Look at Figure 9-2 and you will see that, as you begin Control Review Step 4, you probably have completed Steps 5, 6, and 8 of the system development life cycle. The systems analysis and design effort is about ready to go into Step 9, Sell the System. Control Review Steps 4 and 5 are completed at this stage of the system design effort.

Control Review Step 4 is very easy to describe; but, it is a difficult step because it involves the professional judgment of the entire control review team (the user, data processor, and auditor). It is at this point that each individual cell is evaluated in order to determine whether the controls listed in that cell are adequate to prevent, detect, and correct any occurrence of the threat in relation to its compo-

---

Preventive Controls

☐ *Deterrent* controls discourage or restrain one from acting or proceeding through fear or doubt. They also restrain or hinder an event.

☐ *Preventive* controls mitigate or stop one from acting or an event from occurring.

Detective Controls

☐ *Detective* controls reveal or discover unwanted events and they offer evidence of trespass.

☐ *Reporting* controls document an event, a situation, or a trespass.

Corrective Controls

☐ *Correction* controls remedy or set right an unwanted event or a trespass.

☐ *Recovery* controls regain, make up for, or make good due to the effect of an event or a trespass.

Figure 9-6 Controls to prevent, detect, or correct.

nent (process bubble). In other words, if you look at the cell intersection at which Theft intersects with component 3.0, you will see that there are three controls listed: 3, 16, and 21. Now, you must determine whether those three controls (3, 16, 21) are adequate with regard to preventing, detecting, and correcting theft within the process 3.0, APPLY PAYMENT. In order to help determine whether the three controls listed in that cell are adequate, we have provided a set of criteria to help in that judgment. Figure 9-6 explains the three different criteria of preventive, detective, and corrective controls. Notice that preventive controls may either deter or prevent; detective controls detect and report; corrective controls may correct or recover.

Your task in Control Review Step 4 is to examine each and every cell of the matrix to determine whether the subset of control numbers contained in each cell represents a set of controls that show an adequate level of control. An adequate level of control exists when you have adequately prevented, detected, and corrected the possibility of a threat that can cause damage to, or delay, a specific component (process). Notice that this is very easy to understand, but it is difficult to do because it involves personal judgment on the part of the control review team.

If a given cell does not have an adequate set of controls, then you may recommend that another control be added. This is a point at which you might return to the original controls list (developed during Control Review Step 2) and look for a control that may have been rejected then, but now must be reconsidered because of a serious lack of control in a cell. Notice that we are talking about using the control description for the rejected controls that we documented earlier.

Because the current controls are put onto the matrix using numbers, we suggest that you use alphabetical characters when recommending further new controls. In that way, any cell that has both numbers and alphabetic characters is identified immediately as a cell in which further recommendations have been made, over and above the already agreed upon controls that will be implemented. Once this task is completed, your matrix will look exactly as it did in Figure 9-5, except that there may be some newly recommended controls, represented by alphabetical characters, in a few of the cells.

A control review report must be written immediately after the control review is completed.

Control Review Step 5

The control review and evaluation report usually is written by the auditor because management expects this type of report from the auditor. This is a very short report in that the matrix, with its supporting control numbers and alphabetic recommendations, serves as the basis for the entire report. All that should be required now is a report that shows the matrix with its control numbers and alphabetic recommendations, along with a very short narrative that describes why the further recommendations are necessary.

It is wise to include any conflicting opinions in the same report. In other words, if the auditors feel that a new recommendation should be made and the user department feels either that an alternate recommendation should be made or they have no recommendation, include both the auditor's opinion and the user's opinion in the same report. This is done so upper management can make a quick decision as to whether they will order implementation of the new recommendation. Remember, system design does not stop to wait for a management decision on whether a new recommendation will be implemented.

After management has made its decision with regard to further recommendations, the last step of the control review process is undertaken.

Control Review Step 6

The final step of the control review may not take place for several weeks or months. If you look at Figure 9-2 you will see that Control Review Step 6, verifying and testing the controls, takes place after programming during the tasks of testing and implementing (installing). During the testing task, all of the automated or programmed controls that have been built into the computer application and the systems programs are verified and tested. During the implementation task, you verify and test all of the manual interface controls between the computerized system and the user department personnel who perform whatever manual or semi-automated functions are left in the new system.

The purpose of verifying and testing is to validate whether all of the controls that were accepted by management for implementation (including the newly recommended controls) have been implemented. To *verify a control* means to be sure it exists. To *test a control* means it is tested to be sure it exists, is operational, and does what it was designed to do.

Finally, there might be one more short control review report. Hopefully, this report will confirm that all of the accepted and recommended controls have been implemented and that they are operating properly. If it is necessary to report that some of them have been omitted, it must be done at this time, although we recommend that you do not wait until this short final report. What you really should do is convince the data processing and user departments to implement the controls during system implementation rather than saying nothing and reporting the discrepancies at the close of the project.

To assist in the development of control matrices for your systems, we have included four completed matrices in Appendix 2. These matrices are on Controls for Inputs, Data Communications, Programming, and Outputs. The matrices in Appendix 2 list typical components that exist in computerized systems. The components are not listed as process bubbles from a data flow diagram because the general matrices in Appendix 2 were not built from a Level 0 data flow diagram.

One more control topic needs to be discussed before continuing with the Sunrise Sportswear cumulative case. This control issue is audit trails. The next section presents some ideas on how to build contiguous audit trails throughout either a manual or a computerized business system.

Audit Trails (Transaction Trails)[2]

Whether the analyst is defining the new system requirements or designing for a manual or computer-based system, audit trails must be taken into account. An *audit trail* provides a thread of continuity or traceability between various reports. Audit trails allow the user of the system to trace forward from the source document to the end report or to trace backward from the end report to the original source document. When the analyst is defining the requirements for a system

---

[2] Transaction trails is an alternate term for audit trails. When users, data processors, and auditors work together, the term transaction trails better fits each of their viewpoints and, therefore, is a more acceptable term.

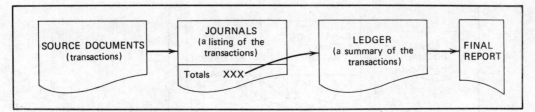

Figure 9-7 Traditional audit trail.

that will have control of the firm's resources, such as money, the firm's auditors will demand that there is an audit trail.

The audit trail in a manual system consists of source documents, journals, ledgers, and reports. This trail enables an auditor to trace an original transaction either forward or backward through the system. Figure 9-7 shows a traditional audit trail which should be present in any system that deals with the firm's resources.

When the analyst is designing a computer-based system, the audit trail may look different than for a manual system. The capabilities of the computer change certain key elements that relate to the audit trail. These possible changes include the fact that source documents once transcribed into machine readable format are no longer used in the data processing cycle, and may be filed in a manner that makes them hard to retrieve. In some systems, such as an on-line real-time system, source documents may be eliminated entirely by the use of direct input devices. Ledgers (a summary of the transactions) may be replaced by direct access files which do not show the amount leading up to these summarized totals. Files kept on magnetic drums, magnetic disks, or magnetic tapes cannot be read except by use of the computer. The sequence of the records and the processing activities cannot be viewed because these activities are taking place within the computer system. It is for these reasons that the analyst, when designing computer-based audit trails, should provide a means for identifying the account from which the transaction was written. The analyst should provide a means for tracing the summary amount back to the individual source document, a regular provision should be made to print out the necessary record, upon request, and there must be a means for tracing any account, even though a regular provision for this trace is not made.

The method by which a systems analyst provides for a computerized audit trail is limited only by the analyst's ingenuity. One example might be that the data recorded on a disk file gives the current balance of that account and also contains reference numbers to all changes that have been made to the account. These reference numbers can then refer back to a batch number or a transaction listing that will lead the auditor back to the record (source document) that

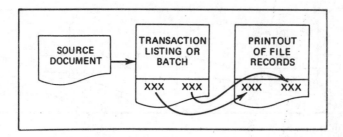

Figure 9-8 Computerized audit trail.

originally was made machine readable and read into the computer. It is this record (source document) that updated the file. This type of audit trail is shown in Figure 9-8. The source document is recorded on a transaction listing, which can be interpreted as a machine readable input, and a printout of the file record refers back to the transaction listing or batch. In summary, the computerized file record gives the current balance in the printout of the file record and it references all changes by transaction listing or batch number. The auditor need only look at the transaction listing or batch in order to determine where the source document is located.

For another type of audit trail, the printout of the file records gives the balance only. This balance is directly traceable, by its unique amount, back to the transaction listing or batch. The auditor then locates the transaction listing or batch by this unique total, checks the individual listings on that transaction listing or batch input, checks the reference number and goes directly to the source document by using that reference number. Figure 9-9 shows this type of an audit trail.

The amount of detail in an audit trail depends upon the organization's particular needs. Several reports that are generated by rearranging a given set of data from a computer file will require a more comprehensive audit trail. The analyst should design the new system for the audit trail so there is a minimum amount of file space used for the audit trail. This minimizes the cost of preparing data, it minimizes clutter in the printout of the file records, and it minimizes the chance that errors will be generated within the computer system. Conversely, a simple error may be fatal to the audit trail because it would end the trail at the point where the error was made.

The auditor uses the audit trail to test the reliability of the system and the dependability of the data it generates. Management uses the audit trail to trace items in order to troubleshoot or find the cause of some problem. Management also uses the audit trail to verify the accuracy of processing. The systems analyst should not make audit decisions alone. The analyst can design the technical aspects of developing and using the audit trail and the related computer programs, but an auditor *must* be called in to assist the analyst in determining what test data are needed and what information is to be obtained.

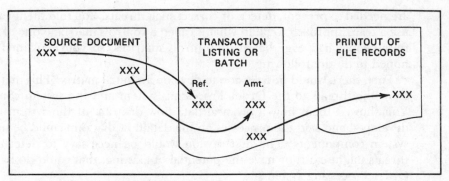

Figure 9-9 Computerized audit trail.

SUNRISE SPORTSWEAR COMPANY

CUMULATIVE CASE: Designing New System Controls (Step 7)

You recognized quite early that the management of Sunrise Sportswear has not been very aware of the need for controls over their Order Processing system. This became evident when you realized that no one could tell you how long it takes to process an order, when you saw the generally lax manner in which incoming customer payments are handled, and when you noticed the apparent lack of concern for the potential for theft by employees. While you laud the fact that the Reynolds family trusts their employees, you recognize that every system must have some controls to make management accountable to the firm's owners. Even a family-owned business such as Sunrise Sportswear must implement some controls as a check and balance against potential problem areas. Stanley Reynolds is a managing owner, but even he is accountable to other family members who have an interest in the business.

While you were gathering general information about Sunrise Sportswear early in the analysis phase of the study, you began making notes about controls that either were lacking or that appeared to need changing. You also learned that Sunrise Sportswear has an auditor whose name is Jessie Call. Even before the drawing of the physical data flow diagram of the existing system was completed, you arranged a meeting with Jessie Call, Valery Brunn, Ann Bull, and Ed Wallace. You arranged the meeting to ask for their participation in a Control Review Team. Even though Ed Wallace is not involved directly in the Order Processing activity, you sought his assistance because of his concern with the incoming customer payments.

At the beginning of this session, you explained that the new Order Processing system at Sunrise Sportswear will require some controls to prevent errors, theft, loss, and other undesirable situations. You further explained that these controls are needed to prevent, detect, or correct such threats. You told them you want to use a team approach to build what is called a controls matrix. None of the other four people had ever heard of controls matrices, so you explained that you hoped to do the following.

First, there would be a session to develop an initial matrix. This matrix would show the threats to the Order Processing system and the system components. You showed them how a physical data flow diagram of the system was being developed and said the processes on the data flow diagram could be used as the system components. The first session would be necessary to determine what threats might exist, or have the potential of existing, that could do harm to the Order Processing system.

Second, there would be a brainstorming session to identify what controls are required to mitigate these threats to the system. It would be a lengthy session because of a need not only to identify the controls, but also to determine whether the identified controls would be implemented into the new system.

The third step would be to document the identified controls onto the matrix. You explained that you needed their knowledge of the system in order to do this step adequately.

The fourth step (evaluation) would occur late in the analysis or early in the design phase. As you explained, their expertise would be needed to evaluate the controls.

You asked Jessie Call to take the lead with the fifth step which would be a control evaluation report. You explained to all of them that it is essential to have the controls identified by the time the control evaluation report is written.

Finally, the last step would be to verify and test the controls. This would be a team effort also, since it would require everyone's cooperation to validate that the controls work properly.

Everyone agreed to be on the Control Review Team. Ed Wallace said he thought it was a good idea from an accounting viewpoint because he knows some customers send cash to pay for their merchandise. He notes that Sunrise Sportswear has been lucky to have honest employees because there does not appear to be any control over the cash that enters the system. Valery Brunn countered with a statement that Jon Gray writes the amount of any cash received on the Order Verification form and on the payment transmittal slip that is sent to Rosemary Dunlap. You see that this could turn into a major confrontation and steer the topic back to Jessie Call by inquiring whether she has been involved in previous control review efforts during the development of a new system. She says this is a first, but is aware that control reviews have become more common in recent years because of the vulnerability of computerized systems to misuse or . error. Ann Bull agrees and says there has been increasing attention to this area in the computer magazines. She tells the group that many of the early computer system efforts were built without realizing how critical a system failure could be to a firm. Even after some major failures were publicized, auditors and users were seldom consulted about the need for controls. Even with today's more enlightened view, many system developers still do not consult others early in the system development project. To make matters worse, computer people often are concerned only with the controls they require to keep the system up and running; these people tend to ignore the fact that other people have requirements for controls as well. She believes this matrix approach is an interesting solution to the problem of defining controls and is anxious to see how it turns out.

After the logical data flow diagram of the proposed system was fairly well on its way toward completion, you met again with the Control Review Team. You showed them the changes that would take place with the proposed system. Although this could have been started as early as the logical data flow diagram of the existing system, you decided it was too early in this particular situation. You also knew that it could wait until the physical data flow diagram of the proposed system, but decided that would not allow enough time for the Control Review Team to get their job done. The logical data flow diagram of the proposed system (Figure 7-15) seemed to be a good point at which to begin. Once the Control Review Team understood the logical data flow diagram, they started developing the initial matrix. The result of their first effort is shown in Figure 9-10.

The Control Review Team wrote the name of each threat across the top of the matrix shown in Figure 9-10. They also wrote a short definition for each of the threats listed across the top of the matrix. Then they began to work out their list of controls. As you had suggested, they wrote down each control as it was discussed and indicated the disposition of each one. Rather than leading the members of the control team, you got them started at each new step by playing devil's advocate. This got them thinking about what needed to be done, and allowed you to continue working on some of the other tasks. About the time you were beginning to work on the physical design of the new system, they were evaluating the controls they had chosen. You helped them evaluate cells on the matrix to be sure there were controls where necessary. They discussed which cells should have higher priority for implementation of the recommended controls.

Now you are nearing the end of the design of the proposed system. You are pleased that the Control Review Team has progressed through their first four control review steps.

Student Questions

1. If you were *not* using structured design techniques, how would you have arrived at the list of components?
2. Do you think you started your controls matrix too early? Too late? Or, just about the right time?
3. Do you think micro matrices will be needed on this project?

COMPONENTS	THREATS					
	ERRORS AND OMISSIONS	THEFT	LOSS OF DATA	BREACH OF PRIVACY	DISASTERS AND DISRUPTIONS	UNAUTHORIZED ACCESS
1.0 ACCEPT TELEPHONE ORDER						
2.0 VERIFY ORDER						
3.0 ASSIGN ORDER NUMBER						
4.0 VERIFY PAYMENT DETAILS						
5.0 VERIFY CREDIT CARD						
6.0 FILL CUSTOMER ORDER						
7.0 PREPARE SHIPMENT						

Figure 9-10 Initial control matrix developed by Sunrise Sportswear's Control Review Team.

Student Tasks

1. This task is accomplished best by small groups of students working together (two or three students per group). Using your knowledge of Sunrise Sportswear, identify as many controls as you can that might apply to the matrix in Figure 9-10. The best approach may be to use Figure 8-3 (Level 0 physical data flow diagram) and think of those controls that prevent, detect, or correct each threat as it relates to each component (process bubble). You may use control lists in Appendix 2. To get you started, we have supplied the first three numbered controls as follows.

   (1) The file server software programs have a password protection scheme that allows each file and/or each application program to be protected against erasure, modification, destruction, and so forth. This five-character password is unique for each employee.

   (2) There is a tape streaming device that is used for backup of all files each evening. This backup tape is placed in a fire-resistant safe.

   (3) Casper Management Consultants will build an edit program that will check each new customer entry to ensure that the person's name is not already in the file. This program will check customer name in association with the street address, city, state, and zip code. It automatically uses similar name search and cross-reference to similar names.

2. Document or place the controls that you have identified onto the matrix. Be sure to ask yourself the two questions that were discussed in this chapter under Control Review Step 2.

3. Evaluate the control matrix that you have developed for Sunrise Sportswear. Use the preventive, detective, and corrective evaluation criteria that were discussed in this chapter.

Selected Readings

1. Campbell, Mary V., and M. Margaret Cermak. "Practical DP Controls for the Small Business," *Journal of Systems Management*, vol. 35, no. 8, August 1984, pp. 16–21.

2. Cockburn, Donald J. "Risk Assessment: An Important Part of the Audit," *CA Magazine* (Canada), vol. 117, no. 7, July 1984, pp. 47–49. [Risk assessment use in planning and evaluating an audit.]

3. FitzGerald, Jerry. *Business Data Communications: Basic Concepts, Security, and Design.* New York: John Wiley & Sons, Inc., 1984. [Chapter 8 discusses the security and control of data communication networks.]

4. FitzGerald, Jerry. *Designing Controls Into Computerized Systems.* 506 Barkentine Lane, Redwood City, Calif.: Jerry FitzGerald & Associates, 1981. [Contains 101 individual

lists composed of over 2,500 specific controls for use when designing computerized systems.]

5. FitzGerald, Jerry. *Internal Controls for Computerized Systems*. 506 Barkentine Lane, Redwood City, Calif.: Jerry FitzGerald & Associates, 1978. [Contains nine completed control matrices based on Figure 9-1 of this chapter.]

6. Helms, Glenn L., and Ira R. Weiss. "Auditor Involvement in the Systems Development Life Cycle," *Internal Auditor*, vol. 40, no. 6, December 1983, pp. 41–44. [Discusses the benefits of having an information systems auditor involved in the SDLC.]

7. Holley, Charles L., and Keith Reynolds. "Audit Concerns in an On-Line Distributed Computer Network," *Journal of Systems Management*, vol. 35, no. 6, June 1984, pp. 32–36.

8. Kahn, Beverly R., and Linda R. Garceau. "Controlling the Microcomputer Environment," *Journal of Systems Management*, vol. 35, no. 5, May 1984, pp. 14–20. [Discusses operating system controls and commands, application system controls, environmental controls, and user controls.]

9. Lord, Kenniston W., Jr. *The Data Center Disaster Consultant, Revised Edition*. Wellesley, Mass.: QED Information Sciences, Inc., 1981. [Contains a checklist of 500 questions and a sample disaster recovery plan.]

10. Mansur, Ovad M. "The Impact of Structured Analysis and Design on EDP Auditing," *Ohio CPA Journal*, vol. 42, no. 1, Winter 1983, pp. 35–42. [Describes how structured methods can be used to make a system auditable.]

11. Parker, Donn B. *Computer Security Management*. Reston, Va.: Reston Publishing Company, Inc., 1981.

12. Perry, William E. "How to Maintain Control in the Data Base Environment," *Journal of Information Systems Management*, vol. 1, no. 2, Spring 1984, pp. 46–54.

13. Ruthberg, Zella G., ed. *Audit and Evaluation of Computer Security, Proceedings of the NBS Invitational Workshop held at Miami Beach, Florida, March 22–24, 1977*. Washington, D.C.: National Bureau of Standards Special Publication 500-19, October 1977.

14. Ruthberg, Zella G., ed. *Audit and Evaluation of Computer Security II: System Vulnerabilities and Controls, Proceedings of the NBS Invitational Workshop held at Miami Beach, Florida, November 28–30, 1978*. Washington, D.C.: National Bureau of Standards Special Publication 500-57, April 1980.

15. Spencer, J. "Documentation is a Control (Auditing)," *Internal Auditor*, vol. 41, no. 1, February 1984, pp. 44–46. [Discusses programmer/analyst documentation, computer operations procedures, and user manuals in terms of control implications for management.]

Questions

1. In today's sophisticated, rapidly changing business environment, what does a new system need to be built upon to be successful?

2. In recent years, organizations have become increasingly dependent upon computer hardware, software, and data processing personnel. How has this fact changed the potential vulnerability of the organization's assets?

3. What factors have increased management's concern about the adequacy of control mechanisms currently in use in the EDP environment?

4. Identify the nine major control components that the typical data processing system may be viewed as having.

5. With reference to the control matrix approach, define the terms "threat" and "component."

6. Identify the six steps that are followed when using the control matrix approach.

7. Why is step two on the control matrix the longest?

8. What is the difference between a logical control and a technical control?

9. In order to place a specific control onto the proper cell of the matrix, what two specific questions must the control review team ask?

10. Of what does the audit trail in a manual system consist?

11. What does an audit trail allow the user to trace?

12. What does the auditor test by using an audit trail?

SITUATION CASES

Case 9-1: *First State Savings Bank*

In this situation case you are to assume that the First State Savings Bank's analyst has completed Control Review Steps 1 and 2. Your task now is to take the following empty matrix and place the controls from the attached controls list into their proper cells. To do this, return to Control Review Step 3 in order to determine the procedure for placing controls. Figure 9-11 is your matrix for the bank's computer operations area. Following that is a description of each of the threats, each of the components, and a list of the controls. Remember, when you place controls onto a matrix, there is no single "best" answer. That is the correct answer. Just do your best at logically thinking about where each control goes. This case is done best in teams of two or three people. Fill in the controls in Figure 9-11, a matrix of the bank's mainframe computer operations center.

Description of Components for Figure 9-11

☐ *Control Reports (off-line).* This involves the control reports that are produced by the off-line system; it specifically includes all reports of a confidential nature or that contain proprietary information.

COMPONENTS	THREATS							
	PHYSICAL ACCESS	UNAUTH. SYSTEM ACCESS	FRAUD	ERRORS	UNAUTH. SOFTWARE CHANGES	UNAUTH. CONFIG. CHANGES	DELAYS	BREACH OF PRIVACY
CONTROL REPORTS (OFF-LINE)								
DISKS/DISKETTES OR TAPES								
DATABASE/NETWORK CONFIGURATION								
PROGRAMS								
HARDWARE								
PEOPLE								
REMOTE CONSOLES								
COMMUNICATION CIRCUITS								
FACILITIES AND POWER								

Figure 9-11 Matrix for computer operations (Case 9-1).

☐ *Disk/Diskettes or Tapes.* Magnetic disks, diskettes, or tapes upon which bank information is recorded temporarily or copied onto for long-term storage.

☐ *Database/Network Configuration.* This includes the basic definition, and all the update methodologies used, with regard to configuring the database files for the system, along with the network configuration with regard to the flow of data.

☐ *Programs.* All of the on-line real-time programs that are utilized in the bank's system during its daily operation.

☐ *Hardware.* The mainframe computer hardware and its associated hardware such as disk units, tape units, and the like.

☐ *People.* This refers to the employees who are authorized to work in the data center, as well as other individuals who are not direct employees but who periodically need to gain access to the data center (such as vendors, maintenance personnel, janitorial staff, and the like).

☐ *Remote Consoles.* The remote consoles, even though they are located physically at the bank's headquarters, are included in the review of controls because they relate specifically to the data center's computer operations complex.

☐ *Communication Circuits.* The communication lines utilized for transfer of data between the computer center and the various bank branches throughout the state.

☐ *Facilities and Power.* The physical facilities that house the computer systems and other equipment, programs, and the electrical power associated with these systems.

Description of Threats for Figure 9-11

☐ *Physical Access.* This includes unauthorized physical access to any of the components listed down the left vertical column of Figure 9-11.

☐ *Unauthorized System Access.* This includes unauthorized access to the Computer Operations Center and/or any of the programs or databases, or tapping into a communication circuit.

☐ *Fraud.* The theft of funds or other valuable information through fraudulent methods.

☐ *Errors.* This includes any errors, omissions of data, or duplicate messages/data that have happened during the preparation of input, processing of data, or transmission of data.

☐ *Unauthorized Software Changes.* The possibility of someone making an unauthorized change to any of the software programs.

☐ *Unauthorized Configuration Changes.* This involves someone making unauthorized changes to the configuration of the system, the databases, or the communication circuits.

□ *Delays.* Any message that is delayed, whether caused by a system bug, power failure, hardware failure, communication circuit failure, or any other catastrophic event.

□ *Breach of Privacy.* This involves someone gaining access to information that either is confidential or proprietary to the bank, or that contains data that is private or confidential to an individual customer.

Controls for Figure 9-11

1. Magnetic tapes that hold the confidential off-line reports are kept under strict physical control until the reports are produced. For delivery to the user department, the off-line report tapes and the reports themselves are placed in locked canvas bags. These bags are given to messengers who deliver the reports directly to the user departments and in accordance with a previously prepared delivery schedule.

2. Report tapes are retained for a 5–10 day cycle (depending on the type of reports contained on the tape) in order to assure a second copy of the report if one should be needed.

3. Tapes and disks that are considered confidential are locked in the computer room cabinets after hours. There is off-premises backup for these tapes and disks.

4. Diskettes for the on-line controller/terminal programs are modified only on an approved change request that emanates from the Systems Development Department. These diskettes also are locked up within the already locked computer room.

5. Any changes to the databases must be authorized by the user department. These authorizations are written on a software change notice form. After the approval signature is verified, they are keyed to magnetic tape by the Systems Development Department.

6. There are various access controls for controlling the physical movement of personnel at the Computer Operations Center. First, there are guards at the building entrance to the Operations Center; second, each employee wears a badge and visitors must be signed in by an authorized employee and be escorted continuously throughout the area; third, the eighth floor has its own "badge reader" that restricts access; and fourth, the computer room has a lock on the door that can be activated by still another badge reader or a key. After hours, there are infrared detectors that detect movement within the area, should anyone make an illegal entry.

7. There are two types of computer passwords that must be used to sign on to the computer system. The computer operator passwords are separate from the sign on passwords.

8. There is a distinction between sensitive and non-sensitive reports. All reports that have been determined to be non-sensitive with regard to bank information are placed in an area that might be called "backup writer." This backup writer stores current reports so they can be re-printed quickly if necessary. Conversely, all of the sensitive reports are not sent to the backup writer. All of these confidential/sensitive reports can be reprinted only by obtaining the original hard copy from the user department or by retrieving the magnetic tapes from the user depart-ment. This tape control/movement was discussed in control 1 above.

9. FEDWIRE and BANKWIRE (nationwide banking telecommunication networks) operating hours are restricted and differ from our computer system. The computer operator is present during the hours in which these two systems are operational.

10. The remote computer console can be disconnected by the central com-puter operator, and this remote console, at the present time, has been disabled for all functions except print only.

11. Changes to the computer operator passwords are made by the security department. Currently, these passwords are changed at irregular time intervals, and there is no set plan in effect for changing the passwords.

12. There is a higher level password (supervisor sign on password) that must be utilized by authorized personnel in order to make any computer con-figuration changes or password changes.

13. Training for the computer people in the Operations Center is segregated by function so that a natural separation of duties occurs. In other words, the training is such that computer operators and other personnel are trained only in the area for which they are responsible; they do not learn the entire system operation.

14. All communication circuits between the computer at the Operations Cen-ter and the controllers for the various remote terminals are controlled by the central computer operator.

15. The test equipment for the data communication network is in a separate room in order to reduce the flow of personnel who do not need access; authorized requests are required for the use of this test equipment. The personnel realize the sensitivity to this equipment and do not use it except for authorized purposes.

16. There is an error message and retrieval program for investigation of errors to determine if these errors were caused by the computer system, software, or the operational people/users of the system.

17. There is a general operational training procedure for all personnel at the Operations Center.

18. The computer system uses an algorithm/test key in order to check the

validity of various messages (this is an automated computer check on validity).

19. All modifications to the system are scheduled; they go through this scheduling routine in order to assure that all modifications are authorized properly.

20. The doors to the computer room have key locks as well as badge readers. These key locks can be used in case the badge reader system fails. Duplicate keys to these doors are located in the guard area.

21. Fallback procedures that can be utilized to back out malfunctioning software, load the prior version of the same software, or load a backup software package have been written and are available. These procedures have been tested.

22. The hardware restart capabilities in the Operations Center are under a dual computer configuration that has been developed and implemented. These procedures also have been tested thoroughly.

23. In key areas within the Operations Center, there are backup personnel, backup data communication circuits, backup modems, and backup telephone lines/hot line.

24. There is an uninterruptible power supply (UPS) in order to ensure that the computers keep operating if there is an electrical failure.

25. The Operations Computer Center is protected by fire detectors, an alarm system, Halon 1301 fire suppressant material, and water in case of fire.

Chapter 10

ECONOMIC COST COMPARISONS

LEARNING OBJECTIVES

You will learn how to . . .

□ Conduct a cost/benefit analysis.

□ Separate planning and opportunity costs.

□ Think in terms of investment, implementation, and operational costs.

□ Utilize a variety of cost analysis methods, such as break-even analysis, payback period, marginal efficiency of investment, and present value.

□ Compare the costs of today's system to those of the proposed system.

□ Appreciate the importance of basic noneconomic/intangible benefits.

□ Develop cost chargeback methods.

□ Develop Request for Proposals (RFPs).

□ Evaluate needs related to hardware and software.

□ Evaluate costs of alternative human–machine boundary proposals.

What Is Cost/Benefit Analysis?

The quality of life depends in large measure upon mankind's wise use of scarce resources. The systems analyst must learn to compare the costs and benefits of system resources, while management must evaluate these costs and benefits in terms of their probable effect on the quality of the organization.

Before we explain the alternate methodologies that are available for comparing the cost of different system designs, let us look at a simplistic cost/benefit analysis that you already may have performed. The usual practice is first to identify the benefits and second, to identify the costs.

Let us assume that you have just purchased a high fidelity stereo/tape deck/ FM radio console. Probably the first thing you did was identify the benefits. For example, you reviewed the frequency response ranges for the high tones and the low tones. While this may be considered a technical capability of the stereo, it is this technical capability that provides the benefits that you desire, e.g., smooth and clear high tones and low tones. You looked at the tape deck to determine whether it played the various types of tapes you wanted to use, and whether it recorded and played in Dolby. The record player may have had an automatic changer, but you wanted just a single turntable that did not allow records to fall on other records. The speaker cabinets, including the number of individual speakers that were in each cabinet, became one of your criterion. The quality of the FM radio and whether it had automatic frequency control (AFC) may have been another criterion. In other words, you decided which component or set of components best fitted your needs with regard to your records, tapes, and radio listening pleasures.

Next (in reality you did this at the same time you were looking at the benefits), you obtained the costs of the various systems. During this evaluation of benefits (what you wanted), you also learned what the costs were, and certain limitations became evident. These limitations were that you probably could not afford a music system that cost $10,000. Alternately, music systems were available that cost less than $100. The point is that somewhere in that range ($100 to $10,000) was a dollar figure that you could afford. Finally, you decided upon the system you wanted. This decision was inspired primarily by the benefits or how the system worked, but it was controlled severely by the amount of money that you could afford to spend.

This cost/benefit analysis example is very similar to what is done during a system study because, as you design the system, you outline all the benefits or needs that must be fulfilled. During the cost analysis portion, you identify the costs of the system or the several alternative systems that you plan to recommend. Notice that costs *do* limit the type of system that will be implemented at a company, just like costs limited the type of music system that you purchased for personal enjoyment.

We suggest that you examine Figure 10-1, which shows cost/benefit analysis factors. This figure shows the costs subdivided into direct costs and indirect

COSTS	BENEFITS
Direct costs	*Direct and indirect cost reductions*
—Computer equipment	—Elimination of clerical personnel and/ or manual operations
—Communications equipment	—Reduction of inventories, manufacturing, sales, operations, and management costs
—Common carrier line charges	
—Software	
—Operations personnel costs	
—File conversion costs	—Effective cost reduction, for example, less spoilage or waste, elimination of obsolete materials, and less pilferage
—Facilities costs (space, power, air conditioning storage space, offices, etc.)	
—Spare parts costs	—Distribution of resources across demand for service
—Hardware maintenance costs	
—Software maintenance costs	*Revenue increases*
—Interaction with vendor and/or development group	—Increased sales due to better responsiveness
—Development and performance of acceptance test procedures and parallel operation	—Improved services
	—Faster processing of operations
—Development of documentation	*Intangible benefits*
—Costs for backup of system in case of failure	—Smoothing of operational flows
	—Reduced volume of paper produced and handled
—Costs of manually performing tests during a system outage	—Rise in level of service quality and performance
Indirect costs	—Expansion capability
—Personnel training	—Improved decision process by providing faster access to information
—Transformation of operational procedures	—Ability to meet the competition
—Development of support software	—Future cost avoidance
—Disruption of normal activities	—Positive effect on other classes of investments or resources such as better utilization of money, more efficient use of floor space or personnel, and so forth
—Increased system outage rate during initial operation period	
—Increase in the number of vendors (impacts fault detection and correction due to "finger pointing")	—Improved employee morale

Figure 10-1 Cost/benefit analysis factors.

costs. It also shows benefits subdivided into direct/indirect cost reductions, revenue increases, and intangible benefits. These items are meant for use during preparation of your cost analysis contrasted to the benefits derived from the proposed computer or the new system.

In this chapter we discuss a variety of methodologies that can be used for cost analysis and for cost/benefit analysis. The reason we discuss different methodologies is that no one methodology is appropriate in all cases.

General Concepts

Usually it is a hindrance to propose cost limitations during the initial development of design alternatives. Notice that we completed the definition of the new system requirements (Chapter 7) *before* we started developing economic cost comparisons. In fact, the system development life cycle that we suggest presents the idea of simultaneously designing the new system (Chapter 8), designing controls (Chapter 9), and developing economic cost comparisons (Chapter 10). If this is not totally clear, review Figure 7-1 in order to see how Steps 6, 7, and 8 are conducted simultaneously or in parallel.

Remember, there always should be an effort to keep costs down; however, costs should not interfere with the definition of the system requirements. The point is that the various alternatives should be identified first, *then* costs should be related to the design configuration alternatives.

Estimating the cost of a system is significantly more complex than estimating the cost of a new piece of hardware. Many variables and intangibles are involved. Nevertheless, estimating the cost of a system is a necessary prerequisite to deciding whether implementation is justifiable. Some of the general questions that must be considered are

☐ What are the major cost categories of the entire system? These may include items such as communication circuit costs, hardware costs, software costs, maintenance costs, personnel costs, and the like.

☐ What methods of cost estimating are available and what accuracies can be achieved?

☐ Can all costs be identified and accurately estimated?

☐ Can the benefits be identified? Which benefits cannot be estimated in dollar terms?

☐ What criteria will management use when evaluating these estimates? You might review the set of evaluation criteria that was discussed in Chapter 7.

Assembling the various costs for a new system usually requires a very detailed analysis, although the methodologies presented in this chapter will give you a wide choice of cost estimation tools.

Two Concepts of Cost Analysis

The first concept is the *planning* type of cost analysis. It is a method based on the analysis of the *opportunity costs* of using a resource for one purpose rather than another.

Suppose that the firm has 10,000 square feet of unused (empty) floor space in its main plant. To determine the opportunity cost of alternate uses for the space, management would develop a list of all the uses to which this floor space could be put. For example, it could be used for

1. Office space
2. Manufacturing a new product
3. Expanding the manufacture of an existing product
4. A new computer center
5. Leasing to an outside firm
6. Nothing . . . let it sit empty

A systems analyst then would estimate the return on the investment for all six of the above uses to which the floor space could be put. Suppose the return on investment turned out as follows.

DOLLARS RETURNED PER YEAR FOR EACH $1,000.00 INVESTED			USE TO WHICH THE FLOOR SPACE WILL BE PUT
$180	or	18% return on investment	Expanding the manufacture of an existing product
110	or	11% return on investment	A new computer center
60	or	6% return on investment	Office space
55	or	5.5% return on investment	Manufacturing a new product
−10[1]	or	−1% return on investment	Nothing . . . let it sit empty
−50[2]	or	−5% return on investment	Leasing to an outside firm

[1] Negative dollars returned because the firm must pay property taxes.
[2] Leasing to another firm might interfere with your own business, giving a negative return.

The opportunity cost of expanding the manufacturing of an existing product is $70 compared with the next best alternative which is to locate a new computer center in that empty space ($180 minus $110 equals $70). If the firm chooses to locate the computer center in this space, it will be foregoing $70 return for each $1,000 investment required.

The second concept of cost analysis is the *budgeting* type of analysis. It is based on the *cash flow* concept, which refers to the amount of money that will be required for a particular project and the dates when that money will be needed. The firm can then budget or set aside the required funds so they will be available when needed.

Cash flow also involves the *speed* of collection of the firm's incomes and the *amount* of collection. In other words, a firm cannot adequately plan budgets unless it knows when it will collect its incomes, the amounts it will collect, and when it will have to pay out funds.

Finally, the analyst should try to determine the similarities or differences in the final estimates that are caused by differences in the system's requirements versus those caused by peculiarities in the different methods used to estimate the costs in each instance.

*T*hree *Major Cost Categories*

When you are estimating or calculating costs, there are three major cost categories that must be taken into account. These three categories are investment costs, implementation costs, and annual operating costs.

Investment costs are nonrecurring capital outlays to acquire or develop new equipment, new software, or some other major new capability. Obviously, if you are buying a new computer or a new software package, the purchase price is the investment cost. Note that the organization can convert investment costs to annual operating costs by renting or leasing the product or new equipment.

Implementation costs are one-time outlays to create or install this new capability. Note here that one-time implementation costs can be converted into an annual operating cost if the product is leased. This is because the lease might include the initial installation in its monthly lease payments. Implementation costs usually are different from investment costs in that your own personnel are used to install the new system. For example, user training and relocating people or equipment are implementation costs.

The *annual operating costs* are the recurring outlays required to operate the system on a month-to-month or year-to-year basis.

In order to combine these three general cost categories into a single system cost figure, use the following formula.

$$\text{Annual cost} = \frac{\dfrac{\text{Investment}}{\text{cost}} + \dfrac{\text{Implementation}}{\text{cost}}}{\begin{array}{c}\text{Estimated system life} \\ \text{in years}\end{array}} + \begin{array}{c}\text{Annual} \\ \text{operating} \\ \text{cost}\end{array}$$

As an example of the three categories, consider an organization that wants to purchase a minicomputer security system to control the door locks of the computer room. This system is to have a minicomputer, software, door lock badge readers on each door, and the electrical wiring to interconnect the door lock badge readers to the minicomputer. Now let us look at this security system with regard to implementation costs, investment costs, and operating costs. Assuming the organization does not lease this equipment, the investment costs are the purchase of the minicomputer, the door lock badge readers, the electrical wiring, and the software. The implementation costs are the installation of the minicomputer, the door lock badge readers, and interconnecting the badge readers to the minicomputer with the electrical wires. Finally, the annual operating costs are the costs of maintenance on the hardware, software, and badge lock door readers, electricity costs, possibly paper costs, and perhaps the repair of broken electric wires between the badge lock door readers and the minicomputer. Also, the individual employee badges are an annual operating cost.

Break-Even Analysis

It is possible to apply the concept of break-even analysis to comparisons between the current system and the proposed system or just between various alternative systems. This is different from the use of break-even analysis in accounting or financial operations of a major organization. In accounting, the cost of a project is compared to the revenues it produces. When the revenues equal the costs, the project is said to be at its break-even point. Instead, we will be comparing the cost of a new system to the current system to determine the point at which the new system costs the same as the old.

Figure 10-2 shows such a break-even analysis, in which the cost of the new system initially would be higher than the current system. By the end of year plus one (next year), the new system would have reached the break-even point and thereafter becomes more economical to operate than the current system. Note that the cost of the new system must include the three major categories of cost: implementation costs, investment costs, and operating costs.

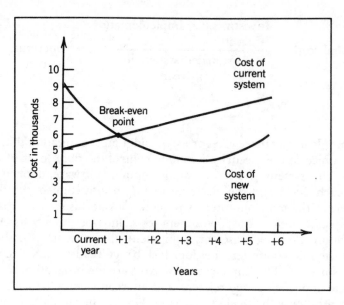

Figure 10-2 Break-even analysis.

Payback Period

A criterion that frequently is used to judge the profitability of a system is the payback period. For example, if a new computer-based information system costs $700,000 and is expected to yield $100,000 per year, its payback period is 7 years (before taxes). The payback period is defined as the number of years required to accumulate earnings sufficient to cover its costs.

The payback period criterion ranks projects in terms of number of years to payback. Two factors that must be examined closely are the rate at which funds flow in, and taxes. Two investments (A and B) each have a 4-year payback period.

PROJECT	ANNUAL RETURN FIRST YEAR	ANNUAL RETURN SECOND YEAR	ANNUAL RETURN THIRD YEAR	ANNUAL RETURN FOURTH YEAR	TOTAL RETURN
A	$10,000	$10,000	$10,000	$10,000	$40,000
B	25,000	5,000	5,000	5,000	40,000

Clearly, project B is preferred because a larger amount of the investment is recovered during the first year. Project B returns the investment money more promptly.

The second factor concerns taxes. Corporate income taxes lengthen the payback period. The payback period calculator is

Before taxes	After taxes
$P = \dfrac{I}{R}$	$P = \dfrac{I}{(1 - T)R}$

where P = payback period, I = investment, R = average annual return on investment, and T = corporate tax rate in percent. For example, if the investment required for a project equals \$22,000 ($I = 22,000$) and the average annual return is \$3,800 ($R = 3,800$) and the corporate tax rate is 48% ($T = 0.48$), then the payback period (after taxes) is

$$P = \frac{22,000}{(1 - 0.48)3,800} = \frac{22,000}{(0.52)3,800} = 11.13 \text{ years}$$

The same project has a before taxes payback period of 5.79 years.

Marginal Efficiency of Investment

The marginal efficiency of investment (MEI) is the rate of return that a potential system is expected to earn after all of its costs (except interest expenses) are recovered.

This method also is called internal rate of return (IRR). It assumes that the cash inflows are reinvested at this internal rate of return. As you will see when you finish reading this section, the MEI or IRR must be equal to, or greater than, the organization's cost of capital from banks or wherever they obtain money.

For example, consider a new system that requires \$10,000 for installation and equipment, \$30,000 in operating expenses, and is expected to return \$41,000 at the end of *one year* of its life. The MEI of this system is 10% because after covering the operating expenses (noncapital costs), the firm had enough left over to replace the original \$10,000 equipment cost plus a net return of \$1,000 ($1,000 \div 10,000 = 10\%$).

The investment may be made if the MEI is greater than the rate of interest that a bank charges the firm to borrow.

\$41,000	estimated benefits at end of year
− 30,000	operating expenses during the year
\$11,000	
− 10,000	equipment and installation cost
\$ 1,000	return on investment

The above example assumes that the system will be obsolete at the end of one year. In order to consider a longer life span, the following formula should be used.

$$\begin{matrix}\text{Fixed} \\ \text{investment} \\ \text{in dollars}\end{matrix} = \frac{\begin{matrix}\text{Return over} \\ \text{operating} \\ \text{expenses} \\ \text{(1st year)}\end{matrix}}{(1+r)^1} + \frac{\begin{matrix}\text{Return over} \\ \text{operating} \\ \text{expenses} \\ \text{(2nd year)}\end{matrix}}{(1+r)^2} + \ldots + \frac{\begin{matrix}\text{Return over} \\ \text{operating} \\ \text{expenses} \\ \text{in last} \\ \text{year (Nth)} \\ \text{of the} \\ \text{asset's life}\end{matrix}}{(1+r)^n}$$

where r equals the MEI

For example, if a new system has a fixed investment of $10,000 and if at the end of the first year of its life it is expected to yield a return on investment of $5,500 and at the end of the second year a return on investment of $6,050, its MEI equals 10%.

$$\$10,000 = \frac{\$5,500}{(1+r)^1} + \frac{\$6,050}{(1+r)^2}$$

Solving this for r, we get $r = 10\%$. This means that if r (MEI) is greater than the current interest rate, the investment may be made. The financial people in the firm should be consulted to get the specific interest rate which the firm must pay to obtain funds. If that is not available, the MEI might be compared with the "prime rate" that banks charge their best customers.

*P*resent Value Analysis

Like the marginal efficiency of investment or internal rate of return method, the present value method is a discounted cash flow approach to determining which investment is best. The chosen system is the one which offers us the most for our money. With the present value method all cash flows are discounted to the present value using the required rate of return. With the previous marginal efficiency of investment/internal rate of return method, we are given the cash flows and allow for the rate of discount that equates the present value of the cash inflows with the present value of the cash outflow. With the present value method, the project is accepted if the present value of cash inflows exceeds the present value of cash outflows.

One way of looking at this is with your own bank account. Assume you have $1,000 and you can deposit it in a bank account at 10% simple interest. This means that, at the end of one year, your $1,000 is increased by 10% or it now is worth $1,100. The 10% simple interest is your required rate of return or the current rate of return that you are able to get from the bank. Now, let us assume that you can loan your money to a friend who is starting a new business. This friend offers to give you $1,200 back at the end of one year. This means that your friend is offering you 20% simple interest. On the other hand, you might decide to take your money and bury it in your backyard, thus receiving zero interest. In this case, assuming equal safety among the three alternatives, your best approach is to loan the money to your friend who is starting a business. This is because at the end of one year, the money in the bank will have a value of $1,100, the money loaned to your friend will have a value of $1,200, and the money that you buried in your backyard will have a value of $1,000. If you choose the bank or burying the money, you might say that you have a lost opportunity cost because you missed the opportunity, or did not take it, to loan the money to your friend.

A common ranking alternative for investment proposals is the method of *net present value*. The following equation presents the formula for the net present value.

$$NPV = \frac{R_1}{(1 + k)^1} + \frac{R_2}{(1 + k)^2} + \ldots + \frac{R_n}{(1 + k)^n} - PV$$

NPV = net present value
PV = cost of the new system
R = cash flow (savings because of the new system)
k = cost of money (interest rate)
n = number of years the savings (cash flow)
     is available

As an example, let us assume that the actual rate of return that we can receive on invested money at a bank is 10% ($k = 0.10$). Also, assume that the cost of the new system is $18,000 ($PV = \$18,000$). Next assume that our cash flow (savings each year because of the new system) is $5,600 ($R = \$5,600$). Another necessary piece of data is how long these $5,600 savings will be available. For our case let us assume it is five years, which means we will let *n* go from 1 to 5. Now let us calculate the net present value, using this data.

$$NPV = \frac{5,600}{(1.10)^1} + \frac{5,600}{(1.10)^2} + \frac{5,600}{(1.10)^3} + \frac{5,600}{(1.10)^4} + \frac{5,600}{(1.10)^5} - 18,000$$

$$NPV = 21,228 - 18,000$$

$$NPV = \$3,228$$

Inasmuch as the net present value of this proposal is greater than zero, the proposal should be accepted, using the present value method. The NPV is greater than zero because the new system provides a rate of return greater than 10% (actual rate of return from the bank).

Compare Current System with the New System

This method of comparing the cost of the current system to the cost of the new system may well be the single most important method of cost comparison. The reason is that everyone wants to know, What does it cost me now? (current system) and What will it cost me in the future? (new system). Therefore, a basic one-to-one comparison of today's cost of the existing system and tomorrow's cost of the new system is mandatory.

In order to prepare an economic cost comparison between the current system and the proposed system, *first* estimate the projected useful life of the proposed system. This is the common basis by which the old and new systems can be compared. Estimate a reasonable life span for your proposed system since no system lasts forever. It might collapse from advances in computer technology or from overuse as company sales increase.

Second, calculate the proposed system's operating costs during the projected useful life of the system (a detailed example of costs is in the next section).

Third, calculate the present system operating costs over the same projected useful life. In this way an accurate cost comparison can be made between the present and proposed systems. It is likely that the present system will not be able to function over the projected useful life of the new system. Estimate when the current system will fail to operate adequately or when it might collapse completely.

Fourth, compare both operating costs (present and proposed) over the projected useful life of the new system. Calculate the fixed investment costs, including any one-time implementation costs. Resources and costs generally are divided into three categories (these were discussed previously in the section Three Major Cost Categories).

1. *Implementation costs* are one-time outlays to create new capability.
2. *Investment costs* are nonrecurring outlays to acquire new equipment.
3. *Operating costs* are recurring outlays required to operate the system.

For both the current and the proposed system, the approximate costs can be estimated from the various documentation sheets, reports, or summaries that were prepared as the systems study progressed through its phases.

Detailed Example of Costs

For both the current system and the proposed system, the following should be determined.

Salaries

The current wage rate for those people operating the system usually can be obtained from the personnel department, but be careful! Rate of pay for non-union jobs is sometimes a well-guarded secret. Settle for estimates if the exact amount is not readily divulged. Departmental budgets may help also.

In projecting costs, do not forget to figure salary increases for personnel in future years. Always include the firm's cost of fringe benefits. Fringe benefits generally are in the area of 20%; that is, company costs (contributions) are 20 cents per dollar of wages paid. If the payroll or personnel department said the company paid 20% in fringe benefits, the wage rate would be multiplied by 0.20 to get the amount the company contributes, per hour, toward fringe benefits.

$$
\begin{array}{rl}
\$14.85 & \text{wage rate per hour} \\
\times 0.20 & \text{fringe ratio} \\
\hline
\$2.97 & \text{fringe cost per hour}
\end{array}
$$

The actual payroll cost is $17.82 per hour ($14.85 plus $2.97) for this job classification. The actual payroll cost is then multiplied by 40 hours per week to get the weekly cost and then by 52 weeks to get the annual cost.

$$
\begin{array}{rl}
\$17.82 & \text{per hour} \\
\times 40 & \text{hours per week} \\
\hline
\$712.80 & \text{per week} \\
\times 52 & \text{weeks per year} \\
\hline
\$37,065.60 & \text{per year}
\end{array}
$$

Assuming this is the annual cost of one computer programmer, and six of them are needed in the proposed system, the annual cost is $222,393.60 for the first year (6 × $37,065.60 = $222,393.60). For the second year, this figure should be increased by the expected salary increases. If the firm averages 7.5% in increases, increase the $222,393.60 by 7.5% when calculating the costs of the system during the second year of its existence. Repeat this entire operation for each different wage rate in the current and new system in order to get the total salary costs.

Space

The cost of floor space should be included. Many firms prorate the cost of floor space on a dollars-per-square-foot basis. Assume, for example, that the cost of floor space is prorated by the accounting department at $14.50 per square foot. Calculate the square footage of space required by the current and the proposed system, then multiply by $14.50 in order to assign a cost to the facilities required for each system.

If space is rented in order to house the system, then the rent is the cost of floor space. Carefully consider the location for the new system. Is it expensive or inexpensive? In a multiplant firm, different buildings have different prorated floor space costs. The new system or computer should be located in a convenient location.

Supplies and Inventories

Evaluate each operation within the system as to the needs and costs of different supplies. Supplies are used to operate the system and should not be confused with inventories. One supply might be paper for the computer's high speed printer, whereas inventory costs have three classifications: raw materials with which to make the product, work-in-progress, and finished goods inventory.

If the system study involves inventories, a calculation should be made to determine whether inventories will increase or decrease because of the proposed system. For example, if inventories are decreased by $10,000, there is a savings. Multiply the $10,000 reduction by the rate of interest that the firm must pay to borrow from a bank.

$$
\begin{array}{ll}
\$10,000.00 & \text{reduction in inventory} \\
\underline{\times\,0.12} & \text{interest rate} \\
\$\;\;1,200.00 & \text{annual savings}
\end{array}
$$

The proper interest figure can be obtained from the financial personnel in the firm. If the system increases inventories, it is an additional cost to be added to the system. The calculation is the same.

Overhead

Salaries, space, supplies, and inventories already have been taken into account, but there might be some other *indirect* cost items that should be taken into account. If the new system reduces overhead, it is a savings; if the new system increases overhead, it is an additional cost. Overhead items include

1. Janitorial and maintenance services.
2. Plant protection.
3. Insurance.
4. Property taxes on a building or land.
5. Heat, light, and power.
6. Specialized services, the cost of which is borne by all departments (company library, duplicating services, etc.).

Implementation Costs

Add one-time implementation costs to the overall cost of installing the new system. Implementation costs include

1. Moving costs for equipment and people.
2. Refurbishing costs.
3. Costs for locating electrical outlets and telephones.
4. Furniture costs.
5. Cost of file conversions, for example, manual to computerized or computerized to a new computerized system.
6. Cost of removing the current system.

Investment Costs

Investment costs include the cost of purchasing new equipment or facilities for the proposed system.

1. Computers.
2. Disks/tapes.
3. Communication network.
4. Software.
5. Special facilities.

Basic Noneconomic Benefits . . . Intangibles

Managers of today's business and government organizations must be very cost-conscious. For that reason the first prerequisite in accepting a new system may be the cost of the system or possibly the future avoidance of cost. Cost avoidance often is not a highly accurate figure; in fact, you may not be able to calculate it at all! This is called an intangible benefit. You, as the systems analyst, must stress the noneconomic benefits (intangibles) because the responsible managers frequently look only at cost savings that are expressed in dollar terms. Remember to explain these intangible benefits thoroughly in your write-up. They may help cost-justify your new system.

Noneconomic benefits can be defined as those benefits which are difficult to estimate in economic terms. The cost of effort to make the estimate may exceed the value of having the estimate. A list of some noneconomic benefits the analyst should look for are

1. Faster response time to inquiries from prospective customers . . . better public relations.
2. Increased employment stability . . . higher employee morale.
3. More accurate delivery promises to customers.
4. Greater stock availability . . . fewer stockouts.
5. Improvement in quality of product or quality of service . . . fewer rejects.
6. Positive effect on other classes of investments or resources, such as more efficient use of floor space or personnel.
7. Better managerial control of the organization.
8. Effective cost reduction, for example, less spoilage or waste, elimination of obsolete materials, and less pilferage.
9. Greater flexibility in dealing with a changing business environment.
10. Future cost avoidance.

The effectiveness of a system is determined by the time and cost required to operate the system versus the benefits derived from the system. Do not base the success of a system solely on economic values. Management must know also about the other important benefits (intangibles) of your proposed system. (Intangible benefits were listed in Figure 10-1.)

Cost Chargeback Method

In some cases it may be desirable to develop a chargeback methodology in order to charge user departments for their use of the new system you are designing. Cost chargeback is quite popular for allocating the costs of a computer center back to each user. It also is a very popular technique for allocating the costs of data communication networks. In other words, chargeback is used for cost recovery.

Figure 10-3 shows a user chargeback method for an interactive system that is

Terminals in California connect with headquarters computer in New York City. During peak day hours, 9 A.M. to 5 P.M., 100 input transactions of 75 characters each and 110 output transactions of 350 characters each are processed.

Other elements of the algorithm include

□ Terminal charge of $243.00
□ Modem charge of $15.00.
□ Administrative overhead charge of 5% on owned equipment
□ Access charge of $400.00
□ Character overhead (message address, special instructions, etc.) of 100 characters per transaction
□ Daytime rate of $0.11/1,000 characters
□ Month equals 22 days

Monthly communications charge would be

1. Equipment		
Terminal	$243.00	
Modem	15.00	
Equipment costs	258.00	
Administrative overhead (5%)	12.90	
Equipment total		$270.90
2. Access charge (based on distance)		$400.00
3. Daytime character rate		
Input Transactions (100 × 75 char.)	7,500	
Overhead (100 × 100 char.)	10,000	
Total input characters	17,500	
Output Transactions (110 × 350 char.)	38,500	
Overhead (110 × 100 char.)	11,000	
Total output characters	49,500	
Total characters per day	67,000	
Daily charge ($0.11/1,000 char.)	$7.37	
Monthly char. charge (22 days)		$162.14
Total monthly charge		$833.04

Figure 10-3 Chargeback of data communication costs for an interactive system.

sensitive to the number of transactions, the number of characters in each transaction, and the distance between the user departments and the location of the central computer. The monthly charges consist of three main elements: the equipment, the access charge (cost of communication circuits), and the number of characters transmitted. Character charges are assessed at daytime, off hours, or nighttime rates. This provides an incentive for users to use the data communication network during non-prime hours.

*R*equest *for Proposals (RFPs)*

With today's high technology systems and with the vast number of available alternatives, you most likely will be involved with Requests for Proposals (RFPs). An RFP is an invitation sent out to prospective vendors (bidders) notifying them of your interest in obtaining hardware, software, and/or complete turnkey systems. RFPs also are used to determine whether you should buy or lease the hardware/software. Another use of RFPs is to determine whether your firm will operate the system with its own personnel or use facilities management. This is when the vendor who supplies the hardware/software also supplies the personnel and operates the system for your organization.

It is important that all vendors are notified at the same time and that they are given a reasonable time within which to respond. You must state clearly how they should respond to your Request for Proposal, and also how you plan to evaluate their responses. There should be a bidders conference which vendors can attend to ask questions in person with regard to the Request for Proposal. This conference should be held well in advance of the date that their responses are due.

Our way of explaining how to use RFPs is by first presenting an outline of the contents of an RFP and second, by presenting a detailed, complete RFP for you to use. Because of space limitations in this chapter, the completed RFP is presented in Appendix 3. Incidentally, the RFP in Appendix 3 is a real one that was used successfully. The name and locations were changed for reasons of privacy.

The following general outline can be used to identify the pieces of an RFP. In other words, you must prepare a written document that clearly covers all of these items.

COMPUTERIZED SYSTEM FOR THE
WHITE MEDICAL CLINIC

I. Preliminary Review
   A. The administration of the medical clinic identifies the potential systems that are needed
   B. Select the systems analyst and/or consultant who will prepare the RFP

    C. The systems analyst and/or consultant and the clinic's administration develop a bid document (RFP)

II. Development of the RFP (bid document)

    A. Joint effort to develop the RFP

        1. Introduction

        2. Statement of intent

        3. Guidelines for the vendors' preparation of their bids

        4. Service bureau requirements (if appropriate)

        5. On-site computer requirements (if appropriate)

        6. General description of the White Medical Clinic systems and the associated transaction volumes

        7. The expectations required from the vendor–bid system

        8. The evaluation procedure to be used by the White Medical Clinic

    B. Organize bidders (vendor) conference

III. Bid evaluation process

    A. Evaluate mandatories

    B. Evaluate exceptions

    C. Evaluate service bureau

    D. Evaluate on-site computer

    E. Evaluate technical items

    F. Evaluate description of system

    G. Evaluate cost section

    H. Evaluate references

IV. On-site visit to vendors for performance and features demonstrations

V. Prepare a report on the results of the on-site visit(s) for use in evaluating vendors (recommend the winner)

Once you have reviewed the above outline, you should go to Appendix 3 to read the RFP. Rather than try to tell you what to do step-by-step, this real-life RFP illustrates the process by example. If you ever need to prepare an RFP, you can use it as a guideline. The next two sections of this chapter can be used when your RFP is to obtain a computer or a software package.

*C*onsiderations if a Computer Is Required

In the previous section we discussed Request for Proposals (RFPs); now let us review some of the considerations when a new computer or microcomputer is required.

The first major item is to decide what applications are to be put on the computer. In other words, to what use do you want to put this computer, and for which business systems? This really involves a study to determine priorities; that is, which applications should be put onto the computer first, second, and so forth. Economic return, the internal political structure, and long-term survival of the firm may be some of the criteria used to determine which applications get developed or purchased first.

After deciding upon applications, the second decision has to do with the computer hardware. This might be a large mainframe computer, a minicomputer, or a microcomputer (which frequently is the case these days). Choose the hardware to fit the application software programs and not vice versa. In reality, you want application programs that will perform the necessary business tasks. You really do not care which computer runs the programs. Of course, in reality you do care because of such items as cost and future maintenance; but your first priority is to identify needed application software and then determine which computers can handle the selected software.

At this point, you probably will have to do some research, visit computer equipment vendors, and/or visit software package vendors (if you are going to purchase or lease the software).

Now you are at the point where the Request for Proposals (RFPs) can be developed. RFP preparation was described in the previous section. Following is a checklist of items that must be taken into account when mainframes, minicomputers, or microcomputers are purchased or leased.

- ☐ Description of all hardware being bid upon.
- ☐ Cost of this hardware (purchase/lease).
- ☐ Any special installation requirements.
- ☐ Which software packages come with the hardware at no extra cost?
- ☐ What is the manufacturer's assistance for training, programming, software, and the like?
- ☐ Who provides the maintenance, at what cost, and for how long will it be available (in years)?
- ☐ Does this computer have any physical or data security features?
- ☐ What type of warranty does this equipment have?
- ☐ Get a description of all the documentation that comes with this hardware.
- ☐ What are the delivery schedules (impose a penalty clause for late delivery)?
- ☐ Are there any one-time computer installation costs?
- ☐ Who performs the initial computer training for personnel, and at what cost?
- ☐ Are there conversion costs, such as from the current file format to a new or different computer format?

- Review the supplies costs, such as magnetic tapes, floppy disks/diskettes, disk packs, paper, and so forth.
- Assuming we prefer to do our own applications programming, what programming languages are available on this computer?
- Where is this computer installed so that we can visit that site to see how it operates?
- Are there adequate internal controls?
- Are there program conversion costs?

Considerations if a Software Package Is Required

We described the methodology of preparing a Request for Proposals (RFP) previously in this chapter. This section is intended to offer further suggestions for the preparation of an RFP when you want to purchase/lease already developed software packages, particularly when the purchase of software for mainframe computers and minicomputers is being considered. Selecting software packages for microcomputers is comparatively less complicated because such packages are relatively inexpensive, ranging from $50 to $2,000. Most software vendors do not modify inexpensive general purpose software packages developed for microcomputers. Only when the software packages start costing in the neighborhood of $15,000 and up can you obtain custom modifications of a package. Further, it is quite easy to load a software package into a microcomputer and test it fully to see if it fits your needs. This is not the case with a complex, on-line, large scale software package that runs on a mainframe or minicomputer.

The initial consideration is whether you have the time and personnel to develop the application software package in-house. Along with that consideration, you also should determine the approximate cost of in-house development. Some of the factors against in-house development may be excessive cost, lack of personnel to develop the software, the system may require technical expertise in which the data processing staff has little or no experience, or the organization may need to use this new application system before it can be developed in-house.

Your next step is research. At this point, you have to search for candidate software packages. When you begin your search for software packages, your first goal is to identify potential sources of software information. This step usually is done at the corporate/agency library, where the librarians can help you locate volumes that list and describe software packages. Once you have narrowed the potential list of packages, the librarians can help you find articles that describe how others have used these same packages, what the packages could do, and what problems were encountered in their use. If there is no library at your place of employment, consider using your purchasing department (they may have trade literature), the public library, a nearby college or university library, or even the library of another corporation (with their prior permission, of course).

Part of your research may include talking to people in other organizations that use similar systems. Sometimes a competitor or other similar organization has a package that it is willing to sell. In any case, you must identify where software packages are available for sale before you can review them for use at your organization.

Finally, once you identify potential application software packages, you can begin developing your Request for Proposal (RFP). During the development of this RFP, some of the key factors to consider are

- ☐ What do we want this application program to perform?
- ☐ What are the volumes of transactions and/or data flows in our organization? In other words, what capacities will this software package have to handle?
- ☐ Consider reviewing performance and features demonstrations.
- ☐ You may want a benchmark "speed" demonstration, although this may be more *apropos* to the hardware than to the software.
- ☐ Is a thorough description of the software package available?
- ☐ Will the package be given to you in object code or can you have it in source code? Source code is superior because you can maintain the package yourself.
- ☐ What will it cost to purchase or lease the package?
- ☐ Who will maintain the package and at what cost?
- ☐ Are future enhancements available? If so, at what cost or are they free?
- ☐ Find a user of the software package and visit that user to see the package in operation. Try to avoid being the "world's first user" of a new package.
- ☐ Get a list and description of the different computers on which this package can operate.
- ☐ Get a description and list of the various operating systems under which this package operates.
- ☐ Get a list and description of the various teleprocessing monitors and/or telecommunication access programs under which this package operates if it is to be run on a real-time data communication network.
- ☐ Obtain descriptions of all "windows" in the package. Windows are where auxiliary operations can be appended if additions must be made to the package. Sometimes windows are called "exits," although exits usually are for normal or error departures from a module in structured programming.
- ☐ Get a list of all programmed security and control features that have been built into the package.

- □ In what language is this package written?
- □ What are the delivery schedules of this package?
- □ What vendor assistance can be expected during installation and in the future?
- □ Are there any special installation requirements or one-time installation costs?
- □ Are the databases or files expandable?
- □ How much quicker can the application be operational if the product is purchased rather than developed internally?
- □ Will the supplier provide any necessary program modifications?
- □ Will the vendor assist in the design of a pilot database?
- □ Does the vendor have a "hot line" telephone for technical support? How quickly can the vendor get to your site?

In closing, let us re-state the single most important factor with regard to purchasing/leasing a software package. Go to a user site where the potential package is installed and operating to see it in operation. Talk to the users to determine their satisfaction both with the software package and the seller of the software package.

SUNRISE SPORTSWEAR COMPANY

CUMULATIVE CASE: Economic Cost Comparisons (Step 8)

You have spoken a number of times with your friend Nancy back at Casper Management Consultants. She not only has expertise in prototyping, but is considered to be CMC's "resident expert" on microcomputer systems. As early as the logical data flow diagram, you spoke with her to confirm that what you planned to propose was realistic in terms of hardware. You sought her advice at that stage because you did not want to propose a system that would not work; even then you were thinking in terms of a local area network. After the discussion with Nancy, you proceeded to finalize the logical data flow diagram and it was approved by Mr. Reynolds.

Now you have worked out three alternatives based on the human–machine boundary. They are the minimal configuration (Alternative A) shown in Figure 8-4 in Chapter 8, the middle-of-the-road approach (Alternative B) shown in Figure 8-5, and the maximum human–machine boundary (Alternative C) shown in Figure 8-6. Serious work can be started now on the cost comparisons of these alternatives. You have invited Nancy out to Sunrise Sportswear to assist with the cost comparisons.

You have shown Nancy the building and personnel layout chart developed early in the project (see Figure 6-7 in Chapter 6). Since then the layout chart has been revised to incorporate the proposed Order Processing system. This revised layout of personnel and equipment is shown in Figure 10-4. You and Nancy have walked through the buildings at Sunrise Sportswear to see exactly how large the proposed local area network is and where the people are to be located. You discuss the types of available microcomputers, the need for off-the-shelf software packages to handle such things as text editing, similar name search capability to be used with customer mailing list software, database software, and packages to handle the local area network's communications and security. With the assistance of Ann Bull, you have determined approximately how many customers are currently in the D7: CUSTOMERS printout and how fast the list is growing. You and Nancy discuss the disk size needed to handle the size of the file and still allow for growth over the next few years. Nancy also reminds you that tape streaming will be required for backup in case anything happens to the hard disk. Finally, you talk about servicing of the equipment, warranties, and user documentation for both the software packages and the microcomputers.

Nancy has gained an understanding of what is needed, and you now sit down to work out the details of the cost estimates. You both came prepared with all types of equipment catalogs to make sure the costs will be realistic. First, Alternative A costs are calculated. The total for this alternative is $24,728 as shown in Figure 10-5. The equipment for process 3.0 is key to the entire proposal because it is the process in which Suzanne Wolfe checks customer names, assigns order and customer numbers, and changes addresses as needed. It is the key process because it must work adequately in order to achieve the overall objectives of lowering order processing time to 48 hours or less. Also, it must be able to provide lookup capability to other processes. Because process 3.0 needs at least a 20–50 megabyte hard disk, this process has the most expensive equipment. Also, it will be the one that is programmed to handle the file server software. Nancy has told you that some custom programming will be required to augment the off-the-shelf packages. Finally, this process requires a letter quality printer, which costs about twice as much as the double density matrix printers that will be adequate for some of the other processes. The cost of equipment and initial supplies for process 3.0 is estimated at $11,615.

Process 7.0 has a much less expensive configuration of $5,863 because its equipment does not require a hard disk or letter quality printer. It does, however, require two printers: one to handle continuous packing lists and another to handle continuous labels.

Alternative A costs include the equipment for both processes 3.0 and 7.0, the custom programming, and the cost of setting up a local area network. When working on the human–machine boundaries, you had considered an alternative of automating only process 3.0. The cost advantage was that it would not require a local area network. Such a configuration would not have been conducive to further automation, however, and the more up-to-date file of customer information could not be used by any of the other processes. You considered this to be such a serious deficiency that you purposely eliminated that configuration and went with one that, while more costly, would provide Sunrise Sportswear with more long-term advantages. As a result of this decision, nearly one-fifth of the total cost of Alternative A is devoted to the local area network.

Use of a local area network allows the people at process 7.0 (see Figure 8-4) to use the information in data store D7: CUSTOMERS that would be unavailable otherwise. In addition, if process 7.0 wants to use any other files that are put into the system later, it will have the capability to do so. The opposite also is true; other processes can use any data stores owned by process 7.0. The installation of a local area network allows Sunrise Sportswear to expand its network of microcomputers either a few at a time, or all at once. The file server software at process 3.0 allows all of the other microcomputers to store their information on the hard disk located at Suzanne Wolfe's microcomputer. In addition, they can have a supply of diskettes (or floppy disks, as they are sometimes called) to handle other jobs.

When satisfied with the completeness of the first proposal, you move on to Alternative B (see Figure 8-5 in Chapter 8). It is nearly double the amount of Alternative A, as shown in Figure 10-6. Processes 3.0 and 7.0 already have been calculated, and their total is at the top of the figure. Next, process 2.0 is shown. It has the least expensive configuration because a printer is not needed at this time. Process 2.0 is anticipated to be a lookup function, which is the reason for excluding a printer. Processes 5.0 and 6.0 are identical, with both needing a letter quality printer, continuous letterhead, and continuous envelopes.

Notice that the custom programming is unchanged from Alternative A. This is because the same programming needs to be done, regardless of the number of workstations that require a microcomputer and access to the local area network. Also, notice that the primary cost of the local area network does not increase all that much after the initial installation. The reason is that the wire pairs (or cabling) needed for the local area network are priced in terms of a reel. Even though the cost is estimated at only five cents per foot, Sunrise Sportswear would need enough to go between Buildings 1 and 3. The number of feet needed would be two or three times the actual footage between the various rooms. This is because the wire pairs must be pulled up and down walls and through ceiling panels. It is quite likely that Sunrise Sportswear will need at least half of a reel or more. The primary cost variables for the local area network, after the initial installation, are how much it costs to perform the wire pulling (which is based on how many rooms need to have a microcomputer connected to the LAN) and how many microcomputers have to be equipped with circuit cards so they can use the LAN.

Finally, Alternative C (see Figure 8-6 in Chapter 8) is calculated. It is a smaller than anticipated increment because Process 4.0 is a minimal configuration with

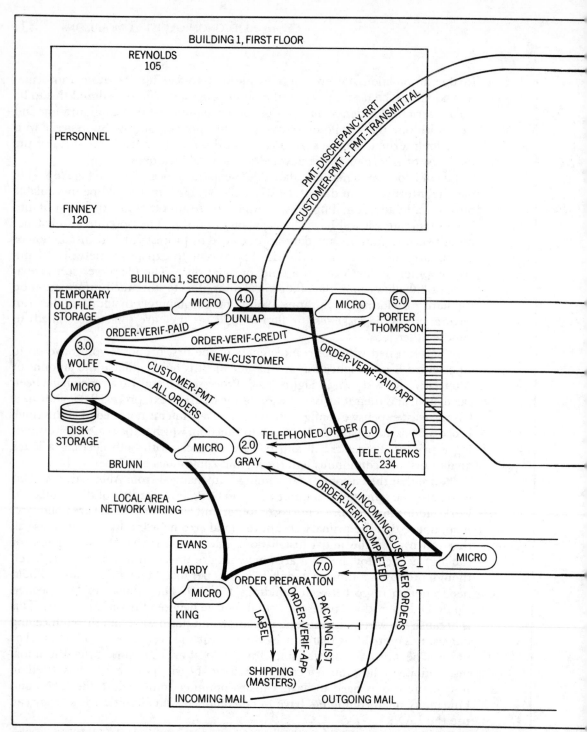

Figure 10-4 Revised building and personnel layout of Sunrise Sportwear. Assumes the maximum human–machine boundary. Accounting has been moved to Building 2. The first five steps of the order processing activity now are in the same building and on the same floor. Contrast this with Figure 6-7 in Chapter 6.

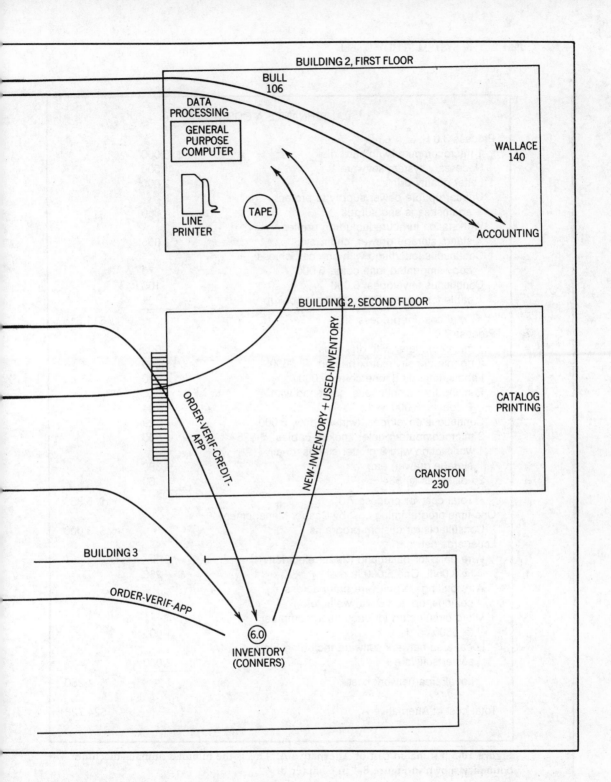

BUILDING 2, FIRST FLOOR

BULL
106

DATA
PROCESSING

GENERAL
PURPOSE
COMPUTER

LINE
PRINTER

TAPE

WALLACE
140

ACCOUNTING

BUILDING 2, SECOND FLOOR

ORDER-VERIF-CREDIT-
APP

NEW-INVENTORY + USED-INVENTORY

CATALOG
PRINTING

CRANSTON
230

BUILDING 3

ORDER-VERIF-APP

6.0

INVENTORY
(CONNERS)

433

ALTERNATIVE A COSTS

Process 3.0

1 microcomputer with hard disk	$ 6,000	
Necessary system software	1,500	
Letter quality printer	2,000	
Uninterruptible power supply to protect against sags and surges	850	
Workstation furniture including printer stand, storage drawer, chair, etc.	1,065	
Continuous letterhead with one carbonless copy, imprinted, one color, 6,000	70	
Continuous envelopes, 6,000	105	
1 cable for microcomputer/printer hookup	25	
Total cost for process 3.0		$11,615

Process 7.0

1 microcomputer with diskettes	$ 3,000	
2 double density matrix printers @ $600	1,200	
Labels, imprinted, one color, 6,000	30	
Packing lists, continuous, screened with 2 copies, 6,000	104	
Continuous envelopes, twin-window, 6,000	29	
2 microcomputer/printer hookup cables @ $25	50	
1 workstation with 2 printer stands, chair, storage drawer, etc.	1,390	
20 diskettes @ $3	60	
Total cost for process 7.0		$ 5,863

One-time programming cost by Casper Management

Consultants for custom programs		$ 3,000

Local area network

Wire pairs for baseband (direct electricity) @ $.05/ft. One 5,000 ft. reel	$ 250	
Wire pulling (to pull wire pairs across ceilings, up and down walls, etc.)	1,000	
Micro circuit card for each microcomputer @ $500/card	1,000	
Local area network software including file server software	2,000	
Local area network cost		$ 4,250
Total cost of Alternative A		$24,728

Figure 10-5 Estimated cost of Alternative A. This is the minimal human–machine boundary shown in Figure 8-4 in Chapter 8.

ALTERNATIVE B COSTS

Process 3.0 total costs		$11,615
Process 7.0 total costs		5,863
Process 2.0		
1 microcomputer with diskettes	$ 3,000	
Workstation with chair, storage drawer,		
no printer stand	807	
10 diskettes @ $3	30	
Total cost for process 2.0		$ 3,837
Process 5.0		
1 microcomputer with diskettes	$ 3,000	
1 letter quality printer	2,000	
Workstation, including printer stand, chair,		
storage drawer, etc.	1,065	
Continuous letterhead with carbonless		
copy, 6,000 @ $69.95	70	
Continuous envelopes, 6,000 @ $104.90	105	
1 microcomputer/printer cable	25	
20 diskettes @ $3	60	
Total cost for process 5.0		$ 6,325
Process 6.0		
1 microcomputer with diskettes	$ 3,000	
Workstation with chair, printer stand,		
storage drawer, etc.	1,065	
1 letter quality printer	2,000	
Continuous letterhead with carbonless		
copy, 6,000 @ $69.95	70	
Continuous envelopes, 6,000 @ $104.90	105	
1 microcomputer/printer cable	25	
20 diskettes $3	60	
Total cost for process 6.0		$ 6,325
One-time programming cost for custom programs		$ 3,000
Local area network		
Wire pairs for baseband. One 5,000 ft. reel	$ 250	
Wire pulling	2,000	
Micro circuit card for each microcomputer	2,500	
Local area network software	2,000	
Local area network cost		$ 6,750
Total cost of Alternative B		$43,715

Figure 10-6 Estimated cost of Alternative B. This is the middle-of-the-road approach to the human–machine boundary shown in Figure 8-5 in Chapter 8.

no need for a printer. Again, the only changes in the local area network costs have to do with the wire pulling and the micro circuit card. Alternative C is estimated at $48,252 (see Figure 10-7).

These are the investment costs of setting up a local area network within Sunrise Sportswear. There are other costs that must be calculated, however. These pertain to the actual implementation of the system. The total investment and implementation costs for the three alternatives are shown in Figure 10-8. Notice that the three investment cost totals are first on the list. Then the implementation costs are considered. Did you notice in the revised layout chart shown in Figure 10-4 that Ed Wallace and his Accounting Department were no longer on the second floor of Building 1? When you were revising the layout of the Order Processing steps, you realized that putting the people in processes 1.0 through 5.0 near one another could have numerous advantages. At that point, you examined the locations of the various departments. You might compare Figures 6-7 and 10-4 to see the revisions.

Because Order Processing is such an important function at Sunrise Sportswear, you talked with some of the managers to obtain their reactions to the possibility of shifting some of the groups around. It was obvious that the Data Processing Department was not a candidate for moving because of the computer equipment and special room needs. Dave Cranston was not receptive to moving the Catalog Printing Department because of its large drafting tables, photography equipment, and so forth. When you approached Ed Wallace, however, he said that he would be willing to have the Accounting Department moved closer to the Data Processing Department because they have to interact so much. Also, he said he was tired of running up and down the stairs for all these years and would love to be on the first floor. His only stipulation was that the whole Accounting Department would have to be located close to one another.

As a result of these discussions, you talked with Mr. Reynolds about the possibility of relocating these departments. Because people had been complaining, he agreed that it might make more sense to get the Order Processing staff grouped in a better way. He wondered, though, if Valery Brunn would be willing to make such a change because she was partial to her current location. Since it was clear that Ms. Brunn's approval was necessary before proceeding further, you approached her with the proposal. At first she was reluctant. You used all of your persuasive powers to convince Ms. Brunn that it was a good idea. Your major argument was that she needed to be closer to her staff in order to observe and control their activities more effectively. Ms. Brunn finally agreed to move to the second floor of Building 1 on the condition that she will have Jon Gray's old area, once the system is running and the files no longer need to be stored there. This was agreeable to Mr. Reynolds, so you proceeded with the remainder of the planning. Because the flow of work could be arranged more suitably, this precluded the need to extend the local area network either to the first floor of Building 1 or to Building 2. Thus, the cost of installing the local area

ALTERNATIVE C COSTS

Process 3.0 total costs	$11,615
Process 7.0 total costs	5,863
Process 2.0 total costs	3,837
Process 5.0 total costs	6,325
Process 6.0 total costs	6,325

Process 4.0

1 microcomputer with diskettes	$ 3,000	
Workstation with storage drawer, chair, no printer stand	807	
10 diskettes @ $3	30	
Total cost for process 4.0		$ 3,837

One-time programming cost for custom programs		$ 3,000

Local area network

Wire pairs for baseband. One 5,000 ft. reel	$ 250	
Wire pulling	2,200	
Micro circuit card for each microcomputer	3,000	
Local area network software including file server software	2,000	
Local area network cost		$ 7,450

Total cost of Alternative C	$48,252

Figure 10-7 Estimated cost of Alternative C. This is the maximum human–machine boundary shown in Figure 8-6 in Chapter 8.

COST TO IMPLEMENT PROPOSED ORDER PROCESSING SYSTEM

	Alternative A	Alternative B	Alternative C
Investment costs	$24,728	$43,715	$48,252
Implementation costs*			
Move Accounting Dept.** from Building 1, 2nd floor to Building 2, 1st floor	0	1,800	1,800
Move Wolfe (3.0) from Building 2, 1st floor to Building 1, 2nd floor	300	300	300
Move Gray (2.0) around the corner to different room in same building and same floor (only current files to be moved)	0	600	600
Move Porter and Thompson (5.0) from Building 2, 2nd floor to Building 1, 2nd floor	0	900	900
Move Dunlap (4.0) from Building 1, 1st floor to Building 1, 2nd floor	0	0	300
Training for 3.0 and 7.0	400	0	0
Training for 3.0, 7.0, 2.0, 5.0, and 6.0	0	1,000	0
Training for 3.0, 7.0, 2.0, 5.0, 6.0, and 4.0	0	0	1,200
Relocate electrical plugs for microcomputers	500	1,000	1,200
Total costs	$25,928	$49,315	$54,552

* Moving costs estimated at $300/person for desks, files and movement of telephone extensions.

** Compare Figure 6-7 to Figure 10-4 to confirm these moves.

Figure 10-8 Comparative costs for implementing the three alternative configurations at Sunrise Sportswear.

network has been minimized, as you can see from Figure 10-4. Incidentally, one other factor in choosing this particular layout had to do with telephones. You wanted the Order Processing staff to be near one another, and this included the telephone order clerks. It was not desirable to add the cost of moving all the telephone lines or disrupting the order clerks. It was more desirable to have the Order Processing people shifted to be near the telephone order clerks.

Returning to Figure 10-8, the Accounting Department does not have to move if the minimal alternative is chosen. Suzanne Wolfe can be moved from Building 2 to Building 1 without disrupting the Accounting Department. If either Alternative B or C is chosen, however, the Accounting Department must move to make room for Order Processing. It is for this reason that moving costs for the Accounting Department are shown only for Alternatives B and C.

Suzanne Wolfe will be moved with any of the three alternatives because process 3.0 is such a key activity and must be closer to the other Order Processing staff.

Jon Gray, Bob Thompson, and Lynn Porter will be moved only with Alternatives B and C, while Rosemary Dunlap only moves with Alternative C. Figure 10-8 reflects these moving costs under the appropriate alternative.

Training will have to be done under all three of the alternatives. The increasing cost of this training is reflected in Figure 10-8 also.

Finally, Nancy reminds you that many people forget to include the cost of relocating electrical plugs that are needed for the microcomputers. Since this is necessary for any microcomputer installation, and because it must be done by an electrician, it must be included as an implementation cost. (Normally the local area network is an implementation cost, but in this case it fits more logically with investment costs.)

Since neither of you can think of any other costs, the alternatives are totaled, as shown in Figure 10-8. As you can see, Alternatives B and C are approximately double that of A, with C being slightly more than B.

You know that Mr. Reynolds is going to need to know why he should spend all this money just to add a couple of microcomputers. Recognizing that it is important to present benefits along with the costs of a proposed system, you calculate the savings that will accrue because of the changes. Although it is difficult to obtain concrete dollar figures because of Sunrise Sportswear's poor recordkeeping, you do your best to assign dollar figures to some of the tangible benefits. These are shown in Figure 10-9. These figures indicate that Alternative A could save $900/month, Alternative B could save $2,100/month, and Alternative C could save $2,300/month. In addition, you list the intangible benefits for which no dollar values can be assigned because you recognize their importance in helping Sunrise Sportswear's management understand why they need to make these changes.

You decide to perform two different cost comparisons. The first of these is the payback period technique. Using the amounts from Figures 10-8 and 10-9, you are able to calculate payback, as shown in Figure 10-10. With "I" as the total

SAVINGS TO IMPLEMENT PROPOSED ORDER PROCESSING SYSTEM

Tangible Benefits	Alternative A	Alternative B	Alternative C
Fewer lost/canceled orders	$500	$500	$500
Provision of packing lists enable customers to have fewer inquiries	200	200	200
Faster label printing	200	200	200
Gray has more efficient file lookup, less filing, reduced storage costs		200	200
Credit rejection letters printed by computer, and overdue accounts reduced almost to zero		300	300
Backorder file more efficient with added information available		500	500
Backorder letters printed by computer		200	200
Dunlap lookup more efficient and faster			200
Total savings	$900*	$2,100*	$2,300*

* Savings calculated on a per month basis

Intangible Benefits

Faster order processing time, reduced from several weeks to 48 hours
Better employee morale
More efficient use of floor space and personnel
Better control over potential threats
Better customer relations
More realistic delivery promises
Future cost avoidance; modernization is inevitable to meet competition
Better managerial control

Figure 10-9 Monthly savings that will be realized with implementation of the proposed alternatives at Sunrise Sportswear. Also indicates intangible benefits.

PAYBACK PERIOD TO INSTALL NEW ORDER PROCESSING SYSTEM

Using the basic formula for after tax payback of:

$$P = \frac{I}{(1 - T)R}$$

where:

I = investment or capital expenditure
T = tax rate (use 48%)
R = annual savings realized by investment

Alternative A

$$\text{Payback} = \frac{25,928}{(1 - 0.48)\ 10,800} = 4.62 \text{ years to payback}$$

Alternative B

$$\text{Payback} = \frac{49,315}{(1 - 0.48)\ 25,200} = 3.76 \text{ years to payback}$$

Alternative C

$$\text{Payback} = \frac{54,552}{(1 - 0.48)\ 27,600} = 3.80 \text{ years to payback}$$

Conclusion: Alternatives B and C are so close in time to payback that they may be considered equal. Alternative A is the least attractive based on years to payback. R was calculated by multiplying the monthly savings amounts by 12.

Figure 10-10 Calculation to show how soon the three investment alternatives will be paid back.

cost to implement each of the alternatives, a corporate tax rate of 48 percent, and the annual savings (R) calculated from the total savings in Figure 10-9, you learn that investment Alternatives B and C provide after-tax payback nearly a year sooner than investment Alternative A. This is true even though they cost more than double that of Alternative A. What this indicates is that the investment Alternatives B and C will produce increased cash flow to Sunrise Sportswear sooner than Alternative A. Since future revenue streams are faced with uncertainty, investment proposals based on the payback method help eliminate some of the uncertainty because preference is given to projects that have an earlier payback. There is one serious drawback to this method, however. The payback method does not take into account the time value of money. That is, it does not help you weigh the value of today's dollars in terms of their future worth.

To do this, you must use the present value method. Figure 10-11 shows your net present value calculations for the three alternatives. These calculations indicate that if Sunrise Sportswear borrows the money to pay for this investment at a cost of 9%, the cost of all three alternatives would be recovered by the end of three years. What is important, however, is that Sunrise Sportswear would be $1,364 ahead at the end of the third year by using Alternative A. By using Alternative B, they would be $14,365 ahead, and Alternative C would be even more advantageous with $15,193. If the money to finance these alternatives costs 9%, then Alternative C is the preferred one. Since the rule in net present value is to accept all proposals that have a positive value, all three of these alternatives may be accepted; however, Alternative C is the best of the three in terms of the cost of raising capital to finance investment.

Since all three alternatives show a positive net present value at the end of three years, you perform one more calculation to determine exactly how soon you would expect Sunrise Sportswear's cash flow to improve. You do this by breaking the third year dollar value into a monthly figure. When you add the first and second year together, the monthly figure is added progressively until the amount of the investment is exceeded. In Figure 10-12 you see that both Alternatives B and C turn positive at the end of 2 years and 4 months, while Alternative A turns positive at the end of 2 years and 11 months.

Although you would like to make some cost comparisons with regard to the present operating costs versus the alternatives chosen for the proposed system, you are unable to do so because Sunrise Sportswear cannot provide enough information on current costs to do this. The only figures you can obtain are salaries, which are not expected to change with the new system unless it is so effective that fewer personnel are needed.

You have one last concern to discuss with Nancy and that is whether to write a Request for Proposals for this system. The conclusion is not to write one in this case. Nancy advises that the system is too small to be worth the effort; RFPs usually are written where the purchase or lease of large mainframe computers is

PRESENT VALUE OF PROPOSED ORDER PROCESSING SYSTEM

Using the basic formula for net present value

NPV = net present value
PV = cost of the new system
R = cash flow (savings)
k = cost of money (interest rate)
n = number of years savings available

$$NPV = \frac{R_1}{(1+k)^1} + \frac{R_2}{(1+k)^2} + \ldots + \frac{R_n}{(1+k)^n} - PV$$

Alternative A (monthly savings of 900 × 12 = 10,800)

$$NPV = \frac{10,800}{(1+0.09)^1} + \frac{10,800}{(1+0.09)^2} + \frac{10,800}{(1+0.09)^3} - 25,928$$

$$NPV = \frac{10,800}{1.09} + \frac{10,800}{1.19} + \frac{10,800}{1.30} - 25,928$$

$$NPV = 9,908 + 9,076 + 8,308 - 25,928$$

$$NPV = 1,364 \text{ at end of third year}$$

Alternative B (monthly savings of 2,100 × 12 = 25,200)

$$NPV = \frac{25,200}{(1+0.09)^1} + \frac{25,200}{(1+0.09)^2} + \frac{25,200}{(1+0.09)^3} - 49,315$$

$$NPV = \frac{25,200}{1.09} + \frac{25,200}{1.19} + \frac{25,200}{1.30} - 49,315$$

$$NPV = 23,119 + 21,176 + 19,385 - 49,315$$

$$NPV = 14,365 \text{ at end of third year}$$

Alternative C (monthly savings of 2,300 × 12 = 27,600)

$$NPV = \frac{27,600}{(1+0.09)^1} + \frac{27,600}{(1+0.09)^2} + \frac{27,600}{(1+0.09)^3} - 54,552$$

$$NPV = \frac{27,600}{1.09} + \frac{27,600}{1.19} + \frac{27,600}{1.30} - 54,552$$

$$NPV = 25,321 + 23,193 + 21,231 - 54,552$$

$$NPV = 15,193 \text{ at end of third year}$$

Figure 10-11 Net present values of Sunrise Sportswear's three alternatives. Alternative C is the most desirable.

YEARS TO REACH POSITIVE NET PRESENT VALUE

Alternative A

NPV = 1,364 at end of third year
Year 1 = 9,908
Year 2 = 9,076
Year 3 = 8,308 ÷ 12 = 692/month
therefore,
       9,908 + 9,076 + 11(692) = 9,908 + 9,076 + 7,612 = 26,596
Alternative A becomes positive (over $25,928) at 2 years, 11 months

Alternative B

NPV = 14,365 at end of third year
Year 1 = 23,119
Year 2 = 21,176
Year 3 = 19,385 ÷ 12 = 1,615/month
therefore,
     23,119 + 21,176 + 4(1,615) = 23,119 + 21,176 + 6,460 = 50,755
Alternative B becomes positive (over $49,315) at 2 years, 4 months

Alternative C

NPV = 15,193 at end of third year
Year 1 = 25,321
Year 2 = 23,193
Year 3 = 21,231 ÷ 12 = 1,769/month
therefore,
     25,321 + 23,193 + 4(1,769) = 25,321 + 23,193 + 7,076 = 55,590
Alternative C becomes positive (over $54,552) at 2 years, 4 months

Conclusion: Assuming Sunrise Sportwear borrows money at 9% to finance this investment, Alternatives B and C are equally attractive since the investment will pay for itself by the end of 2 years, 4 months. Alternative A is the least attractive expenditure of investment dollars.

Figure 10-12 How soon Sunrise Sportswear will be able to reinvest its capital because the amount borrowed has been repaid.

of concern. Further, she has enough familiarity both with the equipment and software to short-cut this process. She has many contacts with vendors and feels that she can obtain prices that are equal to, or better than, what could be obtained with an RFP.

You are not able to identify anything else that is needed, and begin to gather all of the information on the design alternatives, the controls, and the cost comparisons for the presentation to Mr. Reynolds.

Student Questions

1. Can you think of one good reason why the costs of the existing system at Sunrise Sportswear cannot be compared very well with the proposed system even though the text says that comparing the cost of the current system with the new may be the single most important cost comparison?
2. Can you explain one factor that eliminates operating cost analysis of an existing system such as that at Sunrise Sportswear?
3. Name at least one more intangible cost that has been left out of Figure 10-9.
4. Why was the chargeback method ignored with regard to cost analysis at Sunrise Sportswear?
5. What factor or factors would make you change your mind with regard to writing an RFP for Sunrise Sportswear's new system?
6. When it comes time to purchase the new system, what will be your first priority?

Student Tasks

1. For purposes of comparison, let us assume that the annual savings amounts shown in Figure 10-9 really were the "return over operating expenses" for each of three years. The "fixed investments in dollars" are shown in Figure 10-8. Using these assumptions, calculate the marginal efficiency of investment (also called internal rate of return) for our three proposals. What do they tell you?
2. Identify future operating costs for the proposed system. To which ones can you assign dollar amounts?

Selected Readings

1. Behrman, Andrew. "The Art of Purchasing a Computer System," *Journal of the Society of Research Administrators*, vol. 15, no. 4, Spring 1984, pp. 35–39.

2. Cashin, Jerry. "A Procedure for Selecting a 'Standard' Personal Computer for End Users," *Small Systems World*, vol. 12, no. 1, January 1984, pp. 22–25. [Describes the steps of a successful microcomputer acquisition project.]

3. Cross, Philip C. "Reducing Operating Costs: 101 Items to Check," *Journal of Information Systems Management*, vol. 1, no. 1, Winter 1984, pp. 3–15. [Data center cost reduction techniques.]

4. Eaton, Roderic L. "Lease vs. Buy: Careful Evaluation of Alternatives Assists in Optimum Return on Equipment Investment," *Computerworld*, vol. 18, no. 30, July 23, 1984, pp. 76–77.

5. Horr, David A., and William E. Barker. "Choosing Your First Computer System," *Retail Control*, vol. 52, no. 7, March 1984, pp. 46–54.

6. Kirby, H. Roger. "11 Ways to Select Software," *ComputerData* (Canada), vol. 9, no. 8, September 1984, pp. 5–6.

7. Loew, Gary Wayne. "Designing an Effective Request for Proposal," *Small Systems World*, vol. 12, no. 5, May 1984, pp. 34–39.

8. MacQuarrie, J. J. "What to Remember When Selecting Software for Micros," *Canadian Datasystems*, vol. 16, no. 4, April 1984, pp. 65, 67, 69.

9. Mikill, Frederick J., II. "ISD Cost Allocation," *Journal of Information Management*, vol. 5, no. 2, Winter 1984, pp. 15–21. [Describes an actual Information System Department's cost allocation system in which both direct and indirect costs are allocated to users.]

10. Mishan, E. J. *Cost Benefit Analysis, 3rd edition.* Winchester, Mass.: Allen & Unwin, Inc., 1982.

11. Ossi, Richard. "Buying vs. Leasing: Considering the Pros and Cons," *National Public Accountant*, vol. 29, no. 5, May 1984, pp. 50–52.

12. Perry, William E. *Evaluating the Costs/Benefits of Data Bases.* Wellesley, Mass.: QED Information Sciences, Inc., 1982.

13. Rummer, Patricia. "Making the Lease vs. Buy Decision," *Small Systems World*, vol. 12, no. 3, March 1984, pp. 20–24.

14. Shore, Barry. "Identifying and Minimizing the Risks in Software Selection," *Journal of Systems Management*, vol. 35, no. 8, August 1984, pp. 26–31.

15. Stewart, Rodney D., and Ann L. Stewart. *Proposal Preparation.* New York: John Wiley & Sons, Inc., 1984.

Questions

1. Identify the cost categories that are available for comparing the cost of different system designs.

2. Why is estimating the cost of a system significantly more complex than estimating the cost of a new piece of hardware?

3. Identify the two concepts of cost analysis.

4. Briefly describe investment costs.

5. Briefly describe implementation costs.

6. Briefly describe annual operating costs.

7. What is the formula for calculating annual cost?

8. How is break-even analysis applied to comparisons between the current system and the new system that is being planned?

9. How does the payback period criterion rank projects?

10. What is the formula for calculating the payback period after taxes?

11. Define the term "marginal efficiency of investment."

12. Under what conditions should an investment be made using the MEI criterion?

13. Using present value analysis, under what conditions is a project accepted?

14. What four steps should be taken in preparing an economic cost comparison between the current system and the proposed system?

15. There are a number of noneconomic benefits for which the analyst should be looking. Name at least five.

16. For what is the cost chargeback method used?

17. What is an RFP and how is it used?

18. Identify a minimum of 10 items that must be taken into account when preparing an RFP that is directed toward the acquisition of computer hardware.

19. Identify a minimum of 10 items that must be taken into account when preparing an RFP that is directed toward the acquisition of application software packages.

SITUATION CASES

Case 10-1: *Guild Mortgage*

Using the following data, determine which is the best proposal cost-wise for Guild Mortgage to implement.

Costs	Microcomputer-Based Payroll	Central Mainframe Payroll
Investment	$10,000	$6,000
Implementation	$ 2,000	$3,000
Annual Operating	$ 1,000	$3,000
Estimated System Life in Years	4	4

Case 10-2: *Guild Mortgage (continued)*

Using both the data from Case 10-1 and the following data, calculate the after-taxes payback period for the two proposals in Case 10-1. Which system is preferable when using the payback criterion? Annual return is

Year	Microcomputer-Based Payroll	Central Mainframe Payroll
Year 1	$1,500	$9,500
Year 2	$2,500	$7,000
Year 3	$7,000	$5,500
Year 4	$9,000	$5,000

Corporate tax rate is 48 percent.
Annual return does not include annual operating costs.

Case 10-3: *Guild Mortgage (continued)*

Using the data in Cases 10-1 and 10-2, perform a net present value comparison between the microcomputer and mainframe computer payroll proposals (use a 10 percent interest rate). Should you reject either proposal based on its net present value?

Case 10-4: *Gerald Publishing Company*

A college textbook publisher was considering the expansion of its operations, and the need for a new printing press system was being explored. Gerald Publishing retained an analyst to perform an economic cost comparison of the proposed system against the existing system.

The analyst first prepared data with which to predict the projected useful life of the proposed printing system. From this data, a reasonable life expectancy of 12 years was predicted.

Once life expectancy of the new system was predicted, the analyst calculated operating costs during the projected useful life of the system. The analyst first projected the cost of salaries for the new system.

To run the new system, three journeyman printers and two apprentices would be required at a cost of $72,800 per year. The analyst obtained this figure by multiplying the hourly rates by 40 hours, and then multiplying that figure by

52 weeks. This figure then was projected over the estimated life of the new system. Consideration of a 6.5 percent wage increase per year was calculated into the projected figures.

Cost of floor space was then calculated for the new system. It was felt that expansion of the existing printer room would be the best way to obtain the new area needed for the proposed system. Even though some personnel and equipment would have to be moved, management had decided specifically on expansion of the existing room. The space needed for the new system was calculated at 3,200 square feet. Accounting provided the analyst with a cost per square foot of $15. This cost, multiplied by 3,200 square feet, gave a total room expansion cost of $48,000.

Inventory and supply costs for the new system were then estimated. Accounting once again was useful in providing the needed figures. Expanding newspaper subscriptions were considered since they cause increased inventory requirements. It was explained that newsprint was considered to be a raw material and was, therefore, included in inventory. Increased system size also would increase the need for supplies. Inventory costs increased $25,000 for the new system. When calculated against an eight percent interest rate, additional annual costs were projected at $2,000. Supply costs were $99,000.

The analyst also found that overhead would increase under the proposed system. Costs for air conditioning, heating, lighting, and power would increase, and insurance costs would rise because of increased personnel and property protection requirements. The analyst also learned that property taxes (both state and local) would increase, along with maintenance and janitorial costs.

Investment costs were considered for the new system. The cost of the new system was estimated at $474,000. This figure was contained in a bid which had been agreed upon tentatively by management at an earlier time.

The analyst then examined implementation costs. Increased electrical and air conditioning requirements were calculated after consultation with contractors. Air conditioning installation would cost $80,000 and electrical changes would cost $32,000. Additional furniture costs would be $4,000. When the analyst added up implementation costs, the total obtained was $116,000.

At this point, the analyst took the present system into consideration. The operating costs were calculated using the same method as was used for the proposed system. Only two journeyman printers and one apprentice were needed at a salary cost of $44,720 per year. Expected remaining life of the current system was estimated at three years, although the cost comparisons were made on an equal basis.

The existing system required 2,400 square feet of floor space. At a cost per square foot of $15, the total cost was estimated at $36,000.

Inventory and supply costs also were considered for the present system. Supply costs were placed at $92,000, with inventory costs totaling $122,000.

Overhead costs for the existing system were calculated at $71,000 for air conditioning, heating, lighting, and power. Taxes were calculated at $32,000, while janitorial and maintenance costs were placed at $27,000.

When the analyst had gathered all the information, a report was compiled for management. The analyst included a chart to show exact figures for comparison, and it showed other costs incurred. With these facts and figures before them management could see, in dollars and cents, what a new system would cost in comparison with the existing system.

OPERATING COSTS

	New System	Existing System
Salaries	$ 72,800	$ 44,720
Space	48,000	36,000
Inventory (increased cost only)	2,000	
Supplies	99,000	92,000
Overhead		
Air conditioning	104,000	58,000
Heating	8,000	6,000
Lighting	10,000	5,000
Power	2,000	2,000
Insurance	30,000	21,000
Taxes	44,000	32,000
Maintenance–janitorial	34,000	27,000
TOTAL	$453,800	$323,720

IMPLEMENTATION COSTS

Additional air conditioning	$ 80,000
Additional electrical service	32,000
Additional furniture costs	4,000
	$116,000

INVESTMENT COSTS

Cost of new printing press system	$474,000

Questions

1. Did the analyst present an accurate projection of salary costs for both the existing and proposed systems at Gerald Publishing Company?
2. Did the analyst correctly provide management with a clear picture of implementation costs for the new system?

Chapter 11

SELLING THE SYSTEM

LEARNING OBJECTIVES

You will learn how to . . .

☐ Gain self-confidence.

☐ Deal effectively with others.

☐ Pre-identify basic objections to the proposed system.

☐ Prepare a written report that summarizes the systems study.

☐ Give a verbal presentation on the systems study.

☐ Use visual aids.

☐ Close the presentation on a positive note.

☐ Use structured and traditional documentation in presenting the alternative proposals to management.

Selling Yourself

One of the first things you must learn, if you are going to be a successful systems analyst, is to sell yourself. What we are referring to is your personal ability to convince other people that you are a dependable or reliable person. It is through *your* personal actions, written reports, and verbal output that other people receive an image by which they judge your dependability or reliability.

Selling yourself involves some basics that you learned long ago, such as good hygiene, a clean cut appearance that is in accordance with the current dress customs or codes where you work, your posture and how you carry yourself when you walk around the organization, and how *sure* you sound when you speak.

Other specific things that will sell *you* in your systems analysis projects are how well you get along with people while you are gathering data, the physical appearance of your written report, its readability, and the impact of any verbal presentations. Finally, you must not appear as arrogant, self-centered, conceited, or overconfident when dealing with other people.

Please remember, an important phase in the development of any useful product is the communication of that product's utility (usefulness) to the prospective users. You have the responsibility for presenting the system proposal to management in a clear and objective manner, but with enthusiasm for the benefits that can be derived from its use.

Background Knowledge

The systems analyst must realize that in the final presentation an *idea* is being sold to management, not a product. A system is an abstract idea. It rides the thin line between the tangible and the intangible. Management usually has a desire to improve the company's systems, but normally there also is fear of expensive failure. When the analyst replaces fear with reassurance, management's desire is free to express itself and the new system can be accepted.

The analyst should mentally ask many questions in relation to selling the new system to the management of the area under study. Has management had any previous experience with *your* systems studies, and was that experience favorable? Does management have a need for this specific new system? Is management aware of the need? Does management harbor any fears or prejudices of a specific or general nature? Does the management in the area under study have the authority to buy or accept the new system? Is management able to implement the changes called for in the new system? To whom is the management of the area under study accountable (who else needs to be convinced about the new system)?

After answering the above questions the analyst should think about the meanings of a few key words. Whether a written or a verbal report is used, the five key words for successful interaction with people are

1. *Empathy:* mentally entering into the feeling or spirit of other people in order to understand them better.
2. *Tact:* ability to say or do the right thing without offending other people.
3. *Rapport:* a meeting of the minds, or absence of friction.
4. *Sensitivity:* the quality of being readily affected by other people, responding to their feelings.
5. *Integrity:* basic honesty and moral uprightness.

Selling management on a new system is a continuous effort and it should be carried on throughout the entire systems study. The analyst's enthusiasm and positive mental attitude can help sell the system in the beginning. (We assume in this chapter that the analyst genuinely feels a new system is needed and that it will be a beneficial change for the firm.) As the study progresses and each individual's personality unfolds it takes empathy, tact, rapport, sensitivity, and integrity to continue the selling job. Finally, after the design phase, it takes the optimum combination of written reports and verbal presentations to negotiate a change from the old to the new.

*B*asic Objections to Overcome

The analyst will be better prepared during this phase if basic objections to the proposed system are considered ahead of time. Think about them, weigh their importance, and prepare answers to them. Any experienced analyst can tell you that your hands will be full trying to answer the *unexpected* objections. Anticipating and being prepared for as many objections as possible has several important advantages. First, it can help you determine, prior to the final presentation, if any items were overlooked. If so, these omissions can be corrected immediately. Second, it helps you *feel* prepared because you know you are prepared. And third, your obvious preparedness probably will be recognized and appreciated by management, thus inspiring their confidence in your overall design.

You must be prepared for the obvious objections to the proposed system. Some categories of basic objections usually follow along these lines.

1. The cost is too high or it appears too low for what the system is claimed to be able to do. You might respond by offering to go over the costs again, describing an alternate system that was dropped earlier, or ask the person who is objecting what cost would be just right.

2. The performance is not good enough, or it is more than is required at this point in time. Again, you might review the performance and the performance goals that were established previously. You also might inquire as to what level of performance this person feels is adequate.

3. The new system is not in keeping with the goals, objectives and policies of the firm or the area under study. If this is true you are in trouble, although because you reviewed the organization's goals, this should not be a serious objection. Your response might be to present to the objector the actual goals, objectives, and policies of the firm or area under study because the objector really may not understand what they are.

4. The response time or processing time is either too slow or too fast with respect to other operations within the firm. You can respond that we plan to change the processing time in those other operations also; since it has to start with some system, the new one is the most logical. Or, you can point out that this imbalance in processing times does not hurt anything and it builds for the future.

5. The system is not flexible enough. If changes are made in other areas, this system will collapse and the investment will have been wasted. Again, if this is true, you are in trouble. Your response might be to review the flexibility of your system; show them that it is flexible enough to accept changes that are made in other systems. If the questions relate to a specific system interface, be sure to address that concern.

6. The quality, capacity, efficiency, accuracy, or reliability of the new system may not meet the criteria of the management personnel involved. When you wrote the evaluation criteria (back in Chapter 7, Define the New System Requirements), you should have made sure that these criteria matched those of the management personnel involved. Your response should be sure to enumerate each criterion in your report, make sure your system meets that criterion, and then review that criterion with the objecting managers. They might see that your criteria are even higher than their own!

7. Certain management personnel may dislike your motives, personality, or presentation methods. If this is true, it is a major problem. There really is no good response if you have alienated the people for whom you are developing the system. The only solution might be to have another person make the management presentation so the people who must accept the system are not further alienated. Also, go back and read the first section of this chapter, Selling Yourself.

You may ask why the analyst should have to sell the new system to a company that has paid for it, wants it, needs it, and will profit by it. The basic reason is that you have to *prove* to management that it needs the new system and will profit by it. Money is a scarce resource and management usually has more projects on which to spend it than there is money available. Therefore the analyst has to convince management that this new system is more important than the other projects that are under consideration.

Another reason that selling is required is the fact that what the analyst offers is change. Change often is seen as a threat by some personnel. The threat of change may develop insecurity and fears of job loss. When this happens, there will be opposition to the analyst and to the new system that was developed. Only when management agrees that the new system is needed and decrees that it will be implemented will some of these people cooperate. Management, in other words, must impose change. In some cases, change occurs only through directive.

Gaining Acceptance through the Written Report

The final written report is the single most important report of the entire systems study. All systems studies require a final system report. Until now, the other required reports were the feasibility study, problem definition, definition of the new system requirements, data flow diagrams/flowcharts/documentation sheets, and periodic progress reports. (At this point you might want to refer to the section titled Progress Reports in Chapter 18 in order to see a typical progress report.)

An outline is presented below of what might be put into a final written report. It is by no means a definitive statement on the subject since the contents and outline may vary a great deal depending upon the study. It is simply a guide to the basic contents the analyst should consider for inclusion. Amplifying comments follow the outline.

Final Report

   I. Summary of the full systems study.

      A. Statement of events leading up to decision to conduct the study.

      B. Statement of the problem to be solved.

         1. Subject.

         2. Scope.

         3. Objectives.

      C. Statement of the major recommendations only, and justification of the new system.

      D. Summary of the cost and implementation schedules (this may be left until the body of the report).

  II. Body of the report.

      A. Description of the existing system (this section may not be required in some studies).

1. Brief description of the existing system and how it is used.
2. Purpose of the existing system.
3. The "product" of the existing system and whether it has served management effectively.
4. Major control points and responsibilities within the existing system.

B. Description of the proposed system or alternate systems.
   1. The "product" of the new system.
   2. Major control points and responsibilities within the new system. Are they equal to or better than the control framework within the existing system? Include the control matrix.
   3. Display of all reports or forms to be used in the proposed system. Emphasize elimination of nonessential data.
   4. Systems flowchart or data flow diagrams/context diagrams.
   5. Any or all of the documentation of the proposed system. Any not included here can be put in the appendix.
   6. Full list of recommendations.
   7. List of time schedules.[1]
      a. Overall elapsed time required to install the proposed system.
      b. Chargeable time, for example, number of work hours required to install the proposed system.
      c. Operating times for the proposed system.
   8. List of personnel requirements.
      a. Personnel required to install the proposed system.
      b. Personnel required to operate the proposed system.

C. Section on economic cost comparison (see Chapter 10).
   1. Estimated useful life of the proposed system (one method enumerated in Chapter 10).
   2. Cost of the old system over the estimated useful life (from 1 above).
   3. Cost of the new system over the same estimated useful life (from 1 above).
   4. Other areas of cost to be covered.
      a. Salaries.
      b. Space.
      c. Supplies.
      d. Inventories.

---

[1] Notice that some of the time now being estimated pertains to the time required to install the proposed system.

   e. Overhead.

   f. Computer time.

   g. One-time implementation costs.

   h. Cost of capital . . . investment costs.

   i. Other annual operating costs.

   j. Distribute costs back to users (chargeback).

  5. Noneconomic benefits . . . intangibles.

 D. A definite, straightforward, and positive statement relative to why you believe the planned system should be installed.

III. Appendix.

 A. Prior reports (when available).

  1. Feasibility study.

  2. Problem definition.

  3. New system requirements specification.

  4. Progress reports, as necessary.

  5. Summaries of various phases.

  6. Letters/memoranda.

 B. Any items that do not fit into the body of the report.

  1. Charts.

  2. Graphs.

  3. Tables of data.

  4. Controls list for matrix.

  5. Notes.

The preceding outline can be used as a guide when assembling the final report. In the Summary (Section I) all that is required is a couple of paragraphs for each item, A through F. In the Body (Section II) the analyst should be very detailed. This section should answer all possible questions about the proposed system and the economics involved; it may include a description of the existing system so a comparison can be made. The Appendix (Section III) should contain anything that is too bulky or appears to be out of place in the other sections of the report.

There are also a number of possible *faux pas* that the analyst should take into consideration. First, try not to send out a report with spelling and grammar errors. If you cannot correct it yourself, have someone else do it. Second, do not mail the report to the *key* management personnel. Hand it to them personally and include a cover letter pointing out that a meeting about this report already has been arranged. Arrange a meeting, through each manager's secretary, for a week or two in the future. Third, do not have numerous copies mailed to everyone involved. Instead, decide who needs a copy and give them one. Check your list carefully. If one manager receives a copy, another manager also may have to receive a copy (like a dinner party where some people cannot be invited without offending others). The offended manager of today may turn out to be the key person in your next systems study!

Data should be treated consistently. If a report begins by comparing costs with revenue in a particular way, that method of comparison should be continued throughout the report. Financial matters, especially estimates, always should be reported conservatively. This idea of conservatism assures management that it is, in fact, receiving representative cost data. Of course, a conservative estimate is much easier to defend than an estimate that is biased toward your own vested interests in the proposed system.

As you are writing your final report, remember the acronym CATER that was discussed in Chapter 1. Recall that this acronym stands for Consistent, Accurate, Timely, Economically feasible and Relevant. Relate this acronym to your final report so that it will CATER to the needs of the managers who will be using it and, thus, approving or disapproving your recommendations.

Finally, in writing the final systems report, the analyst should take into account all six of the following ideas.

1. Be clear and effective.
2. Be brief; verbose reports usually do not get read.
3. Use the active voice because it portrays enthusiasm.
4. Use short declarative sentences.
5. Check the spelling.
6. Demonstrate good grammar and sentence structure.

Gaining Acceptance through the Verbal Presentation

The verbal presentation can be just as important as the final written report, although it is not always required. Psychologists tell us that almost 90 percent of our impressions come to us through our eyes; therefore anything that can create a positive impression for the audience is advantageous to the analyst. The use of visual aids to demonstrate important points is an especially valuable technique.

Before deciding upon the techniques of presentation, however, the analyst has to determine what information is going to be presented. The written report serves well as the basis for the verbal report; but, of course, there is *nothing so boring* as an analyst who *reads* the report, so a whole new approach should be devised at this time.

A suggested outline for the verbal presentation is shown below. As with the other reports, the outline may vary with the study; but this can serve as a basis. Some approximate times are included for each of the five sections; but these, too, can be adjusted to fit the circumstances. Amplifying comments follow the outline.

Verbal Presentation

    I. Introduction ($\frac{1}{12}$ of time allowed).
-     A. State the problem.
-     B. Explain how the systems study progressed.
-     C. Explain the division of this presentation, for example, what follows the introduction.

   II. The body of the presentation ($\frac{1}{2}$ of total time).
-     A. Describe, very briefly, the existing system.
-     B. Describe the proposed system or alternate proposals.
-     C. Present economic cost comparisons.
  -     1. Be careful not to make unsupported claims.
  -     2. Be conservative.
-     D. Make recommendations.

 III. Summary of the body of the presentation ($\frac{1}{12}$ of total time).

 IV. Open discussion ($\frac{1}{4}$ of total time).
-     A. Answer management's questions.
-     B. Keep lively discussions going; it is more profitable not to cut off a lively question session just because the allotted time has elapsed.

  V. Conclusion ($\frac{1}{12}$ of total time).
-     A. Summarize the points of agreement that were brought out during the open discussion.
-     B. Make a positive statement as to what you are going to do next, such as get more data, install the system, start programming, or conclude the project.

The *introduction* is descriptive and is only concerned with preliminaries. For example, introduce yourself and the subject of your presentation. Explain the purpose of the meeting and make a statement of the problem. Explain how the systems study began, how it progressed, how the presentation will be made, and how much time will be devoted to each section of the presentation. In closing the introduction, the main points that will be covered during the body of the presentation can be noted.

The *body of the presentation* is the heart of the lecture and demonstration. Try to be concise since the audience will lose interest if it is too long. It is desirable to use management terminology rather than systems analyst terminology because management tends to be more interested in *what* is being done rather than *how* it is being done. Use positive concepts, such as cost reduction, faster response time, greater accuracy, more consistency, better control, and so forth. Emphasize the benefits of the proposed system, not its special features. Although it is tempting to forget them, do not omit the major drawbacks. Management must have the most reliable information available, and only by your being honest can they make a good decision. (It may be good to keep in the back of your mind that what is bad for the firm also is bad for you.)

In the *summary*, the body of the report is summarized. The analyst should again stress the benefits of the proposed system. The *open discussion* is where the pressure is on the analyst. The unexpected objections will crop up here, so this is where the proposed system will have to be defended. (It is perhaps desirable to remember that if it is truly a good system, it *is* worth defending!)

Finally, in the *conclusion* the analyst summarizes any points of agreement. The presentation should then close with a positive statement on what the next step will be.

The Presentation Itself

Before giving the verbal presentation, the analyst has certain opportunities that will help assure success. Learn about the individuals who will attend the presentation because the more you know about them, the more the presentation can be tailored toward their interests. The technique of dropping suggestions prior to the presentation is very valuable. Subtle hints can be made to department managers beforehand. This is not to suggest that the analyst should be secretive about the study results. On the contrary, surprise endings are not welcome! Do ask for advice, though. It is a compliment to the person you ask.

Remember to dress up and look businesslike for your presentation. This means that you should be well groomed and wear clothing that matches the business environment, while in keeping with current styles. Your personal appearance, such as hair, makeup, clothing, shoes, jewelry, and the like will have an effect on the people attending your presentation. If anything, tend toward a conservative appearance.

Another point that you must consider is your personal ability to appear before a "hostile group." Can you think on your feet when the audience is hostile and may be attacking your ideas or presentation? The ability to do this cannot be learned from a textbook! Learning to work with a hostile group can only be done through experience. Two excellent ways to gain experience in this area are to join Toastmaster's International (an outside professional organization) and to practice presenting information to other students who will be hostile to your remarks. Remember, *NEVER* be angry back to the group. Your case is lost if you get angry!

The management involved usually decides who will attend the presentation, but the analyst should express a desire that certain personnel be present. Attempt to have present the personnel who have the most to gain from the new system and those who are the most involved. The name and title of everyone who will attend the presentation should be known. Be aware, too, of what their function is within the current system and what their function will be within the proposed system. Prepare a "benefit-list" for the *key* people who will attend. List the items within the new system that will benefit each of these people the most.

As for the actual presentation, it should be *set up early*. Whenever possible, make a trial presentation with another systems analyst; use a tape recorder so you can hear how you sound. Make sure, for instance, that the verbal presentation is coordinated with any charts or graphs. Know the mechanics of any equipment to be used during the presentation. Avoid memorizing the presentation, though. A memorized presentation often seems insincere, and if a question arises halfway through, it is too easy to lose composure. Make sure you understand what you are saying! Above all, be sure that *you* are sold on the value of the new system.

During the presentation, speak from the "you" or "we" viewpoint, rather than "I." In other words, do not refer to the proposed system as "my" system. After all, it is management's system, and management will be paying for it. Explain all charts, graphs, or illustrations, remembering to reveal each visual aid only as it is discussed, not before. When visual aids are shown beforehand, they tend to detract from a presentation because the audience begins concentrating on them rather than on what is being said. Along the same line, speak to the audience, not to the wall or the visual aids. In fact, you should be speaking *with* the audience, not *at* them. Have a conversation with the audience so each individual will feel involved. Maintain that all-important ingredient, eye contact. Researchers have determined that the brain receives 87 percent of its information from the eyes and only 9 percent from the ears. If this is true, eye contact during business presentations is even more important than thought previously. Allan Pease[2] recommends the use of a pen to control a person's gaze. While discussing charts, point to them with a pen and then move it to a point between your eyes and those of a listener with whom you wish to maintain eye contact. This use of a pointer has the effect of "lifting" the other person's head so that eye contact is achieved. Since fumbling with notes or visual aids also is distracting to the audience, any fumbling should be avoided. In summary, the best advice that can be given for the presentation is this: *You are supposed to be a professional, so act like one.*

Throughout the discussion period remember the words empathy, tact, rapport, sensitivity, and integrity. Anyone who asks a question in front of a group of other people generally has a good reason for asking it, no matter how poorly it is phrased. The person asking the question deserves the courtesy of the most accurate reply the analyst can give.

[2] *Signals,* by Allan Pease (New York: Bantam Books, 1984).

In every group, however, there generally is at least one person who is outspoken in objecting to whatever is being proposed. Dealing with such an objector can be a very delicate matter. You may wish to view the objection from one of these two viewpoints.

1. If the objection is of minor importance, it usually is better to concede the point and make whatever revision is requested. This approach demonstrates to those in attendance that you are flexible, and it may pave the way for future cooperation.

2. If the objection would require major changes in the system, tactfully explain to the objector why the system is designed as it is in this area. Explain that you cannot make the changes without consulting others, gathering more data, or doing considerable redesign work. Tell the opposition that you will investigate this aspect and report back later on this point.

Visual Aids

A visual aid is any device used to illustrate what the analyst is talking about. It may be notes on the chalkboard, an object, a model, photographs, charts, graphs, tables, diagrams, lists, maps, flowcharts, or any other device the analyst selects to describe something.[3]

Flip charts are a common device used in business presentations. They are nothing more than a set of graphs, tables, or other visual aids drawn on paper and clamped together onto an easel-type device. As the speaker finishes discussing the top sheet of paper, it is "flipped over" to the next illustration.

Flip charts can be used to help the presentation proceed in a step-by-step fashion. When using charts, remember to write the verbal presentation first and then determine where to include charts and graphs. Each chart or graph should be limited to one major idea, and it should be easy to read. Any sentences on the chart or graph should be short and simple. As mentioned previously, keep the charts and graphs covered until the presentation reaches that point. Before giving any detailed explanations, read any major writing or figures on the chart to the audience.

A chalkboard is another type of visual aid. When using a chalkboard, know beforehand what you are going to draw. Keep the drawings simple, and if talking while drawing, raise your voice when facing away from the audience. Clean the board before presenting a new point and be neat. Take a trial run to

---

[3] There are numerous volumes on technical writing, most of which include a section on graphic presentations. For specific examples, the reader is referred to *Basic Technical Writing*, by Herman M. Weisman (Columbus, Ohio: Charles E. Merrill Publishing Company, 1974), now in its third edition.

look at your own handwriting from the point of view of the audience; perhaps you should print the message rather than write it.

Overhead transparency projectors are easier to use than many other visual aids, but they do require considerably more prior preparation. For example, you should go to the presentation room early in order to check the overhead projector's lighting, the lighting of the room relative to the projector, get the projector in proper focus, ensure that there is a backup bulb available, and check that the projector is placed so people's views are obstructed minimally. Overhead projectors are used with maximum effectiveness by system analysts who also can draw on the transparency; this adds a real-life perspective to the visual aid as they are speaking. You might check off items, use color in certain areas of a graph or chart, or you might extend a current picture to show how it will change over time. Another technique is to write occasional marginal notes (two or three words) with regard to the points you are making. These techniques allow you to fit the presentation to specific personalities in the audience and, even more important, answer basic objections by showing what effect the objection has on the data that is being projected.

Films and slides do not allow the analyst to vary the presentation to fit specific personalities in the audience. Explain the contents of the film just before it is shown. After the film, reserve some time for discussion. Films generally tend to be better for training (during the system implementation phase) than they are for selling the system to management.

Ending the Presentation

At the end of the presentation, the analyst should attempt to get management to agree to implement the new system. Try to get management to say, yes, they want the system. There are three approaches that may be useful for getting management to agree to the implementation. The appropriate one may be used during the conclusion of the verbal presentation.

1. The ask-them-to-buy approach. Boldly ask management to accept the proposed system.
2. The inducement approach. Conclude by pointing out that some outside event will happen if the proposed system is not installed. Or offer a special inducement for acting now. (Be careful, though, not to let this strategy sound like a threat!)
3. The secondary-question approach. Get management to agree on something of secondary importance such as whether implementation should start on the first of next month or next week.

Under most circumstances, the first strategy will be the most appropriate. It is positive, but still respects management's prerogative in making a decision.

The second strategy is appropriate only if some impending event *genuinely* threatens the well-being of the organization. The analyst, while being realistic, must be careful not to exaggerate the significance of the event.

The third strategy should only be used with great caution for it borders on disregard for management's prerogative and ability to make a decision. In this strategy the analyst closes on the assumption that the case already is won—a posture which can be very irritating to line managers.

Although it is desirable to close the presentation on a positive note, for example, a point of agreement, the analyst should assess carefully both his or her own position and that of the audience before choosing a method of ending the presentation. Above all, the analyst must be thoroughly convinced on the proposed system before attempting to sell it to management. Otherwise, any reservations should be explained clearly, along with the various alternatives.

SUNRISE SPORTSWEAR COMPANY

CUMULATIVE CASE: Selling the System (Step 9)

The May 30th deadline imposed by Mr. Reynolds is nearing and you still must write the final report for your study of the Sunrise Sportswear Order Processing system. You also need to prepare for the verbal presentation. These reports are important because you know that selling an *idea* is difficult. Major concerns are to describe why the changes are needed, try to overcome any fears or prejudices held by the management of Sunrise Sportswear, guarantee that your report is received by the people who have the authority to accept or reject it, and submit proposals that you are able to implement.

Throughout the study you have attempted to show as much enthusiasm as possible for the work and to put forth a positive attitude toward needed changes. You know there is still much to be done, however, because these changes must be negotiated. You cannot simply present the alternatives and expect people to fall in love with your ideas; you are going to have to be very convincing in order to make the idea of investing so much money in an unfamiliar system palatable to Stanley Reynolds and his managers. This has been a continuous effort, but you know the most difficult part is still ahead.

Selling the system involves two reports. First, you plan to submit a written report on your study of the Sunrise Sportswear Order Processing system. This report must convey all of the points that can provide useful background for management to make a decision. Second, you plan to back up this written report with a verbal report presentation during which people can ask questions. The verbal presentation is as important as the written report because you know the people who attend will be judging *you* in order to decide whether they can trust your recommendations. In the final analysis, they may make their decision based on written facts, how you come across to them during the presentation, or a combination of both. Knowing this, you recognize that both the written report and the verbal presentation must include everything that is important. With that in mind, you decide to write the report first under the assumption that the presentation will fall into place naturally after everything is in writing.

The first thing you do is gather all of the documentation together. By this time, you have accumulated quite a lot and know it will have to be pared down to what is most meaningful. During the years you have developed the habit of keeping a notebook for each project. These notebooks are arranged with a view toward the final report that is an inevitable part of each study. Sections are labeled as follows: Problems, Existing System, Requirements, New System, Controls, Costs, Recommendations, Implementation, Re-evaluation. You have learned that making notes under these headings is an immense time-saver when each phase is ended and reports to management are needed. You also have the problem statement, context diagram, data flow diagrams (four Level 0, plus each decomposition), the data dictionary, data structure and data access diagrams, system structure charts, minispecifications, and their supporting documentation for each process on the data flow diagrams. This documentation provides a complete model of the proposed system. In addition, you have several alternative system designs, matrices to show system controls, and cost comparisons for each alternative. Finally, you have created mock-ups of some of the inputs and outputs that will be changed when the new system is implemented. You have learned that people respond better to abstract ideas when they have something concrete to view as an example. A picture is worth a thousand words!

Remembering that you want to CATER to the needs of Sunrise Sportswear's management, you begin to develop the outline from which you will develop the final written report.

SUNRISE SPORTSWEAR COMPANY
Order Processing System

I. Summary of study.
  A. Need for study.
    1. Management recognized problem signals.
       a. Customer complaints regarding slow order processing. Customers canceled orders.
       b. Customer complaints regarding Credit Rejection Notices. Considered humiliating.
       c. Credit customers not paying their bills.
       d. Credit verification process too slow.
    2. Management wants solution to problems.

B. Statement of problem.
 1. Credit policy.
   a. Credit is given to any customer who does not have an account more than 60 days overdue.
   b. Credit is given to customers whose credit card purchases are rejected by the credit card companies.
   c. Of 2,000 overdue accounts, 60 percent are those of customers whose credit was rejected by credit card companies.
   d. Overdue accounts are major burden to the Accounting Department.
     (1) More staff to handle.
     (2) More filing.
     (3) More storage of records.
     (4) Overdue accounts are now greater than 10 percent of Accounting's accounts receivables.
   e. Credit risk has not been a factor in the extending of credit. Result is that Sunrise Sportswear has inherited the potential bad debts that were recognized by credit card companies.
 2. Credit Rejection Notices.
   a. Format is a post card (Figure 5-4).
   b. Customer privacy is not protected.
   c. Wording does not exhibit tact or sensitivity. (Caution: Take care in wording this in the report so no one will be offended. Use positive terminology.)
 3. New customer records (Figure 3-15).
   a. Current system requires typing on 3 × 5 cards.
     (1) Time consuming to type.
     (2) Time consuming to file.
     (3) Time consuming to search.
   b. Process has become major bottleneck in system because of increase in new customers.
   c. Estimated 50 percent of orders fall into the category of "new customer."
   d. Result is that 50 percent of orders cannot be processed until new customer record is created.
   e. Process 2.0 (VERIFY ORDER) returns orders directly to customer if merchandise cannot be identified as belonging to Sunrise Sportswear; therefore, orders returned by process 2.0 do not get entered into the new customers file.

     f. Different processes in system use three different sources of information to determine old/new status. No consistency in results.

     g. New customer information is keyed twice.

       (1) In Order Processing (3 × 5 cards).

       (2) In Catalog Printing (key entry to magnetic tape).

4. Backorders.

     a. Handled two different ways at two different steps of Order Processing.

       (1) VERIFY ORDER returns orders to customers for later reorder.

       (2) Inventory puts out-of-stock merchandise on backorder and notifies customer of expected delivery date.

     b. Orders are lost because VERIFY ORDER does not have adequate information to make judgment on inventory stockouts.

5. People who need to interact are far removed from one another (Figure 6-7).

     a. Much time is wasted going from one building to another or up and down stairs.

     b. Involves movement of data, so telephone cannot be used instead.

6. Management does not have adequate records to determine what merchandise is sent to customer.

     a. Depends on customer to notify if there is a problem.

     b. Lack of packing list encourages pilferage.

     c. Shipping Notices inadequate to meet need.

7. Invoices.

     a. Invoices must be prepared for every order in which credit is extended.

     b. Filing of invoice copies time-consuming.

     c. Filing of invoices takes valuable space.

8. Storage of old paper records costly.

     a. Takes up needed floor space.

     b. Labor cost to file.

     c. Labor cost to search.

     d. Old customer orders (filed by name) have never been weeded or discarded because it is major source of old/new customer decision at VERIFY ORDER (process 2.0). Files now take up one large room in Building 1.

C. Subject of problem.
   1. What happens to customer orders during Order Processing.
   2. What delays the filling of customer's orders.
   3. Why there are so many overdue customer accounts.
   4. What causes customer complaints.
   5. What processes can be combined or deleted.

D. Scope of problem.
   1. Every process that handles customer orders.
     a. Order verification.
     b. New customer accounts.
     c. Credit verification.
     d. Customer payments.
     e. Inventory.
     f. Order preparation.
     g. Invoice preparation.
     h. Shipping notification.
     i. Backorder notification.
     j. Returned orders.
   2. Interactions with these processes.
     a. Accounting Department.
     b. Shipping Department.
     c. Catalog Mailing Department.
     d. Data Processing Department.
     e. Credit card companies.
     f. Customers.

E. Objectives of study.
   1. Reduce number of overdue accounts to 5 percent or less.
   2. Reduce the time it takes to handle customer orders to 48 hours or less.
   3. Locate Order Processing system bottlenecks and determine if they can be removed from the main processing stream.
   4. Clarify and streamline credit policy.
   5. Eliminate poor credit risks.
   6. Reduce time order is held in credit verification to one day or less.
   7. Determine more effective method of handling new customer records.
   8. Determine if any processes could be handled more effectively elsewhere than in Order Processing.

F. Major recommendations.

1. Eliminate credit. Maintain check or credit card only policy.
2. Eliminate Invoices.
3. Eliminate Shipping Notices.
4. Centralize backordering at Inventory.
5. Centralize old/new customer checking at one place.
6. Eliminate duplicate keying of new customer records.
7. Send excessively overdue accounts out for collection.
8. Revise Credit Rejection Notices.
9. Initiate use of Packing Lists.
10. Initiate records retention schedule.
    a. Customer orders (Figure 3-3) and letters.
    b. Order Verification forms (Figure 3-4).
    c. Shipping Reports (Figure 2-13).
    d. Need to
       (1) Reduce floor space used for records storage.
       (2) Reduce time used to file old records.
       (3) Reduce time used to search old records.
11. Decrease number of customer complaints.
12. Increase number of customer orders filled.
13. Move Order Processing staff closer together.
14. Eliminate 3 × 5 cards for new customer records.
15. Initiate controls to guard against theft and other unwanted threats to assets.

II. Body of report.

A. Review of existing Order Processing system.

1. What it does.
   a. Context diagram (Chapter 3, Student Task 1).
   b. Physical data flow diagram (Figure 5-6).
   c. Final logical data flow diagram (Figure 7-11).
2. Purpose is to process customer orders.
3. Product is provision of merchandise with good service.
4. No longer effective.
   a. Causing problems that can be eliminated.
   b. Does not meet competitive needs.

B. Proposed system.

1. Input/output requirements (Figure 7-13).
   a. System requirements model (Figure 7-14).

      b. Logical data flow diagram (Figure 7-15).

      c. Statement of changes from existing system to proposed system.

      d. Measurable evaluation criteria

         (1) Reduce overdue accounts to 5 percent or less.

         (2) Reduce order processing time to 48 hours or less.

         (3) Reduce credit verification time to one day or less.

         (4) Reduce active records storage space by 90 percent.

         (5) Reduce time new customer orders are held from approximately two weeks to one day or less.

      e. Data dictionary (Figure 7-12).

      f. Physical data flow diagram (Figure 8-3).

  2. Highlights of proposed system—choice set.

    a. Alternative A (minimal, Figure 8-4).

      (1) Automates customer data collection.

        (a) Assigns order number.

        (b) Assigns customer number (new).

        (c) Creates new customer records.

        (d) Modifies old customer address (new).

        (e) Eliminates 3 × 5 card file.

        (f) Provides customer records that are up-to-date.

        (g) Permits access to customer records by other processes.

      (2) Automates order preparation

        (a) Creates Packing Lists (new).

        (b) Enhances label preparation.

        (c) Permits access to customer records not available previously.

        (d) Eliminates Shipping Notices.

        (e) Eliminates open boxes of merchandise, which are susceptible to pilfering.

        (f) Provides better records to customers.

        (g) Provides better control to management.

    b. Alternative B (middle-of-the-road, Figure 8-5).

      (1) Includes all of Alternative A, plus

        (a) Streamlines order verification.

          (a1) Permits access to up-to-date customer records when needed.

          (a2) Eliminates room full of paper records.

(a3) Transfers backordering to Inventory.

(a4) Permits all orders to be entered into customer records by handling returned orders later in process.

(2) Eliminates internal credit.

(a) Reduces accounts receivables.

(b) Eliminates invoicing.

(c) Permits more personal handling of credit card rejection notices.

(d) Permits access to up-to-date customer records when needed.

(e) Reduces problems in Accounting Department caused by granting credit.

(3) Centralizes backordering.

(a) Automates backorders.

(b) Automates customer notification of backorder.

(c) Enables filling of more customer orders by using more up-to-date information that is centralized in Inventory.

c. Alternative C (maximum, Figure 8-6).

(1) Includes Alternatives A and B, plus

(2) Permits access to more up-to-date customer records when needed.

3. Moves Accounting closer to Data Processing (Figure 10-4).

4. Implementation of local area network (Figure 8-7).

a. Enhances possibility of automating other Order Processing activities.

b. Enhances possibility of automating other departments.

C. Cost comparisons.

1. Investment costs.

a. Alternative A: Minimal proposal (Figure 10-5).

b. Alternative B: Mid-range proposal (Figure 10-6).

c. Alternative C: Maximum proposal (Figure 10-7).

2. Implementation costs (Figure 10-8).

3. Savings realized from investment (Figure 10-9).

4. Payback periods of alternatives (Figures 10-10).

5. Net present value of alternatives (Figure 10-11).

6. Years to reach net present value (Figure 10-12).

7. Marginal efficiency of investment (Chapter 10, Student Task 1).

8. Intangible benefits (Figure 10-9).

9. Summary cost analysis (Figure 11-1).

    a. Recommend Alternatives B or C.

    b. Alternative A least desirable financially.

D. Mock-ups (facsimile reports).

    1. Revised Order Verification form (Figure 11-2).

    2. Revised customer order form (Figure 11-3).

        a. New credit card added.

        b. Space added for signature.

        c. Does not provide for cash (want to discourage).

        d. Does not provide for credit (discontinuing).

    3. New Packing List, computer-generated (Figure 11-4).

    4. Revised backorder letter, computer-generated (Figure 11-5).

    5. Revised return order letter, computer-generated (Figure 11-6).

    6. Revised credit card rejection letter, computer-generated (Figure 11-7).

    7. Change of credit policy letter from Stanley Reynolds, computer-generated (Figure 11-8).

E. Controls matrix (completed as Student Task 1 in Chapter 10).

F. Changes in organization structure.

    1. Old system (Figure 3-9).

    2. Proposed system (Figure 11-9).

        a. New group names based on processes.

        b. Reflects no-credit policy.

        c. People may be shifted around some.

            (1) Credit may need fewer people.

            (2) Customer records may need more people.

            (3) Order Verification may need fewer people.

            (4) Inventory may need more people.

    3. Effort needed to implement system.

        a. Movers to move equipment from one area to another.

        b. Telephone installers to move telephone extensions.

        c. Electrician to install plugs for microcomputers.

        d. Wire pairs (cabling) installers for local area network.

        e. Custom programming (Casper Management Consultants).

        f. Training (Casper Management Consultants).

III. Summary statement as to why proposal should be approved.

A. It will solve problems.

    1. Reduce overdue accounts.

	ALTERNATIVE A	ALTERNATIVE B	ALTERNATIVE C
Investment cost	$24,728	$43,715	$48,252
Total cost	25,928	49,315	54,552
Monthly savings	900	2,100	2,300
Annual savings	10,800	25,200	27,600
Payback period	4.62 years	3.76 years**	3.80 years
Net present value	$1,364	$14,365	$15,193**
Positive NPV	2 years, 11 months	2 years, 4 months**	2 years, 4 months**
Marginal efficiency of investment	13.47%	24.83%**	24.16%

** Most desirable alternative

Figure 11-1 Summary of cost analyses for three alternatives.

ORDER NUMBER _____

ORDER VERIFICATION

ORDER VERIFICATION
- ☐ Order date/time stamped

Inventory check
- ☐ Our mdse.   ☐ Not our mdse.

Price check
- ☐ Correct   ☐ Incorrect

Gift card enclosed
- ☐ Yes   ☐ No

Payment method
- ☐ Check   ☐ Cash enclosed
- ☐ Money order   ☐ Credit card

ORDER NUMBER ASSIGNMENT
- ☐ Assign order number

Check customer information
- ☐ Name
- ☐ Address (change if necessary)
- ☐ Assign customer number
- ☐ Old customer   ☐ New customer

Routed to
- ☐ Batch payments
- ☐ Credit card verification
- ☐ Returned to customer

Reason for return _____

BATCH PAYMENTS
Verification of payment amount
- ☐ Approved   ☐ Discrepancy

Discrepancy amount _____
Batch number _____

Request
- ☐ Invoice   ☐ Refund

CREDIT CARD VERIFICATION
Expiration date _____
- ☐ Expired   ☐ Not expired

Credit card company
- ☐ American Express   ☐ MasterCard
- ☐ Diners Club   ☐ Visa

Credit card number _____

Credit card approved?
- ☐ Yes   ☐ No

Credit approval number _____

Credit card charge slip
- ☐ Yes   ☐ No

Credit action
- ☐ Approved, forwarded to Inventory
- ☐ Disapproved, returned to customer
- Reason for return _____

INVENTORY
- ☐ All merchandise sent
- ☐ Partial order sent
- ☐ Backordered
- Backorder date _____

ORDER PREPARATION
- ☐ Quality check
- ☐ Packing list
- ☐ Label
- ☐ Gift card enclosed (if applicable)

SHIPPING
Date shipped _____
Shipper
- ☐ Federal Express   ☐ Postal Service
- ☐ United Parcel   ☐ NPS

SUNRISE SPORTSWEAR

Form 57 (4/86)

Figure 11-2 Revised Order Verification form. Replaces the one shown in Figure 3-4.

SUNRISE SPORTSWEAR
CALL US TOLL-FREE (800) 555-1212

Sold to:

Place peel-off mailing label here. Please correct if incorrect.

Ship to: (only if different from "Sold to")

☐ Mr.
☐ Ms.   First Name   Initial   Last Name

Address

City   State   Zip Code

Page	Item No.	Description	Size	Color	How many	Price	Total

Total Price of Items

Add 5% sales tax if state resident

Shipping, Packaging & Handling

TOTAL

PAYMENT METHOD

Please check payment method   ☐ Check or money order
☐ American Express   ☐ MasterCard
☐ Diners Club   ☐ Visa

Credit card number _____

Expiration date _____

Signature _____

Form 73 (4/86)

Figure 11-3 Revised Sunrise Sportswear order form. Reflects additional charge card and provides room for credit card signature and expiration date.

Packing List

SOLD TO:

SHIP TO:

	SUNRISE ORDER NO.
	CUSTOMER NUMBER

LOCATION	ITEM NUMBER	COLOR	SIZE	QUANTITY	DESCRIPTION

SHIPPED VIA	DATE SHIPPED	NUMBER OF BOXES	TOTAL WEIGHT

SUNRISE SPORTSWEAR

Form 98 (4/86)

Figure 11-4 Packing List form to be used by Order Preparation.

SUNRISE SPORTSWEAR

(today's date)

Dear *(customer name)*

    We have received your order for the following merchandise which is temporarily out-of-stock:

    It is expected that we will have this merchandise available to ship on or about *(expected date)*.

    Although we hope you will still want to receive this order, we will understand if you wish to cancel it. If this date is unsatisfactory, please check the box below and we will refund your money.

    We look forward to serving you again soon.

Very truly yours,

Sunrise Sportswear
Inventory Backorders

☐ I am sorry, but I must cancel this order. Please refund my money for Order Number *(number here)*.

Figure 11-5 New letter to Sunrise Sportswear customers informing them of a backorder.

SUNRISE SPORTSWEAR

(today's date)

Dear *(customer name)*

We have received your order for merchandise, but have encountered a problem with it.

Based on the information provided, it does not appear that we can fill this order for one of the following reasons:

☐ The merchandise cannot be identified as being that of Sunrise Sportswear

☐ Enough information has not been provided to identify the merchandise

☐ More information is needed on
    ☐ Size or waist
    ☐ Color
    ☐ Quantity
    ☐ Sleeve length or inseam
    ☐ Other (see below)

We will be pleased to provide this merchandise if you will return the order with additional information.

We look forward to serving you again soon.

Very truly yours,

Sunrise Sportswear
Order Verification

Figure 11-6 New letter to return customer order because of inadequate information.

SUNRISE SPORTSWEAR

(today's date)

Dear *(customer name)*

We have received your order for merchandise, but have encountered a problem. We are sure it is an error that can be corrected easily with your help.

When we called for the necessary credit card approval number, the credit card company disapproved the credit purchase for the following reason.

☐ The credit card expired on _____

☐ The name does not match the credit card number. The number we checked was _____ for

     ☐ American Express

     ☐ Diners Club

     ☐ MasterCard

     ☐ Visa

☐ The credit limit has been reached.

We are sure the problem can be corrected and know that you will return the order to us shortly with the corrected information.

We look forward to serving you again in the near future.

Very truly yours,

Sunrise Sportswear
Credit Verification

Figure 11-7 New credit rejection notice sent to Sunrise Sportswear customers. It is a regular letter meant to be sent in an envelope. It replaces the notice shown in Figure 5-4.

SUNRISE SPORTSWEAR

June 23, 1986

Dear (*customer name*)

Because of the increased cost of maintaining our credit accounts, we regret to inform you that Sunrise Sportswear is changing its credit policy.

Starting July 1, 1986 all purchases must be paid for by check, money order, or credit card. We have added another credit card service for your convenience. We will accept any of the following credit cards.

American Express

Diners Club

MasterCard

Visa

Current credit accounts will be phased out as they are paid. No further amounts may be added to them at this time.

We are sorry if this is an inconvenience for you, but we hope that it will not affect your continued patronage as one of Sunrise Sportswear's valued customers.

Very truly yours,

Stanley Reynolds
Managing Owner

Figure 11-8 Letter to be sent to Sunrise Sportswear's current and future credit customers.

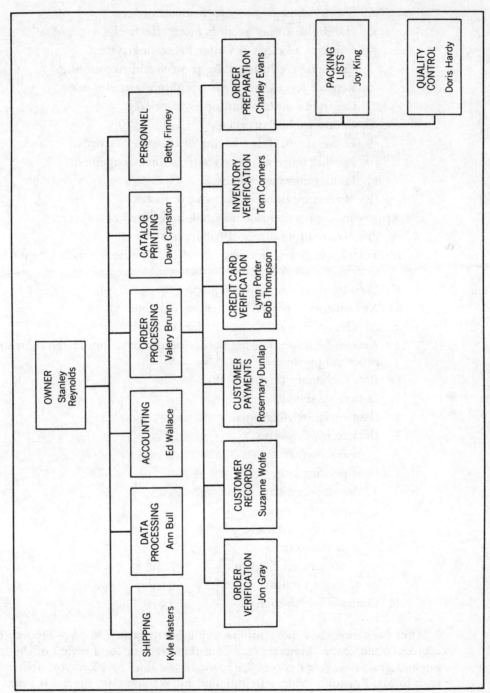

Figure 11-9 Revised Sunrise Sportswear organization chart.

    2. Shorten time to process customer orders.

    3. Handle customer records more effectively.

    4. Enhance all steps of Order Processing system.

    5. Eliminate credit handling problems in Accounting.

    6. Replace less useful records with more useful ones.

    7. Centralize old/new customer records.

    8. Centralize backordering.

    9. Eliminate duplicate keying of customer records.

    10. Provide more effective controls for management.

    11. Reduce storage problems.

    12. Modernize to meet competitive forces.

IV. Appendix (supporting documentation not used elsewhere).

    A. Problem definition report (Chapter 3).

    B. Telephone survey summary of how competitors handle credit to customers (Figure 5-5).

    C. Credit policy alternatives (Chapter 8).

    D. New customer record alternatives (Chapter 8).

    E. Articles on how other mail order houses handle credit.

    F. Articles on how other mail order houses have automated their order processing systems.

    G. Data dictionary (Figure 7-12).

    H. Data store sheets.

    I. Data structure diagrams.

    J. Data access diagrams.

    K. System structure charts.

    L. Minispecifications.

        1. Decomposed data flow diagrams.

        2. Supporting logic.

            a. Decision tables.

            b. Decision trees.

            c. Structured English.

            d. Tight English.

    M. Controls list for matrix.

After preparing the report outline, you use it to write a 36-page report which is given to the Casper Management Consultants editor for a review of the spelling and grammar. After copies are made of the final revision, you deliver one each to Mr. Reynolds, Valery Brunn, and Ed Wallace. Mr. Reynolds wants the presentation on May 30th, even though this does not leave much time for reading the report. He also tells you that he has arranged for all of Sunrise Sportswear's managers to be present at the verbal presentation which he has set for 10:00 A.M. on May 30th. You are pleased that Mr. Reynolds is interested in having the presentation right away, but wish you had more time to prepare for it. With only one day left, you have time for only one dry run of the presentation, which Nancy critiques.

The night before the presentation, you polish your shoes, and make sure your nails are manicured and that your hair is trimmed neatly. That morning you take special care with your appearance and dress conservatively so you will make a positive impression. You arrive at the Sunrise Sportswear conference room early so that you can make sure everything is set up properly.

While the report was being typed, you also had the various data flow diagrams and other documentation prepared into overhead transparencies so that everyone would be able to see all of the supporting documentation. Keeping the word CATER in mind, you make sure there is at least one transparency that will appeal to each person. For Mr. Reynolds, you made a transparency of the quantified evaluation criteria (point II.B.1.d. of your outline) because you know he will want some hard numbers showing what he is going to get for his money. Also, the cost analysis summary (Figure 11-1) was designed for the benefit of Stanley Reynolds. The personnel layout charts are for Valery Brunn. You want her to be able to see how spread out her staff are, as shown in Figure 6-7, compared to how much more efficient they could be if moved closer to one another, as shown in Figure 10-4. Although the list of recommendations (point I.F. of your outline) is for all attendees, you know it will appeal to Ed Wallace because many of the points will reinforce what he has been advocating for some time.

The revised Order Verification form (Figure 11-2) is for everyone since it reflects the new arrangement of processes and will be a more complete record of each customer order. One point you want to stress about this form is that Sunrise Sportswear now will have both the date the order arrives and the date the merchandise is shipped. This will enable management to sample overall order processing time at regular intervals so they will know if expected processing times are being met.

The Packing List form (Figure 11-4) is aimed at Charley Evans. You want him to see how much more effective this form will be when it replaces the present Shipping Notice.

The new letter to inform customers about backorders (Figure 11-5) is for the benefit of Tom Conners. You told him earlier that Jon Gray would no longer be returning out-of-stock orders, and he was concerned about the increased workload for his staff. You feel he will be pleased to see that you have addressed this issue.

Even though the letter to return a customer order (Figure 11-6) will be sent by

Suzanne Wolfe's area, it is important to Jon Gray. If he has a microcomputer, he can input the information with the necessary information for the letter, which will be printed after the customer's name and address has been checked.

Since you suspect that Valery Brunn designed the post card that currently is used as a credit rejection notification (Figure 5-4), you know this subject must be handled with tact. You want to stress how it will help the customer have a favorable impression of Sunrise Sportswear so that the order will be returned when the credit problem is straightened out.

Finally, you have been reassuring everyone throughout the project that the transition will be made as easy as possible. Toward this end, you have designed a letter with Mr. Reynold's signature (Figure 11-8). Since customers must be told about the new credit card/check policy, this letter has been designed to be sent to all current accounts receivable customers and any others who request credit over the next few months. It can be sent by Suzanne Wolfe if an order has not been accompanied by payment or a credit card number. You also plan to submit a credit collection plan so that the excessively overdue accounts can be handled by a collection agency.

People begin to arrive at the presentation a few minutes before 10:00. Mr. Reynolds brings in two people you have never met, his brother Chris and his sister Penny. You are surprised to see Dan, the owner of Casper Management Consultants, arrive with Nancy. You asked Nancy to attend in case there are questions about the local area network or hardware that you cannot answer. Each of the managers is present, as well as the leader of each Order Processing group.

When everyone is seated, you begin the presentation. Since some of the people are unfamiliar with the background of the study, you review the situation that caused Mr. Reynolds to seek a consultant, describe what you learned with regard to subject, scope, and objectives, and what was learned during the problem definition phase. The existing Order Processing system is described using the context diagram and the logical data flow diagram of the existing system. Then you describe how you wish to change the Order Processing system by showing the new logical data flow diagram and summarizing the changes that will take place. The three human–machine boundaries are shown so that the attendees will understand the three alternative proposals. Based on these alternatives, you then make recommendations (these were point I.F. in your outline). Finally, you present the cost comparison tables that you compiled for the three alternatives. You are careful to observe Stanley Reynolds when discussing costs. You have a sinking feeling that he is dismayed by the projected expenditures. Undaunted, you continue by showing how much Sunrise Sportswear will benefit from the proposed changes.

During the open discussion, Ed Wallace is as enthusiastic as you had anticipated. Of all the people in the room, you suspect he has the most to gain from any changes that are made. Valery Brunn does not say very much, but does ask how all these people can be trained to use this equipment (meaning the microcomputers) when none of them have ever seen one except perhaps on television ads. You explain that Michael Allen, who is an Educational and Training consultant with Casper Management Consultants, has taught many people how to use microcomputers. Having observed him in such situations, you express confidence that the Order Processing staff not only will learn how to use the equipment, but they probably will become so proficient with it that they think of new uses on their own.

Ann Bull wants to know about the programming for the local area network. She asks if there is software that can be bought off-the-shelf for it. That question is deferred to Nancy, who replies that there is some, but it will have to be modified to handle the various applications that are unique to Sunrise Sportswear's operations. Nancy explains that CMC's programmer is John Middleton. She has worked with John in similar situations, and the results have been quite good. He is especially good at testing and debugging because he is quick to grasp problem routines.

The Reynolds family have all been listening to the questions and answers. Finally, Stanley Reynolds says that it all sounds very good, but he simply does not see how Sunrise Sportswear can afford to implement such an expensive system. He agrees that they could do a few of the things such as change the credit policy, but he shakes his head over buying all the equipment. He does not see how they can buy even the minimal configuration (Figure 8-4), much less the others that cost twice as much. At this comment, you try not to let your disappointment show.

Suddenly, Penny Reynolds turns to her brother and says, "Oh Stanley. Don't be such an old fuddy-duddy. You never want to spend money on anything, but if you want to make money, you have to spend some to do it. Based on what we've been shown here, I think it's a super idea and we ought to go for it." Stanley is visibly shaken over the comment, but protests that they don't have that kind of money. At that, Chris speaks up and says, "Right, but that is what banks are for. We would have no trouble borrowing enough to do it, and it looks like we'd be able to pay off the loan quickly enough. Stanley, you never take any chances, and it's about time we make some changes around here. You run this operation like we were in the last century. I agree with Penny; you're too conservative."

When you realize that this could turn into a public family argument, you decide to shift the emphasis away from the Reynolds family and ask the group if there are any other questions. Tom Conners wants to know how soon the system could be up and running. He explains that the Inventory group already is experiencing an increase in backordering since Jon Gray no longer returns orders. Since they just changed that a couple of weeks ago, he is beginning to worry about the next few months. You explain that the answer to that question depends primarily on two factors. The first and most obvious factor is how soon the decision is made on whether to proceed with implementation and which choice is made regarding the three alternative designs. The second factor depends on how fast the needed software and microcomputers can be purchased, how soon the local area network can be installed, how quickly the custom programming can be accomplished, and how fast people can be moved from one area to another. If the Inventory area is one of the areas included in the implementation, it might be one of the first to be up and running since no movement of people is involved. You add that this also is true of Charley Evans' group. Because the Accounting Department staff has to be moved out of Building 1 before the others can be moved in, the people affected by that part of the implementation may receive their equipment later. In any event, you tell them that you hope installation can be completed by the end of August. Mr. Reynolds says it would *have* to be done by then because their Fall/Winter catalog is put out in August and they would have to have it done by then.

The discussion seems to have tapered off so you summarize the points of agreement. These are

1. Credit can be eliminated regardless of whether a new system is implemented. It seems that most agree this is a desirable thing to do.
2. Backordering already has been centralized at the Inventory area, but problems already are being encountered and a need to automate is recognized.
3. If credit is eliminated, invoices automatically will be eliminated.
4. If the creation of customer records is not automated, nothing will improve and it is likely the situation will worsen.
5. The revised letters to customers seem to have been well received, and they can be used regardless of any changes that are made to the system.
6. The use of Packing Lists is desirable.
7. Sunrise Sportswear does need to implement more controls to protect its assets.
8. It appears that most of the attendees think the proposed changes would be beneficial.

You summarize by stating that Sunrise Sportswear's management could decide not to make the recommended changes, but you see this decision as being a dangerous one. They already are losing customers, presumably to more efficient competitors. You state that the proposed changes not only are desirable, but reasonable and necessary given today's competitive marketplace. You strongly recommend that Sunrise Sportswear's management should select Alternative C for implementation. In closing, you say that you would like to begin implementation as soon as possible since any delays would mean that the system could not be changed by the time the new Fall/Winter catalog is put out. Mr. Reynolds thanks you for your efforts, but says he wants to think about it for a while. Penny and Chris Reynolds both compliment you on the presentation and Penny whispers that she will work on Stanley to get him to implement the changes. You were not expecting such an ally, but are pleased to learn your proposals have a chance of being implemented.

You have reached another major milestone in this systems analysis and design effort because Phase II of the system development life cycle (Steps 5–9) has been completed. At this point, Sunrise Sportswear's management could decide not to accept any of your recommendations, accept only some of your recommendations, or accept all of your recommendations. This is a very logical point in the system development life cycle for the management of any firm to either accept the lowest cost alternative or possibly terminate the entire project. For this reason, it is very important that you overwhelmingly convince management that your most cost-effective and efficient recommendations are precisely what they need. This is achieved through your written report and the verbal presentation. Your next task is to begin Phase III of the system development life cycle, depending upon the alternative Mr. Reynolds approves. Phase III involves the programming, testing, and implementation (installation) of whatever alternative is accepted.

Student Questions

1. What did you forget to include in the presentation?
2. What mistake did you make in closing the presentation?
3. Did you anticipate objections well enough?

Student Tasks

1. Assume the Reynolds family have agreed to implementation of the maximum human–machine boundary (Alternative C). Set up schedules for implementing it by August 30th. Use a Gantt chart to accomplish this.
2. Form small groups and perform some role-playing in which one of you gives another ending to the verbal presentation. Other members of the group can be any of the characters, including Sunrise Sportswear staff, the owner of Casper Management Consultants, the auditor, or another member of the Reynolds family.

*S*elected Readings

1. Austin, Richard L. *Report Graphics: Writing the Design Report.* New York: Van Nostrand Reinhold Company, 1984.
2. Bromage, Mary C. *Writing for Business, 2nd ed.* Ann Arbor: University of Michigan Press, 1980.
3. Brown, Leland. *Effective Business Report Writing, 4th edition.* Englewood Cliffs, N.J.: Prentice-Hall, Inc., 1985.

4. "Dead Men Don't Use Flip Charts (Or: 17 Things You Can Do with a Flip Chart that You Can't Do with a Carp)," *Training*, vol. 21, no. 2, February 1984, pp. 35–40.

5. Golen, Steven P., C. Glenn Pearch, and Ross Figgins. *Report Writing for Business and Industry*. New York: John Wiley & Sons, Inc., 1985.

6. Grassell, Milt. "The Four Psychological Types of Buyers," *American Salesman*, vol. 29, no. 5, May 1984, pp. 22–26. [How to recognize four types of personalities so you can tailor appropriate sales presentations.]

7. Holmes, Geoffrey. "How to Present Your Message Graphically," *Accountancy* (U.K.), vol. 95, no. 1088, April 1984, pp. 64–71. [How graphics can be used in presenting information, reports, and presentations.]

8. Jacques, Raymond E. "End-User Business Graphics Calls for MIS Attention," *Computerworld*, vol. 18, no. 26, June 25, 1984, Special Report 20. [Issues surrounding end-user graphics.]

9. Malc, Kenneth. "Make the Sale by Perfecting Your Close," *Life Association News*, vol. 79, no. 6, June 1984, pp. 82–86.

10. McMaster, John B. "The Spoken Word Can Be Enhanced by Visual Aids," *Office*, vol. 99, no. 4, April 1984, pp. 50, 52. [How to use flip charts and transparencies for effective presentations.]

11. Smith, Terry C. *Making Successful Presentations: A Self-Teaching Guide*. New York: John Wiley & Sons, Inc., 1984.

Questions

1. Identify at least three factors that can help sell you during systems analysis projects.

2. Identify the five key words that are necessary for successful interaction with people.

3. Why will the analyst be better prepared during this phase if basic objections to the proposed system are considered ahead of time?

4. List some of the basic objections that should be considered.

5. Why should the analyst have to sell the new system to a management that has paid for its design?

6. List some of the factors the analyst should take into account when writing the final system report.

7. Identify five typical kinds of visual aids.

8. What should the analyst consider if a chalkboard is going to be used as a visual aid for the verbal presentation?

9. What factors should be considered when an overhead transparency projector is going to be used?

10. How should the analyst end the presentation for selling the new system?

11. During the presentation to management, what are you selling?

12. What are the five main parts of the verbal presentation? List each and briefly describe what is included in them.

13. Why are films and slides sometimes not very useful during a verbal presentation?

SITUATION CASES

Case 11-1:   Personnel Consultants

Since you must learn to *sell yourself,* try to identify positive words that will help you, such as PMA (positive mental attitude). There are five key words identified in this chapter, starting with empathy. Go to a thesaurus and identify two or three similar words for each of these five key words. Can you find others?

Case 11-2:   Software, Inc.

An analyst, a recent graduate, had been with the consulting firm for only a month when a software developer asked that a systems analyst be sent out to revise their credit operations in order to reduce bad debt expenses.

It was this relatively inexperienced analyst who was sent out to Software, Inc. Previously, the analyst had worked on projects along with a Senior Analyst, who more or less supervised him. On these assignments, the supervisor had handled the verbal presentation while the analyst had prepared the written report. They had collaborated on other aspects of selling the system.

This time the analyst was to be on his own because his ability to conduct a systems study was good in the judgment of his supervising partner. The analyst had proven to be enthusiastic in approaching the study and exhibited quite a bit of self-confidence when he began.

The analyst encountered no insurmountable problems as far as gathering information and revising the old system were concerned.

Near the end of the study, as the analyst was preparing his final draft of the written report, the Software, Inc. Controller approached him with a preliminary bill that had been sent by the analyst's consulting firm. The Controller argued that the bill appeared to be too high for a mere revision of the credit operations. The analyst replied, "I can't give you an answer because my firm does its billing independently. I, as a member of their staff of analysts, conduct the study without regard to cost." After that, the Controller stalked out, commenting as he left that the consulting firm was "robbing" his company.

When the final written report was complete, the analyst objectively examined the document. It was brief and concise, and exhibited no grammatical or spelling errors. Financial estimates were conservative; all in all, a good report.

After determining which company personnel needed a copy of the report, the analyst had the necessary copies made and mailed out immediately, including a cover sheet detailing a future meeting to discuss the report.

The analyst then sat down to prepare for the verbal presentation. He made an outline to be followed while delivering the presentation because he did not want to memorize it word-for-word. Not knowing who would attend the presentation, the analyst had to prepare a rather generalized speech.

A week before the verbal presentation, the analyst contacted the company and reserved a conference room, also asking that an overhead projector be made available for his use.

When the presentation day arrived, the analyst walked into the conference room as the last of the firm's personnel entered. He immediately situated himself at the speaker's podium, introduced himself, and offered a brief overview of what was to come in the speech. Other introductory matters were then presented, and the analyst started the body of the presentation.

He first described the existing system and then prepared to describe the proposed system. For this part of the presentation, the analyst opened his briefcase and produced a set of transparencies to illustrate graphically the proposed operations. While walking to the overhead projector, the analyst realized that it was an unfamiliar model. He had to look around for the switch, then nothing happened when he turned on the machine. He quickly grabbed the plug and plugged it into the nearest outlet. With the overhead projector operating, the analyst proceeded to describe the proposed system without any further complications. He described the proposed system, economic cost comparisons, and outlined his recommendations. Then he summarized the presentation and asked for questions, of which there were many. He defended the new system well, being convinced in his own mind of its inherent advantages.

In concluding the meeting, the analyst summarized the points of agreement brought out during the open discussion and asserted that he would soon conclude the project.

In closing, the analyst attempted to get management's concurrence on whether implementation could commence immediately or start with the beginning of the company's fiscal year which was to begin in three weeks. The firm's president said he would let the analyst know of their decision by the end of the week.

Questions

1. What mistakes, if any, did the analyst make in the preparation and presentation of his verbal report?

2. Outside of the mistakes in the verbal presentation, how could the analyst have been more successful in selling the system?

Case 11-3:   *Micro Printer Company*

The management of the Micro Printer Company decided that they needed either a new system or an enlargement of the existing system because of an increase in their production needs.

For some time the systems analyst had been advocating a new system rather than an enlargement of the old. Enlargement of the old system would be the most economical choice. Although more costly, the proposed system would be faster, smaller in size, and able to perform more functions. Also, it would enable the company to add hardware with little modification, which was impossible with the old system.

After the analyst gave a well-researched, complete verbal report, most members of management tended to prefer the new system; but there was still some opposition because a number of points had not been covered sufficiently. Certain management personnel did not want to invest in the new system because they were afraid it might not work with the same efficiency and reliability as the old system. They had general doubts regarding increased costs the new system would incur.

Management informed the analyst at the close of the verbal presentation that they desired a more in-depth, documented written report concerning all aspects of the new system. At its submission, management would decide if the new system would meet the needs of the company. Management informed the analyst that he had three weeks to prepare the more detailed written report, during which time the analyst would be doing a considerable amount of research.

The analyst's final written report contained the following areas.

   I. Body of the report.
     A. Description of the existing system.
       1. A brief description of the existing system and how it is used.
       2. The purpose of the existing system.
       3. The "product" of the existing system and whether it serves management in an effective manner.
     B. Description of the proposed system.
       1. The "product" of the new system.
       2. Degree of control. Is it equal to or better than the existing system?
       3. Display all reports or forms to be used in the proposed system. Emphasize the elimination of nonessential data.
       4. Data flow diagrams.
       5. Any or all of the documentation of the proposed system (he put bulky items in the appendix).
       6. Full list of recommendations.

    7. List of the time schedules.

       a. Overall elapsed time required to install the proposed system.

       b. Chargeable time, e.g., number of work hours.

       c. Operating time for the proposed system.

    8. List of the personnel requirements.

       a. Personnel required to install the proposed system.

       b. Personnel required to operate the proposed system.

  C. A definite, straightforward, and positive statement relative as to why the planned system should be installed.

II. Appendix.

  A. Any prior reports.

  B. Extra items that do not fit into the body of the report.

At the end of the three weeks, the systems analyst finished his report, but was unable to distribute it to management on a personal basis. The following day, the analyst's vacation began and he left town for a month. About a week later, after management had reviewed the analyst's report, they wanted to meet again with the analyst to discuss some very pertinent points in his report. It was at this time that they discovered the analyst was on vacation. Since there was no address where he could be reached, management was unable to locate him in order to discuss the report. Because the lease on the existing system was about to expire, management had to decide within the coming week whether to enlarge the existing system or to implement the proposed system. With the analyst's location unknown, management's questions and doubts about the analyst's written report remained unanswered. As a result, management decided to enlarge the existing system rather than venture the risk of a new system.

Questions

1. Discuss the final report.

2. Discuss the analyst's vacation plans.

Chapter 12

IMPLEMENTATION

LEARNING OBJECTIVES

You will learn how to . . .

☐ Carry out installation of a computer-based system.

☐ Carry out installation of a manual system.

☐ Conduct the programming.

☐ Conduct the testing.

☐ Conduct the implementation.

☐ Perform the follow-up.

☐ Perform the re-evaluation.

☐ Structure the final system documentation.

☐ Use structured documentation to explain implementation to users.

*P*hase *III: Implementation*

Now that you have completed Phase I (Steps 1–4) and Phase II (Steps 5–9), you are about to embark on Phase III (Step 10) with its three sequential tasks. These three tasks are *program the new system, test the programs,* and *implement the new system.* Figure 12-1 depicts this phase. Notice how the three tasks are shown in sequence. We suggest that you return to Figure 2-1 to review how these tasks fit into the system development life cycle.

This chapter concentrates on converting the conceptual idea that has been approved by management to the reality of an empirical system. While Phases I and II were concerned with *analyzing* and *designing* a proposed system, Phase III is concerned with *building* the new system. Implementation involves building and installing the new system; it emphasizes people. In this chapter, the analyst learns how to implement both manual and computerized systems.

*T*he Implementation Process

The implementation process begins *after* management has accepted the new system. Implementation consists of the installation of the new system and the removal of the current system. It involves hardware (machines), software (computer programs, procedures, forms), and peopleware (personnel). The implementation phase is often the most difficult part of your job. Naturally, the time chosen for the changeover to the new system should be a time when the system is *not* involved in heavy operations. A slack period should be chosen, if possible.

During implementation of the system, problems that had not been anticipated during the study and design effort often appear. Solutions to these problems usually require modification to the original design. The analyst should be willing to accept changes where necessary, but should prevent extreme distortions of the original design.

As an example of implementation difficulty and the long time involved, let us describe an actual situation. A new data communication network was being implemented within a three-story building. The company installing the new cabling (data communication circuits) spent 2½ days cabling the entire building for connection to all desk locations in the areas where terminals, microcomputers, or minicomputers would be located. The next night a second crew of workers arrived; their job was to remove the old cabling. You probably can guess what happened, but let us finish the story. Red tags were on all the new cables so they would be marked clearly for people to connect the modems, terminals, microcomputers, and the like. The new crew thought the red tags on the cables

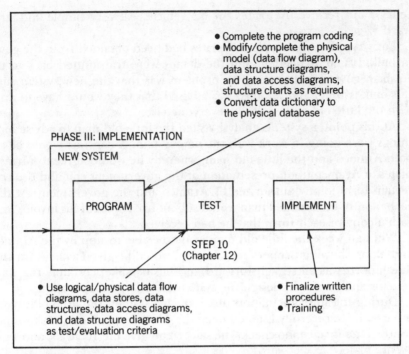

Figure 12-1 Phase III—Implementation.

meant they were the ones to be pulled. So in one evening they pulled all of the new cables that were to be connected to the hardware. What do you think a situation such as this does to your frustration level, let alone your implementation time and cost schedules?

Another situation was described by someone who had worked for the Aramco Oil Company in Saudi Arabia.[1] This anecdote had to do with a system involving the control and licensing of the corporate automobiles and trucks. It all started when the Saudi Arabian government franchised a little old man, who owned a small metalworking shop, to issue automobile license plates for the Eastern Province where the Aramco headquarters are located. Aramco is one of the largest companies in the world, so they own many vehicles.

In accordance with the system, a person acquiring a motor vehicle would bring the pertinent documents to the appropriate government office, register the vehicle, and pay the fee. This person then would be given a chit which permitted him to go to the little old man's shop, pay 10 riyals (the Saudi cur-

---

[1] *Looking Back Over My Shoulder,* by Larry Barnes (1979) describes experiences while living for 30 years in Saudi Arabia (85 Currier Avenue, Peterborough, N.H. 03458).

rency), and receive the plates for his vehicle. All very simple and straightforward.

For years the Aramco license plates had been obtained from the government in bulk, issued as needed, and the details were transmitted back to the Saudi Arabian government later. The problem was that the new system superseded this bulk issuing, and Aramco was advised that they would have to do business with the little old man, just like everyone else.

At this point, a systems analyst visited the little old man to advise him of how things were going to work with the new system. A contract would be signed by both Aramco and the little old man, whereby he would agree to furnish license plates to Aramco upon presentation of the government chit and two copies of a certain form jointly authorized by Aramco and the government. At the end of each month, the little old man would submit five copies of his invoice to Aramco, with a copy of each form that he had received.

Within a week the little old man would be able to stop by the Aramco offices and, upon showing proper identification, would be given a check for the money due him. It was all straightforward and businesslike; certainly the way a good systems analyst would design the system for a large corporation.

During the implementation phase of this system, the little old man was approached. He carefully listened to all the procedures, then shook his head. "No contract, no invoice, no check," he said. "You give me 10 riyals, and I give you a license plate."

This threw the system designers at Aramco into an uproar. A hasty meeting was called with executives from contracts, law, accounting, auditing, government relations, and the systems analysis department. The little old man's refusal to conform cut to the very core of Aramco's excellent accountability system and their business procedures. The little old man had to realize that in a modern, industrial world there must be systems with certain checks and balances for control purposes. He must conform!

How do you suppose it ultimately was settled? Aramco gives the little old man 10 riyals, and he hands over a license plate. Remember, *people* must accept your new system!

Getting a new system to the operational stage involves three separate and distinct tasks that must be performed in sequential order. They are

- ☐ Program the system. This is the point at which application programs are written in order to perform whatever business functions are being computerized. If some of the programs or program modules are being purchased or leased, this task may be shortened.
- ☐ Test the programs. This involves the testing of the programs, a full systems test, and the documentation of the programs. Sometimes analysts think that there will be no "hassle" if programs are purchased or leased. This may not be true because usually there are program changes to purchased or leased software packages.

☐ Implement (install) the system. This is the point at which you run the programs, interface with the different files of data, utilize any telecommunication networks, and interface with the users (the human–machine interface).

Each of these three tasks (programming, testing, and implementation) is described in the sections that follow.

Programming

It is advisable not to start any extensive programming until management fully approves the new system and orders that it be implemented. Prior to management's acceptance, only small test programs should be undertaken. Make it a policy never to spend the organization's money on extensive programming until the system has been accepted formally; this means you must remember Step 9, Selling the System. For this reason, programming commences at the beginning of the implementation phase (Step 10).

If the programs or program modules are purchased or leased, not all of the programming steps may be necessary. In other words, you either will use the programs "as is" or you will integrate the purchased program modules into your own program code. The programming proceeds in the following sequence (amplifying comments follow this list).

1. If you are not familiar with the new system design because you were not a member of the analysis team, you must study the documentation to see how the system is to operate. A lot of documentation is available, including data flow diagrams, minispecifications, data structure diagrams, data access diagrams, system structure charts, written narratives, flowcharts, and other documentation sheets.

2. Develop the final form for the outputs and then the inputs. This includes specific sequences, how outputs will come out of the computer, and how inputs will go into the computer.

3. Develop program flowcharts or Nassi Shneiderman charts of each program's step-by-step logical operations (both of these charts are described in Chapter 13). The Nassi Shneiderman charts are used for structured programming.

4. Determine the file layouts.

5. Write the program code.

6. Desk check (see Glossary) the program by reviewing it.

7. Debug each program. Debugging a program is getting it to compile and run properly using simple data.

8. Run all the programs together. At this stage, the programs/program modules are connected together and the system is debugged. The system of programs now operates as a complete application system using simple test data.
9. Document the program(s).

The programmer must study the design details of the new system in order to understand how the system should operate. The analyst who performed the study should be available for advice. Together they can decide which programming language to use, for example, COBOL, APL, and so forth.

The analyst and programmer analyze the new system requirements and break it logically into cycles and jobs. The frequency of processing must be determined and the appropriate cycles identified, such as daily cycle, weekly cycle, monthly cycle, quarterly cycle, semiannual cycle, and annual cycle. The next step is to identify the job requirements to meet the needs of each cycle. Each job is then broken down into its basic components, that is, the programs required.

For each program, the next step is to lay out the format of the outputs and inputs. First the format of the output reports should be considered. Lay them out based on the information they will contain and on how they should look when they come out of the computer. The outputs and inputs were designed during the system study. Next determine how the inputs will be put into the computer. Where does the input data come from? Who submits it? How will it be converted to machine-readable format? At this point the programmer should know what the output reports will look like and what the input data will look like.

Now develop a program flowchart. A program flowchart delineates the logic of the program. It portrays the step-by-step sequence of the program's instructions, and each decision point is spelled out. The *program flowchart* is a pictorial model of the program. (Flowcharts are discussed in Chapter 13.) Alternatively, Level 2 or 3 data flow diagrams and system structure charts may be used.

The file layouts should be determined next. Use the data dictionary, data structure diagrams, and data access diagrams to develop logical data layouts. The computer-based files can be stored in any of four layouts. *Sequential* files are in sequential order by their primary keys,[2] for example, from the lowest to the highest part number. *Index-sequential* files also are in sequential order by their keys, but an index is created so specific data can be accessed directly without searching sequentially through the file. *Random-access* files are in an order prescribed by a mathematical formula, and can be accessed directly. *Partitioned* files are those in which various areas are partitioned into unique file areas for your specific data only. You must understand the database design in order to determine which layout is best.

---

[2] The primary key is whatever the data are filed by or accessed by, for example, part number, name, or whatever the programmer chooses.

In addition to the above-mentioned files, in today's world you might be required to build database files that are hierarchical, plex/network, or relational. Hierarchical files are those in which some records are subordinate to others, but where each lower level record can have only one parent record. Plex files (also called network structure) involve a relationship between records in which a lower level record can have more than one parent record. Relational files are two-dimensional flat files, quite similar to matrices. Types of files were defined previously in Chapter 7.

Coding the program follows. If the program flowcharts or system structure charts are complete, the coding should be easy. Coding is nothing more than writing the computer program in whatever programming language was chosen.

Desk checking is next and it is the most overlooked step in the sequence of programming. The program is followed through *mentally* with some simple input data. The object is to see if the program logic is in proper sequence and if the output is what is expected. Sometimes the programmer is joined by another programmer, and they perform a program logic walkthrough together. One programmer explains the logic to the other, who serves as a "devil's advocate" by asking questions that challenge the logic.

The program test is made by trying out the actual program on the computer to see whether it will compile and run. A program rarely runs perfectly the first time. Removing the errors to get the program to run correctly is called debugging the program. Test data should be run in the program to see if the program logic develops as it should. All logical paths in the program must be tested during this phase.

For our purposes, when the debugging is completed and the individual programs work, then the programmer has completed the programming step. This is because we have defined the next task as testing. Extensive testing should not be done until the programs run by themselves.

*T*esting

Testing of the debugged programs is one of the most critical aspects of computer programming because, without programs that work, the system will never produce the output for which it was designed. Testing is best performed when user departments are asked to assist in identifying all possible situations that might arise. Another method is to query the internal auditors for their opinions on possible situations that may arise.

One other thing to remember at this time is that this is the point at which Control Review Step 6 commences. Whoever is managing the matrix of controls now begins to verify and test the controls to be sure they were implemented into the new system. Cross reference Figure 12-1 with Figure 9-2.

Along with verifying and testing of the controls, a complete schedule of testing involves the following subtasks.

- □ Testing individual programs.
- □ Creating test data.
- □ Link/string/single-thread testing.
- □ System/multiple-thread testing.
- □ Backup and restart testing.
- □ Complete the documentation.

With regard to *testing individual programs,* remember that this was completed during the programming task. The programmer tested each individual program to make sure it performed satisfactorily.

The next task is to *create an extensive set of test data.* The programmers probably created some test data for testing the individual programs, but now test data must be created for all possible real-life situations. The programmers, systems analysts, user department representatives, and auditors should now get together. They should create test data that contain both valid and invalid data, test normal processing routines, test error routines, check lists (such as maximums and minimums), test variations using different input and output formats, test the addition and deletion of records to files, test the file storage and retrieval algorithms, insert data that will cause problems, and finally, prepare just plain ridiculous out-of-scale data. The point is that your goal is to test all possible situations that might occur in the future. While we all know it is impossible to anticipate everything, the better job you do here, the fewer failures the system will have in the future. Failure to check all conditions may propagate errors that are very hard to locate later.

After the individual programs have been tested and you have created a massive amount of test data, you can do the *link or string testing* (sometimes called single-thread test). For example, you might test an edit program and an update program. The output of the edit program must be properly formatted and contain the correct data in order to be accepted as input for the update program. This testing is what we call the upstream and downstream feeds between different programs or program modules (this is similar conceptually to balancing data flow diagram levels). The reason for testing the series of programs is to ensure that the "job stream" is correct. The job stream consists not only of those job control statements that are necessary to invoke the proper programs to be processed, but it also defines the files that will be created and processed, and it designates the devices that are to be used for the files. Obviously, if the files are defined incorrectly or the programs do not interact properly, the system will not function as it should. For this reason testing of the job stream is as important as testing the individual programs within the system.

After the link or string testing is complete, the entire system must be run through a series of tests called *system or multiple-thread* testing. You probably will have some computer operations people try to run the system tests so they can determine if the system will operate on the organization's computers. The objective of testing the entire system (system testing) is to verify that the programs meet the original programming specifications, to ensure that the computer operations staff has adequate documentation to run the system, to ensure that user departments are able to input data properly, and to ensure that the overall system flow works properly. An even more important basic objective is to make sure that the entire system functions as a whole when all the programs are interconnected with the files and the inputs/outputs. This can be likened to an automobile that has both a very good motor and a very good transmission. Unless the motor is bolted properly onto the transmission the entire system (the automobile itself) will not operate.

The next step of program testing is the *backup and restart testing.* In this task you test the backup of files that may be destroyed inadvertently. The questions you need to answer are, Can I rebuild a file that is inadvertently destroyed, or Can I down-date a file from its data values at, let us say, 2:00 P.M. today to the data values that existed at 10:00 A.M. today? You need to test the restart of the system in case the computer or data communication circuits inadvertently and instantaneously fail. If such a situation occurred, you must determine if the computer system and/or communication circuits can be restarted satisfactorily. The basic goals are to make sure that the files can be reconstructed if they are destroyed totally, that the files can be down-dated to a value from a previous period of time, that the programs are backed up in case they are destroyed, and that the systems can be restarted in case of disaster.

After completion of the testing, you must finish the *documentation* of the program, set of programs, or program modules. This was done partially during the programming task, and now it must be finished. Documentation is necessary for communication of program characteristics to persons other than the programmer, and for the programmer's future reference as well. People come and go, but the programs stay. Documentation provides the written and charted explanations necessary to familiarize new personnel with the program. The documentation package for a computer program may consist of the following.

1. In-line comment or note statements in the program coding itself. For every new logical unit there should be a comment that explains what these instructions do and how these instructions interact with other related areas in the program.
2. Depending on the design methodology used, there may be flowcharts, data flow diagrams, pseudocode, system structure charts, or Nassi Shneiderman charts.

3. One program flowchart for each program; and if there are multple programs, an overall flowchart showing how the various programs interact.

4. For sections of complicated logic or calculations, minispecifications or narrative descriptions of the activity should be prepared.

5. Pictorial layouts (data structure diagrams/data access diagrams) of the files, the outputs, and the inputs.

6. Program run book that contains operating instructions; for example, brief program narrative, computer setup information, tapes, disks, carriage control tapes, special printer forms, or any special restart procedures in case of failure prior to normal program end.

*I*mplementation of a Computer-Based System

After programming and testing, the systems analyst, user department representatives, programmers, and any other necessary personnel should be ready to install the new computer-based system. This is the moment of truth! Can a computer-based system be implemented with the personnel in our organization and within the organization structure that exists today? Will there be political implications that might hurt this system and slow its installation? These questions will be evident now that you are interfacing the user departments, the user personnel, and the computerized system.

Now the decision whether to implement using a parallel conversion or a one-for-one conversion must be finalized (see Figure 12-2). In a parallel conversion, the old and the new systems run simultaneously for at least one cycle using current data. It is costly, but it is the safest method because the old system keeps operating until the new system has proven its accuracy and reliability. In a one-for-one conversion, the new system is installed with simultaneous removal of the old system. For protection during a one-for-one conversion, emulators may be used to process the old programs by the old procedure using current data on the computer.

Actual implementation of the new system can begin at this point using either a parallel or a one-for-one plan, or some blend of the two. It is advisable that both the systems analyst and the programmer observe the following basic principles during any implementation.

1. Avoid disrupting the day-to-day business activities during the implementation process.

2. Do not require excessive overtime work during implementation.

3. Inform management of all changes in the implementation method or time schedule.

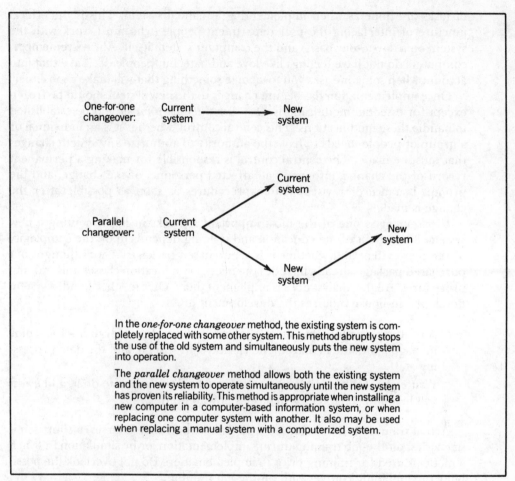

In the *one-for-one changeover* method, the existing system is completely replaced with some other system. This method abruptly stops the use of the old system and simultaneously puts the new system into operation.

The *parallel changeover* method allows both the existing system and the new system to operate simultaneously until the new system has proven its reliability. This method is appropriate when installing a new computer in a computer-based information system, or when replacing one computer system with another. It also may be used when replacing a manual system with a computerized system.

Figure 12-2 Changeover alternatives.

4. Do not give demanding orders; you are functioning as advisory staff, not as a line manager.

One more point should be made with regard to the actual implementation of the interface between the user department, user personnel, other departments, and the computerized system. Identify each subtask of installation and use each as you install the new computerized system. Subtasks like *training users, writing procedures, setting up one central control point, determining time schedules,* and the like, are performed during the implementation phase. Even though a computer system is being implemented, this is a very *human*-oriented task, and the same types of tasks are done as when implementing a manual system. This is the critical juncture of interfacing the user department people (who must work with the system on a day-to-day basis) and the computer system itself. Always remember, computers do not have feelings like love and hate, but people do. Take that into account when someone asks you to change something that will make a job easier.

Once implementation has begun, changes to the new system should be frozen except for essential modifications. *One central control point* should be established to handle these modifications. This central control, whether it is an individual or a group of people, needs to have the authority to authorize any system changes that must be made. The central control is responsible for making a permanent record of the change, informing all affected personnel of the change, and the prompt issuance of revised written procedures as soon as possible after the change is made.

User training is one of the most important subtasks in implementing a new system. The extent of the education and training depends upon the complexity of the new system and whether it is a purchased package. A well thought out purchased package already includes the necessary education classes and training procedures. All the analyst does is implement them. On the other hand, a system developed in-house requires the development of

- [ ] A training schedule that shows the time and duration of training for senior management, line management, clerical staff (users), and the data processing staff.
- [ ] Written procedures explaining *what* is to be done, *who* is to do it, and *how* it will be done (Chapter 17 describes how to do this).

Actual training can be achieved with full- or part-time courses, a short seminar series, on-the-job training during implementation, or by simulation in which a model is used for training prior to implementation. Do not overlook the possibility of combining courses with on-the-job training.

After implementation is complete and the user departments are, hopefully, using the new system successfully, members of the project team can be disbanded and put onto other assignments. This is done so that an individual, or possibly several individuals, can be assigned the task of future maintenance of the new system. This transition from a working system design team into maintenance is considered to begin from the time the implementation phase (installation) ends.

All new maintenance projects and all new system enhancements are treated as separate, new projects. They are scheduled and people are assigned to perform the work. Maintenance and system enhancement projects, therefore become minisystems analysis/programming projects. Remember, if this system design team is not disbanded, it may go on forever, creating its own maintenance projects and its own system enhancement projects, thus becoming a self-perpetuating and costly project group within the data processing department.

Implementation of a Manual System

The steps involved in the implementation of a new system can be very complex and demanding. To make implementation proceed as smoothly as possible, the analyst should work out an implementation plan. The plan should specify who will do what and when they will do it. The best method is to prepare detailed instructions for the supervisors to follow during the system implementation in their departments. The detailed instructions should outline the responsibilities, time schedules, and operating instructions that are required in order to properly implement the new system. Various items that help in organizing the plan are To Do lists or your original plan (see Chapter 3), Gantt charts (see Chapter 4), and job procedures (see Chapter 17).

Actually, the analyst should think of implementation from the very beginning of the project in order to keep the system oriented to all user levels. The users of the new system will have to be taught new methods. Benefits of the new system should be pointed out early to enable the users to understand why their cooperation is needed. They also should be made aware of both the limitations and capabilities of the new system so they can accept it in realistic terms. This avoids later disappointment when users learn that the system cannot handle something they had assumed it could handle. The workings of the new system and its procedures should be explained thoroughly to them.

The personnel also have to be trained to operate the new system. The analyst should assist in the training function and, whenever possible, train each employee individually. The analyst may have to train in small groups, however, dividing similar tasks into separate training groups.

The analyst operates in a staff capacity and, as such, operates without line authority. The analyst, therefore, cannot *order* anyone to do anything. If line authority is required, the manager of the department where the implementation is taking place should be the one to give orders. Since the analyst can only request, methods which will secure the cooperation of the operations employees are vital to the system analyst's success. The analyst should learn the art of dealing with the operations employees in such a way as to secure their goodwill and cooperation right from the start of the project. Learning to deal with employees who have extreme aversion to change or who are obstinate in their attitude toward cooperating is especially important. Needless to say, getting the job done without line authority of any kind can be tricky; but the competent analyst does it.

As with computer-based systems, it is important that changes to the new system be frozen at implementation except for essential modifications. Manual systems also need to have one central control point to handle these modifications. The central control for a manual system has much the same responsibility as the one for a computer-based system, except that it is not dealing with computer programs and programming changes. Instead, it is more forms- and procedures-oriented. As such, any modifications usually are to forms or procedures. All forms used in the new system must be on hand before implementation can begin. Because any changes may affect more than one group of users, the central control should be the only one who can make modifications to these forms.

A time schedule must be estimated for the system implementation. First take into account the overall elapsed time from the start of implementation to its finish. Calculate chargeable time to determine how much it will cost to implement the new system. Then decide *how* the new system will be implemented. There are three basic approaches to starting up the new *manual* system.

1. *All at once.* All operations are started up at the same time (one-for-one changeover).
2. *Chronologically, and in sequence through the system.* Start with the first operation and move through to the last operation.
3. *In predetermined phases.* Similar areas within the system are started up at one time and then other areas are started up.

The first of these three approaches to starting a new manual system, needs further comment. With the all at once changeover, there are two basic options that can be followed. In the first option, the current system ceases and the new system is started with no overlap between the two operations. In the second option, the current system is kept running and the new system is started at the same time. This is a parallel conversion in that both systems are running for a short period of time, let us say an accounting cycle or some other measurable time. By running the two systems in parallel, you can compare the new with the old and reconcile any *differences* that may occur because of the changeover. The differences that may occur are in areas such as financial, procedural, personnel, and time related areas. In a manual system the changeover usually is made without the benefit of parallel conversion. When the operating personnel are busy with one manual system (the old one), they cannot be expected to operate both the old and the new manual systems simultaneously. Even if temporary employees were considered, a physical space problem often precludes parallel conversion of a manual system. As a result of these very real limitations, parallel conversions usually are reserved for computerized systems.

The analyst should help the operating personnel in modifying old data so it will fit the new system. New data sources may have to be located or cross-reference files started. In a system change where both old and new files must be maintained, the analyst should try to help the people make the transition with as little frustration as possible.

For example, if the old system files were indexed by customer name and the new system files are by customer number, the two files are not compatible. The analyst can assign customer numbers and refile the entire old system or have two files: an old file by customer name, and a new file by customer number for all of the current business. If all subsequent reports were to contain *only* customer number, a cross-reference file would be required to use the old system files. The operating personnel would have to look up the customer number in the cross-reference file to get the customer name so they could use the old system files. In time, the old system files would become outdated and would no longer be used because all the current business would be filed in the new customer number file.

The old system must definitely be phased out. Operating personnel must learn to depend on the new system and forget the old one. By some preplanned date, only the new system should be operating. Do not allow a mixture of the old and the new systems unless that mixture was part of the original system design or implementation plan.

In summary, the systems analyst, when installing a *manual* system, does the following.

1. Develops a plan for implementation.
2. Assists line management in understanding their commitment to support the new system, that is, their responsibilities toward the new system.
3. Prepares any required documentation, such as written procedures or instruction manuals.
4. Orients the operating personnel and assists in their training.
5. Coordinates the installation of the new system and the phaseout of the old system.
6. Performs follow-up and re-evaluation as necessary. These are described next.

*P*urpose of the Follow-Up

The follow-up usually is performed within a month or two after the system has been implemented. The analyst should wait this short period of time in order to allow the system to stabilize. In other words, the users are going through a learning process in which they have to learn how to operate the system. Give them time to feel comfortable with it and to find out if everything really is working as *they*, the users, would like it to be working. You have developed a system for the users, not for yourself. They will judge the system by how it works for them. Do not overlook the fact that the system must be accepted by not only the everyday users who operate and use the system to perform their daily work, but also by the management personnel who rely upon the system's information for decision making. Remember, if this is a transition from a manual system to an on-line terminal system, the users will take longer to get used to their new terminals than if you were changing from a terminal-oriented system to a different version of that same system. With the latter, people already are accustomed to using on-line terminals or microcomputers.

During the follow-up, try to make sure that the people are not using the old system in order to check up on, or feel comfortable with, the data that emanates from the new system. Sometimes people do not trust what is new, and they want to hang on to the old ways of doing things. The old system must be terminated because it is not cost-effective for people to collect data for two different systems.

It is during the follow-up that the analyst determines how good the system design really is by returning to observe the actual operation of the installed system. The analyst finds out if the operating personnel are using the new system with its formal procedures or if they have started their own informal procedures. Many observations are required during follow-up. Management wants to know if the objectives of the new system are being accomplished. Management also wants to know whether any anticipated cost savings are being realized, whether the new system is providing the information or "product" that is required, and whether the day-to-day working schedules are being maintained.

The analyst, during the follow-up, should make sure that all parts of the new system actually are operating and that minor activities or operations have not been overlooked. The operating personnel should be observed to be sure they have not reverted back to the old system! Operating costs should be examined to see if they are in line with the estimates and whether the facilities are really adequate, for example, equipment, space, number of operating personnel, and so forth.

The programmer also should be active at this stage to determine if each program is operating correctly and if the program's output is really adequate. Both the programmer and the analyst should collect a list of employee complaints for evaluation and possible corrective action.

Why Re-evaluation Is Required

A re-evaluation is not mandatory, but it should be performed for all major new systems. The re-evaluation might be performed 6 to 12 months after the system is implemented (installed). The purpose of re-evaluation is to determine whether some system enhancements should be made to further improve or refine it.

User departments often automatically request enhancements to their system; this is nothing more than an on-going re-evaluation by the user department. In such a situation, data processing already has all the re-evaluation requests (enhancements) that the users feel are necessary. If this is the case in your organization, a specific re-evaluation may not be required.

The primary reason for re-evaluation of the system after it has been installed is to make whatever changes are needed for the refinement and improvement of the new system. It may be necessary to redesign some portions of the system and revise some of the original recommendations.

Review the list of employee complaints and evaluate the efficiency of the work flow of your new system. Seek out more opinions from the operating personnel. Determine when peak loads occur, the quantity of paperwork flowing through the system, the accuracy, the utility, and the timeliness of the outputs. Using the *evaluation criteria* from the new system requirements phase of the systems study, develop some performance standards. Use the evaluation criteria to monitor the day-to-day performance of the system as well as for possible re-evaluation and change. Do not be afraid to change the system you designed. It is better that *you* do it than someone else who might use the opportunity to your detriment.

*F*inal System Documentation

The final documentation package requires the pulling together of all the documents that were prepared along the way. It is a *mandatory* step. If certain documents were bypassed originally, they must be prepared now. The final system documentation consists of the developmental documentation that was used in defining and analyzing the problem, the documents used to control the whole project, the documents that formally describe the new system, and the documentation that actually is used during the operation of the system. In other words, it consists of all the records showing how the system was designed and how it is operated.

A suggested format for the final documentation package is shown in the following outline. Please note that this outline accounts for both structured and traditional design documentation (i.e., data flow diagrams and flowcharts), whichever was utilized.

FINAL SYSTEM DOCUMENTATION

I. Introduction and table of contents
   A. Name of the system
   B. Why the system was developed
   C. Purpose and objectives of the system
   D. Who uses the system
   E. Where the system fits into the company
   F. Any other pertinent remarks
   G. Describe the design methodology used (structured or traditional)

II. Describe the system and how it operates
  A. Narrative description
  B. Structured documentation
    1. Context diagram
    2. Logical data flow diagram of overall system
    3. Level 0 physical data flow diagram
    4. Lower level data flow diagrams
    5. Data structure and data access diagrams
    6. Data dictionary
    7. Minispecifications for processes, including logic
      a. Decision tables
      b. Decision trees, and so forth
    8. System structure charts
  C. Traditional documentation
    1. System flowchart
    2. Documented flowchart and documentation section
    3. Area cost sheets
    4. System requirements specification
    5. Input/output sheets
    6. Equipment sheets
    7. Personnel sheets
    8. File sheets
    9. Layout charts
  D. Controls matrix and auditor's report
III. Show how the computer programs fit into jobs, how jobs fit into cycles, and how cycles fit into the overall system. Provide a narrative description of what each program, job, and cycle does. Include
  A. A computer listing showing the statement for each program
  B. In-line comment or note statement. Wherever a new logical unit begins, put in a few comments that explain what these instructions do and how these instructions interact with the rest of the program
  C. Structured charts such as Nassi Shneiderman charts
  D. One program flowchart for each program and an overall flowchart showing how the various programs interact with the rest of the program (may be system structure charts instead)
  E. Detailed narrative descriptions and decision trees or decision tables for complicated logic or calculations within each program (minispecifications)

    F. Pictorial layouts (data structure diagrams/data access diagrams) of the files, the outputs, and the inputs

    G. Program run book that contains operating instructions, for example, brief program narrative, computer setup information, tapes, disks, carriage control tapes, special printer forms, or any special restart procedures in case of failure prior to normal programs end.

  IV. Program test plans and the results, including the test data

   V. Implementation plans and the results of the implementation

 VI. The appendix contains all other documentation. Nothing is discarded

    A. Feasibility study report

    B. Problem definition report

    C. The study plan (outline)

    D. Other miscellaneous structured design documentation, such as the normalization documentation

    E. Summaries of various phases (if they were prepared)

       1. General information on the area under study

       2. Interactions between the areas being studied

       3. Understanding the existing system

       4. Definition of the new system's requirements

       5. Designing the new system

       6. Economic cost comparisons

    F. Final written report

    G. Verbal presentation

    H. List of controls for the control matrix

    I. Any significant notes made by the user, analyst, or programmer

The complexity and level of detail will vary with the particular system or firm involved. However, the documentation should be sufficiently complete to enable the reader to understand the essential characteristics outlined above. Such information can become extremely valuable in the future when the inevitable changes are required in the system.

Documentation provides the necessary means of coordinating the procedures, programming, and other operations involved in the system. Proper system documentation refers to a thorough written description of all the component parts and operations of the system. The documentation usually describes the forms used, the personnel required to run the system, the equipment needed, and the sequence of operations from input to output. System documentation should be assembled as the system is being designed, and revised as the system is changed and perfected. Computer programs also must be documented thoroughly.

There are six principal reasons why documentation of a system is of vital importance.

1. Projects that are postponed may be difficult to restart unless there is adequate documentation stating the problem, the system objectives and scope, and the degree of completion.
2. When no documentation of previous work exists, a complete restudy or a complete reprogramming effort may have to be undertaken just to obtain an understanding of the prior effort, before making a change.
3. If documentation is inadequate, conversions from one system to another can result in unnecessary delay and additional cost.
4. When file layouts are changed, the system documentation may not accurately reflect the relationships between all the various file formats.
5. Without proper documentation, effective communication of the who, what, where, when, and how of the system is virtually impossible.
6. Without adequate documentation, auditability and control are hard to achieve.

SUNRISE SPORTSWEAR COMPANY

CUMULATIVE CASE: Implementation (Step 10)

You have returned to Casper Management Consultants after the presentation to wait for Stanley Reynolds' decision. Two days later he calls to say they have decided to accept the new system and have chosen Alternative C, the maximum human–machine boundary. He tells you that he is reluctant to spend so much money, but Penny and Chris persuaded him that it is necessary to modernize. You may begin as soon as he gets the bank loan needed to finance the investment. Mr. Reynolds expects to have the necessary funding within a few days and instructs you to begin scheduling for what must be done, but tells you not to commit funds for equipment until the bank loan is secured.

Even though the new system for Sunrise Sportswear is comparatively small, the three months that Mr. Reynolds has allowed is not much time (remember, implementation must be completed by the end of August, and this is early June). The first thing you do is work out an implementation plan. This plan includes all of the tasks that must be done and how long each task will require. Since many of the tasks will be done concurrently, you set them up in a Gantt chart as shown in Figure 12-3.

Highest priority is given to the purchase of the applications packages, which will be done by Nancy and the programmer, John Middleton. While they are

PROJECT NAME	S or C	JUNE				JULY				AUG				SEPT				OCT				NOV				DEC			
		7	14	21	28	7	14	21	28	7	14	21	28	7	14	21	28	7	14	21	28	7	14	21	28	7	14	21	28
Purchase applications package	S	X	X	X																									
	C																												
Add Diners Club	S	X																											
	C																												
Print Order Verification form	S		X	X						X																			
	C																												
Finalize order form	S		X	X						X																			
	C																												
Install LAN	S			X	X	X																							
	C																												
Install electrical plugs	S				X	X																							
	C																												
Purchase equipment	S		X	X	X																								
	C																												
Purchase workstations	S			X	X																								
	C																												
Purchase supplies	S			X	X	X	X																						
	C																												
Orientation meeting	S						X																						
	C																												
Move telephones	S						X	X	X																				
	C																												
Move Accounting	S						X																						
	C																												
Move Wolfe	S							X																					
	C																												
Move Porter/Thompson	S							X																					
	C																												
Move Dunlap	S							X																					
	C																												
Move Gray	S								X																				
	C																												
Move Brunn	S								X																				
	C																												
Package testing	S					X	X	X	X																				
	C																												
Custom programming	S						X	X	X	X	X	X																	
	C																												
Programmer/trainer	S							X	X																				
	C																												
User training	S									X	X	X	X	X															
	C																												
Write procedures	S									X	X	X	X																
	C																												
Changeover	S													X															
	C																												
Records retention schedule	S														X														
	C																												
File usage forms	S														X														
	C																												
Collection schedule	S														X														
	C																												
Follow-up	S													X	X	X	X	X					X			X			
	C																												
Final documentation	S																									X	X	X	X
	C																												

Figure 12-3 Gantt Chart showing implementation of Sunrise Sportswear's new Order Processing System.

shopping for software, you will be making arrangements to add Diners Club to Sunrise Sportswear's credit card sponsors. This became a higher priority when you learned the next catalog will be in the printing process while the implementation of the new system is underway. You want to be sure the Diners Club arrangements are finalized so that the revised order form (Figure 11-3) can be put into the new Fall/Winter catalog. You also make arrangements for printing the new Order Verification form (Figure 11-2), which must be ready to use on the day of changeover to the new system. Other high priorities are making arrangements to install the local area network cabling and the electrical plugs for the microcomputers.

Once you know all of those things are being handled, you and Nancy can begin purchasing the microcomputers, printers, workstation furniture, and the supplies, such as continuous forms, envelopes, and labels. After firm delivery dates are established, the moving plans can be finalized. Moving of telephones and people is planned for July.

You plan to have an orientation meeting one day during the first week of July. Everyone from Order Processing will attend, as well as Ed Wallace, Ann Bull, Dave Cranston, and Kyle Masters. Although you realize that Sunrise Sportswear activity will virtually cease during this meeting, you feel it is important that they all be present. The purpose of the meeting is two-fold. First, everyone must be informed about the scheduling of the changeover to the new system. Everyone must know who is responsible for what, and who is going to move when. Toward this end, you plan to review both the existing building layout chart (Figure 6-7) and the revised layout chart (Figure 10-4), along with the Gantt chart you have prepared.

The second purpose of this orientation meeting, and the reason why so many people from outside Order Processing need to attend, is to be sure that everyone involved has the same understanding of how the new system is going to work. You plan to explain the differences between the old and the new systems by means of the existing system's logical data flow diagram (Figure 7-11) and the Alternative C configuration (Figure 8-6) selected by Mr. Reynolds. It is vital that people who interact with the Order Processing system understand how it will affect their own areas. For example, Kyle Masters must understand that the Shipping Reports will no longer be returned to Jon Gray and that they will be stored in his area for a designated period of time. Ann Bull must understand how the new customer records are going to be handled, so that she can make the necessary changes in her operation. Finally, Ed Wallace must understand the changes in the handling of customer payments and the fact that invoices are being eliminated. Even though you know this will not be new information to anyone, it is necessary that everyone has the *same understanding* of how the new system is to operate and exactly which alternative was selected.

While you and Nancy are purchasing equipment and so forth, John Middleton will be busy testing software packages and doing the custom programming. Also, when the programming is near completion, John must spend some time with Michael Allen, the trainer. They must go over the routines together so that Michael can understand the system well enough to write the procedures and train the users.

The actual changeover to the new system is planned for the last week of August. Since you are doubtful that you can do such things as the records retention schedule before the changeover, you leave a few tasks until later. Also, you plan to have a continuing follow-up for several weeks after the changeover to make sure that the people know how to use the equipment and that they are able to follow the procedures. Because the people have never worked with microcomputers before, you know they will require more assistance than if they were making the transition from another automated system. You hope that everything will be running smoothly by the end of September, but you plan more follow-ups during November and December. When satisfied that the system is working as it should, you will put the final documentation together into one package. It is reasonable to expect that the Sunrise Sportswear Order Processing system will be operating smoothly and in a "maintenance mode" by the end of the year.

Feeling confident that everything has been taken into account, and with the funding approved, you begin building the new system. Nancy and John are able to locate suitable software. Since the outputs and inputs were developed during the analysis process, you and John can decide almost immediately how and where each fits into the scheme of things. John has the data flow diagram functional primitives and system structure charts. He plans to use them for program coding. In a couple of cases, John develops pseudocode and Nassi Shneiderman charts to be used in programming. You also discuss each of the data stores and the physical data dictionary for each one. You make sure John knows the person at Sunrise Sportswear who is most familiar with the contents of each data store in case questions arise and you cannot be reached. Finally, you discuss file layouts so John can make decisions with regard to the database management system software package that was purchased. Considering the short amount of time in which everything must be accomplished, you congratulate yourself for having used structured analysis techniques. Because you used a top-down hierarchical approach to analysis, you know John will be able to convert the structure charts so that each module can be coded efficiently. The resulting program will be easier to maintain because the structure charts are an index to the code, and each module is short and manageable. You also tell John to contact Sunrise Sportswear's auditor, Jessie Call, when he is ready to begin testing (remember, Jessie was the leader of the Controls Review Team). John will have to have Jessie's concurrence that all the controls from the matrix are implemented.

Nancy makes most of the arrangements for the hardware, workstation furniture, and supplies. Everything is progressing smoothly. The orientation meeting with the Sunrise Sportswear staff has been held, and everyone seems to understand what is expected of them.

It is the last week of July, and Michael Allen has just begun the user training.

Since Suzanne Wolfe's process is key to the entire operation, he works with her first. About mid-way through the first morning, he encounters the first major problem. He and Suzanne have been discussing how the new customer records and address changes will be provided to Catalog Printing and how Suzanne will receive the current list of old customers initially. Michael realizes there is a gap in his knowledge and comes to see you because you have designated yourself as the central control point. When he inquires about how the current customers file is to be put into Suzanne's hard disk, you are appalled at having overlooked a key step in the implementation of the new system. You immediately call Nancy to find out how you can convert the magnetic tape of old customers over to the microcomputer's hard disk. Nancy says she believes it probably can be done by a service bureau, but she does not know of one offhand. She suggests that John Middleton may have a better answer.

When you speak with John he agrees that it could be done by a service bureau. He suggests, however, that you could "fool" Sunrise Sportswear's mainframe computer into thinking it is using a data communication circuit to download the data from the mainframe to the microcomputer's hard disk. To accomplish this, you take Suzanne's microcomputer to the Data Processing area and hook it to the mainframe computer with a null modem cable. This cable is attached to the RS-232 port on each piece of equipment. It is called a null modem cable because it does away with modems, but the computer thinks it is transmitting over data communication circuits, when it is transmitting to another piece of equipment a foot or two away. By doing this, you are successful in transmitting the customer name and address file to Suzanne's hard disk and breathe a sigh of relief when the file actually works. You are dismayed that you overlooked such an important task, but are relieved that such a "quick fix" was available.

The next crisis occurs when Joe, an employee in the Inventory area, is being trained to handle the backorders. They have been working diligently for several days in order to input all of the current backorders onto diskettes, and everything has been progressing well. Inputting has been completed and Valery Brunn has come to observe how the new procedure works. While people are talking and moving around to look at the backorder forms that have been printed using the new equipment, one of the diskettes falls to the floor. No one notices it until they want to reuse the diskette and cannot locate it. As they begin searching for it, Ms. Brunn runs her chair over the diskette, and it is ruined. Since the inputting was just completed, there is no backup diskette and the work must be redone. You know everyone is discouraged by what has happened, but see it as an opportunity to discuss the need for security of diskettes. You use the disaster to impress upon everyone the need for backup diskettes and to have them in a secure place. Nevertheless, the Inventory staff have to work that next weekend to replace the lost data.

Everyone is in their new locations (offices were moved on weekends so work disruption would be minimized), the equipment is in place, everyone has been trained, and the time to change to the new system has arrived. You have decided to automate each step of the process in sequential order, so Jon Gray is the first person to convert to the new system. The first batch of orders are time and date stamped, and Jon attaches the new Order Verification form (Figure 11-2) to each one. He then proceeds to check each order against the INVENTORY printout to determine whether the requests are for Sunrise Sportswear merchandise. When he locates the item in the printout, he verifies the price. So that other people will not have to look up the price again, you tell Jon to indicate the correct price whenever he marks the "incorrect" box on the Order Verification form. With regard to payment method, you also tell him to indicate the exact amount if actual cash is sent as the payment. He is not to check any of the payment method boxes if credit is requested.

You move with the first batch of orders to the next step, which is Suzanne Wolfe's area. Even though everyone was under a lot of pressure, the fact that Mr. Reynolds hired an extra person to help Suzanne type the new customer records means that she caught up and is able to begin the new procedure without a backlog. The first thing she does is assign an order number. This order number uses the first two digits of the current year, two digits for the month, and four numbers that are assigned in sequential order. A typical order number looks like this: 86080001. Next Suzanne looks in the file for the customer's name. If she finds the name, she checks the address to be sure it is the same person. If it is, she then assigns a customer number. This customer number starts with the first letter of the person's surname, uses the two digits for the current year, two digits for the month, and four numbers that are assigned in sequence (for example, K86081234). By looking at a customer's number, anyone will be able to tell the year and month the person became a Sunrise Sportswear customer. Initially the customer number will be assigned to each person's name because the old customer file did not use customer numbers. Eventually they will be assigned only to new customers and those who have not ordered anything from Sunrise Sportswear since the new system was installed.

After inputting the customer information, Ms. Wolfe checks to determine whether it is an old or new customer. You envision a time when this old/new customer designation will no longer be needed, but kept it for now because of management's strong desire to identify with old and new customers. During the follow-up stage, you plan to show them customer printouts that are arranged by date so they can see this is now an extra step that can be eliminated. When the customer information is completed, Ms. Wolfe then checks one of three alternatives. If the customer sent a payment, she checks the Batch Payments box on the Order Verification form, and forwards it to Rosemary Dunlap. If it is a credit card purchase, the Credit Card Verification box is checked and it is forwarded to Lynn Porter and Bob Thompson. If the order must be returned to the customer, she writes the order number on the order and prints out the new letter designed to return customer orders (Figure 11-6).

The next step to observe is that of Rosemary Dunlap, who handles the customer payments. During the analysis phase, you were not able to locate any documentation relating to how payment discrepancies were handled. As far as you could tell, Ms. Dunlap entered whatever the payment amount was into the accounts receivable records, and no one worried about whether it was an overpayment or underpayment. You finally were able to get Mr. Reynolds, Valery Brunn, and Ed Wallace to agree that payment amounts that varied by more than $1.00 should require either a refund or an invoice. It is Ms. Dunlap's job to check for such discrepancies and report them to Accounting for further handling. For the time being, this discrepancy reporting will be handled on paper; however, Ed Wallace already has expressed a desire to join the local area network, and this step may be one of the first in his area to be automated. If this is the case, Ms. Dunlap will be creating her own records from the CUSTOMERS file and then will transmit the discrepancy report to Accounting via the local area network. In the meantime, she is using the same payment discrepancy report form that Jon Gray has been using, but includes the customer number and the order number.

The step that verifies credit cards is next. It has not changed very much, except that the Order Verification form now provides a more complete record of credit card action taken, and there is a fourth credit card company to check. None of this first batch of orders are from the new catalog that was just sent out, so you do not know if any problems will be encountered with the fourth credit card company. You are pleased that one of the orders has to be rejected because the credit card number does not match the name. This allows you to make sure that the new credit card rejection letter (Figure 11-7) is being printed properly and that the staff can handle the equipment. You also remind them that the new form must have the credit customer's signature, which was not required previously.

The Inventory staff recovered from their earlier mishap with the damaged diskette and now have the BACKORDERS file in good shape. None of the orders in this first batch needs to be backordered, so you cannot see how this step will work. Instead, you tell them to let you know when the first backorders are encountered so that you can move on to the next step. Before leaving, Tom Conners tells you he is so impressed with how fast everything prints out that he already is considering getting the purchase orders automated.

When you arrive in Charley Evans' area, there is some confusion. Since the packing lists are new, the staff there has more adjusting to do than in the other areas, in terms of working with unfamiliar things. You walk through each task, from the time the merchandise and order arrives in their area, until it leaves for the Shipping Department. You conclude that they know how to do what needs to be done, and that their problem is based primarily on hesitation over the new equipment and fear that they might somehow destroy a file. You reassure them that this will not happen and tell them that you will return after checking other areas.

Since the new procedure has a direct impact on the Shipping Department, you go there next. Some of the people complain that they now have to file the Shipping Reports, which they do not like. You explain that when the Shipping Reports were returned to Jon Gray's area, they were not of much value. Instead of keeping them for an indefinite period of time, they will be stored in the Shipping Department for a short period of time based on the records retention schedule, which has not yet been devised. You point out that these reports require far less filing in the Shipping Department, since they are filed in the same order in which the merchandise is sent out. This allows quick retrieval in case a customer complains that merchandise has not been received. Since the Shipping Department is responsible for tracking lost merchandise, they can be more efficient because they will no longer have to go to Jon Gray's area to retrieve the record but can begin tracing it immediately.

Ed Wallace is beaming when you arrive at his area. All of his staff are delighted that there will be no more credit orders. Now any invoices that are sent from Sunrise Sportswear will be sent by them, and they will have control of any problems that are encountered. Also, they anticipate an immediate drop in the amount of filing that is done in their area.

Finally, you stop by Catalog Printing. Ann Bull tells you that the new order form got submitted in time to arrive at the printer for the new catalog. She still needs to work out some details about the handling of the CUSTOMERS diskettes from Suzanne Wolfe. These diskettes have to be converted to magnetic tape and sent to the printer so that the printer can address the catalogs and preprinted order form customer labels. Ms. Bull is pleased that they no longer have to key the customer data from the 3×5 cards.

The first day of the new system has proceeded fairly well and without any major problems. You continue working with each group for several weeks until they feel comfortable with the new procedures and equipment. Although it was hectic initially, things seem to have smoothed out and there do not appear to be any major backlogs.

At the end of the new system's fourth week of operation, you decide it is time to check some of the orders to find out how long it is taking them to be processed under the new system. Since the completed Order Verification forms are returned to Jon Gray's area, you go there to examine the latest batch of filled orders. Of the last 50 orders that were filled, 75 percent were filled in five days. This is a considerable improvement over the old system, and you expect to see it improve by the next time it is checked. You report this figure to Valery Brunn and Stanley Reynolds, who are pleased to see that the investment appears to be paying for itself already.

In the meantime, you and Ed Wallace have worked out a schedule for the collection of seriously overdue accounts. By showing Mr. Reynolds the paperwork for some of these accounts, you finally convince him that accounts over 120 days old should be sent out for collection. In the meantime, the number of accounts receivables already is beginning to drop, and Ed Wallace's staff can spend more of their time working on the overdue accounts to get the remaining ones under better control.

You also work out records retention schedules. The old customer orders file has been filed by the customer's name in Jon Gray's area. Recall that when the completed orders were returned for filing, the Order Verification form and the customer's order were separated. Under the new system, it is no longer necessary to separate them. In the new system, they are both filed by the Order Number, which provides a chronological filing sequence. The old file of customer orders is being phased out because its sole purpose was to be able to retrieve customer orders by customer name. Now Jon Gray is using the CUSTOMERS file that is stored on the hard disk in Suzanne Wolfe's microcomputer instead. With it, he can determine the customer's name, address, order number, and customer number. The old customer orders cannot be discarded immediately, however. Since they are filed by customer name, there is no easy way to locate the more recent records. In order to have a reliable means of determining how often the old files are needed, you designed a small form that has been taped to the front of each drawer. On the assumption that most problem orders will have surfaced within a three-month period, starting on December 1st each access to the files will be indicated on this form. It is expected that the files will not be accessed after the new system has been in operation for six months, so you expect that they can be discarded about March of next year (the system was up the last week of August, so a full six months of operation is from September through February). The form on each drawer will provide assurance that records are not disposed of prematurely. Also, it has been agreed that the Order Verification forms older than two years can be discarded immediately. Only the last two months of Order Verification forms were moved to Jon Gray's new area. The same form has been taped to the older Order Verification file drawers, but instead of waiting for a specified period of time, each access to them is to be marked starting immediately. You know that Valery Brunn is anxious to move to her new office (which is larger than the previous one), so you took special care to help her understand how to monitor the usage of the files so they can be discarded as quickly as possible.

The Shipping Department is now required to store the Shipping Reports (Figure 2-13). Some of the file cabinets that have been freed by disposal of old Order Verification forms have been transferred to that area. Again, it is felt that six months probably is adequate for these records, but as a double check Kyle Masters also will use the access form you have designed. It will be used for the second three-month period the system is in operation (December through February), and the records retention schedule may be revised if it is determined that older records are not being used.

Since the BACKORDERS and PACKING LIST data stores are filed on diskettes, the amount of paper storage at Sunrise Sportswear has been reduced substantially. As older records are phased out, you feel confident that your goal of reducing the active records storage of the Order Processing system by 90 percent will be realized.

During the December follow-up, everyone appears to be happy with the new system, and there are fewer questions. Bob Thompson now works with Suzanne Wolfe, since his previous tasks were phased out. The clerk who had done the filing in Jon Gray's area has transferred out of Order Processing to another area. Ed Wallace reports that he has been able to reduce his staff by two; these were the people he had hired specifically to handle the increase in overdue accounts caused by the credit situation.

Enough time has passed so that the evaluation criteria you established can be tested. You document the following changes caused by implementing the new system.

1. Ed Wallace reports that overdue accounts have been reduced to 4 percent. The collection agency has been able to collect 48 percent of the accounts sent to them so far.

2. Sampling of completed Order Verification forms indicates that the overall order processing time has been reduced to 2½ days. Although this is short of the goal by one-half day, nevertheless you are pleased with the figure.

3. Most credit verifications are handled within a half-day, which is well within the acceptable range.

4. Active records storage has been reduced by

   a. Thirty-five percent in Jon Gray's area.

      (1) All Shipping Reports have been eliminated from this area. The latest year was transferred to the Shipping Department with the expectation that these will be pared down to six months in the near future.

      (2) All completed Order Verification forms older than two years have been discarded. It is expected that all completed Order Verification forms older than six months will be eliminated in the near future.

      (3) Tracking of access to old customer orders begins this week. It is expected that all of these files will be discarded approximately in March.

   b. One hundred percent in Suzanne Wolfe's area.

      (1) The file of new customers on 3 × 5 cards has been eliminated.

      (2) The Data Processing Department no longer supplies a customers printout to Suzanne Wolfe.

   c. One hundred percent in Rosemary Dunlap's area.

      (1) The Data Processing Department no longer supplies an accounts receivable printout to Rosemary Dunlap.

    d. One hundred percent in the credit verification area.

        (1) The Data Processing Department no longer supplies an accounts receivable printout for the credit verification process.

    e. One hundred percent in Inventory.

        (1) The paper file of backorders has been eliminated and is stored on diskette.

        (2) The area is beginning to plan for placing purchase orders on diskettes.

    f. No files were maintained in Order Preparation.

        (1) The new file of packing lists is on diskettes.

    g. The Accounting Department has been able to dispose of copies of invoices more than one year old. Ed Wallace estimates that this is a reduction of 75 percent, although this has not been measured.

    h. The number of printouts that have to be printed nightly by Data Processing has been reduced. The result is an unexpected savings. Four hours of overtime pay has been eliminated because the evening computer operator no longer has to run these reports.

After checking each one of the processes to be sure they are all operating as anticipated, you ask Suzanne Wolfe to provide some sample customer printouts by customer name, customer number, date of entry into the system, and ZIP code.

When you are satisfied that everything has been accomplished, you compile a short final report to summarize what has been achieved by modernizing Sunrise Sportswear's Order Processing system. In this report, you indicate the measurable evaluation criteria that you determined early in the study and indicate how well the new system is measuring up to these criteria. You are pleased that the system is nearing the objectives. With this final report, you also submit the final documentation package that has been completed on the Sunrise Sportswear Order Processing system. Your project has been completed successfully.

Student Questions

1. On the first day of operation for Sunrise Sportswear's new Order Processing system, you verbally added four additional procedures. Identify them.

2. Why is it necessary to hold an orientation meeting?

3. Why was Jessie Call notified?

4. Who is the central control point for implementation of Sunrise Sportswear's new Order Processing system?

5. How was Sunrise Sportswear's new Order Processing system implemented?

Student Tasks

1. Draw a context diagram for the new Order Processing system at Sunrise Sportswear. This form of review is nice to give to management. Mr. Reynolds will appreciate having it, and it will serve to emphasize the data flows entering and leaving the new system.
2. List all of the documentation that should be in the final documentation package provided to Sunrise Sportswear.
3. Design a form that can be used to track access to old records in the file cabinets.

Selected Readings

1. Dickie, R. James. "Implementation Demands a Personal Approach," *Data Management*, vol. 22, no. 2, February 1984, pp. 28–29. [Steps to be considered by both data processing and end users when designing an information system.]
2. Er, M. C. "Principles of Program Documentation," *Journal of Systems Management*, vol. 35, no. 7, July 1984, pp. 31–35.
3. Garcia-Molina, Hector, Frank Germano, Jr., and Walter H. Kohler. "Debugging a Distributed Computing System," *IEEE Transactions on Software Engineering*, vol. SE-10, no. 2, March 1984, pp. 210–219.
4. Gilmore, D. J., and H. T. Smith. "An Investigation of the Utility of Flowcharts During Computer Program Debugging," *International Journal of Man–Machine Studies* (G.B.), vol. 20, no. 4, April 1984, pp. 357–372. [Usefulness of flowcharts varies by task and individual programmer characteristics.]
5. Green, Gary I., and Robert T. Keim. "After Implementation What's Next? Evaluation," *Journal of Systems Management*, vol. 34, no. 9, September 1983, pp. 10–15.
6. Hetzel, William. *The Complete Guide to Software Testing.* Wellesley, Mass.: QED Information Sciences, Inc., 1984. [Examples and checklists.]
7. Kull, David. "To Raise Productivity, Work Smarter, Not Harder," *Computer Decisions*, vol. 16, no. 3, March 1984, pp. 164–189. [Discusses standard questionnaires, development notations, documentation techniques, top-down programming, code and design inspections, and other techniques to improve programmer productivity.]
8. McKay, Lucia. *Soft Words, Hard Words: A Common-Sense Guide to Creative Documentation.* Wellesley, Mass.: QED Information Sciences, Inc., 1984. [How to write hardware and software documentation.]
9. Mushet, Mike. "Life After Implementation: Management System Maintenance," *Journal of Information Systems Management*, vol. 1, no. 2, Spring 1984, pp. 55–65.
10. Noll, Paul. *How to Design and Develop COBOL Programs.* Fresno, Calif.: Mike Murach & Associates, Inc., 1984. [Advocates use of structured design techniques to develop COBOL programs.]

11. Parikh, Girish. *How to Measure Programmer Productivity.* Wellesley, Mass.: QED Information Sciences, Inc., 1981.

12. Perry, William E. *The Complete Guide to Installing Personal Computers.* Wellesley, Mass.: QED Information Sciences, Inc., 1984.

13. Perry, William E. *A Structured Approach to Systems Testing.* Wellesley, Mass.: QED Information Sciences, Inc., 1983.

14. Simms, Jed. "Who Will Implement It: The User Managers," *Modern Office* (Australia), vol. 23, no. 5, June 1984, p. 29. [Implementation of office systems by managers who also are end users.]

15. Smith, K., S. Wall, and H. Henry. "Team Approach Mixes Design, Development, Documentation in Cooperative Programming," *Computerworld,* vol. 18, no. 22, May 28, 1984, Special Report 34–35, 40. [Integrating design, development, and documentation into a single structured process.]

16. *System Development: Improving the Productivity of EDP Systems Development.* Phoenix, Ariz.: Applied Computer Research, Inc., 1981–

17. "What Is Training's Role in Designing Computerized Systems?" *Training & Development Journal,* vol. 38, no. 3, March 1984, pp. 18–21.

Questions

1. When does the implementation process begin and of what does it consist?

2. What can the analyst do to make the implementation as smooth as possible?

3. Identify the three basic approaches to starting up a manual system.

4. What does the analyst do when installing a manual system?

5. Identify the three separate tasks that are performed during Step 10 of the system development life cycle.

6. Describe the typical procedures that should take place when a program is being developed.

7. Identify the four computer-based file layouts that can be considered for use.

8. What subtasks would a complete schedule of testing involve?

9. Who should be involved in the process of creating test data?

10. What should be considered when creating test data?

11. What are the objectives of testing the entire system at once?

12. Identify the basic principles that the programmer and analyst should observe during any implementation.

13. What does the documentation package for a computer program normally contain?

14. How does the one-for-one changeover method differ from the parallel changeover method?

15. What should the analyst try to do during the follow-up phase of implementation?

16. Why is re-evaluation required?

17. Identify three reasons why documentation of a system is of vital importance.

SITUATION CASES

Case 12-1:   *Fire Protection Systems*

Assume that you have reached the point of Phase III: Implementation, and you are about to commence on Step 10. During this step you will program, test, and implement (install) the new system. You begin Step 10 by reviewing all of the earlier documentation, file layouts, data flow diagrams, context diagrams, and any flowcharts. After developing program flowcharts for the various program modules, you actually write the code. Your desk check goes very smoothly and the programs compile rather quickly, although there are a few bugs in the early runs.

Next, you completely debug the program with some test data that will check out each of your branches, loops, and prove that the programs are compiling completely and that all mathematical formula/operations are giving correct answers.

At Fire Protection Systems, you are the person who does the testing. You invite the internal auditors and some other experienced members of the user department to assist in this testing task. In reality, you already tested the individual programs during the debugging phase, so you move directly to the link/string/single thread testing. After a thorough link testing, you move on to the backup and restart testing where you want to ensure that the programs are backed up adequately and that complete restarts can be made. Let us assume that the link testing, backup/restart testing, and the actual implementation (installation) went smoothly and were done to perfection.

Question

1. In this case, you overlooked three items during the testing phase. Can you identify these three items?

Case 12-2:   *Telephone Stores, Inc.*

Telephone Stores, Inc. consisted of 10 large stores. For 15 years they had vendors service each of their stores to supply them with merchandise. Inefficiency, cost, diversity of stock, and stockouts forced the company to change this type of ordering system.

Management requested that a systems analyst study the problem and recommend a better system. Rather than try to develop a custom ordering system, the analyst decided to use a ready-made computer-based system that had been used effectively in similar retail stores. It would have to be tailored to fit the company's circumstances, but no major modification was necessary.

With management's approval, the system was designed. Costs and phase-out times also were determined. To change systems, the analyst chose a one-for-one changeover in which all areas would be started simultaneously.

The analyst personally helped familiarize the employees with the new system and its benefits. He verbally explained the way implementation would work and explained each person's job. After their training was completed, implementation began. With the analyst directing all activities, the system changeover went smoothly for a while. Then the changeover began to bog down. The analyst found that the new system was functioning well, but the changeover process was being drawn out, and the employees were confused. He began working overtime and carefully watched all new phases to avoid further confusion. The analyst tried to answer each question completely so the employee would understand the situation; however, he found there was not enough time and the changeover fell further behind. Finally, the changeover was complete. It had taken 30 percent longer and cost 10 percent more than anticipated.

Question

1. What major items did the analyst fail to prepare?

Case 12-3:   *Tool Rental Company*

A new manual system for order processing was given the final approval by management, and implementation was to start at Tool Rental Company.

The analyst began by setting up a plan which specified who would do what and when they would do it. She then made copies of the plans and distributed them to all management personnel and all supervisors involved in the new system.

Next she ordered all the necessary new order forms and had them delivered two weeks prior to implementation. While the new forms were being shipped, the analyst prepared instruction manuals for each involved employee.

When the forms arrived, the analyst set up small training sessions with the various involved departments. After all the training sessions were over, each individual was visited in order to answer any questions.

The analyst had decided to start the implementation in chronological order beginning with the Sales Department and ending with the Accounts Receivable Department. Each department would start the new system one day after the preceding department. By doing it this way, she could be with each department on their first day of implementation.

The analyst began with the Sales Department on Tuesday. Everything went as planned. All new orders were put on the new forms correctly and at the end of the day, all orders were sent to the Credit Department.

On Wednesday the Credit Department checked all orders for proper credit authorization. They then sent the orders to the Shipping Department.

On Thursday the Shipping Department began to have difficulty in distinguishing what products the code numbers represented, and only half the orders were filled that day. At the end of the day the analyst decided to put the new code numbers on the stock shelves next to the product name. A manpower shortage on Friday put the Shipping Department one full day behind in their order filling.

Also, on Friday the analyst was helping the Accounts Receivable Department get started on its implementation of the new system.

Just before closing on Friday the analyst went to the supervisor of the Shipping Department to see if the employees could come in Saturday to catch up on their work. The supervisor agreed to the overtime and on Saturday they caught up.

The following Wednesday the analyst began the follow-up process. She went from department to department, checking to see if the system was operating properly and to determine if the benefits of the system were being realized. After analyzing the entire system at work she determined all goals were being met as expected.

The analyst then sent a report to management informing them that the system was now in operation and all planned benefits were being realized.

Two weeks later the analyst was requested to attend a management meeting. At the meeting she was severely criticized by both the President and Controller of the firm because of the amount of money spent on implementation of the new system. The Controller noted that it would take two years of financial benefit from the new system to break even because of the higher than expected implementation costs. The President let it be known that he would not have approved implementation of the system had he known the costs involved. The analyst had no support material to use as counter-arguments and left the meeting with a sense of failure.

The following week the analyst did her re-evaluation; but, not wanting to spend much time on her failure, she conducted a very hasty re-evaluation. She concluded that the system was working as planned.

She finished by putting together the final system documentation. She gathered all the information thus far and organized it in the following manner

   I. Introduction.
  II. Explanation of how the system operates.
 III. Summary of implementation plans and results.
 IV. Appendix containing all other documentation.

The analyst then filed the documentation for future reference.

Questions

1. How could the analyst have avoided the criticism by management or at least have references with which to back up a counter-argument to the criticism?
2. Was the re-evaluation performed correctly at Tool Rental?

Part Three

THE TOOLS OF SYSTEMS ANALYSIS

*P*art Three describes additional tools that are used by systems analysts. The tools discussed in Chapters 13 through 19 are ones that were not covered in detail during the 10 steps of the system development life cycle (Chapters 3–12) or the Sunrise Sportswear cumulative case. They can be introduced at any point the instructor deems to be appropriate.

Chapter 13

CHARTING

LEARNING OBJECTIVES

You will learn how to . . .

☐ Use *management* charts such as: PERT/CPM, organization, and work distribution.

☐ Use *functional* charts such as: flowcharts, HIPO, I-P-O, bar/pie/line, and Nassi Shneiderman.

☐ Integrate charts into your systems study.

☐ Understand charting categories and guidelines.

How to Use This Chapter

The charts in this chapter have been divided into two groups. All of the management-type charts appear at the beginning of the chapter and the functional-type charts follow.

Management charts are those used for management planning and project control. These include Gantt charts (described in Chapter 4), PERT/CPM, organization charts, and work distribution charts.

Functional charts are those used as aids in understanding or defining a process, such as in determining how something is done or what is being done. These include flowcharts, HIPO, I-P-O charts, layout charts, decision tables, bar/pie/line charts, matrices, Nassi Shneiderman charts, and data flow diagrams. Data flow diagrams and decision tables were presented in Chapter 2, layout charts were presented in Chapter 6, and matrices in Chapter 9.

What Is Charting?

If a picture is worth a thousand words, a chart can be worth even more, for a chart can provide an overview of a situation, as well as the detail of the situation's parts. For this reason, charts are one of the primary tools of the systems analyst. They are used, in one form or another, throughout the systems study. These tools are used during feasibility studies, for specific tasks within the system analysis phase, during system design, and to help plan "what is to happen when" from the beginning of the systems study to its end. They also are used extensively by management for planning, organizing, directing, controlling, staffing, and especially for project control.

Charting is a graphic or pictorial means of presenting data. Charting takes the flow of work and makes a picture of it. Charts can be used to illustrate statistical data, locations of desks or equipment, relationships between people and jobs, sequences of events, work flow, controls, organizational structure, and planning or implementation schedules.

The primary use of charting is for communication and documentation of the system. Charting also is used during feasibility studies, problem definition, understanding the existing system, defining new system requirements, design, cost comparisons, the final report, and implementation. Another major use of charts is during the selling of the proposed system.

General Categories of Charts

Charts and graphs can be separated into four categories. The first is *activity charting*. In activity charting, the analyst pictorially summarizes the flow of work through the various operations of a system. Flowcharts and data flow diagrams are the best examples of activity charting. The second category is *layout charting*. Layout charting pictures the physical area under study. Layout charts show the locations of work areas and equipment before and after the new system design. A layout chart actually combines activity and layout charting because the work flow is shown, as well as the physical locations of work areas and facilities. We discussed layout charting in Chapter 6.

The third category is *personal relationship charting*. Charts in this category depict lines of authority, job responsibilities, or job duties. Good examples are work distribution charts and organization charts. The fourth, and last, category is *statistical data charting*. These charts convert statistical data into meaningful statistical information by graphic portrayal. The analyst can be original in illustrating statistical data. Whatever format conveys the picture in a simple, easy-to-read, and factual manner is acceptable. Columnar tabulations or graphs are examples of statistical data charting. The acronym ALPS might help you remember Activity, Layout, Personal, and Statistical charts.

General Charting Guidelines

Charts and graphs can be used as communication aids and visual devices for the presentation of a new system to management. Charts also provide a means of analysis and evaluation by providing an overall picture of the current system or the proposed system. The area cost sheet from Chapter 6 is a good example of a cost picture of the current system. Charts show what goes on where, and allow comparisons of efficiency, timeliness, and costs between the old and new systems. Grouping data together with charts assists the analyst in spotting duplications, bottlenecks, redundant operations, and many other system peculiarities. Finally, charts can serve as aids in isolating problems caused by imbalanced work assignments.

Before developing a chart, the analyst should know what standard charts are appropriate to the application at hand. This requires a familiarity with flowcharts, Gantt charts, work distribution charts, organization charts, and others.

The analyst first must learn the basic kinds of charts that have developed over the years, along with their usual applications. It then becomes possible to devise creative variations in charting methods and applications. Following this general discussion we present the specifics of the more useful charting methods.

The analyst should, depending on the type of chart, determine the flow of work, job duties involved, responsibilities, or the organization involved. These items can be ascertained during the step Understanding the Existing System, and they may be modified during the step Designing the New System.

Try to picture the system as it really is, when charting the existing system. Remember that the formal organization, with its formal written job procedures, provides only one picture of the system. The informal organization, with its informal and unwritten job procedures, provides another view of the system. These formal and informal procedures may or may not be the same, and neither may be totally correct. The point is that the system should be pictured as it actually is at the time the existing system is being portrayed.

Regardless of what the written procedures say, or what some opinions are about how things *should* be, find out and chart what the system *actually* is doing. The actual system idiosyncrasies usually can reveal the important reasons why things are as they are. The analyst then can study these reasons to gain a more realistic approach to redesigning the system.

PERT/CPM

The acronym PERT stands for Program Evaluation Review Technique and CPM stands for Critical Path Method. Up to this point, we have been using Gantt charts for scheduling tasks within projects. PERT is a more precise method for scheduling tasks. While Gantt charts show sequence and time, PERT charts show sequence by detailed activity and time by hours, days, or weeks. PERT also shows which task of a system development project or implementation may become a bottleneck. In other words, PERT charts enable the planner to determine which task may be the one that could delay the entire project. You should use PERT charting when a more precise and detailed planning methodology is required.

Throughout this section on PERT, it should be noticed that it is always referred to as PERT rather than PERT/CPM. In fact, CPM is automatically included in PERT. The basic difference between PERT and CPM is that in PERT, three time estimates are used, while in CPM only one time estimate is used (this difference will become clear as you read further).

The first question to ask is, what is PERT? PERT is a planning and control tool for defining and controlling the efforts necessary to accomplish project objectives on schedule. PERT is a unique method of graphically illustrating the interrelationships of events and activities required to bring a project to its conclusion. PERT was developed jointly by the United States Navy and the Lockheed Aircraft Corporation; CPM was developed by the DuPont Company.

PERT is a statistical technique. It is both diagnostic and prognostic, and it is used for quantifying knowledge about the uncertainties that are faced in completing all of the individual project activities that lead to the successful conclusion of a major systems project. It is a method of focusing management attention on

1. Danger signals that require remedial decisions in order to prevent the materialization of problems.

2. Areas of effort in which tradeoffs in time, resources, or technical performance might increase the possibility of meeting the major schedule dates of a product.

PERT is a tool that aids the decision maker but does not make the decisions. It is a technique that the systems analyst can use to

1. Establish coordinated and definitive job activities at the lowest organizational responsibility level.
2. Determine relative importance of each activity.
3. Simulate real or proposed changes in the project and show the effect of these changes on the project.

The department manager or the project leader needs a method to organize activities. PERT offers them a method of visually seeing what must be done. PERT provides these management people with

1. An excellent medium for coordinating the various project tasks, particularly if the project tasks are separated geographically.
2. A definitive plan in which each analyst really understands each portion of the whole task, and the relative importance of each activity is easily determined.
3. A basis for determining the time to complete each task within the project, as well as the total time required to complete the entire project.
4. Identification of tasks that will delay the entire project if specific tasks do not meet the planned schedule.
5. The means for rescheduling in order to reduce the total time required to meet the project's objectives.
6. The criteria for measuring the project's progress.

PERT is a management tool for defining and integrating what must be done to accomplish the project's objectives on time. It provides a precise method of planning for the development of a new product, the installation of a new computer, the planning of a major systems study, and many other projects.

PERT can be carried out either by using hand calculation methods or by using a computerized PERT program. When the analyst is using a computerized program, the input format and the specialized output format of the PERT program for whichever computer the company has, must be learned first. In this book computerized PERT programs will not be discussed because they are developed specifically for a certain computer by the computer software programmers.

Instead, we discuss PERT hand calculations. PERT hand calculations are

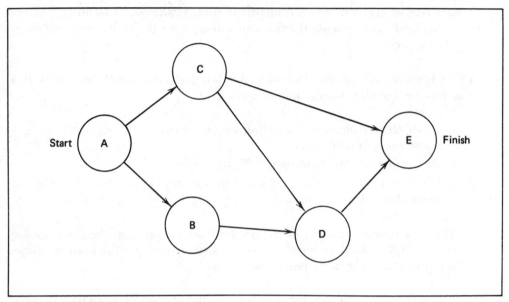

Figure 13-1 PERT network.

often advantageous for small networks of approximately 150 events or less. Even when a computer facility is available, usable results often may be obtained by hand in a shorter overall elapsed time and at less cost than is possible with the use of the computer. The point is, a systems analyst who wants to use PERT for a relatively small network may be able to design the network and perform the hand calculations required to determine the critical path in less time than it would take to use the computerized PERT program. The hand calculation is particularly valuable in small companies or in operations that are performed in the field.

The first definition that the reader must know is *network*. A PERT network is the foundation of the PERT procedure. Figure 13-1 shows a PERT network.

The network consists of events and activities. All of the required events are connected by arrows that indicate the preceding and succeeding events. An *event* (A, B, C, D, or E) is the beginning or ending of an activity. An event is a decision or the accomplishment of a task (activity). An event is looked at as a milestone. Events have no time dimension and usually are represented by a circle or a box. An *activity* links two successive events together and represents the work required between these two events. An activity must be accomplished before the following event can occur. Activities are presented by an arrow.

This example of a PERT network contains five events (lettered A through E) and six activities (represented by the arrows). In summary, each event represents the accomplishment of a task, and each activity represents the time it takes to accomplish that task. The example below expands upon the previous PERT network.

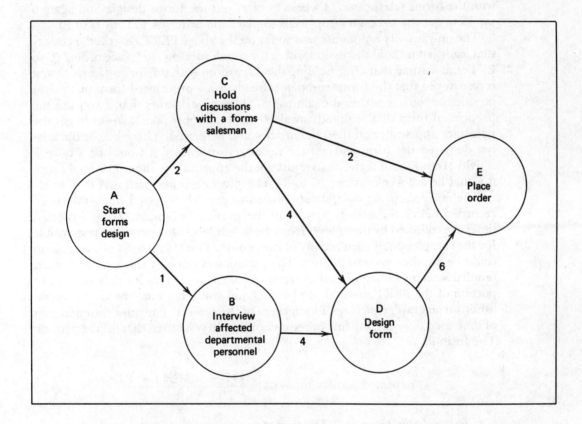

This PERT network represents an overly simplified forms design PERT chart. This PERT chart begins at *start forms design*. The analyst then branches off in two directions. One activity requires 2 weeks while the analyst holds discussions with a forms salesperson (A to C). The other activity requires 1 week while the analyst interviews affected department personnel (A to B). Branching off in both these directions implies that both of the events can take place simultaneously. For example, the analyst can hold discussions with a forms salesperson, and interview the affected department personnel. The next event to look at is D, design form. This event can take place only after the analyst has held discussions with a forms salesperson and interviewed affected department personnel. The point is, if you are drawing a PERT network and one event follows another, it implies that the preceding event must be totally completed before the succeeding event can begin. In the above example, one path takes 1 week to complete the interviews with the affected department personnel, 4 weeks to carry out the forms design, and 6 weeks to get the necessary approvals to place the order (A to B to D to E). Another path shows that it takes 2 weeks to complete the interview with the forms salesperson, 4 weeks to carry out the forms design, and again 6 weeks to get the necessary approvals to place the order (A to C to D to E).

The only activity not mentioned so far on the above PERT chart is the activity that leads from "hold discussion with a forms salesperson" to "place order" (C to E). Let us assume that after holding the discussions with the forms salesperson it is discovered that the forms company already has a preprinted form that might be suitable for use within the company. This activity shows that if you use the preprinted form that is already available, it would only take 2 weeks to get the necessary approval; and then the order could be placed. Therefore, if the analyst designed the form and got the necessary approvals, it would be a 6-week activity (D to E); but if the analyst just got the approval for the preprinted form, it would be a 2-week activity (C to E). Therefore, another path is A to C to E.

The *expected activity time formula* is used to get the expected times that were recorded below the activity arrows in the previous example. These expected times are collected by the analyst from the lowest level of supervision responsible for the completion of each activity of the project. This lowest level of supervision could be another systems analyst. The planning is done by those persons most familiar with the details of that operation of the project. This is a most important portion of the PERT method of planning and collecting times because it establishes a true graphic picture of each event of the project. The most common unit of time used is weeks, but any other unit of time may be used that fits the project. The formula is

$$\text{Expected activity time } (t_e) = \frac{\text{OT} + 4(\text{MLT}) + \text{PT}}{6}$$

- □ *Expected activity time* (t_e). The time in *weeks* calculated for an activity from the three time estimates given.
- □ *Optimistic time* (OT). Time estimate for an activity assuming everything goes better than expected; that is, no unforeseen problems arise.
- □ *Most likely time* (MLT). The time which the responsible manager or analyst thinks will be required for the job. (This is the *only* estimate in CPM.)
- □ *Pessimistic time* (PT). The time required if many adverse conditions are encountered, not including acts of God, strikes, power failures, and so forth.

These three estimates are obtained from the people closest to and responsible for the activity in question. The analyst inserts the optimistic time, the most likely time, and the pessimistic time into the expected activity time (t_e) formula to arrive at the expected activity time (t_e). For example, if OT = 2 and MLT = 3 and PT = 6, then t_e = 3.33 weeks.

$$t_e = \frac{2 + 4(3) + 6}{6} = \frac{20}{6} = 3.33 \text{ weeks}$$

In hand-calculated networks, time usually is written on the activity arrows as shown below.

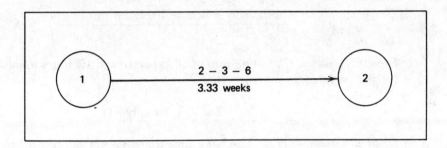

In summary, *events* are shown on the network as meaningful specific accomplishments that do not consume time or resources, but can be identified with a particular point in time. They may be such things as *program go ahead, start forms design, place order, start fabrication,* and so forth.

Activities are the time-consuming elements of the network. The activities are shown by an arrow that connects two events. The arrow indicates the beginning and the ending of the activity. The length of the arrow is unimportant.

The *expected activity time* (t_e) is the calculated time of completion for an activity that links two events. As was stated previously, PERT hand calculations are very advantageous for networks of 100 to 150 events or less. Computers should be used for larger networks. The whole objective of the PERT network is to determine the critical path for the entire project. *The critical path is the longest path through the network.* It is obtained by summing all of the activities for all possible paths. It is the shortest time to complete the entire project even though it is the longest path through the network. For example, the critical path in the previous example, which started out with forms design and ended with placing the order, was 12 weeks unless the management of the operation decided to use a preprinted form.

The following is a list of the various terms that will be used as we develop a larger PERT network for hand calculation.

□ *Activity.* The effort required to accomplish an event measured in time. Represented by an arrow.

□ *Critical path.* The longest path through the network. It is found by summing all activities for all possible paths. It is the limiting factor because the
longest path, in weeks, is the earliest time that the entire project can be
completed.

□ *Event.* A point in time where something has been accomplished. Represented by a circle or a box.

□ *Expected activity time* (t_e). The time in weeks calculated for an activity from
the three time estimates given.

$$t_e = \frac{\text{optimistic} + 4(\text{most likely}) + \text{pessimistic}}{6}$$

□ *Expected event time* (T_E). The sum of all expected activity times (t_e) along the
longest path leading to an event.

$$T_E = \Sigma\, t_e \text{ (See Footnote 1)}$$

□ *Latest allowable time* (T_L). The latest time that an event can be accomplished
without affecting the date scheduled for completion of the entire project
(last event).

$$T_L = T_S - T_E$$

□ *Scheduled time* (T_S). The time in weeks from the starting event to the
planned-for or contractually-obligated completion date (last event).

□ *Slack* (S). The difference between the latest allowable time (T_L) and the
earliest expected event time (T_E) for an activity to be completed. Slack may
be positive (spare time), or negative (predicted slippage), or zero (project
completion on schedule).

$$S = T_L - T_E$$

In order to start the example, a worksheet with seven columns is needed (see
Figure 13-2). The column headings follow the worksheet.

The step-by-step method of determining the critical path and the slack by
hand calculation is as follows.

1. Calculate the expected activity times (t_e) for *all* activities from the formula

$$t_e = \frac{\text{OT} + 4(\text{MLT}) + \text{PT}}{6}$$

[1] Σ means summation, for example, Σa_n means $a_1 + a_2 + a_3 \cdots a_n$.

For example, the activity between events 1 and 2 in Figure 13-3 is

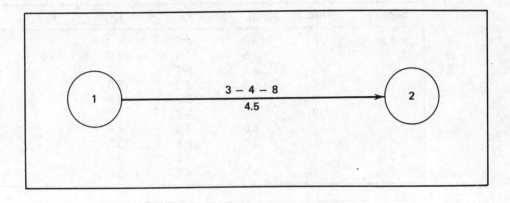

$$t_e = \frac{3 + 4(4) + 8}{6} = \frac{27}{6} = 4.5$$

2. Start with the last event (event 8 in Figure 13-3 and record the event number on the top line of the Successor column (column 1) of the worksheet (Figure 13-2).

3. Record all immediate predecessor events (events 6 and 7) in the Predecessor column (column 2).

4. Record the expected activity time (t_e) for each activity defined by each set of predecessor-to-successor event numbers. For example, record 6 to 8 and 7 to 8 (t_e) in column 3.

5. Record all "last events" if there are more than one. Only in very sophisticated PERT networks will there be more than one last event.

6. When all last events have been recorded, go back to the first event number, listed in the Predecessor event column, and determine the number of succeeding activities from that event. (In this case, events 6 and 7 have only one succeeding activity.)

7. If there is *only one succeeding activity*, record that predecessor event number next in the Successor event column and proceed to record its predecessor events as in step 3 above.

8. If an event has *two or more succeeding activities*, do not record it in the Successor column until it appears in the Predecessor event column as many times as there are succeeding activities.

9. In order to avoid errors, place a check $(\checkmark)$ next to each event number in the Predecessor column as you record that event number in the Successor column.

(1)	(2)	(3)	(4)	(5)	(6)	(7)
Succ.	Pred.	t_e	T_E	T_L	T_S	S
8	√6	3.0	~~16.8~~			
	√7	1.8	17.0	18.0	18.0	1.0*
6	√5	2.2	~~9.7~~			
	4	4.3	13.8	15.0		1.2
7	√4	5.7	15.2	16.2		1.0*
	√3	6.5	~~7.7~~			
5	2	3.0	7.5	12.8		5.3
4	√2	5.0	9.5	10.5		1.0*
3	1	1.2	1.2	9.7		8.5
2	1	4.5	4.5	5.5		1.0*

Column	Abbreviation	Definition
1	Succ.	Successor event number
2	Pred.	Predecessor event number
3	t_e	Expected activity time
4	T_E	Expected event time
5	T_L	Latest allowable time for an event
6	T_S	Scheduled time for an event
7	S	Slack time

Figure 13-2 PERT worksheet.

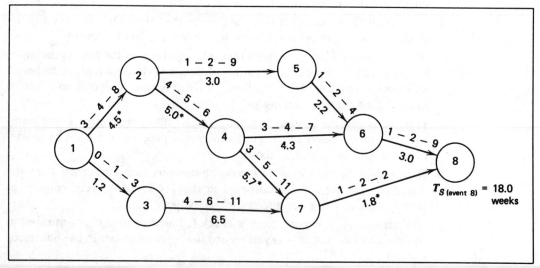

Figure 13-3 PERT network.

10. Record each t_e value as in step 4. The Successor event column (column 1) should have each event recorded once except for the starting event (event 1), which should not be recorded in column 1. The first three columns of Figure 13-2 are now completely filled in.

Calculation of the T_E (Column 4)

The computation of T_E is the sum of the time from event 1 to the predecessor event "in question" plus the activity time from the predecessor event "in question" to its successor event. For example,

---

$$T_E \text{ (successor)} = T_E \text{ (predecessor)} + t_e \text{ (activity)}$$

---

1. Start from the bottom of column 1 in Figure 13-2. The T_E for event 2 is the T_E for event 1 (0.0) plus the t_e of activity 1—2 (4.5).
   T_E (event 2) $= T_E$ (event 1) $+ t_e$ (activity 1—2)
   T_E (event 2) $= 0.0 + 4.5$
   $\quad\quad T_E = 4.5$
2. T_E (event 3) $= T_E$ (event 1) $+ t_e$ (activity 1—3)
   $\quad\quad T_E = 0.0 + 1.2$
   $\quad\quad T_E = 1.2$
3. T_E (event 4) $= T_E$ (event 2) $+ t_e$ (activity 2—4)
   $\quad\quad T_E = 4.5 + 5.0$
   $\quad\quad T_E = 9.5$
4. T_E (event 5) $= T_E$ (event 2) $+ t_e$ (activity 2—5)
   $\quad\quad T_E = 4.5 + 3.0$
   $\quad\quad T_E = 7.5$
5. T_E (event 7) $= T_E$ (event 3) $+ t_e$ (activity 3—7)
   $\quad\quad T_E = 1.2 + 6.5$
   $\quad\quad T_E = 7.7$
6. T_E (event 7) $= T_E$ (event 4) $+ t_e$ (activity 4—7)
   $\quad\quad T_E = 9.5 + 5.7$
   $\quad\quad T_E = 15.2$

   Note: Event times are determined by the *longest* elapsed times; therefore the T_E (event 7) $= 15.2$ is the limiting time. Cross out and disregard the T_E (event 7) $= 7.7$. Use only the 15.2 for T_E of event 7 in any future calculations.
7. Calculate the rest of the T_E values.

At this point, a preliminary evaluation can be made of the project that is being scheduled using a PERT network. The expected time to reach each of the objectives (events) is available in the T_E figure. This time can be compared with any scheduled requirements in order to determine the compatibility of this PERT network plan with the need to meet a scheduled date.

The limiting or critical path is the longest path between the last event and the starting event (event 8 and event 1). Working backward through the network from event 8 back to event 1, one can determine the *critical path* by summing the figures in the T_E column (column 4). For example, start with event 8 in the Successor column (column 1). Go to the Predecessor column (column 2) and note that 8—6 with a T_E of 16.8 has been crossed out; therefore, 8—7 with a T_E of 17.0 is the proper value to use. Now that you have found that 8—7 is the first leg, go to the Successor event column again and find event 7. The proper leg backward from event 7 is 7—4 because its T_E is 15.2 (you already crossed out 7—3 with a T_E of 7.7). Now go to the Successor column again and find event 4. Event 4 has a predecessor event of event 2. The T_E for activity 4—2 is 9.5. Now go to the Successor column again and find event 2. The T_E for activity 2—1 is 4.5. The point is, the critical path for the PERT network in Figure 13-3 is 17.0 weeks long. The critical path itself is event 8 to event 7 to event 4 to event 2 to event 1.

Calculation of the T_L (Column 5)

Start at the top of column 1 in Figure 13-2. A given scheduled commitment date for the completion of the last event (project completion) determines the latest allowable time (T_L) for the last event. Therefore, $T_L = T_S$ for the last event (event 8). If there is no scheduled completion time given (T_S), then let $T_L = T_E$ for the last event. In our example $T_L = T_S = 18.0$ for event 8; but if there were no T_S given, then $T_L = T_E = 17.0$ for event 8. We have assumed that $T_S = 18.0$ was given as a scheduled completion date.

1. The T_L for event 8 is $T_S = 18.0$.

---

2. T_L (predecessor) $= T_L$ (successor) $- t_e$ (activity)

---

3. T_L (event 6) $= T_L$ (event 8) $- t_e$ (activity 6—8)
   $T_L = 18.0 - 3.0$
   $T_L = 15.0$ (record this time under T_L opposite event 6 of column 1)

4. T_L (event 7) $= T_L$ (event 8) $- t_e$ (activity 7—8)
   $T_L = 18.0 - 1.8$
   $T_L = 16.2$ (record this time under T_L opposite event 7 of column 1)

5. T_L (event 5) $= T_L$ (event 6) $- t_e$ (activity 5—6)

$T_L = 15.0 - 2.2$

$T_L = 12.8$ (record this time under T_L opposite event 5 of column 1)

6. When an event has more than one succeeding activity there will be several T_L values. The *lowest* value should be recorded for that event. For example

T_L (event 4) $= T_L$ (event 6) $- t_e$ (activity 4—6)

$T_L = 15.0 - 4.3$

$T_L = 10.7$

T_L (event 4) $= T_L$ (event 7) $- t_e$ (activity 4—7)

$T_L = 16.2 - 5.7$

$T_L = 10.5$ (record the *lowest* time under T_L opposite event 4 of column 1)

7. Calculate the rest of the T_L values. It is not necessary to calculate values for the starting event (event 1).

Slack is the latest allowable time (T_L) minus the earliest expected event time (T_E).

$$S = T_L - T_E$$

1. S (event 8) $= T_L$ (event 8) $- T_E$ (event 8)

$S = 18.0 - 17.0$

$S = 1.0$

2. S (event 6) $= T_L$ (event 6) $- T_E$ (event 6)

$S = 15.0 - 13.8$

$S = 1.2$

3. Calculate the rest of the slacks (S).

Earlier, the T_E column was used to find the critical path. The events with the least slack lie on the critical path. Also note that the slacks are all equal for the critical path. The critical path in this example (Figure 13-3) is marked with asterisks, that is, 8—7—4—2—1.

In summary, the previous example of a PERT network has shown us many things. First, it has forced the analyst to define all of the individual events that must take place from the start of a project to its completion (last event). Second, it has forced the analyst to obtain time estimates for the completion of each activity. Third, it has shown the analyst the critical path, that is, the longest path through the network. This longest path through the network is the shortest time to completion for the entire project because the project will not be complete until all of the events and activities are complete. Fourth, the analyst can see now which paths through the network have slack. The paths that have positive slack show the analyst the activities that will be done in plenty of time. In other words, those activities will not hold up the entire project. Those paths with negative slack show the analyst which activities will need close scrutiny and perhaps some extra effort in order to bring them back to zero slack so the project will not fall behind schedule. Those paths with zero slack show the analyst the activities that are right on schedule and that must be watched so they do not fall behind at all. If they do fall behind, the project will be delayed.

You might find that it helps to insert T_E above each event as you work from the beginning to the end of a PERT network. This shows the cumulative effect of each activity and makes this process much easier since it becomes more graphic. Later, as you work backward, it helps to insert T_L above each event.

PERT/CPM is a very valuable tool to the systems analyst and to the manager of the systems analysts because it can be used to plan individual projects or to plan the workload of an entire department. This simple hand-calculated method can be used quickly and easily by an analyst in order to plan a complicated systems study.

*O*rganization Chart

Organization charts (Figure 13-4) show the structure of the organization in terms of functional units or in terms of superior–subordinate relationships. Organization charts can be designed to portray

1. Levels of authority, from the top to bottom of the organization.
2. The important distinctions between line and staff personnel.
3. Divisional, departmental, or job functional interrelationships in the organization.
4. The lines of formal communication channels.
5. The names and relative prestige of employees.

What the organization chart does not show is often of more interest to the systems analyst than what it does show because the chart shows only the formal organization. It does not show the *informal* organization that may have developed. Therefore it may not show the true relationships between people and between departments, and it may not show the true lines of communications. For example, in the chart shown in Figure 13-4, is Tom Taylor a relative of Phil Taylor? Think about the importance of knowing such relationships. Other

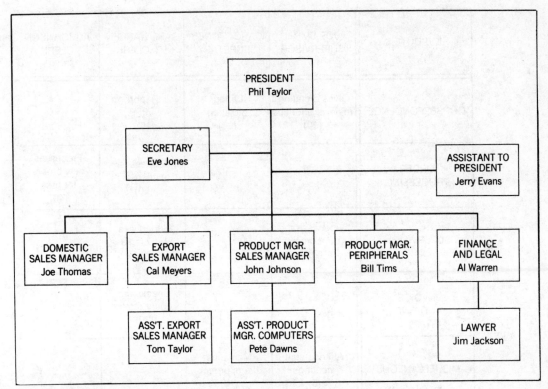

Figure 13-4 Organization chart.

things may be omitted by the organization chart. It may not show the actual degree of authority held by any one person (the person's ability to get the job done through others), and it may not show status and importance.

Nevertheless, organization charts are extremely important to the systems analyst. During the first interviews with management in the area under study the analyst should be sure to obtain an up-to-date chart of the authority and functional relationships of the area. Quite often the analyst will have to draw it as the manager explains the organization, but the manager should verify the accuracy of the final draft. Other examples of organization charts are shown in Figure 1-6 (Chapter 1) and Figure 5-3 (Chapter 5).

Work Distribution Chart

A Work Distribution Chart provides an analysis of what jobs are being performed, who performs them, how the work is divided, and the approximate time

JOB DUTIES	JOE SMITH SUPERVISOR	CAROL JONES SECRETARY	CARL WARREN SR. CLERK	AL JOHNSON CLERK
CORRESPONDENCE	Gives dictation, reviews priorities (10)	Typing, dictation (30)	Report writing (5)	
ORDER PROCESSING			Processes rush orders (10)	Processes new orders for tires (40)
SUPERVISION	Supervises the department (20)		Supervises ten clerks (2)	
INVOICE AUDITING			Checks the dollar totals (20)	
MISCELLANEOUS	Attends staff meetings (5)	Maintains file of orders (10)		

Figure 13-5 Work distribution chart.

required to perform each job. Work distribution charts often are used for analysis when morale problems exist because morale problems frequently are caused by uneven work distribution or some other form of imbalanced work load among the employees.

The work distribution chart for the area under study consists of a list of job duties down the left-hand column and identification of the personnel across the top of the chart. Figure 13-5 shows an example of a typical work distribution chart.

Within the appropriate box the analyst enters a short statement of what the person does in relation to the job duty. In the example in Figure 13-5, under JOE SMITH and to the right of CORRESPONDENCE, the analyst entered "gives dictation" and "reviews priorities." The analyst also entered the number of *hours per week* spent on those tasks. Other units of time can be used; but hours per day is too short a span to include all job tasks, and hours per month is usually too long a span for people to estimate accurately.

The analyst should sum the number of hours in each column to verify that the sum equals the number of hours in the work week for each employee. Summing the hours horizontally shows the total hours being spent per week on each job duty. The analyst should now proceed to study the chart, the work itself, and the employees to determine what changes should be made.

The study might reveal that far too much time is being spent on certain activities, or that certain employees are carrying more than their share of the load. Overburdened employees usually welcome the opportunity to have their performance contrasted with the performance of others who may be doing less than their share. Such imbalanced work loads are often the source of severe employee discontent and frustration. The work distribution chart often can be used to bring such problems to light objectively.

Probably the chart's biggest limitation is the difficulty of using it where the work is highly creative or continuously changing. Even under such circumstances, however, the chart is useful for sorting out the routine tasks.

Flowcharting

A flowchart is a graphic picture of the logical steps and sequence involved in a procedure or a program. Flowcharts help the analyst or programmer break down the problem into smaller, more workable segments and aid in the analysis of sequencing alternative paths in the operation. Flowcharts usually bring to light new areas of the problem that need further study and evaluation. Many laborsaving or timesaving ideas can come from a flowchart.

When developing flowcharts the analyst or programmer should observe the following guidelines.

1. Flowcharts are drawn from the top of a page to the bottom and from left to right.
2. The activity being flowcharted should be defined carefully and this definition made clear to the reader.
3. Where the activity starts and where it ends should be determined.
4. Each step of the activity should be described using "one-verb" descriptions, for example, "prepare statement" or "file customer statement."
5. Each step of the activity should be kept in its proper sequence.
6. The scope or range of the activity being flowcharted should be carefully observed. Any branches that leave the activity being charted should not be drawn on that flowchart. A connector symbol should be used and that

branch put on a separate page, or omitted entirely if it does not pertain to the system.

7. Use standard flowcharting symbols.

Systems Flowchart

A systems flowchart shows the overall work flow of the system. It is a pictorial description of the sequence of the combined procedures that make up the system. A systems flowchart shows *what is being done* in the system. A very simple systems flowchart is portrayed in Figure 13-6 (all of the flowchart symbols are listed later in this chapter).

Another example of a systems flowchart might be as follows: The XYZ Company has found that it can purchase a raw material at a cost of $40 per order. The company has a 10 percent carrying charge on average inventory. They expect to use $20,000 of the raw material within the next year. We want to determine the Economic Order Quantity (EOQ). The systems flowchart portrays only "Data processing determine EOQ" (Figure 13-7). The actual calculations are shown later in a program flowchart.

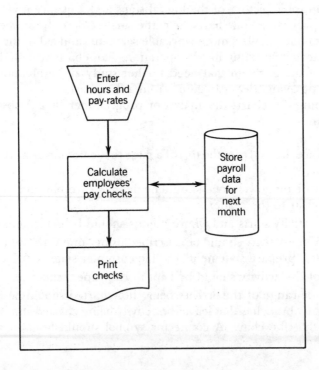

Figure 13-6 Systems flowchart.

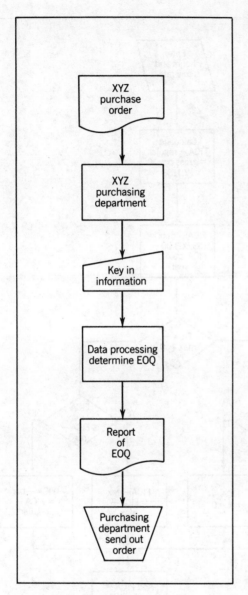

Figure 13-7 Systems flowchart.

*P*rogram Flowchart

Program flowcharts are related to systems flowcharts. A program flowchart is a detailed explanation of *how* each step of the program or procedure actually is performed. It shows *every* step of the program or procedure in the exact sequence in which it occurs. Programmers use program flowcharts to show the

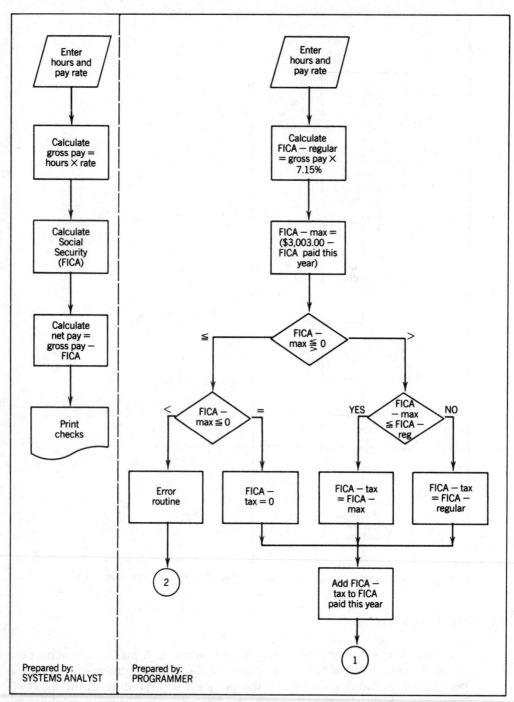

Figure 13-8 Program flowcharts.

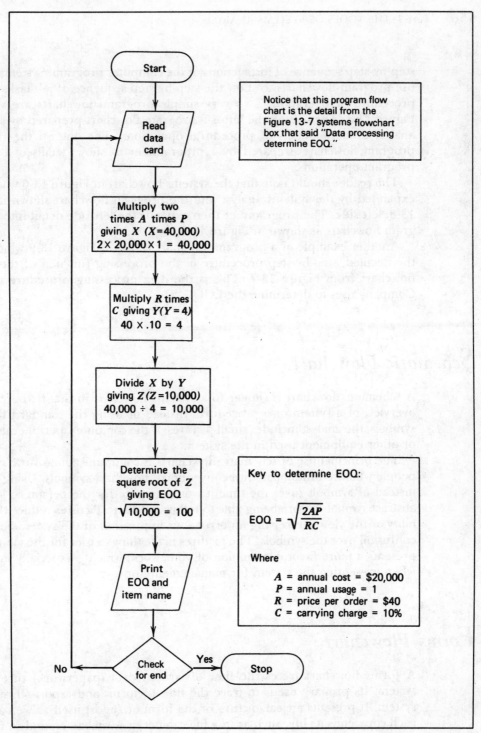

Figure 13-9 Program flowchart.

Start

Read data card

Notice that this program flow chart is the detail from the Figure 13-7 systems flowchart box that said "Data processing determine EOQ."

Multiply two times *A* times *P* giving *X* (*X*=40,000)
2 × 20,000 × 1 = 40,000

Multiply *R* times *C* giving *Y*(*Y* = 4)
40 × .10 = 4

Divide *X* by *Y* giving *Z* (*Z* =10,000)
40,000 ÷ 4 = 10,000

Determine the square root of *Z* giving EOQ
$\sqrt{10,000} = 100$

Print EOQ and item name

Key to determine EOQ:

$$EOQ = \sqrt{\frac{2AP}{RC}}$$

Where

A = annual cost = $20,000
P = annual usage = 1
R = price per order = $40
C = carrying charge = 10%

Check for end — No / Yes — Stop

555

step-by-step sequence of instructions of the computer program. Systems analysts use program flowcharts to show the step-by-step sequence of job tasks within a procedure or operation. Two very simple program flowcharts are shown in Figure 13-8. The one on the left is a program flowchart prepared by a systems analyst to show details of procedural operations. The one on the right is a program flowchart prepared by a programmer to show details of computer program operations.

The reader should note that the systems flowchart in Figure 13-6 was further expanded by the systems analyst into the program flowchart shown in Figure 13-8, left side. The programmer then expands the left side detail into the program flowchart as shown in Figure 13-8, right side.

Another example of a program flowchart is that in Figure 13-9 which shows the detailed, step-by-step procedure of the processing function of the systems flowchart from Figure 13-7. This is the data processing procedure the XYZ Company uses to determine the EOQ.

Schematic Flowchart

A schematic flowchart is similar to a systems flowchart in that it represents an overview of a system or a procedure. Instead of using the standard flowchart symbols, the analyst includes small pictures of the computer, peripherals, forms, or other equipment used in the system.

The principal use of schematic flowcharts is communication of the system to people who are unfamiliar with conventional flowchart symbols. Using pictures instead of symbols saves the time it would require for the person to learn the abstract symbols before being able to follow the chart. Pictures reduce the possibility of the viewer receiving an erroneous impression of the system because of confusion over the symbols. The pictures make things easier for the viewer. This presents a more favorable opinion of your work, which is especially important when presenting the system for management approval.

Forms Flowchart

A forms flowchart traces the flow of written data (paperwork) through the system. Its primary use is to trace the flow of forms and reports through the system. It presents a clear picture of the form or report itself as well as where each copy ends its life, such as in a file cabinet or wastebasket, and so forth. In Figure 13-10, a form is traced through its life cycle.

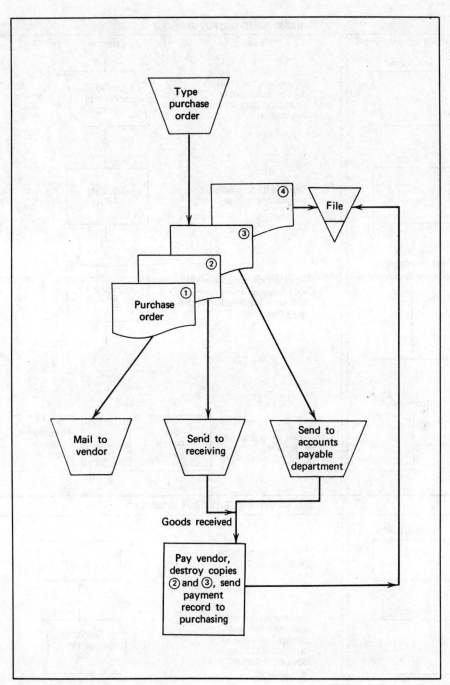

Figure 13-10 Forms flowchart.

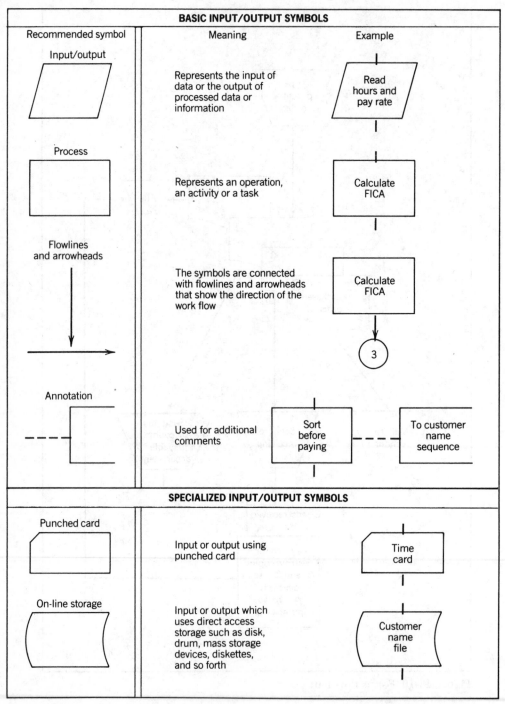

Figure 13-11 Flowchart symbols.

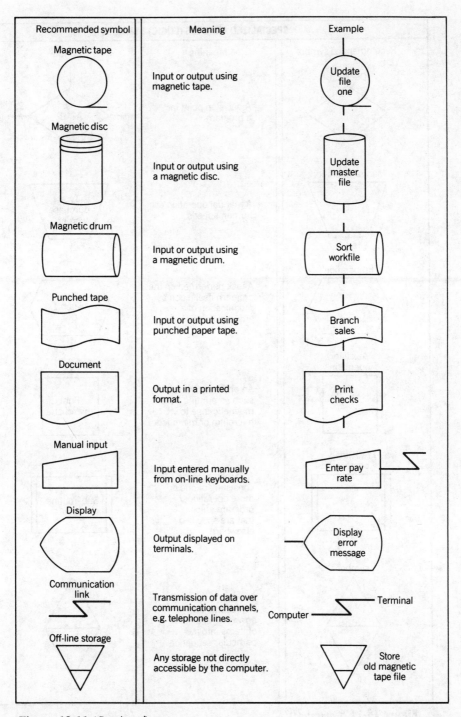

Figure 13-11 (*Continued*)

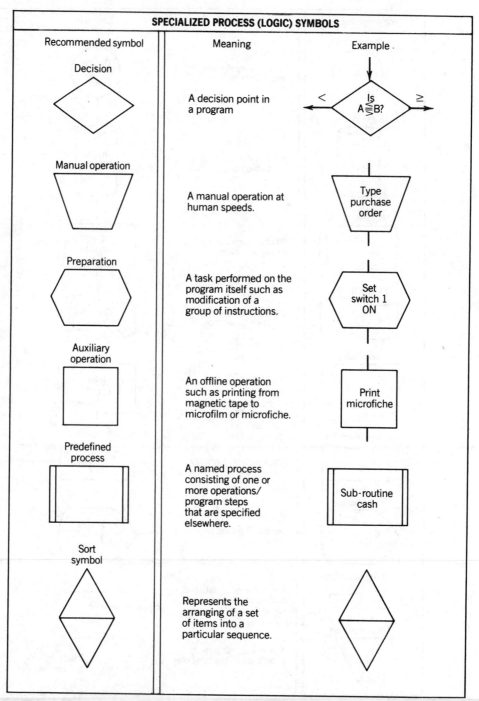

Figure 13-11 (*Continued*)

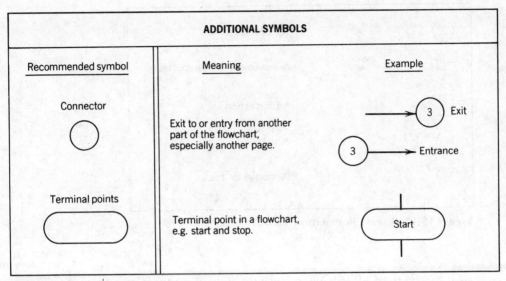

Figure 13-11 (*Continued*)

Standard Flowcharting Symbols

The flowcharting symbols are shown in Figure 13-11. The shape of each recommended symbol appears on the left. Its meaning and an example appear on the right. The flowcharting symbols have been divided into four groups: basic input/output symbols, specialized input/output symbols, specialized process (LOGIC) symbols, and additional symbols. The source of these symbols is the *American National Standard Flowchart Symbols and Their Usage for Information Processing*, ANSI X3.5-1970. The ANSI flowchart standard conforms to the International Organization for Standardization's *Flowchart Symbols for Information Processing*, ISO Recommendation 1028-1969. If you are a user of IBM's flowcharting template, note that IBM's symbols may vary from those of the ANSI and ISO standards.

Process Flowchart

A process flowchart is an industrial engineering charting technique that breaks down and analyzes successive steps in a procedure or system. Process flowcharts use their own special five symbols (see Figure 13-12).

A process flowchart lends itself to industrial engineering where the industrial engineer is studying and improving manufacturing processes. In systems analy-

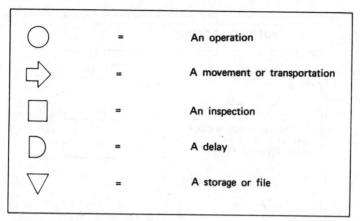

Figure 13-12 Process flowchart symbols.

sis it can be used effectively to trace the flow of a report or a form. See Figure 13-13 for a filled-in process flowchart, then compare Figures 13-10 and 13-13.

HIPO Diagrams

Hierarchy plus Input-Process-Output (HIPO) is a technique for documenting programming systems. HIPO was developed by IBM personnel who believed that if programming systems documentation was created that emphasized function, it could speed up program maintenance by facilitating the location in the code of a procedure to be modified. It might be mentioned that it usually does not speed up program maintenance because the HIPO maintenance package always has been described as optional. When something is described as optional, more than likely it will be omitted and, therefore, the advantage of speeding up program maintenance is lost.

HIPO can satisfy the requirements of a variety of people who use documentation for many different purposes, such as

1. A manager can use HIPO documentation to obtain an overview of the system.
2. An application programmer can use HIPO documentation to determine program functions for coding purposes.
3. A maintenance programmer can use HIPO documentation to locate quickly the functions to which changes will be made.

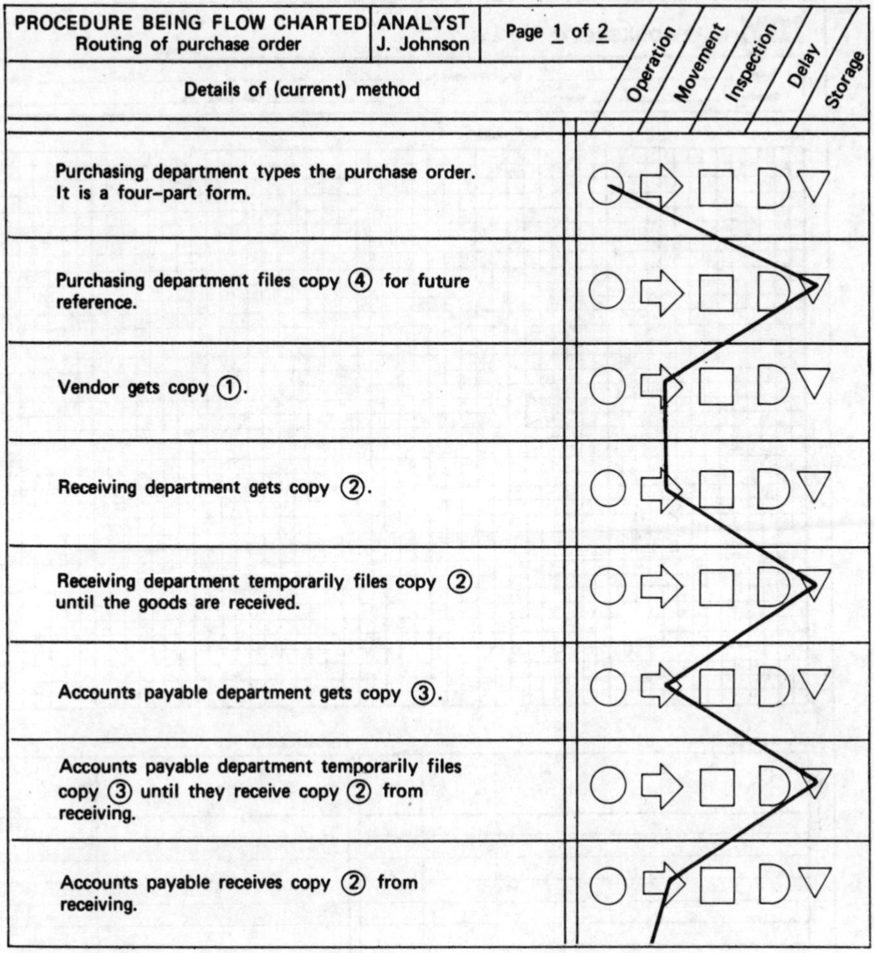

PROCEDURE BEING FLOW CHARTED Routing of purchase order	ANALYST J. Johnson	Page 1 of 2	Operation	Movement	Inspection	Delay	Storage
Details of (current) method							
Purchasing department types the purchase order. It is a four-part form.			○	⇨	□	D	▽
Purchasing department files copy ④ for future reference.			○	⇨	□	D	▽
Vendor gets copy ①.			○	⇨	□	D	▽
Receiving department gets copy ②.			○	⇨	□	D	▽
Receiving department temporarily files copy ② until the goods are received.			○	⇨	□	D	▽
Accounts payable department gets copy ③.			○	⇨	□	D	▽
Accounts payable department temporarily files copy ③ until they receive copy ② from receiving.			○	⇨	□	D	▽
Accounts payable receives copy ② from receiving.			○	⇨	□	D	▽

Figure 13-13 Process flowchart.

HIPO documentation usually is prepared using the HIPO worksheet (see Figure 13-14) and the HIPO template (see Figure 13-15). Although many of the symbols are similar to standard flowchart symbols, there are some new conventions.

As a design and documentation technique, HIPO has three major objectives. The *first* objective is to provide a structure by which the functions of a system can be understood. The diagrams are organized in a hierarchical structure (see Figure 13-16), where each diagram at any level is a subset of the level above it. The *second* objective of HIPO is to state the functions to be accomplished by the program, rather than to specify the program statements to be used to perform

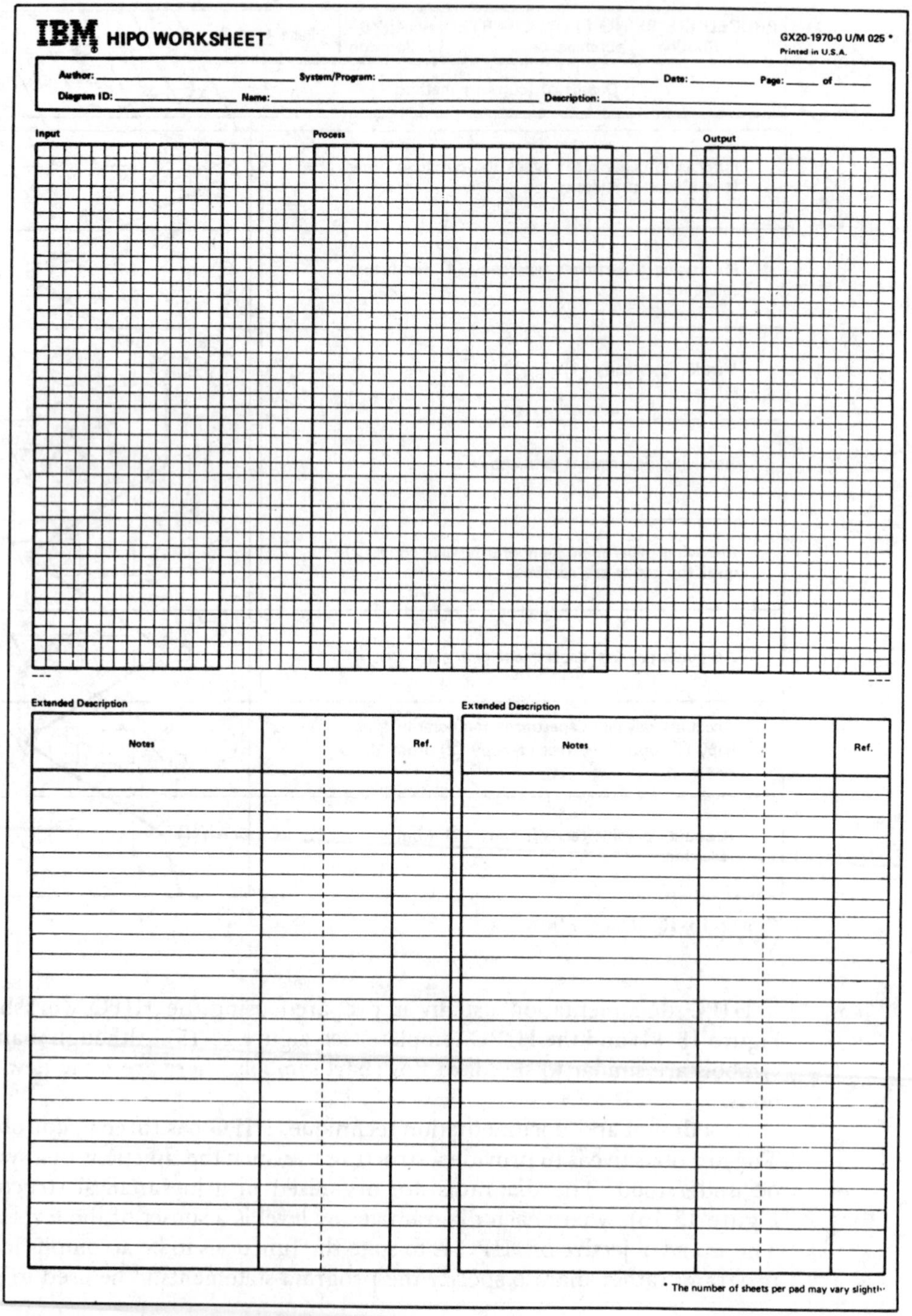
IBM HIPO WORKSHEET

GX20-1970-0 U/M 025 *
Printed in U.S.A.

Author: ______ System/Program: ______ Date: ______ Page: ______ of ______
Diagram ID: ______ Name: ______ Description: ______

Input

Process

Output

Extended Description

Notes		Ref.

Extended Description

Notes		Ref.

* The number of sheets per pad may vary slightly.

Figure 13-14 The HIPO worksheet.

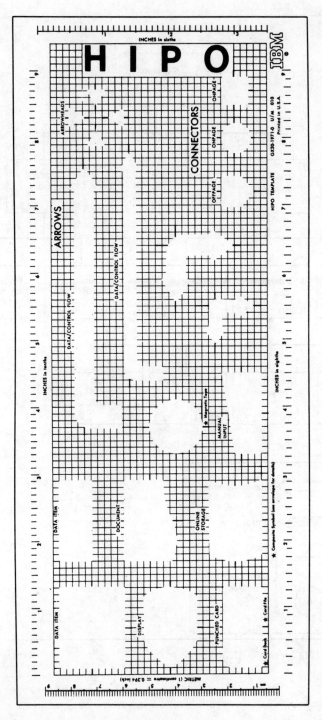

Figure 13-15 The HIPO template.

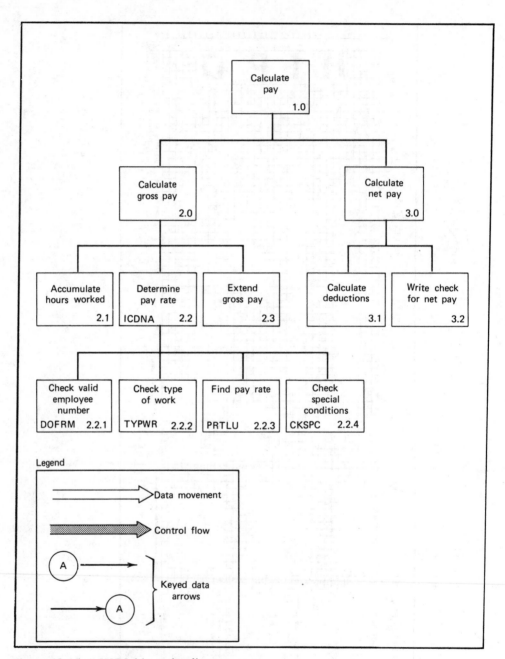

Figure 13-16 A HIPO hierarchy diagram.

the function. The *third* objective of HIPO is to provide a visual description of input to be used and output produced by each function for each level of diagram (see Figure 13-17).

A typical HIPO package contains three kinds of diagrams: a visual table of contents, an overview, and detail HIPO diagrams (see Figure 13-18). The objective of the visual table of contents is to show the major functions to be performed by the system and the relationships between each function (see Figure 13-16). In the visual table of contents, the top box identifies the overall function of the system. The next level of boxes breaks that function down into logical subfunctions. In the case of Figure 13-16, the subfunctions include calculation of gross pay and calculation of net pay. Although four to five levels in the top-down structure are usually all that are necessary, as a general rule it is wise to continue to lower levels until both the designer and user completely understand the functions being described. Each box in the visual table of contents refers to a HIPO diagram, the description and identification number of which are shown in the box. For example, box 2.0, labeled "calculate gross pay," is described further by HIPO diagram 2.0, as shown in Figure 13-17. The visual table of contents should include a legend to describe how the diagrams are to be read and what the various symbols mean.

The objective of the overview diagram (a high-level HIPO diagram) is to provide general information about a particular system. This is accomplished by describing the major functions within the system and referencing the detail diagrams necessary to expand each function to a detail level (see Figure 13-17). The overview diagram describes, in general terms, the inputs, processes, and outputs. The process section contains a series of numbered steps that describe the function being performed. In Figure 13-17, these steps describe the procedure for calculating gross pay. The input section identifies the data items used by the process section, and includes all major input items used in any lower-level diagrams. The input data items are connected to the process steps by arrows. The output section identifies the data items created or modified by the process steps, and includes all major output items shown in lower-level diagrams.

The detail HIPO diagrams contain the basic elements of the system, describe the specific functions, show specific input and output items, and may reference other HIPO diagrams, as well as flowcharts or decision tables of complex logic. The detail diagrams contain an extended description section that is used to amplify the process steps and can reference the code associated with the process steps. The number of levels of detail HIPO diagrams that are required is determined by the number of functional subassemblies, the complexity of the processing, and the amount of information to be documented. Figure 13-19 is a sample detail HIPO diagram with an extended description section. This figure is an extension of box 2.2 in the visual table of contents shown in Figure 13-16, and process step 2 in the overview HIPO diagram shown in Figure 13-17. The specific labels in the input section refer to record names (PAYMSTR) and data

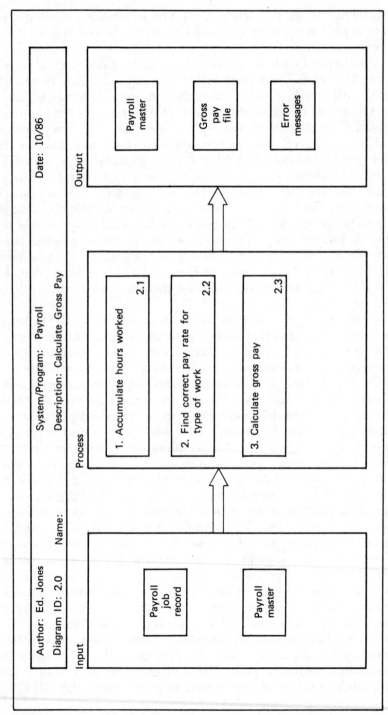

Figure 13-17 A HIPO input-process-output diagram derived from Box 2.0 in Figure 13-16.

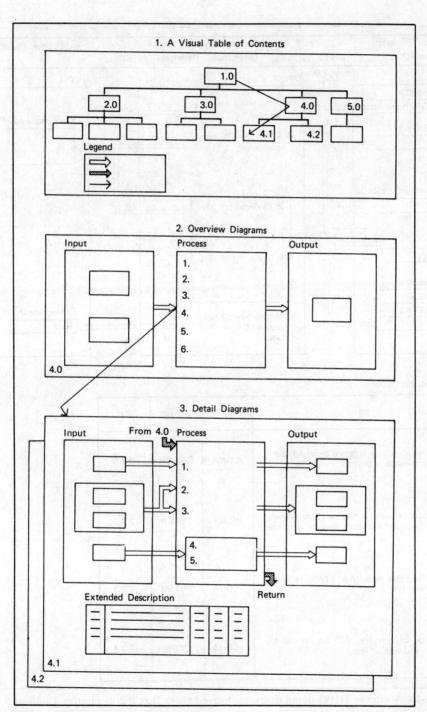

Figure 13-18 A typical HIPO package.

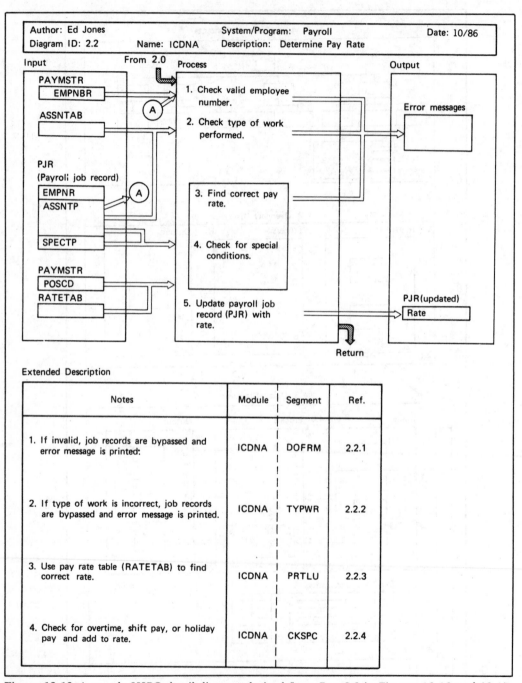

Figure 13-19 A sample HIPO detail diagram derived from Box 2.2 in Figures 13-16 and 13-17.

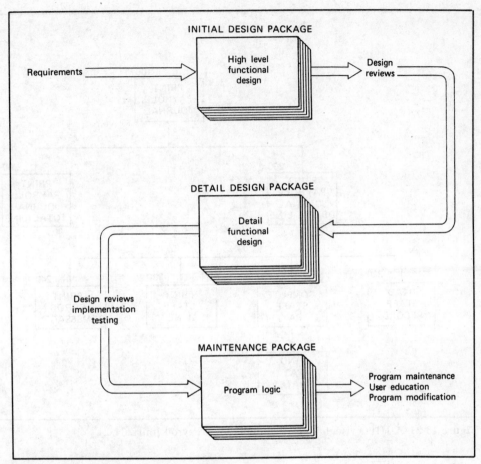

Figure 13-20 The three kinds of HIPO packages.

names (EMPNBR) to be used in the actual coding. The labels referred to in the extended description relate to program modules and segments of code.

There are three major kinds of HIPO documentation packages: the initial design, the detail design, and the maintenance package. Each package contains all three kinds of diagrams, but each package has a distinct purpose, characteristics, and audience (see Figure 13-20). The initial design package is prepared by the design group at the beginning of a project. It describes the overall functional design of the project and is used for design reviews by management and user groups. The detail design package is prepared by the development group. The initial design package is used as a base to specify more detail and add more levels of detail HIPO diagrams. The resulting package then can be used for implementation and comparison with the initial design package to ensure that all require-

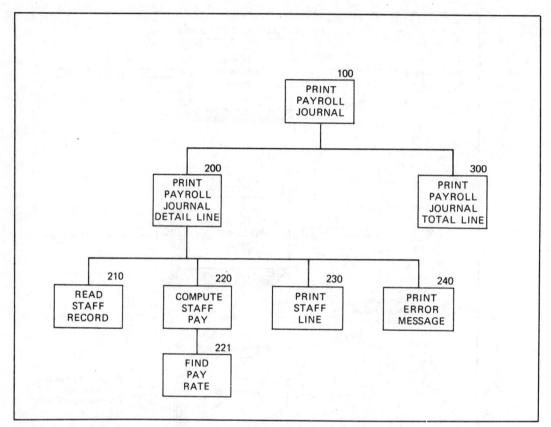

Figure 13-21 A HIPO visual table of contents for a Payroll Journal.

ments have been covered. During the coding process, the extended description area is expanded to include program labels and other pertinent information regarding implementation. This package is good reference material for maintenance programmers, and also may be used to develop user instructions. If a maintenance package is assembled, it is used for corrections, changes, or additions to the system. It is basically the detail design package with some of the lower-level diagrams deleted.

Combining HIPO with the structured analysis and design process and structured programming can provide the analyst and system designer with powerful tools that result in a design and related programs of extreme modularity, both in function and logical structure. HIPO assumes that a system (a collection of related programs) is organized into a hierarchical structure of functions. The structure of HIPO is well suited to a functional design made by starting at the top and subdividing into increasingly lower levels of detail such as the structured

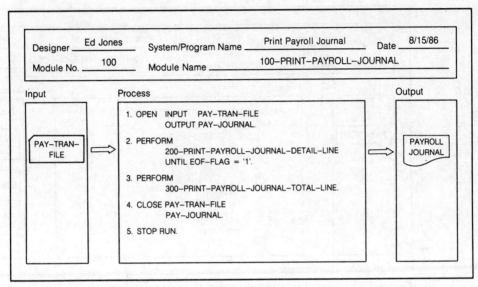

Figure 13-22 Code for module 100 from Figure 13-21.

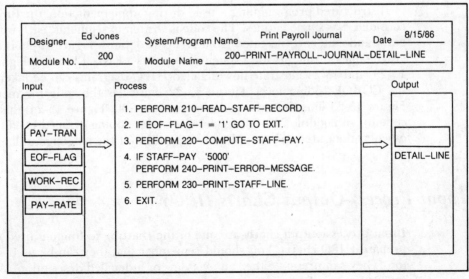

Figure 13-23 Code for module 200 from Figure 13-21.

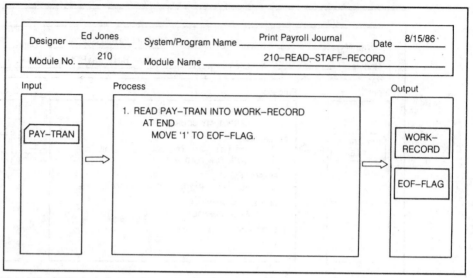

Figure 13-24 Code for submodule 210 from Figure 13-21.

techniques discussed in Chapter 2. In this type of development, the functions are implemented in the same sequence as the structure. The top module contains the highest level of control logic and decisions for each program within the system, and either passes control to lower-level modules or identifies lower-level modules for in-line inclusion.

If structured programming is used during implementation, the functions are considered as single entities. The code is written in segments, each with a single entry and exit, and is created from HIPO programs. Figure 13-21 is the HIPO visual table of contents for a system that prints a Payroll Journal. Figures 13-22, 13-23, and 13-24 illustrate how detailed HIPO diagrams can be taken down to the COBOL coding level. Figure 13-22 illustrates the code for module 100. Figure 13-23 illustrates the code for module 200. Figure 13-24 illustrates the code for submodule 210. The technique of developing detailed HIPO diagrams down to the code level is applicable regardless of the language utilized.

*I*nput-Process-Output Charts (IPO)

Input-process-output charts are one of the charting techniques used when you prepare HIPO charts. You should remember that they can be used separately too. They can present either an overview or a detailed description. We recommend that you first prepare overview IPOs and then prepare detailed IPOs.

Figure 13-22 shows an Input-Processing-Output chart. You can see that an IPO describes, in whatever level of detail is necessary, each input, the sequence of processing steps, and the output. In Chapter 7, we expanded upon IPO charts with our system requirements model (see Figures 7-2 and 7-3).

*B*ar/Pie/Line Charts

The work of a systems analyst is not completed even when the study has progressed to the point where the necessary data has been obtained and analyzed and pertinent conclusions have been drawn. Regardless of whether a study is intended for inclusion in a final report, for publication, or for advertising, the final step consists of making the results as appealing as possible.

All too often, the results of a system study are wasted because the data are not presented in an effective manner. We do not exaggerate when we say that the method of presenting the data often is more important in its acceptance than the nature of the data itself.

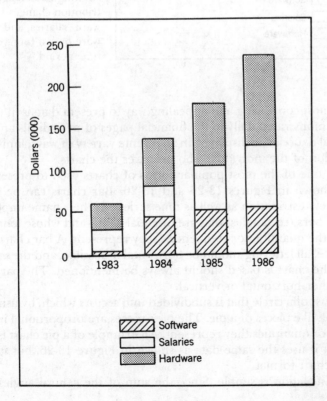

Figure 13-25 Bar chart showing dollar expenditures for software, salaries, and hardware over a four-year time period.

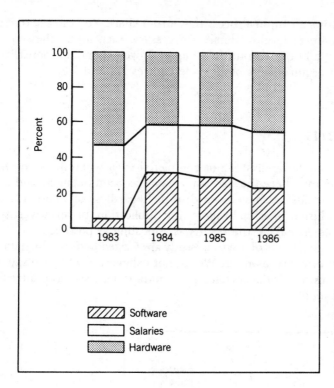

Figure 13-26 Bar chart showing percentage distribution changes for software, salaries, and hardware over a four-year time period.

Perhaps the most convincing and appealing way to present data is in pictorial form. This is demonstrated daily in the financial pages of periodicals and newspapers. Statistical data can be displayed in an infinite variety of ways, limited only by the imagination of the individual who prepares the charts.

Bar charts are one of the most popular forms of charts used to present data. Examples are shown in Figures 13-25 and 13-26. Bar charts can be used to present frequency distribution as well as time series. As their name implies, bar charts consist of bars (rectangles) that are of equal width and whose lengths are proportional to the quantities or frequencies they represent. A bar chart should always have a title, all lettering should be horizontal if possible, and the source of data on which the chart is based should always be mentioned. The bars themselves can be either horizontal or vertical.

Pie charts consist of a circle that is subdivided into sectors which, by using your imagination, look like pieces of a pie. The pie's pieces are proportional in size to the percentages or quantities they represent. An example of a pie chart is shown in Figure 13-27; it uses the same data as shown in Figure 13-26, but it is converted to a pie chart format.

Pie chart construction is simple. Since the sum of the central angles of the

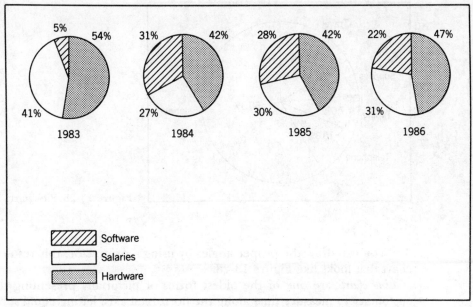

Figure 13-27 Pie charts showing percentage distribution changes for software, salaries, and hardware over a four-year time period. This is the Figure 13-26 bar chart converted to pie charts.

sectors is 360 degrees, and the entire circle represents 100 percent, 1 percent is represented by a central angle of 360/100 = 3.6 degrees. To illustrate the construction of a pie chart, let us use the following data on the expenditures of a small consulting firm.

Account	Expenditures	Percentage Distribution	Central Angles
Salaries	$43,300	60.3%	217.1°
Telephone	7,400	10.3	37.1°
Typing	5,000	7.0	25.2°
Supplies	5,000	7.0	25.2°
Travel	11,100	15.4	55.4°
	$71,800	100.0%	360.0°

The percentages of the pie chart are obtained by dividing each of the dollar values of the first column by their total ($71,800) and then multiplying by 100. The central angles then are obtained by multiplying each of the percentages by

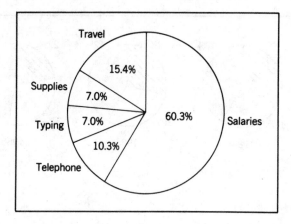

Figure 13-28 Pie chart.

3.6. You can draw the proper angles by using a protractor; this results in a pie chart that looks like Figure 13-28.

Line charts are one of the oldest forms of pictorially presenting data. It is customary to measure time along the horizontal axis, letting equal subdivisions represent successive years, months, weeks, or days. On the vertical axis you measure/record the data, such as dollars, that is being matched against time.

Figure 13-29 Line chart.

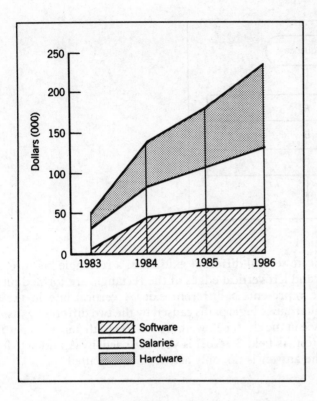

Figure 13-30 Line chart showing total dollar expenditures for software, salaries, and hardware over a four-year time period (same data as in Figures 13-25, 13-26, and 13-27).

Figure 13-29 shows a simple line chart. Figure 13-30 shows a line chart using three sets of data: software, salaries, and hardware.

Nassi Shneiderman Charts

Nassi Shneiderman charts, or Chapin charts, as they sometimes are called, are used primarily for designing *structured programs*. Their purpose is to show complex program logic.

The chart shown below is composed of a series of rectangular boxes. The rectangles may be of any size so they can accommodate whatever activity statements must be placed within them. These activity statements follow a vertical sequence from top to bottom. Successive rectangles are considered to have only one point at which control passes vertically down from one rectangle to the one below it. You can see below this flow of execution from rectangle A to rectangle B to rectangle C. When the activity described in rectangle C is executed, this job is complete.

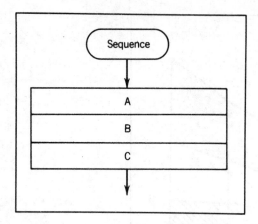

In order to indicate several different exits from a rectangle because of some decision, the right and left vertical edges of the rectangle are formed into triangles. Each triangle represents a different exit. A vertical line in the middle separates the two alternative logic paths caused by the two different exits. For example, as you can see in the chart below, there is a Yes path and a No path. When the answer to the test (Is field 3 zero?) is yes, both activity A and activity B are executed. When the answer is no, only activity C is executed.

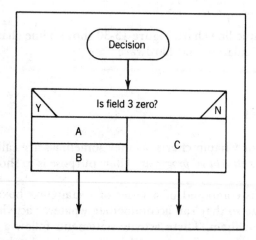

Now that you have seen a simple yes/no decision, let us look at a multiple level decision. In business, when a credit limit has been exceeded, another question is asked to determine if the past payment history of this customer has been adequate. If this past history of payment is acceptable, then the sale is approved. For example, in the chart below, the question is asked, "Has the credit limit been exceeded?" You can see that if the answer is no, you would approve the sale. But, if the answer is yes, you ask another question, "Is there a good payment history?" If the answer to that question is no, you disapprove the sale; but if the answer to that question is yes, you approve the sale.

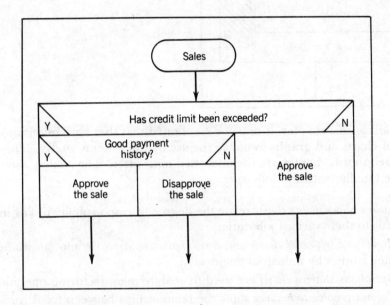

Let us look at one more example, this time with regard to programming loops. The box below demonstrates how a repetitive process (program looping) is shown using Nassi Shneiderman charts. All the program activities within the striped area are executed repeatedly until a certain condition is satisfied. When that condition is satisfied, control passes to the next operation to be executed. Notice in the chart below that the stripes are on the right side of the overall statement. This indicates that Activity 1, Activity 2, and Activity 3 are executed in sequence, before the value X is tested to determine whether it equals 100. If it does not equal 100, then Activity 1, Activity 2, and Activity 3 are executed again. After that, X is tested again to see if it equals 100. This is iterated as many times as necessary until X equals 100, at which point the process is complete and another, separate, task is undertaken.

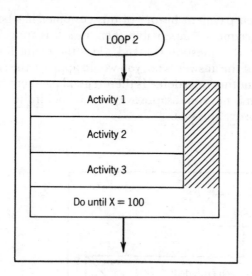

In closing this chapter, it must be mentioned that there are numerous other types of charts and graphs available for use by the systems analyst. The charts presented in this chapter are the ones used most often. The analyst also should become familiar with the following.

1. *Linear responsibility charts* relate the degree of responsibility of key individuals to their various job duties.
2. *Right- and left-hand charts* and *Simo charts* are used for motion studies and time studies by industrial engineers.
3. *Operations analysis charts* are used to analyze manufacturing operations.
4. *Various graphic techniques* show the relationships between fixed costs, variable costs, and break-even points.

Selected Readings

1. Colwell, Phoebe T. "The Use of Charts: A Tool for Management," *Fund Raising Management*, vol. 15, no. 6, August 1984, pp. 52–60, 99. [Illustrates the use of Gantt charts, PERT, and CPM in a six-month fund raising example.]
2. Justice, Karen. "Systems to Keep You on Schedule," *Interface: Administrative & Accounting*, Winter 1984, pp. 25–27. [Discusses project management system software used to plan resource and time constraints.]
3. McMullen, B. "Structured Decision Tables," *SIGPLAN Notices, Association for Computing Machinery*, vol. 19, no. 4, April 1984, pp. 34–43.
4. Moder, Joseph J., and Cecil R. Philips. *Project Management with PERT and CPM, 3rd edition.* New York: Van Nostrand Reinhold Company, 1983.

5. Passen, Barry J. *Programming Flowcharting for the Business Data Processing.* New York: John Wiley & Sons, Inc., 1978.

Questions

1. Why can a chart be worth more than a picture?

2. Define the term "charting."

3. What is the primary use of charting?

4. Identify the four general categories of charts.

5. What do charts in the personal relationship category depict?

6. Identify the guidelines the analyst and programmer should follow when developing flowcharts.

7. What does a system flowchart show?

8. What does a program flowchart show?

9. How is a schematic flowchart similar to, and different from, a systems flowchart?

10. What is the principle use of schematic flowcharts?

11. What is the primary purpose of a forms flowchart?

12. For what is a process flowchart used?

13. What can HIPO documentation be used for and by whom?

14. As a design and documentation technique, what are the three main objectives of HIPO?

15. What is a major flaw in the use of HIPO?

16. What kinds of diagrams does a typical HIPO package contain?

17. What does a work distribution chart provide to the analyst?

18. What can organization charts be designed to portray?

19. Name three ways to present statistical data.

20. What is the basic difference between PERT and CPM?

21. What is the primary use of Nassi Shneiderman charts?

SITUATION CASES

Case 13-1: *Pacific Tire Repair*

Did you ever think about the time required for changing a flat tire on your automobile? As an example of the Program Evaluation Review Technique (PERT), let us review changing a flat tire. Using the following PERT network, the activity description list, and worksheet, answer the following questions.

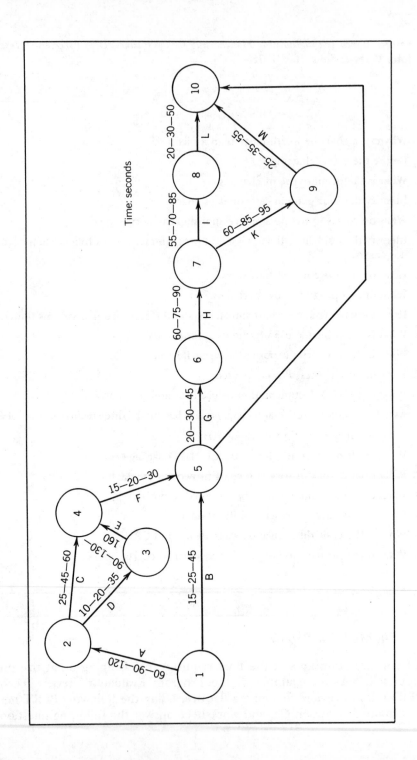

ACTIVITY DESCRIPTION LIST		
Activity	**Description**	**Events**
A	Take out jack and tools	1-2
B	Remove spare tire from trunk	1-5
C	Jack up car	2-4
D	Pry off hubcap	2-3
E	Loosen and remove wheel nuts	3-4
F	Remove flat tire	4-5
G	Place spare tire on car	5-6
H	Replace nuts, tighten with fingers	6-7
I	Tighten nuts with wrench	7-8
J	Replace flat tire in trunk	5-10
K	Lower car and remove jack	7-9
L	Replace hubcap	8-10
M	Replace tools and jack in trunk	9-10

WORKSHEET						
(1)	(2)	(3)	(4)	(5)	(6)	(7)
Succ.	Pred.	t_e	T_E	T_L	T_S	S

Questions

1. Complete the worksheet provided using the information given in the case. T_S (event 10) = 486 seconds.
2. What is the critical path and the latest allowable time for the last event? Disregard T_S (event 10) = 486 seconds.

Case 13-2:   *Eastern Bell Telephone*

An analyst working for Eastern Bell Telephone was assigned a study of the telephone directory white pages system. The analyst had accumulated information concerning the directory system and was planning a systems flowchart of the existing system.

Information the analyst had collected began with the receipt of service orders from the Plant Department which installed new telephones. The service orders contained the names, addresses, and telephone numbers of customers who had recent installation of home telephones. The orders received had to be inspected because the telephone directories have to be completely accurate. The name and address on each service order was checked first for spelling and then for the correct address. This was done manually. Then the telephone numbers were inspected by machine to be sure that no one else had the same telephone number. If an error was found, it was corrected and the order sent to its next location.

After the orders were inspected, the correct information, including name, address, and telephone number, was key entered and sent to the company's computer. Updating the directory records followed; the data was stored on magnetic disks until time to compile the next directory. The analyst noted that the inspection of the service orders came before the updating of the directory records. The reason was simple. If there was an error in the service orders, it was easiest to correct before the data was sent to the computer to update the directory records. Correcting the error in the computer directory records involved a more complicated procedure.

The next step was publication of the telephone directory, which occurred each spring. The list of names, addresses, and telephone numbers were obtained from the stored computer records. Enough telephone books were printed to account for new orders and replacement of those lost or destroyed during the year. Even though the directory was printed during one part of the year, updating directory records and receiving service orders was a continuous, year-round job. Last in the directory system was the distribution of directories to the customer by name and number of telephone instruments at each location.

With the above information, the analyst proceeded to draft the flowchart. He decomposed the gathered information into eight boxes: receive orders from Plant Department; key in the information on the service orders; update directory; store the information on magnetic disks; inspect orders for correct name, address, and telephone number; correct errors on orders; publish directory once a year; and distribute directories. The section "inspect orders for name, address, and telephone number" was further divided into: "inspect name and address" and "inspect telephone numbers." The analyst then decided to use his own judgment and completed the following system flowchart.

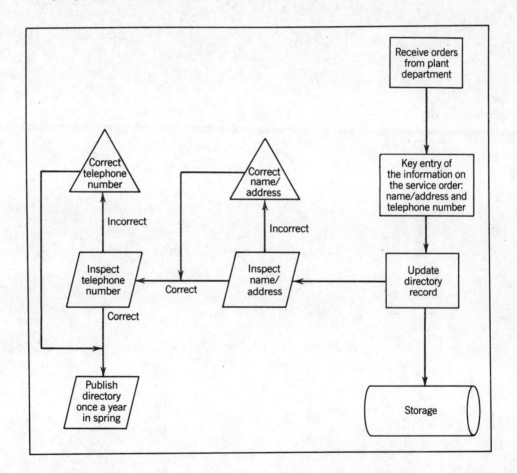

Questions

1. Were the layout and symbols of the flowchart adequate?
2. Were the flowchart sequences correct?
3. Construct a corrected flowchart.

Chapter 14

FORMS DESIGN

LEARNING OBJECTIVES

You will learn how to . . .

☐ Set up a forms control function.

☐ Design paper forms.

☐ Design video screens.

☐ Structure data layouts for the best productivity.

☐ Utilize the best forms design techniques.

☐ Choose from various kinds of forms, types of print, and line widths.

Introduction to Forms Design

It is difficult to imagine the operation of any business without the use of forms. They are the vehicles for most communications and the blueprints for most operations, as well as the documents upon which the organization's historical data are recorded. Although most paper forms may be replaced by electronic data mail or electronic voice mail by the year 2000, the analyst still will have to design electronic video screen form layouts.

Today's business world requires some skills in designing forms for the authorization, transfer, and input/output of data with regard to both manual and computer-based recordkeeping systems. This chapter presents the details of designing business forms, whether they are to be used for paper or a video screen. Even though many of our examples are for paper forms, the same criteria are used to design video screen formats. In Chapter 8 we introduced alternative presentations of video data. The last section of this chapter provides an in-depth examination of video screen data structures.

This chapter should be read when you first encounter the need to design a form during the systems study. This may be as early as the feasibility study or at any time during the 10 steps of the system development life cycle (SDLC).

Objectives of Forms Control

Somewhere in the firm there should be one person, or one functional area, who is responsible for forms. The objectives of centralized forms control are

1. To prevent the introduction of new forms when suitable forms already exist somewhere else in the firm.
2. To offer expert advice on forms design techniques.
3. To reduce the total number of forms by consolidating similar forms already in existence.
4. To ensure a unique forms numbering system with no duplication of form numbers or revision dates.
5. To provide for proper replenishment, storage, and distribution of forms throughout the firm.
6. To consider the design costs, the cost of artwork, and the quantities to be purchased.
7. To coordinate forms design between all users of the form in question.

8. To review the usage of existing forms in order to detect changes in requirements.

9. To assure that forms are well designed and usable for a long period of time.

Forms Control Methodology

The following forms control methodology, which is described as a manual system, can be designed and programmed easily into a microcomputer-based system. This is true especially if your firm has a microcomputer with a 10–20 megabyte hard disk. The design is described below. All you need to do is to adapt it to your microcomputer.

The forms control area does not necessarily approve or disapprove the introduction of a new form or the modification of an existing form. When the forms control area has the authority to disapprove forms, the departments that need design assistance tend to avoid using the form expert's advice. They often fear that getting involved with the forms authorities will result in their form being altered or disapproved. The best organized forms control function then is one which coordinates and assists rather than rules the forms requirements of the organization.

A forms control program can follow the general sequence of first getting the backing of management, then announcing commencement of the program, publicizing the objectives of the program, and collecting one sample of every form (including any written procedures on how to fill out the form). Samples of *all* forms should be collected, whether they were purchased originally from an outside vendor, printed within your firm, or designed as a video screen form.

The collected samples can be filed now into a *form-number file* where all forms are filed numerically by their identification numbers. (Attach any existing instructional procedures to the form before filing it.) Each form should be put into a separate file folder with all appropriate data recorded on the front of the file folder. The analyst should have some file folders preprinted similar to Figure 14-1. The form name(s) should include *all* of its names, the official name of the form, plus any informal names that operating personnel use to refer to the form. List all of the *major* departments that use the form or any of its copies. Circle *all* of the purposes of the form, for example, a form may request a typewriter, authorize the movement of that typewriter, and instruct where to move the typewriter. Circle all of the subjects to which usage of the form is applied.

The next task in the forms control program is to develop a *cross-reference file*. Enter each form name (formal and informal) with its form number on a 3 × 5 card and file them alphabetically (see Figure 14-2). This cross-reference file can

FORM
NAME(S): _____

DEPARTMENTS THAT USE THIS FORM: _____

_____   _____

_____   _____

_____   _____

_____   _____

_____   _____

PURPOSES OF THIS FORM   APPROXIMATE
(CIRCLE ALL THOSE THAT   ANNUAL USAGE: _____
APPLY):

                                       SUBJECT OF THIS FORM (CIRCLE
TO ACKNOWLEDGE   ALL THOSE THAT APPLY):
   AGREE
   APPLY   EQUIPMENT
   AUTHORIZE   FACILITIES
   CANCEL   FILES
   CERTIFY   FINANCIAL
   CLAIM   INVENTORY
   ESTIMATE   MACHINERY
   FOLLOW-UP   MATERIAL
   IDENTIFY   PARTS
   INSTRUCT   PERSONNEL
   NOTIFY   SUPPLIES
   ORDER
   RECORD
   REPORT
   REQUEST
   ROUTE
   SCHEDULE
   TRANSFER

FORM NUMBER: _____

Figure 14-1 File folder for each form.

```
┌─────────────────────────────────────────────────────────┐
│                                                           │
│  FORM                                                     │
│  NAME: _____ PURCHASE REQUISITION _____  │
│                                                           │
│                  FORM NUMBER:   1261                      │
│                                 Rev. 3/87                 │
│                                                           │
│                                                           │
│  Also known as:                                           │
│                                                           │
│    1. pick sheet                                          │
│    2. req. "pronounced wreck"                             │
│    3.                                                     │
│    4.                                                     │
│                                                           │
│                                                           │
│                                                           │
│                                                           │
└─────────────────────────────────────────────────────────┘
```

Figure 14-2 Cross-reference file card.

be used to find a file folder for any form if you know any one of the form names. (Remember that the file folders were filed by form number.) Another method of developing a cross-reference file is to use a Key Word In Context (KWIC) index system on a computer. KWIC may be described as a method whereby the computer lists each title of a form according to all the important words in the form's title. These important words all fall into alphabetical sequence with all the important words from other form titles. The titles are matched back to the form's number so that the analyst can trace either from the key words in the form's title, or from the form's number.

The last task in setting up a forms control program is to develop a forms classification system, the *functional file*. Each form already is classified by name, user departments, purpose, and subject, as recorded on the file folder in Figure 14-1. All that remains is to set up a data retrieval system. Two manual systems are edge-notched cards and superimposable card systems. A good breakdown on these retrieval methods is found in Dykes' *Practical Approach to Information and Data Retrieval.*[1] If you are using a microcomputer, you might consider one of the many database software packages that are currently available, such as dBase III.

At this point you have a *form-number file* (in form number sequence) contain-

---

[1] See *Practical Approach to Information and Data Retrieval,* by Freeman H. Dyke, Jr. (Boston: Industrial Education Institute, 1968).

FORM
NAME(S): _____

FORM
NUMBER: _____

FORM PURPOSES:

1. To Acknowledge	7. To Claim	13. To Order
2. To Agree	8. To Estimate	14. To Record
3. To Apply	9. To Follow up	15. To Report
4. To Authorize	10. To Identify	16. To Request
5. To Cancel	11. To Instruct	17. To Route
6. To Certify	12. To Notify	18. To Schedule
		19. To Transfer

FORM SUBJECT:

20. Equipment	23. Financial	26. Material
21. Facilities	24. Inventory	27. Parts
22. Files	25. Machinery	28. Personnel
		29. Supplies

DEPARTMENTS THAT USE THE FORM:

30. Accounting

.

.

.

52. Warehouse

Figure 14-3 Coding of the form's characteristics.

ing a copy of each form, a *cross-reference file* (by form name) on 3 × 5 cards, and now a *functional file*. This file is used to locate similar forms already in existence.

The analyst takes all of the characteristics from the front of the file folder (Figure 14-1) and codes them 1 to 52 as shown in Figure 14-3. Next, the analyst enters the 52 characteristics of the first form into a database retrieval system. There is one database record for each form, and each form's characteristics are the individual data items or fields for that record (form). When the analyst wants to see if the firm has an existing form, he or she enters the desired characteristics (data items) into the database system and it searches the file. After finding the desired characteristics, such as no. 8 to estimate, no. 20 equipment, and no. 52 warehouse, the database prints out the form number. The analyst then goes to the *form-number file* to check the specific form visually in order to see if it will do the job.

Objectives of Forms Design

An entirely new form often needs to be designed for a new use. When designing such a new form, begin by writing down the purpose of the form as precisely as possible. Of course, a particular form may have many purposes. As more departments become involved in the use of the form, its function becomes more complex. The forms designer should be clear on the form's purposes and should resist any additions or other complexities that might compromise its efficiency. The major cost associated with forms is not the cost of the form itself. Processing the form through the system is by far the most expensive aspect, and the most important concern of the analyst. For example, if a poorly designed form causes each of nine people who handle it to lose 30 seconds of time, then 4½ minutes of time is lost per form. If the firm uses 7,000 of these forms per year, then 31,500 minutes per year are lost (4.5 × 7,000 = 31,500). This amounts to 525 hours of lost time per year (31,500 ÷ 60 = 525), which could have been avoided by a better forms design. Bear in mind that the major objectives of forms design are to have

1. Forms that perform their function as simply and efficiently as possible.
2. Forms that can be filled out easily.
3. Forms that are legible, uncomplicated, and economically feasible.

Know the Machines to Be Used

It is very hazardous to attempt to design a form without knowing the type of equipment that will be used to fill it out. Will the equipment be a human hand or

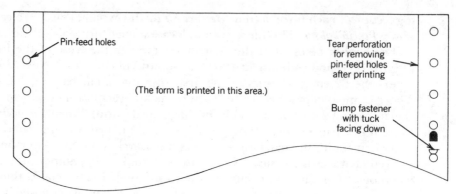

Figure 14-4 Line printer form.

a computer? The standard typewriter is the basic machine used in filling out forms. The analyst should know whether the typewriters to be used have ⅙-inch vertical spacing, elite type (12 letters to the inch horizontally) or pica type (10 letters to the inch horizontally). This is important because the right amount of space must be allowed on the form for each entry. For typewritten forms the analyst also should specify the correct vertical spacing of items. Typewriters have 6 lines per inch vertically. Improper spacing can render a form useless because whenever the typewriter carriage returns, the form must be in a position to accept the next line of typing. If not, the typist will have to realign the form for each line; and the form will be very inefficient and time consuming.

An entire book easily could be written on the various kinds and uses of printing presses, but the analyst should be familiar with the basic processes used to print forms. In the letterpress process, the form is printed from a raised surface of type that is smeared with ink. In the offset (lithography) process the finished drawing of the form is photographed onto a printing surface from which the form is then printed. Offset is a photographic reproduction process. The familiar term "camera-ready copy" refers to the designer's finished, touched-up draft of the form, which is perfect enough to be copied photographically and reproduced as the actual form. Offset is probably the most flexible reproduction method available to the forms designer.

Computer line printers are very important to a forms designer. A form for a computer line printer may require pin-feed holes so the printer's mechanism can move the forms through the printer at high speeds (see Figure 14-4). If you order continuous form letterhead for your microcomputer's letter quality printer, make sure you get the left and right tear-off strips microperforated. This allows them to be torn off, leaving clean cut edges that almost look as if the tear-off strips were never attached to the letterhead.

Multiple copy continuous strip forms can be fastened together with staples, crimping, or can be bump fastened. (When using bump fastening, be sure that the tuck faces down or there may be paper jams in the printer.) A form thicker than one original and five copies may give poor, hard-to-read copies. (Multilith paper, which can be used directly for offset printing, is available whenever a large number of copies are required.) Line printers usually have 80 to 120 characters horizontally across the paper (up to 160) and have 6 or 8 lines per inch vertically. Check these figures, however, for any specific line printer. Line printer forms come in a continuous strip that is continually fed through the printer.

*L*ayout Form for Computer Printers

If your form is to be printed on a computer-driven printer, you should first design the form and then lay it out on a computer printout layout form.

Design the form using the techniques presented in this chapter. Then use the printer layout form (see Figure 14-5) to see how the output is to be spaced. The use of this form is a programmer's tool, as well as an analyst's tool, to clarify how the output is to be spaced; it does not show the original design of the form as desired by the user department.

This print layout sheet is simply a matrix or grid, with each box or cell representing one print position. Using it, you describe, line-by-line and print position-by-print position, the layout of the report. Eventually, a programmer converts each line on the printer spacing chart (e.g., the print layout sheet) to the appropriate set of source language code or to a data structure.

Laser printers use photographic positives (called flash forms) for simultaneous printing of the form and its data. In other words, you draw the form and use a photographic image of it in the laser printer.

*T*ypes of Paper

The type of paper to be used in a form is important because the form must be able to withstand a certain amount of mishandling in addition to fulfilling a definite function. If it fails in either of these two areas, it is not a successfully designed form. Multipart forms use sulfite bond of about 9–12 pounds weight. Letterhead and checks use rag bond of about 16–20 pounds weight. Machine posted ledgers use ledger paper of about 28–32 pounds weight.

Paper is measured in pounds. For example, 16-pound bond paper means that a ream of the particular paper weighs 16 pounds. A ream is 500 sheets of paper measuring 17 inches by 22 inches. Each sheet is usually cut into four standard 8½ × 11 inch sheets.

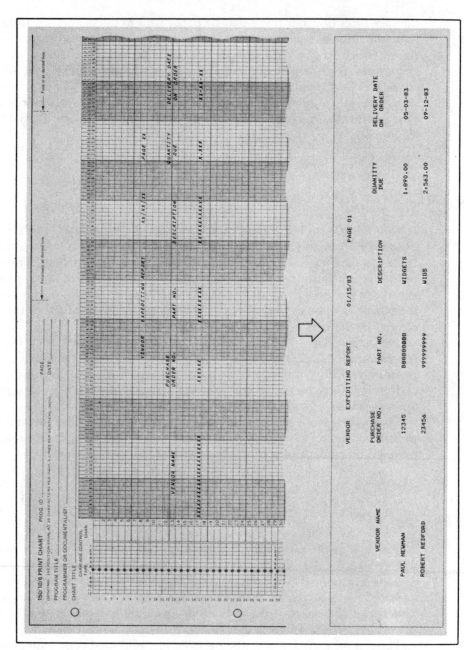

Figure 14-5 Printer layout form with sample report layout.

□ *Bond paper.* Bond paper is high quality paper. Rag bonds are the highest quality because they have 25% or more rag content. Sulfite bonds are inexpensive and usually are durable enough for use in forms. Duplicating bonds are for reproduction (Ditto machines) where ink absorption is required.

□ *Ledger paper.* Ledger paper is a heavier weight bond paper (24–44 pounds).

□ *Index bristol paper.* Heavier than either ledger or bond, it is better known as card stock (60–220 pounds).

□ *Manifold paper.* Manifold paper is a lightweight bond sometimes called onionskin (8–10 pounds).

□ *Safety paper.* Safety paper is paper that cannot be erased without leaving an obvious mark. It is the type used for checks.

The American National Standards Institute publishes standards relating to types of paper. For example, ANSI X4.4-1955(R1972) is *Basic Sheet Sizes and Standard Stock Sizes for Bond Papers and Index Bristols.*

*T*echniques of Forms Design and Layout

The designer of a form should follow certain basic guidelines in order to assure that the form is both usable and used.

When designing a form, first list all the items of information or data to be recorded on the form and the maximum number of characters to be allotted for each. Make a tabular contents list as illustrated in Figure 14-6. If anything is deleted from an existing form, explain the reason for the deletion. The contents list should be checked by the personnel who use the form in order to make sure nothing is omitted. Always have the form users check the contents list *before* giving them a rough draft copy of the form because the draft copy of the form may distract their attention from checking for omitted items. Instead, they may become preoccupied with layout and so on.

Give the form a descriptive title, and make the name as long as necessary to describe clearly how the form is to be used. The name should be placed at the top of the form where it can be seen readily.

Assign a new form number if the form is a brand new one, or a revision date if it is a revised form. Some firms use a form number and revision number instead of a revision date. The best placement for the form number and revision date is in the extreme lower left corner of the form. Be consistent by placing the form number and revision date in the same position on all forms.

Determine what the correct sequence of data should be. Lay out the data on the form either so it is most convenient for whoever fills out the form or for

Information or Data Item	Number of Characters
Ship to: Name Address City, State ZIP	24 alphabetic 24 alphanumeric 24 alphanumeric 10 numeric
Quantity	4 numeric
Drawing number	9 alphanumeric
Description . . . etc. . .	44 alphanumeric . . . etc. . .

Figure 14-6 Contents list.

whoever reads the form and copies from it. This depends on the use of the form. Perhaps a combination of both is desirable. If in doubt, lay out the data so it is most convenient for whoever fills out the form, especially if the form is to be filled out by typewriter.

Use boldface type or double parallel lines to make special information stand out. Screening, a light shading in one area of the form, also can be used to separate the form's sections.

Common variations of ruled lines are

Broken --

One-point _____

Half-point _____

Hairline _____

Double parallel ================================

Provide for a continuous writing flow by the person who will fill out the form. Writing should be from left to right and from top to bottom. Boxed design is favored over caption and a line (see Figures 14-7 and 14-8). In Figure 14-7 it is perfectly clear where the data go, but in Figure 14-8 it is not as clear as you move down the form. For example, does marital status go below or above the caption "marital status"? Compare the two layouts on this point.

When possible use a simple ballot box so all the user has to do is check the box applicable to the transaction (see Figure 14-9). Other important features to consider during the layout phase include

1. In boxes or areas for numeric data, allow sufficient space for the largest probable string of figures.
2. Place filing information near the top of the form so it can be seen easily when looking for it in a file. This varies with the type of file to be used.

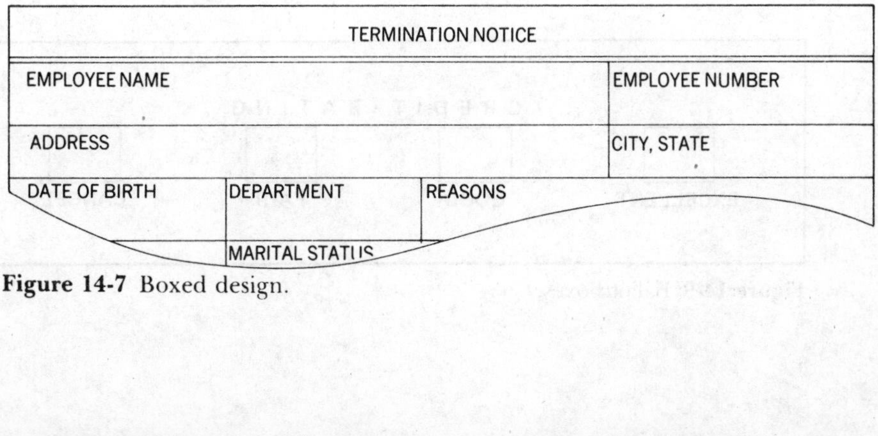

Figure 14-7 Boxed design.

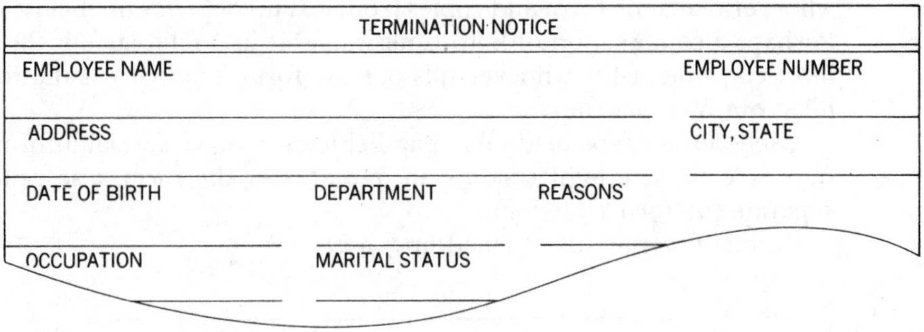

Figure 14-8 Caption and a line.

3. For multiple copies use a different color paper for each copy. Also, print the destination of each copy at the extreme bottom of the copy.
4. Avoid abbreviations. They might have different meanings to different people.
5. Preprint as much as possible. A consecutive document number can be preprinted.
6. Consider printing the form in some ink color other than black in order to make the form stand out.
7. If possible, print the instructions on how to fill out the form on the back of the last copy of the form. Print a message on the glue margin (top of form) stating that the instructions are on the back of the form. Another method of providing instructions is to code each area with a number and have a corresponding instruction sheet. This method was used in Figure 7-9 in Chapter 7 of this book.
8. Group similar data in the same area on different forms, for example, always put form number and revision date in the extreme lower left corner.
9. Put a border around the form to give it a look of balance and professionalism.

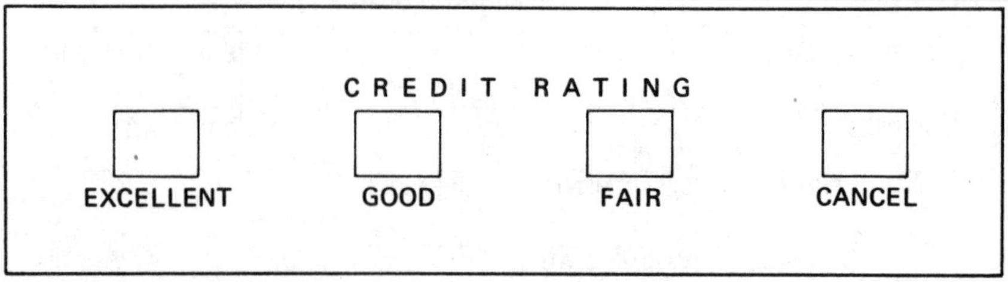

Figure 14-9 Ballot boxes.

Form Width

The overall width of the form is an important dimension in determining horizontal printing space. Remember that for typewritten forms, elite types 12 characters per inch while pica types only 10. For handwritten forms the horizontal space per character should be ⅙ inch. The forms designer should consider the requirements for each entry on the form in terms of these constraints.

Forms costs can be reduced by confining form widths to the standard sizes of paper stock supplied by the forms printer. In addition, standard widths allow for the purchase of binding and filing supplies in standard sizes. This, of course, increases the efficiency of forms handling and filing. If the form must be mailed, consider the width of the firm's envelopes. Always try to use standard sizes. In addition, it is important to consider whether the firm uses plain envelopes or window envelopes. If the latter, the form can be designed so the addressee's name shows through the glassine window. With imagination the forms designer can even indicate by the use of arrows where the form should be folded to efficiently fit into the envelope.

For filing convenience limit form maximum size to 8½ × 11 inches. Smaller than 8½ × 11 may be acceptable, but avoid anything larger since most filing cabinets are built to accept 8½ × 11 paper size. Any larger size will have to be folded before filing or special files will have to be purchased. The analyst has to determine if the form will be filed in cabinets, on shelves, in loose-leaf binders, in tub files, in visible files, and so forth, before determining its size. The filing method can have much to do with the required size of the form.

Vertical lines that separate boxed design are called horizontal spacing lines (see Figure 14-10). They are drawn so each one splits a printing position, that is, splits a character. If they are drawn between adjacent positions, the paper shrinkage and variations in form alignment may prevent satisfactory registration during both the printing of the form and during the filling out of the form, especially if the form is filled out with a typewriter.

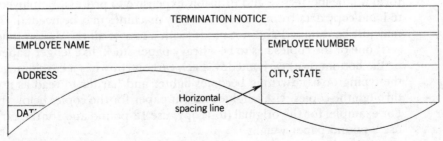

Figure 14-10 Horizontal spacing lines.

Avoid horizontal spacing lines as much as possible because a typist must set a tab stop on a typewriter for each different horizontal spacing line across the form's width. Try to locate horizontal spacing lines on typewriter forms at the same tab position, even though some horizontal spaces will be allotted excessive width. Avoid cutting one shorter than its minimum requirement, though.

Form Length

The overall length of the form is important in determining the number of lines of printing space. Typewriters have six lines per inch vertically, for example, $\frac{1}{6}$ inch per line. Computer line printers have either six or eight lines per inch vertically depending upon the model. Handwritten forms should have a minimum of $\frac{1}{4}$-inch line width vertically for writing. Notice that if there is $\frac{1}{3}$ inch between lines, the form is perfectly suitable for either handwritten entries or typewritten entries because a typewriter set on double spacing indexes $\frac{1}{3}$ inch. Handwritten entries can adapt readily to the larger space.

Forms costs can be reduced by confining form lengths to the standard sizes of paper stock supplied by the forms printer. The same benefits listed for standard form widths will be realized: fewer sizes of binding and filing supplies required, more convenient forms handling, and easy filing. Again, remember that most file cabinets are made for $8\frac{1}{2} \times 11$ inch paper.

As with types of paper, the American National Standards Institute specifies the types of spacing used for forms. For example, see ANSI X4.17-1976, *Character and Line Spacing for Office Machines and Business Forms.*

Carbon Copies and Carbon Paper

It may seem that cost savings should be pursued by reducing the number of carbon copies in a form to a minimum; but if there are not enough copies, the form will be ineffective and probably expensive to process. Employees will need to hand copy data from the form or copy machines may be needed. Or the form may just be dumped and not used—with a loss of all the design time.

If one of the copies has to be a heavy paper stock, like ledger paper, it should be the bottom (last) carbon copy. Each carbon copy has a cushioning effect and the typing or handwriting becomes lighter and harder to read as it goes down through the copies. Use a lighter weight paper for the copies below the original. For example, for the original (top copy) use 12-pound and for the carbon copies use 9-pound paper weight.

When a multipart form with many copies (over eight) is typed, a very hard platen should be put on the typewriter. This gives more legibility to the copies.

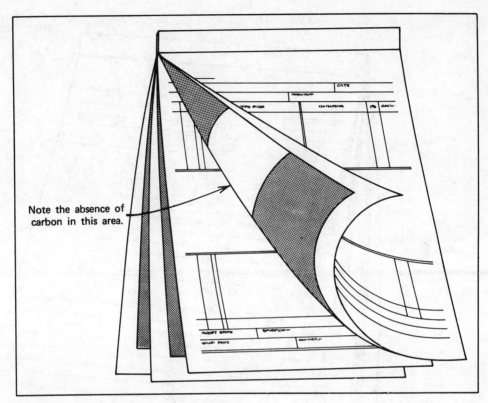

Note the absence of carbon in this area.

Figure 14-11 Blocked-out carbon paper.

When a form is entirely handwritten, softer carbon paper should be used. A softer carbon paper transfers more easily and thus gives more legible copies.

Various methods of transferring the impression between copies are in use. The basic types of carbon paper are

1. *One-time carbon paper.* The carbon paper is interleaved in the form, used once, and thrown away. It is the most economical method for multipart forms.
2. *Carbon-backed paper.* The carbon surface is painted on the back of each copy so it transfers to the next lower copy. This method might be avoided because it is messy when handling the copies from the form.
3. *Chemical-coated paper.* An invisible chemical dye allows an image to be transferred to the next lower copy.

If there is a need to prevent some of the data from printing on all of the copies, the carbon paper can be blocked out (see Figure 14-11). Another method

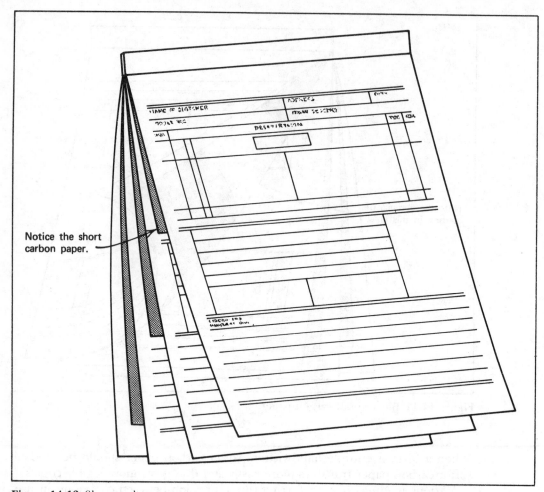

Figure 14-12 Short carbon paper.

is to use short carbons (see Figure 14-12). A third method involves disguising the data by printing a random design on the copy in the area where the data will appear. The random design renders the carbon impression unreadable.

Types of Forms

Flat Forms

Flat forms are single-copy forms, that is, an original only. If copies of the original are required, carbon paper must be inserted between copies prior to filling them

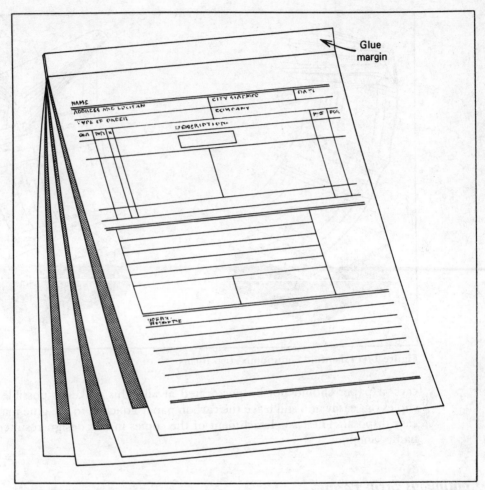

Figure 14-13 Unit-set/snapout forms.

out. Or a copy machine can be used. Often pads of flat forms are printed identically to the original (top) copy of a unit-set. In this way a salesman can write in the data and give it to a secretary for typing onto a unit-set and thus not use the more expensive unit-set for the rough handwritten data.

Unit-Set/Snapout Forms

These forms have an original copy and several copies with carbon paper interleaved between each copy. The entire set is glued together into a unit set (see Figure 14-13). The unit-set should have the carbon paper cut ⅜ inch shorter than the copies. The copies should be perforated at the glue margin and the

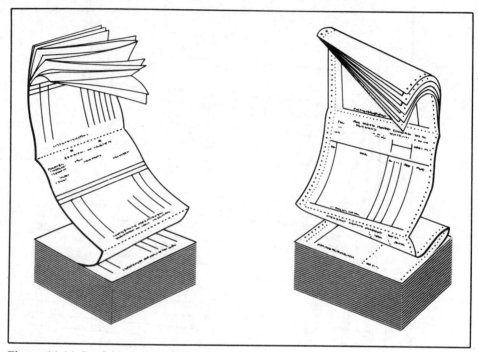

Figure 14-14 Fanfold continuous strip forms.

carbon paper should not be perforated at all. This makes it possible to tear copies out easily and still leave the carbon paper attached to the glue margin for easy disposal. The easy detachment of the copies in this design resulted in the name "snapout."

Continuous Strip Forms

Continuous strip forms are joined together in a continuous strip, with perforations between each form. They are delivered in a fanfold arrangement. Figure 14-14 shows an example. On the left are fanfold forms for a typewriter (no pin-feed holes) and on the right for a computer line printer (pin-feed holes). The analyst should know that, besides forms, the following items are available in a continuous strip for printing on a computer line printer.

1. Envelopes.
2. Fifty-one- or 80-column tab cards.
3. Envelopes already stuffed with a preprinted form. As the envelope is addressed, the form also can have a minimum amount of data simultaneously printed on it by the computer line printer. Chemical-coated paper

causes printing on the form *inside* the envelope because the character impact is transferred through the envelope.

4. Continuous letterheads.

Success Is a Miscellaneous Checklist

Probably the best advice that the analyst could follow is to call in an experienced forms salesman to assist in the design of any major new form, especially if there will be a high usage of the form. Over 500 a month would be considered high usage.

The analyst should be aware of a process called crash imprinting. Most printers have blank unit-sets of forms, already glued together, with different colored copies. You can get a quick unit-set of forms from this blank by printing with inked metal type and crashing the metal type down on the blank unit-set so hard that a carbon impression is transferred to all copies below the original. Crash imprinting costs less than regular printed unit-sets and offers a quicker delivery time. The quality usually is quite good. Another use of crash imprinting is to correct an omission made by the forms designer, or to revise an existing stock of forms with some additional details.

The analyst should always work through the purchasing department. The purchasing agent should arrange any meetings with the salespeople from various forms vendors. Quantities of the form used in the past should be checked to see if the same quantities still are being used. Try to obtain quantity price breaks. Also try to obtain reasonable delivery date promises. It usually takes 60 to 120 days from the time the new form order is placed until the new forms are delivered. Before placing the order have three or four co-workers check the final proofs for errors before approving them for printing. Be sure that you are satisfied that the form will do its job before ordering it in large quantities.

Types of Print

Legibility and simplicity are the primary consideration in the choice of typefaces. Stick with one basic design such as sans serif. The following example shows various sans serif styles.

UNIVERS—11 Pt. Light

ABCDEFGHIJKLMNOPQRSTUVWXYZ
abcdefghijklmnopqrstuvwxyz
1234567890!†+$%/&*()—@¼½¾:'',.;-=?[]

UNIVERS—11 Pt. Medium

ABCDEFGHIJKLMNOPQRSTUVWXYZ
abcdefghijklmnopqrstuvwxyz
1234567890!† + $%/&*()—@¼½¾:",.;-= ?[]

UNIVERS—11 Pt. Medium Italic

ABCDEFGHIJKLMNOPQRSTUVWXYZ
abcdefghijklmnopqrstuvwxyz
1234567890!† + $%/&()—@¼½¾:",.;-= ?[]*

UNIVERS—11 Pt. Bold

ABCDEFGHIJKLMNOPQRSTUVWXYZ
abcdefghijklmnopqrstuvwxyz
1234567890!† + $%/&*()—@¼½¾:",.;-= ?[]

UNIVERS—11 Pt. Bold Condensed

ABCDEFGHIJKLMNOPQRSTUVWXYZ
abcdefghijklmnopqrstuvwxyz
1234567890!† + $%/&*()—@¼½¾:",.;-= ?[]

UNIVERS—10 Pt. Medium

ABCDEFGHIJKLMNOPQRSTUVWXYZ
abcdefghijklmnopqrstuvwxyz
1234567890!† + $%/&*()—@¼½¾:",.;-= ?[]

UNIVERS—8 Pt. Medium

ABCDEFGHIJKLMNOPQRSTUVWXYZ
abcdefghijklmnopqrstuvwxyz
1234567890!† + $%/&*()—@¼½¾:",.;-= ?[]

UNIVERS—7 Pt. Medium

ABCDEFGHIJKLMNOPQRSTUVWXYZ
abcdefghijklmnopqrstuvwxyz
1234567890!† + $%/&*()—@¼½¾:",.;-= ?[]

Character counts are based on the standard unit of printer's measure, which is a pica (no relationship to pica type on a typewriter). There are approximately 6 printer's picas to an inch and 12 points to a pica; thus there are 72 points to an inch, that is, 1 point is ¹⁄₇₂ inch. Type sizes smaller than 6 points are difficult to read.

The following are combinations of ruled lines available to the analyst

Hairline —————————————————————————————

½ Point Rules —————————————————————————

1 Point Rules —————————————————————————

1½ Point Rules ————————————————————————

3 Point Rules ████████████████████████████████████

4½ Point Rules ████████████████████████████████████

6 Point Rules ████████████████████████████████████

Parallel ══

In summary, it is evident that to be a successful form designer one must have knowledge of certain basic information in order to design a form that will be usable. This information includes knowledge of why forms control is desirable, types of machines used to fill out the form, types of paper and carbon that can be used, the types of forms that are available, and the techniques involved in the forms design itself.

Now that you have learned the basics of paper forms design, we can look in more detail at the design of formats for video screens.

Video Screen Data Structures

Video screens can be called either CRTs (cathode ray tubes) or VDTs (video display terminals). Microcomputers and VDTs are being used more frequently as remote input and output devices interconnected to computer systems. As an input device, the terminal can be used in the traditional data entry role or as an on-line medium for data collection. As an output device, the terminal can be used to (1) display traditional reports of financial and operating significance, (2) answer simple queries, or (3) provide sophisticated graphic displays to facilitate management decision making.

The use of VDTs or microcomputers as integral parts of the data entry (system input) function has grown rapidly over the past decade. Initial activities in this area involved the use of standalone data entry systems. This type of system was set up to collect the information entered and then to store it on magnetic tape. The information then was transferred periodically to the central computer. Numerous technological advances in computer hardware and software capabilities, however, have made it possible for the analyst to consider incorporating on-line input and output features into the design of new systems.

When an analyst is considering the use of on-line inputs during the design of a new system, the possible advantages and disadvantages must be weighed carefully.

Advantages

1. The operator can identify and correct immediately manual keying errors by scanning the screen (hopefully errors will be highlighted).
2. Redundant key verification procedures, typically used in punched card data entry, are eliminated.
3. Input data usually is available for processing much sooner. Depending upon the situation, the system can process input data immediately.
4. The data entry function can be dispersed out into the user departments where the information originates. This facilitates the timely entry of data and the immediate correction of data that fails any detailed editing and validation criteria.
5. Microcomputers and VDTs are, in many cases, less expensive than centralized data entry operations.

Disadvantages

1. The communications costs to support on-line data entry may be too high for some organizations.
2. Provision must be made for backup equipment or manual procedures in case the computer is down for extended periods of time.
3. The data entry routines must be programmed and maintained.

The input of information to a computer via on-line microcomputers/terminals can be handled by two basic types of operators; that is, the dedicated data entry operator, and the general information collection and entry operator. The analyst must determine which type of operator approach best fits the needs of the company and the system being designed. A combination of both approaches may be necessary.

When the dedicated data entry approach is used, the operator performs a function similar to a full-time key entry operator. If the analyst decides to use this approach, the following points should be considered carefully.

1. The emphasis should be on facilitating operator ease and speed of entry.
2. Interaction with, and evaluation of, data displayed on the screen should be minimized.
3. On-line editing and validation should be limited to ensuring that (a) all mandatory data fields have been entered (a data field is that part of the input which contains specific information such as an employee name or

employee identification number), (b) data entered does not exceed or overlap the maximum size of the field, and (c) all numeric fields contain only numeric data.

4. The operator should be able to visually scan items entered if a keystroke mistake is suspected.

5. Users should batch documents to be entered (by item count), and establish hash totals on significant data fields.

6. The system should accumulate batch totals automatically and compare them to previously entered manual control totals.

7. The operator should be able to recall the entire batch, if necessary, to locate and correct errors.

In using the dedicated data entry approach, the most common method of identifying fields of data to the system is to have them entered in a fixed sequence. As a part of the detailed system design process, the analyst works with users to establish a fixed entry sequence of data fields for each type of document or transaction type to be entered. As an example, the system could be set up to require that the data on a payroll time card be entered in the following sequence.

1.	Employee name	John Doe
2.	Employee number	1234
3.	Date	8/12/86
4.	Regular hours worked	32.0
5.	Overtime hours worked	0.0
6.	Vacation hours taken	0.0
7.	Sick time hours taken	8.0

If the data fields to be entered must be fixed in length, then either the operator or the data entry program must be able to ensure that the spacing within fields is correct. This may require zero or blank filling fields where no data is entered, or where the data must be right or left justified. Figure 14-15 illustrates how a typical payroll time card entry might look. Note that the name field has been left justified with trailing blanks, and the numeric fields have been zero filled or right justified depending on the value.

If the system design requires that the data fields be set up as variable in length, then the operator can use a field separation character such as '/' to distinguish between the end of one field and the beginning of the next. By using a special character to separate fields, the operator can avoid entering fill characters and can identify which fields have no data by entering dual separators. Figure 14-16 illustrates how the same time card information would be entered in a system using variable length fields and a separation character '/'. Note that the

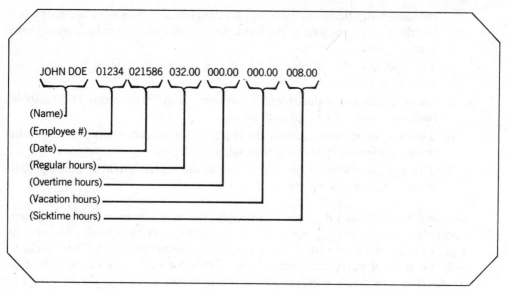

Figure 14-15 Illustrates how a typical payroll time card entry would be entered on-line.

name field does not need to be padded with blanks. The employee number field, the regular hours field, and the sick time field do not need to be zero filled. In addition, the fields for overtime hours and vacation hours were not entered because there was no data. In this case, the data entry program interprets the two consecutive special characters to mean the field was not entered and default values should be assigned.

The typical sequence of events that the dedicated data entry operator goes through include

1. Entry of the batch number and user supplied control totals. (See Figure 14-17.)

2. Entry of the batched transaction data with a symbol that denotes end of batch so the balancing can be done ('*' has been used as the end of batch symbol). (See Figure 14-18.)

3. Scanning the batch control message produced by the data entry program to determine if the computed batch totals match the user supplied batch totals. (See Figure 14-19.) If the batch control totals are in balance, the message example A would be displayed. If an out-of-balance condition is noted, message example B would be displayed.

When an operator has entered a batch of input transactions and an out-of-balance condition is noted, corrective action must be taken immediately. Nor-

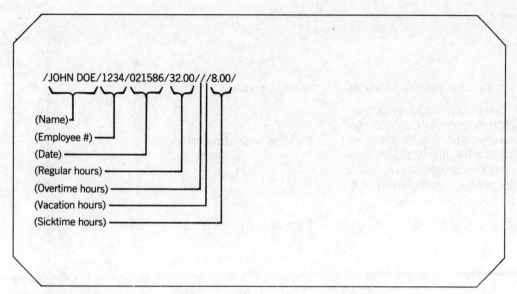

Figure 14-16 Illustrates how the same time card information would be entered on-line using field separators.

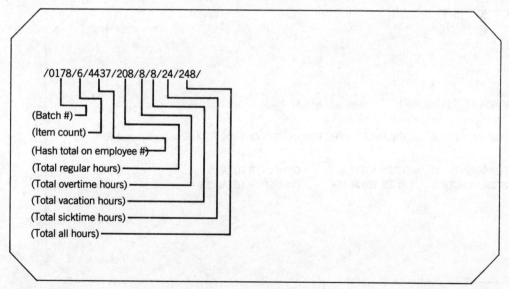

Figure 14-17 Illustrates on-line entry of batch number and user supplied control totals.

```
/0178/6/4437/208/8/8/24/24/248/          (Batch control totals)

/JOHN DOE/1006/021579/40/8///
/BOB JONES/1104/021579/32//8//
/RALPH EVANS/1078/021579/40////          (Individual batch transaction entries)
/TED SMITH/1014/021579/24///16/
/JANET WALSH/192/021579/40////
/NANCY ZEE/43/021579/32///8/*
```

Figure 14-18 Illustrates the on-line entry of a batch of payroll time cards using field separators.

```
BATCH # 178 IS BALANCE.        (Message type A)

BATCH #178 IS OUT OF BALANCE ON THE FOLLOWING CONTROL TOTALS: (message type B)

ITEM COUNT:         USER TOTAL 5          COMPUTER TOTAL 6
REGULAR HOURS:      USER TOTAL 206        COMPUTER TOTAL 208
```

Figure 14-19 Illustrates the two types of batch completion control messages that could be produced by the data entry program.

mally the operator reviews the source documents and the entries on the screen to identify which of the fields noted as "out-of-balance" was entered incorrectly. If an erroneous entry is located, the operator moves the cursor (place marker) across the screen to the incorrect character and writes the correct one over it. The final step would be to signal the data entry program to rebalance the batch, so that the operator can ensure all corrections have been made.

In recent years, the dedicated data entry approach has lost some ground to the general information collection and entry approach. Although the traditional approach will probably always be used to some extent because of its high speed, more and more systems are being designed that incorporate the use of the general approach. Under the general approach the operator probably will have such responsibilities as

1. Collection of information entered directly from customers, users, or from output reports generated by other systems.
2. Entry of the data and immediate resolution of all editing and validation problems.
3. Use of the output reports produced by the system.
4. Provision of immediate feedback to the customer or user after entering the data.

Since the operator in this approach has other duties, his or her level of technical data processing and data entry expertise may be limited. The type of operator used in this approach could include a bank teller, an airline reservations clerk, or even a salesman who wishes to check the status of a customer order. In the general approach, the dialog required between the operator and the terminal/computer system assumes greater importance. The procedures must be as simple and easy to understand as possible. The most popular procedure begins by providing the operator with a menu of possible functions from which to choose (see Figure 14-20). Once the function to be performed has been selected, the analyst must decide what type of dialog best fits the needs of the application and the users. The two most common techniques are (1) the detailed prompting technique, and (2) the simulated forms completion technique.

The detailed prompting technique is relatively slow, but it allows an unskilled operator to be walked through each step required to perform the desired function. Figure 14-21 illustrates how this technique would be applied to opening a checking account. Each field to be entered is prompted individually. If an obvious error is made, the operator can re-enter the data immediately. If editing and validation criteria are exceeded, the operator can be advised and prompted to re-enter the data. When the data is completely entered, the operator is given one last chance to scan the results to be sure they are correct. If everything is accurate, then a Y is entered to complete the session. If a mistake is noted, an N is entered, which allows the operator to make further corrections (see Figure 14-22).

```
BANK TELLER MENU
ENTER LINE NUMBER OF FUNCTION TO BE PERFORMED
1. OPEN CHECKING ACCOUNT
2. OPEN SAVINGS ACCOUNT
3. DEPOSIT IN CHECKING ACCOUNT
4. DEPOSIT IN SAVINGS ACCOUNT
5. WITHDRAW FROM SAVINGS
6. QUERY BALANCE OF SAVINGS ACCOUNT
7. QUERY BALANCE OF CHECKING ACCOUNT
8. TRANSFER FUNDS FROM SAVINGS TO CHECKING ACCOUNT
9. TRANSFER FUNDS FROM CHECKING TO SAVINGS ACCOUNT

"1" (represents the operator's response in selecting function '1')
```

Figure 14-20 Illustrates a displayed menu of possible functions a bank teller or clerk could perform.

The simulated forms completion technique normally is used when the operator is more familiar with the equipment and functions to be performed. In this technique, the operator is presented with a simulated form to fill in. The form identifies the fields to be entered and their relative sizes by initializing them with blanks. The user then moves the cursor to the appropriate place and fills in the

```
FUNCTION '1' SELECTED—OPEN CHECKING ACCOUNT
ENTER NAME:
'JOHN Q. DOE'
ENTER STREET ADDRESS:
'1411 E. MARKET STREET'
ENTER CITY:
'SAN FRANCISCO'
ENTER STATE & ZIP:
'CALIFORNIA, 94014'
ENTER SSN: (xxx—xx—xxxx)
'595—14—3817'
ENTER SPOUSES NAME:
'JANE A. DOE'
```

Figure 14-21 Illustrates the detailed prompting technique in setting up a checking account.

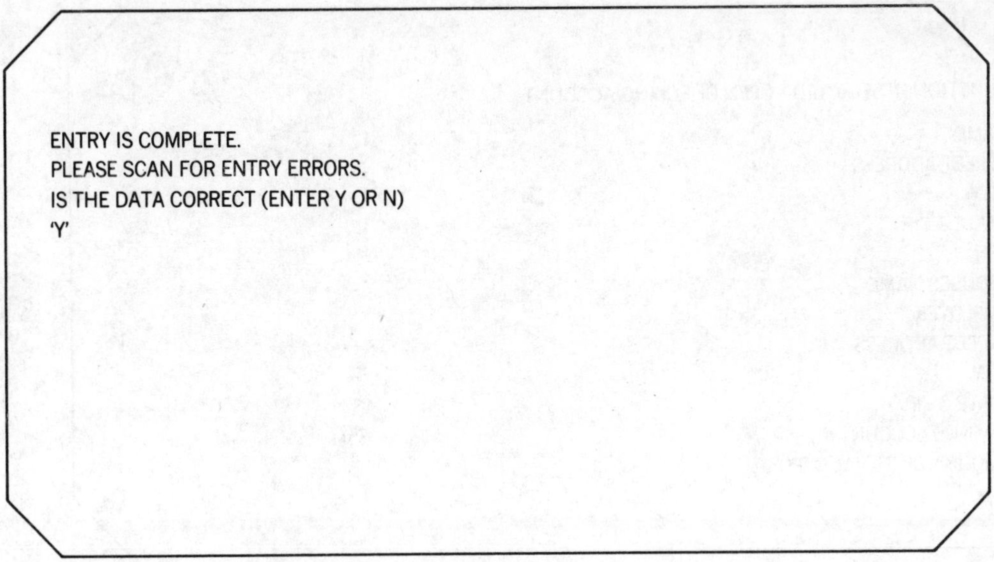

```
ENTRY IS COMPLETE.
PLEASE SCAN FOR ENTRY ERRORS.
IS THE DATA CORRECT (ENTER Y OR N)
'Y'
```

Figure 14-22 Illustrates the dialog the operator must respond with when an entry has been completed and a final check of the data has been made for accuracy.

blanks. Figure 14-23 illustrates a simulated form that could be used for opening a checking account.

As previously mentioned, video terminals are being used more frequently as a medium for system output. The approaches used include (1) the display of traditional type reports, (2) answering user queries about specific data, and (3) providing sophisticated graphic displays. When the design of a system calls for the use of video terminals as a medium for output, the analyst should consider the following questions carefully.

1. Which type of output approach best fits the needs of the intended user?
2. Does the size of the video screen place any limitations on how the output can be formatted?
3. Does the video terminal have sufficient local memory to store extra lines or pages of data when there is too much for one screen?
4. Is the video terminal capable of displaying all the required characters (uppercase and lowercase), symbols, and punctuation marks?
5. Can the microcomputer/terminal distinguish between variable data and protected data? Protected data is a data item that terminal operators cannot change or delete when using their terminal and/or password. Some video screens highlight the intensity of protected data (see Figure 14-24).

If the system design calls for the display of the traditional style output reports, spacing will be an important consideration. The horizontal lines of data should

```
FUNCTION '1' SELECTED—OPEN CHECKING ACCOUNT

NAME
STREET ADDRESS
CITY
STATE & ZIP
SSN
SPOUSES NAME
EMPLOYER
STREET ADDRESS
CITY
STATE & ZIP
SAVINGS ACCOUNT #
AMOUNT OF INITIAL DEPOSIT
```

Figure 14-23 Illustrates the simulated forms fill-in technique for setting up a checking account.

be presented with adequate spacing between fields. This serves to minimize user eye strain in distinguishing field values. If insufficient horizontal space is available, the report may need to be split into two parts. Vertical spacing should be used whenever possible between report ID information, column headings, data, and report totals. Figure 14-25 illustrates how a traditional type report could be displayed.

When the inquiry technique is used, the output may be relatively small in quantity. In this case, the formatting considerations probably are minimal. Figure 14-26 shows an example in which a bank teller inquires about the balance of a customer's checking account. When an inquiry may involve substantial amounts of data, it may be necessary to segment it so that selective portions can be displayed. Figure 14-27 illustrates an example in which the output from a bank teller's inquiry against a customer's checking account is divided into three logical segments. When the teller selects the segment to be reviewed, the number is entered and the segment displayed. Figure 14-28 illustrates how segment 2 would look if selected for display.

The use of graphic displays is the most complex of the output approaches. The techniques employed vary widely. The most common approaches include displaying Gantt charts (described in Chapter 4) and bar graphs (see Figures 14-29 and 14-30). The most important factors for the analyst to consider in using this approach are the

1. Information needs of the user.
2. Level of information required (detailed or summary).

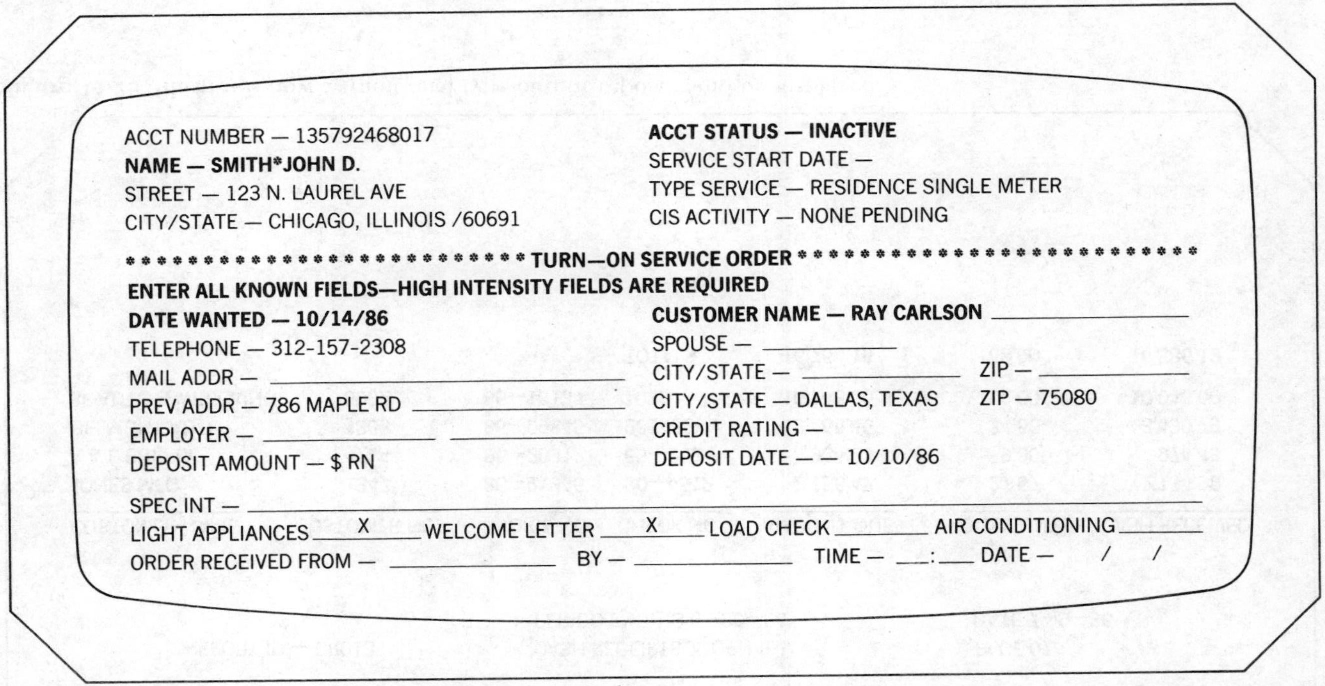

Figure 14-24 Illustrates how some terminals highlight the intensity of protected data.

ACCT NUMBER — 135792468017

NAME — SMITH*JOHN D.

STREET — 123 N. LAUREL AVE

CITY/STATE — CHICAGO, ILLINOIS /60691

* **TURN—ON SERVICE ORDER** *

ENTER ALL KNOWN FIELDS—HIGH INTENSITY FIELDS ARE REQUIRED

DATE WANTED — 10/14/86

TELEPHONE — 312-157-2308

MAIL ADDR —

PREV ADDR — 786 MAPLE RD

EMPLOYER —

DEPOSIT AMOUNT — $ RN

SPEC INT —

LIGHT APPLIANCES —   X   WELCOME LETTER —   X   LOAD CHECK —

ORDER RECEIVED FROM —   BY —   TIME —   :

ACCT STATUS — INACTIVE

SERVICE START DATE —

TYPE SERVICE — RESIDENCE SINGLE METER

CIS ACTIVITY — NONE PENDING

CUSTOMER NAME — RAY CARLSON

SPOUSE —   ZIP —

CITY/STATE —   ZIP —

CITY/STATE — DALLAS, TEXAS   ZIP — 75080

CREDIT RATING —

DEPOSIT DATE — — 10/10/86

AIR CONDITIONING —

DATE —   /   /

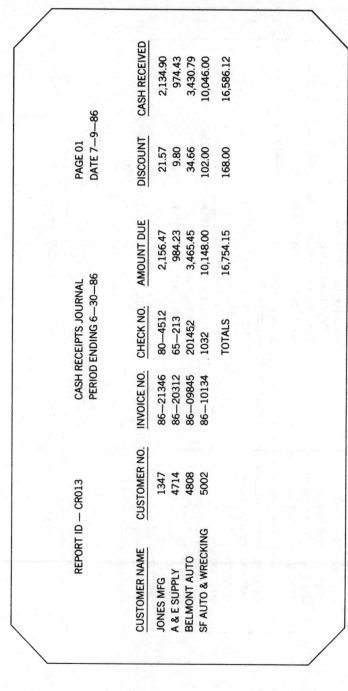

REPORT ID — CR013

CASH RECEIPTS JOURNAL
PERIOD ENDING 6—30—86

PAGE 01
DATE 7—9—86

CUSTOMER NAME	CUSTOMER NO.	INVOICE NO.	CHECK NO.	AMOUNT DUE	DISCOUNT	CASH RECEIVED
JONES MFG	1347	86—21346	80—4512	2,156.47	21.57	2,134.90
A & E SUPPLY	4714	86—20312	65—213	984.23	9.80	974.43
BELMONT AUTO	4808	86—09845	201452	3,465.45	34.66	3,430.79
SF AUTO & WRECKING	5002	86—10134	1032	10,148.00	102.00	10,046.00
			TOTALS	16,754.15	168.00	16,586.12

Figure 14-25 Illustrates how a traditional type output report could be displayed.

'ACCOUNT NUMBER: 12345678'
'BALANCE ?'
CURRENT BALANCE OF ACCOUNT NUMBER 12345678 IS $478.53.

Figure 14-26 Illustrates a bank teller's inquiry as to the balance of a customer's account.

FUNCTION 3 SELECTED — CHECKING ACCOUNT INQUIRY
IDENTIFY SEGMENT OF DATA TO BE DISPLAYED
1 — PERSONAL DATA
2 — HISTORY OF DEPOSITS
3 — CHECKS BEING HELD FOR NEXT STATEMENT
'2' (Teller has selected segment 2 for display)

Figure 14-27 Illustrates the inquiry technique where the data available is too much for a single screen so it has been segmented into three pieces.

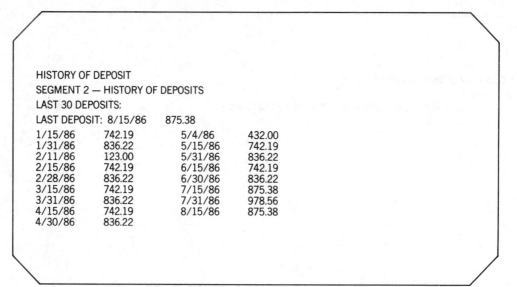

```
HISTORY OF DEPOSIT
SEGMENT 2 — HISTORY OF DEPOSITS
LAST 30 DEPOSITS:
LAST DEPOSIT: 8/15/86     875.38
1/15/86      742.19          5/4/86       432.00
1/31/86      836.22          5/15/86      742.19
2/11/86      123.00          5/31/86      836.22
2/15/86      742.19          6/15/86      742.19
2/28/86      836.22          6/30/86      836.22
3/15/86      742.19          7/15/86      875.38
3/31/86      836.22          7/31/86      978.56
4/15/86      742.19          8/15/86      875.38
4/30/86      836.22
```

Figure 14-28 Illustrates what segment 2 of data would contain for a typical customer.

PROJECT NAME	S or C	JAN 7 14 21 28	FEB 7 14 21 28	MAR 7 14 21 28	APRIL 7 14 21 28	MAY 7 14 21 28	JUNE 7 14 21 28	JULY 7 14 21 28	AUG 7 14 21 28	SEPT 7 14 21 28	OCT 7 14 21 28	NOV 7 14 21 28	DEC 7 14 21 28
A/P SYSTEM DESIGN	S C					X X X X / X X X X							
A/P SYSTEM TEST	S C						X X / X X						
A/P SYSTEM START	S C						X X / X						
G/L SYSTEM DESIGN	S C						X X X X / X X X X						
G/L SYSTEM TEST	S C							X X X X / X					
G/L SYSTEM START	S C												
A/R SYSTEM DESIGN	S C							X X X X / X X X					
A/R SYSTEM TEST	S C								X X X X				
A/R SYSTEM START	S C									X X X X			
	S C												
	S C												
	S C												
	S C												
	S C												

Figure 14-29 Illustrates how a Gantt chart looks displayed as a graph. Gantt charts are described in Chapter 4.

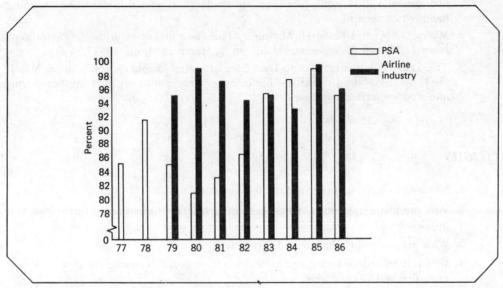

Figure 14-30 Illustrates how bar graphs can be displayed as output for management.

3. Use to which the information is going to be put, that is, information only or timely decision making.
4. Most appropriate method of presenting the data.
5. Method of presentation which may be more important than the data itself with regard to its acceptance by the user.

Selected Readings

1. *Definition of Terms Relating to Carbonless Copy Products.* New York: American National Standards Institute. ANSI/ASTM F549-78a.
2. Erdmann, Glenn. "Laser Forms Make Mark at AAL," *Journal of Forms Management,* vol. 9, no. 2, July/December 1984, pp. 13–16. [Benefits and constraints of laser printers in an actual situation.]
3. Galitz, Wilbert O. *Handbook of Screen Format Design.* Wellesley, Mass.: QED Information Sciences, Inc., 1981.
4. Myers, Gibbs, and Leslie H. Matthies. "Forms Definition and Purposes," *Journal of Systems Management,* vol. 35, no. 4, April 1984, pp. 41–42.
5. Myers, Gibbs, and Leslie H. Matthies. "A Forms Primer," *Journal of Systems Management,* vol. 35, no. 2, February 1984, p. 34.

6. Myers, Gibbs, and Leslie H. Matthies. "New or Revised Forms," *Journal of Systems Management,* vol. 35, no. 5, May 1984, pp. 20–21.

7. Myers, Gibbs, and Leslie H. Matthies. "Pen and Pencil Forms," *Journal of Systems Management,* vol. 35, no. 7, July 1984, pp. 40–41. [Factors to consider when designing handwritten forms.]

8. Myers, Gibbs, and Leslie H. Matthies. "The Place of Forms in the Organization," *Journal of Systems Management,* vol. 35, no. 3, March 1984, pp. 16–17.

9. The, Lee. "The Business-Forms Data Base," *Personal Computing,* vol. 8, no. 3, March 1984, pp. 198–206. [A database file manager program to organize business forms into a computerized database.]

Questions

1. Name five objectives of centralized forms control.

2. Why can giving the forms control area the authority to disapprove forms lead to a problem?

3. What are the major objectives of forms design?

4. Why is it hazardous to attempt to design a form before knowing the type of equipment that will be used to fill it out?

5. What is the advantage of continuous forms with microperforated tear-off strips?

6. How is paper measured?

7. Identify some of the basic guidelines that should be followed when designing a form.

8. What factors should be considered in determining the horizontal printing space?

9. How much space should be allowed for vertical line width in a form that will be handwritten?

10. How many lines per inch do typewriters provide vertically?

11. Name the three types of carbon paper.

12. What aid can be used for designing forms that will be printed on a computer-driven printer? How does it help you?

13. What are the types of forms?

14. Are the principles of designing paper forms and video screen forms the same or different?

15. What is the best sequence of data on a form?

16. In the context of designing a new system, identify some of the advantages and disadvantages that must be considered when weighing the use of on-line input methods.

17. What are the questions that must be considered when the design of a new system favors the use of CRT terminals as an output medium?

SITUATION CASES

Case 14-1: *JFA Consultants*

The following is a work progress report. Can you improve upon the design of this form (note content)?

PROJECT NAME (SUBJECT)	DATE

DATE OF PREVIOUS PROGRESS REPORT	ANALYST	PROJECT NUMBER

BUDGETED AMOUNT TO DATE	COST TO DATE	THIS PROJECT'S COSTS ARE
		UNDER ESTIMATE ON TARGET OVER ESTIMATE

ORIGINAL ESTIMATED COMPLETION DATE	NEW ESTIMATED COMPLETION DATE	THIS PROJECT WILL FINISH
		EARLY ON TIME LATE

NARRATIVE (SHORT WRITTEN DESCRIPTION OF PROGRESS SINCE LAST REPORT)

Case 14-2:   *Software International*

Software International had no centralized forms control. The firm had grown large enough so that it used a considerable number of forms. Each department developed forms for its own use. The result was duplication of forms and confusion within the departments over the correct usage of the available forms. An analyst was asked to remedy the situation.

After obtaining the approval of management, the analyst collected a copy of each existing form but did not explain why she was collecting them. No special effort was made to collect written procedures on how to fill out the forms. The collected samples then were placed in a form number file by their form identification number. Each form was put in a separate folder with cover data showing which departments used the form and the form's purpose. Next a classification system (functional file) was devised. Each form was then sorted by certain characteristics to determine if one form might do the job of other existing forms. It was decided that the existing forms lacked the versatility needed and some new forms were initiated.

The main criteria selected by the analyst for designing a good form were multifunctional use and low cost of printing. She used good forms design techniques and was commended by her supervisor. Bids were solicited for the printing and a small company using letterpress equipment submitted the low bid. The analyst enlisted the aid of the company's art department in making the forms as attractive and as efficient looking as possible. When the new forms were introduced it was decided that the newly established Forms Control Department would approve or disapprove the introduction of any new forms and the modification of existing forms. Each department was to assume responsibility for reordering and distributing its own forms.

After a short time in operation, the new forms system had proven to be as costly as no system, there still was unnecessary duplication, and the department heads showed a reluctance to submit new forms for approval.

Question

1. What are the major flaws in the forms control system at Software International?

Case 14-3:   *Forms Design Associates*

Can you improve upon the following form?

DATE	CUST. NR.

CUST. NME & ADDR.

STATE TERMS: CASH, COD, or CREDIT

QTY.	ITEM NR.	WHLSE. PR.	TOTAL

AUTH. BY   GRAND TOTAL

LESS DISC. _____

NET TOTAL _____

FORM 2013

Case 14-4:   *Nick's Restaurants*

The manager of the Purchasing Department at Nick's Restaurants asked a systems analyst to design a Purchase Requisition form. This was to be a totally new form that had never existed before in the company. The analyst was quite excited about this new project and started immediately. His first step was to design a rough draft of the form. He did this by deciding what information was needed and then placing it on the form in a logical manner. The analyst then took the form out to the involved work areas. He showed the new form design to the managers, the first-line supervisors, and the employees who would use the form in their day-to-day work. He was quite surprised to find that everyone seemed to have a different idea of where information should be placed on this form. After much argument and debate, the analyst decided there was at least a tentative confirmation that all the necessary items of information were, in fact, on the form.

Next the analyst developed a descriptive title for the form and assigned a new form number to it. The form number was placed in the lower left corner as it was on all the other forms in the company.

Using information gained from the earlier discussions with the managers, first-line supervisors, and clerical workers, the analyst laid out the data on the form so that it was most convenient for the clerical workers who would have to fill out the form. Various areas of the form were set off with boldface type in order to make them stand out. The analyst used a boxed design so it was very easy to determine where the information belonged. Also, ballot boxes were used wherever possible. Filing information was placed near the top of the form so it could be seen easily, and all areas for numeric data had sufficient space for the largest possible numbers. There were to be four carbon copies below the original so four different colors of paper were chosen for these copies. The analyst was very careful not to use abbreviations and as much information as possible was preprinted. The form was printed in blue ink; and because it was such a simple form, the analyst decided not to print any instructions. Throughout the design, similar data were grouped in the same area as on other forms within the company. As a final touch, the analyst put a border around the form to give it a balanced and professional appearance.

The form's width and length both conformed to standard paper sizes and to the standard file cabinet sizes used within the company. The forms company made sure that the spacing on the form fit the company's standard typewriters which were elite. As a final check, the analyst made sure that the horizontal spacing lines were above each other so the typist would not have to set very many tab stops.

The analyst consulted an experienced forms salesman, worked through the Purchasing Department, and had three other systems analysts check the final proofs before approving them for printing.

After the form had been in use for several months, it was found to be less than successful. The analyst had done a thorough job, but he overlooked some very important points.

Questions

1. What was overlooked at the start of the project?
2. What two items could improve this form (they were left out during design)?

Case 14-5:   *Airless Paint Company*

A systems analyst had completed the steps of her systems study up to the point of developing video screen formats for inputs. The following is a layout of one of these video screens.

```
_____ — NAME
_____ — STREET ADDRESS
_____ — CITY
_____ — STATE & ZIP
___ __ ____        — SSN
_____ — SPOUSES NAME
_____ — EMPLOYER
_____ — STREET ADDRESS
_____ — CITY
_____ — STATE & ZIP
_____ — SAVING ACCOUNT #
_____ — AMOUNT OF INITIAL DEPOSIT
```

The New Accounts Clerk uses this screen when opening a new account at the savings and loan. Mary, the analyst, has designed a screen for data entry in which there are two protected fields. The two fields that are underlined are protected.

A protected field in this system means that once data is entered into the field by the New Accounts Clerk, the New Accounts Clerk can never modify the existing data. It can be modified only by the supervisor of the area.

The data entry is in a left-to-right format and some of the approximate sizes are 25 characters for name, 25 for street address, 20 for city, and so forth.

Question

1. Can you comment on some of the problems that you might be able to identify in this video screen format?

Chapter 15

RECORDS RETENTION

LEARNING OBJECTIVES

You will learn how to . . .

☐ Evaluate both computerized and manual records.

☐ Understand the magnitude of the records storage problem.

☐ Introduce risk analysis into the firm's records program.

☐ Handle the active, storage, and legal life of records.

☐ Develop a records retention program.

☐ Devise a records retention schedule.

☐ Conduct a records inventory.

☐ File records.

☐ Handle the security of records and their destruction.

☐ Understand microforms/micrographics.

☐ Recognize when optical disks and magnetic media can be used for records.

Computerized Records/Information

Records contain the data/information for the organization. They can be considered as vital extensions of knowledge and memory, the past history or road map of the organization. Business firms and government organizations begin to build records as soon as they enter the business world. Once records are created, it is inevitable that a cost-effective means of handling and storing the records will be sought.

Today's records arrive at a records retention area recorded on paper, cardboard stock, microfiche/microfilm, possibly magnetic media, and in the future they may arrive on non-erasable optical disks. The point is, computerized records are changed only by the format or media upon which they reside. The same basic rules need to be observed with regard to: filing these records so that they can be retrieved, adequate storage so they do not get damaged, and proper disposal policies and procedures to ensure security and privacy, as well as conformance with legal requirements.

Computer systems do not change the basics of records retention. They do make good records retention practices that much more important because today's computer systems create more data than we ever had with manual business systems. To give you an idea of the magnitude of the records storage problem, consider the following. It has been estimated that U.S. business generates about 600 million pages of computer output, 235 million photocopies, and 76 million letters *every day*.[1] With figures such as these, it is not difficult to see why the number of new documents increases at a rate of 20 to 22 percent each year. As computer capabilities have increased, the number of records stored in some type of computerized format has increased geometrically. With significant storage costs, regardless of the storage media used, one of the major business problems is deciding which records must be maintained and which can be eliminated. Keeping or disposing of business records implies that the business exposes itself to a certain amount of risk when making these decisions. This risk can be minimized through the use of risk analysis.

Risk Analysis

Risk analysis is nothing more than a systematic approach to categorizing threats to data and developing appropriate countermeasures to these threats. This risk analysis should result in a plan of action that will implement the countermea-

---

[1] See "Micrographics Shrinks Document Storage Costs," by H. Paris Burstyn. *High Technology*, vol. 5, no. 4, April 1985, p. 64.

sures. Risk analysis is not intended to result in a plan for absolute security of records; but, it *should* result in an optimum plan that balances risk of losses against the cost of the countermeasure controls. The organization may wish to conduct a risk analysis of its records retention area with regard to the data/ information being stored there. With over a dozen methods of performing risk analyses, the analyst must choose the method that fits best with the environment (corporate culture) in which he or she is working.

With regard to the records retention program, a risk analysis can produce the following benefits.

- □ Identify sensitive information and sensitive data items that are contained in seemingly harmless records.
- □ Define segregation parameters for sensitive and non-sensitive data/ information.
- □ Identify potential dollar losses if stored data is lost, stolen, modified, or destroyed.
- □ Identify the necessary controls that are required.
- □ Calculate the cost of the necessary controls.

The records retention risk analysis should result in an explicit security policy that identifies what is to be protected, which threats are significant, and who shall be responsible for the execution, review, and reporting of the security program.

The use of risk analysis implies that the business entity considers its data/ information to be important. Such an analysis also is an indication that the business entity considers its information important enough that it has a formal records retention program. The subject of this chapter is how to organize and maintain a formal records retention program.

*P*urpose of a Records Retention Program

Records retention is a systems technique that provides control over records. It provides for more efficient use of current office space, more efficient use of the space used to store old records, and reductions in paper usage. A formal records retention program provides more effective access to both active and inactive business records. Usually, it also must fit into the firm's information network.

The ultimate goal of a records retention program is to control the records from their source, through their use, on to their inactive storage, and finally, to their destruction. The single most important function of records retention is removing unneeded records from the current office space and moving them to an out-of-the-way storage area. This makes space available for newly created records. The second most important function is to ensure that old records are kept for the proper length of time. Some are needed for longer periods than others. For example, a firm may elect to dispose of all production records on a job as soon as the job is finished. But it might elect to retain a copy of the job contract for 10 years. The records retention system prescribes when the records are to be moved from the current work areas to the storage area, how they will be filed in the storage area, and when they will be destroyed.

*A*ctive . . . *Storage* . . . *Legal Life*

Active records are those records that are used in the day-to-day operation of the firm. Active records are located in the current office space and they are used frequently. Their total retention time might be from 2 or 3 days to 20 years.

Storage life (inactive) begins when the active life ends. Any record that is not referred to more than four times a year should be considered inactive and should go into its storage life. Schedules for retention and disposal provide timetables for the movement of each type of record from active records storage, located in the current office space, to inactive storage. Usually, when records are transferred from active to inactive storage, they should be analyzed to determine whether any of them can be destroyed immediately according to the retention period scheduled for the particular record.

The *legal life* of a record is the retention period that is required by law, or regulatory agencies which have the force of law. While the task of identifying which laws apply to any individual firm is large, it is not impossible. The *Federal Register,* published daily by the National Archives, provides proposed and new regulations that may affect business practices and records retention requirements. Once a year it summarizes these records retention requirements. Further, the National Records Management Council (NAREMCO) maintains an index to federal records retention requirements.

*R*ecord Retention Schedule

A record retention schedule is a timetable governing the retirement and destruction of business records. The schedule shows how long the record should be kept in the active file located in the current office space, and it tells how long the record should be kept in storage. The overall life requirement of the record (both active and storage) may be governed by law (its legal life) rather than the firm's desire.

Many state and federal requirements pertaining to record retention times are vague. For example, suppose one government agency says you have to store a record for 7 years, and a different government agency says it must be held for 20 years. Which requirement do you follow? Another area that causes confusion concerns the retention of records with duplicate information. For instance, a company is required to retain a certain record for 10 years. Now, assume the same information is in another document that also is being stored for 10 years. Do you need to save both documents for 10 years, or can you assume that saving one will be adequate? Perhaps both must be saved because all copies of forms with a specific government identification number must be retained. For example, W-2 Wage and Tax Statements, Form 941 Employer's Quarterly Federal Tax Returns, or W-4 Employee's Withholding Allowance Certificates must be saved for several years. Finally, some of the government regulations are written in a vague fashion. They may say "all legal documents" should be saved for 20 years. Let us say your company has a legal document, the title to an automobile, and the automobile is destroyed totally by fire. The automobile no longer exists. Now, because the title was a legal document, do you still need to save it for 20 years even though the automobile no longer exists? Suppose the *Code of Federal Regulations* says a firm has to keep contracts for three years or until the contract is terminated. If you have a five-year contract, should you count the three years from the first day of the contract and keep it five years, or do you count from the end of the contract and keep it 8 years? The firm often must try to learn the *intent* of the regulations and set its retention schedules accordingly. Never assume the 6- or 7-year statute of limitations is sufficient for the life of all records. Some manufacturing records have a 20-year statute of limitations. There are many exceptions imposed for certain records by customers and by the state and federal governments. The firm itself should consider the value of retaining certain records for extended periods of time, or permanently.

Some of the laws or acts that affect records retention are the Fair Labor Standards Act, Code of Federal Regulations, Armed Services Procurement Regulations, Industrial Security Manual of the Defense Department, insurance company regulations, and the National Records Management Council (New York City).

As we have discussed, the usual route of most records is to go from active to inactive to disposal. As stated, the general rule that can be used to initiate the movement from active to inactive storage is a referral frequency of less than four times per year. Some records may go directly from active use to disposal, of course. Figure 15-1 shows an example of a general retention schedule and some of the codes often found in records control systems.

Records Retention Timetable

LEGEND FOR AUTHORITY TO DISPOSE	LEGEND FOR RETENTION PERIOD
AD—Administrative Decision	AC—Dispose After Completion of Job or Contract
ASPR—Armed Services Procurement Regulation	AE—Dispose After Expiration
CFR—Code of Federal Regulations	AF—After End of Fiscal Year
FLSA—Fair Labor Standards Act	AM—After Moving
ICC—Interstate Commerce Commission	AS—After Settlement
	AT—Dispose After Termination
INS—Insurance Company Regulation	ATR—After Trip
	OBS—Dispose When Obsolete
ISM—Industrial Security Manual, Attachment to DD Form 441	P—Permanent
	SUP—Dispose When Superseded

* After Disposed   ** Normally   † Govt. R&D Contracts

TYPE OF RECORD	RETENTION PERIOD YEARS	AUTHORITY
ACCOUNTING & FISCAL		
Accounts Payable Invoices	3	ASPR-STATE, FLSA
Accounts Payable Ledger	P	AD
Accounts Receivable Invoices & Ledgers	5	AD
Authorizations for Accounting	SUP	AD
Balance Sheets	P	AD
Bank Deposits	3	AD
Bank Statements	3	AD
Bonds	P	AD
Budgets	3	AD
Capital Asset Record	3*	AD
Cash Receipt Records	7	AD
Check Register	P	AD
Checks, Dividend	6	
Checks, Payroll	2	FLSA, STATE
Checks, Voucher	3	FLSA, STATE
Cost Accounting Records	5	AD
Earnings Register	3	FLSA, STATE
Entertainment Gifts & Gratuities	3	AD
Estimates, Projections	7	AD
Expense Reports	3	AD
Financial Statements, Certified	P	AD

Revised and printed by Electric Wastebasket Corp. © 1983

Figure 15-1 Records retention schedule.

TYPE OF RECORD	RETENTION PERIOD YEARS	AUTHORITY
ACCOUNTING & FISCAL (*continued*)		
Financial Statements, Periodic	2	AD
General Ledger Records	P	CFR
Labor Cost Records	3	ASPR, CFR
Magnetic Tape and Tab Cards	1**	
Note Register	P	AD
Payroll Registers	3	FLSA, STATE
Petty Cash Records	3	AD
P & L Statements	P	AD
Salesman Commission Reports	3	AD
Travel Expense Reports	3	AD
Work Papers, Rough	2	AD
ADMINISTRATIVE RECORDS		
Audit Reports	10	AD
Audit Work Papers	3	AD
Classified Documents: Inventories, Reports, Receipts	10	AD
Correspondence, Executive	P	AD
Correspondence, General	5	AD
Directives from Officers	P	AD
Forms Used, File Copies	P	AD
Systems and Procedures Records	P	AD
Work Papers, Management Projects	P	AD
COMMUNICATIONS		
Bulletins Explaining Communications	P	AD
Messenger Records	1	AD
Phone Directories	SUP	AD
Phone Installation Records	1	AD
Postage Reports, Stamp Requisitions	1 AF	AD
Postal Records, Registered Mail & Insured Mail Logs & Meter Records	1 AF	AD, CFR
Telecommunications Copies	1	AD
CONTRACT ADMINISTRATION		
Contracts, Negotiated. Bailments, Changes, Specifications, Procedures, Correspondence	P	CFR
Customer Reports	P	AD
Materials Relating to Distribution Revisions, Forms, and Format of Reports	P	AD
Work Papers	OBS	AD

Figure 15-1 (*Continued*)

TYPE OF RECORD	RETENTION PERIOD YEARS	AUTHORITY
CORPORATE		
Annual Reports	P	AD
Authority to Issue Securities	P	AD
Bonds, Surety	3 AE	AD
Capital Stock Ledger	P	AD
Charters, Constitutions, Bylaws	P	AD
Contracts	20 AT	AD
Corporate Election Records	P	AD
Incorporation Records	P	AD
Licenses—Federal, State, Local	AT	AD
Stock Transfer & Stockholder	P	AD
LEGAL		
Claims and Litigation Concerning Torts and Breach of Contracts	P	AD
Law Records—Federal, State, Local	SUP	AD
Patents and Related Material	P	AD
Trademark & Copyrights	P	AD
LIBRARY, COMPANY		
Accession Lists	P	AD
Copies of Requests for Materials	6 mos.	AD
Meeting Calendars	P	AD
Research Papers, Abstracts, Bibliographies	SUP, 6 mos. AC	AD
MANUFACTURING		
Bills of Material	2	AD, ASPR
Drafting Records	P	AD†
Drawings	2	AD, ASPR
Inspection Records	2	AD
Lab Test Reports	P	AD
Memos, Production	AC	AD
Product, Tooling, Design, Engineering Research, Experiment & Specs Records	20	STATUTE OF LIMITATIONS
Production Reports	3	AD
Quality Reports	1 AC	AD
Reliability Records	P	AD
Stock Issuing Records	3 AT	AD, ASPR
Tool Control	3 AT	AD, ASPR
Work Orders	3	AD
Work Status Reports	AC	AD

Figure 15-1 (*Continued*)

TYPE OF RECORD	RETENTION PERIOD YEARS	AUTHORITY
OFFICE SUPPLIES & SERVICES		
Inventories	1 AF	AD
Office Equipment Records	6 AF	AD
Requests for Services	1 AF	AD
Requisitions for Supplies	1 AF	AD
PERSONNEL		
Accident Reports, Injury Claims, Settlements	30 AS	CFR, INS, STATE
Applications, Changes & Terminations	5	AD, ASPR, CFR
Attendance Records	7	AD
Employee Activity Files	2 or SUP	AD
Employee Contracts	6 AT	AD
Fidelity Bonds	3 AT	AD
Garnishments	5	AD
Health & Safety Bulletins	P	AD
Injury Frequency Charts	P	CFR
Insurance Records, Employees	11 AT	INS
Job Descriptions	2 or SUP	CFR
Rating Cards	2 or SUP	CFR
Time Cards	3	AD
Training Manuals	P	AD
Union Agreements	3	WALSH-HEALEY ACT
PLANT & PROPERTY RECORDS		
Depreciation Schedules	P	AD
Inventory Records	P	AD
Maintenance & Repair, Building	10	AD
Maintenance & Repair, Machinery	5	AD
Plant Account Cards, Equipment	P	CFR, AD
Property Deeds	P	AD
Purchase or Lease Records of Plant Facility	P	AD
Space Allocation Records	1 AT	AD
PRINTING & DUPLICATING		
Copies Produced, Tech. Pubs., Charts	1 or OBS	AD
Film Reports	5	AD
Negatives	5	AD
Photographs	1	AD
Production Records	1 AC	AD

Figure 15-1 (*Continued*)

TYPE OF RECORD	RETENTION PERIOD YEARS	AUTHORITY
PROCUREMENT, PURCHASING		
Acknowledgments	AC	AD
Bids, Awards	3 AT	CFR
Contracts	3 AT	AD
Exception Notices (GAO)	6	AD
Price Lists	OBS	AD
Purchase Orders, Requisitions	3 AT	CFR
Quotations	1	AD
PRODUCTS, SERVICES, MARKETING		
Correspondence	3	AD
Credit Ratings & Classifications	7	AD
Development Studies	P	AD
Presentations & Proposals	P	AD
Price Lists, Catalogs	OBS	AD
Prospect Lines	OBS	AD
Register of Sales Order	NO VALUE	AD
Surveys	P	AD
Work Papers, Pertaining to Projects	NO VALUE	AD
PUBLIC RELATIONS & ADVERTISING		
Advertising Activity Reports	5	AD
Community Affairs Records	P	AD
Contracts for Advertising	3 AT	AD
Employee Activities & Presentations	P	AD
Exhibits, Releases, Handouts	2-4	AD
Internal Publications	P (1 copy)	AD
Layouts	1	AD
Manuscripts	1	AD
Photos	1	AD
Public Information Activity	7	AD
Research Presentations	P	AD
Tear-Sheets	2	AD
SECURITY		
Classified Material Violations	P	AD
Courier Authorizations	1 mo. ATR	AD
Employee Clearance Lists	SUP	ISM
Employee Case Files	5	ISM
Fire Prevention Program	P	AD
Protection—Guards, Badge Lists, Protective Devices	5	AD
Subcontractor Clearances	2 AT	AD
Visitor Clearance	2	ISM

Figure 15-1 (*Continued*)

TYPE OF RECORD	RETENTION PERIOD YEARS	AUTHORITY
TAXATION		
Annuity or Deferred Payment Plan	P	CFR
Depreciation Schedules	P	CFR
Dividend Register	P	CFR
Employee Withholding	4	CFR
Excise Exemption Certificates	4	CFR
Excise Reports (Manufacturing)	4	CFR
Excise Reports (Retail)	4	CFR
Inventory Reports	P	CFR
Tax Bills and Statements	P	AD
Tax Returns	P	AD
TRAFFIC & TRANSPORTATION		
Aircraft Operating & Maintenance	P	CFR
Bills of Lading, Waybills	2	ICC, FLSA
Employee Travel	1 AF	AD
Freight Bills	3	ICC
Freight Claims	2	ICC
Household Moves	3 AM	AD
Motor Operating & Maintenance	2	AD
Rates and Tariffs	SUP	AD
Receiving Documents	2-10	AD, CFR
Shipping & Related Documents	2-10	AD, CFR

Figure 15-1 (*Continued*)

*R*ecords Inventory

A records inventory is the starting point in initiating a records control program. The systems analyst should be given the authority of a project manager. The analyst must be authorized to go into the involved departments to examine their records. Of course, in government work the analyst also may be required to have a security clearance at or above the level of classification of the records being examined. In private industry, the authority given the analyst must be sufficient to overcome reluctance on the part of departments not wishing to allow access to their records.

Begin by taking an inventory of the active records used and maintained in each department of the organization. Instinct will lead you to the various business departments that need and use forms, but do not overlook data processing.

Besides the normal paper forms used in data processing, many data processing departments now use *flash forms*. A flash form is used on the newer, high speed laser printers. A laser printer is so fast that, as it prints the output data to be utilized in the business, it also can print the entire form that the data is printed upon. This way, the form and the data are printed simultaneously and there is no need to purchase forms or store them in a forms storage area. The point is, be sure to determine during the inventory if your data processing people are using flash forms. Further, do not overlook forms that are part of a video screen output or forms developed within a department for its distributed microcomputer-based systems.

This inventory should be performed in person. Later, if the job gets too large, a questionnaire can be designed to complete the records inventory, but it is important that the analyst get the feel of the job before designing the questionnaire. Questionnaires are fast, but an inventory personally performed by the analyst usually is more accurate and realistic. During the physical inventory, use a worksheet such as the one shown in Figure 15-2 to obtain the following.

1. The current filing system of each area. (Do not get involved in improving the current filing methods except as a project separate from the records inventory.)
2. Title of each record (form number if applicable).
3. Type of copy, such as original or carbon copy.
4. Size of the record, for example, $8\frac{1}{2} \times 11$ inches.
5. Quantity of each record (approximate).
6. Inclusive dates of records accumulation.

The analyst then should research the retention requirements imposed by the government, customers, other regulatory agencies, and the firm itself, assigning appropriate retention times to each type of record.

The schedule shown in Figure 15-1 may be used as a guide to the types of records that should be retained. The analyst, however, always should keep in mind that since laws change, any list such as in Figure 15-1, may become obsolete very quickly. This is true especially of personnel records, which are being retained for increasingly longer periods of time. The only *sure* way of knowing how long to keep a record is to check the law governing that record. The corporate lawyer can assist in this, or if the firm is quite small, the nearest municipal or county law library should be visited. Remember, too, that records not covered by a federal law may vary from state to state.

After all record types have been assigned tentative retention times for both active and inactive phases, the analyst should seek the concurrence of the most knowledgeable people in each affected department. The Contracts Department is usually an excellent source of information regarding exception retention re-

RECORDS INVENTORY WORKSHEET

Department	Analyst
Accounting	Robert Buchanan

Title of Record	Form Number
Capital inventory	VS-841-4/86

Type of Copy (original, carbon, etc.)	Size of Record in Inches
Original from computer files/video screen	On video screen

Inclusive Dates of Accumulation in Department	Quantity of Record
From 6/79 to present on disk files	None—generated on demand

Number of Times This Record Is Used Per Year

On a daily basis about 10–15 times per day
(15 × 260 workdays = 390 times/year)

Current Filing System (Active Life Area)

On-line disk files 1/1/85 to present.
Filed by inventory ID tag number and cross-referenced to inventory item name.

Storage Filing System (Storage Life Area)

Magnetic tape files 6/79 to 12/31/84 with a six hour retrieval time.

Active Life + Storage Life = Total Life
(Then Destruction)

Active Life	Storage Life	Method of Destruction
2 years	15 years	☐ Burn ☐ Shred ☒ Local Trash

Remarks (Relationship to Other Records)

Relates to tax forms and loan documents.

Figure 15-2 Records inventory worksheet.

quirements imposed by customers. The Quality Assurance Department is another source of such information.

When the retention times for a department's records are finalized, the analyst should obtain a signature of concurrence from the department manager. When the schedule is finalized for all departments, it should be signed by each department manager, and a concurring signature should be obtained from an executive at general manager level or higher.

Types of Filing Systems

There are many types of filing systems: some good, some bad. When working on a records retention project, it is easy to get sidetracked in the current records area if it has a poorly designed filing system. The analyst should not get involved in the filing system used in the current work area (active life), except as a separate project. The analyst's goal is to develop a records retention schedule, get records moved from active areas to storage areas, and to develop a good retention system in the storage area. The storage area filing system must allow for the retrieval of the records when they are requested and when their destruction date arrives.

The most economical and quickest filing system for the storage area is to file the records by the title of the record. Each record is listed in alphabetical order using the Storage Box Label Form (Figure 15-3). The records are stored in boxes and then marked with the appropriate information. The label in Figure 15-3 is a three-part form. The top copy is a gummed label, the second copy is kept by the sending department (active life area), and the third copy is for the storage area files. The gummed label is put on the box of records before transfer to the storage area. The storage area files its copy, by the title of the record, in alphabetical sequence.

The records in the box are kept in the same filing sequence as they were when sent to the storage area from the active life area. This eliminates any refiling in the storage area. It does, however, result in storing multiple copies of the same record because all records from all departments are stored without trying to consolidate. This has the minor disadvantage of losing some storage space, but has the positive advantage of safety in numbers of copies stored. In addition, the stored copies are in the same filing sequence that was used in the active area. This method, filing by title of the record, allows for quick retrieval because the storage area can quickly send a specific box of records to the requesting department. The requesting department then can locate the needed record, since they will be familiar with the box's filing order.

Other methods of filing are subject classification, record classification, and numeric classification. All three of these methods require the storage area to

Title of Record (Form Number)		Box Location Number
Inclusive Dates Within This Box		Originating Department

How Filed Within This Box

☐ Alphabetic   ☐ Numeric   ☐ Other (explain)

Method of Destruction

☐ Burn   ☐ Shred   ☐ Local Trash

Date to be Destroyed

Enter the Date (Month & Year) and Department Every Time a Record is Requested

Date	Department	Date	Department	Date	Department

Form 186 Rev. 4/86

Figure 15-3 Storage box label form.

refile the records. In subject classification, each record is classified and arranged by subject in alphabetical order. In record classification, only one copy of each record is arranged in alphabetical order; this eliminates the storage of multiple copies of the same record. In numeric classification, all records are arranged in a unique redefined numeric sequence.

Unless the firm is willing to spend the extra money for the refiling of records by storage area personnel, it is recommended that the records be filed by title of the record and kept in the same filing sequence as they were in the active life area, that is, the department from which they came. The cost of storage space for storing multiple copies of the same record from different departments is far less than the labor cost of refiling to eliminate the duplicate copies.

The people who work in the records' active life area are responsible for the boxing of the records for transfer to the storage area. When the records are received at the storage area, they should be checked to make sure they are properly identified and sequenced. A unique *box location number* is stamped on the box and also entered in the upper right corner of the filed copy of the storage box label (see Figure 15-3). The object of the box location number is to enable the storage area to store boxes in the most efficient manner. The boxes are stored in a numeric sequence starting with 1 and going as high as required.

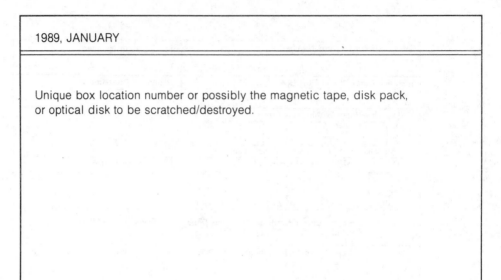

Figure 15-4 Destruction cards.

With this index there is really no need for worrying about whether records with the same title are all in the same area on the storage shelves. To find a record, one looks up the filed copy of the storage box label form to find the unique box location number and retrieves the box.

Before placing the box in its designated shelf area, one other file should be utilized by the storage area. A file box of 5 × 8 inch cards, each with the month and year in consecutive order, must be developed. A 50-year file will require only 600 cards of the kind shown in Figure 15-4. The personnel in the storage area enter the unique box location number on the card that contains the month and year in which the box of records is supposed to be destroyed. A "tickler file" of this type ensures that boxes are retrieved and destroyed. Prior to destruction, the supervisor of the storage area should check the dates of retrieval at the bottom of the storage box label (see Figure 15-3). If these records have been accessed numerous times in the recent past, then their destruction schedule should be re-evaluated. The system should ensure that records still being used are not destroyed.

During the storage life of the records, whenever a box of records is returned to a specific department, the storage area should mark their file copy of the storage box label with the name of the department that has the box of records. When the box of records ultimately is returned, the storage area should then cross out the department listed at the bottom of Figure 15-3.

We do hope you noticed that the above filing system lends itself nicely to the use of a microcomputer. For example, you might put the "destruction cards" (Figure 15-4) onto a database file in the department's microcomputer.

Security of Vital Records

The loss of records may or may not hurt the firm. For this discussion, some records may be classified as "vital." Vital records are those records that would enable the firm to reconstruct its operations after a disaster such as a major fire. Vital records might be stockholder records, articles of incorporation, contracts and agreements, accounts receivable and payable, patents, production drawings, customer name and address files, client project files, and so on.

Copies of such vital records may be destroyed by fire, floods, terrorists, or nuclear destruction. Because of the importance of these records, many firms store them outside the plant in a safe area. The analyst must examine how the files might be destroyed and seek to find a location that will be protected from such events. Some firms store vital records in underground vaults that are available for rent.

Not only must the analyst evaluate where the vital records are to be stored, but a set of priorities also must be established. Generally speaking, those records that are necessary to resume operations after a disaster are given the highest priority (computer tapes should be stored relatively near the computer site in a different building). The priorities assume less importance as they go down the hierarchy to such items as product and price information.

Destruction of Records

The vital records of your organization may be destroyed almost immediately upon their creation or they may be destroyed after 20 or more years of storage. For immediate or almost immediate destruction, the organization should have paper shredders strategically placed so responsible employees can destroy sensitive documents/records. It should be noted, however, that this is not adequate for military (including military contractor) classified documents. These have special requirements.

With regard to the destruction of records that are stored for many years, a formal destruction procedure should be devised. This procedure should ensure that the records are destroyed thoroughly so they cannot be reassembled by anyone. Depending upon the sensitivity of the records, you may wish to shred them, burn them, or even have the paper turned into a liquid paper pulp. Some organizations carry out these tasks themselves, while others contract with a bonded company that guarantees safe destruction.

As a general guideline for business documents, the following items should be higher priority for complete destruction after their useful life has ceased.

□ Sales Reports	□ Sales Forecasts
□ Bids & Quotations	□ Customer Mailing Lists
□ Engineering Drawings	□ New Product Proposals
□ Personnel Records	□ Confidential Memos
□ Confidential Correspondence	□ Contracts
□ Accounts Receivable	□ Cost Estimates
□ Labor Estimates	□ Planning Studies
□ Production Reports	□ Credit Information
□ Purchase Agreements	□ Payroll Data
□ Inventory Reports	□ Canceled Checks
□ Bank Statements	□ Securities
□ Research & Development Data/Reports	

As you consider the items that need positive and complete destruction, do not overlook microfilm, punch tape, tab cards, magnetic and/or optical disk, as well as the normal items such as paper and other card stocks.

There are two types of paper shredders. The first type cuts the paper into long strips. The other uses a "cross-cut" technique in which the paper is cut in both directions, forming confetti. If the need for security is great, paper left in long strips can be reconstructed by someone really interested in your records. Consequently, when greater security is needed, the cross-cut type shredder should be used.

*M*icroforms/Micrographics

Microforms, or micrographics, have been with us since the 1920s, but they did not come into widespread use until the 1960s. Microform proponents have touted their advantages loudly, and rightly so. These include

□ Microforms provide savings in storage space of 98 percent.

□ They are relatively permanent, rarely lost, and seldom mutilated.

- ☐ They provide copies of rare items inexpensively (of concern primarily to libraries).
- ☐ They preserve rare or vital documents that could be destroyed by frequent use.
- ☐ Copies can be made quickly and inexpensively.
- ☐ Distribution of microform copies is simple and much less expensive than mailing the same thing in hard copy.
- ☐ Microforms generally cost less initially.
- ☐ For libraries in particular, binding costs are eliminated.
- ☐ Microforms can be used by most professions, including accounting, purchasing, education, personnel, hospitals, banking, insurance, engineering, retailing, airlines, automotive parts departments, and the like.
- ☐ Updating and retrieval are easy.
- ☐ Microforms that meet government specifications may be used for vital records.
- ☐ If color is needed, it is now available in some formats.
- ☐ Microforms have the added ecological advantage of preserving our forests since less paper is needed.

In short, microfilm has been referred to as the "transistorization of the printed page."[2]

There are a number of disadvantages, too, which must be considered and which often are glossed over by the advocates of microforms. The disadvantages include

- ☐ There is some user reluctance, which varies from claims of inconvenience to claims of illness from watching a moving image on the screen; there is reluctance to depend on a machine for reading.
- ☐ Users cannot browse easily through microforms and usually need to be directed by an index or other secondary reference.
- ☐ File integrity, particularly with some microforms, is not well understood by some systems designers. It may be vital that only people knowledgeable in the system perform manual refiling.
- ☐ The user organization must provide a sufficient number of readers.
- ☐ Machines *do* break down, which can cause major problems.
- ☐ Continuous microfilm means that reel travel time must be experienced in order to arrive at the needed "page."

[2] Refer to *The Microfilm Technology Primer on Scholarly Journals*, by Franklin D. Crawford (Princeton, N.J.: Princeton Microfilm Corporation of New Jersey, 1969), p. 5.

☐ Purchasers of microforms have to choose from hundreds of companies engaged in producing microfilm equipment and services.

☐ Although there have been many National Microfilm Conventions, there is a definite lack of standardization in the industry. For a company concerned only with one application and one format, this may not be a problem. But for companies purchasing microforms from both civilian and government agencies, different equipment may be needed for the various microforms since equipment is often incompatible and not adaptable.

☐ Microfilm may have many advantages in many situations, but it is not always an economic solution to a records storage problem. (On the other hand, economics may be less important than security for vital records.)

☐ Viewers must be used to read microforms. Since it may not be convenient or economically feasible to locate readers in all work areas, there may be an increase in employee lost time because of travel to and from readers.

☐ Each film must be inspected carefully to verify that it is completely readable; faint copies and some tissue copies do not photograph well.

In spite of these disadvantages, the micrographics industry now is an established part of the records retention industry, with sales in the neighborhood of $2.5 billion and an annual growth rate of 10 percent. While the growth rate on the equipment side of the industry has slowed to approximately 2 percent, the microfilming services are booming, with an estimated annual growth rate of about 30 percent.[3] Obviously, many firms concerned with recordkeeping must feel that the advantages of using microforms of one kind or another far outweigh the disadvantages.

Designing a microform information system of any kind is complicated by both the advantages and disadvantages. In addition, a major dimension is added to the system when you interject microforms because humans are habitual animals. For the human to communicate with a machine, the human must learn new thinking habits, and some humans do not adapt well. This human-to-machine interaction often is referred to as the human–machine interface.

The systems analyst follows the same procedures when designing a system of this type; but it generally is more complicated in that one must learn not only what routines are needed, but also the microforms and their equipment capabilities and drawbacks. It is complicated further by the fact that costs often are miscalculated; and since one piece of equipment often leads to another, the *true* costs of the project are often not anticipated fully. Technology also is advancing so quickly that various types of microforms can now be used within the same system. In effect, many new systems are experimental, each one building upon

---

[3] See "Tiny Is Beautiful," *Forbes*, November 4, 1985, p. 12.

previous ones. Robert Bodkin of Microfilm Service Corporation pointed this out when he said

> *Generally, you are asking a customer to change his entire method of recordkeeping and people just don't jump at something like that. . . . When we first started selling microfilm we made something of a mistake by talking about it in general terms. Just about everyone knows you can record documents on microfilm, that you will save space by doing so and that it gives an added measure of security. But those aren't the advantages that sell microfilm. Microfilm has to be sold with a systems approach toward specific applications. It has to be sold as a system that does something better, not necessarily cheaper. If microfilm were being sold as something to make storage easier, it would be next to a nothing market for us.[4]*

Fortunately, a whole new generation of office workers has grown up in an age in which high-reduction microforms and sophisticated micropublishing techniques have made microfilm less expensive than paper. The psychological barriers to the new media are disappearing as the paperless office emerges. The paperless office demonstrates how advanced information management concepts can be applied to practical business situations.

Microfilm is the oldest and best known of the microforms, and the term is used often to describe other microforms. It has been the principal medium for records storage since the 1920s. Microfilm, by reducing storage space by 95 percent, can eliminate the entire inactive storage area because all microfilmed records can be kept in the current office space (active life) and then go directly to destruction when that time arrives.

Microfilm, as used here, is a specific type of photo-optical reduction of a document onto a continuous strip of film that usually is placed on a reel (see Figure 15-5). Historically this film has been 35-mm (millimeter), which meant an optical reduction of anywhere from $10\times$ to $40\times$ ($\times$ means times). This size film had sufficient definition that copies could be made in the original size without appreciable loss of detail.

Now, 16-mm has become increasingly popular (see Figure 15-6). For the many companies subscribing to periodicals microfilmed exclusively in 35-mm, it causes a major equipment problem if a new type of film is introduced. If their equipment cannot utilize the 16-mm film, they must purchase additional equipment. The systems analyst should endeavor to account for such unforeseen developments when designing for such an expensive long-term commitment.

There currently are two types of 35-mm microfilm available: *positive* and *negative*. Initially, positive microfilm was the most widely used because only microfilm readers were of concern. Positive film provided the user a black print

---

[4] "Out of the Desert, Into the Green." *Office Products*, vol. 135, no. 1, January 1972, p. 28.

Figure 15-5 A variety of microforms. Reading left to right, top row: negative microfiche (NMA standard), Recordak Micro-Thin jacket (COSATI standard), aperture card; middle row: 35-mm microfilm roll, Recordak 16-mm thread-easy microfilm magazine, another style of 16-mm magazine; bottom row: Recordak Microstrip holder. (Photograph graciously provided by Eastman Kodak Company, Rochester, N.Y.)

on a white background. The rapid rise of reader-printers has caused a trend toward negative film. Positive film prints look very much like photostats, that is, they have white letters on a black background. Negative film, on the other hand, provides a copy with black print on a white background. Equipment manufacturers have been working on printers for positive film to provide a black print on a white background. Color film, although beautiful in viewing, is still experimental in terms of reproduction.

There is a distinct possibility that standardization of continuous strip film will come with 16-mm microfilm. Its advantages include greatly improved film resolution, storage not on reels but on easy-to-use cartridges (see Figures 15-5 and 15-6), and reader-printers that need no manual threading and have push-button access to the needed page. The latter is made possible by coding each "page" or frame, enabling retrieval through odometer readings or visually (see Figure 15-7). (When a computer is involved, such indexing is referred to as computer-assisted retrieval or CAR.) Further, copies made just by pushing a button save time, money, and errors in copying. Manufacturers claim that the high cost of purchasing this equipment is inconsequential compared with the time saved in retrieval and printout by customers or by highly paid research people.

Figure 15-6 A variety of microforms. Reading clockwise from bottom center: Recordak Microstrip holder, 16-mm microfilm roll, Recordak Micro-Thin jacket, Recordak 16-mm thread-easy magazine, another style of 16-mm magazine, and a positive microfiche. (Photograph graciously provided by Eastman Kodak Company, Rochester, N.Y.)

Microfilm rolls and cartridges generally are considered best for inactive files that no longer need updating. Updating of continuous roll film can be performed by only two methods. The first is to replace the entire roll or cartridge. This replacement often leads to the need for a new index if the cartridge/frame index is used for retrieval. The second method is to add on at the end of individual rolls or at the end of the set of rolls. In this case either the current index or the historical index may have to be revised.

Another storage method is the *aperture card* (see Figure 15-5). This is another use of 35-mm or 16-mm film. An aperture card is simply an 80-column tab card upon which one or more frames of film have been mounted. The aperture card has been used successfully for the storage of voluminous materials, such as

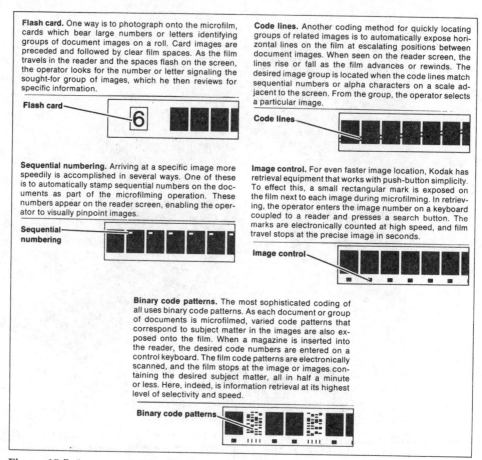

Flash card. One way is to photograph onto the microfilm, cards which bear large numbers or letters identifying groups of document images on a roll. Card images are preceded and followed by clear film spaces. As the film travels in the reader and the spaces flash on the screen, the operator looks for the number or letter signaling the sought-for group of images, which he then reviews for specific information.

Code lines. Another coding method for quickly locating groups of related images is to automatically expose horizontal lines on the film at escalating positions between document images. When seen on the reader screen, the lines rise or fall as the film advances or rewinds. The desired image group is located when the code lines match sequential numbers or alpha characters on a scale adjacent to the screen. From the group, the operator selects a particular image.

Sequential numbering. Arriving at a specific image more speedily is accomplished in several ways. One of these is to automatically stamp sequential numbers on the documents as part of the microfilming operation. These numbers appear on the reader screen, enabling the operator to visually pinpoint images.

Image control. For even faster image location, Kodak has retrieval equipment that works with push-button simplicity. A small rectangular mark is exposed on the film next to each image during microfilming. In retrieving, the operator enters the image number on a keyboard coupled to a reader and presses a search button. The marks are electronically counted at high speed, and film travel stops at the precise image in seconds.

Binary code patterns. The most sophisticated coding of all uses binary code patterns. As each document or group of documents is microfilmed, varied code patterns that correspond to subject matter in the images are also exposed onto the film. When a magazine is inserted into the reader, the desired code numbers are entered on a control keyboard. The film code patterns are electronically scanned, and the film stops at the image or images containing the desired subject matter, all in half a minute or less. Here, indeed, is information retrieval at its highest level of selectivity and speed.

Figure 15-7 Automated microfilm retrieval methods. (Information and pictures graciously provided by Eastman Kodak Company, Rochester, N.Y.)

engineering drawings. In 1966 the U.S. Patent Office contracted to put each patent granted since 1970 on aperture cards. At that time the Commissioner of Patents, Edward J. Brenner, estimated the cards would save $500,000 per year in filling the demand for 25,000 copies of patents every day.[5]

To confuse matters further, there are *opaque microcards*. These cards vary quite a bit in size, including 3 × 5, 5 × 8, 4 × 6, and 6 × 9 inches with equally varying reduction ratios. They, too, are available in both positive or negative form. The cards are opaque, as the name implies, and have the appearance of a black and white photograph.

[5] See "Wallet Libraries," by Lee Berton. *Wall Street Journal*, vol. CLXVIII, no. 62, September 28, 1966, p. 1.

Transparent microforms generally are considered superior to opaque types because they cost less, they are more readable because the image is better, equipment is considerably better, it is easier to use higher reduction ratios thus using still less space, and copies cost less to make and are of superior quality.

A much more popular microform is *microfiche*, the latter part of the word probably derived from the French word "fiche" (pronounced fēesh) meaning card. Microfiche is sometimes referred to as a unitized microform. It is generally a flat sheet of film, 4 × 6 inches in size, with a number of images (anywhere from 60 to 98) arranged in rows (see Figures 15-5 and 15-6). In reality, the "4 × 6 inches" size is known internationally as the ISO A6 size, or as 105-mm by 148-mm. This size is the only one that has been standardized by the International Organization for Standardization (ISO), the National Micrographics Association (NMA), the American National Standards Institute (ANSI), the Department of Defense (DoD), and the Committee on Scientific and Technical Information (COSATI). These organizations have the responsibility of recommending standardized methods for processing and handling microforms. The U.S. organizations must work with the international organizations so that technology can flow easily across national boundaries.

As with the other microforms, microfiche may be either positive or negative. If positive, it appears on the viewer as black print on a white background (see Figure 15-6). Positive "fiche" are good when large numbers of photographs are used because it is easier to interpret positive images. Negative microfiche, or white print on a black background (see Figure 15-5), are used when a paper copy is of major importance. Equipment is improving quickly, however, so this emphasis may soon lose its importance.

Microfiche received its greatest boost when various government agencies began disseminating their technical reports and specifications by this method. Today many engineers have desk-top viewers and store all the documents they need in one small drawer of their desk.

Microfiche advantages include the relatively low cost of the readers, the fact that full-size copies can be made quickly, easily, and inexpensively, and that wide distribution can be handled with little cost. Microfiche also can be used for active storage files since it can be updated just by adding or pulling a microfiche (assuming an open-ended filing system). In addition, microfiche lends itself to a wide variety of applications including manufacturers parts catalogs, in-house reproduction of research and development reports, maintenance information for complex equipment installations, efficient filing of customer invoices, and patient medical records.

Disadvantages include a lack of standardization in reduction ratios and formats with corresponding confusion in equipment. Cost of input equipment is high; one method of producing microfiche is by a step-and-repeat camera which costs more than cameras used for rolls, cartridges, or aperture cards. File integrity is also of major importance. Unless automated equipment is available, a good records administrator must oversee refiling procedures. Few people realize that each misfiled microfiche generally means other microfiche also will be misfiled in a building block fashion. Twenty percent of the file can, for all intents and purposes, be considered unusable when file integrity is lost. On the other hand, users tend to react negatively toward locks, keys, security, and steel cases. Automated retrieval equipment for which no coding systems have been standardized creates further problems for users. Another storage problem is that microfiche curls when improperly stored. If equipment does not have provision for keeping the microfiche packed flat and tightly together, users will soon be pulling out not one but several of the curled and bent microfiche.

Jackets are similar to microfiche. This technique uses roll microfilm, which is cut and placed in a specific sequence within a "jacket." The jacket is usually of mylar film having good optical properties (see Figure 15-6). The advantages and disadvantages of jackets are similar to those of microfiche with one outstanding exception: the capability of adding, deleting, or making frequent changes is good with jackets. Once a jacket is filled and is ready to become a permanent record, it can be filmed and put into regular microfiche format. Two of the most frequent applications of jackets are in medical records and personnel records. Jackets are available in a variety of sizes.

Ultrafiche is the newest of the microforms, and it is surrounded by controversy. The process used by the companies producing ultrafiche is to first film the original on 35-mm and then further reduce it. Since it is still not very well known, reduction ratios are reported by varying sources to be from $60\times$ to $150\times$ and from $100\times$ to $400\times$ ($\times$ means times). One manufacturer claims 3,200 pages to a single 4×6 inch transparency, while another claims 10,000 pages, also on 4×6, while still another puts 1,000 pages on 3×6 using reduction ratios varying from $55\times$ to $90\times$. Generally speaking, ultrafiche images are reduced by at least 90 times.

The advantages of ultrafiche are obvious: they have greatly increased storage capacity, the cost of reducing the whole sheet is very inexpensive once the master is made, they are as easy to handle as microfiche, and manufacturers claim their equipment is inexpensive (always a relative term).

The disadvantages of ultrafiche include the alarming need for still another generation of unstandardized viewing and printing equipment. If a uniform system is to be developed, the existing commonly used reductions would have to be refilmed, or else the equipment would have to be considerably more sophisticated than it is now to accommodate all reductions. Cost of the original master is extremely high since it requires two steps in the process, under "clean-room" conditions. Additionally, the equipment itself is high priced, and the materials are metallic oxides requiring monochromatic light sources. Speculation concerning the tie-in of ultrafiche to data communication/computer facilities has yet to be proven.

No discussion of microform records would be complete without including COM, or *Computer Output Microfilm.* COM can be called the marriage of the computer to microfilm. It is a sophisticated technology which came about because of the computer's ability to overwhelm its users with paper and because of the limited speed of computer line printers. With COM, unwieldy paper is eliminated entirely, if desired. Instead, the information may be put directly onto microfilm, or the information may be put onto magnetic tape to be put onto microfilm later at the convenience of the user.

The COM system design must take into account the accessibility of records, flexibility both in adding and deleting data in future applications, costs of microfilm preparation, recorders and readers, a cost/performance evaluation, and timeliness. It may become necessary to make the tradeoff, or to sacrifice one item for another.

Advances in COM technology are taking place rapidly since it is obvious that to print a page and then microfilm the page is expensive and unnecessary in many cases. Although high speed impact printers will no doubt be in use for many years, the EDP manager may need to select a COM unit when computer usage changes from a high speed reproduction unit to a true information tool. When evaluating a COM system some of the following advantages and disadvantages may need to be considered.

1. Adequate supplies of lumber for paper are getting more difficult to find. As a result, paper costs are rising and a shortage of business forms is on the horizon.
2. COM printers are 100 times faster than impact printers.
3. CPU (Computer Processing Unit) time is significantly reduced over that of other methods.
4. COM equipment is easier to use.
5. COM equipment utilizes both dry and wet processing techniques. Film handling is eliminated in some.
6. It has been estimated that COM can reduce the cost of computer output as much as 80 percent.[6]
7. Labor costs are lower with COM since paper does not need to be decollated, burst, or bound.
8. COM can be updated easily.
9. COM is flexible and can be indexed easily for efficient retrieval.
10. COM has many applications.
11. COM equipment is expensive to purchase, with basic hardware and software costing anywhere from $75,000 to $150,000.[7]
12. Entry of a firm into COM usage is made easy by the use of service bureaus.

[6] See "The New Freedom in Computer Output: Part III, Computer Output Microfilm (COM)," by Dale Rhodabarger. *Computer Decisions*, vol. 2, no. 8, August 1979, p. 48.

[7] Ibid., p. 50.

13. Storage space is reduced since voluminous paper records are no longer needed.
14. Shipping costs are reduced for reports that must be mailed.
15. COM has the ability to produce graphics.
16. COM costs less than a tenth that of equivalent-capacity magnetic tapes and disks.[8]
17. A 5,000 page report that costs $236 to produce on paper and mail, can cost as little as $6 to $8 if COM generated.[9]

Selection of the correct COM unit should take many factors into account and the systems analyst should play a major role in the decision making process. The analyst will want to determine the functions for which the system is designed and for which it will be used. Some of the following steps should be undertaken before selection of a COM device.

1. Check the current system of using microfilm to determine if a COM device is needed; that is, if a COM device will enhance the system.
2. Determine if only alphanumeric or graphic output, or both, are required. (Graphic units produce both kinds of output but are, naturally, more expensive.)
3. Determine if an on-line or off-line operation is required.
4. Check the output that the computer is capable of producing against the input acceptable to COM devices.
5. Check the form of output of COM devices in relation to the form required by the current microfilm usage.
6. Determine the needs for overlays and indexing.
7. Determine the expected quality.
8. Establish speed requirements.
9. Determine the need for special features such as on-line processing and color recording.
10. Check the price range that makes the acquisition of a COM device feasible. Also consider the operating cost.[10]

When COM is selected as the processing medium, the firm must decide whether to implement an in-house COM processing facility or to use an outside service bureau. *Computing Canada,* assisted by Datacrown Limited, has listed the

[8] Burstyn, op. cit., p. 64.

[9] Ibid., p. 66.

[10] Refer to "Selecting the Right COM Unit," by George H. Harmon. *Datamation,* December 1969, pp. 102–106.

following criteria that should be used to determine whether a service bureau should be used.

1. Turnaround. The standard may be 24 hours, but some provide 4 hours.
2. Quality. Either method should adhere to standards set by the National Micrographics Association and the Canadian Micrographics Society. Quality control tests should be conducted at the end of each run.
3. Hours of service.
4. State of the art. Does the service bureau use a minicomputer to do processing that frees time from the host computer?
5. Is professional assistance available for selection of the proper applications and integration with other media for an effective system?
6. Is there a backup facility for emergencies?
7. Are appropriate cost accounting methods used?
8. Cost. Is the cost quotation best in terms of what you get, based on the above factors?

Improved technology has allowed computer-output microfilm to be combined with computer-assisted retrieval. Such combined systems are referred to as CAR/COM. While the microfilm part of the system is old technology, the computerized retrieval portion is very high technology. Kodak's KAR-4400 system is typical for medium- to high-volume users who process 3,000 to 7,000 documents daily and perform 25 or more retrievals. The smallest version, which includes a minicomputer, two display terminals, a 60-megabyte disk drive, and the necessary software, costs $76,000.[11] CAR systems can operate in an independent manner, be linked to a computer network, or be linked on-line to a mainframe computer.

A new development has to do with replacing microforms with optical disks. To retrieve a page of microfilm requires sequential searching. Because optical disks can be searched by direct access, document retrieval is significantly faster. Optical disks also use high resolution display terminals. The two largest microfilm producers, Kodak and 3M, are planning to integrate optical disk technology where possible in their current products. Because users have such a major capital investment in microfilm systems (CAR or COM), these two firms want any optical technology to be compatible with currently installed systems. In 1984, the FileNet Corporation announced a CAR-like system[12] that uses optical disks rather than microfilm. Its double-sided disks hold 40,000 pages. These disks are held in "libraries" that can hold 64 optical disks. Since up to eight libraries can be attached to the system, it has a total storage capacity of 20 million pages. This

---

[11] Burstyn, op. cit., p. 66.
[12] Ibid.

storage capacity, high resolution terminals, and faster retrieval are obvious advantages. The disadvantages are that it is not compatible with current microfilm systems, and its price is $258,000. For the systems analyst, the most important issue with regard to optical disks as a storage medium has to do with whether the firm already has embarked on an expensive microfilming program. If not, perhaps optical disks are a viable alternative.

You may have noticed that we have not been discussing records retention in terms of magnetic media (disks, reels, and so forth). This is because no one really knows how long the magnetic charge on a disk or tape can last.[13] There are various opinions as to how long records should be stored on magnetic media. Joseph Kish, who is well known in records management circles, contends that magnetic tapes and disks should not be used for storage for longer than one year.[14] Part of this is because of signal deterioration from non-usage after one year, and part of it is because of the stringent (and expensive) storage requirements needed for longer term storage. By contrast, Walter says that data stored on magnetic tape generally is considered valid for three to five years.[15] He feels that the problem is more in the wear and "print-through" of the tape than in the fading of the signal.

Diskettes are sensitive and require proper care. Users already are discovering large gaps in data on diskettes that have been stored for a year or less. As you can see, caution must be taken if users intend to store important data on magnetic media for any length of time. Microfilm has a useful span of perhaps 100 years if properly stored; paper lasts about 50 years; magnetic media *may* last as long as five years, but one to two years is more likely. Certainly, magnetic media do not appear to be viable as a permanent storage medium.

There are other drawbacks with magnetic media. First, they are not legally admissible as court evidence; microfilm and paper are. The major problem, however, has to do with the fact that so many legal documents must have signatures. Many applications require signatures, for example, in banking, laboratory notebooks, physician prescriptions for narcotics, and legal documents. We know of one laboratory situation in which the data entry clerks use touch screen data entry. At the end of each shift, the data entry operator prints out what was inputted and signs the paper copy, which serves as the legal record even though the basic information is in the computer. Two magnetic tapes are kept, one on-site and one off-site, in case of disaster.

As you can see, the newer storage media are both interesting and exciting; but, they do have serious limitations, which must be considered by anyone who wants to use them for records retention. One of these problems has been recog-

---

[13] "The Inscrutable Computer," *Forbes*, February 11, 1985, p. 12.

[14] See "Establishing Retention Periods for Magnetic Tape-Based Records," by Joseph L. Kish, Jr., *Information and Records Management*, vol. 15, no. 7, July 1981, p. 45.

[15] Refer to "Optical Digital Storage of Office and Engineering Documents," by Gerry Walter. *Journal of Information & Image Management*, vol. 17, no. 4, April 1984, p. 32.

nized by historians and archivists for the federal government who are alarmed over the loss of computerized data. Complaints from this group indicate that information systems seldom are designed to retrieve historically significant information (such as information that is 30 years old), strong policy direction is lacking at higher government levels with management of federal records by a hodgepodge of agencies, and newer technologies are causing the loss of historically significant drafts. The last problem is caused by word processing software and the growing use of electronic mail. Use of these technologies means that policy document drafts and government memos are less likely to be preserved.[16] Obviously, if these problems are taking place at the federal level, they also must be taking place in the world of corporate records retention. Both business and government depend on such records for their "memory" and for legal purposes. It is imperative that systems analysts recognize and forestall such problems in new systems they develop.

One final comment is in order with regard to any records that are stored on microfilm, magnetic, or optical media. Do not overlook these records in terms of destruction. They often contain personal or sensitive information that can be damaging to your firm if improperly destroyed. Actually, the record itself may not be damaging, but a single data item within the record may contain personal or very sensitive information. For example, while working with an international wire transfer network in banking, we found microfilmed records that contained the secret test key. People who obtained these microfilmed records could have learned the secret test key (encryption) that would enable them to interpret the wire transfers of money. This possibly could enable such a person to illegally change dollar amounts, modify the payee, or create false wire transfers.

Selected Readings

1. Aaron, C. H. "Micrographics for the Automated Office," *Journal of Information and Image Management,* vol. 17, no. 7, July 1984, pp. 29–33. [Discusses merger of "electronic filing" of source documents with micrographics.]

2. Aschner, Katherine, ed. *Taking Control of Your Office Records: A Manager's Guide.* New York: John Wiley & Sons, Inc., 1983.

3. Bernett, William A. "Long Life for Your Tapes," *Computer Decisions,* vol. 12, no. 3, March 1980, p. 81.

4. Burstyn, H. Paris. "Micrographics Shrinks Document Storage Costs," *High Technology,* vol. 5, no. 4, April 1985, pp. 64–67.

5. Caldwell, D. L. "How to Determine Which Records Need Protecting," *Office,* vol. 98, no. 3, September 1983, pp. 200, 202. [Understanding vital records.]

---

[16] See "Federal Historians Alarmed at Loss of Computerized Data," by Mitch Betts. *Computerworld,* vol. 19, no. 38, Sept. 23, 1985, p. 34.

6. Canning, B. "Records Automation," *Office Administration and Automation,* vol. 45, no. 8, August 1984, pp. 93–94. [Introduces new computer-assisted retrieval tools for records management, including personal computers, remote image transmission, and optical image storage.]

7. Carroll, John M. *Computer Security.* Los Angeles: Security World Publishing Co., Inc., 1977.

8. Ciura, Jean. "Corporate Records Scheduling: Systems Design and Planning," *Information Management,* vol. 18, no. 8, August 1984, pp. 21, 28.

9. Ciura, Jean. "Managing Media & Resources: Establishing a Records Retention Schedule for Managing Paper, Microfilm, and Computer Data," *Information Management,* vol. 18, no. 5, May 1984, pp. 12–14, 39.

10. Evans, Sherli. "Shredder Security: Keeping the 'Ordinary' Confidential," *Office Administration and Automation,* vol. 45, no. 2, February 1984, pp. 33–36, 82.

11. *Guide to Record Retention Requirements,* published annually by the *Federal Register.* Washington, D.C.: Government Printing Office number GS4.107/a:R245/981, 1955– .

12. Hill, Marjorie. "Retention Guidelines for Paper, Microfilm, Mag Tapes, Diskettes," *Information Management,* vol. 17, no. 1, January 1983, pp. 17–20.

13. Kesner, Richard M. *Automation for Archivists and Records Managers: Planning and Implementation Strategies.* Chicago: American Library Association, 1984.

14. Kish, Joseph L. "Establishing Retention Periods for Magnetic Tape-Based Records: An Outline of Legal and User Requirements," *Information and Records Management,* vol. 15, no. 7, July 1981, pp. 45–47.

15. McRedmond, John. "How to Maintain Long Life and Quality of Diskettes," *The Office,* vol. 96, no. 5, November 1982, pp. 195, 198.

16. Parker, Donn B. *Computer Security Management.* Reston, Va.: Reston Publishing Company, Inc., 1981.

17. Pennix, Gail B. "Indexing Concepts: An Overview for Records Managers," *ARMA Records Management Quarterly,* vol. 18, no. 2, April 1984, pp. 5–9.

18. Snyder, B. E. "A Cost-Benefit Analysis Method for Various Record Storage Media," *Journal of Information and Image Management,* vol. 17, no. 5, May 1984, pp. 41–47. [Uses a "detail-level window" concept with Warnier–Orr process diagrams to isolate cost centers and variable costs.]

19. Specifications for Copies from Office Copying Machines for Permanent Records. New York: American National Standards Institute. ANSI/ASTM-D3458-75.

20. Walter, Gerry. "Optical Digital Storage of Office and Engineering Documents," *Journal of Information and Image Management,* vol. 17, no. 4, April 1984, pp. 27–35.

Questions

1. In what form do records typically arrive at a records retention center?

2. What is the purpose of a records retention program?

3. Define the terms "active records," "storage life," and "legal life."

4. What does a records retention schedule include?

5. Where can the analyst look to determine what legal regulations affect records retention practices?

6. What is the starting point for initiating a records control program?

7. What methods can be used for storing records in the storage area?

8. Give some examples of the types of records that firms consider vital to recover their operations after a disaster.

9. Name five advantages of microforms.

10. Name five disadvantages of microforms.

11. Identify the two types of available 35-mm microfilm.

12. What is an aperture card?

13. Describe microfiche.

14. Identify some of the advantages and disadvantages of COM.

15. Why are records important to business?

16. Why is it more important today than previously to have a good records retention program?

17. Some records are governed by the statute of limitations. How long is this statute?

18. What is a flash form?

19. What are some of the benefits of conducting a risk analysis for a records retention program?

20. What is CAR/COM?

21. What are the advantages and disadvantages of using optical disk technology for records retention?

22. How long can magnetic media be used for records retention?

23. What is the useful life of microfilm? Paper? Magnetic tapes/disks?

SITUATION CASES

Case 15-1:   *Micrographics, Inc.*

Micrographics Inc. is a manufacturing concern that produces graphic display systems for microcomputers. The company experienced substantial growth for several years, and records retention became a problem.

The retention system was initiated when the company was a small family operation. It consisted of stacks of cardboard boxes filled with old tax forms, invoices, receivables, payables, and so forth, marked "Old Records." As the company expanded, it became obvious that some formal retention system was needed. The time required to find an old record sometimes took days, and frequently the record could not be found at all.

The office manager was assigned the task of developing a new retention system. He carefully analyzed the active, storage, and legal life of each document being used by the company. With the help of other department heads and the company lawyer, a schedule governing record storage and eventual destruction was developed. Records then in storage were analyzed, with most being destroyed.

Records determined as vital to the company were stored in fireproof underground vaults off the company premises. Other records were stored in the basement. They were filed by title of the record and box number location. A file of destruction cards was established to signal when a record was to be destroyed. The box location number was written on the box and on a 3 × 5 card. The card had the box location number, contents of the box, and the name of the originating department.

The new system was approved by the Executive Board (the owner and president of the company) and initiated.

The program progressed smoothly for several years. During that time, the company became a target of civil rights groups. They accused Micrographics of practicing discriminatory hiring procedures. The company found itself being sued after many informal meetings with civil rights representatives over a three-year period. For the last two of the three years, the company repeatedly had presented evidence in the form of job application forms in an attempt to ward off litigation. Micrographics' position was that all applicants who were refused for available jobs were unqualified on the basis of previous experience or education. The company lawyer personally retrieved all records needed from storage just prior to each meeting.

Upon learning of an actual lawsuit, the company's lawyer immediately requested that all job application forms for the previous five-year period be recalled from storage. He discovered that the only applications in storage were for the preceding 12 months. On inquiry, he determined that the other needed records had been destroyed, on schedule, the week before. Application forms were stored by each 12-month period and destroyed after being in storage for 12 months.

Questions

1. What failure in the new program allowed this embarrassing and serious situation to occur?
2. How could the office manager have lessened the chance of design errors in the system?

Case 15-2: *Software Stores Corporation*

The Software Stores Corporation was having difficulty locating records when needed, so the firm's President called a meeting to discuss the problem. During this meeting it was discovered that the firm had no official records retention program. It was decided, therefore, that a systems analyst would be hired to set up a permanent company records retention program.

The analyst who was hired was given the authority of a project manager. The analyst decided to begin by taking a records inventory of all active records being maintained by the company. The analyst, who had performed similar work before, decided to take this inventory by means of a questionnaire. After the records inventory questionnaires were returned and tabulated, the analyst proceeded to set up a records retention schedule. To set up the schedule, the analyst researched all the requirements imposed by government, other regulatory agencies, customers, and the company itself. Upon completion of this research, the analyst assigned the appropriate retention time to each type of record.

The analyst then visited each department manager, introduced himself, and proceeded to determine whether the managers concurred with the records retention schedule that was proposed for their departments. Those who disagreed were told that he would consider making the needed changes after further research. After talking with all the department managers, the analyst went to the Contracts Department to see if they had any other retention requirements. After compiling all the necessary retention information, the final records retention schedule was compiled and sent to the President for final approval.

While gathering information for the records retention schedule, the analyst noticed that the Purchasing Department filed purchase orders by customer name. Having read the company's procedures on active life filing systems, he realized that filing purchase orders by customer name was against the company's active life filing policy. The analyst, therefore, arranged a meeting with the Purchasing Department Manager, during which it was decided that the analyst would set up a new filing system simultaneously for the Purchasing Department.

When the analyst finished the new filing system in Purchasing, he proceeded to set up an inactive storage filing system. He decided to file by record title because it was both the most economic system and the easiest to maintain. The analyst even set up a destruction file which would handle destruction cards for 50 years. As part of the inactive storage system, the analyst decided the company should have two copies of its vital records, one on the premises for potential referral, with the original kept elsewhere. He noted that records stored off the company grounds should be kept in a place free of the threat of fire, flood, or theft.

When the analyst finished setting up the rest of the records retention system, including the new forms that were required, he gave the final presentation to the President and the department managers. To accompany the new system, the analyst prepared a book describing the system and all the procedures necessary for running it.

Questions

1. Did the analyst start the records inventory in the correct manner? Explain fully.
2. What did the analyst fail to do while setting up a records retention schedule?
3. Should the analyst have gotten involved in setting up a new filing system in the Purchasing Department? Explain why or why not.

Chapter 16

REPORT ANALYSIS

LEARNING OBJECTIVES

You will learn how to . . .

□ Review reporting systems.

□ Analyze reports.

□ Conduct a report analysis.

□ Evaluate the characteristics of a good report.

□ Develop exception reports.

*H*ow to Use This Chapter

Report analysis usually is a by-product of other tasks, such as designing output reports, reviewing the interactions of reports between various departments, conducting a feasibility study, or devising a records retention program. Sometimes, however, companies and government agencies schedule a separate project to review the management reporting system, analyze its reports, and make recommendations for modifying or deleting some of them.

You should use the information in this chapter when designing reports, identifying the uses to which reports are made, and especially if you have a separate report analysis project.

Further use can be made of this chapter when you are writing the feasibility study report or the final system design study report. For example, the section titled Characteristics of a Good Report can be a valuable contribution to your writing effort if you utilize its ideas *before* you write the report.

One other use for this chapter might be when you develop a records retention program. Why not get rid of unnecessary reports rather than storing them for many years?

*R*eviewing Management Reporting Systems

Because of the rapidly changing business environment, many management reporting systems have not kept pace with management's needs. In many cases the traditional paper reports (manual or computer generated) could be replaced by, or supplemented with, computer terminal inquiry and display capabilities. As a result there is a need for periodic reviews to keep pace with the changing environment. In addition, there are special circumstances that arise which require a revision in the reporting scheme. For example, a reporting system revision would be warranted by *changes* in

1. The size of the organization.
2. The structure of the organization.
3. Market conditions.
4. Management style or approach to decision making.
5. Management personnel.
6. Operational technology.

Most organizations should plan to review their reporting systems on a scheduled basis, with the time interval between reviews being relatively short. An effective review of an on-going reporting system is composed of three fundamental tasks.

1. Analysis of the information supply and the related demand.
2. Review of the utility of current reports and data collection techniques.
3. Preparation of a report on suggestions for improvement.

After all the reports have been reviewed, the data collection system should be analyzed to determine how it can be utilized best to meet the firm's information reporting needs. Some of the questions that must be considered are

1. Does the system facilitate the summarization of data as it is collected?
2. Is all of the collected data ultimately used in one or more reports?
3. Can the data collection system itself be utilized to meet some reporting requirements?
4. What steps can be taken to reduce errors?
5. Are controls being utilized to provide for the timeliness and accuracy of resulting reports?
6. Is there any way to reduce the manual effort in the reporting system?
7. Is the system properly documented?
8. Are all the reports being used or should some be eliminated?

After the review has been completed, a report presenting the results of the survey should be prepared for top management. The report should comment on the strengths and weaknesses of the existing reporting system, and it should contain specific recommendations for improvement. In order to identify the weaknesses of the existing reporting system, a thorough report analysis must be conducted. The remainder of the chapter is devoted to this subject.

What Is Report Analysis?

The objective of report analysis is the elimination of time and money spent on the preparation and distribution of unnecessary or redundant reports. In small firms, managers can personally gather the information they need for decision making by way of direct observation and contact with operating personnel. As firms grow, however, the report becomes a necessary medium for transmitting information to management. Report quality then becomes a vital factor in the firm's operations. Consistent, Accurate, Timely, Economically feasible, and Relevant (CATER) reports are necessary to assist management in its guidance of the firm. It is vitally important that reports supply information in the most useful form to the people who need it. Reports must be tailored to meet the specific needs of the management team.

Report analysis has become even more important since the advent of the computer because the computer can print reports at thousands of lines per minute. Too many reports can be worse than too few reports, especially when the information needed by management is spread too widely through the reports for convenient reading.

Usually, no single group or person is assigned the responsibility for developing a report analysis function until the firm finds itself in trouble with too many reports. The systems analysis department should handle this function from a central base, similar to the approach recommended for forms control. The report analysis group or analyst performs a coordinating function rather than one of an authoritarian nature. The analyst should obtain a copy of every report, and any instructions that go with it. A report-number file, a functional file, and a cross-reference file should be developed as explained in the section, Forms Control Methodology, in Chapter 14.

Reports can be classified into the following four general categories: *action reports* initiate or control a necessary procedure or operation; *informational reports* provide data or information for further analysis and control; *reference reports* keep the manager informed on operations; *feeder reports* consist of bits of data to be used later in conjunction with other data, another report, or for accumulating data for a decision.

Within each of these four general categories of reports, a specific report might be presented using one of the following formats. First is the scheduled report. A *scheduled report* is one that is prepared and distributed at a fixed time, such as once a week, once a month, or once a year. The person who receives a scheduled report expects the copy at a prescheduled time. Second is the on-demand report. An *on-demand report* is one that is generated upon the user's request. The report may be generated instantly or it may take a few hours or even overnight to obtain the report. The point is that when the user demands a copy of the report, the report is generated and a copy is delivered to the user. Third is the exception report. An *exception report* is a report that is generated only when certain parameters are out of line with what is expected of these parameters. When the exception report is set up, the analyst decides what will be normal, within a given set of parameters. The computer-based system automatically checks the input data against these parameters and a report is prepared only if the data are outside the limits of the parameters. If the data are within the limits that were specified originally when the report was set up, then no report is generated. One of the advantages of a computer-based reporting system is that exception reports are generated easily. An exception report saves the time of management because no report is generated unless the input data are outside of some predetermined parameters. Because of its importance, exception reporting is discussed again later in this chapter.

In summary, scheduled reports appear on a manager's desk at fixed time intervals, on-demand reports are generated only when management asks for a report, and exception reports are generated only when the data is outside of some preset limits that were developed originally by the analyst and the management of the company.

Analyzing Reports

The analyst should proceed to analyze the reports to determine whether any can be eliminated, combined, rearranged, or simplified, or whether new reports are required. The first step is to collect one copy of each report. Next the frequency of each report should be determined, that is, how often it is prepared per week or per month. The distribution of each report (who gets it and why), the total number of copies being prepared, and any other relevant information about the reports have to be evaluated. As mentioned, if the *report analysis* is to be an ongoing program, the analyst should handle it like *forms control* (see Chapter 14). In analyzing each report, the analyst should consider the following points.

1. The amount and level of detail.
2. The effect, or lack thereof, that each piece of information has on management's decision making capability.
3. The extent or completeness of the information provided. In some cases, two ineffective reports can be combined to produce one that is effective.
4. The degree of accuracy.
5. The effectiveness of the presentation. A good report presents information in a manner that aids the decision making process.
6. The clarity of the report format. Proper layout can make a report much easier to read and understand, thus making it more effective.
7. Key information should be highlighted. For example, the use of comparative data helps pinpoint critical information.
8. The report formats should be consistent from one period to another. When report formats are stable, it is much easier to review data from period to period.
9. The report "package" should be organized logically. Summary information should be on the first page. It should provide a clear index to each section of detail that supports the summary.
10. The report should be structured to provide answers to the questions that usually are asked when the report is reviewed.

After each report is studied, the analyst still has to learn the *value* of each report to the ultimate users. This is accomplished best by interviewing the people to whom the report is distributed. Questionnaires do not work well for this because people are reluctant to criticize or order the cancellation of a report in writing. The same people, however, may be quite candid in a discussion of the report. The analyst must be certain to interview every person on the report's distribution list. The analyst might ask the following questions to determine the importance of the report being studied.

1. How is this report essential to the work of your department?
2. How often do you use your copy of this report?
3. How many data or pieces of information on this report are *not* used?
4. How many people use the report? Do you give it to anyone else?
5. Are the data and information on this report necessary for
   a. Making day-to-day action decisions?
   b. Establishing control over your operations?
   c. Checking the accuracy of specific procedures?
   d. Keeping informed on general conditions?
6. What would be the effect on your work if you
   a. Did not receive this report?
   b. Received this report less frequently?
   c. Received less data or information than at the present time?
   d. Received more data or information than at the present time?
7. What other reports, records, or forms are prepared from the data contained on this report?
8. Can the data or information on this report be located in any other sources?
9. Is this report easy to understand and easy to use?
10. How long do you keep your copy of this report?
11. How and where do you file your copy of this report?
12. Do you make copies of this report for anyone else? If so, how many? For whom?
13. How often do you refer to this report after its original distribution and use?
14. The cost of preparing this report has been estimated at $——. Do you consider your use of the report worth this expense?

The analyst now studies all answers to the questions for the report being evaluated. For example, in questions 1 and 2 the analyst is trying to learn the user's ranking of importance for the report. In question 5 the analyst is cross-checking the user's ranking of importance because any report used to make day-to-day action decisions is much more important than a report that just keeps the user informed on general conditions. Questions 3 and 8 show what parts of the report may be eliminated, from that specific user's viewpoint. Questions 4, 7, and 12 may reveal heretofore unknown, bootleg, or unauthorized uses of the report. Questions 6, 9, 10, 11, and 13 are used to get general background on the feelings of the user about the real importance of the report. Finally, question 14 reveals the economic importance of the report. If *all* the users say "It is not worth the expense for me but think of the other users," then perhaps the report should be eliminated.

After careful study the analyst should decide upon some definite recommendations with regard to whether any reports can be eliminated, combined, rearranged, or simplified, or whether new reports should be developed. The analyst should prepare a summary of the report analysis survey. The summary should mention whether interviews and/or questionnaires were used. Also note any discrepancies between actual utilization of a report and the claimed utilization of a report. Make graphic comparisons between the current and any proposed reports, including detailed instructions on how the proposed reports will be prepared. Show the recommended distribution of all reports, even if it is the same as before the report analysis survey. Make recommendations and cost comparisons between the old and any recommended new reports. Remember, economy is usually the best method of justifying change in a profit-oriented firm.

Criteria of a Good Reporting System

A good reporting system generates just the right amount of reports, at the right time, with the right amount of information, and to the right people. All too often a reporting system either buries the manager with too many reports or details, or it does not offer enough *usable* information.

A good reporting system conforms to the company's formal communications structure so that accountability for results is clarified in the organization. For each separate department or functional area, the reporting system reports on all the important controllable elements of performance.

A good reporting system represents a plan of control. The information furnished by each report should tie in with the other reports for good coordination and standardization of concepts. As reports go up through the higher levels of the organization, they should become more condensed. The detail belongs in the lower-level reports.

A good reporting system is under continuous surveillance so it can be modified to meet changing needs. It is very important to have an easy method for managers to use so they can delete unnecessary reports or criticize reports that are not doing what they were designed to do.

As mentioned, a good reporting system puts out reports that are consistent, accurate, timely, economically feasible, and relevant; and the reports are distributed only to those persons responsible for the area being reported upon.

Characteristics of a Good Report

A good report covers an element of performance that has a significant bearing on the goals of the area receiving the report. It measures performance by comparing actual results with the planned or forecasted results. It reports only the essentials so the manager can quickly learn the whole story.

Managers are at the mercy of their reporting system. When they are not given consistent information, decision making is undertaken at reduced confidence levels and intuitive judgment is the order of the day. Managers often get

1. Too much information and information that is not relevant.
2. Too little information and too few specific facts.
3. No information because it is suppressed. This is caused by reluctance to impart information that may reflect unfavorably upon some department.
4. Information that is too late.
5. Information that is unverified. Information of questionable validity may be used, but with the highest risk.

A good report is aimed at controllable items. It segregates controllable and noncontrollable items so the report is easy to understand and easy to use. It focuses attention on out-of-line performance by accenting significant trends.

A good report appears in a format that is easy to understand, and it is expressed in the language of the report user. For example, if the report user wants the figures in person-hours per week, report it in person-hours per week—so long as all managers are able to make conversions to each other's preferred terms and ratios. Or, better yet, let the computer make the conversion.

Weaknesses of Reports

We know that reports are essential to the operation of an organization; however, they generally have their weaknesses. Unfortunately, reports usually are not designed to forecast or promote action; they are designed to report historical actions, such as accomplishments. So, for example, why not publish a "cost increase report" rather than a "cost reduction report"? (Because costs are increasing faster than they are decreasing.) This focuses attention on the costs that are increasing the fastest.

Exception Reporting

Exception reporting is a convenient tool for management control. Although it is not a new technique, it is being used more successfully than ever now that the computer is here to process the huge quantities of data generated by today's complex organization.

Basically, exception reports spotlight only the unusual situations. Situations not reported can be assumed to be normal. Exception reporting facilitates the management-by-exception principle, wherein

1. Management plans are made for operating a program.
2. Milestones and standards are agreed upon for measuring program performance.
3. Valid methods of measuring *actual* performance are devised.
4. Report formats are designed to spotlight only the significant deviations from planned performance.
5. The computer usually is used to process the data and print the reports, so that the information is available in time for meaningful action.
6. The reports are distributed to the personnel responsible for keeping plans on the right track. If a report shows a detrimental deviation from standard, either corrective action is taken to put things back on course, or the plan or standard itself is adjusted.

Exception reporting generally is used as a tool for the control of a function. For example, the *quality* control of a firm's products is becoming an increasingly important focus. Product quality is a vital weapon of business competition, and must be preserved at some economic standard. Anything that deviates from this standard is reported.

A firm may decide to install a system of reports which spotlight unusual situations or trends in the following

1. Customer complaint rate.
2. Warranty claims.
3. Product returns.
4. Gain or loss of customers because of quality.

For each of these items, some rate must be agreed upon as standard, either in economic terms or in whatever terms are appropriate to the product or company. For example, a company may decide that product returns for quality deficiencies are considered normal if they are no higher than 2 percent of sales. Management may decide to apply this standard to several products.

Tools with return rate over 2% of all
tools sales due to quality deficiencies

For the month of October

Problem tools	Return rate (% of sales)	Outlets reporting problem
40162 Wrench	6.4	1 2 3 4 5 6
40671 Pliers	5.2	1 2 3
51611 Clamp	3.1	1 2 3
62361 Hammer	2.7	2 3 5
No other problems	----	--------------------------------

Figure 16-1 Exception report.

Next, a valid means of obtaining the data needed to measure the dollar value of returns at each of six outlets must be found. They may solve this formidable problem with a central computer receiving the data from terminals in the outlet stores. Even though enough data may be collected to present a detailed quality control report for each product, the final report may contain only a handful of problem situations (Figure 16-1) because the final report only reports exceptions to the 2 percent, as stated above.

The report also could contain analysis data related to the problem tools, such as last month's figures, department responsible, actual defects reported, and so on. All of these things relate to the exceptional cases listed on the report. The report should not, however, list the figures for tools that are not causing any problems. Instead the report reads at a glance since only the problems are reported. All other products (there may be 1,000 more) are assumed to be in control (less than 2 percent returns) and require no special attention.

Many problems exist in today's complex organizations, but the serious problems are few and far between. Exception reporting enables management to concentrate its action where it is needed most. Computerized exception reporting allows the organization to make a faster response to trouble than ever before in business history. Some other areas in which it has been employed successfully include: (1) out-of-balance conditions in accounting systems; (2) inventory stockouts and backorders; (3) microelectronic part failures; (4) project delays; (5) excess overtime worked; (6) excess and obsolete inventory reports; and (7) budget overruns.

Our examples above are only a few of the hundreds of exception reporting applications now in common use in business and industry.

Selected Readings

1. Benson, B. A. "Computer Graphics for Financial Management," *Management Accounting,* vol. 65, no. 7, January 1984, pp. 46–49. [Consolidate most important financial reports to fine tune exception reporting.]
2. Hirt, John. "Besting the Paperwork Beast of Burden," *Journal of Forms Management,* vol. 9, no. 2, July/December 1984, pp. 6–7. [Paperwork audit to control cost of forms processing.]
3. Kerrigan, Douglas. "Do You Really Have Control of Your Paperwork System?" *Modern Office* (Australia), vol. 23, no. 2, March 1984, pp. 38–40. [Forms audit to determine essential forms, make them more readable, and lower costs.]
4. King, Donald W., and Edward C. Bryant. *The Evaluation of Information Services and Products.* Washington, D.C.: Information Resources Press, 1971.
5. "Staying in Control: Making the Right Decisions Requires the Right Data," *Small Business Report,* vol. 9, no. 8, August 1984, pp. 37–40. [Effective reports for top management.]

Questions

1. Under what circumstances is a reporting system revision warranted?

2. An effective review of an on-going reporting system is composed of what tasks?

3. What type of questions should be asked when you are undertaking the review of a data collection system?

4. What is the objective of report analysis?

5. Identify the four categories into which reports can be classified.

6. Define the term "scheduled report."

7. What is the analyst's objective in analyzing a report?

8. What should the analyst consider in analyzing each report?

9. Which is the best technique—a questionnaire or an interview—for the analyst to learn of the value of each report from the viewpoint of the user? Why?

10. What are the criteria of a good report system?

11. What are the characteristics of a good report?

12. How does exception reporting facilitate the management-by-exception principle?

13. When conducting the report analysis study, what is the object of asking these two questions: "How many data or pieces of information on this report are not used?" and "Can the data or information on this report be located in any other sources?"

SITUATION CASES

Case 16-1: *Visicon Corporation*

The Marketing Manager of Visicon Corporation was deluged with information in report form that she felt to be irrelevant. Since most of her time was spent reading these reports, she asked the Manager of the Systems Department to evaluate the problem.

Following this request, the Systems Department Manager assigned one of his best analysts to the project with the understanding that he was to eliminate, combine, rearrange, or simplify all possible marketing reports.

The analyst's first step was to determine the frequency of each Marketing Department report. He then checked the distribution of each report to determine who got it and why, the total number of copies prepared, and other relevant information.

After accomplishing these important steps he wanted to learn the value of each of these reports to the ultimate users. By interviewing report recipients the analyst was able to ascertain how users valued the reports. This is a list of questions he asked during interviews.

1. How is this report essential to the work of your department?
2. How often do you use your copy of this report?
3. How many people use this report?
4. Are the data and information on this report necessary for
   a. Making day-to-day decisions?
   b. Establishing control over your operations?
   c. Checking the accuracy of specific procedures?
   d. Keeping informed on general conditions?
5. What would be the effect on your work if you
   a. Received less data or information than at the present time?
   b. Received more data or information than at the present time?
6. What other reports, records, or forms are prepared from the data contained on this report?
7. Is this report easy to understand and easy to use?
8. How long do you keep your copy of this report?
9. How and where do you file your copy of this report?
10. How often do you refer to this report after its original distribution and use?
11. The cost of preparing this report has been estimated at $———. Do you consider your use of the report worth this expense?

When the interviews were concluded the analyst studied all answers. For example, from questions 1 and 2 he learned the users' ranking of importance for the report. In question 4 he cross-checked the users' ranking of importance; any report which was used to make day-to-day decisions was more important than a report that kept the users informed on general conditions. Questions 3 and 6 revealed unknown or unauthorized users of the report. Questions 5, 7, 8, 9, and 10 gathered feelings of the users about the real importance of the report. Finally, question 11 revealed the economic importance of the report.

Feeling confident that he had covered all aspects of this survey, the analyst prepared his summary. The summary included the fact that he had conducted interviews and also noted the discrepancies between actual utilization of the report and claimed utilization. His recommendation was that the reports currently being distributed were important and should continue to be generated. There was no way to combine, rearrange, or simplify the marketing reports.

Questions

1. Was this project started correctly?
2. Were the interviews complete?

Case 16-2: *Electrocomp, Inc.*

Electrocomp, Inc., an electronics firm located on the East Coast, was engaged in selling a wide variety of electronic parts.

The President met with the Sales Manager, who was asked to explain certain situations that had developed in the Sales Department. At the outset, the Sales Manager complained that he was "flooded" with work and did not have time to waste because keeping up with all the paperwork and weekly sales reports consumed most of his time. The President understood this problem and could sympathize with the Sales Manager's burden, but still wanted an explanation of these situations. The Manager explained that although sales in all districts were adequate, there were a number of salespeople who were not "producing." The President questioned this explanation. The Sales Manager mumbled something about it "being buried in the sales report," and that he would have to look it up.

The second problem was that of a high rate of sales rejections because of bad credit. This problem embarrassed the Sales Manager since he had not known it existed. He stated that the credit verification was performed automatically without any supervision or reporting by the Credit Clerk.

Both the President and Sales Manager agreed that the problems appeared to be related to the department's inadequate reporting system. An analyst from the Systems Department was asked to help solve the problem.

Questions

1. What appears to have been the problem in the reporting system with regard to nonproducing salespeople and a high rate of sales rejections?
2. What kind of report was needed in each case?

Chapter 17

PROCEDURE WRITING

LEARNING OBJECTIVES

You will learn how to . . .

☐ Prepare to write a procedure.

☐ Understand why procedures are required.

☐ Write a narrative procedure.

☐ Write a step-by-step outline procedure.

☐ Write a playscript procedure.

☐ Recognize how structured English and tight English can mesh with other procedure writing styles.

☐ Understand the advantages and disadvantages of the various procedure writing styles.

☐ Use procedure writing techniques.

☐ Identify various types of documentation used by organizations.

☐ Avoid the most common mistakes of procedure writing.

*W*hy Write Procedures . . . *Four Basic Reasons*

Before discussing the four basic reasons for writing procedures, the reader should be familiar with the following definitions.

SUBJECT:
: The topic or central theme of the procedure.

SCOPE:
: The area or range that the procedure will encompass.

REFERENCES:
: The titles of any documents that have a governing or otherwise vital bearing upon the procedure. For example, if the procedure is necessary for compliance with a military specification, that specification title should be referenced.

GOALS:
: What the firm is trying to accomplish with the procedure.

POLICY:
: Management guidelines for regulating progress toward the firm's goals. They set rational limitations to manager's actions. Policies are behavioral guides that may be originated by management, appealed to superiors from subordinates to resolve particular problems, or imposed by external forces that demand compliance. Policies set objectives and usually are given as general statements.

PROCEDURE:
: These are guides to action; they are more specific than policies. Procedures seek to avoid disorganized activity by directing, coordinating, and articulating operations. They are a series of step-by-step instructions that explain how to carry out the policies. Procedures explain *what* is to be done, *who* will do it, and *how* it will be done.

SYSTEM:
: A network of interrelated procedures that are joined together in order to perform an activity.

Procedures are the road map of a system. The procedures explain, usually in minute detail, how the system should be operated. Four basic reasons for writing procedures are

1. To record and preserve the company's methods of operation and previous experiences. They record historically what has proven to be good practice and what has failed. They elicit economy in operations by enabling management to avoid the cost of recurrent investigations. By imposing consistency across the organization and through time, procedures help direct all activities toward common goals. The company's methods of operation must be preserved because employees forget the details, purposes, or tech-

nical considerations involved, and so on. Hopefully, recorded experiences ensure that mistakes of the past are not repeated.

2. To facilitate the training of new employees and acquaint experienced employees with new jobs or new systems. Written procedures standardize the job, and they ensure that the employee gets all the details of the job.

3. To establish a basis of control. Procedures serve to delegate authority to subordinates to make decisions within the framework of the policies devised by management. The written procedure gives a standardized basis from which to regulate and evaluate employee performance.

4. To force an examination and evaluation of the procedure or of the system itself. Written procedures help establish a benchmark to compare with past or future operating methods. Written procedures help both management and employees resolve questions about how the job should be performed.

*P*rior to Procedure Writing

There are a few things that you must do prior to writing procedures. You may want to launch right into the writing phase, but you need to think first about the following tasks. They require your attention before you can do any writing.

Make sure you have copies of any procedures that currently are in force or should be in force. Even if these procedures are not followed closely, they should be reviewed.

Try to empathize with the potential reader of this procedure. In other words, determine who will be responsible for its implementation. Try to get to know the potential users of this procedure. Remember that empathy is mentally entering into the feeling or spirit of other people in order to understand them better. When you understand them, you can write procedures that are more acceptable to them.

Make sure you understand how the current system operates and how you want the new system to operate. This helps you write clear and concise procedures. Many systems analysts start writing procedures before they clearly understand the system. This is a mistake!

Make sure you know the jargon of the area for which you are writing the procedure. If you use unknown jargon, the procedure may not be understandable and, therefore, may be rejected (not used or only used partially).

Finally, think through the procedure and try to picture it in your mind. This may appear to be daydreaming, but sit down and try to picture visually the work flow about which you are going to write. You may be surprised to find that, as you imagine the work flow, certain problems may appear with regard to how you plan to write the procedure. In other words, daydream your way through the procedure prior to committing it to paper.

Styles of Procedure Writing

Basically, procedures are written in one of three styles, but it is quite permissible to write a procedure in whatever manner makes it clear and easy to understand. The three basic styles of writing procedures are

- ☐ Narrative.
- ☐ Step-by-step outline.
- ☐ Playscript.

The *narrative procedure* is composed of words that make sentences and sentences that make paragraphs. The overall objective is to write a story that tells what should be done, who does it, when it is done, and how it is done. The narrative should include everything that is important to the procedure, including charts and graphs that simplify things for the reader. Narrative format not only is the hardest to write, but it is also the hardest and most boring to read.

The biggest problem with the narrative style is the smooth transition that is required between various steps of a procedure. Most people can make a smooth transition from one subject to another when they are speaking, but find it extremely difficult to make this smooth transition when writing. For this reason, we propose the following three-step plan for writing narrative procedures.

First, make a two-level outline of the entire procedure. This is done by writing down the point you wish to make (what/how it is to be done), and then just below that, the various ideas or sub-points that support the major point you wish to make. For example, use bullets for the major points or topics, and dashes for the sub-topics that support the major point. Look at the following as an example of what we mean.

- ☐ Refund desk.
  - –Pay refunds.
  - –Checks.
  - –No cash.
  - –Cashier cashes checks.
- ☐ Refunds (preceding day).
  - –Meal tickets.
  - –Seminar tickets.
- ☐ Registrant.
  - –Sign, member number, chapter.
  - –Blue refund card (Form 81-162).

□ Refund desk.
  −Journal (Form 84-180).
  −Cancel or paid.
  −Prepare check (Form 80-10).
  −Send blue card to cashier.

Second, use this outline to dictate your narrative style procedure. We propose that you dictate the draft procedure from the two-level outline because dictating helps you make relatively smooth transitions from one subject to another. As we mentioned previously, this is because people naturally change subjects more easily when they are speaking than when they are writing. Using the outline, dictate the procedure the way you think it should be. Incidentally, if you followed our earlier recommendation of daydreaming to picture the procedure's flow, your dictation following the two-level outline should go extremely well.

Third, after receiving the typed copy back from the word processing center or typist, edit it and have it retyped. This step is to help you polish the procedure after some time has elapsed between dictation and editing. People who write narrative style procedures by first using dictation not only tend to save a lot of time, but also produce a far more readable, understandable, and acceptable procedure.

Figure 17-1 shows an example of original dictation as it was returned from the word processing center after typing. Figure 17-2 shows the same procedure after editing, and Figure 17-3 shows the final narrative procedure. Notice that form numbers were added during the editing process. The dictated version can be shown to users who may question such major omissions or point out statements that are in error.

The *step-by-step outline procedure* walks the reader through the process. Item-by-item the reader sees what each step is. References to various parts of the procedure are made easily because of the roman numeral, letter, or number identification of each step. An example of good outline format appears below.

I. Refund desk.
  A. Pay all refunds by check.
    1. Do not make a direct cash payment.
    2. If registrant wants cash, send person to cashier to cash the check.
  B. Do not pay refunds on
    1. Meal tickets unless surrendered one day preceding the event.
    2. Seminar tickets unless surrendered one day preceding the event.

    II. Registrant.
      A. Sign name, member number, and name of chapter on
        1. Back of seminar ticket.
        2. Blue refund card (Form 81-162).
      B. Member number may be omitted.
   III. Refund desk.
      A. Use refund journal (Form 84-180).
        1. Enter cancellation.
        2. Enter refund paid.
      B. Prepare refund check (Form 80-10) and give refund check to registrant.
      C. Send blue refund card to the head cashier's office.

A step-by-step outline of a procedure is the easiest style of procedure to read because each phase has a roman numeral (I, II, III, etc.). The divisions within these phases (A, B, 1, 2, a, b) spell out the what, who, when, how, and other information required to explain the procedure.

The *playscript method* of procedure writing is also a what, who, when, and how type of procedure. The playscript style uses sequence numbers, actors, action verbs, and a straight chronological sequence of who does what in the procedure. The sequence numbers (1, 2, 3, etc.) list the sequence of steps in their chronological order. The actors are the employees. They are listed by their job function or job title. Action verbs are present tense verbs like those used in data flow diagrams. An example of the playscript method is given below.

1. Refund desk	Pay all refunds by check. Do not make direct cash payment. If registrant wants cash, send person to the cashier to cash the check. Do not pay refunds on meal tickets or seminar tickets unless surrendered one day preceding the event.
2. Registrant	Sign name, member number, and the name of chapter on the back of the seminar ticket and also on the blue refund card (Form 81-162). Member number may be omitted.
3. Refund desk	Enter cancellation and refund paid on refund journal (Form 84-180). Prepare refund check (Form 80-10) and give refund check to registrant. Send blue refund card to the head cashier's office.

In the Chapter 2 discussion of minispecifications, we described how structured English and tight English are used to show the logic of a structured

```
      The refund desk (Mary Johnson) is responsible for

paying by check only.  No cash will be paid out.  If a

student really wants to receive cash they must take their

check to the cashier.

      Refunds are paid only on meal tickets and seminar

tickets on the same day.  They must be surrendered one

day proceding the event.

      The person requesting the refund must sign their

name, member number, and chapter number on thier meal

or seminar tickets.  They must also fill out the blue

refund card.

      After this, Mary Johnson will prepare a check,

journal form 84-180, noting cancellation or refund, and

send the blue card to the cashier's office.
```

Figure 17-1 Original dictation.

analysis process. If you compare the Chapter 2 examples with those just described, you can see that structured and tight English are similar to the step-by-step outline procedure. The difference is that structured English follows very strict rules of logic, syntax, and vocabulary. Tight English is as concise logically as structured English, but it is written in a more familiar manner. Tight English falls somewhere between structured English and the step-by-step outline procedure. It is quite acceptable to use either the structured or tight English styles of

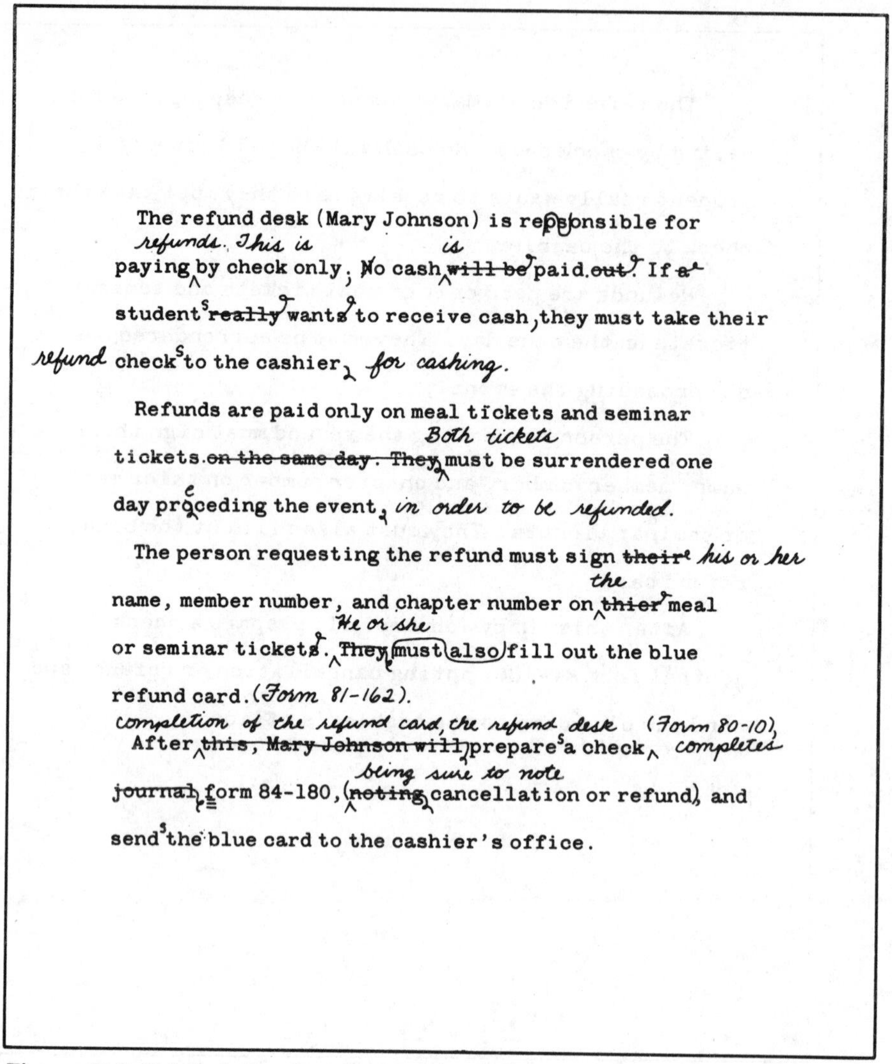

The refund desk (Mary Johnson) is responsible for
~refunds.~ This is
paying by check only; No cash ~will be~ is paid. ~out.~ If a
student ~really~ wants to receive cash, they must take their
refund check to the cashier, for cashing.

Refunds are paid only on meal tickets and seminar
Both tickets
tickets. ~on the same day.~ They must be surrendered one
day proceeding the event, in order to be refunded.

The person requesting the refund must sign ~their~ his or her
the
name, member number, and chapter number on ~thier~ meal
He or she
or seminar tickets. ~They~ must also fill out the blue
refund card. (Form 81-162).
completion of the refund card, the refund desk (Form 80-10)
After ~this, Mary Johnson will~ prepare a check, completes
being sure to note
journal form 84-180, ~noting~ cancellation or refund, and
send the blue card to the cashier's office.

Figure 17-2 Original dictation showing editing.

procedure writing, but they are less familiar to users and may not be accepted by them.

In summary, you may not be able to choose a preferred method because the organization already may use a standard style of procedure writing. On the other hand, if you do have a choice, the step-by-step outline method usually is easiest with regard to writing sentences and developing transitions between ideas. Also, outlining allows you to use short, declarative sentences that are easier to formulate and write.

The refund desk (Mary Johnson) is responsible for
paying refunds. This is by check only; no cash is paid.
If students want to receive cash, they must take their
refund checks to the cashier for cashing.

Refunds are paid only on meal tickets and seminar
tickets. Both tickets must be surrendered one day
preceding the event in order to be refunded.

The person requesting the refund must sign his or her
name, member number, and chapter number on the meal or
seminar ticket. He or she also must fill out the blue
refund card (Form 81-162).

After completion of the refund card, the refund
desk prepares a check (Form 80-10), completes Form 84-180
(being sure to note cancellation or refund), and sends
the blue card to the cashier's office.

Figure 17-3 The retyped procedure after editing and retyping.

Regardless of the method chosen, remember that the purpose of procedures
is to explain what is to be done, who is to do it, and how it is to be accomplished.

Techniques of Writing Procedures

Written procedures do not spell out the *why* of each step in the procedure.
Because of this, they are considerably more simplified and condensed. Written
procedures should specify clearly the actions required by the employee. Writ-

ten procedures may be easier to write and may give the user a much clearer concept of the course of action if the following techniques are adopted by the procedure writer.

Devise a logical outline before writing the procedure. This outline should be a rough draft of the sequence of steps within the procedure. Avoid writing in circles. Instead, follow the step-by-step sequence. Use charts, graphs, and examples of forms when they make the procedure clearer and simpler. Even decision tables or other matrix methods may be used, for example, in an administrative routine. Flowcharts and data flow diagrams are sometimes used, but the analyst should keep in mind that they should be used only for people who thoroughly understand them. Obviously, a person who does not know one symbol from another could not locate needed information through the use of one.

Main headings, divisional headings, and subdivisional headings may be used to break the procedure into separate understandable steps. Write short sentences (10 words or less) or short paragraphs (one idea per paragraph). For simplicity in making necessary changes, structure the outline in an "open-ended" format. For example, a decimal arrangement allows for additions and deletions. The use of boldface print for new subjects helps the user spot quickly what is needed.

There are three essentials to consider in procedure writing. *Layout* is the physical placement of the items on the page. *Style* is the wording that is used. It may be imperative stating who, what, how, when, and so forth; or it may be declarative in the manner of a policy statement. The third consideration is the *format*. This is the logical sequence of events mentioned above.

Indexing is essential for a usable procedure manual, for it is the key to information retrieval. A table of contents is helpful for a general approach to a manual; but an index that uses the vocabulary of the users makes it a unique usable tool. The most frequently cited reason for nonuse of manuals is that "no one can ever find anything." There are usually two main reasons for this lack of utility; either the correct (i.e., needed) information is not included, or if it is included, indexing is inadequate so it cannot be found.

When a form is introduced, include its identification number. Then, in the index to the procedure, list all the forms used in that procedure. List the forms both by form name and form number. Also include a filled-out facsimile of each form in the appendix to the procedure.

Explain the filing systems used for records, reports, forms, or any other paper used in the procedure. Describe the type of filing equipment used and the method of indexing. Give examples if it will make the indexing method more clear to the reader.

Procedures should be direct and to the point. Use present tense verbs and other action words in a straightforward style of writing that moves the reader through the operations smoothly.

There should be a method of disseminating and updating the procedures.

One method is to bind the procedures manual like a book and reprint the entire manual every two or three months. Only *critical* procedure changes are distributed, by memo, between reprintings of the book. With this method, a large, complex organization can feel reasonably sure that its procedure manuals are always current (within three months) and that old manuals are disposed of completely (since all pages are bound together).

An alternate method is to distribute the procedures manual in a loose-leaf notebook. With this method, new or revised procedures are distributed on loose-leaf pages. Users update their own procedure manuals by removing obsolete pages and inserting the updated pages. (If this method is used, all revision pages should be dated.) It is a good policy to have the department secretary keep one copy of a procedure manual updated for the department even though various people in the department have personal copies. This can be the master copy for department use. We suggest this because most people do not like to file new procedures in loose-leaf format. The most common filing methods are to place the procedure in a "to-be-filed" tray where it remains indefinitely, or the new procedure is inserted in the front of the loose-leaf binder where it remains until someone needs to use the procedures and updates them properly.

*T*ypes of Written Documentation

Written procedures are one kind of documentation. Let us take this opportunity to list several forms of documentation which usually are found in medium-size or larger firms.

1. Procedure manuals contain detailed step-by-step information about how a particular operation or activity is to be carried out.

2. Policy manuals contain information on management's attitudes concerning how various phases of the business should be conducted. Policies normally state general guidelines and imply what course of action should be followed.

3. Organization manuals contain information concerning the structure of a business, such as corporate objectives, organization charts, lines of authority, extent of centralization or decentralization, management job descriptions, and so forth.

4. Systems studies contain a review of current systems, system requirements, and new system recommendations.

5. Programming documentation contains program flowcharts, system structure charts, in-line documentation, narrative descriptions, input/output format descriptions, file descriptions, and so forth.

6. Program run descriptions contain information on how a computer program is to be run. They include disk or tape instructions, restart procedures, and checkpoint indicators.

7. Computer library procedures specify magnetic tape and disk storage methods. Also included are computer hardware and software manuals.

8. Standard operating procedure manual "for the data processing area" contains the standard procedures for systems analysis, programming, and computer operations. This manual also may contain the department's organization charts and job descriptions.

9. Structured design documentation, such as context diagrams, data flow diagrams, and so forth.

*P*rocedure Writing in Retrospect

Procedures are unlike policies in that they are more specific and provide detailed instructions for operating activities. Policies imply a general course of action, not a specific set of steps to carry out that action.

When writing or evaluating written procedures there are many general considerations that the analyst must observe in order to get things right the first time. First, the analyst should be clear on the problems and objectives involved. The analyst should be satisfied that sufficient investigation has been performed to ensure that the procedure is realistic and adequate. A hasty approach usually results in an unusable procedure. The analyst must be sure that any relevant contractual requirements are covered, and that management planning and other systems in progress are compatible with the procedure being devised.

The analyst should be alert to the possibility of becoming negatively involved in *departmental interactions* (Chapter 5). Sometimes a manager who seeks control of additional activities requests a procedure that gives him or her control in that area. When this occurs, the analyst usually receives a one-sided view of the proposal and goes to work on changes that may have a considerable impact on another manager's department. The analyst should look for this type of situation by always studying the potential effects of the changes on other departments. Suspicions should be aroused if no clear and objective need can be established for the new or modified procedure.

It is also very important to assess the changes as they relate to other procedures. Sometimes hasty changes are written and implemented before it is learned that they contradict a dozen other important procedures. This kind of backfire is especially bad for the analyst's image and reputation in the firm since it attracts a lot of negative attention. It is wise to remember that people resist change. If they can prove that the changes are detrimental to efficient or effective operations they may attack the analyst's competence. Analysts *cannot* afford to have this happen very often because it is difficult to do any systems work around the firm if the other employees have lost respect for the analyst. The analyst, therefore, should be very cautious in sizing up the potential hazards that exist in any project.

Analysts sometimes think that going on record (by memo to their supervisor or other authority) and predicting a fiasco will protect them from any ill effects that result. However, if the analyst is identified with a poor procedure in the eyes of the rank and file, the damage is already done. What can one do? It is hard to say, but we recommend that the analyst scrutinize such a situation and then try to convince management that the changes will do more harm than good. Unfortunately, a systems analyst can expect to be involved in many such difficulties.

There is a time and place for the fast, patchup procedure job. When an urgent need for change occurs, the analyst should be able to assess the problem quickly and devise a temporary solution that will suffice until a better routine can be devised, or until the emergency is gone. For example, if the normal speed of paperwork in the firm is too slow to keep up with the schedule requirements of a certain customer's orders, the analyst must find a way to expedite the routine for that customer's paperwork. The analyst may shortcut some steps, or design a faster form to process that customer's transaction. In any event, fast action may be required since the customer may be a valuable one whose demands must be satisfied. Such emergencies are called "firefighting" by systems people, and they occur rather frequently. The important step is to follow up after the patch job is done to be sure that either the emergency has subsided, or that an adequate and economic procedure is developed to convert the emergency to a controlled routine. When dealing with firefighting, the analyst has to be careful to avoid a reputation-damaging sloppy job. But the criticism that will follow if one is too cautious and slow in taking action also must be avoided. Again the analyst walks a tightrope!

A procedure should be checked carefully to be sure that it will work on all shifts the firm runs. Usually there are fewer people on evening and graveyard shifts, and there are always fewer authorities and decision makers present then. If the analyst writes a procedure that requires an engineer's signature on a form, the procedure may not operate on a shift when there is no engineer available. There are many differences between the operations of different shifts. The analyst has to learn how these differences will affect the procedure being developed.

The analyst should ensure that the steps of the procedure are not unnecessarily fixed in serial sequence, that is, a rigid sequential order. It is best to design the steps so as many as possible can be performed simultaneously. For example, if certain extra data for future analysis are picked up by a procedural step, do not allow this step to delay the more vital operations by placing it in series order with them. Instead, route a copy to the area that provides the data while the main document continues in the processing stream. Or find some other way of obtaining the data. The point is that the vital line functions of a procedure should be identified and steps designed to get them done with minimal delay. Always explore the possibilities of simultaneous or optional sequences of procedural operations.

The analyst should keep track of the procedure's operating time during the design. There should be a reasonable estimate of the acceptable maximum time. The most effective procedure in the world is useless to the firm if it is too slow.

The analyst should evaluate the operations of the procedure to be sure that none are excessively rigid in their requirements. For example, an analyst might have the impression that a certain checking operation is vitally important to the management of the department. For this reason the procedural step might be written as one that requires the time and signature of some person in the department. This might cause bottlenecks when that person is unavailable. The analyst always should question operations that are liable to be slowed by such circumstances, and the procedure should be designed to run at the lowest possible level of authority in the area.

Briefly, the following checkpoints, if observed with those previously discussed, will bring the analyst and the procedure into the clear in most cases.

1. Are the procedural steps in the *best* order?
2. Can any steps be eliminated?
3. Will the procedure accommodate present and future work volumes as well as management-imposed requirements?
4. Are there enough copies of each form? Too many?
5. Can mechanization be used economically?
6. Will the procedure accommodate unusual transactions?
7. Are any of the steps too complicated for the abilities of operating personnel?
8. Has the procedure been scanned rigorously for potential bottlenecks?
9. Can statistics or sampling be used to shortcut any operations?
10. Are the steps designed for operation at the lowest level of authority possible?

In closing this section we might caution the analyst that all too often systems people insist upon being given a free hand to create what they feel will be a good system or procedure for the firm. This is fine; but the wise analyst seeks advice and concurrence on ideas before getting married to them. And one should stand ready at all times to change personal ideas to whatever form better suits the objectives of the company or the area under study.

Selected Readings

1. Berry, Elizabeth. "A Practical Approach for Standardizing User Documents," *Journal of Systems Management*, vol. 35, no. 7, July 1984, pp. 8–11. [Setting minimum requirements for user guides.]

2. Eischen, Martha. "Documentation for the User," *Modern Office Technology*, vol. 29, no. 4, April 1984, p. 140. [Types of documentation and what they should include.]

3. Herdman, Patricia C. "How to Write Useful Computer Manuals," *Canadian Datasystems*, vol. 16, no. 3, March 1984, p. 67. [Guidelines for writing good manuals.]

4. Lopinto, Lidia. "Designing and Writing Operating Manuals," *IEEE Transactions on Professional Communication*, vol. PC-27, no. 1, March 1984, pp. 29–31.

5. Matthies, Leslie H. *The New Playscript Procedure: Management Tool for Action*, 2nd ed. Stamford, Conn.: Office Publications, Inc., 1977.

6. Price, Jonathan. *How to Write a Computer Manual*. Menlo Park, Calif.: Benjamin-Cummings Publishing Company, 1984. [How to schedule, write, and edit documentation; practical tips to avoid most common pitfalls.]

7. Rubin, Martin L., ed. *Documentation Standards and Procedures for Online Systems*. New York: Van Nostrand Reinhold Company, 1979.

8. Saunders, Susan Furlow, and Lynn Propst. "Documentation: The Automated Approach," *ICP Data Processing Management*, vol. 9, no. 2, Summer 1984, pp. 31–33. [How to provide on-line access to user documentation.]

Questions

1. What should the analyst do prior to writing a procedure?

2. Identify the four basic reasons for writing procedures.

3. Identify the three basic styles of procedure writing.

4. What is the biggest problem with the narrative format?

5. Which type of procedure is the easiest to read?

6. What are the three essentials to consider when writing procedures?

7. List several types of written documentation that usually are found in medium-size or larger firms.

8. What does the analyst have to develop with a procedure's users in order to write more acceptable procedures?

9. Why is dictation recommended as a method of writing procedures?

10. What feature is necessary for a usable procedures manual?

11. What two methods can be used to update procedures as they change?

12. How do departmental interactions affect the new system's procedures?

SITUATION CASES

Case 17-1:   *Electronic Concepts Store*

Two analysts wrote a check cashing procedure for use by the cashier at the Electronic Concepts Store. Each analyst had a different method of procedure writing. Analyst A decided to follow the step-by-step outline format, while Analyst B used the playscript format. The following is the result of Analyst A's procedure

I. Cashier.
  A. Cash checks for store merchandise only.
    1. Stamp the back of the check.
    2. Complete required information in stamped area.
    3. Customer must have a valid driver's license.
  B. Call floor manager when
    1. The check is over amount of purchase.
    2. The check is filled out incorrectly.
    3. The amount is over $25.
    4. There is no purchase of store merchandise.
    5. The check is an out-of-area check.
    6. The check is a payroll check.
  C. Keep checks in a separate slot in the cash register.
    1. Bind checks together at the end of the shift.
    2. Attach your name to the packet.
    3. Give to floor manager.

Since Analyst B was working independently of Analyst A, his results differed. Analyst B wrote the following.

1. Cashier   Cash checks for store merchandise only; we are a merchandising concern, not a bank. Stamp the back of the check and fill in the required information. The customer must have a valid driver's license, since we may have to locate the person if the check is returned to us for insufficient funds. Call the floor manager if the check is over the amount of purchase, incorrectly filled out, there is no purchase of store merchandise, it is a payroll check, out-of-area check, or the amount is over $25. The floor manager has the background to handle these situa-

tions; you do not. Keep your checks bound together in a separate space in your cash register; place your name on them at the end of your shift and give them to the floor manager. This will help our accountant locate any errors in your check cashing procedure.

Question

1. Which is the best procedure? Defend your choice.

Case 17-2: *Digital Data Company*

Digital Data Company had a small internal mail distribution and pickup department. Their job was to pick up, sort, and deliver all intracompany mail from various business offices throughout the company system. The mail terminal was geographically centralized to minimize the distance from one office to another. The department employed about 20 people. Usually 15 were on the road while 5 were left at the terminal to sort incoming mail.

The major goal of the department was to pick up all outgoing mail, sort it into geographic locations, and have it delivered within 24 hours from the time of pickup. It was brought to management's attention that much of the mail was not reaching its destination in the 24-hour period; in fact, it often took two days for mail to travel a distance of only 20 miles.

Each driver had a time schedule to keep so mail could be taken to the central terminal, sorted, and sent back out the same day, or the next morning at the latest. Drivers rotated the runs every week so all drivers knew each run in case of emergency. Procedure manuals were in each truck outlining where to go, how to get there, and what to do at that destination. The procedures were written in narrative form. The drivers read them between stops and/or while driving.

A company analyst was asked to develop and rewrite new procedures for each delivery schedule. Hopefully, this would save time for the drivers, thus speeding up the redistribution process.

The analyst defined the problem and developed an outline for studying the problem. After gathering all the needed background information, the analyst went out on each run until he knew them all. He decided that too much time was lost between stops. The lost time was spent on trying to read the manuals after each stop and continually having to glance at them while driving down the road. Searching through the manuals while driving had caused many drivers to miss turns, which wasted time. Others had been involved in accidents because they were not watching the road.

The analyst rewrote the procedures in the playscript method, allowing the drivers to glance easily at the manuals to pick out specific names, streets, directions, and instructions once they were at the specified location. An example from the new manual is

I. San Bernardino, California   Depart Los Angeles terminal. Turn left onto Ficus Street. Turn left on Reservoir. Enter 405 freeway East. Exit at Euclid Avenue. Left on Euclid to San Bernardino freeway. East on San Bernardino freeway to 8th Street exit in San Bernardino. Turn left at stop sign. Turn right on Ramsey Street. Follow Ramsey to office and park. Pick up mail in front office and deliver mail to receptionist at the front door.

II. Bakersfield, California   _____
_____
_____
_____
_____

Management and the drivers found that the instructions were easier to read and it was faster to pick out specifics while driving. The new procedures were put in the trucks, and the department realized a 45-minute time saving on each run. This was judged adequate by management, but more time was still needed. The analyst felt more time would be saved as each driver became familiar with the new manuals.

Questions

1. Did the analyst use the best style of procedure writing to follow while driving? Can you develop a short example of another style, that could save more time and be less hazardous for the driver?

2. Is there another area in the department in which new procedures could save the entire department more time?

Chapter 18

TECHNIQUES FOR THE SYSTEMS MANAGER

LEARNING OBJECTIVES

You will learn how to . . .

☐ View the three levels of management.

☐ Identify the tasks and responsibilities of the systems manager.

☐ Carry out the planning, organizing, directing, controlling and staffing functions.

☐ Implement project control.

☐ Implement progress reports.

☐ Recognize troubled systems departments.

☐ Decide when to use in-house analysts or consultants.

☐ Conduct a risk ranking for new systems.

*M*anagement Overview

Management is an elusive term because a collection of people, called managers, are the management of the organization. These managers are responsible for the work performed by the people who work for them. The combined effect of the various levels of management are responsible for all of the planning, organizing, directing, controlling, and staffing within the organization (these five responsibilities are defined in the next section). The levels of management range from top management, through middle management, and down to operating management. This pyramid illustrates the levels of management in an organization

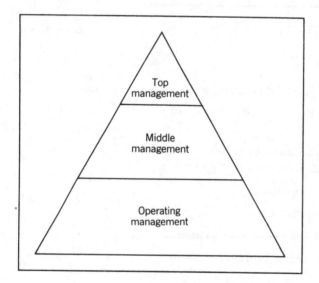

Top management makes decisions with regard to longer-range plans, such as 2–15 years. These decisions have to do with strategic planning, policy making, and the allocation of resources. *Middle management* makes decisions that are in a medium-range time frame, such as 6–24 months. These decisions involve tactical planning, policy implementation, operational planning, and control. Finally, *operating management* usually has a short-range time frame, such as a few days to 6 months. It is interested in the development of procedures, day-to-day operating decisions, and the operation of the firm's daily business activities.

In management there is an information feedback cycle similar to that for the design of a new computerized system. For example, *data* (unrelated facts) are processed to produce *information* (a meaningful assembly of data), which leads to a *decision* that results in taking appropriate *action*. The action taken may produce more data, which means you go through the information feedback cycle a sec ond time. In other words, it is a circular operation that goes from data to information to decision to action, back to data, and so on.

With regard to management organization, look back at Figure 1-6 in Chapter 1 to see the organization structure of the systems analysis department as it relates to the overall organization. This particular organization chart depicts a centralized data processing department.

Data processing departments may be centralized or distributed (decentralized). A *centralized* data processing facility is one in which there is a central computer facility that provides computer services to all users. It is looked upon as an internal service function to the entire organization. On the other hand, there is the *distributed data processing* (DDP) type of computer facility. With DDP, the computers are located in each department and function autonomously, but there is also a central facility that controls and coordinates the activities of each distributed data processing function. There are differences between DDP organizations that tend to relate to the degree of decentralization. Some organizations are very decentralized in that each department has its own systems analysts and programmers. Others may have decentralized computers with distributed data processing, but the systems analysts and programmers are located in a centralized area. Even in organizations that are very decentralized, functions such as data communications probably are centralized because it is the one function that ties together the distributed data processing of the entire organization.

*F*unctions of the Manager of Systems Analysis

The systems department, as an advocate of the best organization and methods techniques within the firm, must set a good example in its own house. It must maintain excellent diplomatic relations with all other areas of the firm. This calls for skillful performance by the systems manager. It has been said that managers who stop growing are *dangerous,* not only to themselves, but to the firm as well. Nowhere is this more true than in the systems department.

Supervision and administration is the manager's primary duty. Good supervision requires a thorough knowledge of the technical skills used by subordinates. Proper administration results in good utilization of personnel and equipment. The five key tasks are *planning, organizing, directing, controlling,* and *staffing.* These are the five basic responsibilities of the manager of the Systems Department (or of any manager, for that matter).

Planning is the rationale that helps the firm allocate its resources. Because planning is concerned with the future, it is never completely finished. The concept of planning has far-reaching implications for the organization because it necessitates looking analytically at all of the organization's operations. Planning activities require forecasting, establishing objectives, scheduling, budgeting, developing policies, and the like.

Organizing is based on the goals and objectives of the organization, which are formulated during the planning process. The important thing to understand is that the organizing activity is impersonal; working relationships are established without regard to the specific people who will function in them. Accepted organization theory rests on several major premises: division of work is essential for efficiency, coordination is the manager's primary responsibility in organizing the work, the formal structure is the main vehicle for organizing and administering work activities, and the span of management control sets limits on the number of people who are responsible to a given manager. Organizing activities require developing organizational structure, delegating to others, establishing relationships, establishing procedures, and so forth.

Directing enables managers to evoke goal-directed actions from others in the organization. Directing is a human resource function concerned with behavior; it is directing people in the use of resources. Sometimes it is called motivating or actuating. This is the very difficult area of superior-to-subordinate relationships. Directing activities require initiating actions, decision making, communicating, motivating, and the like.

Control is the management function that ensures that organizational performance is as close as possible to the objectives, policies, and standards established in the planning process. Control consists of verifying whether everything occurs in conformity with the plan adopted, the instructions issued, and the principles established. Control involves the previously mentioned information feedback cycle. Controlling activities require establishing performance standards, measuring performance, evaluating performance, correcting performance, and so forth.

Staffing is a human resource function that includes recruitment, selection, placement, training, appraisal, and compensation of personnel. The ultimate responsibility for staffing rests with the manager who has direct authority over the performance of subordinates. Staffing is an activity that maintains, develops, and regulates the human resource system of the organization. Staffing activities require interviewing people, selecting people, developing/training people, discharging people, and the like. A later section in this chapter, Job Descriptions, defines the basic job descriptions in a systems department.

As does the firm, the department should develop short-range plans (less than one year in the future) and long-range plans (more than one year in the future) as guidelines for its activities and direction. The systems manager should be a forward thinker. The systems manager also must ensure that high standards of performance are maintained. Work quality standards should be developed, qualified personnel have to be recruited, on-going training programs for employees have to be maintained, job descriptions should be meaningful and kept up-to-date, and employees should get at least one annual performance review to keep them aware of their professional development and job performance.

The systems department must maintain good relations with other departments because departments that do not trust or respect the systems department will avoid it, even when they need help. The systems manager should point out any department limitations before agreeing to do all the projects requested. Mature people can accept being turned down, and it is far better to decline a project than to accept it and fail because the department is overloaded with work. It is vital for the systems manager to know what the systems department's capacity is, to keep track of how it is being used, and work to use it at maximum output. The systems manager has to know when to say yes or no to a project request.

A good system for the translation of technical progress and performance into easily understood reports is required by the systems manager. Project control can be achieved using progress reports that continually report on the progress of all jobs being worked on in the department. The next two sections discuss project control and progress reports.

Project Control

Most systems and programming departments organize their work on a project assignment basis. Analysts are assigned various projects, such as a problem definition project or a full system study, or perhaps a feasibility study. In fact, an analyst might have 8 or 10 projects underway simultaneously. Each project has its scheduled starting date, its scheduled completion date, its own start-to-finish elapsed time, and its own chargeable time.

All projects should be assigned in writing, including small projects. The larger or more vital projects should be described in greater detail than small projects. A Project Assignment Sheet like the one shown in Figure 18-1 can be used to make the written job assignments. It is filled out as follows. (Follow the numbers on Figure 18-1.)

1. The *subject* is the title, topic, or central theme of the project.
2. The *scope* is the area or range that the study will encompass. (Keep the scope within the boundaries of the subject.)
3. The *objectives* are the results that the analyst wants to accomplish.
4. The *project number* is a three-part number: the first box contains the analyst's initials; the second box contains a consecutive number that restarts on January 1 of each year; the third box contains the year.

PROJECT NUMBER	J.F.	01	87
	EMPLOYEE	NUMBER	YEAR

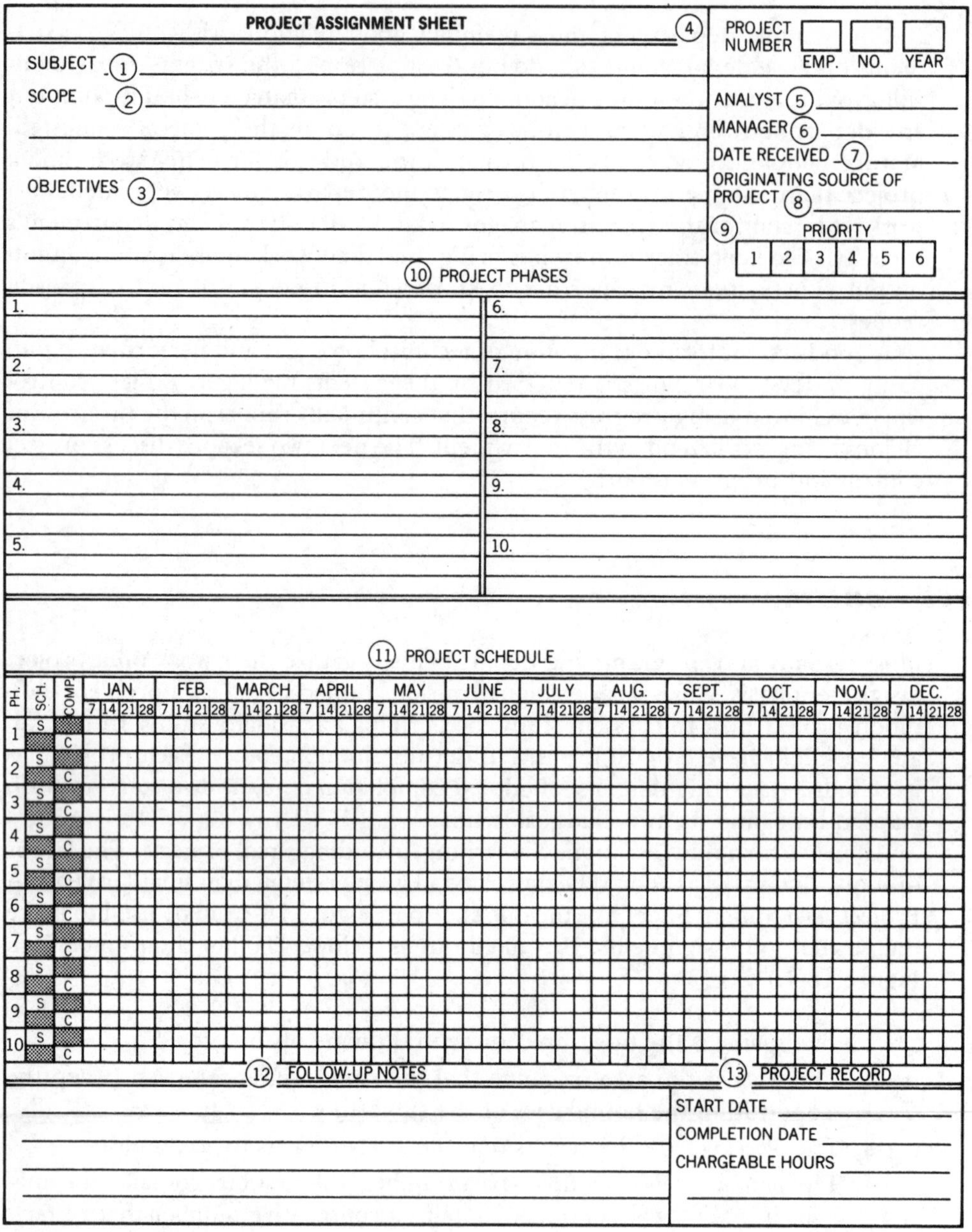

Figure 18-1 Project Assignment Sheet.

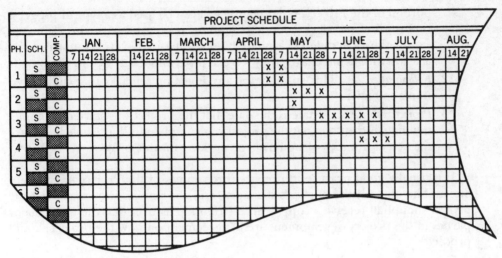

Figure 18-2 Project schedule.

5. *Analyst* is the name of the analyst assigned to this project.
6. *Manager* is the name of the manager of the systems analyst.
7. *Date received* is the date the project was accepted.
8. *Originating source of the project* is the name of the person who requested that this project be undertaken.
9. *Priority.* Check whichever box pertains to the priority assigned to this project, as follows
    a. Emergencies . . . extreme hazards.
    b. Code violations . . . safety . . . labor relations.
    c. Urgent with high economic return—special surveys.
    d. Less urgent and smaller economic return.
    e. Routine projects.
    f. Minor projects with low economic return.
10. *Project phases.* The analyst is expected to divide the project into phases. Each phase is a major task that the analyst completes on the way toward completion of the entire project. When all these tasks are completed, the project is completed.
11. *Project schedule.* Each phase of the project is now scheduled. Figure 18-2 shows phase 1 scheduled for the last week of April and the first week of May; phase 2 is scheduled for the last three weeks of May; and so on. It also shows that phase 1 is completed and only the first of the three weeks of phase 2 is completed. The overall time for this project is from the last week of April to and including the first week in July. The *project schedule*

portion of the Project Assignment Sheet can be used as a type of progress report showing work completed-to-date compared with the estimated completion schedule on a phase-by-phase basis. If you are not familiar already with Gantt charts, they were defined and illustrated in Chapter 4.

12. *Follow-up notes.* This space is for any notes or remarks that the analyst wants to make.

13. *Project record.* Start date is the date that the project was started. Completion date is the date that the project was completed. Chargeable hours are the actual number of hours spent working on this project.

It is usually good practice to prepare three copies of the Project Assignment Sheet. The analyst, the analyst's manager, and the person who requested the project should all receive a copy. This distribution assures that the three major parties in the project development are in agreement on how the project should proceed.

Progress Reports

In order to maintain control over the department, the manager of systems analysis may require periodic progress reports. The manager uses a progress report to monitor the progress of the various systems projects, whereas the analyst uses a progress report to report progress-to-date on a specific project.

Progress reports usually are concerned with work done during the interval since the last report. A typical progress report might contain a very short written description of the progress-to-date, approximate cost-to-date compared with estimated budgeted amount-to-date (Is the estimated budget being underspent or overspent?), and the work completed-to-date compared with the estimated completion schedule (Is the project ahead or behind schedule?). Some financial data, such as actual versus estimated budget, may be reported automatically via the firm's management information system. You should, however, report on *all* unexpected problems as soon as they are encountered.

The progress report is similar to a story told in serial fashion, where the reader is led from the previous progress reports to the current one. The progress reports should be tied together so there is an audit trail to trace back through all previous reports. For example, the first paragraph of the current progress report might point out the previous report's title, date, and accession number if it had one.

Progress reports may be written at irregular times, at the completion of major phases of the system development cycle, or they may be written at time intervals such as once a month. This depends on how often the manager of the systems department wants to see progress reports. In any case, progress reports should

PROGRESS REPORT

PROJECT NAME (SUBJECT)		DATE
Annual budgeting system		7/22/86

DATE OF PREVIOUS PROGRESS REPORT	ANALYST	PROJECT NUMBER
4/30/86	J. Benson	JB–14–86

BUDGETED AMOUNT TO DATE	COST TO DATE	THIS PROJECT'S COSTS ARE		
$4,000.	$2,450.	☐ UNDER ESTIMATE	☒ ON TARGET	☐ OVER ESTIMATE

ORIGINAL ESTIMATED COMPLETION DATE	NEW ESTIMATED COMPLETION DATE	THIS PROJECT WILL FINISH		
12/31/86	12/31/86	☐ EARLY	☒ ON TIME	☐ LATE

NARRATIVE (SHORT WRITTEN DESCRIPTION OF PROGRESS SINCE LAST REPORT)

Four vendors of microcomputer–based budgeting system software packages have been contacted. Our mini–RFP will be returned by 10/31/86 for evaluation.

Form 9204, Rev. 10/86

Figure 18-3 Progress Report form.

be concise and to the point so that neither the time of the reader nor that of the writer will be wasted.

Progress reports may be transmitted both verbally and in written format. Some managers want verbal progress reports, but usually written reports are requested. They are written in many forms: letters, memoranda, or special formats such as a preprinted form. Figure 18-3 shows a progress report that is used as a formal company form.

The previously mentioned Project Assignment Sheet (Figure 18-1) also can be used as a type of progress report. If the analyst updates the Gantt chart on this sheet (let us say on a monthly basis), then the Project Assignment Sheet serves the purpose of showing work completed-to-date compared with the estimated completion schedule.

Progress reports, in one form or another, are valuable aids to the systems manager for they relate in a concise manner the status of each project currently being completed under the auspices of the systems department. In addition, they provide a positive medium through which the manager can evaluate performance of individual systems analysts.

Symptoms of Organizational Problems

A number of symptoms may seem to indicate organizational problems, that is, seem to indicate that the organization structure itself is deficient. The presence of these symptoms may or may not warrant reorganization of the systems department, but each one should be corrected as soon as it is identified.

Since a key function of every manager is to actively receive and give information, communication failures or personality clashes may be at the root of some apparent organization problems. When an apparent organizational problem appears, it is wise to look first into the communications or personality areas for the causes. Internal communication problems may result from personal conflicts among employees or from strained relations among supervisory personnel. Careful observation of employee interactions is the key to discovering the roots of such problems.

Deterioration of "diplomatic relationships" is another symptom of a possible need for reorganization. The systems analysis function is a service function to other departments in the firm. Its image, from the view of these other departments, is crucial to its success. If other departments are unable to respect or trust the systems group, they may be reluctant to cooperate with it. One measurement technique that can be used to detect this symptom is for the manager of the systems department to interview the managers of user departments to learn just how they feel about the department's service function.

A high rate of turnover among the analysts is often a significant indicator of organizational and personnel management ineffectiveness. This symptom of organizational problems should be interpreted with caution because many factors can affect personnel turnover. The causes may be completely external to the department, or firm; however, the systems manager should always look out for the well-being of the analysts. Unfair or imbalanced work loads should be prevented, and the analysts should be informed about their status within the group. The potential damage that can be caused by an analyst's resignation in the middle of a complex project makes good human relations in the systems department essential (along with good documentation, of course). This is a major portion of the manager's duty to the firm.

Continuous scheduling difficulties, such as the failure to meet completion dates or failure to set realistic completion dates may be another indicator of organizational ineffectiveness. It may be that the analysts are not organized enough to monitor their own work load and progress accurately. Or it may be that they are allowing themselves to be pressured into unrealistic commitments and deadlines. Certainly every department that works to maximize its output will have some scheduling problems, but chronic slippage is a symptom that the manager should examine and correct.

*J*ob Descriptions

The following job descriptions are for the tasks typically found in a large systems group. Remember, as we stated previously, staffing is one of the five functions of management.

Manager of Systems Analysis

Plans, organizes, directs, controls, and staffs the activities of the systems analysis department to establish and implement new or revised systems and procedures concerned with either manual or computerized operations. Usually considered to be in command of all systems analysis activities. Responsible for problem definition, feasibility studies, systems design, and implementation. Makes recommendations on the action to be taken. Assigns personnel to various projects, schedules projects, and directs analyst activities. Consults with, and advises other departments on, systems and procedures priorities. Coordinates systems department activities with those of other departments. Prepares progress reports regarding the activities of the entire systems analysis department. Ensures that company policy with regard to system controls has been followed in all projects.

Lead Systems Analyst

Usually considered to be the assistant manager of systems analysis and has full technical knowledge of the activity comparable to a senior systems analyst. Has supervisory duties of instructing, directing, and controlling the work of the other systems analysts, including the senior systems analysts. Assists in planning, organizing, directing, controlling, and staffing the activities of the department. Assists in scheduling the work of the department and the assignment of personnel to various projects. May act as systems department manager in the absence of the manager. May coordinate the activities of the department with other departments. Able to perform all the duties of a senior systems analyst. Reviews and approves the definition of new system control requirements and the design for a framework of integrated controls to meet the needs of the new system.

Senior Systems Analyst

Under general direction, performs problem definition studies, feasibility studies, and full systems studies. Devises procedures for the solution of the problem through the use of manual systems or electronic data processing systems. Usually competent to work at the highest level of all phases of the study while working undirected most of the time. May give some direction and guidance to lower level personnel. Confers with all levels of personnel in order to define the problem. Prepares all types of charts, tables, and graphs to assist in analyzing problems. Utilizes various business and mathematical techniques. Devises logical procedures to solve problems by manual systems and electronic data processing, keeping in mind equipment capacity and limitations, operating time, and form of desired results. Analyzes existing system difficulties and revises the involved procedures as necessary. Prepares the formal definition of the new system control requirements by drawing together the work done by all analysts working on the project. Designs the framework of integrated controls to be utilized in meeting new system needs.

Systems Analyst

Under general supervision, performs problem definition studies, feasibility studies, and full systems studies. Develops procedures to process information by means of electronic data processing equipment, as well as manually. Usually competent enough in most phases of systems analysis to work undirected. Requires some general direction for the balance of the activities. Confers with organizational personnel to determine the problem and type of system to be designed. Analyzes problems in terms of systems requirements. Documents control points and procedures within the existing system. Defines specific control requirements and related control techniques. Proposes groups of related control techniques covering the requirements of major portions of the new system. Modifies the systems design to take maximum advantage of existing data processing equipment. Where necessary, recommends equipment modifications, manual systems, computer systems, or additions to enable efficient and effective systems applications. Defines the problem and makes recommendations for its solution. Confers with a programmer who prepares program flowcharts or system structure charts and machine instructions when the solution requires a computer.

Systems Analyst Trainee

Under immediate supervision, carries out analyses of a less complex nature. Usually works only on a couple of activities, under very close direction, with the work being monitored. Prepares system flowcharts to describe existing and proposed operations. Documents control points and procedures within the existing system, either in flowchart or narrative form. Designs detailed record and form layouts. May assist in the preparation of program flowcharting. This classification usually is staffed by novices who have had sufficient educational background and experience to start in systems analysis.

Programmer Analyst

Depending upon the organization, a programmer analyst must first meet the requirements of systems analyst. Beyond that, an analyst programmer must be able to direct the activities of numerous programmers as well as perform the tasks of writing and testing computer programs. This involves in-depth knowledge of one or more programming languages such as COBOL, APL, PASCAL, FORTRAN, and even fourth generation prototyping languages. Programmer analysts must be able to perform both the activities of a systems analyst and a programmer.

In-House Systems Staff or Outside Consultants?

As discovered earlier, an organization usually does not feel the need for any extensive system renovation until it has some serious growing pains. Then, as often happens, it discovers that the old, overloaded systems simply will not support the projected rate of growth or competitive pressures.

This is commonly the point at which someone suggests using the systems department. In many instances this is the necessary solution to the firm's problems. But all organizations are not the same. Each is characterized by a unique set of operating details and problems. Each one also differs in its approach to objectives, style, and control; therefore, each must have its own approach to systems management.

At this point it might be mentioned that one of the uses of outside consultants is for the development of a Request for Proposal (RFP). How to develop an RFP is described in Chapter 10 on cost analysis, with a completed example in Appendix 3.

Now let us discuss some of the pros and cons of a firm doing its own systems work as opposed to requesting help from outside sources. Should a firm use its own systems department? Or should it rely on periodic help from professional systems consultants? Arguments for both positions are outlined below. The business manager should consider carefully each argument as it relates to the organization in question.

I. Arguments in favor of using an in-house Systems Department.
  A. Growth, present or future, is the reason given most often for using an in-house systems department.
      1. To tie the organization together across departmental boundaries.
      2. To develop and maintain up-to-date systems to control the most vital operations.
      3. To help manage the computer (if there is one).
      4. To plan ahead for change.
      5. To maintain competitive efficiency.
      6. To preserve economies of scale.
  B. Familiarity with the firm's intricacies is another argument in favor of in-house systems personnel.
      1. They know the firm and its management so they can evaluate the feasibility of management's proposals more realistically.
      2. They are always present and can keep the firm abreast of all opportunities that arise in systems methodology.
      3. Confidential company information is kept within the company, rather than carried away by consultants.
  C. Other reasons for using an in-house Systems Department are that
      1. It is more convenient because the personnel are always around when you need a systems problem fixed.

2. If *someone* is not assigned the responsibility for systems maintenance, it does not get done.

3. Since systems personnel are on the payroll, they have a stake in keeping up the good work.

4. With proven staff members, taking chances on unknown outside consultants is eliminated.

II. Arguments for using outside consultants instead of in-house staff are the following.

A. Consultants give an impartial outside viewpoint.

1. They have no vested interest in the *status quo* and are thus free to recommend whatever is best for the firm.

2. They do not get stale and complacent as an in-house staff might if it is not well organized and trained.

3. Members of the firm can be relieved of direct responsibility for unpopular recommendations such as

a. Reorganization or eliminations.

b. Personnel transfers or replacement.

4. They import good ideas from other firms.

B. They have access to any kind of specialist needed to assist with or set up a system, such as

1. Up-to-date accounting systems.

2. Records management systems.

3. EDP hardware and software security.

4. Data communications.

5. Distributed systems.

6. Database.

C. You only pay them while you need them.

D. Use of consultants has proven to be sound practice in professions that were developed long before systems analysis, such as medicine, law, and architecture.

As mentioned, the business manager should consider each item as it relates to the specific firm. It also may pay to learn what the experiences of similar firms have been in this area; but again, since each organization is unique, comparisons should be made only with great care. The success or failure of a particular systems approach in one firm may have been due to circumstances that do not exist in another firm. As any seasoned manager knows, small differences can require very divergent approaches to the "same" problem. On the other hand, there are many general approaches that will fit almost all organizations.

Hopefully, the arguments we have presented will assist the manager in estimating the feasibility, risk, and cost of using an in-house systems staff as opposed to the use of outside consultants. Both approaches have merit. Probably some blend of the two will fit most organizations.

Risk Ranking Systems under Development

The following methodology was developed in order to allow you to risk rank the sensitivity of systems that are planned for development. This risk ranking methodology, called *scoring*, offers the advantage of being able to collect "objective data" that will be ranked by using "subjective" factor values. Unlike other risk ranking methodologies, you do not need to use probabilities of occurrence and annual loss values each time this methodology is utilized.

First let us discuss how to use this methodology; then we will explain its development and how you can fit it into your organization.

Whoever is in charge of the project of ranking the systems under development first talks with the systems design and planning personnel. The purpose of these discussions is to complete a scoring sheet for each system that is scheduled for development. Figure 18-4 shows the scoring sheet. Notice that there are 14 questions that must be answered. All of these questions, called *criteria*, are objective questions that can be answered easily. If your organization does not make estimates for each of these 14 criteria, then delete any that do not apply from the scoring sheet. For example, some organizations do not make estimates with regard to Criteria 7 and 8; therefore, these criteria are deleted. Further, if you are aware of other criteria that would show risk at your organization, it is suggested that these other criteria be added to the scoring sheet.

After answering the 14 questions for each proposed system, the analyst then multiplies the appropriate factor values together. Notice, when you answer Criterion 1, only one of the six boxes is checked. If the check is in the box opposite $10,000–$49,999, then the factor value is 1.2 (factor values will be discussed next). That is, the 1.2 factor value of Criterion 1 is multiplied by the factor value obtained after you answer Criterion 2, the result of that multiplication is multiplied by the factor value you obtain after answering Criterion 3, and so on. In other words, it is a sequential or chain multiplication of the factor values obtained after answering Criteria 1 through 14. Once this multiplication is complete, you have a final system score for the first system. After you complete a separate scoring sheet for each proposed system, there will be a final system score for each one of the systems.

The next step is to list the systems on the comparison worksheet (see Figure 18-5). The systems should be listed in a sequence that starts with the system that has the highest final system score and ends with the system that has the lowest final system score. In using this worksheet, you work backward by first listing the

NAME OF SYSTEM: _ACCOUNTS PAYABLE_

CRITERIA	FACTOR VALUE	CRITERIA	FACTOR VALUE
1. Estimated development cost:		9. ☒ DP uses a formal system development life cycle.	1.0
☐ less than $10,000	1.0		
☒ $10,000–$49,999	1.2	☐ No formal system development life cycle.	2.0
☐ $50,000–$99,999	1.4		
☐ $100,000–$249,999	1.8	10. ☒ Project team includes DP, Audit, and User.	1.0
☐ $250,000–$999,999	2.2		
☐ $1,000,000 or more	2.5	☐ Project team includes any 2 of the above.	1.3
2. Estimated development hours:		☐ Project team includes only 1 of the above.	2.0
☐ less than 200	1.0		
☐ 200–999	1.2	11. ☒ Programs to be written in COBOL (self-documenting).	1.0
☒ 1,000–1,999	1.4		
☐ 2,000–4,999	1.8	☐ Programs *not* written in COBOL (not self-documenting).	1.5
☐ 5,000–19,999	2.2		
☐ 20,000 or more	2.5		
3. ☐ Batch system.	1.0	12. ☐ Nonfinancial system.	1.0
☐ On-line and batch.	1.3	☒ Financial system.	1.5
☒ On-line and real-time.	2.0	13. Access to assets in dollars:	
4. ☒ Does *not* link to other systems.	1.0	☐ $1–$99,999	1.0
☐ Links to other systems (integrated system).	1.3	☐ $100,000–$299,999	1.2
		☐ $300,000–$499,999	1.4
5. ☐ Centralized system.	1.0	☒ $500,000–$999,999	1.8
☒ Distributed system.	1.5	☐ $1,000,000–$9,999,999	2.2
6. ☐ Discrete files.	1.0	☐ $10,000,000–$49,999,999	2.5
☒ Database files.	1.5	☐ $50,000,000 or more	3.0
7. Estimated annual computer hours/CRU^s:		14. ☐ No statutory requirement.	1.0
☐ 1–9	1.0	☒ One statutory body requires output.	1.3
☐ 10–99	1.2		
☐ 100–499	1.4	☐ Two statutory bodies require output.	1.4
☒ 500–999	1.6		
☐ 1,000–9,999	1.8	☐ Over two statutory bodies require output.	1.5
☐ 10,000 or more	2.0		
8. Estimated number of program modules:		**FINAL SYSTEM SCORE**	76.42
☐ 1–5	1.0	Multiply the 14 Factor Values together to get the Final System Score.	
☐ 6–9	1.2		
☐ 10–19	1.4		
☐ 20–34	1.6		
☒ 35–59	1.8		
☐ 60 or more	2.0		

Figure 18-4 Scoring sheet for risk ranking systems planned for development.

SYSTEM UNDER CONSIDERATION	FACTORS														FINAL SYSTEM SCORING
	1	2	3	4	5	6	7	8	9	10	11	12	13	14	
Payroll	—	—	—	—	—	—	—	—	—	—	—	—	—	—	190.50
Accounts Payable	1.2	1.4	2.0	1.0	1.5	1.5	1.6	1.8	1.0	1.0	1.0	1.5	1.8	1.3	76.42
Parts Inventory	—	—	—	—	—	—	—	—	—	—	—	—	—	—	21.35

Figure 18-5 Comparison worksheet.

final system scores in descending order in the right hand column of Figure 18-5. Then write the name of the system that has the highest final system score at the top of the left hand column. Finally list the individual factor values for that system across the middle 14 columns of the worksheet. After this process is completed for each system, the systems will be ranked, with the most sensitive system being at the top of the list (left hand column of Figure 18-5) and the system with the lowest sensitivity at the bottom. If there are any systems that have a questionable rank position, examine the differences by looking at the individual 14 factors of that system and contrast them with the 14 individual factors of the other systems.

Do not use the cardinal numbers in the final system scoring to show how much more sensitive or how many more times sensitive one system is over another. Our system should be used *only* as an ordinal ranking system in which you can say that the system at the top of the list is most sensitive, second place is second most sensitive, third place is third most sensitive, and the last place is least sensitive.

Now we can discuss the all-important *factor values*. These factor values are intended to show the relative sensitivity of each criterion. They may be looked upon as the proxy or replacement for probabilities of occurrence and actual dollar-loss values. This system is not intended to show specific losses or specific probabilities of occurrence; its purpose is to show *relative* risk or sensitivity differences between different systems under development. The factor values presented here are reasonable, but they may be different at your specific organization. In that case, you need to know how to modify or create new factor values that can be added to the original 14 criteria we used in Figure 18-4.

To develop or identify factor values, you need to assemble a Delphi group. A *Delphi group* is a small group of experts, perhaps three to seven people, who assemble in order to develop a consensus in an area in which it may be impossible or too expensive to collect more accurate data. For example, a Delphi group composed of various data processing personnel and user department experts may meet to determine whether a financial system is, on the average, 50 percent more sensitive than a non-financial system. Notice, Criterion 12 in Figure 18-4 shows that non-financial systems have a factor value of 1.0 and financial systems have a factor value of 1.5. To exemplify this, if you work for a bank with financial systems that carry hundreds of millions of dollars, you may want to increase the factor value from 1.5 to 2.0. On the other hand, if you work for a small manufacturer who deals primarily with a single customer, you may feel that financial systems only warrant a 1.3, which is only 30 percent more sensitive than the non-financial system listed in Criterion 12 of Figure 18-4.

The point we wish to make is that there is no textbook or perfectly accurate methodology to calculate indisputable factor values. The Delphi group meets to combine the experience of seasoned managers who use their best judgment in order to determine how much more or less sensitive a particular set of criteria is.

Now review Criterion 13 in Figure 18-4. It says that if there is access to assets of less than $99,999, there is no additional sensitivity. On the other hand, it says if access to assets is greater than $50,000,000, then it is three times more sensitive (3.0). Notice that different criteria have different factor value sensitivities. Criterion 13 ranges from 1.0 to 3.0; whereas Criterion 3 only ranges from 1.0 to 2.0.

By the way, do not worry about factor value accuracy. The Delphi group does its best job and any inaccuracies that exist are insignificant as long as everyone has been reasonable. This is because the current systems under development are ranked only among themselves. You do not compare their sensitivities to other outside systems. Therefore, if one of the criteria has some factor values that are not perfectly accurate (this is probable), the inaccuracy is applied consistently to all of the new systems that are being ranked. It is for this reason that minor inaccuracies in factor values do not invalidate your work. In any event, since there is no known way to gather perfectly accurate, indisputable risk ranking factor values, you have no choice but to utilize a Delphi group of experts in the area for which you are developing these factor values.

This ranking of systems under development can be utilized by management in several areas of the organization. For example

- The manager of data processing may use it to identify especially sensitive systems for close tracking. In other words, this manager may be asked by the Board of Directors or other high level of management about the status of some particularly sensitive systems.
- The manager of the systems department may use such a ranking in order to allocate his or her most experienced analyst to the more sensitive projects.
- The manager of programming may use it to allocate his or her most able programmers to the most sensitive projects.
- The manager of the quality assurance department (internal quality control within data processing) may use it to determine which projects should be followed in order to make sure all the steps of the system development life cycle are done completely and thoroughly.
- The internal audit department (EDP auditors) can use this risk ranking to determine which systems they will follow with regard to ensuring that adequate internal control and security mechanisms have been built into the most sensitive new systems.

Selected Readings

1. Beach, Linda M. "Microcomputer Policy," *Information Management*, vol. 18, no. 3, March 1984, pp. 33–34. [How to set a policy on microcomputer usage, purchase criteria, personnel responsibilities, and related issues.]

2. Bentley, Colin. *Computer Project Management.* New York: John Wiley & Sons, Inc., 1983. [A practitioner's guide with checklists and standards.]

3. Cleland, David I., ed. *Matrix Management Systems Handbook.* New York: Van Nostrand Reinhold Company, 1983. [How to apply matrix management to product development, project management, multi-organization enterprises, international projects, and other tasks.]

4. Cleland, David I., and William R. King. *Project Management Handbook.* New York: Van Nostrand Reinhold Company, 1983.

5. Deutsch, Dennis S. *Protect Yourself: The Guide to Understanding and Negotiating Contracts for Business Computers and Software.* New York: John Wiley & Sons, Inc., 1983.

6. Harrison, F. L. *Advanced Project Management, 2nd edition.* New York: John Wiley & Sons, Inc., 1985.

7. Head, Robert V. *Planning Techniques for Systems Managers.* Wellesley, Mass.: QED Information Sciences, Inc., 1984.

8. *How to Write Job Descriptions . . . the Easy Way.* Madison, Conn.: Bureau of Law & Business, Inc., 1982.

9. Justice, Karen. "The Best-Laid Plans: Systems That Reduce the Risk in Project Management," *ICP Business Software Review,* vol. 3, no. 4, June/July 1984, pp. 50–56. [Automated ways to plan and evaluate project progress.]

10. Lukaszewski, James E. "Working with a Consultant: 10 Steps to a Good Relationship," *Association Management,* vol. 36, no. 8, August 1984, pp. 157–158.

11. Meyers, Kenneth D. "Total Project Planning," *Datamation,* vol. 30, no. 4, April 1, 1984, pp. 143–148. [Actual example of how to manage worldwide introduction of new services or products.]

12. Woolley, Dave. "Avoiding Catch 22: Managing Microcomputers," *ComputerData* (Canada), vol. 8, no. 3, March 1983, p. 26. [Minimum standards governing use of microcomputers in a corporate setting.]

Questions

1. Discuss the differences between a centralized data processing facility and a distributed data processing facility.

2. What are the five basic responsibilities of the systems manager?

3. How does the systems manager's use of a progress report differ from the analyst's use?

4. Identify several symptoms of organizational problems in the systems department.

5. What are the arguments for having an in-house systems staff?

6. How can risk ranking of systems under development be utilized by management?

7. What are the three levels of management and how are they characterized?

8. What is the information feedback cycle?

9. What is the advantage of using the scoring method of risk ranking the sensitivity of planned systems?

10. When risk ranking the sensitivity of systems, how can the identification of factor values be facilitated?

SITUATION CASES

Case 18-1: *Northeast Graphics*

Jerry Martenson, Vice President of Northeast Graphics, met with Yen Lee, the Systems Analysis Department Manager, to discuss a records problem. It appeared that records were kept too long, poorly, expensively, and that too many steps were being taken in the creation and handling of records. In order to control the quality, quantity, and excessive cost of records, the Vice President wanted the Systems Analysis Department to develop a records retention schedule for all departments within the firm. This schedule would tell each department how long to keep the records, when to transfer the records, and when to destroy them. The Systems Analysis Department Manager accepted the project and on January 1, 1986, assigned the project to the Lead Analyst, John Razo.

John, like all good analysts, knew that he should begin the project by preparing the assignment in a written format. He began by filling out a Project Assignment Sheet. John's completed Project Assignment Sheet is shown on page 723. The analyst gave a copy of the completed Project Assignment Sheet to his manager and kept one for himself.

Question

1. Did John use the proper procedures in the handling and carrying out of the Project Assignment Sheet?

PROJECT ASSIGNMENT SHEET

PROJECT NUMBER	JR 01 86

SUBJECT   RECORDS RETENTION SCHEDULE

SCOPE   To evaluate and analyze all records in each department of the firm.

OBJECTIVES   To develop a records retention schedule in order to control the quality, quantity, and cost of records.

ANALYST   John Razo

MANAGER   Yen Lee

DATE RECEIVED   January 1, 1986

ORIGINATING SOURCE OF PROJECT   Jerry Martenson

PRIORITY

1	2	3	4	5	6

PROJECT PHASES

1. Physical inventory: Records inventory sheet to be filled out by authorized clerks in each department on active and inactive records.
2. Appraisal of Value: Administrative
3. Appraisal of Value: Legal
4. Appraisal of Value: Historical
5. Draw up retention schedule including the transferring and disposition of all company records.

6. Get administrative approval on drawn up retention schedule.
7. Distribute the approved retention schedule to the various departments.
8.
9.
10.

PROJECT SCHEDULE

PH.	SCH.	COMP.	JAN.	FEB.	MARCH	APRIL	MAY	JUNE	JULY	AUG.	SEPT.	OCT.	NOV.	DEC.
			7 14 21 28	7 14 21 28	7 14 21 28	7 14 21 28	7 14 21 28	7 14 21 28	7 14 21 28	7 14 21 28	7 14 21 28	7 14 21 28	7 14 21 28	7 14 21 28
1	S	C	X X X X	X X X X	X									
2	S	C			X X X	X X X X	X X							
3	S	C					X X X	X X X X	X X					
4	S	C							X X X	X X X X	X			
5	S	C								X X X X				
6	S	C									X X X X			
7	S	C												
8	S	C												
9	S	C												
10	S	C												

FOLLOW-UP NOTES

PROJECT RECORD

START DATE   January 1, 1986

COMPLETION DATE

CHARGEABLE HOURS

Case 18-2: *Northeast Graphics (continued)*

John Razo, the analyst at Northeast Graphics, filled out his monthly progress report form. This form was the standard one used by Northeast Graphics and all analysts were expected to submit a monthly progress report for each project. The following is the progress report that the analyst submitted reporting on his progress for the month of April, 1986.

PROGRESS REPORT

PROJECT NAME (SUBJECT)		DATE
Records Retention Schedule		5/1/86

DATE OF PREVIOUS PROGRESS REPORT	ANALYST	PROJECT NUMBER
3/1/86	John Razo	JR 01 86

BUDGETED AMOUNT TO DATE	COST TO DATE	THIS PROJECT'S COSTS ARE
$750.00	$735.00	☐ UNDER ESTIMATE ☒ ON TARGET ☐ OVER ESTIMATE

ORIGINAL ESTIMATED COMPLETION DATE	NEW ESTIMATED COMPLETION DATE	THIS PROJECT WILL FINISH
9/14/86		☐ EARLY ☐ ON TIME ☒ LATE

NARRATIVE (SHORT WRITTEN DESCRIPTION OF PROGRESS SINCE LAST REPORT)

The physical inventory (phase 1) took four weeks longer than expected; therefore, the project may not be finished on time. Our firm has 2,900 records that must be evaluated.

The appraisals are progressing on time and in good order.

Question

1. Criticize the analyst's progress report.

Case 18-3: *Beta Software*

Beta Software had a Systems Department consisting of a manager and 15 systems analysts of various levels. The manager of the department, Mrs. Smith, had been in this position for only one year. Prior to that, she had been Lead Systems Analyst with Beta Software for five years. She was well acquainted with the company and possessed a good working knowledge of systems analysis techniques.

The previous Systems Manager had been known to reject certain projects from other departments for a variety of reasons (such as too much work), or postpone them to future dates. These actions had, at times, caused the other departments to feel that they were being slighted, but in no way lessened their respect or trust for the Systems Department. Mrs. Smith, eager to prove herself, decided that this could be one area in which the services provided by the department might be improved.

After reviewing the estimated budget, she judged the work load could be increased within the estimated figures. Subsequently, Mrs. Smith instituted a new department policy in which they would accept all projects requested by other departments, regardless of the current work load. Mrs. Smith did not think it would be much of a strain on the Systems personnel because she had worked with these people for years and knew their limitations. Although there were a few complaints about the increased work load, she shrugged them off as normal gripes of employees.

In an effort to relieve the analysts of some time-consuming details, she reduced the number of progress reports required for each project from weekly to quarterly.

Mrs. Smith used a standard project assignment sheet, assigning to each analyst the projects that she felt that person could best handle. By following this strategy, the manager tended to assign a good portion of the work load, especially the more complex assignments, to two or three highly experienced analysts. She thought these people were the most reliable and did not think they would object to handling a greater share of the work load in an effort to improve department efficiency.

One year after taking over as manager, Mrs. Smith found that the Systems Department was in a desperate situation. All results were the reverse of what she had expected. The department had failed to meet many of its project completion dates, the budget was much more than expected, one of the department's key analysts angrily resigned in the middle of a complex project (complaining of too heavy a work load), and the department quickly was losing the respect and trust of the other departments.

Questions

1. How did the Systems Department get into its present situation?
2. Was it a wise decision for Mrs. Smith to reduce the number of progress reports? Explain.

Chapter 19

RESEARCH NEEDS OF THE ANALYST

LEARNING OBJECTIVES

You will learn how to . . .

☐ Recognize when the library can help you attain your goals.

☐ Utilize computerized literature searching.

☐ Understand the different types of materials found in libraries.

☐ Understand how library resources are arranged for use.

☐ Use indexes of all types.

☐ Use a library card catalog.

☐ Locate needed periodical articles, books, government documents, and so forth.

☐ Utilize librarians to maximize their aid in completion of your system study.

☐ Feel comfortable using libraries.

*I*nformation Needs of Systems Analysts

The systems analyst often has many information needs during the course of a systems study. These needs may vary greatly from study to study. In a Level I study (defined in Chapter 1), the analyst may have to seek out local, corporate, or international data, while a Level IV or Level V study may require very little that is external to the area under study. This need for data can include just about any subject: persons, places, things, methods, legal requirements, and so forth. It also can encompass many different types of materials: periodical articles, books, newpapers, patents, and so forth. While much of this information may be internal to the firm or area under study, more may be located via the library. In this chapter we discuss the types of materials you can expect to find in the corporate or government agency library, how the materials are indexed for retrieval, and how to locate the actual articles cited in various indexes. Both paper and computerized retrieval methods are described.

Before getting into these details, however, you may be asking yourself why you even need to read this chapter. The answer is two-fold. *First,* our experience is that the library is a reasonable place to find much of the information needed during a system study. *Second,* there are many barriers that limit the usefulness of published information.[1] One of these barriers has been shown in numerous studies to be the researcher's lack of familiarity with published information sources and the available information facilities and services.[2-9] Again, our experience has been that systems analysts tend not to consider the library when they

---

[1] "Barriers Limiting the Usefulness of Published Information in the Research Environment," by D. E. Haag. *Special Libraries,* vol. 75, July 1984, pp. 214–220.

[2] "Access and Recognition: From Users' Data to Catalogue Entries," by R. Tagliacozzo, L. Rosenberg, and M. Kochen. *Journal of Documentation,* vol. 26, 1970, pp. 230–249.

[3] "Clinician Search for Information," by J. Friedlander. *Journal of the American Society for Information Science,* vol. 24, 1973, pp. 65–69.

[4] "Faculty Awareness and Attitudes toward Academic Library Reference Service: A Measure of Communication," by J. Nelson. *College and Research Libraries,* vol. 34, 1973, pp. 268–275.

[5] "How Do Scientists Meet Their Information Needs?" *Special Libraries,* vol. 65, 1974, pp. 272–280.

[6] "Measuring Reader Failure at the Shelf," by C. A. Seymour and J. L. Schofield. *Library Resources and Technical Services,* vol. 17, 1973, pp. 6–24.

[7] "Measuring Reader's Failure at the Shelf in Three University Libraries," by J. A. Urquhart and J. L. Schofield. *Journal of Documentation,* vol. 28, 1972, pp. 233–241.

[8] *Pilot Study on the Use of Scientific Literature by Scientists,* by R. R. Shaw. Scarecrow Press Reprints, 1971, 139 pp.

[9] "Scientists and Social Scientists as Information Users: A Comparison of Results of Science User Studies with the Investigation into Information Requirements of the Social Studies," by B. Skelton. *Journal of Librarianship,* vol. 5, 1973, pp. 138–156.

need literature, they often cannot locate materials that are in the library, their knowledge of sources is poor, and they are unwilling to seek assistance from librarians when they need it. The fact is, you may need this reference chapter far more than you might ever suspect. We recommend that you read it even when it is not assigned as part of your systems analysis course.

The Analyst's Most Overlooked Tool

Among the many tools available to the systems analyst, the library is probably the most overlooked and underestimated of them all. The reasons are many, but they can be summarized in one statement: few of us have been shown the vast amount of useful information a library contains, much less how to utilize this very important resource in an effective and efficient manner. Today, however, most larger corporations recognize that the library is an expensive but vital resource. It becomes a wasted resource if not used by the employees for whom it is maintained. As mentioned previously, your own library needs may vary considerably from project to project, but if you become acquainted with this tool early in your career as a systems analyst, you will be prepared when the need arises.

Corporate libraries today vary greatly in size and content, but most firms have some type of library facility available for their employees' use. Smaller firms in highly specialized technical fields may have the basic books relating to their field and some special reports, but the bulk of the collection might be current technical periodicals. These smaller libraries tend to depend on their local public and college libraries for information of a more general nature.

On the other hand, some large firms have libraries comparable to a public library, the only difference being in emphasis on the type of materials. These materials may include not only books, periodicals, and reports, but other highly specialized items such as manufacturers' catalogs and brochures or specifications and standards (these will be discussed later in the chapter). Technical libraries such as these usually have highly trained librarians who also are subject specialists. Additionally, some of these larger libraries, particularly those in the technical fields, have literature searchers whose primary job is to find information in specialized fields for staff members, but this is the exception rather than the rule.

Computerized Literature Searching

One of the primary methods of finding references that are needed during the course of a systems study is to utilize various indexes. These indexes may be to periodical articles, technical reports, government documents, newspaper citations, or to any combination of these or other types of materials. Indexing may be by subject, author, title, report number, or a variety of other indexing points.

There are now two means by which the analyst may go about this searching: manual and computerized. Going through paper copies of these indexes by hand is not only very time-consuming, but it is expensive in terms of the analyst's labor.

Computers have changed libraries as much as they have changed other facilities. Today computers are used in libraries in just about every function: circulation of materials, cataloging (both internally and shared cataloging with other libraries), interlibrary lending of materials, literature searching, and so on. Among the most important of these changes prompted by computers was the increased ability to locate references to relevant articles and retrieve the articles for users. In other words, the advent of computers helped all library users find more efficient methods of using library resources, and primary among these was the computerized method of literature searching. Many of the indexes that are available on library shelves now are available through computerized systems. In addition, many new indexes exist only in a computerized format; that is, they have no paper counterpart. These systems generally are accessed by highly trained librarians or information specialists who not only have an in-depth knowledge of the contents of the various indexes, but who also have specialized training both in the use of the system software and also for the unique capabilities of each individual file within the system. That is, one must have special training in order to know how to get the information out of the computer effectively. (Incidentally, you may be interested to learn that many corporate librarians/information specialists today have at least two master's degrees, one in library science/information handling and one in their subject specialty. Most also attend several seminars a year on the use of specialized materials and systems, so continuing education is considered a high priority for the staff of a corporate library/information center.)

Analysts who work with trained literature searchers will be pleasantly surprised at how quickly and easily the information they need can be retrieved from the computer. In addition, this also is a relatively inexpensive way to proceed. Further, the real advantage to using a computerized index is that the computer can do far more than the human being can in a much shorter period of time, both in terms of the greater number of years of data that the computer can search as well as being able to find more retrieval points. Not only can the searcher search on specific subject categories, but in addition frequently can pinpoint specific terminology that is unique to a particular problem. For example, let us say that the analyst needs to find information on a specifically named system, and wants everything that can be located about that system. The information probably could not be found easily using a subject approach; however, by using what is referred to as "free-text" searching for the specific name of the system, it can be retrieved if there is anything relevant in the particular database that is being searched.

Notice our reference to whether there is anything relevant in a specific database. Today there are hundreds of databases (or indexes) available in dozens of systems. Some of the databases are in several systems. For example, the paper index titled *Government Reports Announcements & Index* is known in its computerized version as NTIS (this is the name of its publisher, the National Technical Information Service, which is part of the Department of Commerce). The NTIS database is in several computerized bibliographic systems, among them DIALOG (Lockheed Retrieval Services), ORBIT (SDC Search Service), and BRS (Bibliographic Retrieval Services). Multiply this one example by hundreds and you will see why knowing where to look for relevant information is very time-consuming and takes a great deal of reading.

Our intent here is not to teach you everything there is to know about libraries and retrieval methods, but to help you gain an understanding of why you need to seek assistance in your search for information. Your job is analyzing systems in an effective and knowledgeable manner; the librarian's job is to help you achieve that goal. One library may have access to 15 or 20 different computerized systems from around the world and these systems might contain 300 or more different databases/indexes. Because this is far more than one person can possibly know, it is not uncommon for the librarians to specialize in certain databases. For example, one librarian may specialize in business databases, while another specializes in engineering, and another in the physical or life sciences (chemistry, biology, and so forth). If your subject is interdisciplinary, more than one librarian may assist you in locating needed information. Each one brings his or her special expertise to solving your problem.

*H*ow to Find Your Library Materials

Once the searcher or analyst finds citations to specific articles, the analyst needs to retrieve some of these in order to get the facts that are needed. While the library of the corporation or agency in which you work may have numerous publications available at hand, there may be many more that are not readily available. Just because the materials are not available in the same facility, however, does not mean that they are totally unavailable.

Today most corporate libraries, and indeed many other types of libraries as well, belong to cooperative networks. These networks tend to emanate from the Library of Congress in Washington, through the various state libraries (such as the California State Library in Sacramento), and down to smaller local level cooperatives in which member libraries are those from the corporate, educational, and public library communities. In practical terms, these cooperatives mean that the systems analyst can ask the corporate librarian to procure material that previously may have been unavailable because no one knew where it might be located. In many cases federal funds to library systems have enabled cooperating libraries to publish joint lists of holdings (called "union lists") so that materials can be located more effectively. Some libraries now have cooperative cataloging, and some even purchase costly items jointly that none could afford alone. One example of such sharing is vividly demonstrated in California where the University of California (a public university) Berkeley campus library and the Stanford University (a private university) library allow their students to borrow directly from one another's library. Not only do they allow interlibrary borrowing, but a bus goes between the two campuses on a daily basis to facilitate such borrowing. Further, Stanford University has developed a computerized library cataloging system, called RLIN (Research Libraries Information Network), in which numerous libraries share their cataloging (there are other shared cataloging networks, for example OCLC in Ohio and WLIN in the state of Washington). In practical terms, this means that if your library is an RLIN participant, you can learn quickly and easily that perhaps three or four other libraries have a book you want. Your interlibrary loan request may be sent via electronic mail to the nearest library, and the book is in your hands within a few days. The days of dusty and unused bookshelves are gone; today's libraries are dynamic!

Cooperative borrowing is done through a formal Interlibrary Loan Request from one library to another (not by individuals). While there is a specific routine to follow in requesting these materials through interlibrary loan, in exceptional cases local librarians cooperate to the extent of providing materials on a same-day or next-day basis when feasible. This, of course, depends on the work load of the various libraries involved. You may be sure, however, that your corporate librarian will do everything possible to help you find the materials you need in order to complete your project on time.

What Your Library Contains . . . Basics[10]

Periodicals

When most people think of libraries, they tend to think of books. To the analyst who needs the latest information on a particular subject, however, periodicals may be the most important resource. This is because books have one inherent disadvantage, which is the time lag it takes to write, publish, and market them. If this process takes two years, it is possible that the book is outdated even before it

---

[10] If you are totally unfamiliar with libraries, there are many books available to guide you. Among them are Gates' *Guide to the Use of Books and Libraries,* Johnson's *How to Use the Business Library,* and Downs' *How to Do Library Research.*

gets to readers. Periodicals, on the other hand, are used as a means of getting new information to others in a relatively short period of time. If you look at professional journals, some indicate when the article was received for review. You then can calculate approximately how recent the information is. In addition, prior to computers, the time lag that it took for a specific article to be received and indexed by one of the indexing services frequently was six months to a year or more. The whole concept of up-to-date information simply did not exist. With the computerization of indexes, this whole area has changed radically. Some services now update their bibliographic citations daily or weekly, which means that it now is possible to obtain references to information that is only days or weeks old. It is for this reason that periodicals often make up the bulk of a special library's collection; it is through them that the analyst keeps up with what is happening currently in a given field. This is true especially in high technology industries. Some libraries maintain interest profiles for regular users. Such profiles are used for generating bibliographic citations of interest to the specific user. These current awareness services sometimes are called SDI or selective dissemination of information.

As a systems analyst, you no doubt will want to read each issue of the *Journal of Systems Management* or perhaps computer-oriented publications such as *Computerworld* if you deal primarily with computerized systems. Also, if your employer is in an industry for which there are several trade journals, you undoubtedly will want to read them on a regular basis.

You may say fine, but what do I do when I need information for a specific project? First, define the subject as well as you can. After that, your task is to locate applicable periodicals. One source that will help is *Ulrich's International Periodicals Directory*. This publication is a guide to journals published in all countries. It provides the name of the journal, publisher information, frequency of publication, price, and whether it includes such items as advertisements or illustrations. Since it is arranged and indexed by subject, it is an excellent means of locating the leading journals in a field. Because it is updated frequently, it is an important tool for locating new journals that may not yet be indexed in other databases. The computer enhances retrieval, since one can obtain the titles of all journals having a particular word in the title. *Ulrich's,* as it is known commonly, not only helps locate relevant periodicals, but it also indicates where they are indexed. You need to know this because it is inefficient and costly to go through periodicals on an issue-by-issue basis. Indexes arranged by subject have been designed to save you time. Some of these are

Business Periodicals Index. This index is perhaps the best known to the business systems analyst because it indexes articles found in most of the major business periodicals. Subject indexing is either by the name of the industry or by a particular subject area such as electronic data processing. Figure 19-1 shows a typical page from this index. It is available both in paper format and via computer. 1958– .

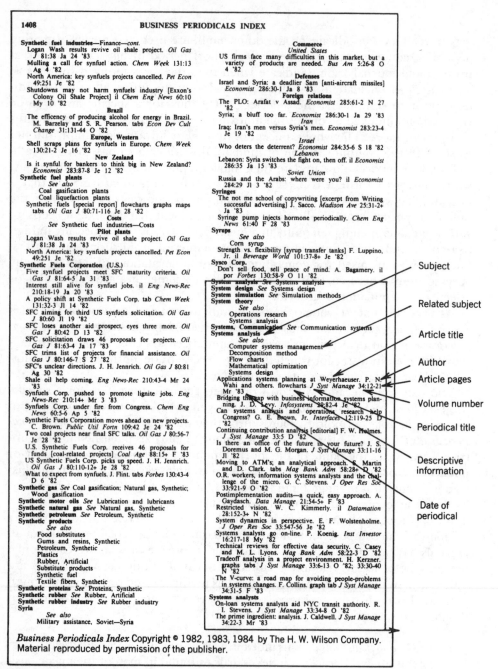

Synthetic fuel industries—Finance—*cont.*
Logan Wash results revive oil shale project. *Oil Gas J* 81:38 Ja 24 '83
Mulling a call for synfuel action. *Chem Week* 131:13 Ag 4 '82
North America: key synfuels projects cancelled. *Pet Econ* 49:251 Je '82
Shutdowns may not harm synfuels industry [Exxon's Colony Oil Shale Project] il *Chem Eng News* 60:10 My 10 '82

Brazil
The efficency of producing alcohol for energy in Brazil. M. Barzelay and S. R. Pearson. tabs *Econ Dev Cult Change* 31:131-44 O '82

Europe, Western
Shell scraps plans for synfuels in Europe. *Chem Week* 130:21-2 Je 16 '82

New Zealand
Is it synful for bankers to think big in New Zealand? *Economist* 283:87-8 Je 12 '82
Synthetic fuel plants
    See also
    Coal gasification plants
    Coal liquefaction plants
Synthetic fuels [special report] flowcharts graphs maps tabs *Oil Gas J* 80:71-116 Je 28 '82
        Costs
        See Synthetic fuel industries—Costs
        Pilot plants
Logan Wash results revive oil shale project. *Oil Gas J* 81:38 Ja 24 '83
North America: key synfuels projects cancelled. *Pet Econ* 49:251 Je '82
Synthetic Fuels Corporation (U.S.)
Five synfuel projects meet SFC maturity criteria. *Oil Gas J* 81:64-5 Ja 31 '83
Interest still alive for synfuel jobs. il *Eng News-Rec* 210:18-19 Ja 20 '83
A policy shift at Synthetic Fuels Corp. tab *Chem Week* 131:32-3 Jl 14 '82
SFC aiming for third US synfuels solicitation. *Oil Gas J* 80:60 Jl 19 '82
SFC loses another aid prospect, eyes three more. *Oil Gas J* 80:42 D 13 '82
SFC solicitation draws 46 proposals for projects. *Oil Gas J* 81:63-4 Ja 17 '83
SFC trims list of projects for financial assistance. *Oil Gas J* 80:146-7 S 27 '82
SFC's unclear directions. J. H. Jennrich. *Oil Gas J* 80:81 Ag 30 '82
Shale oil help coming. *Eng News-Rec* 210:43-4 Mr 24 '83
Synfuels Corp. pushed to promote lignite jobs. *Eng News-Rec* 210:14+ Mr 3 '83
Synfuels Corp. under fire from Congress. *Chem Eng News* 60:5-6 Ap 5 '82
Synthetic Fuels Corporation moves ahead on new projects. C. Brown. *Public Util Fortn* 109:42 Je 24 '82
Two coal projects near final SFC talks. *Oil Gas J* 80:56-7 Je 28 '82
U.S. Synthetic Fuels Corp. receives 46 proposals for funds [coal-related projects] *Coal Age* 88:15+ F '83
US Synthetic Fuels Corp. picks up speed. J. H. Jennrich. *Oil Gas J* 80:110-12+ Je 28 '82
What to expect from synfuels. J. Flint. tabs *Forbes* 130:43-4 D 6 '82
Synthetic gas *See* Coal gasification; Natural gas, Synthetic; Wood gasification
Synthetic motor oils *See* Lubrication and lubricants
Synthetic natural gas *See* Natural gas, Synthetic
Synthetic petroleum *See* Petroleum, Synthetic
Synthetic products
    See also
    Food substitutes
    Gums and resins, Synthetic
    Petroleum, Synthetic
    Plastics
    Rubber, Artificial
    Substitute products
    Synthetic fuel
    Textile fibers, Synthetic
Synthetic proteins *See* Proteins, Synthetic
Synthetic rubber *See* Rubber, Artificial
Synthetic rubber industry *See* Rubber industry
Syria
    See also
    Military assistance, Soviet—Syria

Commerce
        United States
US firms face many difficulties in this market, but a variety of products are needed. *Bus Am* 5:26-8 O 4 '82
        Defenses
Israel and Syria: a deadlier Sam [anti-aircraft missiles] *Economist* 286:30-1 Ja 8 '83
        Foreign relations
The PLO: Arafat v Assad. *Economist* 285:61-2 N 27 '82
Syria; a bluff too far. *Economist* 286:30-1 Ja 29 '83
                Iran
Iraq: Iran's men versus Syria's men. *Economist* 283:23-4 Je 19 '82
                Israel
Who deters the deterrent? *Economist* 284:35-6 S 18 '82
                Lebanon
Lebanon: Syria switches the fight on, then off. il *Economist* 286:35 Ja 15 '83
                Soviet Union
Russia and the Arabs: where were you? il *Economist* 284:29 Jl 3 '82
Syringes
The not me school of copywriting [excerpt from Writing successful advertising] J. Sacco. *Madison Ave* 25:31-2+ Ja '83
Syringe pump injects hormone periodically. *Chem Eng News* 61:40 F 28 '83
Syrups
    See also
    Corn syrup
Strength vs. flexibility [syrup transfer tanks] F. Luppino, Jr. il *Beverage World* 101:37-8+ Je '82
Sysco Corp.
Don't sell food, sell peace of mind. A. Bagamery. il por *Forbes* 130:58-9 O 11 '82
System analysis *See* Systems analysis
System design *See* Systems design
System simulation *See* Simulation methods
System theory
    See also
    Operations research
    Systems analysis
Systems, Communication *See* Communication systems
Systems analysis
    See also
    Computer systems management
    Decomposition method
    Flow charts
    Mathematical optimization
    Systems design
Applications systems planning at Weyerhaeuser. P. N. Wahi and others. flowcharts *J Syst Manage* 34:12-21 Mr '83
Bridging the gap with business information systems planning. J. D. Levy. *Infosystems* 29:82-4 Je '82
Can systems analysis and operations research help Congress? G. E. Brown, Jr. *Interfaces* 12:119-25 D '82
Continuing contribution analysis [editorial] F. W. Holmes. *J Syst Manage* 33:5 D '82
Is there an office of the future in your future? J. S. Doremus and M. G. Morgan. *J Syst Manage* 33:11-16 Jl '82
Moving to ATM's; an analytical approach. S. Martin and D. Clark. tabs *Mag Bank Adm* 58:28+ O '82
O.R. workers, information systems analysts and the challenge of the micro. G. C. Stevens. *J Oper Res Soc* 33:921-9 O '82
Postimplementation audits—a quick, easy approach. A. Gaydasch. *Data Manage* 21:54-5+ F '83
Restricted vision. W. C. Kimmerly. il *Datamation* 28:152-3+ N '82
System dynamics in perspective. E. F. Wolstenholme. *J Oper Res Soc* 33:547-56 Je '82
Systems analysts go on-line. P. Koenig. *Inst Investor* 16:217-18 My '82
Technical reviews for effective data security. C. Casey and M. L. Lyons. *Mag Bank Adm* 58:22-3 D '82
Tradeoff analysis in a project environment. H. Kerzner. graphs tabs *J Syst Manage* 33:6-13 O '82; 33:30-40 N '82
The V-curve: a road map for avoiding people-problems in systems changes. F. Collins. graph tab *J Syst Manage* 34:31-5 F '83
Systems analysts
On-loan systems analysts aid NYC transit authority. R. I. Stevens. *J Syst Manage* 33:34-8 O '82
The prime ingredient: analysis. J. Caldwell. *J Syst Manage* 34:22-3 Mr '83

Subject
Related subject
Article title
Author
Article pages
Volume number
Periodical title
Descriptive information
Date of periodical

Figure 19-1 Sample page from *Business Periodicals Index.*

Abstracted Business Information. This index, which is available only in computerized form, cites references to articles related to all areas of business. It is particularly strong in management. It is in direct competition with *Business Periodicals Index. ABI/INFORM* as it is sometimes known, includes abstracts, however, in addition to the bibliographic information. 1971– .

PROMT and *Funk & Scott Index.* These complementary indexes are essentially the same database. *PROMT* abstracts marketing-oriented articles with a slant toward products, processes, and services for sale by business firms. Indexing is by product, country/state, and "event" (sales, new product/ process, demand, profits, cost per unit, industry structure/members, legal actions, regulatory actions, etc.). Bibliographic information is brief, but abstracts are informative. The *Funk & Scott Index* is strictly an indexing tool; it indexes the same references found in the *PROMT* portion of the index, plus others that are too short for an abstract. The latter would include a one-line announcement indicating that one firm has contracted with another for so many dollars to obtain a certain product. Items that are indexed are international in scope and include journals, trade literature, government documents, and so on. Because of its product orientation, *PROMT* is very useful in locating information on the latest developments in computerized systems. 1972– .

COMPENDEX (COMPuterized ENgineering inDEX). As the title implies, emphasis of this index is on engineering. It is useful especially for determining how others have applied data communications and computers in an industrial or factory-type situation. An example would be an industrial control application. Indexing includes a large number of international journals, technical symposia, reports, government documents, and other materials. References include abstracts. 1970– .

INSPEC. The printed counterparts of this computerized index are *Physics Abstracts, Electrical and Electronics Abstracts*, and *Computer and Control Abstracts*. Because business relies so heavily on computers, and because computers enable the process of data communications, the *Computer and Control Abstracts* portion of this database is an excellent resource. It includes the technical aspects: applications, techniques, hardware, software, technological developments, and architectures. Recently, emphasis has been added in the areas of economics and the practical aspects of implementing such systems. References are international in scope and contain abstracts (see Figure 19-2). 1969– .

Applied Science and Technology Index. This is a subject index to English language periodicals in the fields of aeronautics/space science, automation, chemistry, construction, earth sciences, electricity, and electronics. References do not contain abstracts (see Figure 19-3). Available in both paper format and computerized versions. 1958– .

1850

Computer & Control Abstracts Vol. 19 No. 219 (August 1984)

Continuous recognition of speech. An acoustic-phonetic model ....See Entry 28594

Fast filtering techniques for isolated word recognition ....See Entry 28631

A phonological processor for Italian ....See Entry 29585

An expert system for the production of phoneme strings from unmarked English text using machine-induced rules ....See Entry 29590

Ease-of-use features in the Texas Instruments professional computer ....See Entry 30034

Voice I/O: an effective option for CAD systems ....See Entry 31439

Speech for control of VLSI graphics ....See Entry 31582

Listening cards or speech recognition ....See Entry 31691

Spread the word [talking computers] ....See Entry 31838

55.90 OTHER PERIPHERAL EQUIPMENT

30392   Commander keyboard. A.Leyenberger.
Creative Comput. (USA), vol.10, no.1, p.98-9 (Jan. 1984).
The author presents the detachable Commander keyboard for use with the Atari microcomputers. The author describes the advantages of using the keyboard and the difficulties in installing it. (no refs.)

30393   The PCPI Appli-Card. L.E.Becker.
Creative Comput. (USA), vol.10, no.1, p.100-2 (Jan. 1984).
The author presents the Appli-Card from PCPI, a plug-in card for the Apple II microcomputers. The author reviews the utilities and general features of the card. (no refs.)

30394   Light pens and graphics tablets: new ways to communicate with your computer. K.Yakal.
Compute. J. Prog. Comput. (USA), vol.6, no.5, p.34-8, 42 (May 1984).
This article assesses the worth of light pens and Graphics tablets as input devices. It explains their use and gives details of how they work. In particular, it explains how these devices allow the user to create sophisticated computer graphics easily. (no refs.)

30395   The inside story: how graphics tablets and light pens work. O.R.Cowper.
Compute. J. Prog. Comput. (USA), vol.6, no.5, p.40-2 (May 1984).
Many programmers find graphics tablets and light pens among the most mysterious of peripherals, but the pr_____ ____ _ fairly simple. This article examines the technology _____ __d describes the principles behind their operation. (no ___)

30396   Solid state TV camera. II. _____ _ml. R.Harvey, R.Sargent.
Electron. & Comput. Mon. (GB), vol.4, p.4-6 supl. (May 1984).
For pt.I see ibid., vol.4, no.4 (1984). The hardware of the vision system, described in part I, simply consists of a DRAM chip with its 'lid' removed, and a PIO to interface the DRAM IC to the Spectrum's data bus. The software is presented in two halves. The first routines are concerned with picture acquisition, where timing loops are responsible for interrogating and evaluating the capacitance (and hence the recorded light value) on a particular memory cell. The video image is obtained and placed in STORE. The later routines, specific to the Spectrum, take the information from STORE and display it on the Spectrum screen. The program listings presented are in machine code and assembly language. (no refs.)

30397   300 Mbyte on one cassette: Eurocom-II V7 with video recorder connection. I.Thilo.
Mikrocomput. Z. (Germany), no.3, p.90-2 (March 1984). In German.
A video cassette digital data recording and replay system is described with reference to the Eurocom-II V7 computer. Optocouplers are used in the interface developed for the peripheral interface adapter 6821, and remote operation is possible. PIA software applicable to 6809 microcomputers is briefly discussed. Sub program flow diagrams and listings illustrate record and load procedures in 312 line single field form, with 256 lines being used for data. Single lines correspond to about $^1/_4$ Kbyte, and data transfer rate is 220 Kbit/s. Operating aspects including graph _____ __ ___ are briefly discussed. (2 refs.) H.V.H.

30398   The labour of Hercules. F.Clarl
PC User (GB), p.49-50, 115 (March 1984).
The author presents the 'Hercules' graphic ____ ____ ___ personal computer. The card allows the user to produce high-resolution graphics using the '1-2-3' spreadsheet. (no refs.)

30399   ZX 81 a la carte. IX. Hardware—full sound. Three tone generators in one swoop. O.Merker.
Funkschau (Germany), no.9, p.70-2 (27 April 1984). In German.
For pt.VIII see ibid., no.8, p.71 (1984). The complete circuit diagram of the tone generator is reproduced and described in some detail. The data input selector (DIL 1) permits any of the eight capacitors to be earthed by means of two ICs; a total of 255 different notes can be generated. The customary two drawings of the printed board are included, also advice on calibration and test. Examples of short programs are quoted, with hints on operation via the PIO port. (no refs.) A.L.

30400   Floppy Card III. D.D.Vanmeister, S.Hymes.
Apple Orchard (USA), vol.5, no.2, p.70-1 (Feb. 1984).
The author presents the Burtonix 'Floppycard III' for the Apple III microcomputer. The card interfaces the standard 8-inch double density/double sided disk drives to the Apple microcomputer. (no refs.)

30401   Delay of keyboard typamatic mode. R.E.Chukran (IBM Corp., Armonk, NY, USA).
IBM Tech. Disclosure Bull. (USA), _____ _ec. 1983).
In order to prevent errors in blinc _____ _____ author suggests increasing the apparent delay betwe ____ ____ of a key and the subsequent generation of the first ty_ ___ __ (no refs.)

Portable terminal selection ....See Entry 28310

Analyzers mate with personal computers to lower costs ....See Entry 29696

Joystick for TI99/4A ....See Entry 30105

Keyboard with optically changeable key symbols ....See Entry 30308

The terminal and its peripherals ....See Entry 30314

How to print bar codes and make sure they're scannable ... See Entry 30561

Transport under micro-information technology: on the road! ... See Entry 31157

Input keys for electronic devices of high reliability—comparative investigation on the ergonomics ....See Entry 31694

60.00 COMPUTER SOFTWARE

30402   Software directory.
PC User (GB), p.117-36 (March 1984).
Lists all the new software for IBM personal computer and properly compatible machines—including updates on previous entries. Gives a full listing of software for special applications and special users for the less common PC pursuits. (no refs.)

30403   Programs on TV. G.Moody.
Pract. Comput. (GB), vol.7, no.5, p.102-3 (May 1984).
Discusses broadcast software and accesses the BBC's Ceefax based service and the Acorn/BBC teletext system. Teletext can broadcast software simultaneously with normal programmes. It is therefore possible to transmit software throughout the day, and even to update it, if necessary. (no refs.)

Encyclopedia of computer science and engineering. 2nd edition ....See Entry 28071

Software strategies control micro market ....See Entry 29969

61.00 SOFTWARE TECHNIQUES AND SYSTEMS

30404   A simple measure of software complexity. L.O.Ejiogu.
Computerworld (USA), vol.18, no.14, p.ID10-16 (2 April 1984).
Software engineering needs a metric that can appeal to all software practitioners, irrespective of programming environment or educational background. The tree is used to abstract certain properties of natural relationships, as in genealogy, chain reactions, or organizational personnel structures. In software engineering, the tree models data structures and control structures. The mathematical tradition of modeling with a tree is extended first to reveal some attributes of software structure and then to derive a simple model for measuring software complexity. (no refs.)

30405   Developing a product by an intensive software project. W.A.Swope, S.Zacholi.
Elettron. Oggi (Italy), no.3, p.46-8 (March 1984). In Italian.
The authors discuss the problems of a large team of software experts concerned with microcomputers of complex structure. They deal with the various stages in the development of products and the problems involved. For each problem they discuss the appropriate tool or microprocessor system required for the product producing system and try to evaluate its efficiency. There are four stages. The design and building of the system to make the product (its hardware and software); the prototype hardware and all the tests involved; the debugging of the peripheral equipment; testing the operation of the whole system. Finally, the authors discuss the methods of checking the applications of a system and consider the future prospects for this method of developing projects. (no refs.) G.W.

30406   Development instruments depending on the NS 16000 family. F.Montanari.
Elettron. Oggi (Italy), no.3, p.52-5 (March 1984). In Italian.
The author states that within less than a year after putting their NS 16000 family on the market, National Semiconductor has also provided an ample range of supporting instruments to give the project designer all the help he needs in designing, developing, and debugging software and hardware modules based on this NS 16000 family. This auxiliary equipment includes: a computer card (built on the tiny development system); the software required to handle the three different modes of using the NS 16000; packets of cross software, an emulator ISE 16; the SYS 16 development system and third party software. The functions of each of these auxiliary aids are described in some detail. (no refs.) G.W.

30407   Guidance on software maintenance. R.P.Martin, W.M.Osborne.
Report NBS-SP-500-106, Nat. Bur. Stand., Washington, DC, USA (Dec. 1983), vi+66 pp.
This report addresses issues and problems of software maintenance and suggests actions and procedures which can help software maintenance organisations meet the growing demands of maintaining existing systems. The report establishes a working definition for software maintenance and presents an overview of current problems and issues in that area. Tools and techniques that may be used to improve the control of software maintenance activities and the productivity of a software maintenance organization are discussed. Emphasis is placed on the need for strong, effective technical management control of the software maintenance process. (80 refs.)

30408   An experiment in microprocessor-based distributed digital simulation. D.L.Wyatt, S.Sheppard, R.E.Young (Texas A&M Univ., College Station, TX, USA).
1983 Winter Simulation Conference Proceedings, Arlington, VA, USA, 12-14 Dec. 1983 (New York, USA: IEEE 1983), p.271-7 vol.l.
The design of a distributed simulation system which will utilize off-the-shelf microprocessors in its implementation is discussed. Alternative approaches to the assignment of simulation functions and processes are presented. A project is described which considers the impact of distributed architectures on the design of simulation language support systems. The emphasis in this research project is to produce an operational prototype which can be used to establish the feasibility and utility of distributed simulation. (24 refs.)

30409   Tools for program documentation. C.S.Sankar (Temple Univ., Philadelphia, PA, USA).
1983 IEEE Professional Communication Society Conference Record. The Many Facets of Computer Communications, Atlanta, GA, USA, 19-21 Oct. 1983 (New York, USA: IEEE 1983), p.145-7
The author discusses the tools available to document programs and proposes a new method. This method consists of creating three reports during the development and testing of a computer program. The three reports are: (1) objective of computer program, (2) user manual, (3) detailed description of the outputs, inputs, files, logic and programs. These reports are described, and the items to be included in these reports are outlined. (6 refs.)

Software serial number ....See Entry 28277

On a software availability model with imperfect maintenance ...See Entry 28436

Active logical processes and distributed simulation: an analysis ....See Entry 28466

Performance analysis of a distributed simulation algorithm based on active logical processes ....See Entry 28466

Inductive inference: theory and methods ....See Entry 28479

Callout labels (right margin): Main subject subheading; Abstract number; Periodical title; Country of publication; Article title; Author; Language; Publication date; Pages; Issue number; Report number; Report title; Authors; Publication date; Publishing agency; Pagination; Number of bibliographic references; Paper title; Author; Author affiliation; Book title; Pages of paper; Publisher; Number of bibliographic references; Related article

Callout labels (left, within figure): Periodical article; Report; Conference paper

Figure 19-2 Sample page from *Computer and Control Abstracts.*

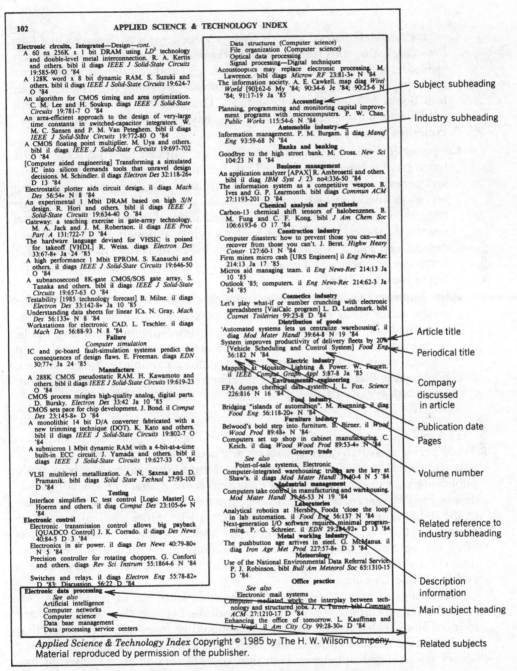

Figure 19-3 Sample page from *Applied Science & Technology Index*.

Computer Literature Index (formerly *Quarterly Bibliography of Computers and Data Processing*). Contains references to periodical articles, books, loose-leaf services, and some reports. Indexing is by subject and author, and citations are arranged in subject groupings. Each subject grouping is divided further into Books & Reports and Periodicals. One feature that is unique to this index is the highlighting of noteworthy articles or books (see Figure 19-4). Published quarterly. 1971– .

Computing Reviews. This publication is not an index in the true sense of the term. Its purpose, as the title reflects, is to provide critical reviews of books and periodical articles in the area of computers. Each review is assigned an accession number which is used to locate articles by specific authors. Arrangement is by a complicated, but well defined, alphanumeric decimal system. As shown in Figure 19-5, H.2.1 is logical design, H.2.2 is physical design, and H.2.3 is data models. This index of reviews is designed for computer specialists and many of the reviews are highly technical. Published monthly. 1960– .

PAIS Bulletin. The *PAIS Bulletin* contains citations to publications in the public sector. It is of special interest to systems analysts who work for municipalities, urban development, rural development, or in any public agency up to the level of the United States government and the United Nations. It cites a wide range of publications including periodical articles, books, pamphlets, and government reports or documents (see Figure 19-6). Published weekly. 1915– .

External sources may be most helpful in locating information on the industry. Trade periodicals often carry articles on new products, developments in technology, and trends in sales, growth, and profit. Most of the major industries' trade publications are indexed by *Business Periodicals Index, Abstracted Business Information,* or *Funk & Scott Index.* In many cases, you need only to look under the name of the industry to locate citations to relevant articles. Since the major business periodicals (*Fortune, Dun's, Forbes,* etc.) are indexed, special industry reports often can be located quickly and easily. In addition, you may find the various financial services helpful. These would include Moody's, Standard and Poor's, and the Value Line series.

This brings us to another type of publication, loose-leaf or ring-binder services. We are including these under periodicals because they sometimes are indexed along with other periodicals. You should be forewarned, however, that most libraries treat them more like books. That is, if the periodicals in your library are arranged alphabetically by title, you will not find them shelved by title in the periodicals section. Instead, they usually are treated like a reference book: located by looking in the card catalog and then found by call number (books are discussed in the next section). These loose-leaf services are serial publications in

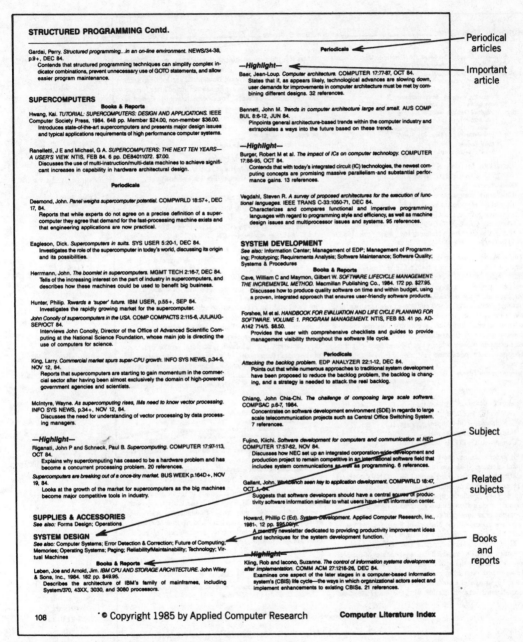

STRUCTURED PROGRAMMING Contd.

Gardai, Perry. *Structured programming...in an on-line environment.* NEWS/34-38, p.9+, DEC 84.
    Contends that structured programming techniques can simplify complex indicator combinations, prevent unnecessary use of GOTO statements, and allow easier program maintenance.

SUPERCOMPUTERS

Books & Reports

Hwang, Kai. *TUTORIAL: SUPERCOMPUTERS: DESIGN AND APPLICATIONS.* IEEE Computer Society Press, 1984. 648 pp. Member $24.00, non-member $36.00.
    Introduces state-of-the-art supercomputers and presents major design issues and typical applications requirements of high performance computer systems.

Ranelletti, J E and Michael, G A. *SUPERCOMPUTERS: THE NEXT TEN YEARS—A USER'S VIEW.* NTIS, FEB 84. 6 pp. DE84011072. $7.00.
    Discusses the use of multi-instruction/multi-data machines to achieve significant increases in capability in hardware architectural design.

Periodicals

Desmond, John. *Panel weighs supercomputer potential.* COMPWRLD 18:57+, DEC 17, 84.
    Reports that while experts do not agree on a precise definition of a supercomputer they agree that demand for the fast-processing machine exists and that engineering applications are now practical.

Eagleson, Dick. *Supercomputers in suits.* SYS USER 5:20-1, DEC 84.
    Investigates the role of the supercomputer in today's world, discussing its origin and its possibilities.

Herrmann, John. *The boomlet in supercomputers.* MGMT TECH 2:16-7, DEC 84.
    Tells of the increasing interest on the part of industry in supercomputers, and describes how these machines could be used to benefit big business.

Hunter, Philip. *Towards a 'super' future.* IBM USER, p.55+, SEP 84.
    Investigates the rapidly growing market for the supercomputer.

John Conolly of supercomputers in the USA. COMP COMPACTS 2:115-6, JUL/AUG-SEP/OCT 84.
    Interviews John Conolly, Director of the Office of Advanced Scientific Computing at the National Science Foundation, whose main job is directing the use of computers for science.

King, Larry. *Commercial market spurs super-CPU growth.* INFO SYS NEWS, p.34-5, NOV 12, 84.
    Reports that supercomputers are starting to gain momentum in the commercial sector after having been almost exclusively the domain of high-powered government agencies and scientists.

McIntyre, Wayne. *As supercomputing rises, IMs need to know vector processing.* INFO SYS NEWS, p.34+, NOV 12, 84.
    Discusses the need for understanding of vector processing by data processing managers.

—Highlight—
Riganati, John P and Schneck, Paul B. *Supercomputing.* COMPUTER 17:97-113, OCT 84.
    Explains why supercomputing has ceased to be a hardware problem and has become a concurrent processing problem. 20 references.

Supercomputers are breaking out of a once-tiny market. BUS WEEK p.164D+, NOV 19, 84.
    Looks at the growth of the market for supercomputers as the big machines become major competitive tools in industry.

SUPPLIES & ACCESSORIES
See also: Forms Design; Operations

SYSTEM DESIGN
See also: Computer Systems; Error Detection & Correction; Future of Computing; Memories; Operating Systems; Paging; Reliability/Maintainability; Technology; Virtual Machines

Books & Reports

Leben, Joe and Arnold, Jim. *IBM CPU AND STORAGE ARCHITECTURE.* John Wiley & Sons, Inc., 1984. 182 pp. $49.95.
    Describes the architecture of IBM's family of mainframes, including System/370, 43XX, 3030, and 3080 processors.

Periodicals

—Highlight—
Baer, Jean-Loup. *Computer architecture.* COMPUTER 17:77-87, OCT 84.
    States that if, as appears likely, technological advances are slowing down, user demands for improvements in computer architecture must be met by combining different designs. 32 references.

Bennett, John M. *Trends in computer architecture large and small.* AUS COMP BUL 8:6-12, JUN 84.
    Pinpoints general architecture-based trends within the computer industry and extrapolates a ways into the future based on these trends.

—Highlight—
Burger, Robert M et al. *The impact of ICs on computer technology.* COMPUTER 17:88-95, OCT 84.
    Contends that with today's integrated circuit (IC) technologies, the newest computing concepts are promising massive parallelism and substantial performance gains. 13 references.

Vegdahl, Steven R. *A survey of proposed architectures for the execution of functional languages.* IEEE TRANS C-33:1050-71, DEC 84.
    Characterizes and compares functional and imperative programming languages with regard to programming style and efficiency, as well as machine design issues and multiprocessor issues and systems. 95 references.

SYSTEM DEVELOPMENT
See also: Information Center; Management of EDP; Management of Programming; Prototyping; Requirements Analysis; Software Maintenance; Software Quality; Systems & Procedures

Books & Reports

Cave, William C and Maymon, Gilbert W. *SOFTWARE LIFECYCLE MANAGEMENT: THE INCREMENTAL METHOD.* Macmillan Publishing Co., 1984. 172 pp. $27.95.
    Discusses how to produce quality software on time and within budget, using a proven, integrated approach that ensures user-friendly software products.

Forshee, M et al. *HANDBOOK FOR EVALUATION AND LIFE CYCLE PLANNING FOR SOFTWARE. VOLUME 1. PROGRAM MANAGEMENT.* NTIS, FEB 83. 41 pp. AD-A142 714/5. $8.50.
    Provides the user with comprehensive checklists and guides to provide management visibility throughout the software life cycle.

Periodicals

Attacking the backlog problem. EDP ANALYZER 22:1-12, DEC 84.
    Points out that while numerous approaches to traditional system development have been proposed to reduce the backlog problem, the backlog is changing, and a strategy is needed to attack the real backlog.

Chiang, John Chia-Chi. *The challenge of composing large scale software.* COMPSAC p.6-7, 1984.
    Concentrates on software development environment (SDE) in regards to large scale telecommunication projects such as Central Office Switching System. 7 references.

Fujino, Kiichi. *Software development for computers and communication at NEC.* COMPUTER 17:57-62, NOV 84.
    Discusses how NEC set up an integrated corporation-wide development and production project to remain competitive in an international software field that includes system communications as well as programming. 6 references.

Gallant, John. *Workbench seen key to application development.* COMPWRLD 18:47, OCT 1, 84.
    Suggests that software developers should have a central source of productivity software information similar to what users have in an information center.

Howard, Phillip C (Ed). *System Development.* Applied Computer Research, Inc., 1981- 12 pp. $95.00/yr.
    A monthly newsletter dedicated to providing productivity improvement ideas and techniques for the system development function.

—Highlight—
Kling, Rob and Iacono, Suzanne. *The control of information systems developments after implementation.* COMM ACM 27:1218-26, DEC 84.
    Examines one aspect of the later stages in a computer-based information system's (CBIS) life cycle—the ways in which organizational actors select and implement enhancements to existing CBISs. 21 references.

Periodical articles

Important article

Subject

Related subjects

Books and reports

Figure 19-4 Sample page from *Computer Literature Index.*

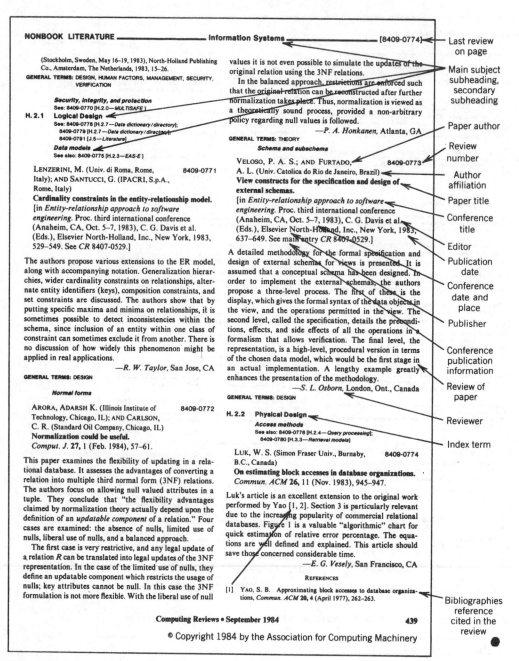

The labels pointing into the figure, from top to bottom on the right:

- Last review on page
- Main subject subheading, secondary subheading
- Paper author
- Review number
- Author affiliation
- Paper title
- Conference title
- Editor
- Publication date
- Conference date and place
- Publisher
- Conference publication information
- Review of paper
- Reviewer
- Index term
- Bibliographies reference cited in the review

The figure content:

NONBOOK LITERATURE ———— **Information Systems** ———— **[8409-0774]**

(Stockholm, Sweden, May 16–19, 1983), North-Holland Publishing Co., Amsterdam, The Netherlands, 1983, 15–26.
GENERAL TERMS: DESIGN, HUMAN FACTORS, MANAGEMENT, SECURITY, VERIFICATION

Security, integrity, and protection
See: 8409-0770 [H.2.0—*MULTISAFE*]

H.2.1　**Logical Design**
See: 8409-0778 [H.2.7—*Data dictionary/directory*];
8409-0779 [H.2.7—*Data dictionary/directory*];
8409-0791 [J.5—*Literature*]

Data models
See also: 8409-0775 [H.2.3—*EAS-E*]

LENZERINI, M. (Univ. di Roma, Rome,　8409-0771
Italy); AND SANTUCCI, G. (IPACRI, S.p.A., Rome, Italy)
Cardinality constraints in the entity-relationship model.
[in *Entity-relationship approach to software engineering*. Proc. third international conference (Anaheim, CA, Oct. 5–7, 1983), C. G. Davis et al. (Eds.), Elsevier North-Holland, Inc., 1983, 529–549. See *CR* 8407-0529.]

The authors propose various extensions to the ER model, along with accompanying notation. Generalization hierarchies, wider cardinality constraints on relationships, alternate entity identifiers (keys), composition constraints, and set constraints are discussed. The authors show that by putting specific maxima and minima on relationships, it is sometimes possible to detect inconsistencies within the schema, since inclusion of an entity within one class of constraint can sometimes exclude it from another. There is no discussion of how widely this phenomenon might be applied in real applications.

—*R. W. Taylor*, San Jose, CA

GENERAL TERMS: DESIGN

Normal forms

ARORA, ADARSH K. (Illinois Institute of　8409-0772
Technology, Chicago, IL); AND CARLSON, C. R. (Standard Oil Company, Chicago, IL)
Normalization could be useful.
Comput. J. **27**, 1 (Feb. 1984), 57–61.

This paper examines the flexibility of updating in a relational database. It assesses the advantages of converting a relation into multiple third normal form (3NF) relations. The authors focus on allowing null valued attributes in a tuple. They conclude that "the flexibility advantages claimed by normalization theory actually depend upon the definition of an *updatable component* of a relation." Four cases are examined: the absence of nulls, limited use of nulls, liberal use of nulls, and a balanced approach.

The first case is very restrictive, and any legal update of a relation *R* can be translated into legal updates of the 3NF representation. In the case of the limited use of nulls, they define an updatable component which restricts the usage of nulls; key attributes cannot be null. In this case the 3NF formulation is not more flexible. With the liberal use of null

values it is not even possible to simulate the updates of the original relation using the 3NF relations.

In the balanced approach, restrictions are enforced such that the original relation can be reconstructed after further normalization takes place. Thus, normalization is viewed as a theoretically sound process, provided a non-arbitrary policy regarding null values is followed.

—*P. A. Honkanen*, Atlanta, GA

GENERAL TERMS: THEORY

Schema and subschema

VELOSO, P. A. S.; AND FURTADO,　8409-0773
A. L. (Univ. Catolica do Rio de Janeiro, Brazil)
View constructs for the specification and design of external schemas.
[in *Entity-relationship approach to software engineering*. Proc. third international conference (Anaheim, CA, Oct. 5–7, 1983), C. G. Davis et al. (Eds.), Elsevier North-Holland, Inc., New York, 1983, 637–649. See main entry *CR* 8407-0529.]

A detailed methodology for the formal specification and design of external schemas for views is presented. It is assumed that a conceptual schema has been designed. In order to implement the external schemas, the authors propose a three-level process. The first of these is the display, which gives the formal syntax of the data objects in the view, and the operations permitted in the view. The second level, called the specification, details the preconditions, effects, and side effects of all the operations in a formalism that allows verification. The final level, the representation, is a high-level, procedural version in terms of the chosen data model, which would be the first stage in an actual implementation. A lengthy example greatly enhances the presentation of the methodology.

—*S. L. Osborn*, London, Ont., Canada

GENERAL TERMS: DESIGN

H.2.2　**Physical Design**
Access methods
See also: 8409-0776 [H.2.4—*Query processing*];
8409-0780 [H.3.3—*Retrieval models*]

LUK, W. S. (Simon Fraser Univ., Burnaby,　8409-0774
B.C., Canada)
On estimating block accesses in database organizations.
Commun. ACM **26**, 11 (Nov. 1983), 945–947.

Luk's article is an excellent extension to the original work performed by Yao [1, 2]. Section 3 is particularly relevant due to the increasing popularity of commercial relational databases. Figure 1 is a valuable "algorithmic" chart for quick estimation of relative error percentage. The equations are well defined and explained. This article should save those concerned considerable time.

—*E. G. Vesely*, San Francisco, CA

REFERENCES

[1]　YAO, S. B.　Approximating block accesses to database organizations, *Commun. ACM* **20**, 4 (April 1977), 262–263.

Figure 19-5 Sample page from *Computing Reviews*.

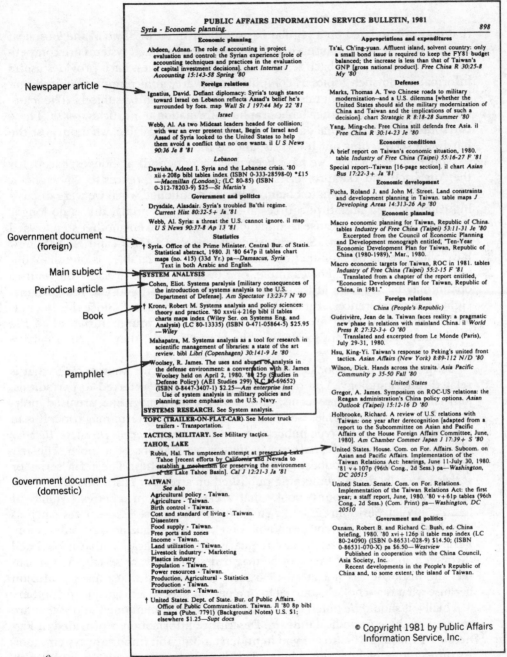

Figure 19-6 Sample page from *PAIS Bulletin.*

that they are updated on a regular basis, usually monthly. Two of the loose-leaf services that you need to use when designing computerized systems are competitors. They are the Auerbach series and the Datapro series. Each provides useful information on such topics as computer hardware, minicomputers, microcomputers, terminals, peripherals, and other hardware-oriented subjects. The material in these series is neither bibliographic information nor articles, *per se*. These two sources contain factual data on what hardware is available, what purpose the hardware serves, how much it costs, and so forth.

Notice that until now, we have been discussing periodical indexes, except for the Auerbach and Datapro series. Once you locate references to, say eight or nine articles, you will want to obtain them. As mentioned when we were discussing computerized literature sources and interlibrary lending, this is no longer the chore it once was because technologically we have taken another step toward total information systems. Several services, notably DIALOG and NEXIS, now have what are called "full-text databases." A full-text database is one that contains the entire article. For example, one or more of the articles you want to obtain may be available in the same system from which you got your original eight or nine references, if that system is a full-text database. Since this is a new and rapidly developing area, be sure to check with your librarian as to the availability of articles not located on the library's shelf; they may be available another way.

Before we go on to books, there is one other point we want to make that is related to terminology. You may have noticed that we referred to periodicals, journals, and series. These terms, along with the word magazine, are used interchangeably by most people. Generally, when we use the term magazine, it is in reference to newsstand-type publications such as *Time, Reader's Digest,* or *Popular Mechanics.* The word journal usually means publications of a more scholarly nature, such as those published by professional societies. The term series or serials generally means something published on a regular basis; however, it can refer either to hard-bound books that are published in a series (Annals of _____, Wiley Series in _____, etc.), ring-binder loose-leaf services (such as Auerbach, Datapro, Moody's, or Value Line), or any magazine-type publication. Periodicals generally refer to any regularly issued publication that is obtained through a subscription; they can be magazines, journals, or serials. As you can see, the distinction is not at all clear, and it is an area that causes confusion because what is a scholarly journal to one person may be a magazine to another.

Finally, it should be noted that all subjects we have mentioned in this text are covered by these periodical indexes. Descriptive information is provided in Figures 19-1 through 19-6 to aid you in understanding this important systems tool. As an example of how you might need these indexes, consider a situation in which your firm has no long-range plans in writing. You will have to try to determine, through interviews, whether any plans or contingencies exist that may affect the area under study. If the study is especially large, you may wish to go beyond your coverage of the firm's long-range plans by studying the periodical literature to determine the industry's long-range outlook and what other firms are doing to prepare for the future.

Books

The approach to books in a library is generally through a card catalog or some computerized version of one. This catalog often is divided into author and title or subject categories, although some special libraries also may use a report number, corporate author (as opposed to personal author), or contract numbers. In practice, the card catalog is the *index* to the library's contents. Each catalog card has a *call number* by which each book in the library is individually identified. Books are placed on the shelves in their call number order. Libraries in the United States tend to use one of two cataloging systems with which to classify their books (determine the call number).

1. The *Dewey Decimal System* is probably the most widely used classification system because it has been in popular use the longest (developed in 1876), and it is the simplest to learn and use. It divides all knowledge into 10 subject classes, each of which is further subdivided. These 10 classes are arranged in numerical sequence.

000–099	General Works
100–199	Philosophy
200–299	Religion
300–399	Social Sciences
400–499	Linguistics
500–599	Pure Science
600–699	Technology (Applied Science)
700–799	Arts and Recreation
800–899	Literature
900–999	History, Geography, and Biography

   Further subdivision is by a well-developed and logical decimal system. Until recently the Dewey system was considered flexible enough to encompass all knowledge.

2. The *Library of Congress System* is taking over quickly as the classification system for academic and technical libraries. Because it is an alphanumeric system, it provides much greater flexibility than the Dewey method. With Library of Congress, all knowledge is classified into 21 subject areas organized on an A to Z basis (the letters I, O, W, X, and Y are omitted). Further subdivision is through the use of alphanumeric designations. See Figure 19-7 for a brief comparison of the two systems.

DEWEY	LIBRARY OF CONGRESS		
000	A	General Books	
	B	Philosophy—Religion	
100		B–BL	Philosophy
200		BL–BX	Religion
900	C	History—Auxiliary Science	
900	D	History (except American)	
900	E–F	America	
		E	America (General) and U.S. (General)
		F	U.S. (Local) and America, except U.S.
	G	Geography and Anthropology	
900		G–GF	Geography
500		GN	Anthropology
300		GV	Physical Education
300	H	Social Science	
		HA	Statistics
		HB–HJ	Economics
		HM–HX	Sociology
300	J	Political Science	
300	K	Law	
300	L	Education	
700	M	Music	
700	N	Fine Arts	
		NA	Architecture
		ND	Painting
	P	Language and Literature	
400		PB–PH	Modern European Languages
800		PN–PZ	Literature
500	Q	Science	
		QA	Mathematics
		QC	Physics
		QD	Chemistry
		QH–QR	Biological Sciences
600	R	Medicine	
600	S	Agriculture	
600	T	Technology	
		TA	Civil Engineering
		TJ	Mechanical Engineering
		TK	Electrical Engineering
		TL	Aeronautics
		TP	Chemical Engineering
		TX	Home Economics
300	U	Military Science	
300	V	Naval Science	
000	Z	Bibliography and Library Science	

Figure 19-7 Comparison of Dewey Decimal and the Library of Congress classification systems.

Neither system has just one number on which the user can rely for a specific subject. It is for this reason that one must learn to use the card catalog or some alternate means of indexing. For example, the systems analyst may think all books on systems analysis are in the 600s if using Dewey or the "Ts" when using the Library of Congress system. In reality, if the book's main emphasis is on mathematical methods of systems, it may be in the 500s or the QAs. If it is on systems analysis in libraries, it may be in the 000s or Zs. A business systems text such as this may be located in the 658s or the HFs.

Users of the Library of Congress system must be particularly wary of being trapped into a favorite shelf area. Incidentally, users seldom can go from one library to another expecting a certain book to have the same classification, or call number. Each library is distinct from others and so are its catalogers! As libraries get more mechanized methods, however, they tend toward shared cataloging, which means more consistency from the viewpoint of the users and librarians alike.

Students sometimes experience the frustration of going to their library to locate a book on a particular subject, only to learn that the library does not have any books on that subject, or perhaps what they do have is not as current as desired. What can be done in this case? As you may have noticed in the discussion of the various periodicals indexes, some of them contain references to materials other than periodicals. The computerization of these indexes has allowed them to expand format-wise into other types of materials than just periodicals. Some have elected to remain as periodical indexes, while others have broadened their indexing scope. The latter sometimes are useful for locating books in such a situation.

There is still the possibility, however, that you need another approach to locating books. One approach is to use a book index. You will recall that we had an index to available periodicals (*Ulrich's International Periodicals Directory*). For books we have one called *Books in Print*. This publication lists books, symposia, and other monographic materials that currently are being sold by publishers in the United States. It is an important tool for learning about what books are available in a particular field. The paper version is available in indexes by author, title, and subject. The computerized version extends its usefulness because terms can be used for which adequate subject indexing is unavailable since the subject is either a narrow one or a new one. Once you have located several books that sound like they will meet your need, discuss with the interlibrary loan librarian how these books can be obtained within your time and cost constraints.

Newspapers

Depending upon the nature of the information you are trying to locate, newspapers may be beneficial. Large dailies such as the *New York Times* have their own indexes; most have none. For the businessperson, the *Wall Street Journal* and its *Index* (divided by corporate name and subject) may be indispensable. See Figure 19-8 for a sample page of the *Wall Street Journal Index*. The advent of computerized typesetting has enabled newspaper publishers to index their newspapers more adequately, so the number of newspaper indexes has proliferated in recent years.

Manufacturers' Literature

These come in a wide variety of formats and are handled in many ways. They may be simple descriptive brochures on anything from a ball bearing to a computer. They may be general or highly technical. They are often the only up-to-date, factual source of information on a given type of equipment or product. Some of these materials will be so important to the library that they will be placed in its reference section and may not be checked out. Other firms maintain all manufacturers' literature in their purchasing department rather than the library. Incidentally, manufacturers' literature is sometimes called trade literature; we have not used this term because people sometimes interpret it as periodicals of the trade.

One note of caution is in order with regard to manufacturers' literature. Although we stated above that they may be the only up-to-date, factual source of information on a product, remember that it is intrinsically sales information. Always remember that the manufacturer wants to sell the product, so deficiencies you may need to know about will not be mentioned. We recommend that you not take this information at face value; always check the facts if their use is important.

Pamphlets

Pamphlets are an ill-defined portion of any library's collection. Most libraries have pamphlets, but each handles them in a different way, depending upon the needs of their users and how important the librarians think each individual pamphlet is to the users. Often they are cataloged, but maintained in upright file cabinets, which librarians refer to as "vertical files." In other libraries, pamphlets are considered to be minor materials and are not considered important enough to catalog. When this happens, they are placed either in vertical files or in boxes on shelves and arranged in broad subject categories. Pamphlet files generally reflect current high-interest topics in which the users of that particular library are interested.

Some pamphlets really may be reports. For example, Auerbach and Datapro both publish, in addition to their loose-leaf services, reports that frequently are

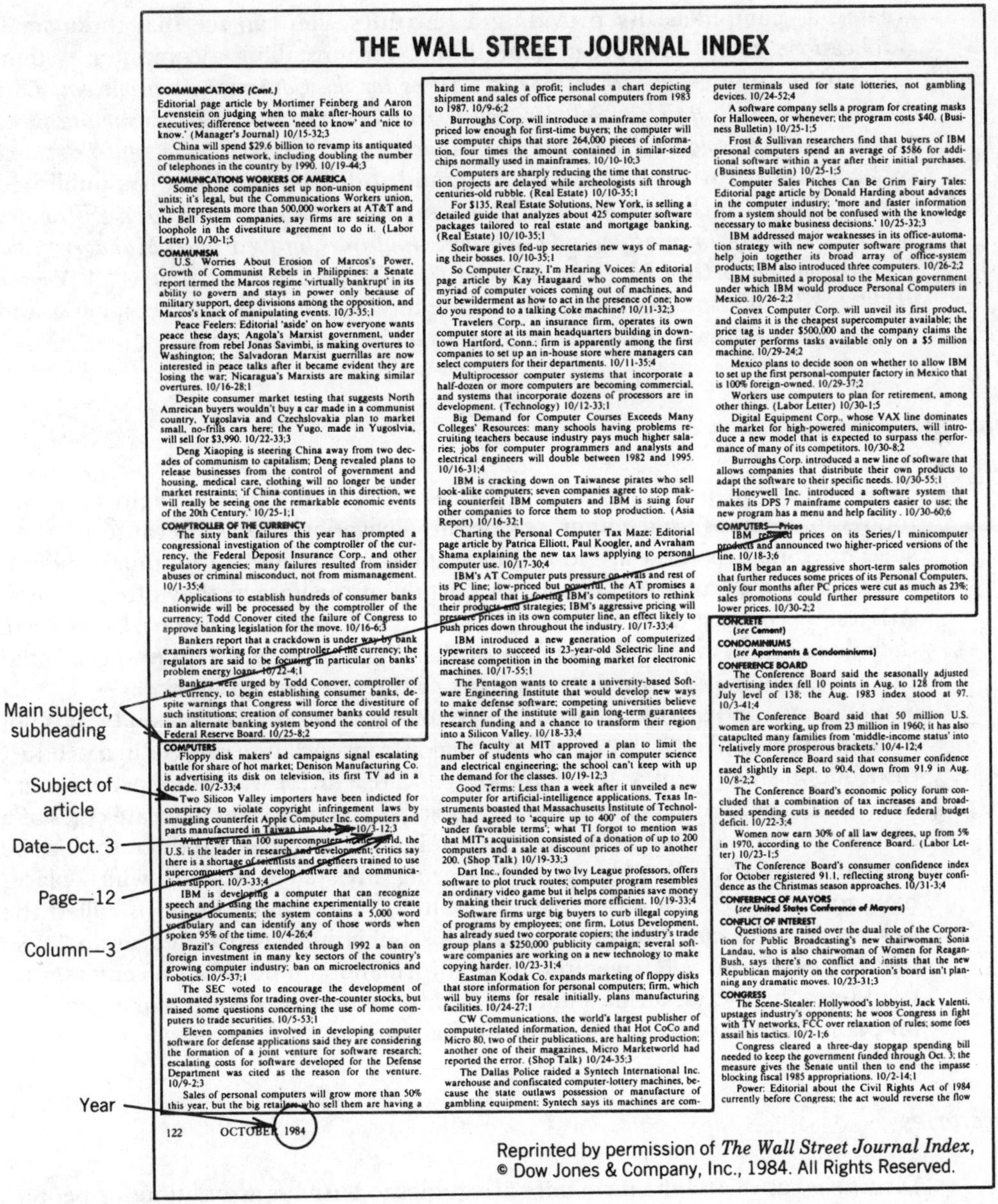

THE WALL STREET JOURNAL INDEX

COMMUNICATIONS *(Cont.)*

Editorial page article by Mortimer Feinberg and Aaron Levenstein on judging when to make after-hours calls to executives; difference between 'need to know' and 'nice to know.' (Manager's Journal) 10/15-32;3

China will spend $29.6 billion to revamp its antiquated communications network, including doubling the number of telephones in the country by 1990. 10/19-44;3

COMMUNICATIONS WORKERS OF AMERICA

Some phone companies set up non-union equipment units; it's legal, but the Communications Workers union, which represents more than 500,000 workers at AT&T and the Bell System companies, say firms are seizing on a loophole in the divestiture agreement to do it. (Labor Letter) 10/30-1;5

COMMUNISM

U.S. Worries About Erosion of Marcos's Power, Growth of Communist Rebels in Philippines: a Senate report termed the Marcos regime 'virtually bankrupt' in its ability to govern and stays in power only because of military support, deep divisions among the opposition, and Marcos's knack of manipulating events. 10/3-35;1

Peace Feelers: Editorial 'aside' on how everyone wants peace these days; Angola's Marxist government, under pressure from rebel Jonas Savimbi, is making overtures to Washington; the Salvadoran Marxist guerrillas are now interested in peace talks after it became evident they are losing the war; Nicaragua's Marxists are making similar overtures. 10/16-28;1

Despite consumer market testing that suggests North Amreican buyers wouldn't buy a car made in a communist country, Yugoslavia and Czechslovakia plan to market small, no-frills cars here; the Yugo, made in Yugoslvia, will sell for $3,990. 10/22-33;3

Deng Xiaoping is steering China away from two decades of communism to capitalism; Deng revealed plans to release businesses from the control of government and housing, medical care, clothing will no longer be under market restraints; 'if China continues in this direction, we will really be seeing one the remarkable economic events of the 20th Century.' 10/25-1;1

COMPTROLLER OF THE CURRENCY

The sixty bank failures this year has prompted a congressional investigation of the comptroller of the currency, the Federal Deposit Insurance Corp., and other regulatory agencies; many failures resulted from insider abuses or criminal misconduct, not from mismanagement. 10/1-35;4

Applications to establish hundreds of consumer banks nationwide will be processed by the comptroller of the currency; Todd Conover cited the failure of Congress to approve banking legislation for the move. 10/16-6;3

Bankers report that a crackdown is under way by bank examiners working for the comptroller of the currency; the regulators are said to be focusing in particular on banks' problem energy loans. 10/22-4;1

Bankers were urged by Todd Conover, comptroller of the currency, to begin establishing consumer banks, despite warnings that Congress will force the divestiture of such institutions; creation of consumer banks could result in an alternate banking system beyond the control of the Federal Reserve Board. 10/25-8;2

COMPUTERS

Floppy disk makers' ad campaigns signal escalating battle for share of hot market; Denison Manufacturing Co. is advertising its disk on television, its first TV ad in a decade. 10/2-33;4

Two Silicon Valley importers have been indicted for conspiracy to violate copyright infringement laws by smuggling counterfeit Apple Computer Inc. computers and parts manufactured in Taiwan into the U.S. 10/3-12;3

With fewer than 100 supercomputers in the world, the U.S. is the leader in research and development; critics say there is a shortage of scientists and engineers trained to use supercomputers and develop software and communications support. 10/3-33;4

IBM is developing a computer that can recognize speech and is using the machine experimentally to create business documents; the system contains a 5,000 word vocabulary and can identify any of those words when spoken 95% of the time. 10/4-26;4

Brazil's Congress extended through 1992 a ban on foreign investment in many key sectors of the country's growing computer industry; ban on microelectronics and robotics. 10/5-37;1

The SEC voted to encourage the development of automated systems for trading over-the-counter stocks, but raised some questions concerning the use of home computers to trade securities. 10/5-53;1

Eleven companies involved in developing computer software for defense applications said they are considering the formation of a joint venture for software research; escalating costs for software developed for the Defense Department was cited as the reason for the venture. 10/9-2;3

Sales of personal computers will grow more than 50% this year, but the big retailers who sell them are having a hard time making a profit; includes a chart depicting shipment and sales of office personal computers from 1983 to 1987. 10/9-6;2

Burroughs Corp. will introduce a mainframe computer priced low enough for first-time buyers; the computer will use computer chips that store 264,000 pieces of information, four times the amount contained in similar-sized chips normally used in mainframes. 10/10-10;3

Computers are sharply reducing the time that construction projects are delayed while archeologists sift through centuries-old rubble. (Real Estate) 10/10-35;1

For $135, Real Estate Solutions, New York, is selling a detailed guide that analyzes about 425 computer software packages tailored to real estate and mortgage banking. (Real Estate) 10/10-35;1

Software gives fed-up secretaries new ways of managing their bosses. 10/10-35;1

So Computer Crazy, I'm Hearing Voices: An editorial page article by Kay Haugaard who comments on the myriad of computer voices coming out of machines, and our bewilderment as how to act in the presence of one; how do you respond to a talking Coke machine? 10/11-32;3

Travelers Corp., an insurance firm, operates its own computer store at its main headquarters building in downtown Hartford, Conn.; firm is apparently among the first companies to set up an in-house store where managers can select computers for their departments. 10/11-35;4

Multiprocessor computer systems that incorporate a half-dozen or more computers are becoming commercial, and systems that incorporate dozens of processors are in development. (Technology) 10/12-33;1

Big Demand for Computer Courses Exceeds Many Colleges' Resources: many schools having problems recruiting teachers because industry pays much higher salaries; jobs for computer programmers and analysts and electrical engineers will double between 1982 and 1995. 10/16-31;4

IBM is cracking down on Taiwanese pirates who sell look-alike computers; seven companies agree to stop making counterfeit IBM computers and IBM is suing four other companies to force them to stop production. (Asia Report) 10/16-32;1

Charting the Personal Computer Tax Maze: Editorial page article by Patrica Elliott, Paul Koogler, and Avraham Shama explaining the new tax laws applying to personal computer use. 10/17-30;4

IBM's AT Computer puts pressure on rivals and rest of its PC line; low-priced but powerful, the AT promises a broad appeal that is forcing IBM's competitors to rethink their products and strategies; IBM's aggressive pricing will pressure prices in its own computer line, an effect likely to push prices down throughout the industry. 10/17-33;4

IBM introduced a new generation of computerized typewriters to succeed its 23-year-old Selectric line and increase competition in the booming market for electronic machines. 10/17-55;1

The Pentagon wants to create a university-based Software Engineering Institute that would develop new ways to make defense software; competing universities believe the winner of the institute will gain long-term guarantees research funding and a chance to transform their region into a Silicon Valley. 10/18-33;4

The faculty at MIT approved a plan to limit the number of students who can major in computer science and electrical engineering; the school can't keep with up the demand for the classes. 10/19-12;3

Good Terms: Less than a week after it unveiled a new computer for artificial-intelligence applications, Texas Instruments boasted that Massachusetts Institute of Technology had agreed to 'acquire up to 400' of the computers 'under favorable terms'; what TI forgot to mention was that MIT's acquisition consisted of a donation of up to 200 computers and a sale at discount prices of up to another 200. (Shop Talk) 10/19-33;3

Dart Inc., founded by two Ivy League professors, offers software to plot truck routes; computer program resembles an ordinary video game but it helps companies save money by making their truck deliveries more efficient. 10/19-33;4

Software firms urge big buyers to curb illegal copying of programs by employees; one firm, Lotus Development, has already sued two corporate copiers; the industry's trade group plans a $250,000 publicity campaign; several software companies are working on a new technology to make copying harder. 10/23-31;4

Eastman Kodak Co. expands marketing of floppy disks that store information for personal computers; firm, which will buy items for resale initially, plans manufacturing facilities. 10/24-27;1

CW Communications, the world's largest publisher of computer-related information, denied that Hot CoCo and Micro 80, two of their publications, are halting production; another one of their magazines, Micro Marketworld had reported the error. (Shop Talk) 10/24-35;3

The Dallas Police raided a Syntech International Inc. warehouse and confiscated computer-lottery machines, because the state outlaws possession or manufacture of gambling equipment; Syntech says its machines are computer terminals used for state lotteries, not gambling devices. 10/24-52;4

A software company sells a program for creating masks for Halloween, or whenever; the program costs $40. (Business Bulletin) 10/25-1;5

Frost & Sullivan researchers find that buyers of IBM presonal computers spend an average of $586 for additional software within a year after their initial purchases. (Business Bulletin) 10/25-1;5

Computer Sales Pitches Can Be Grim Fairy Tales: Editorial page article by Donald Harding about advances in the computer industry; 'more and faster information from a system should not be confused with the knowledge necessary to make business decisions.' 10/25-32;3

IBM addressed major weaknesses in its office-automation strategy with new computer software programs that help join together its broad array of office-system products; IBM also introduced three computers. 10/26-2;2

IBM submitted a proposal to the Mexican government under which IBM would produce Personal Computers in Mexico. 10/26-2;2

Convex Computer Corp. will unveil its first product, and claims it is the cheapest supercomputer available; the price tag is under $500,000 and the company claims the computer performs tasks available only on a $5 million machine. 10/29-24;2

Mexico plans to decide soon on whether to allow IBM to set up the first personal-computer factory in Mexico that is 100% foreign-owned. 10/29-37;2

Workers use computers to plan for retirement, among other things. (Labor Letter) 10/30-1;5

Digital Equipment Corp., whose VAX line dominates the market for high-powered minicomputers, will introduce a new model that is expected to surpass the performance of many of its competitors. 10/30-8;2

Burroughs Corp. introduced a new line of software that allows companies that distribute their own products to adapt the software to their specific needs. 10/30-55;1

Honeywell Inc. introduced a software system that makes its DPS 7 mainframe computers easier to use; the new program has a menu and help facility . 10/30-60;6

COMPUTERS—Prices

IBM reduced prices on its Series/1 minicomputer products and announced two higher-priced versions of the line. 10/18-3;6

IBM began an aggressive short-term sales promotion that further reduces some prices of its Personal Computers, only four months after PC prices were cut as much as 23%; sales promotions could further pressure competitors to lower prices. 10/30-2;2

CONCRETE
(*see* **Cement**)

CONDOMINIUMS
(*see* **Apartments & Condominiums**)

CONFERENCE BOARD

The Conference Board said the seasonally adjusted advertising index fell 10 points in Aug. to 128 from the July level of 138; the Aug. 1983 index stood at 97. 10/3-41;4

The Conference Board said that 50 million U.S. women are working, up from 23 million in 1960; it has also catapulted many families from 'middle-income status' into 'relatively more prosperous brackets.' 10/4-12;4

The Conference Board said that consumer confidence eased slightly in Sept. to 90.4, down from 91.9 in Aug. 10/8-2;2

The Conference Board's economic policy forum concluded that a combination of tax increases and broad-based spending cuts is needed to reduce federal budget deficit. 10/22-3;4

Women now earn 30% of all law degrees, up from 5% in 1970, according to the Conference Board. (Labor Letter) 10/23-1;5

The Conference Board's consumer confidence index for October registered 91.1, reflecting strong buyer confidence as the Christmas season approaches. 10/31-3;4

CONFERENCE OF MAYORS
(*see* **United States Conference of Mayors**)

CONFLICT OF INTEREST

Questions are raised over the dual role of the Corporation for Public Broadcasting's new chairwoman; Sonia Landau, who is also chairwoman of Women for Reagan-Bush, says there's no conflict and insists that the new Republican majority on the corporation's board isn't planning any dramatic moves. 10/23-31;3

CONGRESS

The Scene-Stealer: Hollywood's lobbyist, Jack Valenti, upstages industry's opponents; he woos Congress in fight with TV networks, FCC over relaxation of rules; some foes assail his tactics. 10/2-1;6

Congress cleared a three-day stopgap spending bill needed to keep the government funded through Oct. 3; the measure gives the Senate until then to end the impasse blocking fiscal 1985 appropriations. 10/2-14;1

Power: Editorial about the Civil Rights Act of 1984 currently before Congress; the act would reverse the flow

122 OCTOBER 1984

Main subject, subheading
Subject of article
Date—Oct. 3
Page—12
Column—3
Year

Figure 19-8 Sample page from *The Wall Street Journal Index.*

treated as pamphlets. By providing a few titles, you can see that these small publications could have great value if you were installing a computer system. Datapro has published *How to Select Micros for the Corporate Environment, User Ratings of 222 Proprietary Software Packages, An Overview of 20 Communications Carriers, How to Analyze Your Data Communications Needs, How to Select a Telephone System, All About Remote Batch Terminals*, and so forth. Auerbach has published similar reports such as *Computer Performance Evaluation, Controls for a Distributed System, Designing Transactions and Controls, Guidelines for the Project Manager in the Development of an On-Line Order Entry System, Terminal Security Matrix, 54 Ways to Reduce DP Costs*, and so forth. The guideline for you, the systems analyst and library user, is to ask the librarian how to locate such materials.

Maps and Atlases

Maps appear in many forms in libraries. They may be local highway maps, topographic maps, and either sea or air navigation charts. Because of their specialized nature, these are sometimes cataloged in a library, but unless there is a very large collection that is a major portion of the library, they often are not. Atlases, by contrast, are often what librarians call "oversize" materials. As such, they do not fit in the regular scheme of shelving, so they are kept in special atlas cases. Usually they are cataloged as part of the reference collection.

You may wonder why you would need to use atlases in a system study. It is not at all unusual to need a way of locating major transportation sources in a product distribution study. You would not want to locate a major warehouse where there were no major highways or railroads. Similarly, you may want to locate cities of a certain size to determine where outlets for a consumer product should be located. Atlases can be of great value during any system study in which places have to be located. One of particular value in the United States is called the *Commercial Atlas and Marketing Guide*. This publication is updated annually so that business firms will have up-to-date information on population centers, railroad lines, highways, airlines and other information needed to make decisions on plant location, warehousing, or distribution.

Directories

Directories as we use the term here are guides to business associations or people. They may be membership directories such as for the Association for Systems Management, the American Marketing Association, or similar organizations. Directories to business firms may be either commercially published, such as the publication called *California Manufacturers Register*, or they may be trade association directories listing member corporations. Directories such as these usually are cataloged and frequently are a part of the reference collection. There are, of course, other types of directories such as telephone directories for cities, government agencies, and so on. Sometimes these are cataloged, but more often they are not.

Annual Reports

Corporate annual reports can constitute an important part of a corporate library's collection, if there is a need for information on other corporations. By having these materials available, the analyst has ready access to financial and product information on other corporate entities.

Business Organization Publications

Numerous business organizations publish all types of information. These include the International Chamber of Congress and its affiliates located in various countries (such as the U.S. Chamber of Commerce), the Business Equipment Manufacturing Association (BEMA), Conference Board (formerly National Industrial Conference Board), Electronic Industries Association (EIA), and many more. In addition, many of our Graduate Schools of Business have special publications, such as *MSU Business Topics,* the University of Colorado's *Series in Business,* and the University of California's Institute of Industrial Relations reprint series. The publications of such organizations may be in the form of pamphlets, loose-leaf subscription services, periodicals, or even sets of books. If you need to locate recent information relevant to a specific industry, a good approach is to consult the *Encyclopedia of Associations,* determine one or two relevant trade/industry associations, locate their publications, or contact them directly.

Internal Sources

Internal sources of information are surprisingly numerous. They may be long-range plans, old annual reports, the corporate charter, employee handbooks, speeches made by members of management, the company newspaper (called a house organ), past publications on the company, and the various *Who's Who* (-*In the West, -In Finance and Industry, -In the Computer Field,* etc.). The firm's employees may be a gold mine of information, especially those in management. It is wise to do some background reading on your own first, however, to avoid "foot in mouth disease"!

Suppose, for example, that you have to interview someone in top management. It is important that you know to whom you are speaking, particularly when dealing with upper management personnel. Consult your library's resources to determine ahead of time your interviewee's expertise on the subject, political orientation, or any other factor that might have a bearing on the interviewee's personality. Some firms maintain a file of biographical information on all management personnel. Others maintain files of reprints by authors within the company, while still others maintain newspaper clipping files relevant to their personnel. These files are maintained for just this type of use. With computerized bibliographic indexes, it also is possible to have your librarian perform a quick search on your interviewee as an author.

Incidentally, special collections of materials (such as author reprint files) may not appear in any formal list of library holdings (such as the card catalog). With special files such as these, only the library staff may know of their existence. The best approach is to tell the librarian that you plan to interview Jane Doe for a study you are doing and need background information on her. Let the librarian lead you to potential sources of information.

Two other important areas we will explore in the next section are those of government documents and government reports.

*T*he Topsy-Turvy World of Government Documents

The United States Government is perhaps the largest and most complex system on Earth. Its activities and publications have influence on almost every formal organization in the country. Thus, the systems analyst needs to be familiar with the govenment's system of information dissemination.

To the beginning systems analyst who suddenly may be in the position of needing government documents, one can only advise: take a deep breath and plunge! Even to the experienced practicing librarian who may have worked with these materials for years, the whole procedure often seems impossible. The reason is that, like Topsy, they "just grew that way."

Government Documents

First of all, what is meant by "document"? In this chapter we mean any publication published by any level of government, whether it is international, national (domestic or foreign), state, county, or municipal. Government publications constitute an increasingly major proportion of the world's publishing output. One reason is government's increasing participation in projects too costly on the private level. Another is the need for documentation that can assist others in learning from past mistakes.

Because of the many improvements in information retrieval, such as computerized indexing systems, we also have been made more *aware* of the availability of these publications.

It is essential when working with government document indexes to understand that none of these indexes is totally independent of the others. Or, to put it another way, no agency announces just its own publications in its index; it may announce publications of many other agencies. To complicate matters further, many of these government publications also are announced in commercial indexing services such as *Engineering Index*. To use these indexes intelligently, one should learn and understand the types of information found in the various indexes.

Because so many indexes today actually are printed versions of something that is computerized, one needs to understand some of the odd twists a computerized index can take. If the programmer had little knowledge of library filing procedures, he or she might utilize what could be called the "something before nothing" principle. For example, suppose you have only a National Aeronautics and Space Administration Technical Note number NASA-TN-55. You have seen a reference to this document and you want to find out more about it. Since you do not have NASA's index available, you decide to use the Commerce Department's *Government Reports Announcements Index*. You would expect to find TN-55 between TN-54 and TN-56. Instead (especially in the early computerized index), you may find it between TN-543 and TN-553, thus

NASA-TN-53
NASA-TN-54
NASA-TN-543
NASA-TN-55
NASA-TN-553
NASA-TN-56

In this example, all 54s, regardless of the number of digits, have to be printed before the computer can go on to the 55s.

Another confusing sequence sometimes programmed into indexes might be called alphanumeric reversal. We would expect to find alphanumeric report numbers with the "smallest" alpha designation first; for example

L-6594
LA-4245
LA-TR-70-15

But, if the programmer or systems designer is unaware of library practices, you may instead have the following mixed-up sequence.[11]

LA-TR-70-15
LA-4245
LCI-4
LMEC-10
LMEC-8
L-6594

If these numbers are close to one another, you may be able to find the report number you want; however, if they are separated by pages you may not be able to locate the reference you need.

To further complicate matters, unnoticed and uncorrected input errors also cause problems which you should understand. An extra hyphen, a missed digit, a skipped space, or any other of a dozen possible errors can hamper your use of the index. Using the Technical Note 54 example, assume the key entry operator accidentally hit the space bar when typing TN-54. Depending on how the program is written, you might then have

NASA-TN-53
NASA-TN-543
NASA-TN-55
NASA-TN-553
NASA-TN-56
NASA-T N-54

The alphabetical sequence also may be broken if the people writing the inputs are not consistent: for example, Viet Nam, Vietnam, Viet-nam; or Journal, Jnl, Jl, J, and Jour. Remember that the computer only prints what is put into it; and if no one catches the human errors, you, the user, have problems! Any of these seemingly small errors can cause you to be off by many pages in your searching of paper indexes.

The U.S. Government Printing Office. The Printing Act of 1895 established that the Superintendent of Documents would publish on the first day of each month a list of government publications printed during the preceding month. Today we know this list as the *Monthly Catalog of United States Government Publications.*[12]

---

[11] This example, in shortened form, was taken from *U.S. Government Research and Development Reports Index,* December 25, 1970, pp. AR11–12.

[12] For an in-depth historical analysis, see Schmeckebier and Eastin's *Government Publications and Their Use* (1969), or Kling's *Government Printing Office* (1970).

Its title has varied somewhat over the years, but essentially it announces what the Government Printing Office has printed, instructions for obtaining the items, and the prices. It has often happened that changes in administration or growth of field agencies caused omissions in the *Monthly Catalog,* so it can by no stretch of the imagination be considered complete.

Publications are listed under the issuing agencies, which appear alphabetically. Each publication is assigned an entry number beginning with 1 each January and working consecutively through the December issue. In addition to the title, information given includes date of issuance, number of pages, price, the Superintendent of Documents classification number (by which some libraries file the publications when received), the Library of Congress card number, and other useful information.

Each monthly issue contains indexes by author, title, and report number. Use of the entry number simplifies retrieval. In June and December of each year the index is cumulated for easy use. When using the *Monthly Catalog,* it is useful to note the symbols appearing with each entry. Items marked with an asterisk (*) are available for sale by the Superintendent of Documents. A single dagger (†) indicates the item is distributed by the issuing office. A double dagger (‡) means for official use only (but they often are available anyway). Items marked with a phi (φ) symbol are for sale by the Department of Commerce. A black dot (●) indicates the item is sent automatically to Depository Libraries (a list of which appears in each September issue). See Figure 19-9 for an example of a *Monthly Catalog* page.

Publications announced in the *Monthly Catalog* may be handled in any manner once they arrive in the library. Sometimes they are placed in a separate section and filed by the Government Printing Office designation; sometimes they are cataloged and treated like a book. Some may arrive in microform, and these will be treated in a different manner. Still other libraries have their own unique system for handling these documents, often a system dependent on the knowledge of their first documents librarian.

The *Monthly Catalog* is useful in the identification of most "official" United States Government publications. These include census information, statistics for most industries, many Congressional documents, and documents from agencies that have their own announcing media such as the National Aeronautics and Space Administration. In addition, lists of serials and periodicals currently being published by the government are announced.

Technical Reports

The next major section within the government documents sector is a group of publications referred to as technical reports. These publications are written by corporations, primarily under contract to the various government agencies, both

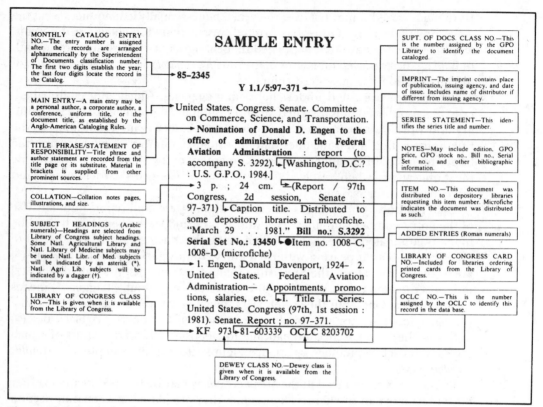

Figure 19-9 Example of an entry from the *Monthly Catalog of United States Government Publications.*

state and federal. These contractor reports frequently are the method by which new techniques or new technologies are transmitted from the private sector to the public sector and vice versa. These reports frequently are part of a systems approach to a problem that needs to be solved. The contractor examines the problem using the various steps within the system analysis framework, and then provides in the contract report recommendations for action that should be taken.

Following is a discussion of the primary government agencies that have contractors perform work on their behalf, and that also provide indexes to these contractor reports. Because most firms today perform government research work, and because the amount of tax money spent on contract research is significant, these reports become essential to business and industry. They are used to determine the state of the art, which can lead to further development. In addition, they can provide important leads to what the competition is doing.

The Department of Defense. The dissemination of Department of Defense

(DOD) documents began in 1945. At that time, what was then called the Air Documents Division of the Intelligence Department loosened wartime classification of research reports. Some of these reports retained their classified status; for example, only those people with the proper security clearance level and "need to know" were permitted access to these classified documents. These classified documents formed one-half of the dissemination program. The second half was composed of declassified reports and captured enemy research documents. These unclassified research reports were announced in the *Technical Information Pilot* (*TIP*), originally begun by the Office of Naval Research (ONR).

In 1947, the *Air Technical Index* took over the announcement of unclassified research reports. Each announced report was identified by a number using an ATI prefix. In the 1948–1950 period there occurred some shifting around of responsibility in the announcement of these reports. Finally, in 1951 the Armed Services Technical Information Agency (ASTIA) was established to handle dissemination of *all* defense-oriented reports. By this time, the unclassified/classified approach was firmly entrenched. One of ASTIA's functions, therefore, was to act as the central document releasing agency for government contractors. ASTIA also continued publication of the *Air Technical Index*.

In 1953 the title was changed to *Title Announcement Bulletin* (*TAB*). This new *TAB* was one of the first indexes to be printed using computerized methods. For approximately a year there were actually three *TAB*s published: an unclassified version announcing unclassified reports, a classified version announcing to military contractors the available classified reports, and a military version. In 1954 the classified version was discontinued and that part which had been classified was "sanitized" to make it available to the public. At this point the unclassified and classified versions were merged.

The previously unclassified reports comprised the first half, a white section. The second half was buff colored, and it announced the still classified or restricted dissemination documents in a "sanitized" style; for example, instead of printing a classified title, it would simply note "Classified Title." Identification of needed reports was by subject arrangement and some descriptors. The new *TAB* used an AD prefix (*ASTIA Document*) with six digits, for example, AD-349 856. This numbering system, with slight modification, still is used today. A new title in 1957 reflected the inclusion of abstracts: *Technical Abstract Bulletin*.

In the meantime, it was ironic that the *TAB* was not truly available to the public at large, primarily because of a statement in small print to the effect that it was not to be given to nationals of a foreign country. For this reason, its use was restricted largely to the military and its contractors. Any library having a *TAB* set was generally associated with a military contractor (such as some university libraries) and kept it in a closed area. For this reason, in 1961 the Department of Commerce began duplicating the *TAB*s white section with its *U.S. Government Research Reports* (see next section for details).

In 1963 ASTIA's name was changed to Defense Documentation Center

(DDC) to reflect more accurately its military orientation. Eventually, in 1967, because the Department of Commerce was duplicating the entire *TAB* white section, the white section's announcement was transferred totally to the Department of Commerce. This was an economical move that should have been taken 10 years earlier. Concurrently, the buff portion was once again classified "confidential" and it officially became available only to military contractors. This move supposedly made the *TAB* more useful to contractors. Since the need to "sanitize" was removed, the contractor could identify more readily the needed reports and, at least theoretically, eliminate the ordering of reports not relevant to the contract.

In mid-1978 DDC was permitted to once again publish the *TAB* in an unclassified format. It is still available, however, only to "authorized users" (e.g., Department of Defense contractors). In 1979, the *TAB* again incorporated the unclassified, unlimited distribution reports that were delegated to the Department of Commerce in 1967. DDC also changed its name to Defense Technical Information Center (DTIC) during 1979.

The later *TAB*s are well indexed (including biweekly, quarterly, and annual cumulations) by personal author, corporate author, title, report number of the company writing the report, report number of the sponsoring military agency, contract number, subject, and AD number. Since 1965 each newly acquired report has been put on microfiche to eliminate the unnecessary cost of paper copies and their accompanying space problem. The reports may be purchased either in paper or microfiche.

To qualify for receipt of classified reports from DDC, one must

- ☐ Have a military monitor to sponsor the activity and to verify the need for the information.
- ☐ Have the military specify in writing the need to know; for example, this contractor needs information on this subject for use on this contract until this date.
- ☐ Send the written need to know to the proper agency (DTIC) requesting registration to receive documents.
- ☐ Signify the exact numerically identified subject areas of interest on the "Field of Interest Register" (FOIR) DTIC sends to you.
- ☐ Send the FOIR to military monitor for approval.

After submitting the FOIR, the following takes place.

- ☐ Military monitor approves all, some, or none of the subject areas on the FOIR and returns the form to the disseminating agency.
- ☐ The agency sets up a file and sends you a copy of the FOIR as it was approved so you may begin ordering reports on that contract.

□ If the military monitor has crossed out a subject area you had indicated, you may not order documents falling into that area unless the monitor agrees to submit a change, following the same procedure as with the original FOIR.

□ The FOIR procedure often takes six weeks, making it virtually useless for short-term contracts. In that case, the military monitor generally provides directly the documents he or she thinks will be needed to fulfill the terms of the contract.

Generally speaking, classified materials

□ Are restricted by law from the public at large under terms of the Internal Security Act of 1950, and the Espionage and Sabotage Act of 1954.

□ When received must be kept in "secure" containers of a type and with locks as specified by the Department of Defense.

□ May be handled only by persons having a proper "security clearance" (which takes from three to six months to obtain) and with a definite "need to know."[13]

The systems analyst who designs for classified materials should know that specific paperwork routines *must* be followed in transferral of classified documents from one person to another; therefore, a document-receiving facility must be prepared for new paperwork routines, as well as special storage equipment.

DTIC estimated that in 1970 alone they processed 42,717 reports. The subject areas are wide-ranging, including aeronautics, agriculture, social sciences, missile technology, and physics, to name a few.

The Department of Commerce. In 1945, the President of the United States established the Office of the Publications Board (PB). Its purpose was to announce research documents available to the public, a function parallel to the Intelligence Department's Air Documents Division. In January of 1946 the Publications Board began its first announcement service, calling it *Bibliography of Scientific and Industrial Reports (BSIR)*. Each report announced was given a Publications Board Identifying number, beginning with PB-1.

The following year the Publications Board was superseded by the Office of Technical Services (OTS), which continued publishing the *Bibliography*, retaining the PB- prefix. The Library of Congress, however, retained the "Publications Board Project" for many years and you often may find PB entries in the *Monthly Catalog* (see the previous section on the U.S. Government Printing Office).

Over the years a number of changes took place in the title, and occasionally indexing changed. Also, in 1961 the *U.S. Government Research Reports (USGRR)*, as it was then known, included the previously mentioned Department of De-

---

[13] Specifics are outlined in *Industrial Security Manual for Safeguarding Classified Information.*

fense's *Technical Abstract Bulletin,* including use of the AD- prefix for accession numbers.

In 1965 the OTS was superseded by the Clearinghouse for Federal Scientific and Technical Information (CFSTI); then CFSTI was superseded in 1970 by the National Technical Information Service (NTIS), which still exists today. In the meantime, users were confused by numerous title changes and problems with the index itself. While the new index had subject, personal author, corporate author, and accession number indexing, it also used *derived* titles rather than *actual* titles, which caused many ordering problems. As was stated in the Foreword of the first issue, the combined index was produced entirely by computer manipulation of data records *prepared for other purposes* by the four contributing agencies. Since these agencies used different rules for indexing and for creating machine-readable records, it was inevitable that format errors, inconsistencies, or duplications would occur. The situation, although improved, has never been fully resolved. This tends to deter all but the most serious user from this very important database. The NTIS index is computerized now, so retrieval has been somewhat simplified.

When the publishing agency became known as NTIS, the new agency was given broader functions. Its current title, *Government Reports Announcements,* reflects this. Today NTIS publishes not only for the Department of Commerce, but also reports of many other government agencies and their contractors. In addition, it includes some journal articles (usually translations), symposia, patents, and theses to aid the Department of Commerce in its mission of transferring technology from the government to the private sector. See Figure 19-10 for an example of a *Government Reports Announcements* entry.

The National Aeronautics and Space Administration. As far back as 1915, the United States had made a formal commitment to aviation, even though by the end of that year only 100 aircraft (both civilian and military) had been built in this country. It was in 1915 that the National Advisory Committee for Aeronautics (NACA) was created by Congress. NACA published numerous reports and memoranda, most of which were announced in the Government Printing Office's *Monthly Catalog.* It was not until 1948 that an index was published. At that time the *Index of NACA Publications, 1915–47* appeared. This was superseded in 1949 by the *Index of NACA Publications, 1915–49.* The reason given for republication was the large number of omissions and the many new reports that had been added. The *Index* continued on an almost-annual basis until 1958. Identification of each report was by its internal NACA number, for example, MR for Memorandum Report, TM for Technical Memorandum, TN for Technical Note, and so forth.[14]

---

[14] This method of numbering was found to be so serviceable that many companies and other government agencies took it over. Today, you will see many numbering sequences like this but with an additional prefix for the name of the corporation or government agency, such as LMSC-TR-78-861 or NASA-TN-5903.

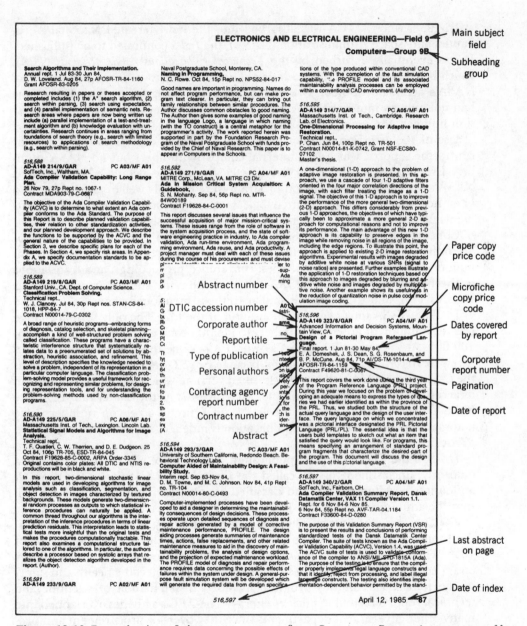

Figure 19-10 Reproduction of abstract entry page from *Government Reports Announcements & Index*.

In 1958, when NACA was absorbed into the newly created National Aeronautics and Space Administration (NASA), the *Index* continued to be published. It was eventually absorbed by the *Technical Publications Announcements (TPA)*, which began as a computerized index. This new index was formatted to reflect NASA's accession number system for computer recognition. Each entry now had not only an internal NASA number, but as primary identification an accession number, for example, N82-100 001.

Use of the accession number eventually facilitated entry into the system of contractor reports, which had internal company numbers but no NASA number. Even to the casual observer, it is clear that the people who organized NASA's document dissemination program were not only well organized but also knew how to set up a user-oriented logical system (as compared with the Departments of Defense and Commerce mentioned previously).

Concurrently the National Science Foundation and the Air Force Office of Scientific Research instituted the *International Aerospace Abstracts (IAA)* to announce and index periodical articles, conference proceedings, and translations in the field of aerospace. The *IAA* followed the same subject arrangement as NASA's *TPA*, and the format is similar to those mentioned above.

In 1963 NASA took over the publication of the *IAA*. The only format change was the addition of accession numbers to identify each entry, for example, A63-100 001. At the same time NASA's own *TPA* became the *Scientific and Technical Aerospace Reports (STAR)*. In reality it became two *STARs*. The second, known as the *C-STAR* was a less well-known classified version, which utilized an X prefix in its accession numbering, for example, X63-100 001. As the reader can see, if one has a publication with any of the A, N, or X prefix accession numbers, one automatically knows where that publication is indexed, for example, in the *IAA*, *STAR* or *C-STAR*.

In 1970 the *C-STAR* ceased publication, but its place was taken in 1972 by a quarterly, unclassified version called the *Limited STAR (L-STAR)*. The *L-STAR* announces both unclassified and classified limited distribution NASA work that must be announced under the Freedom of Information Act.

The Department of Energy. The Department of Energy's earliest predecessor, the Atomic Energy Commission (AEC) was created by the Atomic Energy Act of 1946. The Commission's purpose was to administer programs on atomic energy and special nuclear materials in such a manner as to protect the health and safety of the public. Part of this program included dissemination of scientific and technical reports related to nuclear energy. The AEC's activities overlapped into many other government departments since they oversaw procurement and production of fissionable materials, testing of DOD's nuclear weapons, the development of NASA's nuclear rocket propellants, and development of nuclear reactors. A major purpose of the program was to encourage the development of peaceful uses for nuclear energy.

In 1948 the AEC began publication of the *Nuclear Science Abstracts*, which was an outgrowth of the older *Abstracts of Declassified Documents*. The *NSA* was instituted to announce availability on an international basis of reports, books, translations, proceedings, patents, and journal articles on nuclear science. An accession number system was used to identify each entry, beginning with the number 1 each January. *NSA* had excellent cumulative indexes for subject, corporate and personal authors, and report numbers. Like NASA, the AEC had a network of depository libraries through which many of the reports could be obtained. Many also were available through the National Technical Information Service, mentioned earlier.

The AEC was dissolved in 1975 and replaced by the Energy Research and Development Agency (ERDA) which in turn was replaced by the Department of Energy in 1977. Since the AEC was dissolved, the indexing situation has been very confused. The last issue of *NSA* was in June of 1976 and it was replaced by an ERDA index that changed names several times. The name was changed again in 1977 when DOE took over the ERDA functions. The new *Energy Research Abstracts* is considerably broader than the old *NSA* because it includes all forms of energy including solar and geothermal. The index cites reports, journal articles, conference proceedings and papers, books, patents, theses, and monographs originated by ERDA/DOE laboratories, energy centers, and contractors.

Researchers who wish to study only nuclear energy tend now to use the *INIS Atomindex,* which is published by the International Nuclear Information Service of the International Atomic Energy Agency in Vienna. As with the old *NSA*, this index covers the literature on the peaceful uses of nuclear energy.

The Department of Health & Human Services. The U.S. Office of Education (USOE) also has become interested in the field of systems analysis, so you should be aware of their publications. They too have a distinctive accession numbering process. The Office of Education has a system of clearinghouses, each of which is concerned with a particular aspect of educational research. This clearinghouse system began in 1966 and was called the Educational Research Information Center, now called the Educational Resources Information Center (ERIC).

The ERIC reports are abstracted, computerized, and announced by the Office of Education in the monthly *Resources in Education* (*RIE*). Its accession numbers have an ED (*ERIC Document*) number, for example, ED-010 001. Some entries have an EP (*ERIC PROJECT*) number. Indexing is thorough and is by personal author, institution, subject, contract or grant number, and Office of Education project number.

In 1968 a secondary accession number was added to each entry, although arrangement is still by ED number. The new number indicates which clearinghouse processed the entry. For example

AC = Adult Education
TE = Teaching of English
HE = Higher Education

and so on.

A private publisher in a cooperative venture with USOE began another indexing service in 1969. This one, *Current Index to Journals in Education (CIJE)* complements *Resources in Education,* which tends to announce reports. Each periodical notation has an EJ accession number prefix, and indexing is by personal author, journal title, and subject. Although some entries do not have abstracts, a number of subject terms (called descriptors) are included to help the user decide whether to read the actual periodical article.

Some of the ERIC clearinghouses also publish special abstract journals, such as the *Exceptional Child Education Resources,* which include only their own entries processed for ERIC.

Miscellaneous Documents

Although there are many other types of documents you may have use for as a systems analyst, only a few of the most likely will be included here.

Legal Publications. Legal requirements may be found in the contracts of the company, through the use of loose-leaf services such as the Commerce Clearing House (CCH) *Government Contracts Reporter,* or through the law itself. Official legal pronouncements are of two types. A "statute" is a law passed by Congress or a state legislature. Federal statutes are listed in the *U.S. Code.* State statutes are listed in the various official publications of the states (example: *Statutes of California*). Statutes of the Congress and the various states also are printed by commercial publishing houses and are annotated with citations to interpreting cases and other related materials. For example, the *U.S. Code* in the commercial version is *U.S. Code Annotated* by West Publishing Company, and *Statutes of California* appears as *West's Annotated California Codes.* In addition, they also can be located in the computerized systems called WESTLAW and LEXIS.

The second type of legal pronouncement is a "court decision." Federal Supreme Court decisions are noted in the *U.S. Reports,* the Circuit Court of Appeals decisions are in the *Federal Reporter,* and the U.S. District Court decisions are in the *Federal Supplement.* Again, each state also has its own court decisions (example: *California Appellate Reports*). These court decisions also have commercially printed versions and appear in computerized systems.

Another category, that of "regulations," may play a significant role in a system study since few industries remain free of government regulation. These regulations have the force of law because the agencies that enforce the regulations are created by law and are given an implied legal stature. If you find yourself deeply involved in legal publications, you should be aware that your local librarian may be able to provide only minimal assistance since law librarianship is a highly specialized field requiring special training. The local librarian, however, will be able to help lead you in the most cost-effective and timely direction. As with periodicals and books, there are indexes that specialize in legal publications, such as *Index to Legal Periodicals* (available both in paper and computerized versions).

As noted in Chapter 15, there are many laws that specify lengths of time during which a firm may be required to produce various records. The *Federal Register* publishes a *Guide to Record Retention Requirements*.[15] This publication tells users (1) what federal records must be kept, (2) who must keep them, and (3) how long they must be kept. It is arranged by Departments (e.g., Labor, Postal Service, Transportation, etc.) and contains a thorough subject index. Since each item has its own individual number, finding entries is simplified. Sometimes legal materials appear in unlikely, but useful, places. For example, another records retention publication, Kish and Morris' *Microfilm in Business*,[16] describes for records managers the various types of microforms, how they may be utilized, indexing systems for retrieval, cameras, readers, printers, and storage. This book has two important appendices: the first makes note of the Uniform Photographic Copies of Business Records as Evidence Act and discusses the legal aspects of microfilm for records retention, while the second discusses specifications for microfilm as required by the Department of Defense.

Standards. Although both civilian and military agencies publish standards, the main concept in all standards is comparison. A standard may define a unit of length or define the purity of a piece of metal. The military has two standardization publications; a Military Specification (MIL-SPEC) is intended to establish the necessary characteristics of an item in terms of its expected performance, while a Military Standard (MIL-STD) actually defines dimensions of a particular item for purposes of interchangeability. A Military Handbook (MIL-HDBK) is not a standard but is designed to be used in conjunction with MIL-SPECs and MIL-STDs to aid in their application and interpretation. These specifications and standards are indexed in the *Department of Defense Index of Specifications and Standards.* (See Figure 19-11 for other codes.) You should be aware that shifting to the metric system has affected the military's standards and specifications numbering system. As new standards and specifications are developed, those which are based on the metric system are given a new prefix. Instead of MIL-STD, metric-based standards use DOD-STD; instead of MIL-SPEC, metric-based specifications use the prefix DOD-M. The SPEC part of the prefix is dropped, and letters signifying the first letter of the equipment take its place: for example, M for microcomputer or C for connector. It is anticipated that the dual numbering system will be used for many years because the shift to metrics cannot be accomplished easily.

Federal Specifications (FED-SPEC) and Federal Standards (FED-STD) are

---

[15] "Guide to Record Retention Requirements," published annually by the *Federal Register.* (Government Printing Office number GS4.107/a:R245/981) 1955+ .

[16] *Microfilm in Business*, by Joseph L. Kish, Jr. and James Morris (New York: Ronald Press Company, 1966).

MS	Military Sheet Standard	AR	Army Regulation
MIL-STD	Military Standard	Army TM	Army Technical Manual
MIL-SPEC	Military Specification	Army FM	Army Field Manual
DOD-STD	Military Standard, metric	AMCP	Army Materiel Command Pamphlet
DOD-letter	Military Specification, metric	AMCR	Army Materiel Command Regulation
FED-SPEC	Federal Specification		
FED-STD	Federal Standard	MPD	Missile Purchase Description
QPL	Qualified Products List	ORD M	Ordnance Manual
AN	Air Force Navy Aeronautical Standard	ORD P	Ordnance Pamphlet
		DOD	Department of Defense
AND	Air Force Navy Aeronautical Design Standard	DOD DSAM	Defense Supply Agency Manual
DP	Description Pattern	DOD DSAH	Defense Supply Agency Handbook
MIL-HDBK	Military Handbook	DOD DSAR	Defense Supply Agency Regulation
AFL	Air Force Letter		
AFM	Air Force Manual	NBS	National Bureau of Standards
AFR	Air Force Regulation		
AFP	Air Force Pamphlet	FAA Regs	Federal Aviation Regulation
AFSCM	Air Force Systems Command Manual	CS (GPO)	Commercial Standard
AFSCR	Air Force Systems Command Regulation	USASI	United States of America Standards Institute
AFSCP	Air Force Systems Command Pamphlet	NAS	National Aerospace Standard
AFPC	Air Force Procurement Circular	ASTM	American Society for Testing and Materials
AFTO	Air Force Technical Order	AMS	Aerospace Material Specification
AFPI 71 Series	Air Force Procurement Instruction	ARP	Aerospace Recommended Practice
AF Exhibits	Air Force Exhibit	AIR	Aerospace Information Report
USAF Spec Bul	United States Air Force Specification Bulletin	AS	Aerospace Standard
		AWS	American Welding Society
ANA Bulletins	Air Force Navy Aeronautical Bulletin	AGMA	American Gear Manufacturing Association
Navinst	Navy Instruction		
Navy WR	Weapons Requirement	AISI	American Iron & Steel Institute
Navy WS	Weapons System		
Navy OD	Ordnance Document	NEMA	National Electrical Manufacturers Association
NAVEXOS P	Navy Office Executive Office Pamphlet		
NAVDOCKS DM	Navy-Docks Design Manual	AFBMA	Anti-Friction Bearing Manufacturers Association
NAVFAC DM	Navy-Factory Design Manual		

Figure 19-11 Some common document designations.

similar in format to those of the military. They are published, however, by the General Services Administration which is the "watch-dog" agency of the federal government. The *Index of Federal Specifications, Standards and Commercial Item Descriptions* includes many nonmilitary items because it is intended for civilian usage.

The National Bureau of Standards (NBS) was founded by Congress in 1901 to develop and preserve standards of physical measurement, with effective calibration methods, for use by American industry. The Bureau publishes *NBS Handbooks*, which are recommended codes of industrial and engineering practice. *NBS Handbook 28, "Screwthread Standards for Federal Services,"* is perhaps the most widely used of all the Handbooks. Business systems analysts have been concerned with recent NBS activity in setting standards for secure computer systems through the design of complex algorithms. NBS publications are listed in the *Monthly Catalog of United States Government Publications* and are available from the Government Printing Office.

Other standards are published by the American Standards Association, American Iron and Steel Institute, American Society for Testing and Materials, the Society for Automotive Engineers, the National Electrical Manufacturers Association, and the Underwriters' Laboratories, to name a few. Each has its unique numbering system. Codes, such as the *Uniform Building Code* and the *National Fire Codes,* also may be put in the standards category since they may place a limitation on some part of a proposed system.

Patents. Each country has patents to protect an inventor from having an invention stolen and credited to someone else. All U.S. patents are registered in the Patent Office and announced in the *Official Gazette of United States Patent and Trademark Office.* Since the *Official Gazette* only provides an abstract describing the invention, it is often only a starting point, with the services of a patent attorney being needed for a full-scale patent search. Some patents also may be located through NTIS, *Chemical Abstracts,* Derwent's *World Patents Index,* or the computerized index to U.S. patents called *CLAIMS.* Your librarian should be able to assist with these indexes.

There are some publications that may be considered as supplementing the Printing Office's *Monthly Catalog.* These include the *Monthly Checklist of State Publications* issued by the Library of Congress. It includes official publications of the various states (*if* they are sent to the Library of Congress) and some quasi-official publications of associations of state officials, statistical reports, and so forth.

Many states also have their own announcement services, such as *California State Publications* and the *Checklist of Official Pennsylvania Publications.*

The *United Nations Documents Index* began in 1950. It lists publications of the U.N. and its immediate agencies. Many of these U.N., state, and federal documents also are listed in the commercially published *PAIS Bulletin,* as well as other indexing services.

*A*dvice to the Novice

As you have seen from the preceding discussion, there are so many types of publications that might help a systems analyst, that it is difficult to find a starting point. A hospital systems analyst, for instance, might find *Index Medicus* or the *Hospital Literature Index* indispensable, while the corporate systems analyst may be quite dependent on *Business Periodicals Index, Abstracted Business Information (ABI/INFORM)*, or *Computer and Control Abstracts*. Each reader will find a favorite library resource. In the meantime, the following hints are provided.

1. Read the history of your field. Try to find out the mistakes and accomplishments of others in the field so that you can profit by them. Find out what made the successes.

2. Get to know *your* librarian(s). Find out who knows what is happening in your field. Librarians consider keeping up on various fields to be an essential part of their job (in fact, some companies include "keeping up with the literature" in their performance evaluations). Librarians also like to feel wanted, and a liberal sprinkling of thank-you's can mean a librarian who thinks of *you* when a good article or book is found.

3. While it is not practical for the analyst to learn how to perform literature searching in a detailed way (that is not what you are being paid for!), it is useful to learn what indexes are available and the type of materials they contain. To get the most out of these indexes, ask your librarian to explain them. Only people who use the indexes frequently can keep abreast of changes, so important features may be lost to a novice.

4. Understand that computerization has had a significant impact upon libraries, librarians, and users. With hundreds of indexes readily available to librarians in a computerized form, you can assume a certain percentage of overlap. The key is to select the two or three that will help you solve the problem at hand. Consult with your librarian as you begin a project in a new subject area. This will save frustrations caused by wasting time and in getting caught at the last minute without a plan of action. Most important, it will allow an orderly search of the *best* resources and still allow time to obtain materials via interlibrary loan.

5. In dealing with company and occasionally some government reports, it is useful to remember that there are often restrictions imposed by the company to protect its own designs or processes, or by the government to protect the nation's security.

6. If you have difficulty in using the corporate/agency library, go to the librarian and explain what the difficulty is; librarians *want* people to be able to locate needed information and will be happy to help. Many firms and universities have special orientation tours of the library for new employees and students. Tell the librarian the type of work you will be doing so the

introduction can be tailored to meet your needs. Then spend a few hours examining some of the new tools you have been shown.

7. If you have difficulty locating specific materials in the library, report it. The materials you want may be temporarily on someone's desk, in cataloging, being replaced by a new edition, or just plain lost. In any case, the librarians do not want you to leave empty-handed. Also, they need to know about lost materials, especially those in great demand which may need to be replaced.

8. Finally, and most important of all: librarians sometimes appear to know everything. They don't, but they have been trained to know how to find things. Never hesitate to use their knowledge. It will help you both!

Selections for Further Study

1. *Applied Science and Technology Index.* New York: H. W. Wilson Company, 1958– .
2. *Books in Print.* New York: R. R. Bowker Company, 1948– .
3. Brownstone, David, and Gorton Carruth. *Where to Find Business Information, 2nd edition.* New York: John Wiley & Sons, Inc., 1982.
4. *Business Periodicals Index.* New York: H. W. Wilson Company, 1958– .
5. *Commercial Atlas and Marketing Guide.* Chicago: Rand McNally and Company, 1869– .
6. *Computer and Control Abstracts.* Hitchin, England: Institution of Electrical Engineers, 1969– .
7. *Computer Literature Index* (formerly *Quarterly Bibliography of Computers and Data Processing*). Phoenix, Ariz.: Applied Computer Research, 1971– .
8. *Computing Reviews.* New York: Association for Computing Machinery, 1960– .
9. *Current Indexes to Journals in Education.* New York: CCM-Information Corporation, 1969– .
10. *Department of Defense Index of Specifications and Standards.* Washington, D.C.: Defense Supply Agency, 1970– .
11. *Department of Defense Industrial Security Manual for Safeguarding Classified Information.* Washington, D.C.: Defense Supply Agency, 1970.
12. Downs, Robert D., and Clara D. Keller. *How to Do Library Research, 2nd edition.* Urbana, Ill.: University of Illinois Press, 1975.
13. *Energy Research Abstracts.* Washington, D.C.: Government Printing Office, 1975– .
14. *Engineering Index Monthly.* New York: Engineering Index, Inc., 1884– .
15. Gates, Jean K. *Guide to the Use of Books and Libraries, 4th edition.* New York: McGraw-Hill Book Company, 1979.
16. *Government Reports Announcements* (title varies). Springfield, Va.: National Technical Information Service, 1946– .
17. *Index of Federal Specifications, Standards and Commercial Item Descriptions.* Washington, D.C.: Government Printing Office, 1971.

18. *INIS Atomindex.* Vienna: International Atomic Energy Agency, 1970– .

19. *International Aerospace Abstracts.* New York: National Aeronautics and Space Administration and Institute of Aeronautics and Astronautics, 1961– .

20. Johnson, H. Webster. *How to Use the Business Library, 4th edition.* Cincinnati, Ohio: South-Western Publishing Company, 1972.

21. *Journal of Information Systems Management.* Pensauken, N.J.: Auerbach Publishers, Inc., 1983– .

22. *Journal of Systems and Software.* New York: Elsevier Science Publishing Co., Inc., 1979– .

23. *Journal of Systems Management* (formerly *Systems and Procedures*). Cleveland, Ohio: Association for Systems Management, 1950– .

24. *Monthly Catalog of United States Government Publications* (title varies). Washington, D.C.: Government Printing Office, 1895– .

25. *Monthly Checklist of State Publications.* Washington, D.C.: Government Printing Office, 1910– .

26. *New York Times Index.* New York: The New York Times Company, 1851– .

27. *Official Gazette of United States Patent and Trademark Office.* Washington, D.C.: Government Printing Office, 1872– .

28. *PAIS Bulletin.* New York: Public Affairs Information Service, 1915– .

29. *PROMT* and *Funk & Scott Indexes.* Cleveland, Ohio: Predicasts, Inc., 1972– .

30. *Resources in Education.* Washington, D.C.: U.S. Office of Education, 1966– .

31. Rivers, William L. *Finding Facts: Interviewing, Observing, Using Reference Sources.* Englewood Cliffs, N.J.: Prentice-Hall, Inc., 1975.

32. *Scientific and Technical Aerospace Reports* (title varies). Washington, D.C.: National Aeronautics and Space Administration, 1958– .

33. Tallman, Johanna. "History and Importance of Technical Report Literature, Part II," *Sci-Tech News,* Winter 1962, pp. 164–172.

34. *Technical Abstract Bulletin* (title varies). Alexandria, Va.: Defense Technical Information Center, 1953– .

35. *Ulrich's International Periodicals Directory.* New York: R. R. Bowker Company, 1943– .

36. *United Nations Documents Index.* New York: United Nations Publications, 1950– .

37. *United States Government Manual* (formerly *United States Government Organization Manual*). Washington, D.C.: Government Printing Office, annual.

38. Victorson, Patricia L. "Today Desirable—Tomorrow Essential: Computer Information for Economic Development," *Economic Development Review,* vol. 2, no. 2, Summer 1984, pp. 34–47.

39. *Wall Street Journal Index.* New York: Dow Jones and Company, Inc., 1958– .

ns

1. Describe some of the types of materials a typical corporate or business library might contain. Name at least six. Can you name more?

2. How do most libraries arrange their books?

3. Why do you need to use the card catalog in a library?

4. By what means are journal articles located?

5. Name at least five indexes you might find in a corporate library.

6. Discuss how you might utilize the following tools in a systems study: books, periodicals, newspapers, manufacturers' literature, maps, directories, annual reports, government documents, technical reports, specifications, standards, legal publications.

7. Why might a systems analyst find it important to know about classified documents if the analyst does not need to use these materials in a study?

8. Why should the systems analyst know how to use government documents? Name two reasons.

9. Why should the systems analyst know how to use technical reports? Name three reasons.

10. Name four government agencies discussed in this chapter that disseminate documents and describe the types of materials they handle.

11. Why are accession numbers important in indexing schemes?

12. What is a MIL-SPEC? A FED-STD? A DOD-STD?

13. How can atlases be important to systems analysts?

14. Why do you have to be cautious in using manufacturers' literature?

15. How would your information needs vary between Level V and Level I studies?

16. What are the barriers to effective use of a library? Discuss.

17. What kind of resource is the corporate library?

18. Discuss how computerization of libraries has benefited users.

19. In the context of this chapter, what is the difference between a database and a system?

20. What are RLIN, OCLC, and WLIN? How can they help you?

21. Why may periodicals be more important to your on-the-job activities than books?

22. What is the disadvantage of going through periodicals issue-by-issue when you need literature?

23. When would you use the Auerbach and Datapro series?

24. What is the difference between free-text and full-text?

25. How would you use the library with regard to long-range plans?

26. Name four reasons why computerized literature searching might be used rather than manual searching.

27. How do libraries cooperate to help the analyst do a better job?

Appendices

1. HOW TO EVALUATE FILES
2. CONTROLS FOR INPUTS, DATA COMMUNICATIONS, PROGRAMMING, AND OUTPUTS
3. REQUEST FOR PROPOSALS (RFP): Computerized System for the White Medical Clinic

HOW TO EVALUATE FILES

The following checklist can be used when appraising filing operations. It is taken from U.S. National Archives and Records Service, General Services Administration, "Checklist for Appraising Files Operations in Your Office," Washington: Government Printing Office, 1968. It is subdivided into the following areas.

A. Reduction of quantities being filed.
B. Classification and filing system.
C. Classifying practices.
D. Finding aids.
E. Filing practices.
F. Reference service.
G. Work load.
H. Documentation.
I. Equipment and supplies.
J. Space and work flow.
K. Training.

A. Reduction of quantities being filed.
    1. Does someone in my office determine whether given types of papers being created or received must be filed?

> *General rule:* In every office where files are maintained someone should make this determination; otherwise many papers will be filed which are not worth filing.

    2. Does my office have a policy that the following materials are not to be filed?

    a. Envelopes.

    b. Route slips on which there are no significant notations.

    c. Superseded drafts that show no important substantive changes.

    d. Duplicates of correspondence and reports other than those needed for cross references.

> *General rule:* Every office should have a firm rule that such obviously unneeded papers will not be filed. This prevents wasted effort, filing space, and equipment, and makes needed papers easier to file and find.

3. Does my office have a policy that file copies of form letters will not be made in instances when (a) no retained record is necessary or (b) a notation on incoming correspondence showing the form reply used and the date will suffice or (c) one copy showing distribution will do?

> *General rule:* Such copies serve no purpose, increase the filing work load, clutter files, and so should not be made.

4. Does my office have a policy governing which publications will or will not be filed?

5. Are originators of publications requested to discontinue sending those no longer needed?

> *General rule:* These practices should be followed, because publications rapidly consume filing space and equipment, sometimes require indexing.

6. Does my office, in responding to purely routine correspondence (such as requests for publications, applications, stereotyped inquiries, etc.) reply (a) on the incoming letter, which is returned to the sender or (b) by form letter, printed slip or other readymade answer, returning or discarding the incoming letter?

> *General rule:* Unless policy prohibits, one or more of these practices should be followed. They eliminate preparation of file copies of replies and filing of incoming letters.

B. Classification and filing system.

1. Have I listed the subjects and types of records in my office?

2. Have I compared my list with the subjects and types of records provided for in the filing manual prescribed for my use?

3. Have I defined all subjects on my list which do not appear in the filing manual prescribed for my use?

> *General rule:* These actions should be taken as first, essential steps, if files are not already arranged according to authorized system.

4. Does the filing manual prescribed for my use adequately provide for the records of my office?

> *General rule:* When a filing manual developed for general use does not satisfactorily provide for the records of an office, that office should see that the manual is supplemented to fit local needs by contacting the records management office.

5. Are the manual's subjects logically arranged in relation to the way my office operates?

> *General rule:* Subject outlines work best when they conform to the functions to which they pertain.

6. Do I usually find it rather easy to select the subject under which a paper should be filed (i.e., there are not too many subjects under which a given paper can go)?

> *General rule:* A good filing manual avoids providing an excessive number of subjects from which to choose in deciding where to file a paper. This in turn improves likelihood that all papers on the same subject will be consistently filed and found together.

7. Are the manual's instructions and definitions complete and clear?

> *General rule:* A good filing manual provides clear instructions, definitions, and references not only as general guidance on how to use the manual but also wherever they are needed in connection with subjects.

8. Are the coding symbols that represent subjects short, simple, and easy to remember?

> *General rule:* They should be, to make the marking, sorting, filing, and finding of papers fast, easy, accurate.

9. Are my files actually arranged in accordance with the manual prescribed for my use?

> *General rule:* They should be, unless the manual is believed unsuitable for the office's files, in which event the records management office should be contacted.

C. Classifying practices.

1. Do I assemble directly related papers (e.g., incoming letter and copy of outgoing reply) before determining their file designation?

> *General rule:* By assembling directly related papers, more information is available on which to make a sound decision on the correct file designation.

2. Do I *mark* papers with their file designations (e.g., underlining or checkmarking name, writing file code in corner, etc.)?

> *General rule:* Papers should be so marked to make it unnecessary to re-read a paper when filing it or returning it to file.

3. When I am in doubt regarding the right file designation for a paper do I refer to an index to the files, to papers already filed to verify or reject a tentative choice, or ask the opinion of people who are acquainted with the subject, case, or project?

> *General rule:* These steps, in the order given should be taken, rather than to guess.

4. Do my superiors refrain from marking file designations on papers before sending them to me to file?

> *General rule:* If you are held responsible for finding papers when they are asked for, you should at least participate in deciding how to file them. This is true even if (a) the filing system was devised by a superior and he or she understands it best; (b) he or she is intimately acquainted with the technical content of papers and so feels best qualified to mark them for filing; or (c) he or she feels that certain papers are so important that he or she wants to be certain of their location in the files so he or she can produce them quickly.

D. Finding aids.

1. Are all of the indexes and other finding aids I have really worth the time, effort, and cost of preparing and maintaining them?

> *General rule:* All finding aids are costly and, therefore, should be held to a minimum. Several types of indexes to one kind of file system is a sign of weakness in that system.

2. When a paper covers more than one subject, name, and so forth, do I provide cross-references only for the additional subjects or names by which I feel the paper is likely to be requested?

> *General rule:* Cross-referencing should be restricted to just those which experience has proven are useful. Resist the temptation to cross-reference every subject, name, and so forth, in a paper.

3. When a cross-reference is needed, do I use an extra carbon copy or obtain a "quick-copy" of the paper involved?

> *General rule:* A copy of the paper is preferable to the preparation of a cross-reference form, because it provides the full text of the paper and is usually faster and cheaper to obtain.

4. Do I mark each copy to show (a) that it is a cross-reference, (b) where it should be filed, and (c) where the paper from which it was copied is filed?

> *General rule:* This should be done to clearly identify the nature and purpose of the copy and location of the paper copied.

E. Filing practices.

1. When others release papers to me for filing, do they initial or otherwise mark them to show that their filing is authorized?

> *General rule:* This should always be done; otherwise there is no assurance that a paper has been seen or acted on.

2. Do I sort papers that are ready to be filed, into the same sequence as the files in which they will be placed?

> *General rule:* This should be done. It prevents backtracking and thus saves filing time and effort.

3. Do I fasten papers together which will be asked for as a group?
4. Do I leave papers unfastened which will be asked for singly?

> *General rule:* Whether or not to fasten papers should be governed by the way papers are asked for. The perforating of papers, placing them on fasteners, opening and closing fasteners, and so forth, are tedious, time consuming operations. For these reasons, papers should be fastened only when entire folders are requested.

5. Are my files arranged according to the way they are asked for?

> *General rule:* This should be so, as far as it can be carried, because it makes finding much easier.

6. Have I arranged as many papers as possible into case or project files?

7. Do I clearly understand what constitutes the essential papers that belong in each kind of case or project file, so I can tell when such a file is complete?

8. When a case or project is closed, do I remove the file from among those of still active cases or projects and place it with the files of other closed cases or projects?

> *General rule:* Papers should be arranged into case or project files, if possible, as this is the simplest way to file and find information. Recurrent, repetitive kinds of information that belong in a case or project file should be known to those who maintain such files. Closed files should be separated from active ones.

9. Is file material separated or identified in some way to
   a. Show its age, so that it will be easy to dispose of or retire at scheduled times?
   b. Distinguish that of permanent or long-term value from that of transitory value?
   c. Keep heavily used material from being mixed with and encumbered by seldom used material?
   d. Keep files designated as "official files" apart from those which have not been so designated?

10. If so, is this done in one or more of the following ways?
   a. By maintaining material in (a) separate filing cabinets, drawers, or sections of drawers or (b) separate shelves or sections of shelves, with inclusive dates shown on drawer, shelf, or guide card labels.
   b. By maintaining material in separate file folders, with inclusive dates or values shown on folder tabs.
   c. Color coding to show periods of time or values of papers; for example, yellow label for the current period or for permanent papers, green label for the preceding period or temporary papers, and so forth.
   d. By dividing material within file folders to separate permanent from temporary or to separate heavily used from seldom used material.
   e. By affixing clip-on signals to file folders, using different colors or positions to indicate time periods.
   f. By using staggering positions of file folder tabs to indicate retention periods and methods of disposition.

> *General rule:* Separation of papers for one or more of the purposes listed above should be done, as far as practicable. The method used must depend on the amount, kind, and so forth, of papers, and the advice of the records management person should be requested to help arrive at the right selection in each instance.

11. Are my files neat and orderly in appearance, with file folder and guide card tabs aligned in simple patterns which are easy to scan when locating files?

> *General rule:* Uncluttered, simple arrangement of folder and guide tabs and clear, standardized labeling of such tabs are definite aids to filing and finding papers.

12. Are the contents of my file folders and/or containers limited in volume to avoid overloading them?

> *General rule:* Overloading should be avoided, as it makes filing and finding difficult and can damage papers.

13. Are my files virtually free of empty or nearly empty file folders?

> *General rule:* Only folders for which there is a present or expected need should be established.

14. Is there the right number of file guide cards (dividers) in my files?

> *General rule:* The number of guide cards needed will vary somewhat, due to the number and thickness of file folders, whether the files are subject, name, or number files, and so forth. It is better to have too few than too many, as too many actually slow filing and finding.

15. Do all file drawer or shelf file labels clearly identify the files involved?

> *General rule:* When such labels identify contents of cabinet drawers or shelving sections, filing and finding is expedited.

16. If I have an alphabetical name file of persons or organizations, do I provide for name changes by refiling the papers involved under the new name?

> *General rule:* This should be done, as requests will most likely mention new name. (See also next question.)

17. If name file papers are refiled under a new name is a cross-reference placed under the old name referring to the new one?

General rule: This should be done, since some requests may mention only old name.

18. When I have bulky or oversized file material that cannot be suitably placed with my regular file material, do I (a) mark it with the appropriate file designation and identification of the particular letter, report, and so forth, to which it relates and (b) place it in other equipment suited to its size?

General rule: These steps should be taken, for reasons that are obvious. (See also next question.)

19. If I place bulky material apart from my regular files, do I indicate on the related letter, report, and so forth, in the regular files where the bulky material has been placed?

General rule: This should be done, for reasons that are obvious.

20. When I must remove papers from an earlier group of files to combine them with current papers, do I replace the earlier papers with a cross-reference showing their new location?

General rule: This should be done; otherwise location of earlier papers is uncertain.

21. Do I maintain a suspense (tickler, reminder) file on (a) correspondence to which replies are due or on which action should be taken by a given date or (b) files needed by someone on a predetermined date?

General rule: Such a file is extremely useful, and should be established if supervisor approves.

22. Do I regularly straighten and tamp down papers in folders, crease expansion folds (scoring) on bottom of folders to keep papers from hiding labels, and check for misfiles?

General rule: These practices should, of course, be followed to make files easier to use and to ensure that papers are where they belong.

23. Do I remove paperclips, rubber bands, spring clips, and pins from papers, and staple those which should be stapled before filing?

General rule: These actions should be taken to prevent papers being inadvertently attached to others or separated as clips slip off, and to reduce bulk.

24. Do I keep my current files free of records that should be disposed of according to authorized schedules?

> *General rule:* This should be done to the fullest practicable extent, to save filing space and equipment, making filing and finding easier.

25. Do I periodically dispose of records (by retirement or destruction as authorized) according to schedules provided by my records management office?

> *General rule:* These things should be done, to save filing space and equipment and make filing and finding easier.

26. Do I file security-classified papers in separate file containers from papers not security-classified or papers marked "For Official Use Only"?

> *General rule:* This practice should be followed. However, in most firms, security regulations permit filing unclassified papers with classified ones when they are needed together for reference purposes. Such interfiling should be restricted to papers which directly support, explain, or document a decision or transaction. Be sure to check this point with your records management office or your security officer.

F. Reference service.

1. When records are removed from my files for use are they replaced by a charge-out form?

> *General rule:* This should be done, unless the users are in the same room or within a very limited distance from your files, so that location of records is known.

2. When additional papers arrive for inclusion in a file that is charged out, do I take these additional papers to the person who has the file?

> *General rule:* This should be done, so that he or she will have the benefit of the additional information.

3. Do I periodically contact persons to whom files are charged, after a reasonable period of time, to see if files can be returned?

> *General rule:* This should be done, to make these files available to other persons, and lessen chance of their being misplaced.

4. Over a period of, say, one year, would the total "can't finds" in my file be less than 3%?

> *General rule:* Three percent is regarded as the break-off point between efficient and inefficient reference service.

G. Work load.

1. Do I keep my classifying and filing up-to-date?

> *General rule:* Classifying and filing should, of course, be kept up-to-date; that is, done daily, so that backlogs do not accumulate. If this is not possible because the volume of papers is too great or other duties are given priority, and so forth, this should be discussed with supervisor.

2. Am I able to attend to requests for files or information from files as such requests are received?

> *General rule:* Requests for files service should be handled when they are received, not backlogged. If this is not happening, determine cause and discuss with supervisor.

H. Documentation.

1. Are my files complete, free of information gaps?
2. Do other offices or organizations always supply information due my office (such as periodic reports, requested data, and so forth)?
3. Do other persons in my office always turn papers over to me for my files?
4. Do other persons in my office always tell me when they remove papers from my files during my absence?

> *General rule:* Files should completely document, as far as possible, the office's role in a transaction, decision, project, and so forth. This is not possible if the answer to questions 2, 3, or 4 is "no," in which case you should consult your supervisor.

5. Do I fully understand regulations and procedures for the protection of security-classified files?

> *General rule:* All such policy and instructions must be thoroughly understood.

I. Equipment and supplies.

1. Am I using legal-size equipment and supplies only when the amount of legal-size papers is 20% or more?

> *General rule:* Because legal-size equipment and supplies cost more and take up more space, their use should be held to a practical minimum.

2. Am I using five-drawer filing cabinets?

> *General rule:* These should be used when available and when modern shelving should not be used, because of their greater capacity and saving of floor space.

3. Have I explored the advantages of using modern shelving instead of filing cabinets?

> *General rule:* Unless there are strong reasons why they should not be used, such shelves offer benefits, particularly in floor space savings. Their use should be considered.

4. Am I using fire resistant insulated file equipment and security type file equipment only for records that require this protection?

> *General rule:* Such equipment costs more than regular equipment, occupies more floor space, and is a greater floor load. It should be used only for records that warrant the degree of protection it affords.

5. Am I keeping filing cabinets free of stocks of blank forms, office supplies, stocks of publications, and so forth?

> *General rule:* Filing cabinet space should not be wasted on such items. Materials of this kind should be stored in nearby supply cabinet, shelving, or other suitable housing.

6. Am I using the right kind of file folders?

> *General rule:* Choice of folders should be governed by the kinds of papers, frequency of use, kind of container, and so on, involved.

7. Am I using the right kind of file guide cards (dividers)?

> *General rule:* Here, too, choice should be based on the kind of file, the tab position prescribed, whether color coding is to be used, and so on.

8. Am I using the right kind of file folder labels?

> *General rule:* Pressure-sensitive (self-adhesive) labels are easiest to apply. Their size, color, and other features should be chosen according to the kind of file, amount of information on label, and so on.

9. Do I use such aids as a sorter, hook-on shelves to hold papers as I file into containers, filing stool, tiered desk tray, and so on?

> *General rule:* Such devices make classifying, sorting, and filing easier. They should be used unless volume of papers is quite small.

J. Space and work flow.

1. Are my filing aids and file containers and their contents so arranged that steps are saved and filing moves progressively forward (e.g., from top to bottom of containers, left to right, etc.)?

> *General rule:* They should be so arranged, so that filing can be accomplished with least effort and in least time.

2. Are file containers placed so that I can get to them easily?
3. Are they placed so they do not interfere with the flow of other work and movement of other personnel?
4. Are they placed so they do not expose files to damage?
5. Are they placed so they do not unnecessarily expose my files to unauthorized access?
6. Are they placed so they are not a safety hazard?
7. Are they placed so they are in an area of good light?

> *General rule:* Naturally, as many of these objectives should be realized as possible.

K. Training.

1. Does my firm (a) present files workshops or other files training courses or (b) encourage attendance at such courses when presented by other sources?
2. If so, have I attended one recently (within the past two years)?

> *General rule:* Such courses should be given or supported, and be attended by all who maintain files. Only in this way can skills be improved, and the latest techniques, equipment, and supplies be introduced.

CONTROLS FOR INPUTS, DATA COMMUNICATIONS, PROGRAMMING, AND OUTPUTS

Completed Matrices

In Chapter 9 we defined how to utilize the six steps of the matrix approach in order to develop a matrix of controls using either general components or the process bubbles from the data flow diagrams for the system being designed. In this appendix, we present four generalized matrices; they show controls for inputs, data communications, programming, and outputs.

There is one small difference between the terminology of Chapter 9 and that of the four controls matrices we present here. Originally THREATS were called concerns/exposures and COMPONENTS were resources/assets. In Chapter 9 we changed this terminology because it is less confusing to call the unwanted events *threats* and the pieces of the system *components*. Users tend to understand threats and components better than they understand concerns/exposures and resources/ assets.

These four matrices are an excerpt from a larger book containing nine matrices. The book, titled *Internal Controls for Computerized Systems*,[1] contains over 650 controls.

[1] Published by Jerry FitzGerald & Associates, 506 Barkentine Lane, Redwood City, Calif. 94065.

© Copyright Jerry FitzGerald 1978

Input Control Matrix

The Matrix Approach

The control area to be reviewed using this matrix covers inputs to the computer system. These inputs may involve transaction origination or transaction entry and will be somewhat oriented toward batch computer systems. When reviewing the input controls, match each resource/asset with its corresponding concern/ exposure as listed in Figure A-1 (Input Control Matrix). This matrix lists the resources in relation to the potential exposures and cross-relates these with the various controls/safeguards that should be considered when reviewing inputs to computer systems.

To provide further meaning to this matrix, there is a complete definition provided for each of the concerns/exposures (threats) and also for each of the resources/assets (components). On the matrix, these threats and components are listed by name only. A numerical listing and description of each of the control numbers recorded in the cells also is provided.

Concerns/Exposures (Threats)

The following concerns/exposures are those that are directly applicable to the inputs (transaction origination and transaction entry) of a computer-based system. The definition for each of these threats, listed across the top of the matrix, is as follows:

- Authorization—The proper authorization either prior to the input (source document) or during input into the computer system.
- Source Document Origination—The procedures and methods used to ensure the proper and timely recording of data. The data may be recorded directly in a machine-readable form, or it may be recorded initially on a human-readable document.
- Source Document Error Handling—The procedures and methods used to ensure that all manual transactions rejected at any point in the system are corrected and re-entered in a timely manner.
- Source Document Retention—The procedures and methods used to ensure the proper retention of source documents, including the adequate

CONCERNS/EXPOSURES/THREATS

RESOURCES/ASSETS/COMPONENTS

	AUTHORIZATION	SOURCE DOCUMENT ORIGINATION	SOURCE DOCUMENT ERROR HANDLING	SOURCE DOCUMENT RETENTION	DATA ENTRY	TRANSACTION DATA VALIDATION	TRANSACTION ENTRY ERROR HANDLING	NEGOTIABLE DOCUMENT CONTROL	PRIVACY
INPUT DEVICES		6, 10			10, 43, 41	10	39, 43		57
OPERATIONAL PROCEDURES	5, 7, 9, 11-19, 25, 58	2, 4, 5, 7, 8, 10, 13, 14, 20-25, 31-34, 41, 44, 55, 57, 59-62	4, 5, 15, 21, 27, 34, 38, 40-42, 46, 49, 50, 54, 56, 59, 64	15, 16, 29, 47, 48, 61, 63	1-8, 14, 20, 23, 24, 27, 28, 30, 31, 33, 34, 40, 42, 44, 45, 54, 55, 57, 59, 60, 62, 67, 68	1-3, 6, 8-10, 12, 25, 28, 31, 33, 35-38, 40, 53, 56, 67, 68	21, 24, 28, 34, 39, 40, 42, 49-56, 64	15-18, 26, 57	4, 9, 11, 15, 18, 20, 32, 46, 57, 58, 60, 61
PEOPLE	5, 7, 9, 11-19, 25, 28	4, 5, 9, 10, 12-14, 20, 44, 45, 57, 59-62, 66	4, 15, 45, 46, 49, 50, 56, 59, 64, 65	15, 16, 29, 47, 48, 63	2, 4, 5, 7, 14, 20, 23, 24, 27, 28, 40, 44, 45, 54, 55, 57, 59, 60, 62, 66	9, 10, 12, 25, 53, 56	24, 28, 49-56, 64, 65	15-18, 26, 57	4, 9, 11, 15, 18, 20, 32, 46, 57, 58, 60, 61
FILES (MANUAL OR MAGNETIC MEDIA)		3, 4, 8, 9		15, 16, 29, 47, 48, 61, 63	3		51		
RECORDS STORAGE				15, 16, 29, 47, 48, 61, 63					
FORMS		22, 23, 30, 62	56	15, 16, 61	26, 62			15, 17, 18, 26	

Figure A-1 Input control matrix.

backup of source data maintained to provide audit trails or to be used for recovery should the computer data be inadvertently destroyed.

☐ Data Entry—The procedures and methods used to ensure the proper collection of data for recording as well as the transcription of that data to a machine-readable form for input to the computer system. This begins after the source documents have been originated and authorized. At this point it is necessary to prepare the data further for data processing input.

☐ Transaction Data Validation—The validation of data as it enters the computerized system.

☐ Transaction Entry Error Handling—The methodologies and controls for handling errors after they have been entered into the system, correcting these errors, and re-entering the corrected data into the system.

☐ Negotiable Document Control—The manual handling and use of negotiable document forms, either before, during, or after the use of these negotiable documents within the data processing department.

☐ Privacy—The accidental or intentional release of data about an individual, assuming that the release of this personal information was improper to the normal conduct of the business at the organization.

Resources/Assets (Components)

The following resources/assets are those that should be reviewed during the input control review. The definition for each of these components, listed down the left vertical column of the matrix, is as follows:

☐ Input Devices—Any or all of the input devices used to interconnect with the computer system. This would specifically include (without excluding other devices) key punches, key-tape/disk units, card readers, tape and disk units, optical readers, local terminals, microcomputers, and the like.

☐ Operational Procedures—The written procedures to be followed during the origination, preparation, and inputting of data to the computerized system.

☐ People—The individuals responsible for preparing and inputting data, operating and maintaining the equipment, following the operational procedures, and performing any other operations during the input of data to the computerized system.

☐ Files (Manual or Magnetic Media)—The manual files of source documents and the data once it is stored upon magnetic devices such as magnetic tapes or disks.

□ Records Storage—The long-term storage of various source documents or other types of data or programs that may be needed at some time in the future. This resource also includes the long-term storage of data that has been written onto microforms.

□ Forms—Any of the specially designed and preprinted forms that might be utilized prior to or during the inputting of data to the computerized system.

Controls

The following controls/safeguards should be considered when reviewing the inputs (transaction origination and transaction entry) of a computer-based system. This numerical listing describes each control.

It should be noted that implementation of various controls can be both costly and time consuming. It is of great importance that a realistic and pragmatic evaluation be made with regard to the probability of a specific threat affecting a specific component. Only then can the control be evaluated in a cost-effective manner.

The controls, as numerically listed in the cells of the matrix, are as follows:

1. When keypunching or keytaping, use verification techniques to ensure minimum errors. The operators might verify the entire data record or just critical fields.
2. Consider inputting critical fields twice when entering the data. In this way the computer system can match these two fields to ensure correctness.
3. When using magnetic tape or magnetic disk as an input device, consider using both internal and external labels on the tape and disk media devices.
4. When source documents are passed between various departments for manual processing, log in these documents as to time received and from whom received as they move between these manual operations.
5. Perform a manual check of source documents for items such as control figures, prior editing, signature authorization, and the like.
6. Whenever self-checking numbers are used, consider building hardware into keypunch or key-tape equipment to automatically verify these self-checking numbers during the input function.
7. Review the current operating procedures and verify that the handling procedures, signature authorization, and items similar to these are being followed during the manual handling of source documents or data input.
8. Log all inputs in sequence for on-line systems.

9. Use passwords for people and lockwords for files to protect from unauthorized data entry.

10. Restrict the access to various input devices.

11. Whenever feasible, segregate the functions of the generation of the transaction, the recording of the transaction, and the custody of the assets.

12. Consider establishing an independent control group to verify the authorization of transactions.

13. Ensure that the function responsible for inputting the transaction verifies authorization signatures by comparing them to an authorized signature list.

14. Establish batch controls close to the point of input preparation to prevent introduction of unauthorized input between the source and the entry into the computerized system.

15. Store source documents in a locked cabinet to prevent unauthorized modifications or unauthorized use of the data prior to its entry into the system.

16. Restrict access to blank input forms and especially to negotiable documents.

17. Keep negotiable documents under lock and key and control them through the use of prior serial numbering.

18. Control sensitive documents and especially negotiable documents by using a dual custody method where two people must be present when the documents are being used. These two people should also perform a manual count, which would be reconciled by a third person back to the serial numbers that were preprinted on the negotiable documents.

19. Ensure that the authorized individual does, in fact, sign source documents where this authorization is required.

20. Separate the computer operations functions from the transaction-generation and the transaction-recording functions.

21. Clearly describe the coding requirements, the batching requirements, and the scheduling requirements in the operations procedures manual.

22. Whenever possible, record data on a preprinted form to ensure against errors and omissions.

23. When designing forms, ensure that the data is recorded in a predetermined and uniform format in order to minimize errors and omissions.

24. Clearly describe the input keying requirements, response/error checking interpretation, and any special requirements in the operations procedures manual.

25. Ensure that the personnel who input data either initial, sign, or identify the data that they prepare.

26. Design source documents with preprinted sequential serial numbers for control and to ensure against lost documents.

27. Impose restrictions on batch size to allow ease of correction and control.

28. Record and/or maintain the identification number of the source document on the transaction to be processed.

29. Maintain the file of source documents by identification number or subject so it is readily retrievable. The identification number can be a preprinted sequential number or an assigned number such as employee number, part number, and the like.

30. Design and utilize precoded forms which contain information common to all given transaction types in order to reduce continual re-keying of the same data.

31. Include either the business date or processing date as a field in the input transaction.

32. Verify correctness of source documents prior to their conversion to a machine-readable form.

33. Include the Julian date as part of the transaction number.

34. Match transactions by processing cycle, and maintain uniqueness of batch and transaction numbers.

35. Assign transaction types to reflect the update process and desired update sequence.

36. Publish processing cycles to allow users to control cutoff dates.

37. Identify business or processing cutoff dates with specific logical accounting cycles.

38. Clearly define in the operations procedures the control points at which batch controls should be reconciled in the movement of data between and/or through various departments.

39. Establish backup processing procedures in case of a total and lengthy computer failure. These procedures should encompass alternative computers and/or manual data handling and processing procedures.

40. Ensure that every department that handles data reconciles its batch controls, verifies the processing schedule to ensure meeting cutoff points, and maintains a log of transactions passed between its department and other departments.

41. Try to centralize key-tape or key-disk operations close to the information source in order to ensure against lost source documents.

42. Compare computer-produced batch totals, hash totals, transaction totals, sequence numbers, and the like to predetermined manually prepared totals.

43. Incorporate the batch-balancing comparison process into the key-tape or key-disk equipment.

44. Stamp the source document at the time of inputting to ensure against inputting the same source documents twice.

45. Consider having a data control clerk visually verify all transactions prior to input, anticipate input, research missing input, and the like.

46. Consider having a data control clerk maintain a log of all source documents returned to the user for correction. This log should be reviewed frequently to ensure that the corrected document has been returned and re-entered into the system.

47. Store source documents in a safe place. Filing of these documents should provide for rapid access to the documents.

48. Assign a retention date to each source document, and ensure that it is placed in long-term storage which can be accessed at any time in the future.

49. Clearly outline the correction procedures in the operations manual. These procedures should include the types of errors that occur, correction procedures for all errors, and recycling of input and balancing of output reports.

50. Establish a central data control group responsible for error detection, correction, and re-submission.

51. Suspend the rejects on a file. Remove the file when the re-entered corrected version is verified and accepted for processing.

52. In addition to the original error message, regularly print the overdue suspended items and their messages so follow-up can be done on errors that have not been corrected in a timely manner.

53. When re-entering new transactions, edit the correction with the same module used to edit the original transaction.

54. Provide adequate user manuals and operations procedure manuals that cover items such as how to prepare the documents, regulate document flow, adhere to cutoff schedules, describe input keying requirements, and the like.

55. Ensure that each transaction to be entered into the computer system either has its own transaction identification or the batch identification from which it came.

56. Whenever possible, utilize a cross-reference field, in which the source document number might be part of the transaction identification. That will provide a cross-reference useful in tracing information to and from the source document.

57. Ensure that there is adequate separation of duties during the data preparation and data inputting to the computer system.

58. Ensure that there is evidence of approval (stamp the document) with regard to written authorizations and/or signatures.

59. Develop a control desk function to monitor the timely receipt of transactions and/or batches and to maintain proper source transaction schedules and compliance with requirements to the cut offs.

60. Utilize a transmittal document to control the movement of paperwork between various users and the data entry function.

61. Physically secure input during the transportation of source documents and/or source data between work areas.

62. Utilize source turnaround documents to ensure proper turnaround times. The turnaround portion of the document contains prerecorded data that can be used as the input medium for computer processing.

63. Develop a source document retention schedule and maintain a cross-index system in order to know how long to keep source documents and when to dispose of them. This can also be used for source document retrieval and for changing the retention dates, should it become necessary.

64. Develop written error-handling procedures to provide user personnel with comprehensive instructions for source document error detection, error correction, and corrected data re-submission.

65. Ensure that the operations personnel receive adequate job training.

66. Periodically rotate the duties between the operations personnel to reduce boredom and to give new job duties to different personnel.

67. Ensure that there are run-to-run totals so as not to lose data or information between jobs.

68. Cross-reference data input to record counts, control totals, hash totals, batch totals, and the like.

---

*D*ata Communication Control Matrix

---

*T*he Matrix Approach

The control area to be reviewed using this matrix covers the data communication links between the computer and the input/output terminals. These data communication-oriented controls may involve hardware controls, software controls, and personnel controls. When reviewing the data communication controls, match each resource/asset with its corresponding concern/exposure as listed in Figure A-2 (Data Communication Control Matrix). This matrix lists the re-

CONCERNS/EXPOSURES/THREATS

RESOURCES/ASSETS/COMPONENTS	ERRORS AND OMISSIONS	MESSAGE LOSS OR CHANGE	DISASTERS AND DISRUPTIONS	PRIVACY	SECURITY/THEFT	RELIABILITY (UP-TIME)	RECOVERY AND RESTART	ERROR HANDLING	DATA VALIDATION AND CHECKING
CENTRAL SYSTEM	1-4,7,39,41-43, 47,48	1-5,7,37,39, 48,49,89	1,8,11,13,16, 29,40,48,50, 51,54,57,58, 64,65,79,85	6,8,24,35,53, 56,60,62,68, 70,72-74, 78-80	6,8,24,35,53, 56,60,62,68,70, 72-74,77-80	1,13,16,29,38, 40,50,51, 63-65,68, 81,88	50,51,63-65, 68	48,85,89	6,24,39,41, 47,88
SOFTWARE	1-4,7,39,41-43, 46-49,52	1-5,7,37,39, 41,42,48,49, 52,54,89	1,8,16,40,48, 50-54,57-59, 63,85	6,8,24,35, 53,56,60,62, 68,70,72-74, 78-80	6,8,24,35,39, 53,56,60,62, 68,70,72-74, 78-80	1,38,40,50, 51,56-59, 61,63,68,88	50-52,61,63, 64,68	48,61,85,89	6,24,39,41, 47-49,52,53, 55,60,88
FRONT-END COMMUNICATION PROCESSOR	1-4,7,34,39, 41-44,46-48	1-5,7,34,37, 39,41,42,49, 89	1,8,13,16,29, 40,44,48,50,51, 54,57,58,64, 65,79,85	6,8,24,35,37, 45,60,62,68, 70,72-74, 78-80	6,8,24,29,35, 37,39,45,60, 62,68,70, 72-74,78-80	1,13,16,29, 30,34,36,40, 43,44,50,51, 63-65,81,88	37,50,51, 63-65	43,48,85,89	6,24,39,41, 45,47,48,88
MULTIPLEXER, CONCENTRATOR SWITCH	1-4,7,37,39, 41,44,46,47	1-5,7,37,39, 41,42,49,89	1,8,13,16,29, 30,32,33,40, 44,48,50,51, 54,57,58,65, 79,85	6,8,24,35,37, 45,60,62,68, 70,72-74, 78-80	6,8,24,29,35, 37,39,45,60, 62,68,70, 72-74,78-80	1,13,16,29,30, 32,34,36,40, 44,50,51, 63-65,81,88	37,50,51, 63,64	48,85,89	6,24,39,41, 45,47,48,88
COMMUNICATION CIRCUITS (LINES)	12,26	28,70,91	10,15,16,18, 26,63,64,66, 75,76,79,91	25,28,68,70, 75,76,78-80, 91	25,28,68,70, 75,76,78-80, 91	15,16,20,21, 23,26,27,63, 64,66-68, 88	63,64,66, 68	85	
LOCAL LOOP	12	25	25,75,85	25,76	25,29,75,76	68,88	63,64,68	85	
MODEMS	12,18	18,24	8-11,13-16, 18	24	24,29	9-11,13-18, 20,21,23, 36,88	9-11,14,15, 63,64	18-20,22, 23	
PEOPLE	5,39	5,7,31,39, 70	79-87	6,8,24,53, 69-71,74, 77,79,80	6,8,24,29, 53,69-71, 74,77,79,80	81,82, 85-87	50,51,86,87	49,86,87, 89,90	6,88
TERMINALS/ DISTRIBUTED INTELLIGENCE		2		6,8,24,45, 53,56,62, 70	6,8,24,29,45, 53,56,62,70	1,40,88	63,64		6,24,45

Figure A-2 Data communication control matrix.

sources in relation to the potential exposures and cross-relates these with the various controls/safeguards that should be considered when reviewing the data communication controls.

To provide further meaning to this matrix, there is a complete definition provided for each of the concerns/exposures (threats) and also for each of the resources/assets (components). On the matrix, these threats and components are listed by name only. A numerical listing and description of each of the control numbers recorded in the cells also is provided.

Concerns/Exposures (Threats)

The following concerns/exposures are those that are directly applicable to the data communication network review of an on-line system. The definition for each of these threats, listed across the top of the matrix, is as follows:

- □ Errors and Omissions—The accidental or intentional transmission of data that is in error, including the accidental or intentional omission of data that should have been entered or transmitted on the on-line system. This type of exposure includes, but is not limited to, inaccurate data, incomplete data, malfunctioning hardware, and the like.
- □ Message Loss or Change—The loss of messages as they are transmitted throughout the data communication system, or the accidental/intentional changing of messages during transmission.
- □ Disasters and Disruptions (natural and man-made)—The temporary or long-term disruption of normal data communication capabilities. This exposure renders the organization's normal data communication on-line system inoperative.
- □ Privacy—The accidental or intentional release of data about an individual, assuming that the release of this personal information was improper to the normal conduct of the business at the organization.
- □ Security/Theft—The security or theft of information that should have been kept confidential because of its proprietary nature. In a way, this is a form of privacy, but the information removed from the organization does not pertain to an individual. The information might be inadvertently (accidentally) released, or it might be the subject of an outright theft. This exposure also includes the theft of assets such as might be experienced in embezzlement, fraud, or defalcation.
- □ Reliability (Up-Time)—The reliability of the data communication network and its "up-time." This includes the organization's ability to keep the data communication network operating and the mean time between failures

(MTBF) as well as the time to repair equipment when it malfunctions. Reliability of hardware, reliability of software, and the maintenance of these two items are chief concerns here.

☐ Recovery and Restart—The recovery and restart capabilities of the data communication network, should it fail. In other words, How does the software operate in a failure mode? How long does it take to recover from a failure? This recovery and restart concern also includes backup for key portions of the data communication network and the contingency planning for backup, should there be a failure at any point of the data communication network.

☐ Error Handling—The methodologies and controls for handling errors at a remote distributed site or at the centralized computer site. This may also involve the error handling procedures of a distributed data processing system (at the distributed site). The object here is to ensure that when errors are discovered they are promptly corrected and re-entered into the system for processing.

☐ Data Validation and Checking—The validation of data either at the time of transmission or during transmission. The validation may take place at a remote site (intelligent terminal), at the central site (front-end communication processor), or at a distributed intelligence site (concentrator or remote front-end communication processor).

Resources/Assets (Components)

The following resources/assets are those that should be reviewed during the data communication control review. The definition for each of these components, listed down the left vertical column of the matrix, is as follows:

☐ Central System—Most prevalent in the form of a central computer to which the data communication network transmits and from which it receives information. In a distributed system, with equal processing at each distributed node, there might not be an identifiable central system (just some other equal-sized distributed computer).

☐ Software—The software programs that operate the data communication network. These programs may reside in the central computer, a distributed-system computer, the front-end communication processor, a remote concentrator or statistical multiplexer, and/or a remote intelligent terminal. This software may include the telecommunications access methods, an overall teleprocessing monitor, programs that reside in the front-end processors, and/or programs that reside in the intelligent terminals.

- Front-End Communication Processor—A hardware device that interconnects all the data communication circuits (lines) to the central computer or distributed computers and performs a subset of the following functions: code and speed conversion, protocol, error detection and correction, format checking, authentication, data validation, statistical data gathering, polling/addressing, insertion/deletion of line control codes, and the like.

- Multiplexer, Concentrator, Switch—Hardware devices that enable the data communication network to operate in the most efficient manner. The multiplexer is a device that combines, in one data stream, several simultaneous data signals from independent stations. The concentrator performs the same functions as a multiplexer except it is intelligent and therefore can perform some of the functions of a front-end communication processor. A *switch* is a device that allows the interconnection between any two circuits (lines) connected to the switch. There might be two distinct types of switch: a switch that performs message switching between stations (terminals) might be located within the data communication network facilities that are owned and operated by the organization; a circuit or line switching switch that interconnects various circuits might be located at (and owned by) the telephone company central office. For example, organizations perform message switching and the telephone company performs circuit switching.

- Communication Circuits (Lines)—The common carrier facilities used as links (a link is the interconnection of any two stations/terminals) to interconnect the organization's stations/terminals. These communication circuits include, not to the exclusion of others, satellite facilities, public switched dial-up facilities, point-to-point private lines, multiplexed lines, multipoint or loop configured private lines, WATS services, and many others.

- Local Loop—The communication facility between the customer's premises and the telephone company's central office or the central office of any other special common carrier. The local loop is usually assumed to be metallic pairs of wires.

- Modems—A hardware device used for the conversion of data signals from terminals (digital signal) to an electrical form (analog signal) which is acceptable for transmission over the communication circuits that are owned and maintained by the telephone company or other special common carrier.

- People—The individuals responsible for inputting data, operating and maintaining the data communication network equipment, writing the software programs for the data communications, managing the overall data communication network, and those involved at the remote stations/terminals.

- Terminals/Distributed Intelligence—Any or all of the input or output devices used to interconnect with the on-line data communication network.

This resource would specifically include, without excluding other devices, teleprinter terminals, video terminals, remote job entry terminals, transaction terminals, intelligent terminals, and any other devices used with distributed data communication networks. These may include microprocessors or minicomputers when they are input/output devices or if they are used to control portions of the data communication network.

Controls

The following controls/safeguards should be considered when reviewing the data communication network review of an on-line system. This numerical listing describes each control.

It should be noted that implementation of various controls can be both costly and time consuming. It is of great importance that a realistic and pragmatic evaluation be made with regard to the probability of a specific threat affecting a specific component. Only then can the control be evaluated in a cost-effective manner.

The controls, as numerically listed in the cells of the matrix, are as follows:

1. Ensure that the system can switch messages destined for a down station/terminal to an alternate station/terminal.
2. Determine whether the system can perform message-switching to transmit messages between stations/terminals.
3. In order to avoid lost messages in a message-switching system, provide a store and forward capability. This is where a message destined for a busy station is stored at the central switch and then forwarded at a later time when the station is no longer busy.
4. Review the message or transaction logging capabilities to reduce lost messages, provide for an audit trail, restrict messages, prohibit illegal messages, and the like. These messages might be logged at the remote station (intelligent terminal), they might be logged at a remote concentrator/remote front-end processor, or they might be logged at the central front-end communication processor/central computer.
5. Transmit messages promptly to reduce risk of loss.
6. Identify each message by the individual user's password, the terminal, and the individual message sequence number.
7. Acknowledge the successful or unsuccessful receipt of all messages.
8. Utilize physical security controls throughout the data communication network (see Chapter 8 of the book *Internal Controls for Computerized Systems* for the Physical Security Control Matrix). This includes the use of locks,

guards, badges, sensors, alarms, and administrative measures to protect the physical facilities, data communication networks, and related data communication equipment. These safeguards are required for access monitoring and control to protect data communication equipment and software from damage by accident, fire, and environmental hazard either intentional or unintentional.

9. Consider using modems that have either manual or remote actuated loopback switches for fault isolation to ensure the prompt identification of malfunctioning equipment. These are extremely important in order to increase the up-time and to identify faults.

10. Use front panel lights on modems to indicate if the circuit/line is functioning properly (carrier signal is up). This may not be a viable alternative with organizations that have hundreds of modems.

11. Consider a modem with alternate voice capabilities for quick troubleshooting between the central site and a major remote site.

12. When feasible, use digital data transmission, because it has a lower error rate than analog data transmission.

13. For data communication equipment, check the manufacturer's mean time between failures (MTBF) in order to ensure that the data communication equipment has the largest MTBF.

14. Consider placing unused backup modems in critical areas of the data communication network.

15. Consider using modems that have an automatic or semiautomatic dial backup capability in case the leased line fails.

16. Review the maintenance contract and mean time to fix (MTTF) for all data communication equipment. Maintenance should be both fast and available. Determine from where the maintenance is dispatched, and determine if tests can be made from a remote site (for example, in many cases modems have remote loopback capabilities).

17. Increase data transmission efficiency. The faster the modem synchronization time, the lower will be the turnaround time and thus more throughput to the system.

18. Consider modems with automatic equalization (built in microprocessors for circuit equalization and balancing) in order to compensate for amplitude and phase distortions on the line. This will reduce the number of errors in transmission and may decrease the need for conditioned lines.

19. With regard to the efficiency of modems, review to see if they have multiple-speed switches so the transmission rate can be lowered when the line error rates are high.

20. Utilize four-wire circuits in a pseudo-full duplex transmission mode. In other words, keep the carrier wave up in each direction on alternate pairs

of wires in order to reduce turnaround time and gain efficiency during transmission.

21. If needed, use full duplex transmission on two-wire circuits with special modems that split the frequencies and thus achieve full duplex transmission.

22. Increase the speed of transmission. The faster the speed of transmission by the modem, the more cost effective are the data communications, but error rates may increase with speed, and therefore you may need more error detection and correction facilities.

23. Utilize a reverse channel capability for control signals (supervisory) and to keep the carrier wave up in both directions.

24. Consider the following special controls on dial-up modems when the data communication network allows incoming dial-up connections: change the telephone numbers at regular intervals; keep the telephone numbers confidential; remove the telephone numbers from the modems in the computer operations area; require that each "dial-up terminal" have an electronic identification circuit chip to transmit its unique identification to the front-end communication processor; do not allow automatic call receipt and connection (always have a person intercept the call and make a verbal identification); have the central site call the various terminals that will be allowed connection to the system; utilize dial-out only where an incoming dialed call triggers an automatic dial-back to the caller (in this way the central system controls those telephone numbers to which it will allow connection).

25. Physically trace out and, as well as possible, secure the local loop communication circuits/lines within the organization or facility. After these lines leave the facility and enter the public domain, they cannot be physically secured.

26. Consider conditioning the voice-grade circuits in order to reduce the number of errors during transmission (this may be unnecessary with the newer microprocessor-based modems that perform automatic equalization and balancing).

27. Use four-wire circuits in such a fashion that there is little to no turnaround time. This can be done by using two wires in each direction and keeping the carrier signal up.

28. Within an organizational facility, fiber optic (laser) communication circuits can be used to totally preclude the possibility of wiretapping.

29. Ensure that there is adequate physical security at remote sites and especially for terminals, concentrators, multiplexers, and front-end communication processors.

30. Determine whether the multiplexer/concentrator/remote front-end hard-

ware has redundant logic and backup power supplies with automatic fall-back capabilities in case the hardware fails. This will increase the up-time of the many stations/terminals that might be connected to this equipment.

31. Consider logging inbound and outbound messages at the remote site.

32. Consider uninterruptible power supplies at large multiplexer/concentrator type remote sites.

33. Consider multiplexer/concentrator equipment that has diagnostic lights, diagnostic capabilities, and the like.

34. If a concentrator is being used, is it performing some of the controls that are usually performed by the front-end communication processor and therefore increasing the efficiency and correctness of data transmissions?

35. See if the polling configuration list can be changed during the day in order to exclude or include specific terminals. This would allow the positive exclusion of a terminal as well as allowing various terminals to come on-line and off-line during the working day.

36. Can the front-ends, concentrators, modems, and the like handle the automatic answering and automatic outward dialing of calls? This would increase the efficiency and accuracy when it is preprogrammed into the system.

37. Ensure that all inbound and outbound messages are logged by the central processor, the front-end, or remote concentrator in order to ensure against lost messages, keep track of message sequence numbers (identify illegal messages), and to use for system restart should the entire system crash.

38. For efficiency, ensure that the central system can address either a group of terminals (group address), several terminals at a time (multiple address), one terminal at a time (single address), or send a broadcast message simultaneously to all stations/terminals in the system.

39. See that each inbound and outbound message is serial numbered as well as time and date stamped at the time of logging.

40. Ensure that there is a "time out" facility so the system does not get hung up trying to poll/address a station. Also, if a particular station "times out" four or five consecutive times, it should be removed from the network configuration polling list so time is not wasted on this station (improves communication efficiency).

41. Consider having concentrators and front-ends perform two levels of editing. In the first level the front-end may add items to a message, reroute the message, or rearrange the data for further transmission. It may also check a message address for accuracy and perform parity checks. In the second level of editing, the concentrator or front-end is programmed to perform specific edits of the different transactions that enter the system.

This editing is an application system type of editing and deals with message content rather than form and is specific to each application program being executed.

42. Have the concentrators, front-ends, and central computers handle the message priority system, if one exists. A priority system is set up to permit a higher line utilization to certain areas of the network or to ensure that certain transactions are handled before other transactions of lesser importance.

43. See that the front-end collects message traffic statistics and performs correlations of traffic density and circuit availability. These analyses are mandatory for the effective management of a large data communication network. Some of the items included in a traffic density report might be the number of messages handled per hour or per day on each link of the network, the number of errors encountered per hour or per day, the number of errors encountered per program or per program module, the terminals or stations that appear to have a higher than average error record, and the like.

44. Ensure that the front-ends and concentrators can perform miscellaneous functions such as triggering remote alarms if certain parameters are exceeded, performing multiplexing operations internally, signaling abnormal occurrences to the central computer, slowing up input/output messages when the central computer is overburdened due to heavy traffic, and the like.

45. Ensure that the concentrators and front-ends can validate electronic terminal identification.

46. Ensure that there is a message intercept function for inoperable terminals or invalid terminal addresses.

47. See that messages are checked for valid destination address.

48. Ensure adequate error detection and control capabilities. These might include echo-checking, where a message is transmitted to a remote site and the remote site echoes the message back for verification, or it might include forward error correction, where special hardware boxes can automatically correct some errors upon receipt of the message, or it might include detection with retransmission. Detection with retransmission is the most common and cost-effective form of error detection and correction. This may include identification of errors by reviewing the parity bit or utilizing a special code to identify errors in individual characters during transmission. A more prevalent form is to utilize a polynomial (mathematical algorithm) to detect errors in message blocks. Whichever way is used, when a message error is detected, it is retransmitted until it is received correctly.

49. When reviewing error detection in transmission, first determine whatever error rate can be tolerated, then determine the extent and pattern of errors on the communication links used by the organization, and then review the error detection and correction methodologies in use and determine if they are adequate for the application systems utilizing the data communication network. In other words, a purely administrative message network (no critical financial data) would not require error detection and correction capabilities equal to a network that transmits critical financial data.

50. Ensure that there are adequate restart and recovery software routines to recover from items such as a trapped machine check, where instead of bringing down the entire data communication system, a quick recovery can be made and only the one transaction need be retransmitted.

51. Ensure that there are adequate restart and recovery procedures to effect both a warm start and a cold start. In other words, a data communication system should never completely fail so the user has to perform a cold start (start up as if it is a new day, all message counters cleared). The system should go into a warm start procedure, where only parts of the system are disabled and recovery can be made while the system is operating in a degraded mode.

52. Ensure that there is an audit trail logging facility to assist in the reconstruction of data files and the reconstruction of transactions from the various stations. There should be the capability to trace back to the terminal and user.

53. Provide some tables for checking for access by terminals, people, database, and programs. These tables should be in protected areas of memory.

54. Safe store all messages. All transactions/messages should be protected in case of a disastrous situation, such as power failure.

55. Protect against concurrent file updates. If the data management software does not provide this protection, the data communication software should.

56. For convenience, flexibility, and security, ensure that terminals can be brought up or down dynamically while the system is running.

57. Make available a systems trace capability to assist in locating problems.

58. Ensure that the documentation of the system software is comprehensive.

59. Provide adequate maintenance for the software programs.

60. Ensure that the system supports password protection (multilevel password protection).

61. Identify all default options in the software and their impact if they do not operate properly.

62. For entering sensitive or critical systems commands, restrict these commands to one master input terminal and ensure strict physical custody over this terminal. In other words, restrict those personnel who can use this terminal.

63. Ensure that there are adequate recovery facilities and/or capabilities for a software failure, loss of key pieces of hardware, and loss of various communication circuit/lines.

64. Ensure that there are adequate backup facilities (local and remote) to back up key pieces of hardware and communication circuits/lines.

65. Consider backup power capabilities for large facilities such as the central site and various remote concentrators.

66. Consider installing the capabilities to fall back to the public dial network from a leased line configuration.

67. When utilizing multidrop or loop circuits, review the up-time problems. These types of configurations are more cost-effective than point-to-point configurations, but when there is a circuit failure close to the central site, all terminals/stations downline are disconnected.

68. Review the physical security (local and remote) for circuits/lines (especially the local loop), hardware/software, physical facilities, storage media, and the like.

69. For personnel who work in critical or sensitive areas, consider enforcing the following policies: insist that they take at least five consecutive days of vacation per year, check with their previous employers, perform an annual credit check, and have them sign hiring agreements stating that they will not sell programs, and so forth.

70. With regard to data security, consider encrypting all messages transmitted.

71. Develop an overall organizational security policy for the data communication network. This policy should specifically cover the security and privacy of information.

72. Ensure that all sensitive communication programs and data are stored in protected areas of memory or disk storage.

73. Ensure that all communication programs or data, when they are off-line, are stored in areas with adequate physical security.

74. Ensure that all communication programs and data are adequately controlled when they are transferred to microfiche.

75. Lock up telephone equipment rooms and install alarms on the doors of those telephone equipment rooms that contain the basic data communication circuits.

76. Do not put communication lines through the public switchboard unless it

is a new electronic switchboard (ESS) and the intent is to gain verbal identification of incoming dial-up data communication calls.

77. Review the communication system's console log that shows "network supervisor terminal commands" such as: disable or enable a line or station for input or output, alternately route traffic from one station to another, change the order and/or frequency of line or terminal service (polling, calling, dialing), and the like.

78. Consider packet-switching networks that use alternate routes for different packets of information from the same message; this would offer a form of security in case someone were intercepting messages.

79. Ensure that there is a policy for the use of test equipment. Modern-day test equipment may offer a new vulnerability to the organization. This test equipment is easily connected to communication lines, and all messages can be read in clear "English language." Test equipment should not be used for monitoring lines "for fun"; it should be locked up (key lock or locked hood) when it is not in use and after normal working hours when it is not needed for testing and debugging; programs written for programmable test equipment should be kept locked up and out of the hands of those who do not need these programs.

80. Review the operational procedures, for example, the administrative regulations, policies, and day-to-day activities supporting the security/safeguards of the data communication network. These procedures may include:

   □ Specifying the objectives of the EDP security for an organization, especially as they relate to data communications.

   □ Planning for contingencies of security "events," including recording of all exception conditions and activities.

   □ Assuring management that other safeguards are implemented, maintained, and audited, including background checks, security clearances and hiring of people with adequate security-oriented characteristics; separation of duties; mandatory vacations.

   □ Developing effective safeguards for deterring, detecting, preventing, and correcting undesirable security events.

   □ Reviewing the cost-effectiveness of the system and the related benefits such as better efficiency, improved reliability, and economy.

   □ Looking for the existence of current administrative regulations, security plans, contingency plans, risk analysis, personnel understanding of management objectives, and then reviewing the adequacy and timeliness of the specified procedures in satisfying these.

81. Review the preventive maintenance and scheduled diagnostic testing such as cleaning, replacement, and inspection of equipment to evaluate its

accuracy, reliability, and integrity. This may include schedules for testing and repair, adequate testing of software program changes submitted by the vendor, inventories of replacement parts (circuit boards), past maintenance records, and the like.

82. Determine whether there is a central site for reporting all problems encountered in the data communication network. This usually results in faster repair time.

83. Review the financial protection afforded from insurance for various hardware, software, and data stored on magnetic media.

84. Review the legal contracts with regard to the agreements for performing a specific service and specific costing basis for the data communication network hardware and software. These might include bonding of employees, conflict of interest agreements, clearances, nondisclosure agreements, agreements establishing liability for specific security events by vendors, agreements by vendors not to perform certain acts that would incur a penalty, and the like.

85. Review the organization's fault isolation/diagnostics, including the techniques used to ascertain the integrity of the various hardware/software components comprising the total data communication entity. These techniques are used to audit, review, and control the total data communication environment and to isolate the offending elements either on a periodic basis or upon detection of a failure. These techniques may include diagnostic software routines, electrical loopback, test message generation, administrative and personnel procedures, and the like.

86. Review the training and education of employees with regard to the data communication network. Employees must be adequately trained in this area because of the high technical competence required for data communication networks.

87. Ensure that there is adequate documentation, including a precise description of programs, hardware, system configurations, and procedures intended to assist in the prevention of problems, identification of problems, and recovery from problems. The documentation should be sufficiently detailed to assist in reconstructing the system from its parts.

88. Review the techniques for testing used to validate the hardware and software operation to ensure integrity. Testing, including that of personnel, should uncover departures from the specified operation.

89. Review error recording to reduce lost messages. All errors in transmission of messages in the system should be logged and this log should include the type of error, the time and date, the terminal, the circuit, the terminal operator, and the number of times the message was retransmitted before it was correctly received.

90. Review the error correction procedures. A user's manual should specify a cross-reference of error messages to the appropriate error code generated by the system. These messages help the user interpret the error that has occurred and suggest the corrective action to be taken. Ensure that the errors are in fact corrected and the correct data re-entered into the system.

91. Consider backing up key circuits/lines. This circuit backup may take the form of a second leased line, modems that have the ability to go to the public dial-up network when a leased line fails, or manual procedures where the remote stations can transmit verbal messages using the public dial-up network.

---

*P*rogram/*Computer Processing Control Matrix*

---

*T*he Matrix Approach

The control area to be reviewed using this matrix covers program/computer processing controls. These program/computer processing controls involve those automated controls that can be built into computer programs and into computerized systems. When reviewing the program/computer processing controls, match each resource/asset with its corresponding concern/exposure as listed in Figure A-3 (Program/Computer Processing Control Matrix). This matrix lists the resources in relation to the potential exposures and cross-relates these with the various controls/safeguards that should be considered when reviewing the programmed controls in a system.

To provide further meaning to this matrix, there is a complete definition provided for each of the concerns/exposures (threats) and also for each of the resources/assets (components). On the matrix, these threats and components are listed by name only. A numerical listing and description of each of the control numbers recorded in the cells also is provided.

*C*oncerns/*Exposures (Threats)*

The following concerns/exposures are those that are directly applicable to the program/computer processing of either on-line or batch systems. The definition

CONCERNS/EXPOSURES/THREATS

RESOURCES/ASSETS/COMPONENTS	PROGRAM ERRORS AND OMISSIONS	UNAUTHORIZED PROGRAM CHANGES	SECURITY/THEFT	DATA VALIDATION	HARDWARE ERRORS	RESTART AND RECOVERY	AUDIT TRAILS	COMPUTER PROGRAM GENERATED TRANSACTIONS	ERROR HANDLING
APPLICATION PROGRAMS AND SYSTEMS	1-9, 16-20, 63, 71-74, 86, 89, 90	13, 22, 23, 25, 30-33, 35, 38, 43, 44, 49-51, 70, 85, 88, 90, 92	24, 25, 30-35, 38, 43, 49, 62, 70	2-8, 16, 69, 72-74, 89	70, 72-74, 89	20, 76, 77	6, 16, 22, 23, 25-28, 30, 32, 33, 35, 43, 49	1, 5, 7, 43, 44, 51, 64, 65, 67, 68, 70, 71, 90	9-15, 45, 71, 78-81, 83
DATA RECORD INTEGRITY	1, 3-7, 16, 17, 27, 69, 71, 73, 74, 80, 81	30-33	24-26, 29, 30-35, 36, 39, 48, 49	1-5, 7, 10, 12-14, 16, 17, 24, 25, 27, 28, 63, 69	41, 46, 47, 72, 87	20, 21, 28	6, 16, 25-28, 31, 32, 49, 64, 66, 80-82	64-68	10-15, 45, 79-83
OUTPUT INTEGRITY	2-4, 6, 7, 16, 18-20, 27, 69, 71, 73, 74, 80, 81	39	24-26, 29-35, 38, 39, 48, 49	2, 4-7, 9, 10, 16, 28, 69		21, 28	17	64, 65, 67, 81	15, 71, 75, 78-83
CENTRAL SYSTEM	16, 40-42, 46, 47, 69, 76, 77, 91	36-39, 48, 49, 51-53, 85, 86, 91	36-39, 42, 47-49, 51-53, 55, 62, 84, 91	16, 40, 69	46, 54-61, 87	42, 76, 77	30, 33, 42, 84, 91		91
SOFTWARE PROGRAMS	1, 86, 87, 90	13, 22, 23, 25, 30-33, 35, 38, 44, 49, 50, 51, 70, 85, 88-90, 92	24, 25, 30-35, 38, 49, 62, 70	89	70, 87, 89			51, 70, 90	

Figure A-3 Program/computer processing control matrix.

for each of these threats, listed across the top of the matrix, is as follows:

☐ Program Errors and Omissions—The accidental or intentional creation of an error during the processing of the data or the running of the application programs, including the accidental or intentional omission of data (loss) during the processing of a computer program. This type of exposure includes, but is not limited to, multiprogram code, trapped machine checks where programs just quit processing, loss of data during the running of a program, and the like.

☐ Unauthorized Program Changes—The temporary or permanent change of program code by individuals who are unauthorized to make these changes, as well as by individuals who are so authorized but who make illegal program changes for whatever reason.

☐ Security/Theft—The security or theft of information or programs that should have been kept confidential because of their proprietary nature. In a way, this is a form of privacy, but the information removed from the organization does not specifically pertain to an individual. The information or computer programs might be inadvertently (accidentally) removed from the organization or might be the subject of outright theft.

☐ Data Validation—The computer program editing of data prior to its processing and the preprogrammed specific actions that should be taken when erroneous data is discovered (this may also include the discovery of omissions in certain data that should have been included).

☐ Hardware Errors—The malfunctioning of the computer hardware so it appears that a program has made some sort of an error in processing. The concern here is that a hardware malfunction may cause erroneous data, data omissions, loss of specific data, and the like.

☐ Restart and Recovery—The restarting of computer programs that have failed during their normal course of processing and the recovery that should take place so no data is lost, erroneously processed, or processed twice because of the failure (the failure may have been caused by program failure or computer hardware failures).

☐ Audit Trails—Ensure that the processing of the data can be traced backward and forward through the entire computer processing cycle.

☐ Computer Program Generated Transactions—Ensure that any transactions that are automatically generated within an on-line system are adequately controlled. In other words, some on-line systems automatically create transactions during the time they are being run and these transactions should have adequate controls to prevent errors, erroneous transactions, and illegal transactions.

☐ Error Handling—The procedures and methods used to ensure that all transactions or data that are rejected during the computer processing are, in fact, corrected and re-entered into the system in a timely manner. This involves accounting for and detecting data errors, loss, or the nonprocessing of transactions, as well as the reporting of these errors, error correction, and the corrected data re-submission.

Resources/Assets (Components)

The following resources/assets are those that should be reviewed during the program/computer processing control review. The definition for each of these components, listed down the left vertical column of the matrix, is as follows:

- □ Application Programs and Systems—Any or all the computer programs that are utilized in the data processing operations. This resource should also be viewed as the overall macrosystems that operate within the organization (these systems may be made up of a group of computer programs). This is far and away the most valuable asset of the organization because, in the long run, the computer programs are more costly than the hardware upon which they operate.
- □ Data Record Integrity—The data that is stored in the computer files or databases and is used in the everyday processing of the organization's computerized recordkeeping system.
- □ Output Integrity—The believability and integrity of the output reports from the system. The auditor should review this resource to ensure that the output reports are Consistent, Accurate, Timely, Economic, and Relevant to the intended purpose (reports that meet these criteria will CATER to the needs of the organization).
- □ Central System—Most prevalent in the form of a central computer in which the computer programs operate. This asset may be in the form of a central computer system, or it may be in the form of numerous computer systems spread around in a distributed network.
- □ Software Programs—The software programs that run the overall computerized systems. These may include the operating system software (usually supplied by the computer vendor) as well as the software programs utilized to maintain and operate the data communication network, or the database system (data management software). These software programs usually operate at the "systems control level" because any controls that are built into, or programmed into, this level of software affect all application programs. For example, a control that is built into the operating system software, data communication control software, or data management soft-

ware would have its effect upon any incoming transaction that passed through that level of software programs without regard to whether it was a payroll transaction, inventory control transaction, financial balancing transaction, or the like.

Controls

The following controls/safeguards should be considered when reviewing the programs or computer processing of either on-line or batch systems. This numerical listing describes each control.

It should be noted that implementation of various controls can be both costly and time consuming. It is of great importance that a realistic and pragmatic evaluation be made with regard to the probability of a specific threat affecting a specific component. Only then can the control be evaluated in a cost-effective manner.

The controls, as numerically listed in the cells of the matrix, are as follows:

1. Transactions that are consecutively numbered by the station transmitting (these might be computer generated transactions) to the computer should be sequence number checked by the computer programs. In other words, the computer programs should verify the unbroken sequence of input or output transactions and take corrective action, should there be a break in sequence. One form of corrective action would be to notify the terminal operator and to close down the transmitting station's ability to transmit data until the remote station takes some sort of corrective action.

2. Have the programs compare the total count of input transactions to a predetermined total count or to a count of output transactions.

3. Let the program perform automated and/or preprogrammed editing for all input after it gets into the computer. Some of the editing that the program can perform might be as follows:

   □ Count the number of fields in a record and compare that with a predetermined number of fields.

   □ Check for the reasonableness of the input data with regard to some set of pre-established boundaries.

   □ Test the data for blanks, sign (plus or minus), numeric, or alphabetic, and compare that with a pre-established criteria.

   □ Check for consistency between fields of an input transaction (this would be a specific control with regard to a specific application input).

   □ Conduct a limit test, and reject data or take corrective action whenever the data falls outside of some limit or predetermined range.

- ☐ Check for completeness of data, for example, the zip code field should be full, and it should contain numeric data only.
- ☐ Conduct sequence checking in order to ensure correct sequence.
- ☐ Conduct date checking in order to ensure that the dates are correct whenever this is applicable.
- ☐ Use self-checking numbers that pinpoint erroneous entry of account numbers or whatever type of number the organization is using.
- ☐ Enter critical data twice on one transaction input and have the computer programs cross-check these two inputs to ensure that, first it was entered correctly, and second there was no error during transmission.

4. Let the computer programs compare or crossfoot predetermined control figures such as:
   - ☐ Record counts.
   - ☐ Control totals.
   - ☐ Hash totals.
   - ☐ Batch control totals.

5. Have the program recompute various totals of significant financial or accounting figures and transmit these totals back to the original input station.

6. Have the programs prepare specific reports that will display the contents of batch controls, header controls, and any other types of control totals that can be sent back to the original station that inputted the data.

7. Have the programs compare the current data totals with historical totals in order to maintain a logical relationship over time.

8. Have the programs perform logical relationship tests. Logical relationship tests are solely dependent on a specific application because there may be logical relationships within a specific application system.

9. Have the programs look for duplicate entries of data. Whenever duplicate entries are suspected, the original station inputting the data should be immediately notified.

10. Design systems so, upon the discovery of erroneous data during processing, the original entry station is immediately notified so correction can take place as soon as possible.

11. Ensure that whenever the program edits an incoming record and it finds an error, it continues editing the entire record to see if there is more than one error. This is to avoid the possibility of the program rejecting an input transaction because of an error, and after correcting that error and re-entering the correction into the system, finding a second error in the original input. This control reduces the cycling of erroneous input messages.

12. Where feasible, incorporate the editing/validation routines into the remote areas of a distributed or data communication network to reduce transmitting erroneous data.

13. Do not provide users with the capability of overriding computer program edits.

14. Do not allow fall-through comparison tests when editing.

15. Have the system produce a report containing all erroneous transactions and identify the invalid data, out-of-balance data, and the like.

16. Maintain an opening day transaction count record and a closing day transaction count record. These should be equal and should be compared between the central system and the remote data input stations.

17. Have the programs compare transaction date to the cutoff date table. Transactions entering after the cutoff date should be suspended until after closing. The totals of significant fields of the suspended items are to be reported. These suspended items will not be included in the closing balance because they are for the following period.

18. Ensure that the data management program (the scheduler) determines potential conflicts between two users attempting to access the same file and keeps these two separate.

19. See that the data management system can prohibit two programs from simultaneously updating the same record but not the same file.

20. Have the master file update program (especially data management—database) log the after-image of each database update. This may not be necessary if the database is a small one that can be copied over each day.

21. Maintain a file that reflects all updated master records and that can be used to recover from a master file loss.

22. Develop and maintain a formal system to control program changes. This system should control and log the changes to any computer program (application software or operations software).

23. Maintain a program that will control the various computer program libraries and will show whenever modifications have been made to these computer program libraries that reside within the computer.

24. See that there are various tables within the computer programs to validate and verify individual user security codes (passwords), unique terminal identification codes, transaction security codes, and any other type of verification of input data that might be necessary. This verification involves verifying prior to allowing entry to the system.

25. See that there is a cross-correlation between the individual user's security code (password) and the transactions, computer programs, computer systems, or other areas that that individual user is allowed to access.

26. See that there are reporting programs that can be used to identify all transactions entered by a specific user (password).

27. Ensure that all transactions are dated, time stamped, and logged immediately upon entry into the system. Output transactions should be handled in a similar way.

28. Retain all input and output transactions on an independent file that is backed up.

29. Whenever computer programs or data are to be copied over to microfiche, ensure that the handling and storage procedures for the microfiche at least equal the security and control within the data processing operations.

30. Maintain a special log of all unscheduled or unusual interventions by computer operations personnel. This should include location, date, time, type of intervention, and action taken.

31. Maintain a file of all changes to any security tables. There should be a formal procedure to be followed when changing the "up-front" security tables. These are the tables against which the individual users' passwords are compared. All resident tables that require periodic update should be created and maintained external to the system.

32. See that the update program that produces changes to tables also produces a report containing the changes and the corresponding table entry, both before and after the change.

33. Make sure that all table changes receive appropriate authorization external to the system before the change takes place. This should be a written form approval and it should be reviewed before the change takes place.

34. Restrict the master commands to the computer system to one physical terminal. These master commands should also be restricted to as few computer operators as possible.

35. Have the computer programs accumulate data for a periodic report showing any unauthorized attempts to access the system, special security-type programs, the operating system software, restricted "up-front" tables, and the like.

36. Limit computer operator intervention to system and/or port start up, terminal backup assignments, emergency message broadcasting, system shutdown, communications debugging, and the system or job status reporting.

37. Design application programs so they do not display messages on the system console or accept data from the system console.

38. Establish access restrictions on system utilities and other sensitive programs that might be utilized to manipulate the system.

39. Consider assigning security codes to files (lockwords) to restrict their access to only certain programs and/or users.

40. Utilize disk and tape labels (internal) and check them with the various programs or program modules.

41. Have programs check the position of various computer console switches if there are any.

42. Log all interruptions by computer operations personnel, and especially save the computer console printing log for review by other personnel.

43. Keep a count on the number of program instructions executed, run time, or any other data for sensitive programs. This can be compared periodically with similar data from a prior period to uncover irregularities.

44. Use a check-sum methodology to control or detect unauthorized program changes. A check-sum count on computer programs can be compared with similar data at a later date to determine if a change was made to a program.

45. Immediately write errors, scuttles, or suspense accounts to eliminate computer operator intervention.

46. Consider using a read-after-write option on magnetic recording devices (especially real-time database updates).

47. Use program software protection keys to safeguard data in memory, on tape, or on disk.

48. Internally store data in the computer and on magnetic tape/disk using cryptographic techniques. This will protect the organization from a computer memory dump.

49. Whenever a "program control" is overridden or bypassed, note the event on an exception report.

50. Consider using a program that compares a controlled duplicate copy of the source/object program with the program currently being used. This is time consuming and probably should only be used on very sensitive programs, whether they are application programs or system software programs.

51. Consider including a listing of the job control language with the output to ensure that unauthorized programs have not been executed.

52. Consider having the computer operations personnel insert all job control so computer programs cannot illegally execute programs by manipulating the job control on valid jobs.

53. Consider cataloging the job control language cards so it is more difficult to illegally enter unauthorized job control and also to ensure fewer errors from erroneous job control.

54. Consider having hardware that carries the parity bit into memory and throughout the entire system to more readily detect hardware memory or parity errors.

55. Consider hardware that has memory protection areas that separate parts of memory through hardware controls rather than software controls.

56. Use tape units that have write-ring protection, parity, and read-after-write.

57. Use disk units that allow file protect areas and read-after-write.

58. Use card readers that read twice and compare before entering the data.

59. Use specially equipped key disk/tape/punches and verifying machines that automatically provide for self-checking numbers (if applicable).

60. Use hardware that has circuit diagnostic routines to detect errors.

61. When using optical readers, ensure that they read twice and compare before transmitting the data to the central system.

62. Allow for lower privilege levels for users as contrasted with the operating system. This may be accomplished either through hardware or software, depending on the computer manufacturer.

63. Have the computer programs programmed so they look for a unique identifier such as a transaction code to direct the transaction to the proper portion of the application program for processing.

64. Have all computer program generated transactions printed out in a listing and sorted to whatever is appropriate for direct feedback to users. This control provides for the use of computer program generated transaction control at the user level.

65. Control computer program generated transactions by putting severe limits or other preprogrammed restrictions on them so they cannot exceed certain values. Any transactions that exceed these values are automatically rejected and are printed out on a special report.

66. Control computer generated transactions by keeping a count of them, and on a daily basis graphing this and comparing it with other co-related variables. As time goes by, the operations personnel will get to know what is a reasonable quantity of computer generated transactions.

67. Control computer generated transactions by developing a daily report of the 10 largest, 10 smallest, average number of, average dollar value per transaction, and any other averages or quantities that make sense with regard to the specific application being run. In this way the users get a feel for the types and quantities of computer program generated transactions in their system.

68. Control computer generated transactions by building in balance controls between program modules. These balance controls are automated inter-

nal cross-checks. Such controls may take the form of reasonableness checks, who entered the transactions, program-to-program control totals, and the like.

69. Have control totals passed between jobs and job steps during the running of on-line programs. A system of automated controls should include balancing of the entire system as well as balancing between different program modules and/or the final file (database) control totals.

70. Consider developing default tables for computer programs that have numerous options. This is where a program has several decisions and there is a standardized action for most or all of these decisions. When developing a default table, make sure that one of the options is to report that none of the options fits the specific situation at hand.

71. Consider anticipation controls. These controls are used as a method of ensuring accountability of input. Sequence-checking is a common example of such a control, but the general thought here is to have the programs anticipate what might be coming next.

72. Consider having the computer hardware use techniques such as double arithmetic, arithmetic overflow checks, and reverse multiplication. These checks would only be used at very critical points in the application program calculations.

73. Ensure that programs perform a file completion check to determine that the application file has been completely processed and includes all transactions and all items on a master file.

74. See that programs balance computer files and/or database record changes. The number of records on the opening of a file should be balanced against the changes made during the day and the closing balance. On a regular basis the total of the detail records might be compared to the total in the control records.

75. See that erroneous data is written out to an error file and returned to the user as soon as possible (preferably immediately for immediate correction). Dummy records should never be used to hold erroneous data.

76. Have a specific set of computer operator instructions developed and in use for each application program.

77. Use computer program run books for the specifics of each application program. These would cover items such as console message instructions, error message instructions, program halts, rerun procedures, checkpoint and restart instructions, checkpoint control totals, job control setup, and the like.

78. See that the information on error reports indicates all data fields that are in error in a transaction or record.

79. Maintain an automated error suspense file that indicates all rejected

transactions. These files should be used for follow-up and to correct and re-enter the transactions. These files should be aged so it is evident when certain data has not been corrected and re-entered.

80. Issue special discrepancy reports to ensure that the handling of errors results in their correction and re-entry in a timely manner.

81. Automatically assign unique serial numbers to transactions entered into the automated error suspense files. Such serial numbers are used to control subsequent updating, correction, or re-entry of the data that was in error.

82. Never allow destructive updates to correct error conditions without first logging both the before and after image of the update. Debit and credit type entries should never be deleted or erased. Debit and credit type of entries should be corrected by instituting the opposite debit and credit rather than deleting or erasing.

83. Ensure that there is an automatic program to re-enter erroneous data and to correct the error suspense listing so it is brought up-to-date in a timely fashion.

84. See that computer operations personnel are rotated between various job functions periodically, and that there is a segregation of duties, within reasonable limits, within large data processing operations facilities.

85. Have signature authorizations thoroughly checked with regard to the external formal paperwork approvals that are required for program changes and special runs and other items that are out of the ordinary.

86. Keep both source and object copies of programs (applications and systems) under secure custody so they cannot be easily removed from the organization. The same is true for various historical records whether they reside on magnetic tapes or in database systems.

87. Test the default options of vendor-supplied operating system software to determine what would happen if the default option itself failed.

88. Be sure that all programs, application programs, and vendor-supplied operating system programs are adequately documented.

89. Have computer programs conduct an overflow check on all numeric fields for which there could be a data overflow.

90. Ensure that any fictitious branches or other fictitious entities that are incorporated into the on-line programs for testing or other training purposes are adequately separated from the "real" records and/or computer programs. Ensure that these systems cannot contribute to errors and omissions, fraud, or any other serious types of problems such as disasters, system crashes, and the like.

91. Ensure that there are adequate manual controls to duly record whenever

computer operations personnel are called in at odd times or for an emergency.

92. Downline load new programs to distributed computer sites periodically to ensure program code integrity.

---

*O*utput Control Matrix

---

*T*he Matrix Approach

The control area to be reviewed using this matrix covers outputs from the computer system. These outputs may be directly affected by input controls, program/computer processing controls, and on-line terminal controls. When reviewing the output controls, match each resource/asset with its corresponding concern/exposure as listed in Figure A-4 (Output Control Matrix). This matrix lists the resources in relation to the potential exposures and cross-relates these with the various controls/safeguards that should be considered when reviewing the outputs from computer systems.

To provide further meaning to this matrix, there is a complete definition provided for each of the concerns/exposures (threats) and also for each of the resources/assets (components). On the matrix, these threats and components are listed by name only. A numerical listing and description of each of the control numbers recorded in the cells also is provided.

*C*oncerns/Exposures (Threats)

The following concerns/exposures are those that are directly applicable to the outputs of an on-line or batch type of computerized system. The definition for each of these threats, listed across the top of the matrix, is as follows:

▢ Output Balancing and Reconciliation—The responsibility for the monitoring of data processing related controls. This concern sometimes manifests itself as a quality assurance function within the data processing department, ensuring that the integrity of the data has not been lost during the data processing cycle.

CONCERNS/EXPOSURES/THREATS

RESOURCES-ASSETS-COMPONENTS	OUTPUT BALANCING AND RECONCILIATION	PRIVACY	SECURITY/ THEFT	OUTPUT DISTRIBUTION	USER BALANCING AND RECONCILIATION	RECORDS RETENTION AND DESTRUCTION	NEGOTIABLE DOCUMENTS	OUTPUT ERROR HANDLING
OUTPUT DEVICES	9, 31-34, 41	9	9, 31, 33	9, 25, 34	41			9, 27, 31, 41
PEOPLE	1-3,8,9,11,12, 14, 16, 28, 30, 31, 36-38	4-6, 14	4-6, 14, 21, 37	1,4,6,10,12-15, 17, 21, 30, 34	1, 2, 4, 8, 11, 27, 28, 36, 37	5, 7, 10, 15, 19, 26, 35, 43	5, 7, 20-23, 43	3, 8, 16, 27-31, 36-38
RECORDS STORAGE AND DISPOSAL		7, 43	7, 37, 43			5, 7, 15, 19, 26, 35, 43	5, 7, 43	35, 39
OPERATIONAL PROCEDURES	1-3,8,9,11,12, 14, 16, 28-34, 36-42	4-7, 14, 18, 19, 24	4-7, 14, 18, 19, 21, 24, 33, 37, 40	1,4,6,10,12-17, 21, 24, 30, 34	1, 2, 4, 8, 11, 27-29, 36, 37, 40, 41	7, 10, 19, 26, 35, 43	20-23, 43	3, 8, 16, 27-30, 36-41

Figure A-4 Output control matrix.

☐ Privacy—The accidental or intentional release of data about an individual, assuming that the release of this personal information was improper to the normal conduct of the business at the organization.

☐ Security/Theft—The security or theft of information that should have been kept confidential because of its proprietary nature. In a way, this is a form of privacy, but the information removed from the organization does not pertain to an individual. The information might be inadvertently (accidentally) released, or it might be the subject of an outright theft. This exposure also includes the theft of assets such as might be experienced in embezzlement, fraud, or defalcation.

☐ Output Distribution—A review to ensure the delivery of complete and accurate reports to the authorized recipients in a timely manner.

☐ User Balancing and Reconciliation—Ensure that the integrity of the data has not been lost during the processing by the application system. This concern involves the final users' reviewing, scanning, balancing, and reconciling of the data that they have received.

☐ Records Retention and Destruction—The controls that are used to guide the retention and disposal of confidential or private computer system output. In this context, the disposal may be immediate, or it might come after some years of retaining computer output. This concern should include paper documents, magnetic media, microforms, and so forth.

☐ Negotiable Documents—The handling of negotiable documents (blank check stock, etc.) and prevention of their loss. This concern may also involve accountable documents which are not negotiable, but whose loss would be injurious to the organization.

☐ Output Error Handling—The procedures and methods used to ensure that all transactions rejected during the system processing are corrected and re-entered. The object here is to ensure that any output documents found to be in error are corrected.

*R*esources/Assets (*Components*)

The following resources/assets are those that should be reviewed during the output control review. The definition for each of these components, listed down the left vertical column of the matrix, is as follows:

☐ Output Devices—The peripheral devices connected to the central computer system (also including the computer itself) and the types of errors that might be made by this hardware. The output devices for any controls, their current usage, operational procedures, and any written documentation pertaining to them should be reviewed.

© Copyright Jerry FitzGerald 1978

□ People—The individuals responsible for reconciling the output data, operating and maintaining the output devices, writing operational procedures, and managing the output quality assurance function. This may also include user department personnel.

□ Records Storage and Disposal—The storage of output data (hard copy or microform) as well as the disposal of this data. This includes reviewing the storage area and the disposal techniques.

□ Operational Procedures—The written operational procedures on how to obtain data, verification, reconciliation, and those other aspects of delivering output data from data processing (whether it is centralized or distributed) to the various users.

Controls

The following controls/safeguards should be considered when reviewing the outputs of an on-line or batch type of computerized system. This numerical listing describes each control.

It should be noted that implementation of various controls can be both costly and time consuming. It is of great importance that a realistic and pragmatic evaluation be made with regard to the probability of a specific threat affecting a specific component. Only then can the control be evaluated in a cost-effective manner.

The controls, as numerically listed in the cells of the matrix, are as follows:

1. Visually scan output reports for completeness and proper formatting.
2. On a random basis, thoroughly check a specific output report for correctness.
3. Always review all errors and the reason for these errors in order to determine if there is a program bug or input problem.
4. Control the distribution of reports so they are sent only to the proper and authorized personnel.
5. Keep all sensitive reports in a secure area so unauthorized personnel cannot obtain copies.
6. Verify that the current handling procedures for output reports are being followed.
7. Immediately destroy aborted output runs (paper shredder) for sensitive outputs.
8. Print out computer generated control totals and cross-relate these back to the manually inputted control totals, for example, verify record counts, hash totals, batch totals, and the like.

9. Periodically review computer console error messages and system output error messages to try to determine if there are program bugs.

10. Institute an overall report analysis program to determine whether any reports can be eliminated, combined, rearranged, simplified, or whether new reports may be required.

11. Manually maintain an output log of expected results and compare the actual output to the expected output.

12. Consider developing an independent control group within the data processing function that is responsible for the quality control of output reports.

13. Maintain a job schedule desk with appropriate cutoff times so it can be determined when jobs are to be run and so the output control group can ensure timely report delivery.

14. Determine the number of output documents received and ensure that it agrees with the number of documents the program reported as producing. This may manifest itself as a page count routine.

15. Try to include the following elements in the heading of each report: date prepared, processing period covered, a descriptive title of the report contents, the user department, the processing program's identification job number, how to dispose of the report, and its confidentiality.

16. Number the pages consecutively, and indicate that the report came to a normal ending with a positive statement as to such.

17. Label the cover of all reports to indicate the recipient's name and location.

18. Identify any confidential reports as being confidential and proprietary information.

19. Label any reports that must be positively and completely destroyed as to their disposal procedures. In other words, a report that should be returned to a central destruction area should be labeled as such, or it should be labeled to be destroyed in a paper shredder or whatever.

20. At regular intervals, take an inventory of any prenumbered negotiable documents.

21. Consider having a processing program print an additional sequence number on prenumbered forms. The differences between the beginning and ending preprinted number and the beginning and ending of the computer generated number must agree. The output control group should reconcile these two numbers.

22. Maintain all negotiable documents in a secure location and control access to this location.

23. Maintain signature stamps (such as for payroll) in a different physical location from the negotiable documents themselves.

24. Produce only the required number of output reports.

25. Clearly describe in the operations procedures manual what type of paper stock and/or forms should be used in the print devices.

26. Consider filing output reports by date so at the end of a calendar year they can be discarded when their retention date has been reached.

27. When reviewing output reports that are in error, indicate all data fields in error on the report, and submit them to the programming department for possible evaluation and correction of programs.

28. Produce control totals for all rejects and pass these control totals back to the input area for correction and re-entry.

29. Clearly define in the operations procedures manual the procedures for error correction and re-entry responsibility.

30. The output control totals for each application should be reconciled with the input totals before the release of the output report from the data processing to the user department.

31. Compare any transaction log maintained by the computer system with a transaction log maintained at each output device. These totals should be verified against individual application control totals established at other steps in the processing stream to verify that everything has been properly processed to its final step.

32. In order to monitor process flow, maintain a record that indicates the average time between the input of user data and the actual starting of each application run. One of the sources that might be used for this purpose is the automatic job accounting routines in some vendors' system software.

33. Develop and review an automated job accounting system. This type of control can be utilized to review the time utilized to process jobs, which files and/or programs were used by the jobs, the time it took to print jobs, and other valuable pieces of information. Vendors' accounting record job routines (for example, IBM has Systems Management Facilities) can be utilized for many unique output control tasks.

34. Consider reviewing the job control used for specific jobs whenever there is a discrepancy in the output.

35. Ensure that there are appropriate waste disposal procedures for the immediate disposal of certain paper products (sensitive output reports).

36. Consider obtaining a list of all transactions that went into a specific report whenever there are discrepancies.

37. Consider maintaining an independent history file of errors, which is independent of all processing files, and is regularly analyzed to report error trends and statistics by type, source, and frequency of errors within an application system.

38. Ensure that all data rejected from a processing cycle of an application is entered in an error log by a control group. This log is then used to ensure the correction and re-entry of data.

39. Ensure that error correction procedures are defined in the operations procedures manual.

40. Ensure that header and trailer labels/record counts are printed out at the end of each output report.

41. Even though some on-line systems are individual transaction oriented, consider having the remote terminal operators enter their data in small batches of 2 to 10 transactions.

42. Ensure that lengthy output reports have checkpoint and restart capabilities so an entire report need not be printed if there was an error near its end. In this way, the outputting of this report can go back to a prior partition and all the processing time is not lost.

43. When decollating a sensitive job, ensure that the carbon paper is disposed of in a secure manner.

Appendix 3

REQUEST FOR PROPOSALS (RFP): Computerized System for the White Medical Clinic

CONTENTS

Introduction

This section of the Request for Proposals contains some of the methodologies, points of procedure, and/or legal requirements.

Any modifications or requests for bid must be received by the White Medical Clinic prior to the date of the bid opening. No oral or telephone modifications of any bid will be considered.

All bids must be received by noon, August 6, 1986.

If the final bid dollar amounts differ in any way from the individual sums of the component items, the individual sums of the component items shall be used.

Any bidder may withdraw their bid, either personally or by written request, at any time prior to the scheduled closing time for the receipt of bids.

Clarifications to the bid will be made at a bidders' conference to be held July 6, 1986. Any further clarifications must be submitted in writing to Mr. Frank Evans at the White Medical Clinic.

The White Medical Clinic reserves the right to reject all bids if none of them are deemed suitable.

If any bidder utilizes subcontractors, that bidder shall submit a list of the proposed subcontractors and the services to be performed by them.

The White Medical Clinic will make no payments for the preparation of this bid.

The award of the contract will be made solely upon the information contained in the bid and not from any other, implied or oral, type of information. The only deviation to this will be the demonstration of the performance and features that will be conducted by the bid winner or costs we add.

It is assumed that all software application programs are legally owned by all bidders/vendors.

Statement of Intent

This section of the RFP is the general statement of intent of the White Medical Clinic. For example, this section should be used as the overall guideline as to what the White Medical Clinic hopes to achieve through the use of this data processing system.

The White Medical Clinic wants to improve its data processing capabilities by contracting with an outside service bureau or contracting for its own in-house data processing system or some combination of both of these items. The basic philosophy in doing this is to purchase, lease, or rent the appropriate hardware, software, application programs, and data communication facilities so it does not have to write its own application programs or develop any of its own software. In other words, the White Medical Clinic seeks a data processing "turnkey package."

This turnkey package might be handled totally by an outside service bureau or it might be implemented by the purchase or lease of a computer that has the appropriate turnkey software and application programs so the Clinic will be operating only the system and not developing new systems.

The application systems that the Clinic is most interested in are as follows.

- □ Phase I—Accounts receivable/billing and a patient database (mandatory operational date January 1, 1987).
- □ Phase II—An on-line, real-time patient appointment scheduling system (targeted implementation started by March 1, 1987; this can be done by phases).
- □ Phase III—Accounts payable, payroll/personnel records system and a general ledger accounting system (targeted implementation date October 1, 1987; this can be phased by system).
- □ Phase IV—Future medical or scientific applications (targeted implementation date unknown).

The above shows the desired implementation schedule for Phases I, II, and III upon which you will be bidding in this proposal. In the future sub-section of this proposal called "Exceptions to the Bid" you should note whether you can meet these dates or if you wish to propose alternate dates.

One of the basic criteria for this proposal is that the White Medical Clinic is not interested in developing software or application programs. We do not want to build a programming and system development staff; although, we do recognize that if we go with an in-house system, we will have to hire a qualified data processing manager, computer operator or operators, and possibly a person knowledgeable in programming for *small* maintenance and debugging jobs (the key to any in-house programming commitment is the word small).

Guidelines for Preparing the Bid

This section of the proposal lists the basic guidelines that should be followed in preparing your bid. It covers both the service bureau concept and the in-house computer concept.

(A) The first section of your bid should be the *introduction*. The intent is for you to have a couple of paragraphs or a one- to three-page description of the overall system that you will be presenting. If you have large system brochures and vendor literature on the whole package, these should be placed in the appendix and not in this first section. We prefer that you prepare a short, concise description of your system so that it can be compared easily with the other short, concise descriptions from the other bidders. We will take into account the vendor literature that is placed in the appendix, but we will draw heavily on this concise overall description of your system.

(B) The next part of the bid includes your response to the *mandatory items*. We want you to tell us whether you can or cannot comply with the following list of mandatory items. This list takes into account both service bureaus and in-house computers; therefore, if one of them does not pertain to you, state that the item pertains to a service bureau or an in-house system and that you are not bidding on that particular system. The following mandatory items are highly desired.

- ☐ The bidder shall supply a turnkey software package and turnkey application programs that require no further programming or development.
- ☐ The bidder shall bid a system that will meet or exceed 150% of the volumes listed in this proposal.
- ☐ The system bidder will offer on-line, real-time data processing of accounts receivable/billing, inquiries and updates to the patient database, and the patient appointment scheduling system. (The White Medical Clinic does not want to have a Central Appointment Desk.)
- ☐ The on-line, real-time system shall be able to support up to 100 Cathode Ray Tube (CRT) terminals.
- ☐ The off-line (batch) reports shall be available by the next morning (6 A.M.).
- ☐ Any vendor hardware to be bid on this project shall be supported for a period of five (5) years from the implementation date of this bid.
- ☐ The successful bidder shall set up a demonstration visit with a clinic that uses their system. That clinic shall be approximately the same size as the White Medical Clinic, process approximately the same volume of transactions, have a similar number of physicians, CRTs, patients, and the like, or be capable of simulating the same size clinic and number of transactions.
- ☐ The bidder shall state the programming languages that are available through its system (be it a service bureau or an in-house computer) so the White Medical Clinic will know the programming languages that are available for their future Phase IV (medical or scientific applications).
- ☐ The bidder should state specifically whether its current database management system and its current data communication protocols will handle 150% of the volumes contained in this Request for Proposals.
- ☐ The system should allow for interactive programming so the doctors can develop specialized medical or scientific applications (Phase IV). This programming should be available utilizing a higher level language, such as BASIC.

□ For an on-site system, the bidder and/or computer vendor must be able to provide two-shift, on-site, field engineering support with spare parts and unscheduled service available within four (4) hours of the request for service. Also, scheduled preventive maintenance must not require more than eight (8) hours per week and the maintenance must not be scheduled during the prime shift.

□ The bidder selected must be a proven, reliable, and financially stable bidder and/or vendor of computers, peripheral equipment, terminal systems, and/or data processing service bureau services.

□ The bidder must provide a list of nearby sites that are candidates for backup to the final installed systems.

When you are preparing the bid, please respond to each of the above mandatory items in sequence.

(C) *Exceptions to the bid:* You should list in a separate paragraph any exceptions that you may have to this bid. In other words, if you cannot meet the implementation dates, or if there is some other part of the RFP that you are bidding on in a materially different fashion, please note it here. This will help in our evaluation and allow us to be fair to all bidders.

(D) *Description of your bid:* This is the main part of your proposal. In this part we want you to describe the various systems and/or hardware that you are bidding. We recognize that some of the bidders may bid as a service bureau and some to deliver an on-site computer. For that reason, those bidders who are bidding as a service bureau should go to the next section of this proposal, "Service Bureau Requirements," and use those requirements as their guideline. Those bidders who are bidding as an in-house computer system should go to the section entitled "On-site Computer Requirements" and use that section as a guideline for their bid. Whichever you use, please comment on each of the items listed in the appropriate section for service bureau requirements or for on-site computer requirements.

(E) The next item to comment upon is the *delivery* of the turnkey system. We would like you to detail your proposed implementation dates for each of the above Phases I, II, or III. You may even break out some of the systems within a phase; for example, in Phase III, we list accounts payable, payroll personnel, and general ledger (you may propose up to three different dates for these systems).

(F) The bidder and/or computer vendor should supply appropriate *references* to users of the current systems they have installed and to their financial stability. One of these referenced sites may be used for the performance and features demonstrations.

(G) At the end of your proposal, in a section marked *Appendices,* you may supply any items that you think will help us in evaluating this bid; however, please do keep in mind that we cannot read 10,000 pages of literature for each of the bidders. Specifically, the appendices should contain any vendor literature that you think will help us, as well as anything else regarding vendor qualifications.

(H) *Price* was left until the last part of this section on "Guidelines for Preparing the Bid" because we prefer that you detail each price on an item-by-item basis and write it up as a separate portion of this bid. Then, place this price bid in a sealed envelope. When you deliver the bid, we want the technical bid separate from the price bid. The price bid should be in a sealed envelope so we do not see prices when we evaluate the technical bids in terms of how well they meet the needs of the White Medical Clinic. This methodology will be mentioned again in the last section of this Request for Proposals, "Evaluation Procedure."

Service Bureau Requirements

The following list depicts the various areas in which each bidder should make some comments with regard to the specific "Description of Their Bid." This section is for those bidders who are bidding a service bureau-type environment.

1. Each bidder of the service bureau services shall supply a copy of their standard contract for our review.
2. In case of failure, the bidder should comment on their standard operating procedures to backup such areas as a loss of software or application programs, a loss of the White Medical Clinic data, a failure in the computer equipment or peripherals, and a failure of the communication lines between the White Medical Clinic and the service bureau.
3. Each bidder should identify the response times that you intend to meet for the on-line, real-time systems, such as the Patient Appointment Scheduling System, the Accounts Receivable/Billing System, and the Patient Database when all systems are operational.
4. The bidder should comment on the average turnaround time for batch processing of the end-of-day reports (sometimes called off-line processing). These are the reports that the Clinic wants by 6 A.M. the next morning.
5. The bidder should comment on who maintains programs. Specifically, who maintains the computer software and who maintains the application programs used by the Clinic? This maintenance refers to areas such as a programming bug or a newly discovered problem.
6. Should the Clinic be desirous of having some special programming done, will the service bureau do this programming and, if so, what will be the charge for writing special programs for the White Medical Clinic? Can the Clinic contract with a "third-party" programmer for enhancements?

7. Will the White Medical Clinic have the authority to audit the service bureau system? State specifically whether this authority will allow the management of the White Medical Clinic and their Certified Public Accountant or other specialist to audit the service bureau with regard to security/privacy and the general operations as they pertain to the specific operation and running of the White Medical Clinic system.

8. The bidder should comment on the type of security (both physical and data) that is used in order to protect the data and programs of the White Medical Clinic.

9. The bidder should comment on the procedures in effect to assure privacy of the data from the White Medical Clinic.

10. The bidder should comment on whether there is any warranty or a type of penalty, should there be a failure to perform, excessive lateness in the batch reports, or poor response times.

11. The bidder should define the system performance capabilities and state specifically whether they can meet 150% of the volumes contained in this bid. If possible, define some of the run timings with regard to running the systems you are bidding upon.

12. The bidder should comment on the type of training they plan to conduct or any other way they will assist the White Medical Clinic in training its staff to utilize the bid-for system.

13. The bidder should set forth clearly the availability of documentation. Please specify the types of manuals or user training that are available to the White Medical Clinic.

14. Do you have a standard "Termination for Nonperformance" agreement? If not, do you have any preference on wording for anything such as this? Please supply your agreement or preferences here.

15. The bidder should list any on-site costs (approximate) that must be made in order to install any hardware that the White Medical Clinic will need and any special site-preparation costs, such as air conditioning or electrical. Please list these costs in the *separate price proposal.*

16. If any of the bidder's equipment or other property is on the premises of the White Medical Clinic, who is responsible for the insurance?

17. If you offer mailing services such as folding, stuffing, bursting, mailing, etc., please detail these services. Also list the cost of these services in your *separate price proposal.*

On-Site Computer Requirements

The following guidelines are to be used, when preparing your "Description of the Bid," for any bids that delineate an on-site computer. Please note that we are interested in turnkey packages so the White Medical Clinic does not have to write software programs or application programs. We recognize that, with an on-site computer, we would have to hire a data processing manager and computer operator(s) with some programming knowledge, but we do not want to get into the system development and programming process.

1. The bidder should identify clearly the computer being bid and its basic capabilities. We are more interested in the hardware maintenance and run timings of the application system that you will supply than in specific details such as CPU cycle time, channel transfer times, and the like. Remember, we will be operating this computer (ease of operation would be an advantage) rather than developing software or application programs for this computer.

2. The bidder should list all required peripherals that would be necessary to meet 150% of the volumes listed in this proposal. You may list peripherals from a different vendor than the computer manufacturer if this assists you in achieving a lower price in your separate price proposal (see subcontractor paragraph in the Introduction). Again, we will be operating the peripherals. For this reason, hardware maintenance and the proximity of the manufacturer to the White Medical Clinic could be a positive factor; although, all of the larger computer vendors have adequate maintenance in the greater Los Angeles area.

3. The bidder shall list the specific items that must be performed in order to prepare a site for the computer and its peripherals. We need to evaluate both the square footage of space needed and the site preparation for the central computer. Do not include, however, the space required for the remote terminals throughout the Clinic because you would need space in a Clinic area for an input/output terminal regardless of whether you bid an on-site computer or a service bureau. List approximate site preparation costs in your *separate price proposal.*

4. The bidder should detail the software support and technical support that will be available should a problem arise after the system has been implemented.

5. The vendor shall list here the various application programs (including the programming language) that will be available to meet the application systems of Phases I, II, and III. These include accounts receivable/billing, the patient database inquiry and update system, the patient appointment scheduling system, accounts payable, payroll/personnel, and the general ledger accounting system.

6. The bidder should list some of the run timings for the application programs/systems being bid. We are more interested here in the response times of the on-line real-time accounts receivable/billing, patient inquiry

and update, and the patient appointment system, plus any of the batch or off-line report programs (these report programs are the ones that would prepare the off-line reports that we want by 6:00 A.M. the next morning).

7. The bidder should comment specifically on their database capability and whether it can meet 150% of the volume requirements listed in this proposal while still meeting the on-line real-time update.

8. The bidder should comment on program maintenance and the cost of having the bidder and/or computer vendor perform program maintenance.

9. The bidder should describe whether they will perform program enhancements and/or make custom modifications to the software or application programs used by the White Medical Clinic.

10. The bidder should comment on the type of security (both physical and data) used to protect data and programs of the White Medical Clinic.

11. The bidder should comment on the procedures in effect to assure privacy of the data from the White Medical Clinic.

12. The bidder should comment on the type of training that they will conduct or any other way they will assist the White Medical Clinic in training its staff to utilize the bid-for system.

13. We would like the vendor to define the system performance capability. In other words, will the entire package of data communications, computer, peripherals, software, and application programs meet the needs of the White Medical Clinic with regard to 150% of the volumes listed in this proposal? Will the system operate without constant need for the White Medical Clinic to write and rewrite application programs and/or system software? Any further discussion on system performance capability that would serve to clarify your system should be inserted in this section.

14. The bidder should set forth clearly the availability of documentation to the White Medical Clinic and the types of manuals and/or user training that are available.

15. Any and all warranties that pertain to hardware, software, or application programs should be detailed and inserted at this point in your proposal.

16. The bidder should list clearly who will perform the hardware maintenance and the various times required to do hardware maintenance (please note that there were two mandatories listed earlier in this proposal with regard to hardware maintenance).

17. The bidder should describe procedures for failure of (how to backup) hardware, software, application programs, database, data communications lines, etc.

18. If the bidder on this project either is a vendor for mailing equipment or can supply mailing equipment, please list the type of mailing equipment

that you can supply with regard to folding, stuffing, bursting, etc. We do not expect vendors who want to deliver an on-site computer system to be involved in mailing equipment. It is mentioned here only because it was mentioned for the various service bureau bidders.

General Description of the White Medical Clinic Systems and the Associated Volumes

At the present time the White Medical Clinic is using a service bureau to process our Accounts Receivable/Billing System and a Patient Database (termed indexing). In addition, we are using Security Pacific National Bank for Payroll, Personnel Records, and Accounts Payable. Scientific applications currently are being processed by dedicated minicomputers in Electron Therapy, EMI Scanner, CAT Scanner, Nuclear Medicine, and in the Clinical Laboratory. Specific medical statistical applications generally are achieved by the individual efforts of the interested physician who goes outside of the Clinic's current systems.

The Clinic has experienced a very slow growth rate over the last 8 to 10 years, and because of the very limited growth potential of the Clinic's service area, the Clinic is expecting a continued growth factor of about 1% per year.

Volumes being experienced by the Clinic in the Accounts Receivable and Indexing system are as follows.

Transactions (Debit or Credit)	104,000 monthly
Active Accounts	55,000
Statements	36,000 monthly
Statements Mailed	28,000 monthly
Charge Off Accounts (In Collection)	10,000
New Patients	100 daily (5-day week)
Charts Pulled	2,200 daily (5-day week)
Appointments	1,800 daily
Address Changes (estimated)	600 weekly

The Clinic's Business Office is using 20 CRTs to perform all functions related to the Accounts Receivable and Patient Indexing systems.

The Patient Appointment Scheduling System needs to provide scheduling for 140 physicians and nonphysician medical providers and 30 departments such as X-ray, Laboratory, Physical Therapy, etc. Some facilities such as the Student Health Services and the San Diego office probably will not be incorporated into the Patient Appointment Scheduling System. The Patient Appointment Scheduling System will involve about 30 stations with approximately 40 CRTs. Even without growth in the Clinic's volume, we can foresee the potential demand for additional CRTs (everyone will want their own), therefore, the system must be capable of expanding to approximately 100 CRTs.

The Clinic has approximately 600 employees in the computerized Payroll System provided by Security Pacific National Bank. Employees are paid by check twice a month. All government reporting forms are prepared by the system, as well as the Clinic's Personnel Statistical Records.

The Accounts Payable System currently lists about 1,700 different vendors. Although the General Ledger is not computerized, provisions should be made to accommodate the General Ledger System. We now have approximately 400 General Ledger accounts. We are using the Medical Group Management Association's Basic Chart of Accounts and plan to expand the system to accommodate more detailed cost accounting when this new computerized system is implemented.

Computer applications should be phased as follows.

Phase I	Accounts Receivable/Billing System
	Patient Indexing or Database
Phase II	Patient Appointment Scheduling System
Phase III	Accounts Payable System
	Payroll/Personnel Records System
	General Ledger System
Phase IV	Medical or Scientific Applications

Expectations of a System

The goal of the White Medical Clinic is to have a fully integrated on-line real-time system with the following features and with capabilities for enhancements and growth. These should be available daily, including Saturdays and Sundays, from 7:00 A.M. to 10:00 P.M.

1. Patient Database System
   A. On-line real-time integrated with A/R systems, with other sub-systems such as medical statistics, tumor registry, credit screening and credit applications, general ledger, etc.
   B. Data items should include:
      □ Patient's name
      □ Responsible party's name

    □ Address
    □ Date of birth
    □ Sex
    □ Medical record number
    □ Social Security number
    □ Family connections
    □ Status of account
    □ Date last billed
    □ Date last paid
    □ Amount paid year-to-date
    □ Year-to-date balances
    □ Account number
    □ Miscellaneous information field
    □ Marital status
    □ Telephone number
    □ Insurance coverage
    □ Financial classification code
    □ Primary physician for patient (HMO)
    □ Dunning series code
    □ Type of account (MediCal, Medicare, Prepaid, HMO, etc.)
    □ Phonetic/Soundex name search

2. On-Line Inquiry System
    □ Phonetic/Soundex search
    □ Responsible party search
    □ Scheduling data
    □ Financial/credit data
    □ Insurance data
    □ Detailed transactions for 13 months of activity

3. Accounts Receivable/Billing System
    □ On-line batch mode
    □ Real-time data entry
    □ Interface with appointment scheduling
    □ Tracking missing charges—inpatient and outpatient
    □ Tailored production reports—including allocation of bookings
    □ Superbill and/or insurance forms—printing of diagnosis codes on superbill plus verbage on insurance forms

- □ Finance charges—ability to delete finance charges selectively
- □ Aging of accounts
- □ Demand itemizations and insurance forms
- □ Cycle billing
- □ Thirteen months of transactions on CRT
- □ Microfiche production for storage of long-term data
- □ Printing of charge tags
- □ Remote CRT utilization
- □ Service codes, RVS numbers, modifiers
- □ ICDA codes
- □ Computer pricing of input
- □ Balance forward statements
- □ Ability to hold statements selectively
- □ Service description
- □ Collection notices and reports—ability to be selective
- □ Statement preparation
- □ Interface with plastic card patient identification system
- □ Edit error listings
- □ Daily A/R summary reports
- □ HMO management reports and analysis
- □ Security system limiting access
- □ Inpatient control
- □ Tape-to-tape potential
- □ Common language—adaptable to various hardware (COBOL or similar)
- □ End of year statement showing year-to-date finance charges and medical expenses paid for the year

4. Patient Appointment Scheduling System
   - □ Real-time interface with patient master files (database)
   - □ Real-time interface with Accounts Receivable System
   - □ Scheduling requirements/instructions by doctor and type of appointment
   - □ Dual or split screen display—doctor and patient data
   - □ Future appointments—multiple appointments
   - □ Past appointments in last six months
   - □ Automated appointment reminders

- □ "First doctor" available
- □ "First doctor" by department available
- □ Credit data
- □ Printout of CRT display
- □ Interface with patient plastic identification cards
- □ Backup for "downtime"
- □ Hard copy capabilities
- □ Automatic "out cards"
- □ Recall messages
- □ Common language (COBOL or similar)
- □ Census

5. General Ledger Applications
   - □ Twenty-four months of detail data
   - □ Tailored reporting
   - □ Budgeting ability
   - □ Automatic allocation of transactions

6. Accounts Payable System
   - □ Automatic posting
   - □ Interface with General Ledger

7. Payroll System
   - □ Complete reporting system
   - □ Interface with General Ledger

8. Personnel Records System
   - □ Complete reporting system including items such as salary review, EEO reports, current employment verification, address list, and the like.

9. Medical Applications System
   - □ Tumor registry
   - □ Research capabilities
   - □ Laboratory determinations
   - □ EKG–EEG–EMG—capabilities
   - □ Various medical determinations such as electron therapy determination and scanning interpretation

10. Medical Records

11. Inventory

12. Fixed asset accounting

Evaluation Procedure

The following is a statement of the evaluation procedure that will be utilized by the White Medical Clinic when it assesses bids.

Each bidder should submit separate technical and price bids. The price bid should be in a separate sealed envelope so it cannot be seen until after the technical bids have been reviewed.

The technical bid will comprise approximately two-thirds (⅔) of our evaluation decision criteria. Specifically, we will target our evaluation upon

☐ The mandatory items.

☐ Your description of the bid (how turnkey it is) as taken from your responses to either the "Service Bureau Requirements" or the "On-site Computer Requirements."

☐ The references and/or vendor qualifications you supply (remember, one of these references may be the demonstration site that we plan to visit).

☐ Your ability to meet closely the implementation dates in Phases I, II, and III. Remember, we are interested specifically in application systems that already are developed and operational; we are not interested in systems that are under development.

☐ Any specific exceptions that you have listed to this bid.

The price proposal will constitute approximately one-third (⅓) of our evaluation decision criteria. After completing the evaluation of the technical proposal and ranking the various bids in a most favorable to least favorable technical sequence, we will open the price proposal envelopes and list the various bidders in a highest to lowest (most favorable) cost sequence. At this point, we will make an overall evaluation and determine the specific bidder and/or computer vendor that best meets the needs of the White Medical Clinic for the most reasonable price (not necessarily the lowest price and not necessarily the highest price). After this vendor is selected, we will send evaluator personnel to a user site demonstration.

The last part of our evaluation procedure will be the demonstrations of performance and features at a site that is utilizing the same system, software, application programs, data communication facilities, database, etc., as was bid in the proposal. At the end of the performance and features demonstration, if the evaluation team feels that the vendor can perform the tasks required by the White Medical Clinic, then this bidder and/or vendor will be awarded the overall contract. It should be noted that the evaluation team may visit only one site for demonstrations of performance and features. The evaluation team would visit a second site (the next best vendor judged by the technical proposal and price proposal) only if the first vendor did not perform adequately the demonstrations of performance and features for the system that they bid.

The overall intent in writing this as a "Nontechnical Bid" is to ensure that the White Medical Clinic gets a turnkey system that will meet its needs today and also some four to six years in the future when the various volumes might be 50% higher than they are today. Our overall requirements are to meet the business needs of the White Medical Clinic and to have a computerized system that is reliable, on time, and does not require the development of a complete staff of data processing professionals. We are more interested in meeting our data processing needs than we are in developing an extensive staff of data processing professionals.

Glossary

Access method. A technique for moving data between a computer and its peripheral devices.

Access time. The time that elapses between an instruction being given to access some data and that data becoming available for use.

Accession number. The number or alphanumeric designation assigned to any individual piece of information or document by which it becomes machine retrievable.

ACM. Association for Computing Machinery.

Active file life. Those records that are being used in the day-to-day operation of the firm.

Activity. In PERT/CPM, an activity links two successive events and represents the work required between these two events. It must be accomplished before the following event can take place.

Algorithm. A formula, or series of steps, for defining a problem and describing its solution mathematically.

Aperture card. A type of microform in which a frame of 16-mm or 35-mm film is placed on an 80-column tab card.

Area cost sheet. Documents the formal organization and economic data pertaining to the area under study and fits each area under study into its proper context.

Area under study. That part of the firm for which a new system is to be designed. It may be a small functional area of one department or the whole firm. See also: *Level I study.*

Artificial intelligence. See: *Decision support system.*

Attribute. A field containing information about an entity. Also called data element, data item, or field.

Audit trail. The documentation that provides for traceability among various reports. It may trace either from the source document to the end report or from the end report to the original source document.

Audit trail, computerized. Used by the auditor to test the reliability of a computerized system and the dependability of the data it generates. Each transaction may have an identifying number to print out the record upon request.

Audit trail, manual. The documentation provided by journals, ledgers, or reports that enables an auditor to trace an original transaction either forward or backward through a manual system.

Backup file. Separately retained duplicate physical copy of a transaction file or historic master file, used for reconstruction and recovery of destroyed files.

Ballot box design. A type of form designed in such a way that all the user has to do is check the applicable box.

Batch mode. Application programs run on the computer one at a time. For example, in batch processing, data is gathered up to a cutoff time and then processed. The user receives the output after some period that usually is measured in hours or days.

Batching. A procedure that involves the grouping of like documents to be submitted to the computer as input. Control totals usually are established on document count and one or more significant data fields.

Benchmark approach. A benchmark is a surveyor's mark that is used as a reference point during subsequent measurements; analogously, the analyst's understanding of the current system is a benchmark in determining how much improvement can be made with the new system.

Benchmark test. The test run on a recommended computer to see how long it takes to run one of the firm's selected applications or a standard instruction mix.

Benefit list. A list prepared for each key person who attends the verbal presentation of the proposed system. It lists the items within the proposed system that will benefit each of these people the most.

Black box. A process in a system that has known inputs and known outputs, but how the inputs are transformed into outputs is unknown. Users tend to view systems in terms of a black box because they do not necessarily know the functions that take place in a system. From a user viewpoint, a computer also may be a black box. Users tend to be concerned only with what they must put into the system or what they get out of the system, but not what happens within the system in terms of logic, programming code, and so forth.

Blocking. The combining of two or more records so that they are jointly read or written by one machine instruction.

Bottom-up. Proceeding from the particular to the general or from the detailed to the broad view.

Boundary. Used in system design in reference to the human–machine boundary. This boundary is shown on data flow diagrams to describe the interface of automated processes with manual processes. In data flow diagramming, the automated processes have a circle drawn around them. The encircled processes are described by the data dictionary and minispecification, while those processes outside the circle are described through written procedures for the manual system. The human–machine boundary on data flow diagrams can be used to demonstrate various design alternatives that can be accepted by management.

Box location number. One of the most important pieces of information put on the storage box label form because it identifies exactly where the box will be located physically.

Boxed design. A type of form on which each item is clearly in its own box so there is no question as to where the information is to be filled in.

Break-even analysis. In systems analysis, the comparison of the current system costs against those of the proposed system. The break-even point is the point at which the new system costs the same as the old one.

Bubble. Circular graphic representation within a data flow diagram. It depicts a process within a system at which incoming data flows are processed, or transformed, into outgoing data flows.

Bubble chart. A data flow diagram.

Buffer. An area of storage which holds data temporarily while it is being received, transmitted, read, or written. It often is used to compensate for differences in speed or timing of devices. Buffers are used in terminals, peripheral devices, storage units, and in the CPU.

Byte. A small group of bits of data that are handled as a unit. In most cases it is an 8-bit byte and it is known as a character.

Caption and line design. A type of form in which the items are not boxed in. See also: *Boxed design*.

CATER. An acronym for *C*onsistent, *A*ccurate, *T*imely, *E*conomically feasible, and *R*elevant. These are the features of any good system development effort.

Central transform. The primary process of the functional data flow diagram set. It is the process or processes that performs the major data transforming function within the data flow diagram or diagrams being used. Further, it is that portion of the data flow diagram that remains after the input, editing, and output streams of data have been removed. It is the most important bubble or bubbles in the data flow diagram, and all other bubbles feed data, prepare data, or check data with regard to the bubble or bubbles that comprise the central transform.

Centralized data processing. Data processing performed at a central location on data obtained from several geographical locations or managerial levels. See: *CIS*.

Certificate in Data Processing (CDP). A professional certificate offered by the Institute for Certification of Computer Professionals, 35 East Wacker Drive, Chicago, Illinois, 60601.

Changeover, one-for-one. The existing system is replaced completely with some other system; the old system is stopped and the new begins.

Changeover, parallel. The old system and the new system are operated simultaneously until it is proven that the new system is reliable and can do the job for which it was designed.

Character. An individual letter, numeral, or special character. Synonymous with byte.

Charting. A graphic or pictorial means of presenting data.

Charts, activity. A type of chart in which the analyst pictorially summarizes the flow of work through the various operations of a system.

Charts, flow. See: *Flowchart*.

Charts, functional. Charts that are used as aids in understanding or defining a process, or to show how something is done.

Charts, Gantt. Used for scheduling. Gantt charts portray output performance against a time requirement.

Charts, layout. A type of chart in which the physical area under study is pictured. Work areas and equipment are shown both before and after the new system.

Charts, linear responsibility. A chart that relates the degree of responsibility of key individuals to their various job duties.

Charts, management. Charts used for management planning and control.

Charts, Nassi Shneiderman. Charts that show complex program logic; used in the design of structured programs. They do not use any specific programming language. Their sole purpose is for use by the programmer who must know exactly what is to be programmed.

Charts, operations analysis. Charts used to analyze manufacturing operations.

Charts, organization. A chart that shows the official structure of the organization in terms of functional units or in terms of superior–subordinate relationships.

Charts, personal relationship. A type of chart that depicts lines of authority, job responsibilities, or job duties.

Charts, right-hand and left-hand. Charts used in motion and time studies by industrial engineers.

Charts, Simo. Charts used in motion and time studies by industrial engineers.

Charts, statistical data. A type of chart that converts statistical data into meaningful statistical information by graphic portrayal.

Charts, system structure. A chart that defines and illustrates the organization of a system on a hierarchical basis in terms of modules and submodules, which are used by the programmers to write code.

Charts, work distribution. These provide an analysis of what jobs are being performed, by whom, how the work is divided, and the approximate time required to perform each job.

Checkpoint/restart. A means of restarting a program at some point other than the beginning, used after a failure or interruption has occurred. Checkpoints may be used at intervals throughout an application program; at these points, records are written giving enough information about the status of the program to permit it to be restarted at that point.

Choice-set. The alternatives that the systems designer has to work with.

CIS. Computer Information Systems is the organization which encompasses the combined data processing operations, the database file storage systems, the data communications, and all of the personnel aspects and policies of the overall business data processing operations. This organization used to be called the data processing department.

An alternate meaning to the acronym CIS is the computer information systems curriculum that has been adopted by the Data Processing Management Association as the standard curriculum for universities and colleges.

Coding. Writing the program in whatever programming language was chosen.

Company background. Characteristics of the firm, including management ideas, attitudes, and opinions, and the company's goals and style.

Component. One of the individual parts or pieces of the system that, when assembled together, comprise the system. In structured analysis, the components are the processes (bubbles) from the data flow diagrams.

Computer hardware. The major electronic components in a computer system, including the central processing unit, disk drives, and tape drives.

Computer output microfilm (COM). Microfilm produced as computer output, either directly or first on magnetic tape to be put onto microfilm later.

Concatenate. To link together end-to-end. A concatenated key is composed of more than one data element that uniquely identifies a data structure. A concatenated file is a collection of logically connected files.

Context diagram. Graphic model of a system that shows a flow of data and information between the system and external entities with which it interacts. The top-level diagram of a leveled set of data flow diagrams.

Continuous form. Paper that is used on printers and accounting machines. Can represent checks or any type of preprinted forms.

Control matrix. A two-dimensional matrix that shows the relationship between all of the controls and the specific threats and components.

Control Review Team. A knowledgeable group of users, data processors, and auditors who identify all of the threats and components (as well as possible) that face the new system. This task is performed during Control Review Step 1.

Conversion, parallel. See: *Changeover, parallel.*

Corrective controls. These either correct a situation or recover from a situation. Correction controls remedy or set right an unwanted event or a trespass. Recovery controls regain, make up for, or make good due to the effect of an unwanted event or a trespass.

Cost analysis. That phase of the system design in which the cost of the proposed system is determined in order to decide whether implementation is justified.

Cost analysis, budgeting. The method of cost analysis based on the cash flow concept, which refers to the amount of money that will be required for a particular project and the dates when that money will be needed. The firm then budgets the required funds so they will be available when needed.

Cost analysis, planning. A method of cost analysis based on the analysis of the opportunity costs of using a resource for one purpose rather than another. In other words, how much more can be gained by using a resource in one area rather than in its second best alternative area.

Cost chargeback. The allocation of system or computer center costs back to the users. A popular means of cost recovery.

Costs, implementation. A one-time outlay to install a new capability.

Costs, investment. Nonrecurring outlays to acquire new equipment.

Costs, operating. Recurring outlays required to operate the system.

Court decision. The result of a legal controversy which has been interpreted in a court of law based upon the statutes under the court's jurisdiction.

CPU (central processing unit). The heart of the general purpose computer that controls the interpretation and execution of instructions. Synonymous with mainframe.

Critical path. The longest path through a PERT network.

Critical path method (CPM). See: *PERT.*

Critical success factors. The key items of information or action areas where the system must work in order for management of the organization to meet its goals.

CRT display device. A television-like picture tube used in visual display terminals on which images are produced on a cathode ray tube.

Culture. The environment, customs, values, mores, and so forth that affect how the firm behaves or reacts in given situations. May be legal, political, economic, regulatory, religious, and so forth.

Cycle. One month's business, one quarter, or whatever period of time is thought necessary to convert from one system to another.

Data. (1) Specific individual facts, or a list of such items. (2) Facts from which conclusions can be drawn.

Data access diagrams. Graphic or pictorial representation of each individual data structure, the corresponding relationships between data structures, and the access paths between them. A data access diagram shows a more detailed relationship between data structures than does a data structure diagram.

Data aggregate. A named collection of data items within a record.

Data communications. The overall system of hardware and circuits which permits one or more users to access a remotely located computer or to be interconnected among themselves.

Data dictionary. A set of definitions of data flows, data stores, data elements, data structures, files, databases, and processes referred to in a data flow diagram.

Data element. Synonymous with Data item or Field.

Data flow. The path along which information (data) flows between processes to other processes or data stores.

Data flow diagram. Graphic representation and analysis of data movement, processing transformation functions, and the data stores. A network of related functions showing all interfaces between processes; a partitioning of a system and component parts. Also called a bubble chart.

Data item. The smallest unit of data that has meaning in describing information; the smallest unit of named data. Synonymous with Data element or Field.

Data primitive. An element of data that does not need to be defined further. Data primitives refer to data flows and data stores. Data primitives are most often each individual data element.

Data processing. The conversion of data to information.

Data set. A named collection of logically related data items, arranged in a prescribed manner, and described by control information to which the programming system has access; a file.

Data store. A file or database in which data is stored. It may be a temporary storage position within the system. In a working system, it may be a storage file within a computer system, or a manually accessed file, such as a set of file drawers or microfilm.

Data structure. One or more fields, data items, or data elements grouped together to become a meaningful and logical piece of business information. You might view this as a record or a subset of a record.

Data structure diagram. Graphic representation of the relationships among data structures. It shows the possible access paths between the data structures and various data stores.

Database. A collection of interrelated data stored with controlled redundancy to serve one or more applications; the data are stored so that they are independent of programs which use the data; a common and controlled approach is used in adding new data and in modifying and retrieving existing data within a database.

Database administrator. An individual with an overview of one or more databases, who controls the design and use of these databases.

Database management system (DBMS). The collection of software that is required for using a database.

Debugging. Removing errors in a computer program to get the program to run correctly.

Decentralized data processing. Involves processing at various managerial levels or geographical points throughout the organization.

Decision making. The process of choosing the best solution to a problem.

Decision point. A point in a system where some person or automatic mechanism must react to input data and make a decision.

Decision support system. Real-time system that allows managers to ask questions and get answers to business problems. In some systems, the decision actually is made by the computer system, based on a built-in knowledge base. Also known as artificial intelligence.

Decision table. (1) A tabular format showing all possible criteria that might be involved in an operation, along with the action to be taken in each situation. (2) A method of describing the logic of a computer program that tells what action must be taken when a given condition is either met or not met.

Decision tree. Graphic representation of all possible conditions or processing alternatives and outcomes. It resembles the branches of a tree.

Decomposition. The expansion of a data flow diagram, through partitioning, in which the analyst develops more detailed data flow diagrams. Taking a specific bubble (process transformation) and decomposing it into a more detailed data flow diagram.

Defense Technical Information Center. The primary distributor of classified government documents, sponsored by the Department of Defense. Commonly known as DTIC.

Degradation. A slowdown in computer response time, usually caused by a large number of simultaneous requests for processing or the failure of one or more of the system components.

Delphi group. A small group of experts (three to seven people) who meet to develop a consensus in an area in which it may be impossible or too expensive to collect accurate data. For example, a Delphi group of communication experts might assemble in order to reach a consensus on the various threats to a communication network, the potential dollar losses for each occurrence of each threat, and the estimated frequency of occurrence for each threat.

Dependence, random. When a procedure is required because of some other procedure.

Dependence, sequential. When one procedure must precede or follow another.

Dependence, time. When a procedure is required at a set time with regard to another procedure.

Descriptor. An identifying word assigned to a report so that potential users can determine whether it is within their field of interest. Also, the word the indexer uses to identify a report within a computerized index.

Design. A creative process that plans or arranges the parts into a whole that satisfies the objective involved.

Desk checking. Consists of checking for errors and checking the program code against the program flowchart.

Destruction card. A tickler file, arranged by date, that tells the records storage personnel which boxes are ready for destruction in any given month.

Detective controls. These detect that a threat has occurred and report that occurrence to whichever system or person will take action. Detective controls reveal or discover unwanted events and they offer evidence of trespass. Reporting controls document an event, a situation, or a trespass.

Dewey Decimal System. A subject classification system that divides all knowledge into 10 subject classes which are arranged in numeric sequence and further subdivided by a decimal system. Used in libraries to arrange books by subject.

Direct-access storage device (DASD). A data storage unit on which data can be accessed directly at random without having to progress through a serial file such as tape. A disk unit is a direct-access storage device.

Directory. A table giving the relationships between items of data. Sometimes a table (index) giving the addresses of data.

Distributed data processing (DDP). A method of processing designed to incorporate the benefits of both centralized and decentralized data processing. A minicomputer or remote processing equipment is used to process data at a specific location and feed it into a large-scale mainframe. Numerous users have access to the database using a network of terminals and minis linked to one main CPU.

Document. (1) A verb meaning to outline a program so others know how it operates. (2) A noun meaning any publication published by any level of government or government contractors.

Documentation. A thorough written description of all the component parts and operations of the system. Includes forms, personnel, equipment, and input/output sequence. Communicates to other people the system characteristics. Both written and charted explanation is used.

Domain. The term used in place of data element when describing a relational database.

DPMA. Data Processing Management Association.

Empathy. Mentally entering into the feeling or spirit of other people in order to understand them better.

Empire builder. The type of person who seeks personal power, prestige, and recognition through authority and control.

Emulation. An emulator processes the old program by the old procedure using current data. It enables one computer to process computer instructions from another computer.

Entity. Something about which, data is recorded. Also called data structure or record.

Environment, external. The sources outside of the firm that may influence the firm's operations, such as unions, customers, competition, and so forth.

Environment, internal. Sources within the firm that may influence the firm's operations, such as auditors, budgets, the informal organization, and so forth.

Equipment sheet. A documentation form used to describe needed equipment for various operations in the system.

Estimate error. An error involving time or money, which may be avoided through a feasibility study.

Estimating. The art of predicting by utilizing all available information in a systematic and informed way.

Estimating, comparison. By meeting with individuals, inside or outside the firm, the analyst is able to evaluate comparable operations and make an estimate.

Estimating, conglomerate. Representatives from each functional area within the area under study confer to develop estimates based on past experience.

Estimating, detailed. The analyst makes a detailed study of the costs, times required, and any other pertinent factors for each step of each procedure within the system.

Evaluation criteria. Performance standards through which management can have a valid measurement to evaluate the new system's performance.

Event. In PERT/CPM, the beginning or ending of an activity; a milestone.

Exception report. Specially produced report indicating exceptions. Used to identify conditions that require decisions, items that cannot be processed, or out-of-balance situations. It is created only if an exception point is exceeded.

External entity. A source or destination of data. It can be a person, supplier, department, or another system that supplies data to, or receives data from, a system.

Feasibility study. A study undertaken to determine the possibility or probability of improving the existing system within a reasonable cost.

Feasibility study report. The written documentation of the feasibility study that tells management what the problem is, what its causes are, and makes recommendations for solving the problem.

Field. See: *Data item.*

File. An organized, named collection of records treated as a unit. Also called a data set.

File integrity. A term used in database and records retention. In database, when erroneous data enters the database itself, file integrity is lost. In records retention, records are in their proper location and file integrity is lost if the records are misfiled.

File maintenance. The activity of keeping a file up-to-date by adding, changing, or deleting data.

File organization. Concerned with the view of the data as perceived by the application programmers.

File sheet. A documentation form describing a collection of information in the system.

Files, external. Files maintained outside the area under study but which affect the area's systems in various ways.

Files, index-sequential. Computer files are stored in sequential order by their key, but an index also is created so specific data can be accessed directly without searching sequentially through the file.

Files, internal. Files maintained by the area under study, usually containing up-to-date forms and data that are used by the area.

Files, partitioned. Computer files in which various areas are partitioned into unique file areas for some specific data only.

Files, random access. Computer files stored in an order (prescribed by a mathematical formula) which can be accessed directly.

Files, sequential. Computer-based files stored in sequence by their key; the key may be part number, name, or whatever the data are filed or accessed by.

First normal form (1NF). Any data structure without internal repeating groups.

Flat file. A two-dimensional array of data items like the matrix in Chapter 9.

Flow approach. A method of analyzing the system in which the analyst studies the flow of physical entities and builds a model that simulates the flow of these items through the business organization.

Flowchart. A graphic picture of the logical steps and sequence involved in a procedure or a program.

Flowchart segment. A form of documentation that describes in flowchart format a specific operation.

Flowchart, documented. This chart traces the flow of a single activity through its sequence of operations. A number in each box of the flowchart is used to cross-reference each flowchart box back to the documentation section.

Flowchart, forms. A flowchart that traces the flow of written data or paperwork through the system.

Flowchart, layout. This type of flowchart shows the floor plan of an area, including file cabinets and storage areas, and indicates the flow of paperwork or goods.

Flowchart, paperwork. A type of flowchart tracing the flow of written data through the system.

Flowchart, process. A type of flowchart used by industrial engineers to break down and analyze successive steps in a procedure or system. Five special symbols are used.

Flowchart, program. This flowchart may be derived from a systems flowchart. It is a detailed explanation of the program or procedure being performed. It tells how the work is being done.

Flowchart, schematic. This systems flowchart presents an overview of a system or an overview of procedures. Pictures of the equipment are used in place of standard flowchart symbols.

Flowchart, systems. A pictorial or graphic representation of a system, showing the flow of data or transactions (control) during computer processing at the job level. It represents the transition from the physical model (how it is done) to a set of program specifications to be used for programming flowcharts.

Follow-up. After implementation, the analyst returns to observe actual operation of the installed system to find out if the system really is working as planned.

Forms control. The coordination of forms design and usage among all users of all forms in the firm.

Forms design. Designing the format of the form so that it performs its function simply and efficiently, and is easily completed, legible, uncomplicated, and economically feasible.

Forms, continuous strip. A type of form in which the original and carbons are joined together in a continuous strip with perforations between each form.

Forms, flash. A form that is printed by a high speed laser printer. The printer is so fast that it can print both the form and the output data at the same time. It eliminates the purchase and storage of unused paper forms.

Forms, flat. A single-copy form; that is, there are no carbon copies.

Forms, unit-set/snapout. A type of form which has an original and several copies with carbon paper interleaved between each copy.

Functional approach. A method of analyzing the system in which there are no observable flowing entities through the system, but the analyst studies the sequence of events and builds a model that simulates the sequence of events as they happen throughout the business organization.

Functional primitive. A process that does not need to be decomposed to a lower level. It is the point in data flow diagramming at which the lowest possible level of detail has been reached.

Gantt chart. Graphic representation of a work project showing start, elapsed time, and completion dates of work units in a project. Used to control schedules as part of project management.

Goals. In systems analysis, goals are what the system must be able to do. Major goals are the reason the system is being designed. Intermediate goals are gains the system can make while serving its major purpose. Minor goals are things that would be nice to have, but not at great expense. In management, goals are the objectives of the firm or what management wants to achieve. The goals of systems analysis must meet management's goals or the system will be considered a failure.

Handbook. A manual used in conjunction with specifications and standards to aid in their application and interpretation.

Hardware. The machines utilized in a system. Generally refers to the computer and its peripheral equipment within a system.

Hash total. A meaningless total developed from the accumulated numerical amounts of non-monetary information from a batch of records (used for control purposes).

Heuristic. Something that aids or leads toward discovery, or encourages further investigation.

Hierarchical. Division into successively smaller increments. A tree structure file in which some records are subordinate to others. Each subordinate record can have only one parent. See also: *Tree structure.*

High level language. These are the ones you are most likely to hear about, such as COBOL (for business applications), FORTRAN (for mathematical work), PL/1, and BASIC (a simple, easy to use language). These languages originally were intended to be "machine independent," but it has not worked out that way, and variations are common. High level languages allow the programmer to express operations in a less direct form that is closer to the normal human language representation of the procedures the computer is to perform. Such languages are usually problem-oriented or procedure-oriented programming languages, as distinguished from machine-oriented and/or mnemonic languages.

HIPO. Hierarchy plus Input–Process–Output. A documentation technique that graphically represents functions in charts from a general level down to the detailed level. The technique was developed by IBM.

HIPO detail design package. A HIPO documentation package prepared by a development group using the initial design package. The analysts and programmers specify, in detail, more levels of HIPO diagrams, and use the resultant package for implementation and comparison with the initial design package to ensure that all requirements have been satisfied.

HIPO detail diagrams. Lower level HIPO diagrams that describe the specific functions, show specific input and output items, and refer to other detail diagrams.

HIPO initial design package. A HIPO documentation package prepared by a design group at the start of a project. It describes the overall functional design of the project and is used as a design aid.

HIPO overview diagrams. High level HIPO diagrams that describe the major functions of a system and reference the detail HIPO diagrams needed to expand the function to the described level of detail.

HIPO visual table of contents. A HIPO diagram that contains the names and identification numbers of all the overview and detail HIPO diagrams in a documentation package, and shows the structure of the diagram package and relationship of the functions in a hierarchical fashion.

Human–machine boundary. See: *Boundary.*

Implementation. Consists of the installation of the new system and the removal of the current system.

Index. A table used to determine the location of a record. An essential ingredient in any information storage and retrieval system; the index is a filter to let through to the user the wanted information while keeping back the unwanted information. A listing that is: (1) a guide to primary information (such as that at the end of a book); (2) a guide to periodicals by subject, author, title, and so forth; (3) a guide to a specific page or frame within a microform system.

Indexed-sequential storage. A file structure in which records are stored in ascending sequence by key. Indices showing the highest key are used for the direct access retrieval of records.

Industry background. That part of the systems study which places the firm in perspective within its environment, or looks at how this firm performs in comparison with firms of like nature.

Information. (1) A meaningful assembly of data telling something about the data relationships. (2) A meaningful aggregation of data.

Information storage and retrieval. A field concerned with the structure, analysis, organization, storage, searching, and retrieval of information.

Input/output cycle. That part of the system which consists of inputs, processing, and outputs.

Input/output sheet. Describes inputs and outputs that will be different from those used in the existing system. It contains a functional description of the input or output and describes its purpose and use. A sketch of the input or output may be included.

Inputs. The raw data, raw materials, paperwork, processed computer files, reports, or semifinished products which are used to make up the finished product, or output. The energizing element that puts the system into operation. May be either verbal or written. See also: *Outputs.*

Intangible benefit. A benefit that cannot be measured in economic terms, but which has value. Includes better customer relations, better employee morale, better delivery promises, fewer stockouts, better quality control, and so forth. Some intangible benefits can be measured, but not in dollar terms.

Integrity. Being possessed of basic honesty and moral uprightness.

Interactions. The relationships to be studied between employees, departments, management personnel, or any combination of these elements.

Interactive. Pertaining to an application in which each entry elicits a response, as in an inquiry system or an airline reservation system. An interactive system also may be conversational, implying continuous dialog between the user and the system.

Internal accounting controls. Defined as the plan of the organization, its procedures, and the records that are concerned with safeguarding assets and ensuring the reliability and consistency of financial records.

Internal control. Refers to all the methods, policies, and organizational procedures adopted within a business to reasonably ensure the safeguarding of its assets, the accuracy and reliability of accounting controls, and promotion of operational efficiency and adherence to management standards.

Interview. The most important tool for gathering data about the area under study is to talk with people in an organized, systematic way.

ISAM. Index sequential access method (IBM). See: *Files, index-sequential.*

Iteration. The process of repeating or iterating through a step. In analysis, it is the successive repetition of a step to refine it. In a process, it is task repetition.

Jackets. A jacket usually is made of mylar film and is manufactured in such a way that strips of microfilm can be placed in rows, one frame at a time if desired. It looks similar to microfiche, but the film is removable.

Job control language (JCL). A programming language used to code job control statements. These statements supply information to the operating system and the operators about the program (e.g., name of user, how much memory is required, estimated run time, priority, tapes required, other programs, etc.).

Key data entry devices. The equipment used to prepare data so that the computer can accept it, including old, faithful keypunches (card punches) plus the newer key-to-tape and key-to-disk units.

Key, primary. A key which uniquely identifies a record (or other data grouping).

Key, secondary. A key which does not uniquely identify a record (i.e., more than one record can have the same key value). A key which contains the value of an attribute (data element) other than the unique identifier.

Key verification. A procedure for checking the accuracy of data, which involves rekeying the data and comparing it to the original data entered.

Lateral thinking. The method of thinking, described by de Bono, that explores all the different ways of looking at the system. It often begins with the end of the system (outputs) and works backward through the system.

Ledger. A summary of transactions to document an audit trail.

Legal life. The retention period of a record that is required by law.

Legal requirements. The laws of local, state, or federal government which affect company operations. Some help the company, some restrict the company, while others affect the firm's recordkeeping practices. They may affect a proposed system.

Letterpress. The type of printing press that prints the form from a raised surface of type covered with ink.

Level I study. The systems study that involves the whole firm and in which management has the greatest stake.

Level II study. The systems study that involves one division of the firm, and one in which management is vitally interested.

Level III study. The systems study that involves department interaction; the "middle management" area that involves exacting detail.

Level IV study. The systems study that involves functions within a specific department.

Level V study. The smallest systems study, generally dealing with a specific problem within a specific area of the department.

Level 0. See: *Levels of detail.*

Levels of detail. Data flow diagrams are constructed to show various levels of detail in which each lower level is a more detailed data flow diagram. For example, the highest level (most general) is the Level 0 data flow diagram. That level data flow diagram is decomposed, or partitioned, to more detail through the Level 1 diagram, Level 2 diagram, Level 3 diagram, and so forth.

Library of Congress System. A subject classification system that classifies all knowledge into 21 subject areas. Subdivision is by alphanumeric designations. Used in libraries to enable arrangement of books by subject groupings.

Line printer (computer). A high speed printing device that is attached to a computer.

Logical control. One that pertains to the logical framework of the business system being computerized. User personnel are good at suggesting logical controls because a logical control pertains to the business activity as contrasted with the data processing activity or technical control.

Logical database. A database as perceived by its users; it may be structured differently from the physical database structure. A schema is a logical database.

Logical model. A pictorial representation of the system that shows what processes must be performed, the flow of data through the system, and the data stores that are required.

Long-range plans. The plans for the future of the firm. These plans may affect or make obsolete a proposed system.

Man–machine boundary. See: *Boundary.*

Management information system. A system in which management or others having an established need to know are provided with historical information, information on current status, and projected information appropriately summarized. A decision making tool. Also called an MIS.

Management-proposed control. Those controls that are mandated by middle and upper management. They can be financial controls, legal obligations, and controls that will enhance the operation of a system to make it more efficient.

Manuals. A form of documentation to guide employees in doing their tasks. See also: *Procedure.*

Marginal efficiency of investment. The rate of return that a potential new system is expected to earn after all of its costs are covered, excluding interest.

Matrix of controls. A two-dimensional matrix that shows the relationship between all of the controls and the specific threats and components.

Maximize. To get the highest possible degree of use out of the system without regard to other systems.

Microcard. A term generally used for the type of microform that is opaque as opposed to transparent. These vary a great deal in size and reduction ratio.

Microfiche. A unitized type of microform with a number of images arranged in rows on a transparent card.

Microfilm. A continuous strip of film, usually either 16-mm or 35-mm, with all the "pages" placed in order. The film usually is placed on some type of reel for easy wind and rewind.

Microform/micrographics. A miniaturized record in which the original record has been reduced photographically in order to save space.

Micro matrix. A more detailed matrix that is built using the threats or components from one of the cells of the original matrix. A micro matrix also may be constructed from one of the lower level data flow diagrams, such as Level 1, Level 2, and so forth. The micro matrix shows the control relationships at a much more detailed level, perhaps even at the functional primitive level.

Microprocessor. A single or multiple chip set that makes up a microcomputer.

Minispecification. Defines the policy rules that govern the process of data transformation. These policy rules can be specified in procedure manuals, decision tables, decision trees, structured English, tight English, pseudocode, and so forth.

Model. A pictorial representation of a system. See also: *Logical model, Physical model.*

Modules. When applied to computer programs, it is the process of subdividing a particular program into separate modules that can be written as individual but interconnecting subprograms. When all of the modules are interconnected, you have the overall program required to perform whatever task is being programmed. Also applies to computer equipment as the ability to add to the basic computer system to increase its power, either through more data storage or more input and output devices.

Narrative. A description written in story form. A verbal model in which the analyst details the sequences of steps involved in necessary operations.

National Technical Information Service (NTIS). The primary distributor of unclassified government documents, sponsored by the Department of Commerce.

Need to know. A term originated by the military to identify a person who has a legitimate need to use a specific bit of information for a specific purpose. Also used within a firm to indicate who may have access to sensitive corporate information.

Net present value (NPV). A discounted cash flow approach based on the present value of money. It is a common ranking alternative to determine which of several investments is best. If the NPV is greater than zero, the alternative may be accepted because the system provides a rate of return greater than the rate of return a bank would pay if the money was placed in the bank instead.

Network. Events and activities in PERT/CPM or a database structure (see: Plex structure) or a data communication network.

Network structure. See: *Plex structure.*

Normal form. See: *First normal form, Second normal form,* or *Third normal form.*

Normalization. The decomposition of more complex data structures into flat files (relations). This forms the basis of relational databases. It is the process of replacing existing files with their logical equivalents, thereby deriving a set of simple files containing no redundant elements.

Objectives. As used in systems, what one intends to accomplish in the problem definition phase or during a full systems study.

Offset. The type of printing press that photographs the finished drawing of the form onto a printing surface from which the form is then printed.

On-line. Pertaining to equipment or devices under the control of the central processing unit, or pertaining to a user's ability to interact with a computer.

On-line system. A system in which the input data enters the computer directly from the point of origin or in which output data is transmitted directly to where it is used.

Operations. The procedure or activity that must take place to transform inputs into outputs.

Optimize. To get the most favorable degree of use out of a system, taking into account all other systems.

Organization, formal. The organization that is built around the firm's goals, upper management's policy statements, and the written procedures that carry out the policies. Visually shown on the firm's organization chart.

Organization, informal. The organization that is built around the job at hand as the employees see it, as opposed to the manner in which management wishes the job to be performed.

Outline. The detailed plan of action by which the systems study will be carried out.

Outputs. The end product of the area under study. Outputs can be completed-paperwork, processed computer files, reports, semi-finished products, or finished products. See also: *Inputs*.

Outside interface. See: *External entity*.

Page, database. A block is the physical unit of data transfer between a database and the CPU, and it is referred to as a page.

Paging. Data and programs are divided into fixed size blocks (pages) and are loaded into real storage (computer memory) for access when needed during processing.

Paper, bond. High quality paper. Types include rag, sulfite, and duplicating.

Paper, index bristol. Paper that is heavier than ledger or bond; also known as card stock.

Paper, ledger. A heavyweight bond paper used for machine posted ledgers.

Paper, manifold. A lightweight bond paper; sometimes called onionskin.

Paper, safety. A special type of paper that cannot be erased without leaving a mark.

Parameter. Elements of an activity or job procedure that almost always are constant. Defines the limits of a system or its phases.

Partitioning. See: *Decomposition*.

Password. A unique word or string of characters that a program, computer operator, or user must supply to meet security requirements, before gaining access to data.

Payback period. A criterion used to judge the profitability of a system. The number of years required to accumulate earnings sufficient to cover the cost of the proposed system.

Peopleware. The operating personnel of a system, and the most essential ingredient in the workability of a system.

Periodical. A regularly issued publication, usually oriented toward one specific subject, through which the specialist keeps abreast of new developments. Often used synonymously with magazine or journal.

Personnel sheet. A documentation form specifying the job description, job title, and approximate pay range for each needed position in the system.

PERT. *Programmed Evaluation Review Technique* is a planning and control tool for defining and controlling the efforts necessary to accomplish project objectives on schedule.

Phase out. By some pre-planned date the old system should no longer be operating. Phasing out can pertain to parallel conversion where the old and new systems are operated simultaneously until the new system has been proven. The old system generally is phased out then.

Physical model. A pictorial representation of the system, showing how the job is performed physically, including the sequence of operations, the people, computer processing, paper forms, and so on.

Plex structure. A relationship between records (or other grouping) in which a child record can have more than one parent record.

Policy. Management guidelines for regulating progress toward the firm's goals.

Politics, company. The maneuvering of personalities within the informal organization, which is the individual's strategy to achieve success.

Polling time. Polling is a situation in which each terminal is given permission to send a message one at a time. The polling time is the time between polls or how often each terminal is polled, such as once every 150 milliseconds.

Present value. A discounted cash flow approach to determining the best investment. The project is accepted if the present value of cash inflows exceeds the present value of cash outflows.

Preventive controls. These are controls that either will deter or prevent a threat from occurring. Deterrent controls discourage or restrain one from acting or proceeding because of fear or doubt. They also restrain or hinder an unwanted event from occurring. Preventive controls mitigate or stop one from acting or an unwanted event from occurring.

Primary key. See: *Key, primary.*

Problem. A question proposed for solution or consideration.

Problem definition report. A short report that sets the stage for an advanced feasibility study or a major systems study. It includes subject, scope, and objectives.

Problem flow. The directional flow of a problem from either the internal or external environment to the systems analysis department.

Problem report form. A form to be filled out, which formally reports the existence of a problem and the circumstances in which the problem occurs.

Problem reporting machinery. An expression used to describe the method by which the systems analyst learns of problems. It may be either a written or verbal message.

Problem solving. The process of recognizing a problem, specifying exactly what the problem is, determining what is causing the problem, and providing a solution to the problem.

Procedure, formal. A precise series of written instructions that explain what is to be done, who will do it, when it will be done, and how it will be done.

Procedure, informal. The tasks performed by an individual that are not in writing but which the individual performs to "get the job done."

Procedure, narrative. A procedure composed of words, sentences, and paragraphs; a story form.

Procedure, playscript. A procedure that uses sequence numbers, actors, action verbs, and a straight chronological sequence of who does what in the procedure.

Procedure, step-by-step outline. A procedure in which the reader sees item-by-item what each step contains.

Process. An activity on a data flow diagram that transforms input data flow(s) into output data flow(s).

Processing. The activity in the input/output cycle that transforms the input into an output.

Product. The output of a system or the output of the firm.

Program run book. Operating instructions for the benefit of others who may run the program; included are special restart procedures in case of failure prior to normal program end.

Programming. Writing the software or program modules that will implement the newly designed computer system.

Programming languages. The major kinds of programming languages are as follows: (1) Assembly or symbolic machine languages with symbols and mnemonics as aids to programming, (2) Macroassembly languages, which are the same as assembly or symbolic machine languages, but permitting macro-instructions used for coding convenience, (3) Procedure-oriented languages for expressing methods in the same way as expressed by algorithmic languages, and (4) Problem-oriented languages for expressing problems.

Project assignment sheet. A form indicating not only who will perform a systems study and its priority, but its subject, scope, objectives, phases, schedule, follow-up notes, and record of times spent. An integral part of project control.

Project control. The primary function of the systems analysis manager is to assign projects to each analyst and to ensure that the assigned projects are completed in the specified length of time.

Project schedule. Each phase of a systems project is put on a Gantt chart to indicate the length of time allotted to each phase.

Prototyping. A systems development technique using application software development tools that make it possible to create all of the files and processing programs (a working model) for a business application in a matter of days.

Pseudocode. A method of documenting how a computer program should operate using programming-type logic in an English-like form. It does not conform to any one programming language and thus pseudocode cannot be input directly into a computer. It must be converted to an actual computer program language. Tight English or structured English can be used as pseudocode.

Random access. To obtain data directly from any storage location regardless of its position with respect to the previously referenced information. Also called Direct access.

Rapport. A meeting of the minds, or absence of friction.

Real-time. The processing of transactions as they occur, rather than batching them. Pertaining to an application in which response to input is fast enough to affect subsequent inputs and/or guide the process. On-line processing is used for real-time systems; however, not all on-line processing is real-time.

Record. A group of related fields of information treated as a unit by an application. Also called a data structure.

Record retention schedule. A timetable governing the retirement and destruction of all company records.

Records inventory. The starting point in initiating a records control program, when the analyst makes an inventory of the active records being maintained by each department.

Records retention. A systems technique that provides control over records.

Records, vital. Those records that would enable the firm to reconstruct its operations after a disaster.

Re-evaluation. After implementation and follow-up, the analyst makes whatever changes are needed for the refinement and improvement of the new system. Some portions may be re-designed and others may be revised.

References. The titles of any documents that have a governing or otherwise vital bearing upon the procedure.

Relation. A flat file. A two-dimensional array of data elements. A file in normalized form.

Relational database. A database made up of relations (as defined above). Its database management system has the capability to recombine the data elements to form different relations, thus giving great flexibility in the usage of data.

Report analysis. A function similar to forms control, in which the analyst examines the reports being generated to determine which can be eliminated, improved, or added.

Report, final. The most important report of the systems study. It summarizes the work to date, presents the new system, specifies cost comparisons, describes the existing system, and makes recommendations.

Reports, action. A report that initiates or controls a necessary procedure or operation.

Reports, exception. A report that is generated only when certain parameters are out of line with what is expected of those parameters.

Reports, feeder. A report that consists of bits of data to be used later in conjunction with other data, another report, or for accumulating data for a decision.

Reports, information. A report that provides data or information for further analysis and control.

Reports, on-demand. A report generated upon the user's request.

Reports, progress. A report that delineates the work done during the interval since the last progress report.

Reports, reference. A report that keeps the manager informed on operations.

Reports, scheduled. A report that is prepared and distributed at a fixed time on a regular basis.

Request for Proposals (RFPs). An invitation to prospective bidders (vendors) notifying them of your interest in obtaining hardware, software, and/ or complete turnkey systems. They are used to determine whether hardware/software should be purchased or leased, or whether the firm will operate the system or use facilities management.

Requirements. The objectives as set during the problem definition phase. These are determined in terms of outputs, inputs, operations, and resources.

Resources. Items used in the day-to-day operation to convert inputs to outputs.

Resources, facilities. The resources of the area under study, consisting of land, buildings, data processing equipment, or other capital equipment.

Resources, financial. The assets of the area under study, consisting of the budget for the area and the area manager's ability to get financial backing for new projects and systems.

Resources, inventory. (1) The "stock-in-trade" resources such as materials, parts, supplies, semi-finished products, and finished products. (2) The "files of information" or data collected over the years.

Resources, personnel. The assets of the area under study in terms of key managers and other skilled and able personnel. They include personalities and talents.

Response time. The elapsed time between the last terminal operator data entry and the display of the response from the computer onto the screen.

Retrieval, data. A type of information storage and retrieval system in which the user is provided with data displayed as words or numbers. Commonly known as "lookup" and not truly information storage and retrieval.

Retrieval, document. A type of information storage and retrieval system in which the system ultimately provides the user with the full text of the document.

Retrieval, reference. A type of information storage and retrieval system in which the user is given citations to document locations.

Risk analysis. A systematic approach to categorizing threats to data and developing countermeasures to those threats.

Risk ranking. A method of ranking the relative sensitivity of systems that are planned for development. It allows developers to determine which system is the most vulnerable when compared to other systems that also are under consideration.

Sampling. The collection of a limited quantity of data from the total data available, for the purpose of studying that fraction to infer things about the total.

Satisfice. To choose a particular level of performance for which to strive and for which management is willing to settle.

Schema. A description of the overall database structure as perceived by the users and which is employed by the database management software. The schema is the logical database description.

Scope. The area or range that the systems study will encompass.

Scoring. A risk ranking methodology that eliminates the need to assign probabilities of occurrence and annual loss values, but still uses objective criteria. The system that has the highest factor value score is the most vulnerable. Scoring indicates relative risk or sensitivity of different systems under development.

Second normal form (2NF). A data structure in which all non-key data elements are fully functionally dependent on the primary key. A data element is fully functionally dependent only if it is dependent on the entire key.

Self-defining term. Any data element that is understood fully by everyone who is involved with the system.

Sensitivity. The quality of being readily affected by other people; responding to their feelings.

Simulation. A mathematical model which is programmed into a computer and which represents the system through all its phases.

Software. The programs that control the operation of the computer. Also can refer to application programs.

Sources, external. Secondary sources of information that aid the analyst in understanding the area under study, such as periodical articles or special industry reports.

Sources, internal. Primary sources of information that aid the analyst in understanding the area under study, such as long-range plans or employee handbooks.

Specification. Establishes the necessary characteristics of an item in terms of its expected performance.

Standard. Defines the dimensions of a particular item for purposes of interchangeability.

State-of-change approach. A method of analyzing the system in which no specific sequence can be observed in a large number of interdependent relationships. Various checkpoints of the model are monitored to determine what, if any, changes occur as the inputs to the subsystem are varied.

Statute. A law passed by Congress or a state legislature.

Storage box label. The form used to identify each box of records put into storage.

Storage file life. The time during which records that are inactive or no longer in current use are stored where they can be located if needed.

Structured analysis. A systematic, top-down technique that refines goals and objectives that are presented through the use of layered models of the system's requirements. It is an orderly approach that works from higher level overviews to lower level details in which user needs are presented through the use of data flow diagrams.

Structured design. The physical implementation of the structured analysis. It involves the use of physical models and utilizes hierarchical partitioning of a modular structure in a top-down manner. It is the natural extension of the structured analysis process.

Structured English. A tool that is used for describing a system. It is a subset of the English language (with a restricted syntax and vocabulary), embedded in the procedural constructs of structured programming.

Structured specification. The end product of structured analysis (description of a new system of automated and manual procedures) made up of data flow diagrams, data dictionary, structured English process descriptions, data structure diagrams, decision tables/trees, and so forth.

Subject. The topic or central theme of a system study or problem definition study.

Subschema. A map of a programmer's view of the data. It is derived from the global logical view of the data, or the schema. It is also viewed as a chart of one user's or one application's view of the data stored in a database.

Summation. The verbal summary of an interview with a person. It mentions the points covered and verifies any agreements reached on important or controversial points.

System. A network of interrelated procedures that are joined together to perform an activity.

System, closed. A system that automatically controls or modifies its own operation by responding to data generated by the system itself.

System, conceptual. A system existing only in thought.

System, empirical. A working system.

System, existing. The current system with all its faults and inadequacies.

System, open. A system that does not provide for its own control or modification. It needs to be supervised by people.

System, proposed. The newly developed system designed to replace the existing (current) system.

System design specification. Comprehensive proposal for a new system, encompassing both user specification and all updated and/or additional detailing of hardware, software, procedures, and documentation needed for actual implementation. Same as Structured specification.

System development life cycle. Organized, structured methodology for developing, programming, and installing a new or revised system. The methodology in this book (see Figure 2-1) has three phases and 10 steps.

System requirements model. A model illustrating the relationships between inputs, operations, resources, and outputs.

System structure charts. See: *Charts, system structure.*

Systems analysis. The approach to a system that is the opposite of trial and error. All influences and constraints are identified and evaluated in terms of their impact on the various parts of the system.

Systems department. A staff activity that renders service to all other departments. The staff takes a complex problem, breaks it down, and identifies the possible solutions.

Systems design. The art of developing a new system. The 10 steps outlined in Figure 2-1 portray the system design cycle. It is concerned with the coordination of activities, job procedures, and equipment utilization in order to achieve organizational objectives.

Tact. The ability to say or do the right thing without offending the other person.

Technical control. One that pertains to the computer hardware, software, application programs, data communication networks, or any other data processing facilities utilized in the new computerized business system.

Telecommunications. See: *Data communications.*

Test a control. Means a control is tested to be sure it is operational and does what it was designed to do.

Testing. The critical phase of computer system development in which debugged programs are tested to ensure a working system.

Theory X. A form of managerial style explained by McGregor, which assumes that humans naturally avoid work, are irresponsible, desire security above most other things, and that tight controls are needed to keep humans working properly.

Theory Y. A form of managerial control explained by McGregor, which assumes that humans actually seek work and responsibility, that humans are self-motivated, and that the human being has a capacity for a high degree of ingenuity and creativity, under proper conditions.

Third normal form (3NF). A data structure in which the following two conditions are met: All non-key data elements are fully functionally dependent on the primary key (e.g., 2NF) and no non-key data element is functionally dependent on any other non-key data element in the system (including any other data store). In other words, no data element can be derived from another data element.

Threat. An adverse occurrence, or any event that we do not want to occur.

Tight English. Follows the logical constructs of structured English, but eliminates the clumsy and unfamiliar notations in favor of more familiar, but logically tight, English. Tight English is derived from structured English.

Time, calendar. The overall time in terms of days, months, or years that it takes to complete a new system from start to finish.

Time, chargeable. The actual number of hours to be spent in developing a new system. Each activity or phase fits into a timetable.

Time, expected activity (PERT). The time in weeks calculated for an activity from the time estimates given.

Time, expected event (PERT). The sum of all expected activity times along the longest path leading to an event.

Time, latest allowable (PERT). The latest time by which an event can be accomplished without affecting the date scheduled for completion of the entire project.

Time, most likely (PERT). The time that responsible managers or analysts think will be required for the job.

Time, optimistic (PERT). The time estimate for an activity, assuming everything goes better than expected.

Time, pessimistic (PERT). The time required if many adverse conditions are encountered, not including acts of God, strikes, or power failures.

Time, scheduled (PERT). The time in weeks from the starting event to the planned-for or contractually obligated completion date.

Time, slack (PERT). The difference between the latest allowable time and the earliest expected time for an activity to be completed.

To Do list. (1) A list of all the tasks that you plan to accomplish tomorrow. (2) An outline of how you plan to carry out the problem definition project. It notes the tasks to be accomplished and how you plan to go about them.

Top-down. Proceeding from the general to the particular or from the broad to the detailed.

Transaction. Any element of data, event, or change of state that causes, or initiates some action or sequence of actions. Usually an input.

Transaction analysis. When the data flow diagram is cut into smaller data flow diagrams based on separate transactions. Each smaller data flow diagram represents one transaction that the system must process.

Transaction trail. See: *Audit trail.*

Transform analysis. When a data flow diagram is converted to a system structure chart; depicts the transformations that take place on the data.

Tree structure. A hierarchy of groups of data such that (1) the highest level in the hierarchy has only one group, called a root; (2) all groups except the root are related to one and only one group on a higher level than themselves (only one parent). A simple master/detail file is a two-level hierarchy. Also called a hierarchical structure.

Tuple. An individual data structure or record in a relational database.

Turnkey system. A system in which the manufacturer takes full responsibility for complete system design and installation, and supplies all necessary hardware, software, and documentation elements.

Ultrafiche. One of the newer types of photoreduction onto microform. Similar to microfiche in that it is transparent; but because of the method of reduction, many more frames can be "packed" onto a single 4 × 6 inch or 3 × 6 inch transparency.

User. The personnel in various parts of an organization who prepare data for input to the computer; also those personnel who receive and use the output.

Variable. Those elements of an activity or job procedure that are subject to change or variation.

Verify a control. Means to be sure that a control exists.

Vertical thinking. The method of thinking described by de Bono where thinking begins with the most promising method of approaching the problem and proceeds from that point to a solution.

Video display. Visual data display terminal. Usually called a VDT (video display terminal), but sometimes called a CRT (cathode ray tube).

Visual aid. Any aid the analyst uses during the verbal presentation, which helps demonstrate what the analyst is talking about.

VSAM. Virtual sequential access method, an IBM volume independent indexed sequential access method.

Walkthrough. A technical quality review of a newly designed system. The review is conducted by systems analysts, users, and auditors in order to ensure that both the logical data flow diagrams and the physical data flow diagrams are correct. An alternate meaning is when a programmer has other programmers review his or her program code that was written during the structured design stage. In either case, a walkthrough is a situation in which people play the role of devil's advocate and review the work of another person or group of people.

Work modules. The bottom level functions (modules) of a system structure chart. These are the real workers of the system and may be called worker modules.

Work sampling. Consists of a large number of observations taken at random intervals, noting what the employee does and recording it into a predefined category. The information gained from work sampling can be used to evaluate the existing system or as a benchmark for comparison with the new system design.

Index

Printed by
Fong & Sons Printers Pte Ltd